Rethinking European Modernity

Also available from Bloomsbury

Chinese and Indian Ways of Thinking in Early Modern European Philosophy,
by Selusi Ambrogio
Finding Locke's God, by Nathan Guy
Locke on Knowledge, Politics and Religion,
edited by Kiyoshi Shimokawa and Peter R. Anstey
Spinoza in Twenty-First-Century American and French Philosophy,
edited by Jack Stetter and Charles Ramond

Rethinking European Modernity

Reason, Power, and Coloniality in Early Modern Thought

Hans Schelkshorn

Translated by Paul Bowman

BLOOMSBURY ACADEMIC
LONDON • NEW YORK • OXFORD • NEW DELHI • SYDNEY

BLOOMSBURY ACADEMIC
Bloomsbury Publishing Plc
50 Bedford Square, London, WC1B 3DP, UK
1385 Broadway, New York, NY 10018, USA
29 Earlsfort Terrace, Dublin 2, Ireland

BLOOMSBURY, BLOOMSBURY ACADEMIC and the Diana logo
are trademarks of Bloomsbury Publishing Plc

First published in Great Britain 2024
This paperback edition published 2025

Copyright © Hans Schelkshorn, 2024
English language translation © Paul Bowman 2024

Hans Schelkshorn has asserted his right under the Copyright,
Designs and Patents Act, 1988, to be identified as Author of this work.

For legal purposes the Acknowledgments on p. x constitute
an extension of this copyright page.

Cover image: Map of the world 1800/THEPALMER/Getty Images

This work is published open access subject to a Creative Commons Attribution 4.0 licence (CC BY 4.0, https://creativecommons.org/licenses/by/4.0/). You may re-use, distribute, reproduce, and adapt this work in any medium, including for commercial purposes, provided you give attribution to the copyright holder and the publisher, provide a link to the Creative Commons licence, and indicate if changes have been made.

Bloomsbury Publishing Plc does not have any control over, or responsibility for, any third-party websites referred to or in this book. All internet addresses given in this book were correct at the time of going to press. The author and publisher regret any inconvenience caused if addresses have changed or sites have ceased to exist, but can accept no responsibility for any such changes.

A catalogue record for this book is available from the British Library.

A catalog record for this book is available from the Library of Congress.

ISBN: HB: 978-1-3502-6677-3
PB: 978-1-3502-6681-0
ePDF: 978-1-3502-6678-0
eBook: 978-1-3502-6679-7

Typeset by Integra Software Services Pvt. Ltd.

To find out more about our authors and books visit www.bloomsbury.com
and sign up for our newsletters.

Contents

List of figures	vii
Preface	viii
Acknowledgments	x
List of abbreviations	xi
Introduction: A self-critical reinterpretation of European modernity in a global context	1

Part I Reason, power, and coloniality: Three paradigmatic interpretations of modernity

1	Modern reason as syndrome of power: Martin Heidegger, Max Horkheimer, and Theodor W. Adorno	17
2	The Enlightenment as an unfinished project: Karl-Otto Apel and Jürgen Habermas	33
3	The challenge of decolonial philosophies: The case of Latin America	49
4	Summary and preview	69

Part II Transcending the boundaries of the cosmos and the ecumene: A retrospect on the thought of the Renaissance

5	The de-limitation of the cosmos and the revaluation of insatiable curiosity: Nicholas of Cusa	77
6	Freedom as self-creation: Pico della Mirandola's *Oratio de hominis dignitate*	117
7	The conquest of the Americas and the foundations of global cosmopolitanism: Francisco de Vitoria and Juan Ginés de Sepúlveda	139
8	Experimental self-fashioning in an unlimited world: Michel de Montaigne	215

Part III Foundations of modern science, politics, and economy in the philosophy of the seventeenth century

9 Francis Bacon's vision of modern science and limitless technological progress — 257
10 Thomas Hobbes: The foundation of modern politics amid escalating social conflicts — 299
11 John Locke: The justification of an unlimited market economy — 343
12 Epilogue: The future of modernity and the search for new self-limitations — 389

Notes — 403
References — 413
Name Index — 451
Subject Index — 460

Figures

1 Map of the world, according to Ptolemy — 145
2 Frontispiece of Francis Bacon's *Instauratio magna*, 1620 — 267

Preface

In the late 1980s, by coincidence, I came across Latin American philosophy of liberation, which was hardly known in Europe at the time. At the same time, Franz Martin Wimmer and a few other colleagues in Vienna were beginning to focus their attention on contemporary non-European philosophies, including those developed in Africa. In the 1990s, motivated by our shared interest in overcoming the Eurocentric narrowing of the study and discussion of philosophy in European institutions, we founded the Vienna Society for Intercultural Philosophy and the journal *Polylog*, which is exclusively devoted to the global dialogue between the philosophies of the different regions of the world. Ever since, my thought, up to that point Eurocentric, has become irreversibly decentered.

The idea of a philosophical reinterpretation of European modernity arose out of the dialogue between European discourse ethics and Latin American liberation ethics, in which Enrique Dussel and Karl-Otto Apel were both personally involved. A series of conferences, organized by Raúl Fornet-Betancourt and taking place alternately in Europe and Latin America between 1989 and 1997, focused on identifying a universal foundation for ethics. Besides a number of conference contributions, I presented a systematic comparison of discourse and liberation ethics in my book *Diskurs und Befreiung* (Rodopi, 1997). Through intensive discussions with Dussel and Apel spanning a number of years, and also with a number of other colleagues from Europe, Latin America, and other regions of the world, it become increasingly clear to me that the cross-cultural debates on ethical and political topics and issues are interwoven with different interpretations of modernity.

In the years that followed, the focus of my research shifted from ethics to theories of modernity. My lectures on early modern philosophy at the University of Vienna had already explored Renaissance thought and its importance for modernity. The colonialism debates in Spanish sixteenth-century philosophy, which as a European I had paradoxically become acquainted with first through my encounter with Latin American philosophy, fitted almost seamlessly into this new interest.

In tandem with this turn to theories of modernity, the perspective of my interests also changed. As important as it is for European philosophy to be open to non-European philosophies and self-critique, dialogue between philosophies remains alive and fruitful only when a reciprocal exchange of ideas and criticisms takes place. Thus, two questions became increasingly important: What conception of European modernity can I still advocate as a European philosopher in the wake of the Conquista of the Americas and the atrocities of the Holocaust? And: Which specific constructive contributions could European philosophy offer today to the global discourse about modernity without suppressing the colonial past and its still reverberating consequences? From this background I began the project of a philosophical reinterpretation of European modernity. Because modernity is the object of fierce controversies not only in decolonial thought but also within Western philosophy since the eighteenth century, controversies entangled with one another in diverse ways, a reinterpretation of the philosophical sources of European modernity is forced to move within a dense network of completely different and overlapping discourses.

In this sense, the present set of studies on early modern European thought is a first, and thus also foundational, component for a new self-critical interpretation of European modernity, which I aim to develop in the future and clarify within a global dialogue about modernity. This is no false modesty. On the contrary: the lesson I have learned from my decades of engagement with non-European philosophies can be encapsulated in the following thesis: Because European modernity has had numerous histories due to its global dissemination to all regions of the world, and was and continues to be critically engaged, interpreted, and rejected in some cases by philosophies in "local" and "colonial" contexts, European philosophy can only understand "modernity" or "modernities"—and itself—in dialogue with non-European philosophies.

Hans Schelkshorn

Acknowledgments

This book is a translation of my study *Entgrenzungen. Ein europäischer Beitrag zum philosophischen Diskurs über die Moderne* (Velbrück Wissenschaft, 2009; second edition, 2016), which I have extensively reworked for its English edition. I am extremely grateful to my colleagues for their many-faceted suggestions and critical remarks. With respect to the German edition, Mathias Lutz-Bachmann, Paul Richard Blum, Maximilian Forschner, Gerhard Luf, and Harald Schwaetzer all contributed critical and constructive comments on individual chapters at various stages, some of them also commenting on the whole book. For preparing the English edition I would like to thank Paul Bowman for his commitment and patience in translating such a lengthy manuscript that, moreover, was being constantly revised. I am greatly indebted to my friend Eduardo Mendieta who has continuously accompanied and advised me during all phases of this project, generously sharing his philosophical acumen and organizational competence. I would also like to thank my staff at the Department of Intercultural Philosophy of Religion in Vienna, Agnes Leyer, Stefan Witek, and Kohki Totsuka, for their support, above all in the arduous search for English source texts, the compiling of the references, and the formal organization of the manuscript.

Finally, I wish to express my thanks to Bloomsbury for including this study in their program, and to Colleen Coalter and Suzie Nash for their professional support, not least in the quest for a new title.

Abbreviations

Titles of ancient Greek and Latin texts are abbreviated according to the *Oxford Classical Dictionary* (Oxford University Press, 2003). For bibliographic details of all works listed below, see the list of references at the end of this volume.

Adv. Learn.	Francis Bacon, *Of the Proficience and Advancement of Learning, Divine and Human* (*Works of Francis Bacon*, vol. 3)
DDI	Nicholas of Cusa, *De docta ignorantia/Of Learned Ignorance*
De augmentis	Francis Bacon, *De dignitate et augmentis scientiarum libri IX*
DE	Max Horkheimer and Theodore W. Adorno, *Dialectic of Enlightenment*
E	Michel de Montaigne, *Essais*
Elem.	Thomas Hobbes, *The Elements of Law, Natural and Politic*
Essay	John Locke, *Essay Concerning Human Understanding*
Essays	Francis Bacon, *Essays, or Counsels Civil and Moral* (*Works of Francis Bacon*, vol. 6)
EW	Thomas Hobbes, *The English Works of Thomas Hobbes of Malmesbury*
G	Pico della Mirandola, *De hominis dignitate*, ed. and trans. E. Garin
Lev.	Thomas Hobbes, *Leviathan*
H	*Complete Philosophical and Theological Treatises of Nicholas of Cusa*, ed. and trans. J. Hopkins
LP	Francisco de Vitoria, *Political Writings*, ed. A. Pagden, trans. J. Lawrance

N.O.	Francis Bacon, *Novum organum* (*Works of Francis Bacon*, Latin version vol. 1, English trans. vol. 4)
Oratio	Pico della Mirandola, *Oratio de hominis dignitate*
TTG	John Locke, *Two Treatises of Government*
Val. Term.	Francis Bacon, *Valerius Terminus of the Interpretation of Nature, with the Annotations of Hermes Stella*
works	Francis Bacon, *The Works of Francis Bacon*, ed. J. Spedding, R. L. Ellis, and D. Heath

Introduction: A self-critical reinterpretation of European modernity in a global context

As Immanuel Kant emphasized in his *Critique of Pure Reason*, humanity is "burdened with questions" and, moreover, while the answers to them "transcend every capacity of human reason," those questions nonetheless cannot be dismissed "since they are given to it as problems by the nature of reason itself" (Kant 1999: 99). Although modernity may not be one of those perennial questions of philosophy inseparably tied to the nature of reason itself, it steadfastly remains an unavoidable question. Kant noted that philosophy had become entangled in "endless controversies" (1999: 99) while seeking to resolve the dilemmas of metaphysics; similarly, modernity has become the subject of countless theories. The debates about God, the world, and the soul at least found a "battlefield" (1999: 99) in metaphysics; there is still no one established discipline for discussing the controversies over modernity. Numerous disciplines and approaches have tackled the question of modernity, primarily history, the social sciences, aesthetics, and not least philosophy. The result is a veritable potpourri.

Depending on one's specific interests and discipline, the definition of modernity spans an enormous range of possibilities and chronological frameworks. Aesthetics focuses on the emergence of Modernism in the late nineteenth century; history and sociology position the breakthrough to modernity mostly in the mid-eighteenth century (Bayly 2004). Such signposts are never clear-cut, however. The rudimentary beginnings of social differentiation in various subsystems, akin to a standard theory in the social sciences, are traced back historically to the Reformation and in some cases even the Middle Ages. In contrast, philosophical discourses take a decidedly normative perspective and interpret modernity in the light of theories of rationality. Because the normative concept of "enlightenment" is also employed to designate a specific historical epoch, descriptive theories of modernity formulated in sociology and historical studies become amalgamated with normative perspectives.

The resulting nuances create a complex tableau. Some historians distinguish between a radical enlightenment, characterized by an atheistic critique of religion and the idea of modern democracy, from more moderate currents, foremost in Germany, where religion was still very much a concern and to be integrated (Porter 2000; Israel 2009). Normative theories of modernity can end up running contrary to the epochal definitions of when the modern age begins. When democracy and human rights are posited as core elements of a single normative modernity, then nineteenth-century conservatism and twentieth-century fascism appear as aberrations and not in any way constitutive for the modern epoch. But this also pertains to progressive movements inspired by the Enlightenment, most notably positivism and Marxism. While Auguste Comte formulates the ideal of a hierarchical society based on science, Karl Marx envisions a dictatorship of the proletariat.

To minimize, at least to a certain degree, such counterintuitive exclusions by (or of) normative interpretations of modernity, I wish to follow Hans Blumenberg and proceed from an epochal consciousness that emerged in Europe with the erosion of the predominant Christian theology of history. The consciousness of living in a radically new era generated the need to find historical orientation points, to gain an assurance based on identifying what exactly constituted the new in this era: "The modern age [*Neuzeit*, literally 'new time'] was the first and only age that understood itself as an epoch and, in doing so, simultaneously created the other epochs" (Blumenberg 1983: 116). In short, despite the overarching philosophical intention, my starting point is not a predetermined concept of "modernity" but rather the *discourse* about modernity.

The epochal consciousness that new times have dawned was not a sudden realization in Latin Christianity. The erosion of the Christian theology of history is a centuries-long process that commences with the urban revolution of the thirteenth century, which triggered far-reaching social and intellectual upheavals. Although in the Renaissance there is a perception of a break with the past, out of which the idea of a middle age or lifetime (*aetas media*) is developed, the idea of a "new age" remains alien. The transoceanic expansion of Europe beginning in the fifteenth century marks an important stage in the erosion process. Under the impression of the "discovery" of the Americas, Jean Bodin had already criticized the Christian teaching of the four kingdoms, which goes back to a prophecy in the book of Daniel. The newly discovered Aztec and Inca empires could no longer be fitted into the Christian teaching on the succession of world kingdoms (Babylonians, Persians, Alexander the Great, Romans), which through the *translatio imperii* doctrine was extended to include the

Christian kingdoms (Klempt 1960: 42–61). While the four kingdoms doctrine then experiences a revival in the Reformation, the Christian time horizon, namely the 6,000 years since the creation of the world and its impending end, is irreversibly prized open by the encounter with China, whose histographies burst the confines of the biblical division of time, and above all the advancements in geological knowledge. As a result of the erosion, a question crystallizes in Europe—in which age of the earth is humankind presently? It is in this context that, revealingly, Protestant church historians introduce the concept of the "new age" (*nova aetas*) in the seventeenth century (Jaeger 2009: 160). Concurrently, philosophy in the seventeenth century is permeated with the enthusiasm of a radical new beginning. Bacon, Descartes, and Hobbes all see themselves as the founders of a new thinking, instigating a radical break with tradition. Against this background, the idea of an open future, one that humans can shape and determine, becomes a main characteristic of a new historical consciousness that is at the same time a consciousness of a new or a modern age. In the eighteenth century, the sociocultural changes that have reverberated since the late Middle Ages are perceived retrospectively as the dawning of a "new age." As Reinhart Koselleck has shown, the epochal consciousness of the new age arises out of the overwhelming experience of the "new," which cleaves the traditional correlation between the "space of experience" and the "horizon of expectation":

> What was new was that the expectations that reached out for the future became detached from all that previous experience had to offer. Even the new experience gained from the annexation of lands overseas and from the development of science and technology was still insufficient for the derivation of future expectations. From that time on, the space of experience was no longer limited by the horizon of expectations; rather, the limits of the space of experience and of the horizon of expectations diverged.
>
> (Koselleck 2004: 266f.)

As Michel Foucault's reflections on Kant's essay "What is Enlightenment?" show, the traditional questions on the essence of humanity, truth, knowledge, and morality are joined by another—the interpretation of the present is elevated to a vital issue for philosophy. It is in the "Age of Enlightenment" that the question "What are we at present?" becomes the fulcrum of philosophical reflection, a thread that extends beyond the Kantian juncture: "Kant, Fichte, Hegel, Nietzsche, Max Weber, Husserl, Heidegger, the *Frankfurterschule*," notes Foucault, naming almost all the important European philosophies since the eighteenth century, "have tried to answer this question" (Foucault 1988: 145).

This reflection on the present's place in history is the very quintessence of the discourse about modernity, a discourse that, along with philosophy, several disciplines have taken part in, initially historical studies and then over the course of the nineteenth century the emergent social sciences and theories of culture.

In the eighteenth century, intellectuals in England and France interpreted their present—not modestly—as the dawning of an age of enlightenment or reason, an interpretation that scores of historians have since followed. Nonetheless, "enlightenment" cannot be simply identified with modernity; "enlightenment" is itself already a specific interpretation of the new age, meanwhile queried by historical studies (Pečar and Tricoire 2015). Even philosophical postmodernism, as Jean-François Lyotard explains while attempting to straighten out oversimplifying misconceptions, is not the proclamation of a new age *after* the modern one, but in fact criticizes specific promises and claims made by the earlier self-interpretation of the new age *as* an age of *enlightenment*:

> Postmodernity is not a new age, but the rewriting of some features claimed to be modernity, and first of all modernity's claim to ground its legitimacy on the project of liberating humanity as a whole through science and technology. But as I have said, that rewriting has been at work, for a long time now, in modernity itself.
>
> (Lyotard 1991: 34)

Interpreting the new age as an epoch of enlightenment was already disputed in the eighteenth century. When criticizing the Enlightenment, Rousseau and Herder were not taking aim at reason but at the excessive hopes or problematic constrictions of the historical processes of enlightenment in their age. By the time of Nietzsche at the latest, a rupture cleaves the discourse of modernity. In contrast to Marx, who criticized violence and exploitation in modern societies in the name of the ideals of the French Revolution, for Nietzsche "power" is no longer an irrational counterinstance *to* reason but itself anchored *in* the essence of reason. Thus, in the late nineteenth century the discourse of modernity splits into two main strands: aligned on one side are the proponents of theories of power which unmask "enlightened" reason, most prominently articulated in the mid-twentieth century by Heidegger, Horkheimer and Adorno, and then Foucault; aligned on the other side of this divide are attempts to present a self-critical defense of the heritage of the Enlightenment articulated by Apel and Habermas, Blumenberg and Taylor, to mention some prominent representatives. The frontlines between these two currents are by no means rigid. Because unsparing self-criticism is part of enlightened thinking, Nietzsche's critiques of morality and reason can also be understood as a radical version of enlightenment (Reschke 2004). Conversely, the defenders of the Enlightenment are not blind to the limits and dangers that the processes of modernization can have on societies.

While philosophical postmodernism continues to elaborate central motifs from the theories of power that are critical of modernity, a number of postmodern thinkers seek to avoid the rigid "power versus reason" standoff and trace instead constellations of plurality, difference, and alterity. In this spirit, Lyotard countered Kant's call for an autonomous use of reason with the fourfold imperative of postmodern thinking: "war on totality. Let us attest to the unrepresentable; let us activate the differends and save the honor of the name" (1992: 16). Richard Rorty took another path, and his critique of the universalist claims of enlightened reason led to a culturalist interpretation of Western modernity. The idea of human rights is for Rorty a contingent product of occidental culture that cannot be ultimately justified by the Platonic or Kantian idea of a rational subject. Although avowedly ethnocentric, Rorty rhetorically commends the human rights of other cultures that allow us to image a larger "we" (1998).

The discourse of modernity has not only attracted the voices of defenders and critics of modern Enlightenment. With colonial expansion, modernity became akin to a destiny for all peoples of the globe, and already in the nineteenth century the modernity discourse was transcending the boundaries of Euro-American philosophy. For a long period, the Asian, Latin American, and African discourses were hardly noticed in the centers of European philosophy. The voices of postcolonial thinkers gradually came into earshot only after the Second World War, as Europe's sense of superiority was deeply shaken, and large parts of Africa and Southeast Asia cast off the colonial yoke. In the 1960s, Jean-Paul Sartre turns to the texts of Frantz Fanon and the earlier political and literary current of *négritude*. In his preface to *The Wretched of the Earth*, Sartre emphasizes that the unheard element in Fanon's thought, its new tone, resides not in the critique leveled at modern Europe. Wearily Sartre notes that the self-critical diagnosis that "the country is done for" was a lament heard "almost every day since 1930" and never went beyond "emotional talk," a "threat followed by a piece of advice." Fanon's tone is different, however: "when Fanon says of Europe that she is rushing to her doom, far from sounding the alarm he is merely setting out a diagnosis" (Sartre 1963: 9). Indeed, what is emerging here with this more sober tone is an amalgamation of the cry for liberation with a new type of critical discourse, discernible in the shift of the addressee. As Sartre observes, Fanon "speaks of you often, never to you ... and speaks to the colonized only: 'Natives of all underdeveloped countries, unite!' What a downfall! For the fathers, we alone were the speakers; the sons no longer even consider us as valid intermediaries: we are the objects of their speeches" (Sartre 1963: 10).

As well as being an object of criticism for numerous intellectuals in the "third world," he was also an important discussion partner. His philosophy of freedom strongly influenced Fanon's thought. Nonetheless, his appreciation of how Europe was now an object of non-European philosophies identifies a significant change in the modernity discourse. Since the eighteenth century, whenever European philosophy crossed the boundaries marking out the occidental tradition, the direction was always historical, back to ancient traditions, both in strict rejection and in admiring recognition. One example of this was Confucian ethics, admired by Leibniz and Christian Wolff, while for Hegel they were nothing but popular morals, superficial without any philosophical substance. With Fanon, the entire setting changes and a discourse of self-understanding is initiated among the victims of colonialism. Picking up resonances with Fanon, Sartre notes that "the Third World finds *itself* and speaks to *itself*" (1963: 10). Due to the cultural and social fissuring of global society, philosophical texts, by thinkers in and outside Europe, cannot speak to everyone in the same way. Sartre's clear-sighted appraisal of these new rules of the discourse moved him to precisely determine the "place" of the speaker and the addressees in his writings on *négritude*. Acutely aware that the texts of Aime César, Frantz Fanon, and Léopold Sédar Senghor are not written for them, Sartre deliberately speaks *about négritude to* European readers. Crucially, Sartre's thought is thus no longer located in a specious universality. In effect, the emergence of an autonomous discourse within the (post-)colonial world compels a decentering of European philosophy. Europe can no longer be the exclusive gravity point for a global discourse about modernity.

The "third world" was, however, engaged in dialogue with itself long before Fanon, a fact that Sartre sidesteps. Already in the nineteenth century, currents of thought are arising in various regions of the world, which attempt to mediate between the challenges presented by European civilization and respective local cultural traditions. There is thus a whole host of non-European contributions to the "discourse about modernity"—the neo-Hinduist philosophies from Raman Mohan Roy through to Mahatma Gandhi, reformists in China since the late nineteenth century, the Kyoto School in Japan, the stirrings of philosophical reflection in the Islamic world after Napoleon's Egyptian campaign, and the tradition of a *filosofia americana* founded in the nineteenth century in South America. The modernity discourses of Asia, the Arab world, Latin America, and in more recent times Africa, have been generally ignored by European philosophy. Important intercultural dialogues were, though, initiated at the end of the nineteenth century and in the early twentieth. In 1883, Ernest Renan enters a much-acclaimed dialogue with Jamal al-Din al-Afghani (Norman 2011). The speech by Swami Vivekananda, the founder of the Ramakrishna mission, at the Parliament of the World's Religions in Chicago in 1893, and his subsequent lecture tours through the United States, attract enormous attention in Western societies. In 1913, Rabindranath Tagore becomes the first Indian to be awarded the Nobel Prize and then enters into dialogue with Albert Einstein. Within the framework of the League of Nations, important islands of global dialogue between philosophies surface in the Committee on Intellectual Cooperation, an initiative strongly supported by Paul Valéry and involving intellectuals from India, China, and Latin America (Valéry 1989). These incipient steps toward a global discourse about modernity are truncated by fascism and the east–west divide from 1945.

It is only after the end of the East–West conflict in 1989 that intercultural discourses intensify in Western philosophy. Over the last few decades several authors in German-speaking countries have sought contact with philosophers mainly in Asia, but also Africa and Latin America, forming a current known as "intercultural philosophy" (Fornet-Betancourt 1994; Mall 2000; Wimmer 2004). Overall, these "world philosophies" have meanwhile evolved into an important field of discourse in Euro-American philosophy.

A similar development is also observable in Western sociology, with Shmuel Eisenstadt and Johan P. Árnason lending vital impetus to the shift from a Eurocentric to an intercultural theory of modernity. In distinction from "classical" modernization theories, for Eisenstadt, the history of modernity can no longer be described merely as the spread of the cultural pattern inherent to European civilization since the fifteenth century. Instead, the different waves of globalization have produced multiple modernities, a process that began with the conquest of the two Americas (Eisenstadt 2000b: 83–5). The thesis of multiple modernities, as Eisenstadt and Árnason emphasize, is not blandly limited to empirical describable differences between modern societies in different regions of the world; it also involves the theoretical debates accompanying this process: "The appropriation by non-Western societies of specific themes and institutional patterns of original western modern civilization societies entailed continuous selection, reinterpretation, and reformulation of these imported ideas" (Eisenstadt 2000a: 15). The sociological version of civilization theory is therefore an important innovator for the intercultural reorientation of Western philosophy.

According to Ram Adhar Mall, at least four discourses need to be distinguished in the broad field of intercultural philosophy. "First is the way in which Europeans understand themselves. Second is the European understanding of non-Europeans. Third is the way in which non-Europeans understand themselves, and fourth is the way non-Europeans draw a picture of Europeans." The decisive change in the global dialogue between the philosophies stems from the last discourse type, as Mall notes in agreement with Sartre: "The fact that Europe itself is now an object of interpretation is quite astonishing, primarily, of course, for the European mind" (2000: 3).

The different discourses within intercultural philosophy are not strictly isolated from one another. The traumatic experiences of European colonialism are present in numerous self-understanding discourses of non-European philosophies. For this reason, self-understanding discourses within a specific culture can also become a source of inspiration for debates on identity in others. To name a prominent example: the *négritude* movement provided impetus for intellectuals in other regions of the Global South, to such an extent that a South–South dialogue has developed (Dussel 2015). Taking up a suggestion from Wimmer, the ideal vanishing point for an intercultural philosophy is polylog, i.e., as reciprocal dialogue between the philosophies of *all* regions of the world (Wimmer 2004: 66–73).

For a European, however, the self-understanding discourses of colonized peoples inevitably turn into a tribunal, a fact that Sartre had already noted. By articulating the trauma of colonial repression and the agonizing struggles by those repressed to regain their human dignity, the *négritude* authors plunge European readers into an abyss of deep shame: "By this steady and corrosive gaze, we are picked to the bone" and "I want you to feel, as I, the sensation of being seen" (Sartre 1976: 9f.). Sartre does, however, find a bonding potential here, for colonialism destroys not only the humanity of the victims but also that of the colonial masters, and thus Africans and Europeans face a common challenge, to rediscover human dignity: "We shall be able to rejoin the human hegemony only in tearing off our white underclothing and in attempting simply to be men" (Sartre 1976: 11).

This background to the various discourses enables us to now give a more precise definition of the "location" and trajectory of the present contribution to the global discourse of modernity. The studies on Renaissance and seventeenth-century philosophy can be conceived as part of a critical self-understanding discourse about European modernity that has emerged since Europe itself has become interpretable. However, as Hans Blumenberg rightly emphasizes, "talk of the 'legitimacy' of the modern age makes sense only to the extent that that legitimacy is disputed" (1983: 61). Blumenberg himself was defending the legitimacy of the modern age against Karl Löwith and Carl Schmitt, both of whom criticized the modern age as an illegitimate secularization of Christian theologies. As already mentioned, the legitimacy of this modern age as an age of enlightenment has been questioned by many currents of thought since the late nineteenth century. Early critical theory and Heidegger, taking up Nietzsche's thread, criticize modern reason in terms of a power syndrome that pervades all sectors of modern societies. Jürgen Habermas then takes a different tack, upholding the legitimacy of the European Enlightenment with a new theory of reason, specifically a theory of communicative rationality. At the same time, however, another front has opened and any attempt to defend the project of the Enlightenment is now the target of post- and decolonial philosophies. And, in fact, the ambivalences of modernity differ greatly depending on whether we are talking of highly industrialized zones or the Global South. This means in effect that the end of or the future completion of one single modernity can no longer be proclaimed from New York, Paris, or Frankfurt. The interpretation of European modernity must now be reconfigured, for it can only be determined when taking the long path of global intercultural dialogue.

Faced with this vast array of critical voices in and outside of Europe, any serious defense of the legitimacy of European modernity can deal only with a limited spectrum of the criticism. For this reason, I shall limit my considerations to a few pivotal motifs often encountered in twentieth-century Latin American philosophy, specifically the *historia de las ideas* movement, the philosophy of liberation, and decolonial thought.

As sketched above, since the nineteenth century Euro-American philosophy has seen the formulation of a triad of theories on modernity, respectively those inspired by the Enlightenment, those focusing on perceived innate power mechanisms, and, finally, those culturalist in orientation, with all three also present in the post- and decolonial discourses. These three paradigms of discourse each contain far-reaching implications for the relationship between Europe and other regions of the world. Theories drawing on the legacy of the Enlightenment, characterized by their claims to universality, exert enormous pressure on other cultures to imitate the European example. When pivotal ideas and institutions of European modernity, revolving around and stemming from discourses of human rights, democracy, and science, are in fact taken to be the result of an epochal Enlightenment process, then other cultures and nations are faced with a stark alternative—to either follow and complete in some way this European path of development or to stray from the path of reason. Power theories radically challenge the universalist claims of European modernity. Modern reason is no longer perceived as a medium emancipating humanity from impotent bondage to nature and premodern systems of domination, but as integral to a new logic of power, a logic that drives humanity into totalitarianism and ecological disaster. Culturalist theories in turn consider European modernity to be a singular civilization existing alongside others. Their vision is thus neither to Europeanize the world nor to radically negate the idea of Europe, striving instead to create conditions and relations conducive for the coexistence, based on legal equality and mutual recognition, of different civilizations.

Post- and decolonial theories appropriate pivotal motifs from the self-critiques of European modernity that focus on power or take a culturalist stance and integrate them into their critique of modern colonialism and imperialism. How non-European cultures are to interact with a modern Europe that has moved out of its colonial shadow is a question that has spawned a broad spectrum of perspectives, ranging from constructive exchange through to rigid isolation.

As serious as the suspicion of Eurocentrism may be with respect to the universal claims of the European Enlightenment, the power-oriented and culturalist theories of modernity are themselves not beyond criticism. Certainly, the unmasking of the forms of power at work in modernity opens the possibility for cultures outside of Europe to contribute accounts of the bitter experiences of colonial history and the inequalities of contemporary global society to the modernity discourse. On the other hand, the critical fixation on the power syndrome that has driven modernity, in which the ethics of human rights and the idea of a democratic rule of law are radically devalued, power theories and culturalist theories open the door to secular and religious forms of authoritarianism. Moreover, post- and decolonial philosophies are faced with the awkward question of the normative foundations behind their radical critique. If human rights and the idea of a democratic constitution are merely imports of "Western" culture, then the human rights movements in the South campaigning against fundamentalism, torture, and political terror are normatively on the same level as the authoritarian rulers. Thus, we seem to arrive at a standoff. Theories of modernity oriented in the Enlightenment are suspected of cultural imperialism, while culturalist theories of modernity appear to have a latent tendency toward moral relativism.

From this background it is possible to roughly outline the main thrust of the philosophical dimension of the present study. In the genesis of European modernity—and here I am in full accord with the defenders of the project of the

Enlightenment—significant epochal shifts toward a more rational interpretation of the world occur. The early modern era is most certainly not the first age of reason; enlightenment movements and currents had already existed in all axial civilizations, i.e., in the occident as well as China and India (Jaspers 1953: 1–21). Nevertheless, modern science and the dual ideas of constitutional democracy and human rights mark crucial epochal advances in rationality. At the same time, modern science and the political ideals of the Enlightenment, as various critiques of modernity since the nineteenth century have shown, are entwined with processes of power generating repercussions no less significant: the unleashing of technological power to dominate nature, the centralization and enlargement of the state and its bureaucracy, and colonial expansion.

Important currents of Euro-American philosophy have analyzed the ambivalences of European modernity, identifying the workings of a regressive dialectic in enlightenment or a partial and lopsided realization of its goals, or they have disclosed exclusivist power mechanisms in the name of reason's "other." To adequately describe the interweaving of advancements in rationality, power syndromes, and particularistic cultural or indeed even irrational aspects in European modernity, I intend to trace the lineaments of what I would like to term de-limitations (*Entgrenzungen*). Stated simply, my thesis is that the heterogenous aspects of European modernity emerge out of a multilayered complex process of various de-limitations, for which Copernicus and Columbus have remained the defining symbolic figures down to the present day.

The genesis of European modernity is determined essentially through a twofold de-limitation of space. The revolution in astronomy replaces the ancient notion of a limited cosmos with the idea of an infinite universe, while the voyages of Vasco da Gama and Columbus irreversibly breached the boundaries of the *oikumene*, i.e., the world known and considered inhabitable by Europeans. Because the classical ancient conceptions of the cosmos and the *oikumene* are closely tied to ontological, anthropological, political, and economic ideas, the early modern de-limitations of space spark a radical cultural revolution, which progressively engulfs, much like a domino effect, all areas of human life. In short, from the fourteenth through to the seventeenth century a complex play of de-limitations develops in European philosophy, with the intertwinement of advances in rationality, emerging power syndromes, and particularistic cultural visions impacting on all disciplines, from cosmology, anthropology, and ethics to political philosophy and economics. At the same time, the de-limitations of the cosmos and *oikumene* represent an important proprium of early modern thought in comparison to classical ancient and medieval traditions.

The three main parts of this study ensue from this backdrop. Serving as an introduction, Part I presents some paradigmatic interpretations of European modernity in the twentieth century which are oriented on Enlightenment ideals and power theories. For our purposes, they take precedence because they offer the perspective necessary for the philosophy of the Renaissance (Part II) and the early modern period (Part III). The first sketch in Part I is devoted to two fundamental critiques of modernity: the thought of Martin Heidegger, and Max Horkheimer and Theodor W. Adorno's *Dialectic of Enlightenment*. A second sketch then outlines a defense of the Enlightenment, namely the Frankfurt discourse theory of Jürgen Habermas and Karl-Otto Apel. The third and final sketch takes up motifs from contemporary Latin American philosophy, notable for the attempts to creatively fuse both these dimensions, the unmasking of power and the robust defense of Enlightenment-inspired modernity. The three sketches are a reconnaissance of the terrain, i.e., the explication of pivotal questions and problems in the philosophical discourse about modernity in recent decades.

The twofold revisiting of the historical origins of early modern thought then follows. With respect to the Renaissance (Part II), the example of Nicholas of Cusa shows how the de-limitation of the cosmos leads to an affirmation of limitless or *insatiable* curiosity, always a contentious issue in classical ancient and Christian thought. A brief inquiry into Pico della Mirandola then traces how the affirmative revaluation of humanity's creative power overcomes the teleological paradigm of philosophical anthropology. The third study looks at how the boundaries of the geographical–political worldview in classical antiquity and the Middle Ages are dissolved by the early modern voyages of discovery, which in turn serve to influence Francisco de Vitoria's vision of a new global cosmopolitanism, later expanded on by the debate between Ginés de Sepúlveda and Bartolomé de las Casas on the humanity of the "Indians." As the Renaissance ends, Michel de Montaigne lays the foundation for a type of modern subjectivity that stands apart from that of Descartes, i.e., without recourse to a *fundamentum inconcussum* nor relying on an anthropological dualism.

In Part III I will return to seventeenth-century philosophy, which since Hegel is often seen as the beginning of modern philosophy. Our interest here revolves around the genesis of the key ideas behind the main subsystems of modern societies, namely modern science, the territorial state, and the market economy. This theme of subsystems determines the authors chosen: Francis Bacon, Thomas Hobbes, and John Locke. Despite the rhetoric of the new beginning, all three thinkers remain under the influence of Renaissance philosophy. Thus, the motif complexes of the Renaissance—limitless universe, insatiable curiosity, creative freedom, global cosmopolitanism—enter, variously modified and in some cases dialectically inverted, into the early explications of the ideas steering the subsystems of modern societies. Bacon combines the notion of limitless curiosity about the world with the vision of an unleashing of the productive forces of humanity and nature; in his theory of the natural condition, Hobbes bases the founding of the modern state on the scenario of unfettered power relations; and Locke justifies the idea of a limitless economy. These *Leitideen* (guiding ideas) of modern science and technology, of the territorial state and of the market economy, are developed in the context of an emerging global society and hence the colonial expansion of Europe. Thus, the respective types of rationality are interwoven with power syndromes and particularistic/cultural elements in the guiding ideas of the subsystems.

The main thesis of this study on modernity can thus be encapsulated in the following formula: modernity is *at once* a process of enlightenment, a globally expansive power syndrome, and an ensemble of particularistic and cultural projects. To avoid the impasses of a naive defense of modernity as an age of enlightenment or to assume a radical antimodernist position, the heterogeneous aspects of European modernity need to be carefully differentiated despite their complex intertwining. The difficult and arduous task of precisely identifying and disentangling these heterogeneous aspects, which are still the signature of European modernity today, requires historical study. For Renaissance and early modern philosophy, the various de-limitations, merging into the idea of limitless progress in the eighteenth century, can be analyzed *in statu nascendi* with respect to their specific constitution as well as initial modifications and interconnections.

Part I

Reason, power, and coloniality: Three paradigmatic interpretations of modernity

1

Modern reason as syndrome of power: Martin Heidegger, Max Horkheimer, and Theodor W. Adorno

1.1 Martin Heidegger: the *ego cogito* as will to power

For the early Heidegger, modern science was still a legitimate mode of being-in-the-world, embedded in the practical caring relationship to the world of everyday being-there (*Dasein*) (Heidegger 1996: 326–33). The dictum "that science itself does not think and cannot think" (Heidegger 1968: 8) is not aimed at discrediting science as such, but at drawing attention to the peculiarity of philosophical thinking in contrast to the compartmentalization of the different disciplines of science. Heidegger's turn to a radical critique of modernity takes place in the context of Nietzsche's lectures in the late 1930s. After initially speculating on a transition to a different beginning for occidental thought in *The Age of the World Picture* (1938) Heidegger sees in Nietzsche the consummation of modern metaphysics, in which the essence of modern technology reveals itself to be the empowerment of the world (Zimmermann 2006: 98). This interpretation is then elaborated in Heidegger's writings on the philosophy of technology in the post-war years.

Heidegger's examination of modernity builds critically on Hegel. According to Hegel, the foundation of the modern world is the idea of a rational subject posited by Descartes, a subject that frees itself from the supports offered by religion and radically relies on an independent reason: "The principle of the modern world as such is freedom of subjectivity, the principle that all the essential aspects present in the spiritual totality are now coming into their right in the course of their development" (Hegel 2008: §272, addition). The freedom of subjectivity is the intellectual principle that sustains all areas of modern societies:

the right of subjective freedom, is the pivot and centre of the difference between antiquity and modern times. This right in its infinity is given expression in Christianity and it has become the universal principle ... effective principle of a new form of the world. Among the more specific shapes which this right assumes is love, romanticism, the quest for eternal salvation of the individual, etc.; next come moral convictions and conscience, and, finally, the other forms, some of which come into prominence in what follows as the principle of civil society and as moments in the constitution of state, while others appear in the course of history, particularly the history of arts, science, and philosophy.

(Hegel 2008: §124)

Like Hegel, Heidegger identifies Descartes to be the founder of the modern age. At the same time, however, when Heidegger identifies the major key in Descartes's thought, he devalues the emancipatory idea of a subjective freedom focused on the search for absolute certainty: "The question 'what is being?' is transformed into a question about the *fundamentum absolutum inconcussum veritatis*, the absolute, unshakable ground of truth. This transformation is the beginning of a new thinking, whereby the old order passes into the new and the ensuing age becomes the modern" (Heidegger 1982a: 97). The Cartesian subject is no longer the foundation stone for the development of modern freedom, as for Hegel, but the seat of a threatening power dynamic, which, once unleashed, manifests in various phenomena: in the compulsion to dominate inherent to modern science and technology; in how aesthetics has changed into expressive art; in value-based cultural politics; and, not least, in the de-deification of the world (Heidegger 2002: 70f.).

Descartes—and here Heidegger agrees with Hegel—initiates a radical disengagement of enlightened reason from religious authority, with the self-certainty of the modern subject supplanting the believer's certainty of salvation. The loss of authority suffered by religious orientations is not a specifically modern experience. Ancient philosophy also emerges out of a radical criticism of myths. However, as Heidegger sees it, modern thought reacts to how religious traditions have become questionable in a qualitatively different way than classical ancient philosophy. The modern human takes on the role of judge and lawmaker, placing humanity above all the rights and standards of tradition, and indeed nature as well, encapsulated in how Kant attributed the capacity of "self-legislation" to the rational subject: "If we say pointedly that the new freedom consists in the fact that man himself legislates, chooses what is binding, and binds himself to it, then we are speaking Kant's language; and yet we hit upon what is essential for the beginning of the modern age" (Heidegger 1982a: 97f.). The freedom opened by

Descartes becomes manifest in various determinations of what constitutes the essence of a human being, for example in Kant's law of reason, in the objectivity ideal of positivism, in the classicist idea of humanity, and in the self-assertion of the nation or the proletariat.

> The essence of the history of the modern age consists in the full development of these manifold modes of modern freedom. Because such freedom implies man's developing mastery over his own definition of the essence of mankind, and because such being master needs power in an essential and explicit sense, the empowering of the essence of power as fundamental reality can therefore become possible only in and *as* the history of the modern age.
>
> (Heidegger 1982a: 98)

For Heidegger, the idea of freedom, understood as gaining mastery over the self-given determination of essence, is the foundation of eighteenth- and nineteenth-century humanism. The power syndrome of the modern subject is already tangible in Descartes's *cogito*. Indeed, instead of *cogitare* Descartes at times uses the term *percipere*, which Heidegger derives from *per-capio*, i.e., "to take possession of a thing, to seize something in the sense of presenting-to-oneself by way of presenting-before-oneself, *representing*" (1982a: 104f.). Re-presenting implies, as Heidegger further explains, a commanding or mastering that aims at overcoming any uncertainty and ambiguity:

> *Cogitare* is the presenting *to* oneself of what is representable. In such presenting-to lies something definitive, namely, the necessity of a designation for the fact that the represented is not only generally pregiven but is also presented to us as available. The presented-to, the represented—*cogitatum*—is therefore something for man only when it is established and secured as that over which he can always be master unequivocally, without any hesitation or doubt, in the radius of *his own* power to enjoin.
>
> (Heidegger 1982a: 105)

In contrast to the astonishment of Greek philosophy, i.e., the wondering about what is manifesting, according to Heidegger, Descartes's doubt is "understood as essentially connected with the indubitable, with the undoubted and its securement" (1982a: 106). Doubt aims to arrive at a realm "whereupon thinking as deliberative doubting is at the same time 'finished' and the account is closed" (1982a: 106). Thus, modern thought finds its adequate expression in the program of the *mathesis universalis*: "The mathematically accessible, what can be securely reckoned in a being that man himself is not, in lifeless nature, is *extension* (the spatial), *extensio*, which includes both time *and* space" (Heidegger 1982a: 116).

The "decisively new" in Descartes's theory of the subject, in relation to premodern explications of self-consciousness, lies in how "this relation *to* the one who is representing and thereby the latter *as such* assumes a definitive role for what should and does come to pass in representation as the placing alongside of beings" (Heidegger 1982a: 108). For Heidegger, this marks nothing less than a momentous change to humanity's position in the cosmos: "The essential decision about what can be established as a being now rests with man as *subiectum*" (1982a: 121). Descartes's *cogito ergo sum* expresses a specific relationship between *cogitare* and *sum*: "It says that I am as the one representing, that not only is my Being essentially determined through such representing, but that my representing, as definitive *repraesentatio*, decides about the being present of everything that is represented; that is to say, about the presence of what is meant in it; that is, about its Being as a being" (1982a: 114). But Descartes's *ego cogito* is not the consequence of boundless hubris but rather the symptom of an epochal turn in the history of being: "Surely, we do not stand 'above' history, least of all 'above' the history of metaphysics, if it is really the essential ground of all history" (Heidegger 1982a: 149).

Although the technocratic will to power of the modern subject is traced back to the *techné* model of ancient philosophy, as Heidegger attempts to show in his interpretation of Protagoras' *homo mensura*, every effort must be made to avoid blurring the differences between ancient and modern thought. At first glance, Protagoras appears to anticipate the Cartesian subject. But for Heidegger this appearance is deceptive: "For in every essential respect, what determines the two fundamental metaphysical positions with equal necessity is different" (2002: 79). Despite its orientation on *technai*, Greek thought is still very much informed by the ethics of moderation based on the measure. Human beings do not posit the law themselves but receive the measure from what is manifesting: "For Protagoras, man is the measure of all things in the sense of a measured restriction to the radius of the unconcealed and to the boundaries of the concealed" (Heidegger 1982a: 122). In contrast, the human subject in Descartes is elevated to the measure of all being: "For Descartes, man is the measure of all things in the sense of the presumption of the de-limitation of representation for self-securing certitude" (1982a: 122).

Because, as for Hegel, the modern subject is the fundamental principle of the modern world as such, then the logic of power, already discernible in Descartes's *ego cogito*, penetrates into and pervades all areas of society, whether it be modern science or Kant's ethics: "The standard of measure is the presumption of measure, through which man is grounded as *subiectum* in and as the midpoint of beings as a whole ... the 'subject', which means that man is progressing toward a limitless representing and reckoning disclosure of beings" (Heidegger 1982a: 121). Indeed, because a will to disposing is always structurally inherent to re-presenting, the de-limiting of represented worlds triggers an unleashing of the human will to power on a planetary scale, i.e., "the institution of absolute dominion over the earth" (1982a: 117). The typical modern relationship that humanity has to things resides in "a domineering proceeding into the conquest and domination of the world" (1982a: 121), which, drawing on Nietzsche, can be described as the advent of the over-man: "in its absolute form the modern 'machine economy' ... the machine-based reckoning of all activity and planning, demands a new kind of man who surpasses man as he has been hitherto" (1982a: 116). The will to power inherent to the *cogito*, still concealed in Descartes's conception, now comes out into the open.

> What is happening here? Nietzsche refers the *ego cogito* back to an *ego volo* and interprets the *velle* as willing in the sense of will to power, which he thinks as the basic character of beings. *But what if the positing of this basic character became possible only on the basis of Descartes' fundamental metaphysical position?*
> (Heidegger 1982a: 129)

In Nietzsche's "will to power"—as Heidegger's central thesis would have it— the essence of the modern subject reveals itself and, along with it, modernity as a whole with all its social objectivations.

Heidegger had also traced the positive dimensions of Nietzsche's concept of power in his earlier deliberations, emphasizing for instance the play of power quanta and perspectivism; with the 1930s, however, the essential repressive feature of the will to power comes more and more to the fore as Heidegger explores nihilism and formulates a philosophy of technology: "The absolute essence of subjectivity necessarily develops as the *brutalitas* of *bestialitas*. At the end of metaphysics stands the statement *Homo est brutum bestiale*" (Heidegger 1982a: 148).[1]

In *Contributions to Philosophy*, written between 1936 and 1938 and published posthumously, Heidegger describes fully the "machinations" of modern reason, which elude any integration into overarching moral purposes: "Every kind of (transcendental) laying of foundations that stems from a theory of science has become as impossible as a 'meaning-conferral' which assigns an ethnic-political or any other anthropological purpose to the objectively present (and, in its essential content, thereby unalterable) science and its pursuit" (Heidegger 2012: 111). As if this were not grave enough, even modern morality is contaminated with the "aimlessness of the unconditional will to will ... which was incipient in Kant's concept of practical reason as pure will. Pure will wills itself, and as the will is Being" (Heidegger 2003: 101). For this reason, even reform-oriented movements remain imprisoned in the spirit of modern technology: "The counter movements to this metaphysics belong *to* it" (Heidegger 2003: 89). But without any positive reference to the universalist morality of modernity, then the criteria for a differentiated analysis of social relationships vanish. The ideological conflicts of the twentieth century descend into the undifferentiated sameness of the machinations driven on by the modern spirit. The consequences are dire. Because democracy and human rights are also incapable of evading the domineering clutches of the modern subject, in the 1930s Heidegger saw National Socialism as a countermovement to the nihilism of modern technology, and not as the spawn of the *bestialitas* of the modern subject.

In light of the history of being, overcoming modern technology is not however simply a matter resolved by a human decision, for technology "as an ordering revealing is ... no merely human doing" (Heidegger 1982b: 19). Thus philosophy has just one option: to prepare the passage to a different beginning of Western thought. The key notion now in Heidegger's "twisting" (*Verwindung*) of metaphysics and technology is the event (*Ereignis*), which is approached from a variety of angles, for example release (*Gelassenheit*), the fourfold (*Geviert*), and the mystery (*Geheimnis*). And then there is the significance of art, which as a mode of bringing-forth is especially close to technology (Zimmermann 1990: 222–47).

When all is shrouded in the mists of the universal power syndrome emanating from modern subjectivity, Heidegger inevitably fails to discern the differences between the technological domination of nature, the logic of economic utilization, and Kantian morality. Heidegger's thought thus reveals a dangerous blindness toward the emancipatory achievements of modernity, in particular democracy and human rights, which he continued to disparage even after 1945. At the same time, however, Heidegger expresses a sense of dread and dismay over the destructive power of modern science and technology, a concern which, given recent developments in human genetics, the ecological crisis, and the climate catastrophe, has lost none of its lucidity.

Elaborating on Hölderlin's dictum that "where the danger is, there grows the saving power," Heidegger then reapproaches the question of technology: "Accordingly, we must once more question concerning technology. For we have said that in technology's essence roots and thrives the saving power" (Heidegger 1982b: 29). Here Heidegger disengages somewhat from the mesmerizing spell of an interpretation of modernity based solely on a theory of power. With a view to Aristotle's *poieses*, Heidegger now contends that science and technology are concurrently "a way of revealing" and a "bringing-forth" (1982b: 12f.). The power character of modern science and technology remains indisputable. The revealing performed by modern technology is "a challenging [*Herausforderung*], which puts to nature the unreasonable demand that it supply energy," i.e., "toward driving on to the maximum yield at the minimum expense." Although "regulating and securing" still remain "the chief characteristics of the challenging revealing", as Heidegger now emphasizes, modern technology is still at least subliminally connected to ancient *poiesis*:

> The essence of technology is in a lofty sense ambiguous. ... On the one hand, Enframing challenges forth into the frenziedness of ordering that blocks every view into the coming-to-pass of revealing and so radically endangers the relation to the essence of truth. On the other hand, Enframing comes to pass for its part in the granting that lets man endure—as yet unexperienced, but perhaps more experienced in the future—that he may be the one who is needed and used for the safekeeping of the coming to presence of truth. Thus does the arising of the saving power appear.
>
> (Heidegger 1982b: 33)

Though modern technology "drives out other possibilities of revealing" and indeed even conceals "its own fundamental characteristic from appearing," it nonetheless "must harbour in itself the growth of the saving power" (Heidegger 1982b: 27f.), for a return to premodern forms of life is simply no alternative. Although discerning this ambiguity of modern technology, Heidegger fails to pursue it any further. On the contrary, the ambivalences of modern science and technology are themselves shrouded in the mists of the history of being and the prophecy it induces. In this way the lucidly diagnosed ambiguity of modern technology remains historically unexplained.

For a differentiated interpretation of modernity, two important perspectives crystallize out of Heidegger. Firstly, it is imperative to look candidly and unsparingly at the destructive dimensions of modernity without however denouncing its emancipatory potentials by relying on a holistic theory of power. Secondly, Heidegger's tentative mentioning of the ambivalent character of modern science and technology needs to be taken up and elaborated. Guided by this dual perspective, I aim to identify and examine in Francis Bacon's

1.2 Max Horkheimer and Theodor W. Adorno: *Dialectic of Enlightenment*

Early critical theory adopts a positive attitude toward science and enlightenment. In "Materialism and Morality" (1933) Max Horkheimer notes: "It is not the ideals of the bourgeoisie, but conditions which do not correspond to them, which have shown their untenability. The battle cries of the Enlightenment and of the French Revolution are valid now more than ever" (Horkheimer 1993a: 37). At this juncture, in contrast to Heidegger, Horkheimer identifies the crisis of science not in the power-fixated objectification of what exists, but in a complicity with the capitalist system: "At the present time, scientific effort mirrors an economy filled with contradictions. The economy is in large measure dominated by monopolies, and yet on the world scale it is disorganized and chaotic, richer than ever, yet unable to eliminate human wretchedness" (Horkheimer 1989: 56).

Just a few years later, however, in *The Authoritarian State* (Horkheimer 1978), the idea of such complete and thorough planning, once promising to overcome social anarchy, suddenly seems to epitomize instrumental reason. Together with Theodor W. Adorno, in *Dialectic of Enlightenment* Horkheimer then develops a radical critique of modernity, with science itself, and not solely the idea of a planned society, the target (Adorno and Horkheimer [1947] 2002; abbreviated *DE*). The bitter experiences of fascism and Stalinism had opened their eyes to the totalitarian character of a state apparatus based on modern science and technology: "The absurdity of a state of affairs in which the power of the system over human beings increases with every step they take away from the power of nature denounces the reason of the reasonable society as obsolete" (*DE*, 30f.). And because criticizing enlightenment is no longer to be left to its enemies, enlightened reason needs to prove itself when consideration is given "to the destructive side of progress" (*DE*, xvi). To be able to discern a moment of enlightenment amid seemingly total repression, Horkheimer and Adorno fall back on Hegel's thesis of the unity of reality and reason. Because fascism and Stalinism are the dialectical reversals of unfettered capitalism, the voice of objective reason is still audible even in the current regression to barbarism (Schmid Noerr 1997: 28). At the same time, with Marx, history remains open in its future trajectory. Despite all the excesses of power, the project of the Enlightenment must be continued: "We have no doubt—and herein lies our *petitio principii*—that freedom in society is inseparable from enlightenment thinking" (*DE*, xvi). Enlightened reason, once an instance of critical self-reflection, is disempowered in positivism and, recast as a value-free ascertainment of facts, rendered serviceable to terror. The positivistic reduction of modern reason is not a sudden aberration manifesting in modernity, however; it is in fact inherent to the earliest stages of modern science, specifically in the thought of Francis Bacon:

> Although not a mathematician, Bacon well understood the scientific temper, which was to come after him. The "happy match" between human understanding and the nature of things that he envisaged is a patriarchal one: the mind, conquering superstition, is to rule over disenchanted nature. Knowledge, which is power, knows no limits, either in its enslavement of creation or in its deference to worldly masters.
>
> (*DE*, 2)

For Horkheimer and Adorno, the main moments of positivistic science are already discernible in Bacon: contempt of tradition, calculability and utility as the criteria of knowledge, the glorification of discipline and power, the idea of universal science (*DE*, 3–5), and not least the *verum factum* principle, upon which the modern obsession with technological reproduction rests: "Enlightenment stands in the same relationship to things as the dictator to human beings. He knows them to the extent that he can manipulate them. The man of science knows things to the extent that he can make them" (*DE*, 6). The roots of this compulsion to master, evident in modern science, reach back beyond Bacon and are traceable to the Judeo-Christian religious tradition and Greek mythology: "In their mastery of nature, the creative God [of Christianity] and the ordering mind [of ancient philosophy] are alike. Man's likeness to God consists in sovereignty over existence, in the lordly gaze, in the command" (*DE*, 6). The example of Odysseus, who has himself bound to the mast of his ship to prevent himself from succumbing to the allure of the Sirens, shows how the rational subject is constituted through dominating inward and outward nature (*DE*, 24–8). The compulsion to master and dominate ultimately originates from archaic fear, which connects, for all their differences, the mythical age and modern civilization: "Enlightenment, understood in the widest sense as the advance of thought, has always aimed at liberating human beings from fear and installing them as masters" (*DE*, 1). Under the motto of "myth is already enlightenment" (*DE*, xviii), Horkheimer and Adorno transform the eighteenth-century philosophy of progress into a negative philosophy of history. As Turgot and Condorcet traced the beginnings of enlightenment back to the early times of humanity, in *Dialectic of Enlightenment* the power effects generated by enlightened thinking are discerned in Homeric myths. In short, Horkheimer and Adorno develop a negative philosophy of history in their critique of enlightenment—a philosophy, though, that itself threatens to turn into mythology (Schnädelbach 1989).

Conversely, the structures of mythical worldviews, as Horkheimer and Adorno attempt to show through numerous examples, return in modern science. The idea of a unified science mirrors mythical thinking about origins; the unity of discipline and power perpetuates the strictness of ritual and magic; unequal exchange reflects the sacrificial rite; the idea of natural laws echoes the mythical idea of the cyclical nature of all things (*DE*, 5–8). Insofar as a veil of stringent necessity is cast over the compulsions of a capitalist global economy, i.e., if there seems to be no viable alternative, then the spell of mythical fate itself recurs in a new form in modernity. In short, the thesis of the mythical origin of enlightenment needs to be complemented by a reversal, "enlightenment reverts to mythology" (*DE*, xviii).

Once positivism has relegated moral purpose to the realm of the subjective, the principle of self-preservation is now the sole orientation point of otherwise goalless rationality processes: "Spinoza's proposition: 'the endeavor of preserving oneself is the first and only basis of virtue' contains the true maxim of all Western civilization, in which the religious and philosophical differences of the bourgeoisie are laid to rest" (*DE*, 22). With nature stripped of all its qualities and the integration of reason into the *telos* of a good life suspended, the modern subject is compelled to engage in endless self-optimization, which now becomes an end in itself. But because this optimization merely serves to preserve and perpetuate the capitalist system, the eternal cycle of nature, once conjured in magic, rituals, and myths, returns in modernity: "Any attempt to break the compulsion of nature by breaking nature only succumbs more deeply to that compulsion. That has been the trajectory of European civilization" (*DE*, 9). According to Heraclitus, opposites are held together in tense unity by the *logos*, which remains obscure to the many: "They do not apprehend how being at variance it agrees with itself … there is a back-stretched connexion, as in the bow and the lyre" (KRS, fr. 212). In the same tenor and to the same effect, Horkheimer and Adorno posit enlightenment and myth as an indivisible unity: "The curse of irresistible progress is irresistible regression" (*DE*, 29). Or in Heraclitus' words: "The path up and down is one and the same" (KRS, fr. 203). In short, in so far as the capitalist system is envisaged as without alternative, then the citizens of modernity slip under a spell that, in its gravitational force, fully matches the pull exerted by belief in a mythical fate. In terms of Horkheimer and Adorno's intention, this unsparing exposure of the destructive force in progress is to prepare the way for a positive concept of enlightenment. Ultimately, however, Horkheimer and Adorno make do with vague suggestions. The dictum of a "remembrance of nature within the subject" (*DE*, 32) may mark the possibility of a radical reversal of the will to power by initiating a mimetic reconciliation with nature, whereby the contours of the self-empowered subject become blurred. The idea that humans can unify their inner natures with outward nature is nothing other, however, than the simplifying counterpart to a configuration of instrumental reason reduced to stifling purpose and suppressing drives. Whether the mimetic relationship to nature may even still be considered a figure of *reason* is questionable at the very least.

The preparation for a positive concept of enlightenment is hindered by another factor: the criticism of reason stemming from a theory of power is not solely directed against its positivistic perversion but also its argumentative performance, i.e., how this reason proceeds *per se*. Even the principle of an unbiased weighing up of different arguments is suspected of perpetrating the repressive amalgamation of the individual to the general: "The impartiality of scientific language deprived what was powerless of the strength to make itself heard and merely provided the existing order with a neutral sign for itself" (*DE*, 17). At this point, as Habermas has critically noted, *Dialectic of Enlightenment* threatens to become entangled in a performative self-contradiction. With argumentative reason now also inescapably embedded in the universal nexus of delusion, Horkheimer and Adorno seem to become entranced and "now want only to develop this aporia [of instrumental reason]," no longer seeking the means to "lead the way out" (Habermas 1990b: 68). Whether this is a cogent criticism is itself questionable, however, for at least in terms of their own intention, Horkheimer expressly acknowledges in a letter to Friedrich Pollock from May 1943 that argumentative reason is the ineluctable instance of enlightened self-criticism. "We have to understand this development and we can understand it only if there is something in us which does not submit to it. Such an attitude is shown in each of your discussion remarks, particularly when you are in a somewhat desperate defensive, but in no word of the two other interlocutors" (quoted from Wiggershaus 1994: 332).

The obvious question, *why* Horkheimer and Adorno refrain from integrating the structures of rational argumentation into an affirmative idea of enlightenment, directs our attention to a dubious premise of *Dialectic of*

Enlightenment. Without betraying the slightest trepidation at their proximity to conservative critics of enlightenment, Horkheimer and Adorno frankly admit that discursive reason systematically erodes the binding force of moral standards: "By virtue of its principle, enlightenment does not stop short at the minimum of belief without which the bourgeois world could not exist" (*DE*, 73). Because every form of devoutness is denounced as a regression to mythology, argumentative reason prepares the ground for an unleashing of power, and this occurs not only on the social but also the individual level: "The work of the Marquis de Sade exhibits 'understanding without direction from another'—that is to say, the bourgeois subject freed from all tutelage" (*DE*, 68). And indeed, that is barely the beginning, for Nietzsche and de Sade rightly "did not hush up the impossibility of deriving from reason a fundamental argument against murder, but proclaimed it from the rooftops" (*DE*, 93).

This means in effect that enlightenment, even *prior* to its reversal into positivism, did not possess the competence to provide moral orientation, for a materialist theory of reason can neither furnish a cogent argument against murder, nor offer a criterion for distinguishing moral from unmoral action. Materialism finds no transcendent authority over human beings which would distinguish between goodwill and the lust for profit, between kindness and cruelty, between avarice and self-sacrifice. Logic likewise remains silent and grants no pre-eminence to moral conviction. All attempts to ground morality in terms of temporal prudence rather than in terms of a view to a hereafter—as the cited examples show, even Kant did not always resist this inclination—are based on harmonistic illusions. First of all, in most cases morality and prudence diverge. Morality does not admit of any grounding—either by means of intuition or of argument (Horkheimer 1993a: 33).

Because a reason decoupled from religious and metaphysical horizons of meaning cannot furnish any moral standards itself, Horkheimer's criticism of modernity is based on pre- or trans-rational motifs. In the demystification of the world, Horkheimer and Adorno lament the loss of animism and the sacred: "There shall be neither mystery nor any desire to reveal mystery" (*DE*, 2). The rigor of scientific methodology suppresses freely wandering curiosity: "Power and knowledge are synonymous. For Bacon as for Luther" (*DE*, 2). The fear of the overwhelming and new is very much an essential feature of reason: "The arid wisdom [of Enlightenment] which acknowledges nothing new under the sun, because … all the great thoughts have been thought, *all possible discoveries can be construed in advance*, and human beings are defined by self-preservation through adaptation ... That is the verdict which critically *sets the boundaries to possible experience*" (*DE*, 8; emphasis mine).

The entwinement of myth and enlightenment returns in the resistance to the new because both make "the new appear as something predetermined which therefore is really the old" (*DE*, 21). With the spirit of positivist science pervading all areas of society, enlightenment produces a profound "impoverishment of thought no less than of experience" (*DE*, 28). The suppression of experiential possibilities is exacerbated by the fateful alliance between science and capitalism: "The elimination of qualities, their conversion into functions, is transferred by rationalized modes of work to the human capacity for experience, which tends to revert to that of amphibians" (*DE*, 28). The compulsions produced by the ever-advancing division of labor and automated processes of production threaten to strangle individual freedom, without which it is impossible to conceive of experience even intellectually. In the end, people regress to "mere examples of the species, identical to one another through isolation within the compulsively controlled collectivity" (*DE*, 29). The dominant system produces in the masses an "inability to hear with their own ears what has not already been heard, to touch with their hands what has not previously been grasped" (*DE*, 28). It is in this context that the grim and rigorous conclusion is drawn: "For enlightenment is totalitarian as only a system can be" (*DE*, 18).

The systematic repression of new experiences continues unimpeded in the area of morality, which has always forced humans into controlling their passions and limiting their needs. Moderateness was elevated to the measure of morality as early as the *mesotes* teaching in antiquity, i.e., "nothing in excess." But even modern hedonism has failed to overcome the impoverishment of affects and emotions.

> Its hedonism was moderate, extremes being no less repugnant to enlightenment than to Aristotle. The bourgeois ideal of naturalness is based not on amorphous nature but on the virtue of the middle way ... By subordinating life in its entirety to the requirements of its preservation, the controlling minority guarantees, with its own security, the continuation of the whole. From Homer to modernity the ruling spirit has sought to steer between the Scylla of relapse into simple reproduction and the Charybdis of unfettered fulfillment; from the first it has mistrusted any guiding star other than the lesser evil.
>
> (*DE*, 24)

This means that Horkheimer and Adorno confront the ancient ideal of conducting life based on reason with the vision of a hedonistic de-limitation of needs, morality with the idea of experimental ways of living wherein rational criteria, such as the principle of the lesser evil, are denounced as illegitimate limitations. On the ontological level, the unfettered fulfillment of hedonist ways of life corresponds to the notion of a wild, chaotic nature, its immanent plurality yet to be tamed and grinded down by civilizing interventions.

As Horkheimer and Adorno repeatedly try to demonstrate, the plurality and wild savageness of nature has been maimed by the civilizing will to establish order for thousands of years. In particular the concept (*Begriff*), the "idea-tool" of instrumental reason, "separates the world, as something chaotic, multiple, and disparate, from that which is known, single, and identical"; in effect—and quite literally—it is a tool that "fits into things at the very point from which one can take hold of them" (*DE*, 31). It is solely in mimetic remembrance that nature returns as a presence, albeit mutilated: "In mind's self-recognition as nature divided from itself, nature, as in prehistory, is calling to itself, but no longer directly by its supposed name, which, in the guise of *mana*, means omnipotence, but as something blind and mutilated" (*DE*, 31). On the basis of such a holistic concept of nature, both rational subordination and mimetic reconciliation appear as self-relations of nature: "Enlightenment is more than enlightenment, it is nature made audible in its estrangement" (*DE*, 31).

In summary, we may say that Horkheimer and Adorno gauge enlightenment as twofold, in the light of an idea of an archaic merging with nature (mimesis) or the dissolution of the subject, and in the anticipation of a utopia, the glimmer of a potentially unlimited plurality of relations to the world. The destructive drive in enlightenment is paradoxically unmasked through a complex of transrational motifs, with an emphatic longing for the new, a secular sympathy for the sacred, an excessive hedonism, and an experimental practice of ways of living coming together to form a unity, one as dubious as it seems dazzling. But precisely here is where the serious questions need to be posed as to the genealogy of the normative instances deployed to criticize enlightenment. The affirmation of plurality and openness, as well as the option for de-limiting needs and extending passions, hardly stem from the spirit of archaic societies. The affirmation of limitless curiosity about the world is, as Hans Blumenberg has shown, a specifically modern achievement (Blumenberg 1983: 229–453). The unfettering of needs, as Horkheimer and Adorno themselves indicate, still alien to Epicurus, is first elevated to a condition for creating new ways of life in modern hedonism. Against this background, a strong, almost irrepressible suspicion crystallizes—that Horkheimer and Adorno criticize modernity in the light of motifs drawn from modernity itself, which, however, under the spell of their own fixation on power, are not identified and remain truncated at source. The potential self-contradiction of their critique marks, unwillingly, an extremely important signpost to be followed. Modernity is more than simply a rationalization process; it contains motifs that are trans- and irrational. The idea of an experimental practice in ways of living, whereby rational criteria are consciously suspended, probably, as Horkheimer and Adorno indeed concede, no longer "communicates with the utopia contained in the concept of reason" (*DE*, 73). This means that in their tracing of the dialectic of enlightenment Horkheimer and Adorno seek to prepare the way not only for a positive concept of enlightenment, but also for an integral idea of modernity, one in which trans- and irrational motifs are assigned constitutive importance. In the retrospective on the philosophy of the Renaissance in Part II of this book we will pick up the threads of a genealogy of the non-rational dimensions of modernity, which are seemingly inextricably tied to processes of rationalization.

2

The Enlightenment as an unfinished project: Karl-Otto Apel and Jürgen Habermas

The totalitarian systems and extreme violence of the twentieth century profoundly shook, but did not completely strangle, Enlightenment-inspired hopes for an age of reason. On the contrary: victory over the Nazi regime and imperial Japan, the economic recovery after 1945 and the boom that followed, as well as the establishment of stable democracies in West Germany, Austria, Italy, and Japan, breathed new life into the political ideals of the Enlightenment. In 1949, addressing the United States Congress, President Truman proclaimed an age of development, an ideal that also addressed the hopes of the Global South for a viable future. A new optimism and belief in progress was also pervading the social sciences, which Gunnar Myrdal had sensed and diagnosed even before the Second World War came to an end: "The world catastrophe places tremendous difficulties in our way and may shake our confidence to the depths. Yet we have today in social science a greater trust in the improvability of man and society than we have ever had since the Enlightenment" (1944: 1024).

In post-war European philosophy, particularly in Germany, where Heidegger and Adorno dominated debates, the radical critique of progress continued to prevail. At the same time, the new upsurge in the fortunes of democratic processes and economic growth in the post-war years could less and less be construed to fit in with Heidegger's critique of the modern subject and Adorno's negative philosophy of history. Against this background, Karl-Otto Apel and Jürgen Habermas committed themselves to defending the Enlightenment project. In addition to the radical critique of Heidegger and Adorno, Apel and Habermas saw the heritage of the Enlightenment also threatened by political ideologies and diverse philosophical tendencies.

According to Habermas, the Enlightenment ideal of deliberative democracy is undermined by neoconservative ideologies and sociological theories of modernization. Neoconservatism traces the pathologies of advanced societies back to cultural modernity. While public criticism voiced by intellectuals corrodes the stability of institutions, the cosmopolitanism of the Enlightenment erodes the mores and customs of nations. The repression of a reflective-critical position toward social institutions goes hand in hand with a fatalistic acceptance of the internal dynamics driving capitalist market economies and the concentration of power in the modern administrative state. From a neoconservative perspective, "a self-sufficiently advancing modernization of society has separated itself from the impulses of a cultural modernity that has seemingly become obsolete in the meantime; it only carries out the functional laws of economy and state, technology and science, which are supposed to have amalgamated into a system that cannot be influenced" (Habermas 1990b: 3). But the modernization theories formulated in the post-war period, which presented technocratic models to accelerate the development of science, technology, and market economies, making them implementable for the states of the Global South, also have a corrosive effect on the emancipatory ideals of the Enlightenment. The theory of modernization "dissociates 'modernity' from its modern European origins and stylizes it into a spatio-temporally neutral model for processes of social development in general" (Habermas 1990b: 2).

Apel and Habermas saw the project of Enlightenment also challenged by contradictory currents in philosophy, namely postmodernism, post-structuralism, and neo-positivism. In the direct lineage from Nietzsche and Heidegger, philosophical postmodernism unmasks the power machinations seemingly inherent in modern reason (Habermas 1990b: 83–105; Apel 1996b). In contrast, neo-positivist philosophies elevate the objectivity ideal of modern science to the standard for all forms of human knowledge. In both cases, the enlightened idea of a universally valid, rational morality is dismissed.

With Apel, we find ourselves in a paradoxical problem situation. Given the consequences and side effects of modern science, technology, and economics, which impact on all humans and meanwhile even threaten the earth's biosphere, a rational macro-ethics is the need of the hour. At the same time however, numerous philosophies have been calling into question the universality of ethical reason since the early twentieth century, from existentialism, phenomenology and hermeneutics through to older versions of Critical Theory and postmodern, post-structural, neo-pragmatic, and finally postcolonial approaches. Ethics now has more to do with feelings, subjective decisions or culturally conditioned preferences. In short: the liberal West is snared in an ideological complementarity system between value-free procedural rationality in science and politics and a prerational decisionism in private and public life (Apel 1996a: 1–4; 2001: 27–38).

This background enables us to define more closely the core themes in the theories of modernity formulated by Apel and Habermas. Starting from a communicative transformation of modern subject philosophy, they delineate the contours of an Enlightenment-inspired theory of modern societies and place Kantian rational morality on new ground. This constellation is intended to avert a renewed regression into barbarism while at the same time consolidating the historically achieved level of reason through philosophical reflection.

2.1 Enlightened society based on communicative reason: social differentiation and the rationalization of the lifeworld

With a critical side-glance toward older critical theory, Habermas sees his voluminous *Theory of Communicative Action* as "the beginning of a social theory concerned to validate its own critical standards" (1984: xxxix). The concept of communicative rationality is to identify and explicate the standpoint of reason, ultimately left obscure by Horkheimer and Adorno, from where it is possible to exercise a *rational* critique of the destructive features of modern Enlightenment.

To begin, Habermas identifies the structures of communicative rationality in everyday practical life, more precisely in those situations where "the actions of the agents involved are coordinated not through egocentric calculations of success but through acts of reaching understanding" (Habermas 1984: 285f.) For Habermas, the process of understanding is composed of interactions through which the participants come "to an agreement concerning the claimed validity of their utterances, that is, through intersubjectively recognizing the validity claims they reciprocally raise" (Habermas 1984: 99). With the validity claims to truth, rightness, and sincerity, the speech actors are simultaneously referring to three "worlds," namely the objective world of facts, the social world of legitimately regulated intersubjective relationships, and the subjective worlds to which each has privileged access (Habermas 1984: 100). Communicative actions do not produce understanding *ex nihilo*, but are performed against the background of the lifeworld, the horizon of which is only intuitively known by the actors, i.e., it evades a complete objectification while still containing a culturally ingrained preunderstanding (Habermas 1984: 100).

However, "when disagreements can no longer be repaired with everyday routines," then "the rationality proper to the communicative practice of everyday life points to the practice of argumentation as a court of appeal that makes it possible to continue communicative action with other means"

(Habermas 1984: 17f.). This means that "the rationality inherent in this practice is seen in the fact that a communicatively achieved agreement must be based in the end on reasons" (Habermas 1984: 17). Since "being susceptible of criticism and grounding" (Habermas 1984: 9) is a pivotal attribute of rationality, then for Habermas we may speak not only of communicative actions but also of a communicative rationality, which proves itself in the argumentative and consensus-oriented fulfillment of validity claims.

The relations to the world and the validity claims of communicative reason emerge first in their full plurality and uniqueness in modernity, arising out of attempts to overcome the "world pictures" conceived in ancient mythology and the Axial Age (Jaspers 1953). The theory of communicative action is thus embedded in a macro-sociological theory of the history of humankind, recently complemented by a comprehensive history of philosophy (Habermas 2019).

A "world picture" (*Weltbild*) in the general sense arises when people step out of their everyday routines and create a "picture" about the whole of the everyday world and themselves. In a far-reaching and certainly contestable thesis, Habermas claims that when constructing world pictures, an objectifying totalization of the lifeworld background, by definition not objectifiable, takes place (Habermas 1984: 469).

In mythological world pictures, the structures of communicative action are projected unfiltered on to the objective world, with nature itself then appearing to be a network of interactions between humans and supernatural powers. In magical action, through which humans attempt to influence the spirits, communicative understanding and an instrumental morale, or nature and culture, are therefore mingled together (Habermas 1984: 470). This means that "in mythical thought diverse validity claims, such as propositional truth, normative rightness, and expressive sincerity, are not yet differentiated" (Habermas 1984: 50).

It is first in the world pictures of the Axial Age, i.e., the period when the dominant philosophies and world religions arose in India, China, and the Occident, that the horizontal world of myth, wherein human and superhuman powers clash, is supplanted by a transcendent principle, whether the ontological being of Greek philosophy, Tao in China, or the otherworldly god of the Judeo-Christian tradition (Habermas 2019: 1.464f.). The Axial Age movements initiate an epochally significant desacralization of nature and politics, so that the incipient stages of a differentiation process between a theoretical observation of nature and practical reason become discernible. But because the ideas of transcendence are bound to specific salvation doctrines, in which the world appears as the manifestation or creation of a transcendent principle, the world pictures of the Axial Age remain stuck halfway in the objectification of the world (Habermas 2019: 1.466). Habermas comes to this conclusion because in his post-metaphysical thought, the evaluative contents of nature are nothing other than projections of the lifeworld, through which the reality of the universe, in itself qualityless, is presented as a place habitable for humans.

Starting from the various ideas of transcendence, significant steps toward an objectification of nature and a post-conventional morality are initiated in the Axial Age. But due to the union with specific salvation doctrines, intellectual awakening remains confined within a dogmatic mode of thought (Habermas 2019: 1.474). In addition, the breakthroughs to an ethical universalism are constrained, painfully, through ongoing affiliation to specific religious communities (Habermas 2019: 1.470).

Against this background, Habermas interprets modernity as overcoming the metaphysical and religious world pictures of the Axial Age. With the dissolution of the religious-metaphysical ideas of transcendence, the Enlightenment also leaves behind the dogmatism of the Axial Age movements: "modern modes of thought do not recognise any such preserves, any such exemptions from the critical power of hypothetical thought, either in ethics or in science" (Habermas 1984: 214). But what is of even more importance is how the Enlightenment sees through the Axial Age projections of the non-objectifiable horizon of the lifeworld on to the world at large—this enables the unfettered differentiation of validity claims and formal worlds of communicative action in modernity:

> Reason has split into three moments—modern science, positive law and post-traditional ethics, and autonomous art and institutionalized art criticism ... the sons and daughters of modernity have progressively learned to differentiate their cultural tradition in terms of these three aspects of rationality such that they deal with issues of truth, justice, and taste discretely rather than simultaneously. At a different level, this shift toward differentiation produces the following phenomena: (1) The sciences disgorge more and more elements of religion, thus renouncing their former claim to being able to interpret nature and history as one whole. (2) Cognitivist moral theories disgorge issues of the good life, focusing instead strictly on deontological, generalizable aspects of ethics, so that all that remains of "the good" is the just.
>
> (Habermas 1990b: 17)

Through the differentiation of the validity claims of communicative action and their institutional objectification in value spheres (science, morality, law, and art), in which expert cultures form in turn, a consolidating learning process begins, which for Habermas amounts to an epochally significant "increase in rationality" in modernity (Habermas 1987: 145). The gains in rationality are the result of advances in learning, which, as Habermas emphasizes, are not to be elevated into the idea of a necessary and irreversible progress, and to which visions philosophies of history had succumbed in the eighteenth century (Habermas 1987: 383).

With the differentiation of the value spheres, which form "cultural modernity," the process of modern Enlightenment is not yet completely delineated, however. The rise of capitalist economies and administrative states spawn social systems in which the coordination of action no longer takes place primarily through communicative reason but is subject to media-steered interactions: "Steering media such as money and power attach to empirically motivated ties. They encode purposive-rational dealings with calculable amounts of value and make it possible to exert generalized strategic influence on the decisions of other participants while bypassing processes of consensus formation in language" (Habermas 1987: 180–1).

The interactions in the systems of the market economy and the administrative state do not abstract from language itself but relieve the interactions of the complicated processes involved in gaining the consensual fulfillment of the validity claims made by communicative reason:

> Delinguistified media of communication such as money and power, connect up interactions in space and time into more and more complex networks that no one has to comprehend or be responsible for. If by "responsibility" we mean that one orients one's actions to criticisable validity claims, then a "deworlded" coordination of action that is unhinged from communicatively established consensus does not require that participants be responsible actors.
> (Habermas 1987: 184)

The rise of the market economy and the modern administrative state can therefore be described as an "uncoupling of system and lifeworld" (Habermas 1987: 153–89).

Of crucial importance here is to note that, for Habermas, the rise and seemingly inexorable growth of a capitalist economy and a modern administrative state do not yield an irrational instance erupting in modernity; modern subsystems can be understood as institutional objectifications of purposive rationality which serve the material reproduction of the lifeworld (Habermas 1987: 138–45; cf. Habermas 1990b: 350). Moreover, the legal framework conditions upon which the administrative state and market economy are constitutively reliant are accessible to public criticism.

At the same time, however, Habermas—herein following the older generation of critical theorists—does not leave it to the enemies of Enlightenment to criticize the destructive elements of progress. Indeed, Habermas believes that two major criticisms pertaining to modernity, the loss of meaning and reification, can be reformulated within the scope of his theory of communicative action without succumbing to antimodernist biases.

The loss of meaning is not simply the consequence of value-free science, as Habermas emphasizes contrary to Weber and Husserl—it stems rather from how the cultures of expertise have become increasingly decoupled from the everyday world. When traditions are solely devalued and no longer regenerated, then despite spectacular gains in rationality, the lifeworld is culturally impoverished. By calling for expert cultures to remerge with the lifeworld, Habermas is evoking the project of eighteenth-century Enlightenment. While this project basically facilitated the development of science, morality, and art "in accord with their own immanent logic," at the same time it also "results in releasing the cognitive potentials accumulated in the process from their esoteric high forms and attempting to apply them in the sphere of praxis, that is, to encourage the rational organization of social relations" (Habermas 1997: 45).

In light of our contemporary situation, however, the extravagant hopes for progress held by the eighteenth-century thinkers, namely "that the arts and sciences would promote not only the control of natural forces, but also interpretations of the world and of ourselves, moral progress, the justice of social institutions, even the happiness of humankind," most certainly need to be met with skeptical sobriety, for the experiences of the twentieth century have "left little of this optimism intact" (Habermas 1987: 326). The goal of progress cannot be the attainment of happiness for humankind but, more modestly, a certain rationalization of our lifeworld:

> The vanishing point of these evolutionary trends are: for culture, a state in which traditions that have become reflective and then set aflow undergo continuous revision; for society, a state in which legitimate orders are dependent upon formal procedures for positing and justifying norms; and for personality, a state in which a highly abstract ego-identity is continuously stabilized through self-steering.
>
> (Habermas 1987: 146)

Because the systems of market economies and bureaucratically burdened administrative states are not harmoniously integrable into the life of modern societies, the modern rationalization process leads, secondly, to a reification of communicative everyday practice: "the rationalization of the lifeworld makes possible a heightening of systematic complexity, which becomes so hypertrophied that it unleashes system imperatives that burst the capacity of the lifeworld they instrumentalize" (Habermas 1987: 155). The tendencies of the subsystem imperatives to colonize the lifeworld (Habermas 1987: 318) threaten this defense of the Enlightenment project, for the question now is "whether the rationalization of the lifeworld does not become paradoxical with the transition to modern societies. The rationalization of the lifeworld makes possible the emergence and growth of subsystems whose independent imperatives turn back destructively upon the lifeworld itself" (Habermas 1987: 186).

To ward off the danger of modernity consuming itself through the differentiation of decoupled subsystems, Habermas brings two normative categories into play. A critical theory of society is dependent, firstly, on the criterion of an intact lifeworld, without which "increases in complexity achieved at the expense of a rationalized lifeworld cannot be identified as costs" (Habermas 1987: 186). From a sociological perspective, the lifeworld appears as a "subsystem that defines the pattern of the social system as a whole. Thus, systematic mechanisms need to be anchored in the lifeworld: they have to be institutionalized" (Habermas 1987: 154).

Secondly, Habermas counters the self-destructive tendencies of modern societies with the idea of a balance between lifeworld, value spheres, and subsystems: "The yardstick thus used intuitively to measure the deformation of forms of life consists of the idea of the free interplay of the cognitive-instrumental with both the moral-practical and the aesthetic-expressive, within an everyday practice which must be open to an uninhibited and balanced interpenetration of cognitive interpretations, moral expectations, expressions and valuations" (Habermas 1991: 225f.).

Accordingly, pathologies break out in modernity not because of a dialectic of "the" Enlightenment *per se*; they express rather the deviations of an imbalance, "the one-sided rationalization, and the preponderance of one complex of rationality, to the uneven exploitation of the resources for rationality made available culturally" (Habermas 1991: 225). The idea of an equilibrium between value spheres and subsystems emerged already in the eighteenth century, as "*an appearance of posttraditional everyday communication* suggested by the structures of the lifeworld," which however was still limited to the bourgeois class. Nevertheless, "*this* utopia *of reason, formed in the Enlightenment,* … was [already], so to speak, a transcendental apparition, determining bourgeois ideology, while yet surpassing it. In it, communication was represented as standing on its own feet, setting limits to the inner dynamics of autonomous subsystems, bursting encapsulated expert cultures, and thus as escaping the combined threat of reification and desolation" (Habermas 1987: 329).

The normative ideas of an intact lifeworld and a balance between subsystems and value spheres are criteriologically extremely vague. As Karl-Otto Apel has noted, an empirical concept of the lifeworld cannot support the universal claims of an Enlightenment-inspired idea of modern societies (1992). But the notions of a balance between value spheres and subsystems are also dependent to a high degree on culturally conditioned interpretations of nature and culture (Kettner 1995: 98). Moreover, the question arises as to whether morality, science, art, economics, and politics, i.e., the components which have to be balanced, can be interpreted merely as the institutionalization of different types of rationality.

Against this background, David Owen, among others, has criticized Habermas for his "Eurocentric bias" (2002: 246; see also Jamme 1991: 148f.). Habermas has responded to the criticism of Eurocentrism. In the postcolonial age, he concedes, his post-metaphysical theory of modernity must also be defended within the scope of a global intercultural dialogue (Habermas 2019: 1.111). In this context, Habermas draws on Árnason's civilization theory, according to which current global society can be pertinently described neither in terms of the advancing globalization of European modernity, nor as merely a clash between different civilizations. For Árnason, rather, modernity is

> a civilizational formation sui generis, both more and less than a civilization in the more conventional sense: the modern constellation is marked by civilizational traits which distinguish it from its historical background and constitute an effective challenge to all preexisting civilizational identities, but it is also in some degree adaptable to civilizational contexts which differ more or less radically from its original source.
>
> (Árnason 2003: 42)

On this basis, Árnason formulates a theory of multiple modernities, going beyond the ideas of both Fukuyama and Huntington: "Civilizational frameworks, more or less selectively reconstructed and pragmatically readjusted, can serve to legitimize modernizing projects and mobilize social support for them, without translating into sustainable variants of modernity" (Árnason 2003: 43). As Habermas expressly admits, Árnason's civilization theory opens the possibility "to correct a certain constriction of the *Theory of Communicative Action* through evolution theory" (Habermas 2019: 1.118, note). In contrast to Árnason, however, Habermas distinguishes among three levels in his theory of global modernity: global system mechanisms, especially the triad of capitalism, modern science, and technology, and the bureaucratic state; the identity discourses referring to the traditions of axial civilizations; and a post-metaphysical normative setting that enables the political ideals of European Enlightenment (democracy, human rights, and the law of nations) to be applied to global modernity through cross-cultural discourses (Habermas 2019: 1.118–20). Although the mention of cross-cultural discourses broadens the perspective to philosophies outside Europe, several important questions remain open in Habermas's normative theory.

Firstly, Habermas's theoretical architectonic begs the question if these three levels of global modernity can even be strictly separated. Árnason, at any rate, seems to undermine the dichotomy between system imperatives and cultural patterns:

> a civilizational approach assumes that cultural premises are relevant to the autonomization of economic and political processes; the operative cultural definitions have to do with visions of mastery over nature as well as with new horizons of institutional differentiation, and they call for broader and more complex interpretations than those involved in traditional accounts of the spirit of capitalism or ideas behind the modern state.
>
> (Árnason 2003: 42f.)

This means that the codes or *Leitideen* (guiding ideas) of modern value spheres or subsystems are not merely the result of an anonymous process of functional differentiation; rather, they arise out of epochal cultural changes reflected and promoted by philosophies. From this point of view, the at times sweeping reproach of Eurocentrism leveled at Habermas's theory of modernity can be made specific: ultimately, the decisive question boils down to whether the value spheres and subsystems may be interpreted as the institutionalization of rationality types or are other power syndromes and even particularistic cultural factors already embedded in the *Leitideen* of modern science, morality, politics, and economics.

The second question revolves around the universal validity of the normative core of post-metaphysical thought, i.e., the rational morality which, according to Habermas, continues the political ideals of the Enlightenment but also lays the foundation for intercultural discourses. Habermas sees the rational morality of Enlightenment, in discourse ethics liberated of residual metaphysics and reformulated, as the result of an occidental learning process that is offered to and shall serve other cultures. For this reason, Habermas has deliberately reviewed the question of the normative premises for peaceful coexistence in a multicultural world in a monological, i.e., inner-European, thought experiment

(Habermas 2019: 1.110–35). The problem of Eurocentrism in Habermas's thought therefore leads inevitably to an engagement with discourse ethics, which form the normative foundation of his theory not only of modern societies but of modernity overall.

2.2 The reconstitution of the Kantian idea of ethical reason: the project of discourse ethics

Discourse ethics was established by Karl-Otto Apel and Jürgen Habermas in the early 1970s (Apel 1996a; Habermas 1990a) and subsequently developed in a variety of directions by the founding fathers and other thinkers (Niquet 2002: 42–116; Gottschalk-Mazouz 2000). There is therefore not one discourse ethics but several distinct variations, some of them extremely controversial. Although, despite key differences, they together refined and extended discourse ethics, even Apel and Habermas irreconcilably parted ways after the latter's work *Between Facts and Norms* (1996).

Despite all the controversies, the different variations of discourse ethics are all involved in the same project: the transformation of Kant's cognitive and deontological ethics, with the fulcrum for this transformation being the reformulation of the categorical imperative into a dialogical principle of universalization. While for Kant the individual reviews the suitability of maxims to function as laws in an inner monologue, employing the categorical imperative as the criterion, discourse ethics postulates that all norms and interests are to be tried and tested in real practical discourses (Apel 2001: 55–65). Discourse ethics thus revolves around "the regulative principle of striving for a solution (of moral problems) that could be acceptable by a consensus of all affected persons as possible partners" (Habermas 1990a: 54). It is from this perspective that Habermas encapsulated the distinctive idea of discourse ethics "in the Principle of Discourse (D)", i.e., that "only those norms can claim to be valid that meet (or could meet) with the approval of all affected in their capacity as participants in a practical discourse" (Habermas 1990a: 66). As distinct from Kant, who anchors the moral quality of actions solely in good will, discourse ethics attempts to integrate the valid objective of utilitarianism into deontological ethics, that is, to take into consideration the consequences of an action. Habermas has thus replaced Kant's categorical imperative with the principle of universalization (U)—a norm is only then valid if "all affected can accept the consequences and the side effects its general observance can be anticipated to have for the satisfaction of everyone's interests (and these consequences are preferred to those of known alternative possibilities)" (Habermas 1990a: 65).

With this turn away from Kant, post-metaphysical thought can no longer rely on "pure reason" and a new way must be found to establish the principle of universalization. According to Habermas, (U) is based on two elements: the rules of discourse and "a weak idea of normative justification" (Habermas 1990a: 92). The rules of discourse are implicit norms of argumentative practice, above all impartiality, truthfulness, recognition of the equality of all discourse partners, and a renunciation of violence. The rules of argumentation cannot be questioned without performative self-contradiction—even a radical sceptic arguing against (U) unavoidably acknowledges the pragmatic presuppositions of argumentation. Whereas discourse norms are reasoned through transcendental-pragmatic reflection, i.e., through a performative self-contradiction, the second element of (U), the weak conception of justification, is assigned the status of a semantic preunderstanding, and as such is not justified through reasoning but merely explicated. This means that the principle of universality is justified by the rules of discourse "in connection with an explication of the meaning of normative claims to validity" (Habermas 1990a: 114).

This is the point where, at an early stage within discourse ethics, criticism was leveled at Habermas's theory of morality. As William Rehg has objected, the idea of a discursive justification of norms is still too vague for a moral principle: "(D) is both more and less than a moral principle. It is more in that it covers more areas of social action, less in that it does not tell us what distinguishes the validity of moral norms from that of other kinds of action norm" (Rehg 1997: 31), with legal norms a salient example. For Habermas, (D) and (U) aim to form a "general will" or a "common interest" (1990a: 63; 65). This begs the question whether it is generally understood that the discursive justification of norms does indeed already contain a morally substantial idea of the "equal interest of everyone" (1990a: 66). Even earlier, Seyla Benhabib had raised the suspicion that Habermas's justification of (U) is either viciously circular or rests on hidden normative premises (1986: 307f.).

The criticism leveled against (D) and (U) moved Habermas to make an internal differentiation in *Between Facts and Norms*:

> In my previous publications on discourse ethics, I have not sufficiently distinguished between the discourse principle and the moral principle. The discourse principle is only intended to explain the point of view from which norms of action can be impartially justified; I assume that the principle itself

reflects those symmetrical relations of recognition built into communicatively structured forms of life in general.

(Habermas 1996: 108f.)

The general and morally neutral principle of discourse is the basis of the moral principle, which relates to humankind, and the democratic principle, the norms of which relate—through the medium of law—to a specific society with a specific sociocultural tradition (Habermas 1996: 109). For Habermas, this new differentiation in discourse ethics means that no new justifications are necessary. Just like the earlier concept of (D), the principle of discourse reflects the inherent structures of the lifeworld. Because Habermas understands the lifeworld as not only a transcendental but also a sociohistorical horizon, a defense of the reason-based morality of the Enlightenment through discourse ethics threatens to unravel in the contingencies of European history. Indeed, for Habermas any ultimate justification of discourse ethics would be nothing other than a relapse into a philosophy of consciousness (1990a: 77f.; 96–8).

This is where Karl-Otto Apel's aims his criticism of Habermasian discourse ethics. If regression to a moral culturalism is to be avoided, then discourse ethics simply cannot be anchored in the lifeworld, a point Apel had vehemently made at an early stage in the controversy (1992). Indeed, the consequences are even graver: the idea of a morally neutral discourse principle, preceding morality and law, leads to a disintegration of discourse ethics (Apel 1998).

According to Apel, to defend the universality of discourse ethics it is necessary to start with the transcendental pragmatic justification of the norms of discourse, which Habermas also draws on. At the same time, however, Apel's discourse ethics is not formulated from considerations of communicative everyday practice, but rather a metaethical querying of the very possibility of universally valid ethics. Apel's justification therefore revolves around the validity claim to truth, which even the radical skeptic can only dispute at the cost of a performative self-contradiction. In the argumentative redeeming of truth claims, four normative principles must be acknowledged *a priori*: truthfulness, universal equality, the renunciation of violence, and, as Apel adds in extension to Habermas, the requirement "to bear equal co-responsibility of identifying and solving problems of the lifeworld through argumentative discourse" (Apel 2001: 48).

The general or primordial principle of discourse is not morally neutral, as Apel emphatically counters Habermas, but the universal core of a rational, universally valid ethics, for "together with serious *thinking as arguing*, we always already presuppose the *existence and cooperation of discourse partners*" (Apel 2001: 46). Indeed, the rules of discourse are the orientation for all argumentative practices, whether in the scientific community or in the conflicts of interests manifest in the lifeworld. Therefore, "the distinction between *theoretical* and *practical* discourse is not yet relevant on this primordial ethics" (Apel 2001: 47).

Apel's identification of the rules of argumentation with the moral principle of discourse ethics found an early critic in Albrecht Wellmer. While not denying "that the practice of arguing is, so to speak, imbued with moral obligations," Wellmer believes it is "questionable ... whether those norms of argument which we cannot dispute without committing a performative contradiction actually betoken obligations of a moral nature" (1991: 184). For Wellmer, the "must" entailed in the rules of discourse is not identical with the "must" of moral obligations: "Obligation to rationality refers to the acknowledgement of arguments, moral obligations to the acknowledgement of persons" (1991: 185). Wellmer's criticism identifies an Achilles' heel in Apel's ethics, which Habermas appears to have addressed in his later distinction between the principle of discourse and the moral principle. Apel subsequently described the differences between theoretical and practical discourse more precisely: with the "switch from a theoretical to a practical discourse indeed some differences become visible ... on the level of pure theoretical discourses of the sciences, all vital interests of the human participants, except the interest in truth, should be bracketed." On the level of moral discourses, however, "together with the thematization of rightness-claims concerning moral norms, the vital interests of the discourse partners come to the fore" (Apel 2001: 59).

Questions remain open despite the pivotal differentiation. The distinguishing, for example, between theoretical and moral discourses obviously arises out of the difference between the validity claims, namely those of truth and moral rightness. To clarify the uniqueness of truth claims, Apel analyzed diverse theories of truth in a comprehensive study, focusing on the correspondence, evidential, and coherency theories of truth. Surprisingly, for Apel the consensus theory of discourse ethics is not merely another theory of truth but a regulative idea, guiding the discourse about truth theories, i.e., theories *about* the relations between human knowledge and reality (Apel 1987). The consensus theory of truth therefore explicates only *one* aspect of truth, namely the claim of intersubjective validity, but not the intuitive claim to an adequate knowledge of things themselves.

Apel has not pursued the other side of the coin, however, to define the claim to moral rightness by analyzing different moral theories. This is no oversight or coincidence—after all, Apel identifies the fundamental norms of morality with the normative presuppositions of argumentation, and herein lies the fallacy of Apel's justification of ethics. At the same time, however, Apel's distinction between truth, in the sense of the relationship between knowledge and reality, and the consensus principle can be made useful in the correction of his own discourse ethics. As in the theoretical discourses, the rules of discourse and the postulate of consensus explicate the claim of the intersubjectivity of moral norms—but not the specific content of morality as such.

The distinction between the principle of discourse and morality has far-reaching consequences for attempts to renew rational morality through discourse ethics (Schelkshorn 2004). Because the transcendental-pragmatic justification of discourse norms does not yet determine what is to be understood by "morality," dissent over the concept of morality is legitimate from the perspective of discourse ethics (Gottschalk-Mazouz 2004: 194).

On the one hand, explications on the purport of morality refer to deep-seated morals, for example the prohibitions on killing, stealing, and lying; on the other hand, they are related to the moral traditions in the various cultures, the meaning and significance of which have to be extrapolated hermeneutically. In terms of justification, two levels must be strictly differentiated, namely the transcendental-pragmatic justification of discourse norms and the hermeneutical explication of moral concepts, which cannot be reasoned with the instrument of the performative self-contradiction. Against this background, discourse ethics are in fact called upon to open up to the diversity of moral traditions in the various cultures of the world.

This background makes it understandable why discourse ethics has been suspected of Eurocentrism despite the dialogical reformulation of Kant's categorical imperative. Both Apel and Habermas introduce *de facto* specific moral concepts into discourse ethics: for example, restricting morality to interpersonal relations, the distinction between an ethics of the good life and the morality of justice, etc. The elements of and differentiations in the concept of "morality" are not introduced as *contributions* to a global discourse between different moral philosophies, but as constitutive factors of ethical reason as such under the conditions of modernity. Whether moral responsibility relates merely to the welfare of humans or that of animals, or more broadly to maintaining the integrity of nature as a whole, is not something that can be decided by reflecting on the norms of argumentation. Conversely, with the discovery of the morally substantial discursive norms, discourse ethics introduces a discriminating minimum standard for culturally different explications of morality, which, as reason dictates, should not be undercut. When moral theories bypass the rules of discourse in the name of an overriding purpose, whether it be for religious salvation, secular utopias, or the utilitarian principle of maximizing happiness, then they arouse suspicion of authoritarianism.

Discourse ethics should not therefore be sweepingly criticized as "Western" ethics. Rather, discourse ethics, operating specifically under the conditions of modernity, brings to bear the criticism of tradition that has intermittently erupted in all axial civilizations since antiquity, and this includes China and India. In Europe, issues surrounding how to conduct life and coexist with others are already discussed by Socrates in the framework of an argumentative dialogue, as Apel acknowledges (1989). In this sense, other cultures can certainly absorb from discourse ethics this impulse to deepen their reflective relationship to their own moral traditions.

A twofold task—and this may serve as a concluding summary—ensues from this critical scrutiny of how Apel and Habermas defend the project of Enlightenment.

Firstly, there is the question whether the codes or the *Leitideen* of values spheres and subsystems can in fact be interpreted as objectivations of rationality types. At least Árnason in his civilization theory proceeds from cultural patterns in tracing the lineaments of social differentiation. Because the question of the rational status of modern subsystems unavoidably discusses normative levels of meaning, sociological analysis is never enough—philosophical reflection is indispensable. This is where discourse ethics plays a key role in defending the Enlightenment project. The dilemma is, however, that it is precisely discourse ethics that, by intensifying reflection on justification, has unwittingly revealed a fundamental limit to the rational morality of the Enlightenment: although the self-reflection of argumentative reason can justify a normatively substantial principle of discourse, it is incapable of reaching or furnishing a distinct and genuine concept of morality. The unresolved problems of discourse ethics thus enable a critical perspective on the history of moral philosophy in the European Enlightenment.

These considerations form the background to our retrospective of Renaissance and early modern philosophies, undertaking a dual reconstruction: on the one hand, the genesis of the differentiation of science, politics, and the economy, in tandem with the constitution of their respective guiding ideas; on the other, the genesis of modern cosmopolitanism on the level of philosophy, focusing on the debates about the Conquista. This historical perspective enables us to analyze, in their *statu nascendi*, central pillars of European modernity, aware of their achievements and ambivalences.

3

The challenge of decolonial philosophies: The case of Latin America

In Western discourses about modernity, Latin American philosophy has remained glaringly absent down to the present day. Hegel's dictum that America is "the echo of the Old World" (1956: 87) continues to reverberate, and not only in Europe. As Eduardo Mendieta has noted, until recently a peculiar "silence about Latin American philosophy and philosophers" (2003: 1) has prevailed in North America. This silence extends even further to South America itself, where—unlike in China and India, today reflecting self-assuredly on their millennium-old traditions—any mention of a "Latin American philosophy" becomes entangled in controversy.

Four main strands of philosophical thought can be roughly distinguished. Firstly, Latin American philosophy can be understood as the presence of European philosophies *in* Latin America. Only a few decades after the Conquista, in the sixteenth century, the Spaniards founded the first universities in Mexico and Lima, with scholasticism the primary philosophy. Since the eighteenth century, almost all of the European philosophies have been adopted and adapted in Latin American academic circles. Secondly, in the mid-nineteenth century, the special current of *filosofía americana* emerged, which later variously characterized itself as Hispano, Ibero, or Latin American philosophy. *Filosofía (latino-) americana*, founded most notably by Juan Bautista Alberdi, positions itself emphatically as a political philosophy, acutely aware of its socio-historical context and involved in strengthening the fabric of postcolonial societies and providing orientation in the search for identity in southern America (Beorlegui 2004). The philosophies and theologies of liberation, which attracted enormous interest worldwide in the twentieth century, thus stand in the tradition of the *filosofía americana*. Thirdly, Latin American philosophy may refer to indigenous currents of thought before the Conquista. The debate as to whether the thought of the Amerindian peoples can be categorized as "philosophy" also reaches back to the sixteenth century and—primarily through the work of Miguel León-Portilla, who speaks of a *filosofía nahuatl*—has received new impetus since the mid-twentieth century (1963; cf. Maffie 2014). Finally, also to be included among Latin American philosophies is the thought of the indigenous peoples after the Conquista, who creatively combined their traditions with European intellectual currents. In the rebellion against colonial domination, Túpac Amaru II, for example, drew on elements from Christianity and the European Enlightenment (Serulnikov 2013). The philosophy of indigenous peoples, i.e. *pueblos originarios*, is at the center of the diverse currents of de-colonial thinking, where the idea of "Latin America" is also problematized (Mignolo 2005).

Despite their differences, the boundaries between these four main currents of Latin American philosophy are fluid. To name one example: amid the long-lasting influence of scholasticism, in the seventeenth and eighteenth centuries important philosophers such as Carlos de Sigüenza y Gongoras intensively studied the thought of indigenous peoples (Beuchot 1996). This hybrid perspective has found resonance in a comprehensive history of philosophy in Latin American from 1300 to 2000 edited by Enrique Dussel, Eduardo Mendieta, and Carmen Bohórquez (2009), a collection of studies that present indigenous and European intellectual traditions, notwithstanding their autonomy, in their diversely manifold interdependencies.

In this chapter I will limit my considerations to the strain of Latin American philosophy founded by Alberdi. As a first step I will look at the *historia de las ideas* movement, which initiated an extensive reappraisal of the history of philosophy in Latin America after the Second World War. While the movement can be seen as installing a discourse of self-understanding in Latin American thought, in the sense described by Ram Adhar Mall (2000: 3), post-colonial philosophies always reflect on the repression of colonial rule, and hence the work of the *historia de las ideas* thinkers poses serious questions relevant for European philosophy, exemplified in the debate between Augusto Salazar Bondy and Leopoldo Zea. As a second step I will then turn to the main themes addressed by Enrique Dussel, one of the prominent representatives of Latin American philosophy of liberation, in his theory of modernity.

3.1 "Latin American philosophy"? The debate between Augusto Salazar Bondy and Leopoldo Zea

Juan Bautista Alberdi's project of a *filosofía americana* was continued by numerous authors throughout the nineteenth and twentieth centuries across the whole of Latin America. Nonetheless, Hegel's characterization of America as "the echo of the Old World," internalized by Latin American intellectuals, cast a shadow over these diverse philosophical stirrings. When Samuel Ramos proposed to establish a chair for the history of philosophy in Mexico in 1941, his own colleagues quickly expressed their profound skepticism. In his preface to *Historia de la filosofía en México* (1943), Ramos claims that most Mexican intellectuals did not even believe in the "existence of a rich philosophical past that deserved to be dealt with in the framework of a special history" (Ramos [1943] 1985: 99). But Ramos was not so much concerned with an archive-like history of ideas; his focus was undoubtedly on the importance of philosophy for the genesis of Mexico's national culture, i.e., how philosophical ideas were assimilated and converted into vital elements of that culture (Ramos [1943] 1985: 101). For this reason, Ramos sees the history of Mexican philosophy as being comprised of contributions made not just by philosophers but also by humanists, scientists, politicians, educators, and the wisdom teachings of the indigenous peoples (Ramos [1943] 1985: 101). Without knowledge of the cultures of the Mayans, Aztecs, and other indigenous peoples, the uniqueness of the transformations of European philosophy in Mexico remain incomprehensible. The *Historia de la filosofía en México* is thus a striking testimony to the self-assertion of Latin American philosophy, a vehement defense against the disparagements expressed by European philosophies. The legend that the people of Latin America—and Spain—are barely capable of rational thinking, or are indeed incapable of appreciating it, is rejected by Ramos, who sees claims like these as nothing but "unjust exaggeration [*exageración injusta*]" (Ramos [1943] 1985: 100).

After the Second World War, the philosophical traditions of the various regions of Latin America were researched systematically under the authoritative guidance of Leopoldo Zea, a former pupil of José Gaos. As part of the *historia de las ideas* movement, Zea established committees to undertake this research in numerous countries across the continent. In his lecture series *En torno a una filosofía Americana* (Toward a [Latin] American Philosophy, 1945; Part I translated in Zea 2022), which drew on an earlier series he had given at the

Colégio de México in 1942, Zea emphasizes the historical context of the *historia de las ideas*. Despite the wars of independence in the early nineteenth century and the Mexican Revolution at the beginning of the twentieth, Latin America had essentially remained in the shadow of Europe. It was only with the First World War and then above all the Nazi regime's fall into barbarism that the image of Europe as the model civilization was irrevocably shattered. By the mid-twentieth century, Europe's crisis and loss of geopolitical power forced Latin America into a new philosophical reflection on its own history and culture, as Zea calls for: "Latin America, until yesterday the echo and shadow of European culture, has to procure for itself firm ground and to solve of its own accord the problems of its circumstances … Latin America needs a philosophy, based on an original meditation on, and solution to, its problems" (Zea 2022: 888).

Methodologically, in his conception of a history of Latin American philosophy Zea broadly adopts the *circumstancialismo* of José Ortega y Gasset and his follower José Gaos. Philosophy does not move and change in terms of purely rational or immanent logic but is driven along through a continuous dialectical interaction with its sociohistorical contexts, i.e., the "circumstances." Zea's thinking does not, however, fall prey to a simplifying relativism, as Jorge J. E. Gracia has claimed (1992). Like Ortega y Gasset before him, Zea stands by the universality of reason despite the insight into the contextual contingency of all philosophy:

> Thus, a Latin American philosophy will not be justified as such by the Latin American situation but by the amplitude of the effort to seek solutions. It is necessary to do Philosophy with a capital "P" and not simply philosophy of a determinate country. It is necessary to solve circumstantial problems, but with a view to solutions to the problems of all men.
>
> (Zea 2022: 895)

The appropriation of its own intellectual history by the *historia* movement is undoubtedly a milestone in the self-constitution of Latin American philosophy. Nonetheless, this undertaking could not completely allay deep-seated self-doubt. On the contrary, in fact. At the end of the 1960s, Augusto Salazar Bondy, who had already written important works on the history of philosophy in Peru, revived the question of the very existence and authenticity of an Iberian-American philosophy in his book *¿Existe una filosofía de nuestra América?* (1968). After the studies produced by the *historia* movement, Salazar Bondy looks forward and asks if a Latin American philosophy of the future can build on its own philosophical traditions or not (Salazar Bondy [1968] 1988: 20).

The main flaw of Latin American philosophy, or more accurately the thought inspired there by Europe since the sixteenth century, is not its often lamented epigonic character. After all, European philosophy has been transformed and creatively developed further in many ways (Salazar Bondy [1968] 1988: 74). America was never a mere "echo of the Old World." The decisive problem of Latin American thought has its root elsewhere, in the complex situation of an alienation from its own sociocultural context. Philosophy in Latin America has "begun from a zero point, i.e., without the supports provided by a homegrown intellectual tradition, for indigenous thought was not integrated into the process of forming a Hispano-American philosophy"; Latin American philosophy thus resembles "a transplanted tree [*un árbol transplantado*]" (Salazar Bondy [1968] 1988: 27) that has yet to firmly take root in its new soil. While philosophy was always seen as a natural part of cultural life in Europe, philosophy in Hispanic America has never found the support of an established historical community. That philosophy finds itself in this alienating situation is a consequence of the colonial past. "Philosophy was *brought* by the Spaniards because they *came* to conquer and dominate the American land and *imported* with them the intellectual weapons of domination. It can therefore hardly surprise us that to a large extent the examination of Spanish-American philosophy turns into accounts of the *arrival* of occidental philosophy in our countries" (Salazar Bondy [1968] 1988: 27f.). Moreover, Salazar Bondy sees the perverting of philosophy into an ideology of domination as continuing to have an effect in the period after the wars of independence, particularly in the late nineteenth century, when positivist-oriented dictatorships striving to implement development ruled in numerous Latin American states. Referring to "dependency theory", or the "theory of the development of underdevelopment" of the 1960s, Salazar Bondy emphasizes how Latin American philosophy in the contemporary age is part of a global neo-colonial power syndrome: "We are living alienated because of underdevelopment combined with dependency and domination, which we are subjugated to and to which we were always subjugated" (Salazar Bondy [1968] 1988: 93). Down to the present day, Hispano-American philosophy remains worryingly estranged from its own sociocultural context. Indeed, due to its fixation on European paragons, philosophy has intensified the cultural alienation Latin American societies find themselves in after centuries of colonial rule. As Salazar Bondy's clearsighted diagnosis identifies, alienated thinking is itself self-alienating ("*una conciencia enajenada y enajente*"; Salazar Bondy [1968] 1988: 85), i.e., ever turning in on and against itself; it is at once the victim and the perpetrator.

Because the alienation of Hispano-American philosophy is an effect of global power relations, which have condemned the peoples of the Americas to a life in unfreedom and dependency now lasting centuries, the "constitution of genuine and original thinking" inevitably requires the "transformation of our society through removing underdevelopment and domination" (Salazar Bondy 1988: 93). Only a radical restructuring of power relations in society could pave the way for a future "philosophy of our America [*de nuestra América*]" (Salazar Bondy 1988: 28). Here, it is my impression that Salazar Bondy is alluding to José Martí's essay "Nuestra América" ("Our America", 1891), a work in which Martí calls on the political and intellectual elites to break free from their imitative fixation on European culture. As Martí describes it, the indigenous cultures are, for all peoples living on the continent—i.e., also for the creoles—the mother cultures, even if they obstinately deny it: "These men born in America who are ashamed of their mother that raised them because she wears an Indian apron, these delinquents who disown their sick mother and leave her alone in her sickbed!" (Martí [1891] 2002: 289). Without reconciliation with the indigenous peoples, any modernization project is doomed to failure, a painful lesson to be drawn from the liberal and positivist reforms of the nineteenth century. In short, (Latin) America "must save herself through"— and not against—"her Indians" (Martí [1891] 2002: 289).

Salazar Bondy's trenchant criticism of the history of Hispano-American philosophy triggered a fierce controversy in the *historia de las ideas* movement. In *La filosofía americana como filosofía sin más* ("Latin American Philosophy as Simply Philosophy", 1969), Leopoldo Zea vehemently rejects Salazar Bondy's verdict. Today, the ensuing exchanges between the two are rightly considered the "Great Debate" in the recent history of Latin American philosophy (Sánchez 2019).

Zea begins by endorsing Salazar Bondy's diagnosis of the alienation of Hispano-American philosophy. The importing of European philosophies served, as Zea himself had clearly demonstrated in *El positivismo en México* (1943–4), to legitimate the rule of specific power groups, in this case a small group of bourgeois elites. Nonetheless, philosophers in Latin America have frequently shown that they can engage creatively and critically with European philosophy. Indeed, to give just one example, the Jesuit Francisco Javier Clavijero, who could speak Nahuatl, described Mesoamerican cultures in formidable detail in his work *Historia antigua de México* ([1781] 1991) while incisively criticizing the racial theories of the European Enlightenment formulated by de Buffon and de Pauw, which had influenced both Kant and Hegel. According to Zea, since Alberdi at the latest, numerous philosophies have consciously attempted to anchor their modes of thinking in the reality of Latin America. These initial attempts to contextualize European philosophy have, as Zea readily concedes and illustrates through the example of Alberdi, paradoxically yielded new estrangements. A member of a liberal reform movement, the Generación 1837, Alberdi perceptively recognized that the European model of progress could not simply be adopted as it was but needed to be adapted to fit the unique social conditions of southern America. But firmly under the spell of European liberalism, in which the racist ideology of the Enlightenment maintained an influence, Alberdi saw the Amerindian cultures—and also the mestizos and the creole farmers—only as still under the thrall of the colonial mind and a hindrance on the path of progress. Thus, in the late nineteenth century, campaigns to exterminate the indigenous population were launched in Argentina in the name of liberalism (Zea [1969] 1989: 252-7).

The reasons for the failure of the early attempts to establish a *filosofía americana* resided not only in racist thought but, for Zea, also in the theoretical foundations of the European Enlightenment itself. Kant's ahistorical concept of reason had precluded *a priori* the contextual rootedness of philosophy. It was historicism, which revealed the sociocultural situatedness of human reason, that first opened the possibility for Latin American philosophy to constitutively integrate the cultural context into its own thinking, context that had hitherto been overlooked in favor of a questionable universality of reason. As Zea describes it, the result is a paradoxical situation, wherein "historicism, expression of Europe's cultural crisis, would be for Latin America akin to the constitutive act of its philosophical independence" (Zea [1969] 1989: 69f.).

This means that, while concurring with Salazar Bondy's criticism of Latin American philosophy in many points, Zea "disagrees with Bondy's underlying claim, namely, that authenticity in philosophy is possible only after underdevelopment is overcome" (Sánchez 2019: 686). Moreover, crucially Zea places the contemporary controversy over the authenticity of Latin American philosophy in the broader horizon of the Conquista and the colonial debates of the sixteenth century:

> Our philosophizing in America begins with a polemic over the essence of the human ... This strange philosophy begins in the polemic Las Casas launches against Sepúlveda, a philosophy that will ask itself in the twentieth century whether it possesses a philosophy or not. In the polemic not only the right to the word, the logos, or language is set in parenthesis, but the whole nature of human beings from this America.
>
> (Zea [1969] 1989: 12)

Before the Conquista, the Amerindian peoples, like all other cultures, had used language to communicate and create, and then to transform the world into a human "habitat [*hogar*]" through myths. The arrival of the Spaniards brought with it not only the perishing of the Aztec and Inca empires but also the denial of the Amerindian peoples' right to use their own languages to express themselves. Humanist Europe in the fifteenth century is very much entangled in a paradox: on the one hand, numerous tractates were being written enthusiastically praising the dignity of the human being; on the other, Sepúlveda and Las Casas were embroiled in a discussion *about* the humanity of the Amerindians.

Europe's hubris continued, according to Zea, now targeting the mestizos and indeed even turning on the descendants of the European colonizers. In the early nineteenth century the creoles, inspired by the spirit of the European Enlightenment, demanded the right to codetermination in the Cortes of Cádiz. This demand for equality with the other provinces of the Spanish empire was brusquely rejected in the period of the Napoleonic Wars by both sides of the political spectrum, the monarchists and the republicans. Ever since, in Zea's assessment, a deep doubt as to their own humanity has sunk into the hearts of the creoles. In other words: after the indigenous peoples and the mestizos, at the beginning of the nineteenth century the creoles are also turned into an "object of the very same question mark" (Zea [1969] 1989: 13). Given this historical background, Salazar Bondy's question of whether there is an authentic philosophy in America seems to be nothing other than a much belated aftereffect of the sixteenth-century colonial debates.

This means that Latin American philosophy is—despite all the efforts to adopt and adapt—severed from European philosophy by the bitter experience of this querying of humanity: "in this history there was never once the case that it was investigated whether there was a capacity or the right to the word, to the logos, or to language, although the investigation itself already implies the use of this right" (Zea [1969] 1989: 10). The irresolvable difference between Hispano-American and European philosophy thus lies in the problem of being human, more precisely in the doubt as to being part of humanity, and not in a lack of originality. Thus philosophy must also redefine the concept of "authenticity," for it becomes inauthentic whenever it "creates the idea of a human, which is quite the negation of the human" (Zea [1969] 1989: 113). For this reason, European philosophy itself must look sternly at the problem of inauthenticity.

3.2 The coloniality of power as the dark underside of modernity: from Enrique Dussel and Aníbal Quijano to Walter Mignolo

In the 1960s, a broad and diverse liberation discourse emerged in Latin America, encompassing *dependencia* theories, theologies of liberation, "Pedagogy and Theatre of the Oppressed" (Paulo Freire, Augusto Boal), and finally philosophies of liberation. The idea of liberation grew out of the hopes of social revolutionary movements in Latin America, which had gained new impetus following the Cuban Revolution; the other key source was the decolonization taking place in Africa and southeast Asia. The historical roots of these liberation philosophies lie mostly in Argentina; but important representatives from the *historia de las ideas* movement, notably Leopoldo Zea and Arturo Andrés Roig, developed their own theories of liberation in the 1970s (Cerutti Guldberg 2006). These philosophies of liberation stand in the tradition of the *filosofía americana*, while however also staying forthrightly away from Alberdi's liberalism. Reflecting on the Latin American context, focus is drawn to the liberation of marginalized groups, specifically the landless (*campesinos*), the mestizos, and the indigenous peoples, still seen as hindrances to progress by the liberal elites of the Generación 1837.

In the early 1970s, Enrique Dussel presented one of the most detailed and broadest conceptions for a Latin American philosophy of liberation. As Dussel explains, drawing on Salazar Bondy, Latin American philosophy can only overcome its (self-)alienation through a radical critique of global economic power structures and an expression of its engaged solidarity with the social causes of the marginalized masses. From this background, two focal points emerge in Dussel's philosophy, namely an ethics of liberation[1] and a criticism of European modernity, which in his view has its starting point in the Conquista: "Modernity came to birth in 1492—that is our thesis" (Dussel 1995: 138).

In his theory of modernity, Dussel primarily takes aim at the Hegelian philosophy of history, wherein modern Europe is posited as the summit of world historical progress in the consciousness of freedom. According to Hegel, world history moved from east to west, i.e., from oriental despotism via Hellenic democracy and early Christianity, before reaching its high point in the Germanic world and modern Europe. The Reformation prepared the way for modern freedom. Liberating the Christian believer from scholastic dogmatics and cultic acts, the "Lutheran faith is then that a human being stands in this relationship with God, appears in it as this person only, and must exist in this relationship exclusively" (Hegel 2009: 77). Nonetheless, it was first with Descartes that Luther's discovery of subjective inwardness was detached from its religious context, so that human reason is now radically on its own: "In accordance with this [Lutheran] principle of inwardness it is now thinking, thinking on its own account, that is the purest pinnacle of this inwardness—thinking is what now establishes itself on its own account. This period begins with Descartes" (Hegel 2009: 104).

Despite the diverse criticisms subsequently leveled against Hegel and his philosophy of history, key motifs have remained influential in European thinking down to the present day. Habermas, pointing to "three monumental events around the year 1500", names not only the Reformation and the Renaissance but also the "discovery of the 'new World'," suggesting that these three events "constituted the epochal threshold between modern times and the Middle Ages" (1987: 5). As Dussel critically notes, however, in Habermas's philosophical interpretation of modernity the markers change, with the Conquista once again—as in Hegel—simply cast aside: "The key historical events in establishing the principle of subjectivity are the Reformation, the Enlightenment, and the French Revolution" (Habermas 1987: 17; cf. Dussel 1995: 25f.).

Dussel takes a different tack from the postmodernists in relation to the "grand narrative" (Lyotard) of Hegel's philosophy of history. Rather than replacing it with a plurality of local histories, he offers an alternative interpretation of world history. According to Dussel, himself known as the "Hegel of Coyoacán" (Alcoff 2021), world history moves unilinearly from east to west. Neolithic civilizations arose not only in Egypt and Mesopotamia but also in India (Indus), China (Shang), and America (Chavín, Olmec). From antiquity, empires developed out of the cultural centers of the archaic epoch, each of which then spread outward (Dussel 1995: 73–81). Before 1491, world history is marked by the coexistence of various empires (Persian, Roman, Chinese, the Dar-al-Islam, Aztec, Inca). Although the boundaries between the various *oikumenes* were partially permeable—for example, as the spectacular expansion of the Mongols created an interregional zone (Dussel 2013: 3–24)—overall human history was polycentric in its structure. Indeed, for Dussel, in 1491 Europe, India, and China possessed comparable cultural levels. Until the end of the fifteenth century, Latin Christianity was on the periphery of the Islamic empires (Dussel 1995: 88–90).

This background enables a precise determination of the epochal significance of early modern European expansion. With the circumnavigation of Africa and the conquest of the Americas, the Iberian powers not only established a new interregional system among previously independent *oikumenes* but also laid the foundation for the genesis of a world society, one that all peoples and cultures are part of for the first time in human history: "In my opinion, Western Europe's bursting the bounds within which Islam had confined it, gave *birth* to *modernity*" (Dussel 1995: 90).

Although Europe's conquering of the giant expanses of the Americas meant that it became a powerful center of the emerging world society, even after 1492 the Chinese empire remained at least its equal until the eighteenth century (Dussel 2011: 129–55). The situation first changed with the advent of the industrial revolution, which enabled Europe to finally attain global hegemony.

Although focusing on colonial expansion, the slave trade, and the spreading of a capitalist market economy, Dussel does not simply reduce modernity to a global power system. With the emerging natural sciences and ethics of human rights, an epochal process of enlightenment also begins to crystallize in Europe in the fifteenth century, one "that opens up new possibilities for human development" (Dussel 1995: 136). Dussel thus distinguishes strictly between two dimensions in European modernity. Firstly, all forms of regressive criticism are rejected: "For its first and positive conceptual content, modernity signifies rational emancipation" (Dussel 1995: 136). Philosophy of Liberation philosophy "intends neither a premodern project, nor a folkloric affirmation of the past, nor the antimodern project of conservatives, rightists, Nazis, fascists, or populists" (Dussel 1995: 138). Secondly, in an allusion to Horkheimer and Adorno's *Dialectic of Enlightenment*, the emancipatory dimension of modernity is overlaid by a new sacrifice myth that transfigures the subjugation of the non-European world: "But, at the same time, in its secondary and negative *mythic* content, modernity justifies an irrational praxis of violence" (Dussel 1995: 136). The will to power of modern reason is not—as Dussel emphasizes, now countering Horkheimer and Adorno—directed against outward nature, only to then in the twentieth century revert to the domination of humans over other humans. The dominant disposition to exert power, the main characteristic of the modern subject, in fact turns against other humans at the very birth of modernity, i.e., the Conquista of the Americas and the early modern slave trade.

The emancipatory and power-driven dimensions of modernity are already discernible "in certain medieval European cities under the impetus of the Renaissance proponents of the *Quattrocento*" (Dussel 1995: 138). As Dussel illustrates through the figure of Hernán Cortés, the Conquista is only understandable when approached from Renaissance culture. With Cortés the ego of modernity takes to the stage, i.e., the "free, violent, warlike, politically adept, juvenile modern ego," wielding military technology that mirrors Machiavelli's analytics of power (Dussel 1995: 43). On the other side of the equation stands Moctezuma, who "was absolutely determined by the auguries, sorceries, astrological definitions, myths, theories, and other sources that revealed the designs of the gods" (Dussel 1995: 43).

However, two phases need to be distinguished in the philosophy of the Renaissance, namely before and after the Europeans' discovery of the Americas. For without that discovery, the Italian Renaissance would have ultimately remained a regional phenomenon, like cultural flowerings in other regions of the world. And indeed, as Peter Burke has already point out, in China and Japan there are "a cluster of cultural achievements and innovations at least as remarkable as the cases of Renaissance Italy and the Netherlands." Parallel to the important trend of secularization in the arts, "Japanese Confucians of the period, like the humanists of the fifteenth century, shifted their emphasis from knowing heaven to knowing man" (Burke 1987: 246f.). For Dussel, it is only first by placing them against the broader horizon of emerging global society that we see the enlightenment processes of the Middle Ages and the Renaissance transform into the typical modern processes of rationalization. Hence, "modernity could only take off when sufficient historical conditions were in place: 1492, its empirical spreading over the world, its organization of colonies, and its usufruct over the pragmatic, economic lives of its victims" (Dussel 1995: 138).

A crucial connection emerges against this background. Dussel assigns to Spanish Renaissance humanism a fundamental role in constituting modern thought, initiating a comprehensive and, moreover, a critical reflection on the historical novelty of a global society just a few years after Columbus's voyage.

> The first Hispanic Renaissance and humanist Modernity produced a theoretical or philosophical reflection of the highest importance, one that has gone unnoticed in so-called modern philosophy (which is only the philosophy of the second Modernity). The theoretical-philosophical thought of the sixteenth century has contemporary relevance because it is the first, and only, system of thought to live and express the originary experience of the period of the constitution of the first world system.
>
> (Dussel 2013: 34)

Amid all the justifications for conquering the Amerindian peoples, in the sixteenth century Spanish philosophy provocatively raises the question of the moral legitimacy of European expansion: "What right has the European to occupy, dominate, and *manage* the cultures that have recently been discovered and militarily conquered, and that are now in the process of being colonized?"

(Dussel 2013: 34). As early as the sixteenth century, as Dussel makes clear by drawing on the debate between Ginés de Sepúlveda and Bartolomé de las Casas, both the victim myth of modernity and the central motif of the ethics of modern human rights are developed.

For Dussel, Sepúlveda is not a premodern thinker who applied the Aristotelian theory of natural slavery to the Amerindians, but one of the very founders of modern political philosophy. As Dussel perceptively notes, in his criticism of Aztec culture Sepúlveda presupposes the emancipatory ideal of modernity, namely the principle of "subjective liberty (*suae libertati*), autonomously resistant to the arbitrariness of rulers" (Dussel 1995: 65). In the next step of the argument, however, "Sepúlveda passes from the concept of modernity to its myth" (Dussel 1995: 65), deducing from the thesis that the Europeans have attained a higher degree of freedom—which Dussel incidentally does not dispute in principle in his interpretation of Cortés and Moctezuma: the right to violently civilize the Amerindian cultures. Because of the superiority of European culture, even "the violence inflicted on the Other is said to serve the emancipation, utility, and well-being of the barbarian who is civilized, developed, or modernized" (Dussel 1995: 64). Indeed, this justification can go so far as to claim that since people are exposed to arbitrary violence in a despotic regime—Sepúlveda draws on Oviedo's grim accounts of the Aztec empire—conquest can seem like a liberating process. As Dussel puts it: "Conquest emancipates by enabling the barbarian to depart from (Kant's *Ausgang*) immaturity" (1995: 65). In this sense, Sepúlveda's thought is "typically modern" (1995: 64). Moreover, Sepúlveda laid the cornerstone for the myth of modernity: "Thus, after the innocent Other's victimization, the myth of modernity declares the Other the culpable cause of that victimization and absolves the modern subject of any guilt for the victimizing act" (Dussel 1995: 64). The victim myth of modernity, which Sepúlveda had developed within the framework of Christianity's claim to universality, continues in secular modernity, only the signatures of the age have altered: "Modernity as myth always authorizes its violence as civilizing whether it propagates Christianity in the sixteenth century or democracy and the free market in the twentieth" (Dussel 1995: 71).

For Dussel, a radical critique of colonialist modernity emerges directly in the sixteenth century itself with the thought of Bartolomé de las Casas. Unlike Sepúlveda, whose judgment was based on reports about the Amerindians, Las Casas considers the lifeworld of the people in Mesoamerica. Christian missionizing can only be effective based on persuasion through reasoning (Dussel 1995: 70f.). Any subject going through a civilizing process will transform into a barbarian if violence and coercion are used, for these methods force it to leave the path of reason (Dussel 1995: 71f.).

As Dussel sees it, in contrast to the colonialism debates in the sixteenth century, wherein prophetic voices such as that of Las Casas unmasked and challenged imperial claims, the criticism of European colonialism based on morality falls silent with the onset of the second phase of modernity, i.e., in seventeenth-century philosophy. Echoes of Las Casas's critical voice are perceptible only in Montaigne. Dussel concluded his 1992 Frankfurt lectures with a dictum from Montaigne's essay *Of Cannibals*: "We can call them barbarians with respect to our rules of reason, but not with respect to us, who exceed the entire species in barbarity" (Dussel 1995: 139). After Montaigne's critique, the situation becomes bleak, the thinking of the founding figures of modernity obviously imbued with the logic of colonial power. Before Husserl and Heidegger, it was first and foremost Hegel who had emphatically extolled Descartes as the founder of modern reason's autonomy in the *Lectures on the History of Philosophy*:

> Now we come for the first time to what is properly the philosophy of the modern world [*neuen Welt*], and we begin it with Descartes. Here, we may say, we are at home and, like the sailor after a long voyage, we can at last shout "Land ho" ....
> The principle of this new era is thinking, the thinking that proceeds from itself.
> (Hegel [1825–6] 2009: 104)

Although Hegel considers the age of discovery to be part of the Middle Ages, his assessment of Descartes' importance for modern philosophy alludes, probably subconsciously, to Europe's transoceanic expansion. Hegel slips into the role of Columbus, who on his "long voyage" had discovered the "new world." For Dussel, however, Descartes' thought is not only metaphorically related to the violent expansion of the new world, as in Hegel's portrayal; the connection is very real, the two are interrelated. In the lineage of Nietzsche and Heidegger (see section 1.1 of this book), Dussel de-constructs Descartes' *ego cogito, ergo sum* to reveal its basis in *volo*, which against the background of European expansion is described as an "I conquer."

> Before the *ego cogito* there is an *ego conquiro*; "I conquer" is the practical foundation of "I think." ... From the "I conquer" applied to the Aztec and Inca world and all America, from the "I enslave" applied to Africans sold for the gold and silver acquired at the cost of the death of Amerindians working in the depths of the earth, from the "I vanquish" of the wars of India and China to the shameful "opium war"—from this "I" appears the Cartesian *ego cogito*.
> (Dussel 2003: 38)

Drawing on Heidegger, Dussel identifies the essence of colonial violence in an objectifying re-presentation of the other: "Europe constituted other cultures, worlds, and persons as objects, as what was thrown [*arrojado/jacere*] before [*ob/ante*] their eyes" (Dussel 1995: 35). While Heidegger primarily criticizes the objectification and exploitation of nature by the modern subject, Dussel shifts attention to how colonial violence instrumentalizes the other:

> Modern European philosophy, even before the *ego cogito* but certainly from then on, situated all men and all cultures—and with them their women and children—within its own boundaries as manipulable tools, instruments. Ontology understood them as interpretable beings, as known ideas, as mediations or internal possibilities within the horizon of the comprehension of Being. Spatially central, the *ego cogito* constituted the periphery.
>
> (Dussel 2003: 2f.)

As noted, for Heidegger, the peak of the *cogito*'s power syndrome resides in the freedom that "implies man's developing mastery over his own definition of the essence of mankind" (Heidegger 1982a: 98). It is in this sense that Dussel sees how Europeans have spread their dominion to the point of domination, where it now decides on the humanity of other peoples and cultures, bolstering its own burgeoning sense of self: "The modern ego was born in its self-constitution over regions it dominated ... The Other is Oviedo's beast, Hegel's future ... rustic mass discovered in order to be civilized by the European being [*ser*] of occidental culture. But this Other is in fact covered over [*en-cubierta*] in its alterity" (Dussel 1995: 36).

Against this background, Dussel draws a line from Descartes to Hobbes, in whose thinking the European will to power, unleashed in the "new world" since Cortés, finds its unadulterated expression: "*Homo homini lupus* is the real—that is, political—definition of the *ego cogito* and of modern and contemporary European philosophy" (Dussel 2003: 9).

In contrast to Descartes and Hobbes, in whose thought the colonial violence of early modern Europe is mirrored, for Dussel Las Casas overcomes "the limitations of *emancipative reason* via a *liberating reason*" (Dussel 1995: 137), attaining "the maximal critical consciousness by siding with the oppressed Other and by examining critically the premises of modern civilizing violence" (Dussel 1995: 72). Indeed, the precursor role of Las Casas extends even further: in Las Casas's critique of the sacrifice myth of modernity, Dussel sees the contours of his own conception of liberation preconfigured, supported by the vision of a "transmodernity" (1995: 136-9; 2018: 29-60). The idea of transmodernity enables Dussel to distance himself from both regressive anti-modernity and a postmodernism that is disdainful of rationality. In contrast to the subsumption logic of the Western system, in which the other, i.e. the non-European peoples, is negated, transmodernity pursues a different trajectory—to creatively transform modernity by integrating the peoples of the postcolonial Global outh: "In transmodernity the alterity, coessential to modernity, now receives recognition as an equal. Modernity will come into its fullness not by passing from its potency to its act, but by surpassing itself through a co-realization with its once negated alterity and through a process of mutual, creative fecundation" (Dussel 1995: 138).

Dussel's critique of the sacrifice myth of modernity has been elaborated and detailed by Latin American decolonial thinkers. In his interpretation of modernity, Aníbal Quijano, countering theories emphasizing the dimension of enlightenment, reassesses the rational achievements of cultures usually tagged as "premodern." Science and the secular interpretation of humanity and society are not a European monopoly; rather, "one must admit that it is a phenomenon possible in all cultures and historical epochs. With all their respective particularities and differences, all the so-called high cultures (China, India, Egypt, Greece, Maya-Aztec, Tawantinsuyo) prior to the current world-system unequivocally exhibit signs of that modernity, including rational science and the secularization of thought" (Quijano 2000: 543). The specificity of modernity resides primarily in how a new global power system is established, one that radically changes notions of time and space:

> And since "modernity" is about processes that were initiated with the emergence of America, of a new model of global power (the first world-system), and of the integration of all the peoples of the globe in that process, it is also essential to admit that it is about an entire historical period. In other words, starting with America, a new space/time was constituted materially and subjectively: this is what the concept of modernity names.
>
> (Quijano 2000: 547)

At this point, Quijano introduces the term "coloniality of power" and uses it to describe the different social spheres of the new global system of power, specifically the sphere of human labor and its relation to nature, gender and the reproduction of the species, and subjectivity and its products, including knowledge and authoritarian social relations (Quijano 2014: 236). Furthermore— and this is of crucial importance—according to Quijano, a distinction must be drawn between colonialism and coloniality, although the two are linked. The concept of colonialism refers to structures of domination and exploitation by one power over another. Colonialism already existed in premodern times and does not necessarily imply racist relations of power. Coloniality, however, is, as Quijano emphasizes, "one of the constitutive and specific elements of the global pattern of capitalist power. It is based on the imposition of a racial/ethnic classification of the world population as cornerstone of such a pattern of power, and it operates on each of the, material and subjective, planes, spheres, and dimensions of quotidian existence and at the social level" (2014: 236; translation in Mendieta 2020: 10). The new Eurocentered world system that emerges with the conquest of America conceives and imposes a racist worldview where "new social identities of coloniality (indigenous, black, brown, yellow, white, mestizo), and the geocultures of colonialism (America, Africa, Far East, Near East, West, and Europe) were configured" (Quijano 2014: 268; translation in Mendieta 2020: 10).

This means that the modern system of the capitalist market economy subjugates all peoples and all social relations, from work itself to forms of knowledge, to an all-encompassing and racist control system (Quijano 2000: 544f.). Consequently, Quijano, and for that matter Mignolo too, shift epistemic coloniality, of which Dussel's thought offers an initial consideration, to the very center of their critique. Quijano distinguishes between several forms of colonializing knowledge, for instance the appropriation of the colonized group's cultural discoveries; the repression of their forms of knowledge production, including the creation of a symbolic universe; and not least the compulsion to adopt the culture of the dominators and their Judeo-Christian religion (Quijano 2000: 541).

Epistemic coloniality is based on Eurocentrism, itself sustained by "two principal founding myths: first, the idea of the history of human civilization as a trajectory that departed from a state of nature and culminated in Europe; second, a view of the differences between Europe and non-Europe as natural (racial) differences and not consequences of a history of power" (Quijano 2000: 542). Eurocentrism thus elevates the "idea of race" into the "basic criterion for a universal social classification of the world's population" (Quijano 2000: 551). Although "the Aztecs, Mayas, Chimus, Aymaras, Incas, Chibchas, and so on" were the most developed peoples in the age of the conquest, three hundred years later all of them become "merged into a single identity: Indians. This new identity was racial, colonial, and negative" (Quijano 2000: 551).

Walter Mignolo first analyses the colonialization of knowledge and Eurocentric racism on the cultural level. In *The Darker Side of the Renaissance: Literacy,*

Territoriality, Colonization (2003), Mignolo impressively traces the relations between humanism and colonialism, for so long almost fully disregarded in the European vision of the period. In the sixteenth century, the humanist ideal of an alphabetical literate culture was posited as the standard to judge and communicate with both Amerindian cultures and the great Asian empires. The result is a denigration of cultures that use oral traditions and pictographic writing systems. Further, the newly "discovered" peoples are integrated into Eurocentric maps of the world. And finally, transcending the boundaries of the *oikumene* leads to a new racist imperialism, which Mignolo characterizes by drawing on Carl Schmitt (Mignolo 2011: 77–117). In *The Nomos of the Earth*, Schmitt criticizes the modern idea of the law of nations as a *jus publicum Europaeum*, the legitimacy of Europe's geopolitical hegemony from the sixteenth through to the early twentieth century. The law of nations governs merely relations between the European powers, not their relations to colonies and zones of influence: "Thus, the second nomos of the Earth became Euro-centric" (Schmitt 2003: 352). Parallel to Schmitt, Mignolo sees Francisco de Vitoria more as the founder of the racist ideology of coloniality than of global international law: "We can locate the founding moment of both imperial and colonial differences in the canonical work by the legal theologian Francisco de Vitoria" (Mignolo 2011: 86). Mignolo concedes, though, that Vitoria rejects the claims to world dominion of both the emperor and the pope, and within the framework of his *ius gentium* doctrine affirms the humanity of the Amerindians:

> To cut off the authority of the pope and the monarch, he stated that all nations on the planet (but in this case, the Spanish nation and the Indian nations in the New World) were endowed with *ius gentium*, the rights of nations. Since Indians belong to the human community and were endowed with *ius gentium*, neither the pope nor the monarch could have *dominium* over them.
>
> (Mignolo 2011: 86)

In a second step however, Vitoria then justifies the violent Spanish expansion through denigrating views of the Amerindians: "Francisco de Vitoria ended up, after recognizing that Indians had the rights of nations, demonstrating their deficiencies in rationality (although they possessed reason) and maturity (although they were human). Once de Vitoria determined Indians to be somehow inferior (although people with rights), he built up his argument on racial epistemic hierarchies" (Mignolo 2011: 87).

This brief look at a few motifs from decolonial philosophy in Latin America presents new challenges to a European theory of modernity. At least three impulses emerge from the debate between Salazar Bondy and Leopoldo Zea, which reveals the deep-seated and painful problems inherent to how Latin American philosophy became constituted. Firstly, the history of *filosofía americana* makes it acutely obvious that modernity has long been critically reflected on from its peripheries. The discourse of modernity was not first fragmented with Fanon, as Sartre assumed, but indeed has been for centuries. Secondly, Latin American philosophy mirrors back to European philosophy the aporias of the "other side of modernity" in its own categories of thought. The creoles and mestizos reflect on their experiences with the modern world in the medium of European philosophy. Thirdly, as Zea most notably pointed out, European and Latin American philosophy are bound together in a tragic relationship, a knot tied by the "problem" of humankind. The debate about the existence of a *filosofía de nuestra América* may seem strange at first for European philosophy. But if the self-doubt of Latin American philosophy, as Zea so clear sightedly demonstrates, is a repercussion of the racist debates in sixteenth-century Europe, then the question posed by Salazar Bondy can no longer simply be dismissed as a regional issue in southern America—it is eminently "our" issue as well, a question for European philosophy.

In contrast, Enrique Dussel engages comprehensively with European thought in articulating his philosophy of liberation. Dussel begins by examining two major thematic discourses of European philosophy, ideas of enlightenment and theories of power, which he then modifies and enlarges upon from the perspective of decolonial societies. This perspective also includes, however, configurations of modernity's self-critique within European philosophy, specifically the deconstruction of the *ego cogito* through the *volo* undertaken by Nietzsche and Heidegger, pursuing the aim of revealing the entwinement between modern reason and colonialism in the figure of the "I conquer." At the same time, Dussel locates and excavates the emancipatory potential of pre-Kantian thinkers such as Las Casas, who, considered solely as premodern theologians, have been largely excluded from the discourse about modernity in European philosophy. For their part, the decolonial approaches of Quijano and Mignolo are far more critical of Renaissance humanist and Christian thought and the rational achievements of European modernity than Dussel, with Mignolo even going so far as to declare Vitoria the founding figure of coloniality. But this is precisely the point where the possibility of constructive dialogue opens up for European philosophy. Modernity is simply inconceivable without a thoroughgoing consideration of colonialism, and this is a point postcolonial Latin American philosophies rightly insist on: "There would be no Europe without the discovery and conquest of America and the colonial matrix of power. That is why modernity/coloniality are two sides of the same coin" (Mignolo 2011: 66).

At the same time, in European modernity, as Dussel uniquely points out, there are significant rational and emancipatory breakthroughs worth integrating into a future transmodernity. Against this background, European philosophy is called upon to undertake its own rereading of its modernity discourses and identify and investigate the colonial and rational elements in its own genesis.

4

Summary and preview

Euro-American philosophies have reconstructed the signature of modernity in light of early modern thought. Heidegger locates the genesis of the modern power syndrome in Descartes' *ego cogito*, Horkheimer and Adorno in Bacon's synthesis of knowledge and power. In contrast, Habermas and Apel, while criticizing the solipsism of the Cartesian subject, constructively draw on early modern Enlightenment. The future of enlightened thought, so they argue, can only be secured when the differentiation of value spheres and subsystems, which begins in the early modern period, is maintained, while at the same time modern theories of rationality are replaced with a concept of communicative reason. The post- and decolonial philosophies of Latin America identify a different historical origin, positioning the genesis of modernity in the era of Europe's transoceanic expansion. In this setting, the colonial debates of the sixteenth century are of course assigned a key role in modern thought. Moreover, as Dussel puts it, one consequence is that seventeenth-century philosophy is in fact a "second modern age" that has Europe's colonialist expansion as its prerequisite. As both Dussel and Mignolo emphasize, Francisco de Vitoria lays the foundation for colonial ideology, i.e., for coloniality. Descartes' *ego cogito* is inconceivable without the *ego conquiro* of Cortés. Sepúlveda is regarded, even before Hobbes, as the founder of modern political philosophy. In turn, Las Casas, prior to the Enlightenment, formulates the basic tenets of modern human rights.

Against this background, any self-critical defense of European modernity needs to reread the philosophy of the Renaissance and the early modern epoch. From the overwhelming and fascinating diversity of the cultural, social, and scientific upheavals that took place in Europe from the fourteenth century through the sixteenth, I would like to focus on three motif complexes which are vitally important for the further development of modernity:

1. The de-limitation of the cosmos and the affirmation of an insatiable curiosity about the world.
2. The de-limitation of essentialist anthropology through the idea of creative self-fashioning.
3. The de-limitation of the geographical worldview through the discovery of the Americas and the formulation of the fundamental principles of a global cosmopolitanism.

The overcoming of the geocentric worldview is generally regarded as one of the most significant achievements of modern science. Copernicus stands as the symbol of the superiority of modern thought over classical ancient and medieval science. As Alexander Koyré traces in his study, the revolution in astronomy in the early modern period marks and completes the transition from the closed cosmos to the infinite universe (Koyré 1958). For Hans Blumenberg, the de-limitation of ancient cosmology corresponds to an epoch-making rehabilitation of an insatiable curiosity about the world, without which modern science is simply inconceivable (Blumenberg 1983: 229–453). In short, corresponding to the astronomic worldview of the early modern period is a new configuration of reason, the essence of which resides in "transgressing boundaries and limits already drawn and set, recognized, and then finally scarcely still perceivable" (Blumenberg 1983: 418).

The thought of Nicholas of Cusa serves as my example to elaborate the motif complex of the de-limitation of ancient and medieval cosmology and the affirmation of limitless curiosity. In his early main work *De docta ignorantia*, Cusa develops the idea of a limitless universe, and does so precisely within the framework of a negative theology still resonant with Augustine's strong reservations toward curiosity. In Cusa's later works, in particular the *Idiota* dialogues, he presents a reevaluation of insatiable curiosity, now within a philosophy of the mind, which thus culminates in setting aside both the restrictive classical ancient and Christian stances on *curiositas*. This constellation in the development of Cusa's thought enables us to study the relationship between the de-limitation of the cosmos and the affirmation of curiosity about the world as if in a laboratory.

The second motif complex, an interpretation of human freedom through the idea of self-creation, is part of the de-limitation of classical ancient essentialist anthropology. From the fourteenth century onwards, Renaissance humanism, in a pathbreaking shift of perspective, revalues the creative power of human freedom, which finds its most radical expression, at least in terms of its rhetoric, in Pico della Mirandola's *Oratio de hominis dignitate*. Pico perceives the *vis creativa* not simply in humanity's relationship to the world, but also within humans—it is possible for humans to fashion their own "nature." Thus, in Pico the motif surfaces that Heidegger later describes as "mastery over his own definition of the essence of mankind" (1982a: 98).

The third motif complex relates to the connections between the de-limitation of the *oikumene*, a consequence of the transoceanic expansion of the Iberian powers in the fifteenth and sixteenth centuries, and modern thought. The Conquista of the Americas—as both defenders and postcolonial critics of modernity agree—set off a globalization process, whereby for the first time in the history of humankind the cultures of every region of the world became interconnected. This means that, alongside the opening of the closed world into an infinite universe in cosmology, the advent of the new age also witnessed an overcoming of the boundaries of the *oikumene* and an expansion into a global society. Globality is thus an essential feature of modernity.

Whereas prominent eighteenth-century thinkers celebrated the voyages of Columbus and Vasco da Gama as the spectacular justification of their geographic worldview, in Latin American post- and decolonial thought the protagonists of Europe's transoceanic expansion are the very symbol of colonialist modernity. Indeed, in this perspective, modernity is amalgamated with colonialism to the point that the Salamanca School is taken to be the origin of the racist ideology of coloniality.

This third motif underlines that it is absolutely necessary for any serious self-critical defense of European modernity to independently engage the colonial debates of the sixteenth century. From this perspective I thus reconsider the thought of Francisco de Vitoria, who in his lectures on the Amerindians (*De Indis*) presents what is probably the first philosophically discerning analysis of the challenges emerging out of the de-limitation of the *oikumene*. Influenced by the extreme violence of the Conquista, Vitoria laid the foundation for a new global cosmopolitanism, one that, as shown by a comparative analysis of the ethical universalism and universalist political philosophies of classical antiquity and Latin Christianity, defies its reductionist construing as the ideological groundwork for coloniality. Rather, for the first time in European intellectual history Vitoria formulated a law of nations and an ethic that is globally applicable. Vitoria's cosmopolitanism is analogous to Cusa's enhanced assessment of the urge for knowledge. Just as overcoming the Ptolemaic worldview leads to an affirmation of insatiable curiosity about the world, the politico-geographic de-limitation of classical ancient and medieval world conceptions becomes the fertile substrate for a global cosmopolitanism in which moral responsibility is extended to embrace all of humanity.

At the same time, however, Vitoria's innovative conception for a law of nations is not immune from particularistic cultural aspects, especially of a Christian provenance, which can be exploited to justify colonialism. Vitoria's thought is thus an instructive example of how rational progress and power syndromes become amalgamated in the pivotal ideas of European modernity.

Into the sixteenth century, the motifs of the limitless universe, insatiable curiosity, creative self-formation, and global cosmopolitanism were variously modified and interconnected. Ginés de Sepúlveda developed the theory of enforced civilizing, based on both Vitoria's cosmopolitan ethics and Pico's dynamic anthropology. Although Sepúlveda undoubtedly formulated the most elaborate justification of colonialism, his debate with Las Casas revolved around an explosive question still discussed heatedly today—how can universal ethical norms be implemented and enforced in global modernity? Consideration of this issue means that Sepúlveda's thought cannot be entirely reduced to an irrational sacrifice myth (Dussel).

In contrast, Michel de Montaigne exposed all the de-limitations of the Renaissance to a whirlwind of estranging perspectives. Through skeptical self-observation Montaigne explored both the capabilities and the abysses of early modern humanity. The *Essais* thus articulate a sobering assessment of the idea of human self-creation, of the exuberant hopes for humanity's cognitive faculties resulting from the reevaluation of curiosity, and of the European sense of superiority over other peoples and cultures. In short, Montaigne describes a subject that cannot be merely reduced to forming the skeptical foil to Descartes' founding of modern philosophy, but one that in fact marks the starting point for an independent strand of modern subject philosophy which, through Nietzsche, is still influencing many areas of contemporary thought.

In Part II of this book, I venture back to seventeenth-century philosophy, specifically approaching the theory of social differentiation from a philosophical perspective. According to Habermas, the substantive reason of religious and metaphysical world pictures differentiates into various value spheres and subsystems in an anonymous universal process, and the guiding ideas are interpreted as objectifications of different types of rationality. But the genesis and guiding ideas of modern subsystems are not merely an anonymous historical process. As I intend to show in my studies of Francis Bacon, Thomas Hobbes, and John Locke, such subsystems are very much a key thematic concern and project of seventeenth-century philosophy.

In these studies I identify and discuss the guiding ideas of modern science, politics, and economics. It is already possible to give a detailed analysis of the ambivalences of the emerging subsystems in the thought of the philosophical founding figures of European modernity, where the de-limitations proclaimed in Renaissance philosophy undergo new transformations. The entwinement of reason, power, and coloniality is also mirrored in the still ongoing debates on seventeenth-century philosophy. Bacon was long considered the founder of modern science; since the twentieth century, however, Baconian science has become synonymous with the power obsessions of science and the destruction of nature through the use of modern technology. Hobbes is considered the founder of modern political philosophy on the one hand, and on the other as the ideologue of capitalist possessive individualism, responsible for reducing political reason to a tool subservient to the logic of power. Since the eighteenth century, Locke has been celebrated as the author of modern ideas on human rights, democracy, and tolerance. Karl Marx and more recently postcolonial thinkers have perceived a very different Locke, his theory of property as one part of a triad—along with Bacon's idea of modern science and above all Hobbes's *Leviathan*—ideologically justifying capitalism and modern colonialism. As I aim to show in detailed interpretations of their main works, the thought of Bacon, Hobbes, and Locke is characterized by the mingling of advances in rationality, the crystallization of problematic power syndromes, and colonial ideologies. In short, Baconian science, Hobbesian politics, and Lockean economics reveal, each in its own way, the complex amalgamation of reason, power, and coloniality.

Part II

Transcending the boundaries of the cosmos and the ecumene: A retrospect on the thought of the Renaissance

5

The de-limitation of the cosmos and the revaluation of insatiable curiosity: Nicholas of Cusa

Nicholas of Cusa's position between the Middle Ages and modernity has been discussed frequently since the nineteenth century. In his study on the philosophy of the Renaissance, Ernst Cassirer assigns Cusa a key role in preparing the way for Kant's epistemology and philosophy of freedom (Cassirer ([1927] 1963). Alexandre Koyré and Hans Blumenberg take a different tack, anchoring Cusa's idea of an unlimited universe more firmly in medieval thought; his thinking, so they conclude, is marked by ambivalences and inner contradictions. Finally, in recent times, Cusa has been seen as the founder of an alternative Christian modernity (Casarella 2013; Hoff 2013). Countering these attempts to fit Cusa into rigid epochal schemas, Kurt Flasch argues for a thoroughgoing historical contextualization, believing that Cusa's thought can only be understood in terms of the intellectual debates of the late Middle Ages (Flasch 2003: 81–153).

And indeed, with all these historical categorizations, one critical question is paramount: which type of modernity or which idea of the "modern subject" is Cusa seen as preparing the way for, intentionally or not? Since our retrospective of Renaissance philosophy is guided by the *question* as to what is new about the modern age, the following considerations on Cusa will pick up only two central themes, namely the de-limiting of the cosmos and the enhanced status assigned to curiosity, and will then trace their repercussions in the sixteenth and seventeenth centuries. Thus, the following is neither an overall interpretation of Cusa's thought nor a positioning of it in relationship to an already defined idea of "modernity." At the same time, however, a thorough historicization, as claimed necessary by Flasch, simply cannot nullify the hermeneutic circle that accompanies any discussion of historical philosophies. The interpretation of themes in Cusa's thinking thus remains within the context of the paradigms of the discourse on modernity in the twentieth century.

Cusa was already undertaking the radical de-limitation of the geocentric worldview in his early main work *De docta ignorantia* (*Of Learned Ignorance*) (1440). Aristotelian cosmology, upon which Ptolemy builds, was first considered fully in Christian thought by Thomas Aquinas and Albertus Magnus, both of whom wrote commentaries on *De caelo* (*On the Heavens*). Later reception ignited hefty criticism, which drew on Islamic theology. According to al-Ghazali, the teaching that the world is eternal (as opposed to created) contradicts the creation theology of the Abrahamic religions. This was the perspective adopted in 1277 when the Bishop of Paris, Etienne Tempier, evoking God's omnipotence, condemned the Aristotelian theory of the impossibility of multiple worlds (Grant 1994: 53–5; Bianchi 1997). In his criticism of Aristotelian cosmology, however, Cusa does not refer to the idea of the *potestas absoluta* or the arbitrary will of God who could have created other worlds, which according to Blumenberg triggered the self-assertion of modern reason (Blumenberg 1983: 125–8). The foundation supporting the idea of a limitless universe is not a theological absolutism but a Christian neoplatonism. Since Cusa's criticism of the geocentric worldview does not present any new astronomic observations and calculations, the significance of his cosmology for the genesis of the Copernican world has remained controversial down to the present day (Koyré 1958: 5–27). Despite this empirical lacuna, Cusa's thought was present in early modern astronomy debates and probably known to Copernicus (Meier-Oeser 1989: 190–212).

The epochal significance of Cusa's theory on the limitless universe lies in the radical revision of the metaphysical foundations supporting the Aristotelian-Ptolemaic worldview. As Cusa emphasizes repeatedly, the new cosmology can only proceed from the "instruction in ignorance [*doctrina ignorantiae*]" (*DDI* II, Prol., n.90; H 1.57).[1] And as Cusa is only too aware, the insight into the limits of human knowledge is an achievement of Socrates. Crucially, this means that understanding the doctrine of the limitlessness of the universe obviously requires an appreciation of the difference between the *Socratic* knowledge of not knowing and the *docta ignorantiae*. As Cusa claims, the classical ancient philosophers were not able to attain the new cosmological view because "they lacked learned ignorance" (*DDI* II.12.n.162; H 1.92).

Because metaphysics, cosmology, and epistemology are inseparably entwined in Aristotle, Cusa's transformation of Aristotelian metaphysics leads not only to the idea of the limitless universe but also to a justification of the limitless striving for knowledge. Cusa thus prizes open the ancient-medieval world along two fault lines: firstly the idea of a limitless universe, transcending heliocentric cosmology, and secondly by affirming insatiable curiosity, according to Blumenberg a main characteristic of the modern age.

5.1 An astronomical revolution through speculative reason: from the cosmos to the infinite universe

An initial consideration of the cosmological sections in *De docta ignorantia* encounters a somewhat confusing situation. On the one hand, Cusa speaks of an "infinite universe" (*DDI* II.1.n.81; H 1.58); on the other hand, it is stated that the universe is not infinite but "unbounded [*sine termino*]"; and finally, Cusa emphasizes that the universe is "neither finite nor infinite" (*DDI* II.1.n.97; H 1.61). Similar contradictions are to be found with respect to the center of the universe. On the one hand, there is no absolute center of the universe (*DDI* II, 11, n.157), although the earth lies close to the center of the world (*DD* III.11.n.160). The cosmology presented in *De docta ignorantia* is thus regarded as ambivalent and vague (Hill 1997: 23), while for Blumenberg, Cusa was unable to break completely with the geocentric worldview (Blumenberg 1983: 524). To gain an understanding of Cusa's new cosmology it is necessary to go back to Aristotle.

Aristotle's theory of the limited cosmos

Aristotle establishes cosmology in the "First Philosophy," i.e., the discipline that studies being as being. All being strives toward its ultimate end (*telos*), i.e., its completed state. The complete and the whole (*teleion kai holon*) is defined as that which has nothing outside itself (*Phys.* 3.6.207a8–9). In turn—and this is crucial— the completed is determined as a limit (*peras*): "And 'whole' and 'complete,' if not absolutely the same, are very closely akin, and nothing is complete [*teleios*] unless it has an end [*telos*]; but an end is a limit [*peras*]" (*Phys.* 3.6.207a4–15). For Aristotle, "limit" does not mean a restriction or indeed even a barrier that needs to be overcome; instead, it is a state of untranscendable perfection. Thus, the theory of the limitedness of the cosmos is not expressing a deficient state but its very perfection. Against this background, Aristotle categorically rejects Democritus' teaching of the multiplicity of worlds: "The ancient metaphysics of the cosmos was," as Blumenberg has rightly pointed out, "consummated precisely by the success of Plato and above all Aristotle in eliminating the problem of actually infinite space and infinitely numerous worlds" (1983: 79).

In criticizing Democritus, Aristotle draws on his theories of motion and matter. Every being strives to attain its natural place. Since what is heavy moves toward the middle and what is light to the periphery (*Cael.* 1.2.269b18–270a13), the natural place of a body, where it comes to rest, arises out of the respective mixture of the elements: "Similarly therefore fire and earth do not move to infinity [*apeiron*], but toward opposite points; and in speaking of place, the opposition is between top and bottom, so that these will be the limits [*perata*] of their movement ... There must therefore be an end, and motion cannot go on to infinity" (*Cael.* 1.8.277a21–6). Because completion means that a body has its limit in, and not outside, itself, Aristotle assigns the orbital movement of heavenly bodies precedence over the straight movement of bodies on earth. As such, there is a qualitative distinction between the stellar and the terrestrial world. Heavenly bodies and their element, ether, are complete due to their orbital motion. From this completion there follows for Aristotle the eternity (*Cael.* 2.1.283b26–36) and the immutability and uniformity (*Cael.* 1.288a 22–8) of the orbits of the heavenly bodies. Although positioned at the center of the cosmos, the earth is an ontologically inferior place in comparison to the heavens because earthly bodies are subjected to generation and corruption. This does not mean, however, that the terrestrial is chaotic and random. The movement of bodily things is regulated by their form (*morphé*, *eidos*) and the immanent directional movement of the elements.

Assuming that the number of movements is limited, and each element strives toward its natural place, for Aristotle there cannot be, as Democritus proposes, multiple "worlds [*kosmoi*]." Moreover, because Democritus believes that other worlds are composed of the same elements as the earth with its heavenly bodies, then the question of multiple worlds culminates in an alternative: "Either, in fact, we must deny that the simple bodies of the several worlds have the same natures, or if we admit it, we must, as I have said, make the centre and the circumference one for all." But because the elements in the various worlds (*kosmoi*) strive toward their natural place, it must be inferred "that there cannot be more worlds than one" (*Cael.* 1.8.276b18–22).

Aristotle also demonstrates the oneness and limitedness of the cosmos with the concept of matter. The starting point is the thesis that the world "is composed, not of a portion of matter, but of all matter whatsoever" (*Cael.* 1.9.278b 4f.). In contrast to the pre-Socratics, who explained the cosmos as originating from a limitless primal matter (water, fire, or air), or like Anaxagoras from the *apeiron*, the cosmos, because it is made up of limited things, cannot be formed out of the unlimited. Every division of the unlimited would bring forth, in turn, another unlimited (*Phys.* 3.5.204a20–7). But because there are several elements, not one of them can be unlimited. For instance, "if fire were limited, the air unlimited in quantity ... then obviously the unlimited volume of air must vanquish and destroy the limited" (*Phys.* 3.5.204b18–20). Only prime matter (*prote hyle*), which underlies all the four elements, could be unlimited. But the notion of a prime matter is a limiting concept; in *realiter*, the *materia prima* is only present in the four elements (Buchheim 1999: 125). The conclusion drawn is thus: if the cosmos is made of matter and the primal matter exists only in the different elements, then the cosmos must be limited. "The world in its entirety is made up of the whole sum of available matter (for the matter appropriate to it is, as we saw, natural perceptible body), and we may conclude that there is not now a plurality of worlds, nor has there been, nor could there be. This world is one, solitary and complete" (*Cael.* 1.9.279a 8–12).

Although Aristotle categorically excludes the notion of an actual unlimited universe in his cosmology, the ontological status of the "unlimited [*apeiron*]" is analyzed further in the *Physics* (*Phys.* 3.6). The unlimited is to be correlated not to reality (*energeia*) but possibility (*dynamis*). The concept of the potential infinite implies infinite divisibility or extensibility; its application must be limited to mathematics and spatial dimensions (*Phys.* 3.7). The unlimited "is not that 'beyond which there is nothing' but 'what is always beyond'" (*Phys.* 3.6.207a1 2). Because the completed is the limited in the sense of untranscendable fullness, the unlimited, since something can always be added or it can be divided in an endless number of operations, belongs to the incomplete. Therefore, as Aristotle emphasizes, Parmenides, who taught the limitedness of being, is correct vis-à-vis Melissus' doctrine of the infinity of being (*Phys.* 3.6.207a15–17; Rapp 2004).

The concept of the potential infinite alters depending on whether it is applied in mathematics or to space. A numerical series can be extended infinitely but cannot be endlessly divided; mathematical operations of division encounter their limit in the number one, which is indivisible (*Phys.* 3.6.207b 5–10). In determining spatial dimension, the opposite pertains. Space can be endlessly divided, but not endlessly extended, because the dimension depends on possibility (*Phys.* 3.7.207b). The potential infinite is thus—as Aristotle emphasizes with respect to the numerical series—*limitless/infinite* on the one hand, but at the same time also finite, because a further number can always be added to each number (*Phys.* 3.7.207b11–13; Buchheim 1999: 111).

The metaphysical fundament: *Doctrina ignorantia*

As with Aristotle, Cusa's cosmology is only understandable in the light of his metaphysics, the contours of which are roughly outlined in the first chapter of his early main work *De docta ignorantia*. The starting point is the Aristotelian dictum that all humans strive intrinsically for knowledge (*Metaph.* 1.1.980a1). The naturalness of the urge to know, as Cusa explains with reference to Aristotle, is part of a comprehensive teleological ontology. God has implanted a natural desire in all things (*desiderium naturale*) that channels movement in a specific direction. So that the natural striving avoids coming to nothing, all living creatures are equipped with the capability to understand the purpose given by nature, so that they can then find fulfillment and composure by realizing their essence (*DDI* I.1.n.2). In this sense, humanity is also part of the teleological order of the universe. In distinction from animals, however, as a rational being a human strives not merely to secure self-preservation but to attain truth. As every animal perceives what is beneficial to it, a "sound, free intellect knows to be true that which is apprehended by its affectionate embrace. (The intellect insatiably desires to attain unto the true through scrutinizing all things by means of its innate faculty of inference.)" (*DDI* I.1.n.2; H 1.5).

At first glance, Cusa appears to classify the human striving for knowledge seamlessly into Aristotelian metaphysics, with all existing things striving to attain their ends (*telos*). But in a surprising turn, Cusa radically alters the scope of Aristotle's teleological ontology, describing the alignment toward the *telos* with a remarkable formulation, that every single existing thing is given a natural desire: "ut sint meliori quidem modo, quo hoc cuiusque naturae patitur condicio" *(DDI* I.1.n.2). Various translators, Hopkins among them, have understood this in the sense of Aristotelian ontology: "there is present in all things a natural desire to exist in the best manner in which the condition of each thing's nature permits this" (H 1.5). But the Latin formulation, "meliori quidem modo," when read as "in a better way," expresses, not unintentionally, an intensification. Creatures strive to realize not merely their immanent but, as Offermann had shown in elaborating on Gerda von Bredow's study, an ever-greater improvement of their respective nature (Offermann 1991; Bredow 1967). This ontological principle, also described as "perfectior esse posset" (*DDI* II.12.n.164), recurs in all themes addressed by Cusa, not least in cosmology.

In a next step, Cusa turns to the cognitive capability of humanity. Knowing is gained through comparison, with something known used to infer the unknown (*DDI* I.1.n.2). Cusa takes mathematics as an example, noting that knowledge is derived from evident axioms. Knowledge resides in comparison (*DDI* I.1.n.2); the medium of all comparison is the number, which encompasses every possible relation wherein a noun is assigned or denied a predicate. The number is therefore the principle of knowledge of not only quantitative but also qualitative relations, for example the relationship of substance and accident (*DDI* I.1.n.3; Herold 1975: 87f.; Velthoven 1977: 153–96).

For Cusa, the definition of knowledge as a comparative operation provides an initial insight into the limits of human reason: "Both the precise combinations in corporeal things and the congruent relating of known to unknown surpass human reason—to such an extent that Socrates seemed himself to know nothing except that he did not know" (*DDI* I.1.n.4; H 1.5). The problem of precision (*praecisio*) is explained through reference to the concept of equality (*aequalitas*), understood in the sense of a gradual ontology (*gradualis aequalitas*): "Therefore, number, which is a necessary condition of comparative relation, is present not only in quantity but also in all things which in any manner whatsoever can agree or differ either substantially or accidentally" (*DDI* I.1.n.3; H 1.5). In so far as things belong to the same kind or species, they are similar; but because a thing can never exhaust *all* potentialities *hic et nunc*, individual things remain dissimilar at the same time. A singular thing that would bring into being all the possibilities of its species would not only be the most complete, i.e., perfect, but it would also actually erase the diversity from the individual realizations of its species. From the plural constitution of the mundane world, Cusa draws a surprising conclusion—the individual thing can never reach its *telos* completely but only approach it gradually.

> Therefore, just as in accordance with the nature of contracted things the individual is positable only within the limit of its species, so too no individual can attain to the limit of its genus and of the universe. Indeed, among many individual things of the same species, there must be a difference of degrees of perfection ... Therefore, no [individual thing] reaches the limit of its species.
> (*DDI* III.1.n.184; H 1.113)

This provides us with an access to the thesis presented at the beginning of *DDI*, namely that all things strive "to be in a better way [*meliori quidam modo*] than the condition of one's own nature allows." Because there is no thing that can completely exhaust its potentialities, its truth lies beyond what it attains. The formula *meliori quidem modo* does not imply, however, that the individual strives to exceed the limits of its species, a point Cusa emphasizes through the example of humans: "A man wishes to be only a man—not an angel or any other nature" (*De pace fide* XIII.n.44; H 1.656). Rather, all things strive to fulfill and attain their species "in a better way," in other words, in a process of infinite approximation. Thus, in the physical world, the principle pertains that "we cannot find two or more things which are so similar and equal that they could not be progressively more similar *ad infinitum*. Hence, the measure and the measured—however equal they are—will always remain different" (*DDI* I.3.n.9; H 1.8).

Cusa draws far-reaching epistemological consequences from this insight into the indissoluble dissimilarity between finite things. The human mind must accept that, in the physical world, the truth of things can never be determined precisely (*DDI* I.3.n.10; H 1.5). The imprecision in knowledge is not because of a lack of refinement in our perceptual senses or the inaccuracy of measuring instruments but lies in the very plural constitution of the world. Secondly, what ensues from the principle of *perfectior esse posset* is that every instance of knowledge depends on a specific standpoint. Because there is no perfect measure in the finite, every comparison between physical things must begin with a degree—greater or lesser—of perfection. For this reason,

> in each species—e.g., the human species—we find that at a given time some individuals are more perfect and more excellent than others in certain respects. (For example, Solomon excelled others in wisdom …) Nevertheless, a difference of opinions—in accordance with the difference of religions, sects, and regions—gives rise to different judgments of comparison (so that what is praiseworthy according to one [religion, sect, or region] is reprehensible according to another); and scattered throughout the world are people unknown to us.
>
> (*DDI* III.1.n.189; H 1.115)

In the realm of sensory perceptible things, humans, because no individual perfectly fulfills the species, are compelled to infer conclusions about an unknown from something relatively certain. In other words: knowledge is perspectival. Perspectivity does not, though, merely imply an insight into the limitedness of one's own standpoint; by recognizing the limits of human knowing, humanity effectively moves beyond the conditionality of the individual perspective: "to think a perspective as a perspective is to be in some sense already beyond it, is to have become learned about limitations" (Harries 2001: 42).

At this point, the question arises as to which concept of truth serves to support the thesis of the perspectivity of human knowledge. Plato had set the immutable truth of mathematics and ideas against the perspectivity of sensory perception. For Cusa, too, there is no doubt that mathematical axioms enable far greater precision than empirical concepts: "No one fails to know that truth is more assuredly attained in mathematics than in the other liberal arts" (*De theologicis complementis* II.1–2; H 2.747), for "perceptible things are in a state of continual instability because of the material possibility abounding in them" (*DDI* I.11.n.31; H 1.18). Mathematical knowledge therefore appears to fulfill the ideal of absolute precision. Nonetheless, mathematical knowledge can by no means guarantee this absolute precision because it is not "free of material associations" and is "subject to the possibility of changing" (*DDI* I.11.n.31; H 1.18f.).

Ultimately, though, the imprecision of mathematical knowledge stems from how Cusa understands divine truth, where plurality, the more or the less, is contained in a non-differentiated unity: "For truth is not something more or something less but is something indivisible. Whatever is not truth cannot measure truth precisely" (*DDI* I.3.n.10; H 1.8). The imprecision of mathematics is therefore due to the finiteness of the human mind. Because human beings have not posited themselves in existence, a difference inheres to all thinking operations: in Cusa's terminology, an "imprecision" between the measure and the measured. Absolute precision (*praecisio*) is only possible through sublating otherness (Beierwaltes 1980: 108).

Divine truth thus sheds light on the relationship between the ontological formula of *perfectior esse posset* and the insight into the perspectivity of human knowledge. From the absolute, that all is what is and can be, it is understandable why things, why what exists, is not all that it can be; perfection can only be striven for in a process of endless approximation, without ever being reached. In the same vein, an awareness of how *all* knowledge is perspectival presupposes a move beyond all perspectives, i.e., the finite. In short, thinking the absolute and insight into the perspectivity of all human knowledge depend on one another.

From this background, it is possible to specify the distinction between the Socratic-Platonic knowing of not knowing and Cusa's *docta ignorantia*, a distinction of eminent importance for understanding the new cosmology. As Cusa saw it, the "ancients" had lacked—as Harries (2001: 31–3; 42–5) has identified astutely—the insight into the perspectivity of human knowledge. But the awareness of perspectivity articulated by Cusa—and this is where we may expand on Harries—is anchored in the ontological indeterminacy of the creaturely world, which is based in turn on a concept of truth wherein in all differences are held within an unsurpassable fullness of being (Herold 1975).

But in which sense can humanity surpass, cognitively, the many in the direction of a oneness without difference when knowing takes place by comparing finite things? As Cusa pointedly emphasizes, thinking the absolute, the main theme of *De docta ignorantia*, confronts humanity with a completely new epistemological challenge. Whereas in the act of comparative knowing the human mind can at least depend on a relative measure, once in the infinite, the human urge to know threatens to become mired in an undifferentiated oneness: "it is self-evident that there is no comparative relation of the infinite to the finite [*infiniti ad finitum proportionem non esse*]" (*DDI* I.3.n.9; H 1.7). If knowing is always an act of comparing, then as Cusa logically concludes, it is simply impossible to know the absolute: "Hence, the infinite, *qua* infinite, is unknown; for it escapes all comparative relation" (*DDI* I.1.n.3; H 1.5). The fulfillment of the innate striving for knowledge, guaranteed by God, thus resides paradoxically in non-knowing, more precisely knowing that the absolute cannot be grasped through the comparative. "Therefore, if the foregoing points are true, then since the desire in us is not in vain, assuredly we desire to know that we do not know" (*DDI* I.1.n.4; H 1.6).

In exceeding limits and moving to the absolute, which can be thought only *incomprehensibiliter*, i.e., by relinquishing comparative knowing, all opposites holding thought in comparative relations must be overcome. The absolute can only be touched (*attingere*) through the coincidence of opposites (*coincidentia oppositorum*), but not known (Leinkauf 2006: 89–102).

In *De docta ignorantia* Cusa uses the concepts of maximum and minimum to explain the idea of a coincidence of opposites. When a finite thing, and even in an infinite number of repetitions, is again and again exceeded toward something larger, then thinking remains entrapped in comparative knowing. Despite the trajectory of endless progression, thinking never escapes the relation of either a more or a less, i.e., the medium of finite comparison: "Therefore, it is most clear that where we find comparative degrees of greatness, we do not arrive at the unqualifiedly Maximum [*maximum simpliciter*]; for things which are comparatively greater and lesser are finite; but necessarily, such a Maximum is infinite" (*DDI* I.3.n.9; H 1.7f.). The analysis of the minimum arrives at the same conclusion. This means that thinking arrives at the absolute minimum and maximum not by following an operation of enlarging or reducing a specific magnitude, because in relation to the absolute minimum and maximum nothing larger or smaller can be thought, and in as far as the notion of "more or less" is nonsensical with respect to the absolute, the smallest, the minimum, must coincide with largest, the maximum (*DDI* I.4.n.11). But that is not all: in the absolute without difference, the tension between reality and possibility is overcome: "Hence, since the absolutely Maximum is all that which be, it is altogether actual" (*DDI* I.4.n.11; H 1.9). Maintaining the Neoplatonic tradition, for Cusa, the absolute, as unbounded fullness, is absolute union (*unum*) and necessity (*absoluta necessitas*) (*DDI* I.5).

Finitude and limitlessness of the universe

In the second book of *De docta ignorantia* Cusa turns to cosmology, to "those things which are all-that-which-they-are from the Absolute Maximum" (*DDI* II.n.90; H 1.57f.). Although finite being only *is* in so far as it originates from the absolute, the finite is not simply the other of the absolute, for the infinite, in the sense of the *coincidentia oppositorum*, is at the same time the finite. Accordingly, the finite needs to be understood as a mode of the absolute. At this point, Cusa introduces the concept of *contractio*. The universe *is* the absolute in the mode of contraction, it is *maximum contractum*. Conversely, the finite in the absolute is in the mode of enfolding (*complicatio*), while the finite itself is the unfolding (*explicatio*) of the absolute maximum (*DDI* II.3–6).

It is in this framework that Cusa formulates the momentous idea of a limitless universe. Since the universe encompasses, *per definitionem*, the totality of finite being, the question as to the existence of other worlds outside the universe is meaningless, which, as Cusa emphasizes, is still in full accordance with Aristotle. As God in his absolute fullness bears all within, the universe, as *explicatio Dei*, has nothing outside itself. In contrast to Aristotle, however, the insight that the universe is all that is, and thus cannot be limitedly defined by anything else, prompts Cusa to make a surprising move—the universe is limitless: "And so, [the universe is] unbounded; for it is not the case that anything actually greater than it, in relation to which it would be bounded, is positable" (*DDI* II.1.n. 97; H.1.61).

The reason why Cusa comes to contrary conclusions to Aristotle although proceeding from the same premises lies in how they divergently understand perfection, measure, and limit. For Aristotle, the measure, i.e., the end (*telos*), of each natural being resides within itself. Perfection thus means bringing the immanent end into reality (*entelecheia*). When no external hindrances stand in the way, then all natural things can attain perfection. Therefore, a precise measure exists for Aristotle *in* the different realms of being that thinking can rely on. For Cusa, however, strictly speaking, perfection is ascribable solely to the absolute. Perfection means the absolute identity of a thing with itself, in which all otherness is eliminated. Because the absolute, i.e., God, is the sole measure of all earthly things, created beings cannot bear their measure within themselves. At this point, Cusa once again brings the principle of *perfectior esse posset* into play: "clearly, there must always be positable a greater and a lesser—whether in quantity or virtue or perfection, etc.—than any given finite thing, since the unqualifiedly Maximum or Minimum is not positable in [finite] things" (*DDI* II.1.n. 96; H 1.60). The principle of an endless approximation toward perfection holds valid not just for individual things, genera, and species—it also holds for the universe as a whole.

> Therefore, there is only one Limit of species, of genera, or of the universe. This Limit is the Center, the Circumference, and the Union of all things. And it is not the case that the universe exhausts the infinite, absolutely maximum

power of God so that the universe is an unqualified maximum, de-limiting the power of God. Hence, it is not the case that the universe reaches the limit of Absolute Maximality; genera do not reach the limit of the universe; species [do not reach] the limit of their genera; and individual things [do not reach] the limit of their species. Thus, all things are that-which-they-are in the best way [possible for them] and between a maximum and a minimum; and God is the Beginning, the Middle, and the End of the universe and of each thing, so that all things—whether they ascend, descend, or tend toward the middle—approach God.

(*DDI* III.1.n.185; H 1.113)

Because the universe is also subject to the principle *perfectior esse posset*, two concepts of the infinite emerge, namely the infinity of the universe and the absolute infinity of God, which Cusa summarizes in the "rule of learned ignorance": "This is the gist of the rule of learned ignorance: viz., that with regard to things that admit of more and less we never come to an unqualifiedly [*simpliciter*] maximum or to an unqualifiedly minimum, even though we do come to what is actually [*actu*] maximal and to what is actually minimal" (*De venatione sapientiae* 26.n.79; H 2.1328). In the absolute, all limits and opposites, including the antithesis between the finite and infinite, coincide. What still needs to be explained, however, is how the limitlessness of the universe can even be thought. Because the created world is ontologically subject to the measuring of a "more or less," the concept of the potential infinite, which Aristotle had limited to the numerical series, can be applied to the universe as a whole:

> Therefore, if in ascending the scale of numbers we actually arrive at a maximum number, since number is finite, still we do not come to a maximum number than which there can be no greater number; for such a number would be infinite. Therefore, it is evident that the ascending number-scale is actually finite, and that the [arrived at maximum number] would be in potentiality relative to another [greater] number.
>
> (*DDI* 1.5.n. 13; H 1.10)

Against this background, the contradictions in Cusa's theory of a limitless and, at the same time, finite universe can be resolved. As Cusa emphasizes in accord with Aristotle, the numerical series is at once infinite and finite; its infinity resides in the never-ending possibility of iterative addition, its finiteness in the fact that there *will* always be more: "Thus the universe is finite although it is 'termless' [*interminatum*] like an actually enumerated series of natural numbers: the greatest number we reach in this enumeration is finite, but the series is capable of being continued" (Lai 1973: 164).

To sum up: as potentially infinite, the universe is finite in so far as it, in distinction from the absolute, is not everything that it can be. For this reason, Cusa distinguishes between the infinity of the world, to be understood in the sense of the potentially infinite, and the absolute in the sense of the *impliciter maximum*. Both concepts of the infinite are then also contrasted terminologically in *De docta ignorantia* II.1 through the distinction between the "negative infinite [*negative infinitum*]" and the "privative infinite [*privative infinitum*]" (*DDI* II.1.n.97; cf. Enders 2002: 410f.).

Enhancing the position of humans through the stellarization of the earth

From the starting point of the speculative theory on the limitless and simultaneously finite universe, Cusa transforms Aristotelian cosmology, proceeding step by step, without ever rejecting it completely. This has frequently stirred the suspicion that Cusa remains imprisoned in the ancient worldview. Cusa himself, however, has no doubts as to the new ground he is breaking with his cosmology: "Perhaps those who will read the following previously unheard of [doctrines] will be amazed, since learned ignorance shows these [doctrines] to be true" (*DDI* II.11.n.156; H 1.89).

Through the rule of learned ignorance, Cusa does in fact radically query central premises of classical ancient cosmology, for example the teaching that the earth is at the center of the universe and that the heavens move in circular orbits. Because "it is not the case that in any genus—even [the genus] of motion—we come to an unqualifiedly maximum and minimum," the idea that the earth forms the center of the universe must be at least qualified and a different perspective taken: "For, with regard to motion, we do not come to an unqualifiedly minimum—i.e., to a fixed center. For the [unqualifiedly] minimum must coincide with the [unqualifiedly] maximum" (*DDI* II.11.n.156; H 1.89f.). If no absolute center can be determined in the universe, then the idea of a fixed circumference also loses all meaning (*DDI* II.11.n.156; H 1.89f.).

What ensues from the negation of a fixed center in the universe is the axial rotation of the earth, a thesis that Nicholas Oresme had already brought forth against Aristotle in the fourteenth century (Zimmermann 1979: 131; Grant 1994: 443–6; Hoyer 2003: 28f.). "Therefore, the earth, which cannot be the center, cannot be devoid of all motion. Indeed, it is even necessary that the earth be moved in such a way that it could be moved infinitely less" (*DDI* II.11.n.157, 1–3; H 1.90). If the earth moves like the stars and other heavenly bodies, then the distinction between the stellar and sublunary world, of such fundamental importance for ancient cosmology, collapses. The earth is—as Cusa puts it—just one star among others, "terra quasi stella" (*DDI* II.11.n.160). But this is merely the first move: Cusa also calls into question the circular motion of the heavenly bodies, a thesis at the very heart of ancient cosmology since Plato. Like all things, stars approach their ideal—concretely here: the circular motion of their orbiting—in an infinite manner without ever reaching it (*DDI* II.12.n.163). However, the ancient cosmologists were fully aware that the movements of the stars deviated from the ideal of uniformity and circularity. Ptolemy had thus attempted to salvage the ideal order of the cosmos by formulating the theory of epicycles and assuming an immaterial center of the world (*punctum aequans*) that lies close to the earth (Nagel 1986: 236–9). Cusa takes a different tack, solving the problem of empirical deviations from the ideal premises of ancient cosmology with a speculative argument—because absolute precision is solely ascribable to God, then the order of the spheres and stars is "without complete precision [*sine omni precisione*]" (*DDI* II.13.n.178; H 1.100).

The stellarization of the earth and the assumption that the earth moves have dramatic consequences for human knowledge. With the earth as the standpoint, then only a limited view into the limitless universe is possible. As Cusa emphasizes, however, the insight into the perspectivity of human knowledge is constantly disrupted by our inclination to elevate the earthly standpoint to the center of the universe:

> And because of the fact that it would always seem to each person (whether he were on the earth, the sun, or another star) that he was at the "immovable" center, so to speak, and that all other things were moved: assuredly, it would always be the case that if he were on the sun, he would fix a set of poles in relation to himself; if on the earth, another set; on the moon, another; on Mars, another; and so on.
>
> (*DDI* II.12.n.162; H 1.93)

In antiquity, however, it was not just Aristotle who developed the idea of a hierarchically ordered cosmos; it was also prevalent in neoplatonism and closely tied to the teaching of the world soul. For this reason, Cusa questions the mediating function assigned to the world soul in the relationship between the one and the universe. Without mediation, the absolute is present in all things of creation in the same intensity (Strunk 2019: 323): "Therefore, He who is the center of the world, viz., the Blessed God, is also the center of the earth, of all spheres, and of all things in the world. Likewise, He is the infinite circumference of all things" (*DDI* II.11.n.157; H 1.91).

Nonetheless, for Cusa, the world is thus not dispersed into a limitless sphere. The rule of *docta ignorantia* only excludes the idea of an absolute center. The ancient notion that heavy bodies have an innate propensity to move downwards or to a center, while lighter bodies move upward, is not negated but merely qualified. And what is more: the reinterpretation of the ancient teaching on mechanics opens the way for a broad field of cosmological suppositions, in which metaphysical reflections are now tied to empirical observations.

That the earth moves follows directly from the metaphysical thesis that an absolute point of motionlessness is not possible in the finite for ontological reasons. *How quickly* the earth moves, however, can only be calculated through empirical comparisons. Comets and stars, possessing a high degree of fiery elements—for example the planets of Mercury and Venus, and most predominately, of course, the sun—move more rapidly than the moon; in turn, the moon seems to move quicker than the earth. Cusa draws the conclusion that "the earth is moved even less than all [these] others [stars]" (*DDI* II.11.n.159; H 1.91). Because there is no absolute minimum in the universe, the earth cannot be a body that describes "a minimum circle around a center or a pole" (*DDI* II.11.n.159; H 1.91). For this reason, it is justified to suppose that, from all stars and bodies, the earth is closest to the center and thus moves very slowly, leading us to believe that it is at complete rest.

By connecting metaphysical reflections and empirical observations Cusa ultimately rebuts the traditional devaluation of the earth in relationship to the celestial spheres. In the second book of *De docta ignorantia*, all the arguments used to prove the inferior status of the world in the geocentric worldview are refuted one by one.

The ancient notion that the earth is located in the lower domain of the universe is refuted by the thesis of the limitlessness of the universe, because the categories of "above" and "below" are annulled: "And because in the world there is no maximum or minimum with regard to perfections, motions, and shapes ... it is not true that the earth is the lowliest and the lowest" (*DDI* II.12.n.164; H 1.93). At the same time, though, the earth may be counted among the lower stars, for it, in comparison to other stars, e.g. Venus or the sun, demonstrates a lower portion of fiery elements. Cusa refutes the argument of blackness, frequently cited in antiquity as a sign of the earth's inferiority, through a bold thought experiment: if viewed from the standpoint of the sun, the earth too would no longer appear dark but as a bright star. Conversely, closely observing the body of the sun reveals that it, like the earth, possesses different elements, namely an earth-like kernel, a cloud of steam and bright air, and a fiery periphery (*DDI* II.12.n.164). The argument that the earth is ranked beneath the stars because of its smallness is refuted with astronomical data. As Cusa explains, the earth cannot possibly be the smallest star because it, like the phenomenon of the moon eclipse shows, is larger than the moon, and indeed perhaps than Mercury (*DDI* II.12, n.167). The ancient notion that the heavenly bodies influence generation and corruption on earth, but that the converse influence does not pertain, has become moot with the thesis that the earth itself is a star. Even if an empirical verification appears impossible, for Cusa it must be assumed that stars mutually influence one another: "For being a star, perhaps the earth, too, influences the sun and the solar region, as I said" (*DDI* II.12.n.168; H 1.95). As for the assumption that the inhabitants of the earth—humans, animals, and plants—are of lower rank than the inhabitants of heavenly bodies, Cusa points out the perfection of the human's spirit-nature (*DDI* II.12.n.169). Moreover, the inferiority of the earth's inhabitants must be proven by a comparison with the inhabitants of other stars, for which we simply lack the necessary knowledge (*DDI* II.12.n.171). At the same time, though, the assumption that solely the earth, which is possibly one of the lesser stars, is inhabited while the rest of the universe remains empty contradicts the notion of a wise creator (*DDI* II.12.n.169). Finally, Cusa refutes the thesis that solely earthly creatures are subject to rising and passing as an argument for the inferiority of the earth. Because we have no way of knowing about the reciprocal influences exerted by the stars, then it remains unknown how the decomposition and composition of varying natures proceeds in other areas of the universe (*DDI* II.12.n.172–3).

Cusa's cosmology is—in summary—the result of a transformation of the metaphysical premises of the Ptolemaic worldview through the application of the rules of *docta ignorantia*. The decisive step beyond Plato and Aristotle lies in understanding the absolute as the sole measure of all reality, against which the universe appears to be the asymptotic approximation toward the divine fullness of being.

As the twelfth chapter of the second book of *De docta ignorantia* so strikingly shows, the de-limitation of the universe goes hand in hand with a comprehensive affirmative revaluation of the earth, a stark contrast to the geocentric system. Elevated to the ranks of the heavenly bodies, the earth now shares their perfection, namely their spherical form and steady, uniform circular movement; at the same time, the earth elevated to a star does not escape the principle of *perfectior esse posset* (*DDI* II.12.n.164). Like all stars, the earth is also only ever approaching the ideal spherical form and circular motion, without ever achieving them completely (*DDI* II.12.n.163).

Fritz Nagel has illustrated the epochal importance of Cusa's transformation of ancient cosmology through a comparison with Copernicus and Ptolemy. Into the eighteenth century, Copernicus was considered not the discoverer of a new astronomical worldview but a restorer of the heliocentric model of Aristarchus of Samos (Meier-Oeser 1989: 193). Although not presenting any mathematical data, with his idea of a limitless universe, wherein the sun is no longer the center, Cusa opens the way for astronomy to embark on new discoveries. Ptolemy had blunted the friction between the ideal principles of ancient cosmology and the factual inconstancy of the movements of the stars through two theories, namely the epicycle theory and the assumption of an immaterial center of the world that lies close to earth. Copernicus then replaced the *punctum aequans* theory with the postulation that the sun is at the center of the universe, while the looping movements of the stars were explained by assuming that the earth moves. Thus, Copernicus remains loyal to the ideal principles of ancient cosmology—the constancy and circularity of the movements of stars. Cusa, however, fundamentally questions the normative premises of classical ancient-medieval cosmology. Crucially, he did not fully exploit the possibilities afforded by his new theory of the universe on the empirical or the metaphysical level. Circular movement and spherical form remain criteria of ontological perfection, even if they can only be realized asymptotically in the finite. First Johannes Kepler, drawing on the data of Tycho Brahe, replaced the ideal circular movements with elliptic curves. Thus, Kepler's astronomy is the adequate empirical theory for the overcoming of ancient cosmo-ontology initiated by Cusa.

5.2 Justification of the limitless striving for knowledge of the world: humanity as the creative measure of all things

In the modern age, according to Hans Blumenberg's thesis, theoretical curiosity is rehabilitated to an epochally significant extent (1983: 229–453). The formulation "*re*habilitation" is misleading, however. The modern affirmation of the urge for knowledge is, as Blumenberg himself emphasizes, "just not the mere renaissance of a life ideal that had already been present once before and whose devaluation, through the interruption of its general acceptance, had only to be reversed" (1983: 233). What arises in the modern age is a completely new ideal of knowledge, namely the ideal of an *insatiable* striving for knowledge of the *world*.

As Blumenberg depicts it, the historical roots of curiosity about the world lie in the late Middle Ages and the Renaissance. "As one of the great moments that oscillate indecisively between the epochs, I would like to mark April 26, 1336, when Petrarch ascended Mont Ventoux—'purely out of the desire', as he writes, 'to see the unusual altitude of this place'" (1983: 341). But during his ascent, Petrarch opens the *Confessions* of Augustine, "in which amazement at the heights of the mountains, the tides of the sea and flooding of streams, and the paths of the stars is set in sharp contrast to man's self-forgetfulness" (Blumenberg 1983: 341; cf. August., *Conf.* 10.6). Manifesting in Petrarch is nothing less than the tension between the Augustinian warning against becoming engrossed in amazement at the world and the curiosity about the world that was gestating in the early modern age. As Blumenberg emphasizes, however, it was Cusawho took the most important step for a "recognition of the human craving for knowledge, in its unrestrictable dynamics," albeit still combined "with the humility of finitude that was specific to the Middle Ages" (1983: 355). But it is precisely because of this entwinement of the old and new that Cusa's thought offers profound insight into the argumentative relationships which led to an epochally significant revaluation of insatiable curiosity about the world in the fifteen and sixteenth centuries. Thus, instead of primarily reiterating the lack of modernity in his thought in the light of the subsequent limitless curiosity about the world, I wish to give prominence to the justification of the insatiability of human craving for knowledge, setting the classical ancient and Christian reservations toward curiosity as the contrastive background.

Retrospective: problematizations of curiosity in ancient and medieval thought

The idea of a theoretical investigation of the world, initiated in European thinking by the pre-Socratics, is connected to ethics by Plato and Aristotle and affirmatively revaluated as a mode for achieving the self-perfection of humans. In Hellenistic and Christian thinking, however, this close connection between knowledge of the world and *eudaimonia* once again separate. Striving for knowledge itself could obviously not be integrated into the new ideas about happiness without friction, in particular friction with the Roman ideal of the citizen and the Christian hope of the afterlife. In this context, Cicero introduces the concept of curiosity (*curiositas*), which emerged from the translation of the Greek *oxypeinos* (ravenous, voracious), into Latin (Labhardt 1960: 209); the noun *curiositas*, which corresponds to the Greek *periergía* (exaggerated care, Latin *cura*), is recorded for the first time by Cicero (Bös 1995: 12). It is also Cicero who combines *curiositas*, which, in the language of everyday life, covers the craving for sensation, the lust for gossip, an unflagging interest in the new, strange, and outlandish or monstrous, with the philosophical striving for knowledge. Because the aspect of insatiability is fused with *curiositas*, tension with Plato, where striving for knowledge stands in a fundamental contradiction to the immoderateness and insatiability of desires (*De rep.* 442), is present from the outset. Undoubtedly the most important criticism of curiosity in terms of its impact and history is that articulated by Augustine. However, Augustine already takes up Hellenistic and Roman problematizations of *curiositas*, specifically those brought forward by Cicero and Seneca, before then complementing them with Christian arguments.

Like Aristotle, Cicero assumes that the quest for knowledge is natural (*De off.* 1.4.13), commencing when our senses perceive something beautiful before ultimately finding fulfillment and coming to rest in the intellectual intuition of the harmonious order of the cosmos. Similar to Plato, whatever is perceivable through the senses is capable of awakening us to true wisdom (*De off.* 1.5.15; cf. *Rep.* 493e; *Symp.* 209e–212c). As Cicero explicitly states in *Somnium Scipionis*, human knowledge is to be directed to the divine (*De rep.* 6.9.9–6.26.29). Although Cicero orientates on the ancient maxim of contemplating the heavenly and holding the earthly in contempt (*De rep.* 6.19.20), Cicero by no means advocates an ethos of radical scorn for the world. As long as we are living on earth, then we are obliged to care for family and secure the safety of the fatherland (*De rep.* 6.26.29). Intuiting the divine order of being in fact consolidates the virtues of self-control, moderation, and justice:

> We alone of living creatures know the risings and settings and the courses of the stars, the human race has set limits to the day, the month and the year, and has learnt the eclipses of the sun and moon and foretold for all future time their occurrence, their extent and their dates. And contemplating the heavenly bodies the mind arrives at a knowledge of the gods, from which arises piety, with its comrades justice and the rest of the virtues, the sources of a life of happiness that vies with and resembles the divine existence and leaves us inferior to the celestial beings in nothing else save immortality, which is immaterial for happiness.
>
> (*N.D.* 2.153)

Since studying nature is only legitimate when it leads to emulating the gods and conducting a virtuous life, Cicero distinguishes between the striving for knowledge of the truly valuable and worthwhile things and *curiositas*, which immoderately seeks to know everything: "A passion for miscellaneous omniscience no doubt stamps a man as a mere dilettante; but it must be deemed the mark of a superior mind to be led on by the contemplation of high matters to a passionate love of knowledge" (*De fin.* 5.49).

At the same time, however, Cicero displays great sympathy when describing the immoderateness of human curiosity about the world, asking why is it that "children cannot be deterred even by punishment from studying and inquiring into the world around them?" (*De fin.* 5.48). For the sake of knowledge, scholars willingly accept enormous privation, renouncing wealth and at times even risking their health. Cicero sees the fascination that burgeons out of the insatiable human craving for knowledge depicted in the mythical symbolism of the Sirens, whose alluring song are to prevent Odysseus from returning home: "Homer was aware that his story would not sound plausible if the magic that held his hero enmeshed was merely an idle song! It is knowledge that the Sirens offer, and it was no marvel if a lover of wisdom held this dearer than his home" (*De fin.* 5.49).[2] Even Pythagoras and Plato, fully devoted to the highest and divine, "in their passion for learning [*cupido discendi*] travelled through the remotest parts of the earth! Those who are blind to these facts have never been enamoured of some high and worthy study" (*De fin.* 5.51–2). Inquisitiveness impels us to study "all the obscure and secret realms of nature [*quae naturae obscuritate occultantur*]" (*De fin.* 5.51) and delights in the richness of histories, indeed even fabricated stories (*De fin.* 5.51–2). For Cicero, great happiness grows out of the purposeless studying of the rich diversity of the world: "For what is more delightful than leisure devoted to literature? That literature I mean which gives us the knowledge of the infinite greatness of nature, and, in this actual world of ours, of the sky, the lands, the seas" (*De fin.* 5.105).

The irresistible fascination exerted by the diversity of things destabilizes the hierarchical structure aligning knowledge of the divine, the fulfillment of social obligations, and curiosity about the world. To avoid open conflict between the different objects and goals that provide us with orientation and meaning, it is necessary to restrict the leeway afforded to the human craving for knowledge. Insatiable curiosity is only permissible in specific situations, namely when we are partly or temporarily released from the obligation to fulfill social duties—for example when we reach old age, are in unfamiliar surrounds or strange lands, or in exile—and this explains "the numbers of men who when they had fallen into the power of enemies or tyrants, or when they were in prison or in exile, have solaced their sorrow with the pursuit of learning" (*De fin.* 5.53f.). It is only after death, however, that humans can fully and completely enjoy the delights of curiosity, for we are relieved of all duties serving earthly well-being:

> we feel the wish for an object of our observation and attention, this will happen much more freely then, and we shall devote our whole being to study and examination, because nature has planted in our minds an insatiable longing to see truth [*insatiabilis quaedam cupiditas veri videndi*]; and the more the vision of the borders only of the heavenly country, to which we have come, renders easy the knowledge of heavenly conditions, the more will our longing for knowledge be increased
>
> (*Tusc.* 1.44; see also *De fin.* 5.53).

At the same time, Seneca sees humans encountering limits when seeking to fulfill their original definition as *contemplator mundi*: "though he guards his hours with most miserly care, and attains to the utmost limit of human life, though Fortune wrecks no part of that which Nature has appointed for him, yet man is too mortal to comprehend things immortal" (*De otio* 5.7f.).

In the *Naturales quaestiones*, Seneca thus resolves the tension between the determination as *contemplator mundi* and the limitation of the individual's capacity to understand through the idea that humankind is involved in a transgenerational knowledge process: "How many animals we have learned about for the first time in this age; how many are not known even now! Many things that are unknown to us the people of a coming age will know. Many discoveries are reserved for ages still to come, when memory of us will have been effaced" (*QNat.* 7.30.5). The limitedness of the contemporary state of knowledge does thus not preclude orientating the cosmos tohumanity. On the contrary: "Our universe is a sorry little affair unless it has in it something for every age to investigate" (*QNat.* 7.30.5). However, as Seneca concedes with respect to comets, humanity will never fully know the universe: "How many other bodies besides these comets move in secret, never rising before the eyes of men! For god has not made all things for man. How much a part of god's immense work is entrusted to us?" (*QNat.*7.30.3). And so much remains hidden from human eyes forever, above all else the divine foundation of the universe, which can only be inferred through thinking (*QNat.*7.30.3):

> Moreover, many things related to the highest divinity or allotted a neighbouring power are obscure. Or perhaps—which may surprise you more—they both fill and elude our vision. Either their subtlety [*subtilitas*] is greater than the human

eye-sight is able to follow or such a great majesty conceals itself in too holy a seclusion.

(*QNat.* 7.30.4)

It is in this context that Seneca's frequently cited warning needs to be understood—not to strive for more knowledge than is necessary for individual improvement and perfection, because the "desire to know more than is sufficient is a sort of intemperance" (*Ep.* 88.36). Given this warning against the immoderate and indulgent urge to know more and more, the seemingly modern idea of a progressive, transgenerational study of nature would appear to be again subordinated to the ancient ethics of temperance. But Seneca by no means fully retracts the affirmation of limitless curiosity about the world; rather, like Cicero, he seeks to find and maintain a balance between the distinct goals of life that humans are assigned by nature. Along with *curiositas*, humanity is also directed toward a moral-practical perfection, the "*scientia bonorum ac malorum inmutabili*" (*Ep.* 88.28), for which *ataraxia* is the gauge. "Nature has begotten us," emphasizes Seneca, for both purposes, "for contemplation and for action" (*De otio* 5.2). Against this background, Seneca's critical remarks on the *artes liberales* gain their precise meaning. Incapable of leading the soul to the highest perfection, the liberal arts merely prepare the way for attaining this goal (*Ep.* 88.20). Indeed, for Seneca it is conceivable to attain moral perfection *without* the liberal arts (*Ep.* 88.32). This devaluation is not the consequence of a principal reservation about curiosity, however, but a realistic consideration, stripped of illusions, of its actual impetus. Given the disorderly accumulation of questionable knowledge in the various specialist disciplines, for Seneca the individual faces an insurmountable task—to distinguish what is important from the unimportant (*Ep.* 88.35). For this purpose, the mind must be directed toward the goal of moral perfection. This means that studying nature must serve the appraisal of the true value of things, i.e., the knowledge of the divine, while studying history is to make us familiar with suitable moral role models. The art of the wise is not to indiscriminately accumulate more and more knowledge, but to acquire morally relevant, i.e., better, knowledge: "Study, not to add anything to your knowledge, but to make your knowledge better [*Stude, non ut plus aliquid scias, sed ut melius*]" (*Ep.* 89.23).

Without the orientation provided by the ideal of moral perfection, Seneca sees the mind as erring off course into misguided forms of inquisitiveness. One example mentioned is Didymus' collection of 4,000 books, dealing with countless historical and literary questions, often enough verging on the trivial, such as where Homer was born or whether Sappho was a prostitute (*Ep.* 88.37). Studying philosophical writings can also endanger the goal of moral perfection. Merely to know the answers given to all those issues concerning humanity and the divine would hopelessly overwhelm every individual. And that is before consideration is given to the dizzying quarreling between the philosophical schools:

> Protagoras declares that one can take either side on any question and debate it with equal success—even on this very question, whether every subject can be debated from either point of view. Nausiphanes holds that in things which seem to exist, there is no difference between existence and non-existence. Parmenides maintains that nothing exists of all this which seems to exist, except the universe alone. Zeno of Elea removed all the difficulties by removing one; for he declares that nothing exists.
>
> (*Ep.* 88.43)

In short, unnecessary ballast needs to be cast aside when studying philosophy. Because the misguided forms of curiosity deflect humans from fulfilling their true determination, Seneca repeatedly calls for careful reflection on one's moral orientation. More important than immersion in musical harmonies is caring for the harmony of the soul (*Ep.* 88.9); instead of precisely mapping out landholdings and the like, one should be learning how to map oneself and thus recognize how much knowledge is necessary for leading a fulfilled life (*Ep.* 88.10). Misguided curiosity plunges humans into a state of agitation and disorientation. In contrast, true inquisitiveness, soundly attuned to the harmonious order of the cosmos, leads to tranquillity, the infallible measure of a happy life (Bös 1995: 54).

Antiquity was—and I hope that these sketches on Cicero and Seneca illustrate this—generally familiar with the fascination of limitless curiosity. The primacy of the eternal over the transitory and the orientation on the ethical ideal of *ataraxia* meant, however, that the affirmation of a limitless—and hence restless—curiosity could not be assigned a fundamental meaning in humanity's relation to the world. While Seneca primarily warns of the dangers from indulging immoderately in curiosity, for Marcus Aurelius the progressive study of nature and moral perfection are quite simply mutually exclusive. Investigating the universe when motivated by curiosity leads inevitably to a loss of the self:

> Nothing can be more miserable than the man who goes through the whole round of things, and, as the poet says, pries into the things beneath the earth, and would fain guess the thoughts in his neighbour's heart, while having no conception that he needs but to associate himself with the divine genius in his bosom, and to serve it truly.
>
> (*Med.* 2.13)

Augustine's criticism of *curiositas* has gained paradigmatic status for Christian thought. Although taking up motifs from Cicero and Seneca, the context of his investigation is completely different from the outset. For Augustine, *curiositas* is no longer the expression of a natural striving for knowledge but the symptom of *concupiscentia*, i.e., the evil desire of human nature depraved through original sin (*Conf.* 10.35). In distinction from the desire of the flesh (*concupiscentia carnis*), which attains its fulfillment in the immediate enjoyment of things, the desire of eyes (*concupiscentia oculorum*), under which Augustine places all kinds of sensory perception, strives for knowledge and experience (*Conf.* 10.35.55). Within ocular desire Augustine draws a further distinction, between *voluptas*, a desiring for the beautiful, melodious, fragrant, and flavorful, and *curiositas*, which inclines to the gruesome, e.g., a mutilated corpse, and useless things like magic, theater performances, and astronomy. Curiosity "sets in motion investigation into the secrets of nature (which are beyond our ken [*preater nos*])" (*Conf.* 10.55). The crucial point for Augustine is that curious people are longing for knowledge "not to help their own salvation but rather solely for experience's sake [*non ad aliquam salutem, sed ad solam experientiam desiderat*]" (*Conf.* 10.55). Salvation, however, can be attained only through returning to the inwardness of the soul guided by God's self-revelation in the Bible.

Nonetheless, Augustine's problematization of curiosity does not culminate in radical contempt for the world. On the contrary, as part of his reflections on the Manichaean Faustus of Mileve in Book 5 of the *Confessions*, Augustine develops a critical but thoroughly differentiated view of curiosity about the world (Blumenberg 1983: 309–23; Feldmann 1989). Augustine confesses candidly that he has adopted numerous truths about the creaturely world from the philosophers, in particular calculations of the solstices, equating day and night, etc. (*Conf.* 5.3.4). For Augustine, curiosity only then becomes problematic when humanity fails to penetrate to the very foundation of earthly things, the Creator: "They speak many truths about creation, but do not devoutly seek him who is Truth, the maker of creation" (*Conf.* 5.3.5.) Thus a Platonic motif, which had also shaped Cicero's deliberations on curiosity, returns in a Christian transformation: the human being is not to stand still upon comprehending earthly beauty but is to aspire to move toward the eternal.

The call to keep advancing toward the divine in knowledge is the fulcrum Augustine uses to determine more closely the relationship between knowledge of the world and happiness. True happiness resides in knowing a transcendent God. Because intuiting the divine fulfills the human spirit completely, Augustine refrains, unlike Cicero, from speculating about the liberated curiosity about the world in a post-mortal state; rather, like Socrates and Marcus Aurelius, Augustine decouples happiness from studying nature: "But blessed are those who know you, even if you are ignorant of such things" (*Conf.* 5.4.7). And conversely: "How unfortunate [*infelix*] are those who know all such things and yet do not know you!" (*Conf.* 5.4.7). Studying nature is thus solely legitimate under the condition that God is recognized as the only source of human happiness, whereby Augustine once more underlines that it is not curiosity about the world as such that contributes to human happiness: "Anyone who knows about both them and you is not more blessed for knowing them, but they are only blessed in respect of you" (*Conf.* 5.4.7). Similar to Seneca and Marcus Aurelius, Augustine warns urgently of the danger of losing oneself in and through excessive immersion in nature: "People go off to marvel at the height of mountains and the great waves of the sea and the broad courses of rivers, and the flow of the ocean, and the circuits of the stars: but they neglect themselves" (*Conf.* 10.8.15).

Even if knowledge of God is uncoupled from studying nature, Augustine's thought does not lead to an inwardness without a relationship to the world, for "in the fields and the grand palaces of my memory ... there are treasure stores of countless impressions brought there from every imaginable kind of thing that my senses perceived" (*Conf.* 10.8.12). The infinite diversity of the world is suddenly present in a new way, namely in the medium of human consciousness, where "heaven and earth and sea are present to me, together with everything they contain that I have been able to encounter with my senses, except for what I have forgotten" (*Conf.* 10.8.12). Thus, the temptations of curiosity also return suddenly in the contemplation of the inner self: "O my God, what a powerful force memory is, something awe-inspiring, a deep and boundless complexity! And this is the mind, and this is what I am" (*Conf.* 10.17.26). Just as the scientific study of nature may not remain attached to things perceived through the senses and come to a standstill, it is also denied to humanity to wander through the limitless space of memory out of pure curiosity. The goal of self-examination always remains knowledge of God.

Augustine's considerations on curiosity are not solely limited to recasting the Platonic maxim of an ascent from the visible to the eternal into a Christian teaching. Along with *concupiscentia*, one of the new motifs Augustine introduces to the problematization of *curiositas* is pride (*superbia*), in Christian doctrine the original human sin: "and you draw near only to the broken-hearted and are beyond the perceiving of the proud, even if they had the searching intelligence to tell the number of the stars and the grains of sand and to measure out the starry vault of heaven and to track the paths of the constellations" (*Conf.* 5.3.3). With the inclusion of curiosity in the catalogue of vices (Blumenberg 1983: 309–23), Augustine appears to go beyond identifying problems it causes, rejecting it altogether. However, it is not the urge for knowledge itself that gives Augustine cause for concern, but solely "vain" inquisitiveness. But because natural scientists are held in such admiration by the uneducated, they are particularly susceptible to vainly accepting kudos and basking in fame; in the end, "they do not seek in a godly way what is the source of that intelligence by which they make their investigations" (*Conf.* 5.3.4).

Augustine takes up the relationship between curiosity and pride in *The Literal Meaning of Genesis*. While pride (*superbia*), and not *curiositas*, caused the Fall of Adam, "Bold, shameless curiosity... was moved to transgress the commandment" of God (Augustine 2002: 453; cf. *De civ. D.* 14.13). This placement of curiosity in the Bible's narrative of the Fall is the decisive culmination of Augustine's considerations on it (Bös 1995: 129).

Justification of insatiable curiosity about the world in *De docta ignorantia*

Cusa undertook an epoch-making revaluation of curiosity. At the same time, however, Christian thinkers had already begun to increasingly value the study of nature. Arguing against Augustine, Thomas Aquinas defends the Aristotelian teaching of the naturalness of the urge for knowledge (Blumenberg 1983: 336; Bös 1995: 205). As for Aristotle, because things are *limited* through their respective forms, the progressive investigation of nature cannot lead to restlessness or agitation: "The principle of the thoroughgoing rationality of a finite reality excludes the concept of a theoretical curiosity that is essentially restless and not to be satisfied by an attainable amount of knowledge and cuts the ground from under its demonization" (Blumenberg 1983: 337). For Aquinas, as for Aristotle, striving for knowledge—within the confines of perceiving and rationally understanding the causes of what exists—must, at some point, come to rest.

The particular importance of Cusa in the history of curiosity thus lies in his justification of a *limitless* striving for knowledge of the *infinite world*. While the affirmation of insatiability may find significant support in the idea of a limitless universe, the reservations of Augustine are still present in the *De docta ignorantia*. It is only in the progressive elaboration of his thought that Cusa, step by step, refutes the millennia-old objections leveled at excessive curiosity about the world. Two developments appear to have been crucial in facilitating this turning point: firstly, the new philosophy of mind, commencing with *De coniecturis*; and secondly, the theological teachings of God's self-revelation, which were used to then oust negative theology. The affirmation of limitless curiosity about the world that crystallizes in the early modern period thus has as its prerequisite nothing less than a multilayered restructuring of traditional metaphysics, a shift that is exemplified in the development of Cusa's thinking.

Like Aquinas, Cusa begins his considerations with the Aristotelian teaching of the naturalness of the striving for knowledge. Immediately discernible, though, is how Cusa integrates elements of curiosity into his concept of knowledge: "Unusual things, even if they be monstrous [*rara quidem, et si monstra sit*], are accustomed to move us" (*DDI* 1.1.n.1; H 1.4). The contrast with the classical ancient and Christian problematizations of the insatiability of curiosity is striking, with Cusa considering any further comment unnecessary: "The intellect insatiably [!] desires to attain unto the true through scrutinizing all things by means of its innate faculty of inference" (*DDI* I.1.n. 2; H 1.5). Indeed, even more emphatic is how the insatiability inherent in and the restlessness resulting from the urge to gain knowledge—harnessed and subdued in Hellenist and Roman philosophy through the relationship to the eternal order of the cosmos and the ideal of *ataraxia*—is suddenly given a metaphysical foundation through the philosophy of the absolute and the idea of a limitless universe.

Since the principle of *perfectior esse possit* also holds valid for the human mind, for Cusa the human striving for knowledge is principally never-ending: "Hence, the intellect, which is not truth, never comprehends truth so precisely that truth cannot be comprehended infinitely more precisely" (*DDI* I.3.n.10; H 1.8). With the idea of an infinite approximation, restlessness enters the relationship between thinking and being, a point that Johannes Wenck, a fifteenth-century Aristotelian critic of the *Docta ignorantia*, identified. The notion that the human intellect could never attain precise knowledge of things inevitably leads to a dangerous frustration of the inner striving and ultimately, according to Wenck, the very destruction of science (Vansteenberghe 1910: 29; Herold 1980: 162, n. 95).

Despite Cusa's positive revaluation of the limitless striving for knowledge, the traditional reservations toward curiosity remain present in *De docta ignorantia*. Initially, Cusa returns to the Stoic teaching of the human being as *contemplator mundi*: "He [God] even wills for us to be brought to the point of admiring so marvellous a world-machine" (*DDI* II.13.n.179; H 1.101). But then, like Augustine, Cusa suspects that the turn to the world brings with it an idolization of the earthly. To ensure that humanity is not content with the visible world, God has concealed the order of the universe: "Nevertheless, the more we admire it, the more He conceals it from us; for it is Himself alone whom He wills to be sought with our whole heart and affection" (*DDI* II.13.n.179; H 1.101). The *docta ignorantia* is therefore primarily a method for investigating theological questions (*DDI*, Prol. n.1; H 1.101). As Cusa unequivocally states, the overriding task of humanity is to cultivate a sense of admiration through knowledge, and less to relentlessly pursue an endlessly progressive study of the universe. Echoes of Augustine's warning against excessive inquisitiveness are even apparent in Cusa's rhetorical flourishes: "the intellect—immortal and incorruptible—is not satisfiable until it attains unto God, for it is fully satisfied only by an eternal object" (*DDI* III.10.n.240; cf. *Conf.* 1.1.1).

Another Augustinian motif featuring in *De docta ignorantia* is the inquiry into creation. In Augustine's version, things "cried aloud with a great voice, 'it is he who has made us'" (*Conf.* 10.6.9), while for Cusa things point toward their creator. Cusa, however, refrains from following the turn back to oneself as described by Augustine: "I turned my gaze to myself" (*Conf.* 10.6.9). Since God is the absolute measure of all creatures, the key to humans attaining knowledge of self and the world lies in the non-knowing thinking of the absolute. To illustrate this, Cusa had the personified *docta ignorantia* speak to humanity: "'See to it, says our learned ignorance, that you discover yourself in Him. Since in Him all things are Him, it will not be possible that you lack anything'" (*DDI* II.13.n.180; H I.101). Provisional knowledge of both self and the world are only possible through the non-knowing insight into the concealed absolute: "He made us; He alone knows what we are, in what manner we exist, and for what purpose. If you wish to know something about us, seek it in our Cause and Reason, not in us. There you will find all things, while seeking one thing. And only in Him will you be able to discover yourself" (*DDI* II.13.n.180; H 1.101).

Despite the promise of becoming immersed in an unlimited fullness of being when encountering the absolute, according to *De docta ignorantia* humanity is ultimately in a precarious situation: "The universe that this phrase evokes is one of discontinuity and estrangement, in which man suffers from a metaphysical and epistemological *disjunction*. Man can never know God directly, nor can he know God's creation directly" (Watts 1982: 25). This metaphysical and epistemological alienation can only be resolved through a philosophical Christology, which Cusa presents in the third book of *De docta ignorantia*.

The creative power of the human mind: the turn since *De coniecturis*

Just a few years after the publication of his first major work, Cusa returns to the problematic of human knowledge in *De coniecturis* (1442/3). Although the subject of the treatise—the nature of conjectures and the art of their use—is already prefigured and announced in the *De docta ignorantia*, Cusa by no means merely extrapolates on a few details from the main work. Quite the opposite—*De coniecturis* marks an important turn in this thought, one he elaborates further in *Idiota de mente* (1450) (Koch 1956; Flasch 1998: 143–65; Miller 2003: 68–109). Probably the most significant innovation resides in his enhanced view of the creative power of the human mind. Already in the first chapter Cusa, in the tone of a programmatic statement, draws an analogy between human reason and the creative power of God:

> It must be the case that surmises originate from our minds, even as the real world originates from Infinite Divine Reason. For when, as best it can, the human mind (which is a lofty likeness of God) partakes of the fruitfulness of the Creating Nature, it produces from itself, qua image of the Omnipotent Form, rational entities, [which are made] in the likeness of real entities. Consequently, the human mind is the form of a surmised [rational] world, just as the Divine Mind is the Form of the real world.
>
> (*De coniecturis* I.1.n.5; H 1.164)

In Christian anthropology, as is evident in Aquinas, any analogy between divine creative power and human freedom is constantly avoided (*Sth* I, q. 45, a.5 ad 3). For Cusa, though, the human being is *homo creator* in an emphatic sense (Alvarez-Gómez 1978; Berlinger 1994); this is not, however, a leveling of the difference between God and humans. As Cusa clarifies in *Idiota de mente*, the power to call things into existence remains reserved for God. Humanity is given merely the capacity to come up with concepts that the mind can use to approximate things: "The Divine Mind is a reifying power; our mind is an assimilative power [*Divina mens est vis entificativa, nostra mens est vis assimilative*]" (VII.n.99; H 1.556). In distinction to the nominalism of the late Middle Ages, Cusa still assumes universals *ante rem*, while however taking up the *verum factum* principle: i.e., the teaching founded by Philo that God can only ever have complete knowledge of the world *as* the creator of all things (Peréz-Ramos 1988: 54f.). For Cusa, humanity can only formulate provisional ideas or notions (*notiones*) or imagery of similarity and resemblance (*assimilationes*) with respect to the hidden order of things (*Idiota de mente* III.n.72; *De venatione sapientiae* XXIX.n.86). As the author of ideas, the human being is nonetheless the creator of language worlds: "Accordingly, man makes deliberations about such matters; and from [the use of] *signs* and *words* he formulates a systematic knowledge of things—even as from *things* God [formed] the cosmos" (*Compendium* IX.n.26; H 2.1400).

In *De docta ignorantia* Cusa had repeatedly pointed out the limitations of human knowledge and warned of excessive curiosity. The difference in *De coniecturis* is stark, with an all-encompassing knowledge of the world postulated openly: "Since mind supposes that it encompasses, surveys, and grasps all things, it infers that it is so present in all things, and all things in it, that it asserts that there can be nothing which is beyond it itself and which escapes its purview" (*De coniecturis* I.4.n.12; H 1.168). In *Idiota de mente* Cusa compares human reason with a "living measure" capable of marking out the limitless cosmos with its potentially infinite number of angle settings (IX.n.124f.125; H 1.569).

Unlike *De docta ignorantia*, however, knowing that this measured-based comparison has no end is no longer a reminder of the limitedness of humanity's cognitive capacities; instead, it is now to serve as a spur and to prompt human beings to permanently extend the scope of their knowledge. In the *Compendium* Cusa expresses this enhanced view of progressively exploring and studying things with the *homo kosmographus*, "who dwells in a city that has the five gateways of the five senses. Through these gateways messengers from all over the world enter and report on the entire condition of the world" (*Compendium* VIII.n.22; H 2.1398). To be able describe the whole sensorily perceivable world (*totius sensibilis mundi descriptionem*; *Compendium* VIII.n.22), then not a single messenger may be dispensed with. A neglect of just one single sense, for example the sense of smell or of taste, both since antiquity considered inferior or base senses (Jütte 2004: 54–71), would endanger the goal of a comprehensive description of the world: "Therefore, [the geographer] endeavours with all his effort to keep all the gateways open and to continually receive the reports of ever-new messengers and to make his description ever more accurate" (*Compendium* VIII.n.22; H 2.1398).

The sense impressions require, however—based on the *imaginatio*—the ordering power of reason (*ratio*), more precisely the *vis assimilativa*, which Cusa illustrates with the metaphor of the slab of wax, previously used by Plato to explain the mode of knowledge of belief (*pistis*) in physical entities, that is in the hierarchy of cognitive abilities within the mind (*dianoia*) or the knowledge of ideas. Because sensory things imprint themselves in the psyche as if it were a wax slab, they are recognizable at a later point in time (*Tht.* 190e–192d). In contrast, Cusa uses the imagery of the wax slab not to describe a passive receptivity but the ordering regulatory power of reason (*ratio*) which, no longer furnished with pre-existing ideas, aligns and adapts to things, i.e., assimilates them, with its self-created concepts: "Therefore, suppose that a slab of wax were conceived of as being in-formed with a mind. In that case, the mind existing within the wax would configure the wax to every shape presented to that mind" (*Idiota de mente* VII.n.100; H 1.557). Since the different cognitive capacities (*sensus, imaginatio, ratio*) form a complex unity (Bormann 1975; Kremer 1998), Cusa can describe human cognition as a process integral to a self-activating *self*-assimilation:

> Mind is so assimilative that in the sense of sight it assimilates itself to things visible, in the sense of hearing it assimilates itself to things audible, in the sense of taste to things tasteable, in the sense of smell to things that can be smelled, in the sense of touch to things touchable. In the senses [mind assimilates itself] to things perceptible, in the imagination to things imaginable, and in reason to things accessible by reasoning.
> (*Idiota de mente* VII.n.100; H 1.557)

At this point, Cusa once again broadens the analogy between the human and divine mind. Unlike other creatures, "Our mind is not the *unfolding* of the Eternal Enfolding [Being] but is its *image* [*mens nostra non est explicatio, sed imago complicationis aeternae*]" (*Idiota de mente* IV.n.74; H 1.543). For Cusa, therefore, the creation of concepts can be compared to the divine power of the *creatio ex nihilo*.

> For, indeed, this [mental] spirit—which of its own power goes forth unto all things—examines all things and creates the concepts and likenesses of all things. I say "creates" inasmuch as [this spirit] makes the conceptual likenesses of things from no other thing—even as the Spirit which is God makes the quiddities of things not from another but from itself, i.e., from Not-other.
> (*De non aliud* XXIV.n.112; H 2.1160f.)

All concepts are already enfolded in the mental spirit of humanity; what humans seek is thus already in our mind: "Thereupon, by the operation of its intellective life, mind finds described within itself that which it is seeking" (*Idiota de mente* V.n.85; H 1.549). Against this background, the surprising turn rendered in the image of the geographer in the *Compendium* becomes understandable. As Cusa explains, when the world map is drawn, then suddenly the gates, i.e., the senses, which provide the mind with countless accounts about things, are closed. The human mind turns back to itself and discovers itself to the image of divine creative power: "During his speculation he notices that no brute animal ... could have made such a map" (*Compendium* VIII.n.23; H 2.1399). After receiving the sense data, the human mind, through its own effort, orders the world. The human mind is not essentially passive, but a "mapmaker who, through his inventive art, creates his own visualization of the order he observes in the external world" (Watts 1982: 214).

Despite the extreme comparison with the divine *creatio ex nihilo*, Cusa does not completely dissolve the Platonic world of eternal ideas into ideas designed by the inhuman mind. Quite the contrary—already in the definition of human reason (*ratio*), Cusa clearly differentiates the creative power of the mind according to different areas of knowledge. With respect to the ideas of handcrafted products (*artificialia*), human reason imitates the divine *creatio ex nihilo* in an eminent sense, which Cusa illustrates with the example of the carved spoon, precisely because the idea of the spoon is to be found nowhere in nature (*Idiota de mente* II.n.62f.). The opposite is the case with mathematical ideas. Although the human mind produces mathematical ideas itself, as Cusa emphasizes in opposition to Plato (*DDI* II.3), it is however bound to their inner logic. The empirical concepts of reason (*ratio*) represent a domain in between these two poles, serving to order sensory perceptions. On the one hand, understanding needs to heed the sensory material and the essential structures endued in things; on the other, concepts (*notiones*) are created by reason (*ratio*) in creative freedom. In contrast to these concepts of the reason (*ratio*), the intellect (*intellectus*), no longer directly related to or in contact with the diversity of sensorily perceivable things, encounters in self-reflection innate ideas which are already guiding and directing the activity of the *ratio*: "Moreover, [man has] the innate [intellectual] forms of the imperceptible virtues of justice and of equality, in order that he may know what is just, what is right, what is praiseworthy, what is beautiful, what is delightful and good (and may know the opposites of these)" (*Idiota de mente* IV.n.78; H 2.1394; Velthoven 1977: 105). The ideas of the true, the good, and the just, taken to be likenesses of absolute equivalence (*aequalitas*) (*Compendium* X.n.34), function as ultimate orientations for creatively conceived acts of understanding and must not be confused with the revisable concepts of the *ratio*. Thus, the *via iudiciaria* contains, as Cusa concedes, ideas in a Platonic sense: "If by 'concreated concept' Plato meant this power, then he did not at all err [in this respect]" (*Idiota de mente* IV.n.77; H 1.546). This means that the creative power of the *ratio* does not have absolute freedom to form concepts; rather, in reflecting upon itself, it discovers immutable criteria, in the light of which the concepts of understanding may be evaluated.

Following the demand for comprehensive knowledge of the world through the creative power of the human mind, Cusa increasingly dilutes the Augustinian reservations toward curiosity that still echo in *De docta ignorantia*. In contrast to Augustine, who sees the progressive investigation of nature to be fertile ground for pride and conceit, with humans goaded on to claim mastery over the world and deny the Creator, Cusa sings a paean to the power of the human mind in *De coniecturis*. In the limitless striving for knowledge, humanity discovers not only the beauty and harmony God has endowed the world with, but also—as Cusa now expressly affirms—the power of the human mind. And what is more, the interplay between the different cognitive capacities of humans now becomes the primary source for philosophical astonishment, indeed the *mirabile* of all of creation: "Marvelous is this work of God in which the discriminating power is conducted, progressively, from the center of the senses upwards unto the very lofty intellectual nature!" (*De coniecturis* II.14.n.142; H 1.236). The creative power of the mind enables humanity to pry open, cognitively, both the limitless universe and the absolute, for example in a *docta ignorantia*. It is in this sense that the dictum from *De coniecturis* can claim that the human is a "human god [deus humanus]" (*De coniecturis* II.14.n.143; H 1.237).

But where does pride draw its impetus from, if no longer from the striving for limitless knowledge? According to Cusa, it now resides in the exaggerated claim to be able to precisely grasp the very essence of things. The antidote to the pride induced by curiosity is thus not to restrict the urge to gain knowledge but stems from the *docta ignorantia*, i.e., the realization that only God can precisely know the order of the cosmos, while humans can only approximate things infinitely through the art of conjecture:

> Layman: Perhaps the difference between you and me is the following: you think that you are someone knowledgeable, although you are not; hence, you are haughty. By contrast, I know that I am a layman; hence, I am quite humble. In this respect, perhaps, I am more learned [than you].
>
> (*Idiota de sapientia* I.n.4; H 1.468)

On the foundation of this new philosophy of mind, aiming to elevate the rank of humanity and in some respects pointing ahead to Gianozzo Manetti and Pico della Mirandola (Colomer 1978), Cusa also rebuts Augustine's second reservation about insatiable curiosity, namely that by turning to the world the human threatens to lose the self. For Cusa, as God is at once origin and goal of creation, so too is the human mind not only the origin but also the goal of its own conceptual and language worlds: "Therefore, there is no other goal of humanity's action of creating than humanity itself. For when humanity creates, it does not pass beyond itself; rather, when it unfolds its power, it arrives at itself" (*De coniecturis* I.1.n.5; H 1.237). Thus, the converse holds true—instead of losing the self, it is in fact in the investigation of the limitless universe that humanity, as expressly emphasized in *De mente*, discovers not only the world through the unlimited act of measuring but also, and above all else, itself.

> Philosopher: Since as you say, O Layman, mind receives its name from measuring, I wonder why it proceeds so eagerly to measure things.
> Layman: [It does so] in order to attain the measure of itself. For mind is a living measure that attains unto its own capability by measuring other things. For it performs all [its operations] in order to know itself. But when seeking the measure of itself in all things, mind finds it only where all things are something one. There resides its precise truth, because there is present the adequate exemplar of itself.
>
> (*Idiota de mente* IX.n.123; H 1.569)

While the new philosophy of mind disarms the Augustinian criticism of curiosity with its dual targets of pride and self-loss, the third reproach, namely that curiosity about the world reverses the hierarchy between the transitory and the eternal, remains open. Cusa turns to the theological teaching of God's self-revelation in the world to reject this objection, which reaches as far back as Plato. In his later writings, Cusa elaborates the teaching on the universe as an *explicatio Dei* by resorting to the motif of self-communication: "From Intellect all things come into existence in order for Intellect to manifest itself; for it delights in manifesting and communicating the light of its own intelligence" (*De beryllo* III.n.4; H 2.793).

Cusa employs diverse imagery to illustrate the motif of God's self-communication. In *De visione Dei* the Creator appears as a painter who "mixeth divers colours that at length he may be able to paint himself" (*De visione Dei* XXV.n.116); in *Idiota de sapientia* (I.n.4) Cusa takes up the metaphor of the world as the book of God. Translated into the relationship between God and the universe, this means "that He knows Himself from the Word begotten from Him. In creatures, which are signs of the Uncreated Word, the Former reveals Himself in various ways in the various signs; and there cannot be any [created thing] that is not a sign of manifestation of the Begotten Word" (*Compendium* VII.n.21; H 2.1397).

As manifestation of the absolute, the multiplicity of the universe is no longer—as with Plotinus and Augustine—a source of distraction but rather a site for experiencing God, which Cusa surprisingly underlines with the *homo mensura* proposition of Protagoras. Already in antiquity Plato had defined God as the true measure of all things, countering Protagoras (*Lg.* 716c). Aristotle also criticized Protagoras' proposition, for in trying to know things humans measures themselves rather than the objects of their cognitive efforts (*Metaph.* 10.1.1053a35–1053b4). For Cusa there is no doubt that God alone is the absolute measure of all things; but in knowing the created world, the human, as Cusa emphasizes more markedly since *De coniecturis*, is not merely being measured but is also the creative measurer: "With the senses man measures perceptible things, with the intellect he measures intelligible things, and he attains unto supra-intelligible things transcendently" (*De beryllo* V.n.6; H 2.793). In measuring things, humanity may set created notions to be the measure of things, but humans do not elevate themselves into the position of masters of the world. What ensues rather from the premise of God's self-revelation is something different—by creating worlds through notions and language, humans become capable of an *approximating assimilation* of things. From this perspective, Cusa can give Protagoras' *homo mensura* theorem a new turn—because God has created the world with a view to human beings, things, once they become objects of knowing, find their "measure" through humans. Humanity is thus not the "measure" in the sense of a prescriptive criterion but as the end (*finis*) of things (*De beryllo* V.n.6; Flasch 2001: 66).

For Cusa, it is in the light of God's self-revelation that the chasm separating humans and world, riven in *De docta ignorantia*, can close. Since the self-revelation of the divine guarantees a pre-stabilized harmony between humanity and the world, human cognitive faculties *must* correspond to specific realms of being.

> For when he knows that the cognizing soul is the goal of things knowable, he knows on the basis of the perceptive power that perceptible things are supposed to be such as can be perceived. And, likewise, [he knows] regarding intelligible things that [they are supposed to be such] as can be understood, and [he knows] that transcendent things [are to be such] as can transcend.
>
> (*De beryllo* V.n.6; H 2.793f.)

Against this background, the *homo mensura* theorem accrues yet another meaning for Cusa—humans are the measure of all things because they find the "measure" of all that is created within themselves, i.e., in the species-specific cognitive faculties (*De beryllo* V.n.6).

With the motif of God's self-revelation, there is a shift in importance from negative to positive theology. If God has created the world solely to reveal himself to humans, then his power cannot remain hidden in inaccessible light. Thus, in *De apice theoriae*, Cusa looks back self-critically at the epistemological skepticism of *De docta ignorantia* (Watts 1982: 219–22, Flasch 1998: 36–43): "I once thought that truth is better found amid the obscure." Now, however, he is convinced that "truth, in which Possibility itself shines forth very brightly, is of great power. For it proclaims [itself] in the streets, as you have read in my book about the Layman. Most assuredly, truth shows that it is everywhere easy to find" (*De apice theoriae* n.5; H 2.1425). Above all else, it is the notion of the *posse ipsum* that opens for Cusa an inlet to the absolute. The absolute, or more precisely the power underpinning all being and thus the source for everything that is, is always ascertainable reflectively, for it is the ineluctable presupposition of life and thought:

> What boy or youth is ignorant of possibility [*posse ipsum*]? For each of them acknowledges that he can eat, can run, can speak. And there is no one with a mind who is so ignorant that he does not know, without [the aid of] a teacher, (1) that nothing exists that is not possible to exist and (2) that without possibility nothing whatsoever can either exist or possess or act or be acted upon.
>
> (*De apice theoriae* n.6; H 2.1425)

Unlike Descartes, in the self-reflection of reason Cusa encounters not the *cogito ergo sum* but the absolute as *posse ipsum*.

For whoever would question whether Possibility exists sees as soon as he thinks about it that the question is not germane, since without Possibility no question could be posed about Possibility. Still less can one ask whether Possibility is this or that, since the possibility-of-existing and the possibility of being this or that presuppose Possibility itself. And so, it is evident that Possibility itself precedes all doubt that can be entertained. Therefore, nothing is more certain than is Possibility itself, since [any] doubt [about it] can only presuppose it.

(*De apice theoriae* n.13; H 2.1429)

Cusa poses a rhetorical question to encapsulate just how far the idea of God's self-revelation has shifted the basic constellation of *De docta ignorantia*: "Therefore, unless the mind could see from afar the goal of rest and of [fulfilled] desire and of its own joy and happiness, how could it hasten to reach [that goal]?" (*De apice theoriae* n.11; H II.1428). There could hardly be a more marked distinction from the programmatic sketches at the opening of *De docta ignorantia*.

Conclusion

From *De docta ignorantia* via the *Idiota* dialogues and through to his late philosophy, an epochally important revaluation of *limitless* curiosity about the world takes place in the thought of Nicholas of Cusa. With the transformation of Neoplatonic conceptions of oneness and the de-limitation of ancient cosmotheology, insatiable curiosity—for which a fascination had already shimmered through in antiquity. in Cicero and Seneca for example—now gains a metaphysical foundation. Although the idea of an incompletable approximative process of knowing emerges in *De docta ignorantia*, the decisive step toward an unequivocal affirmation of limitless curiosity can only be taken when new ground is in place, namely that of the new philosophy of mind and the idea of God's self-revelation in the world.

The philosophy of mind in *De coniecturis* and *De mente*, initiating a radical enhancement in how the creative power of human reason is judged, not only marks a turning point within Cusa's thought but indeed, as Kurt Flasch rightly emphasized, heralds the "beginning of another philosophy" (1998: 149). The idea of the self-revelation of the absolute suddenly endows the infinite diversity of things with a dignity that liberates insatiable curiosity from the suspicion of godlessness and self-forgetfulness in the mundane mire of the world. Because, in the opening to the infinite abundance of the world, humanity is pointed to the divine fullness of being—the sole source for a human's measure—the *insatiabilis curiositas* no longer needs to be banished to the beyond, as in Cicero, or exiled into the unpolitical niches of the mundane world, as with Seneca.

This cognitive process of gaining knowledge comes to fulfillment and repose in the absolute, which is "incomprehensible by any intellect, unmeasurable by any measure, unlimitable by any limit, unboundable by any bounds, disproportional in terms of any proportion, incomparable in terms of any comparison" (*Idiota de sapientia* I.n.9). In contrast, the universe is only knowable in an incompletable process of comparison. Thus, by affirming insatiable curiosity, Cusa renders the ancient ideal of *ataraxia* inoperative, at least in theoretical philosophy. And indeed, any premature easing of the striving for knowledge, succumbing to a finite calm (*finibilem quondam quietem*; *Idiota de sapientia* I.n.12), endangers knowledge. Cusa's justification of limitless curiosity about the world therefore refrains from calling into question the primacy of knowing the eternal. An autonomization of worldly curiosity—for Blumenberg a *conditio sine qua non* of modern science—is outside the horizon of his thought: "The fact was still concealed from him that this privative, indefinite infinity could fail in its 'Platonic' effect of referring to the ideal infinity of God and, precisely in its lack of definiteness, could become the compelling motive of cognitive movement for man" (Blumenberg 1983: 529). Cusa's justification of insatiable curiosity is achieved not by dimming theological referential contexts but by transforming the millennia-old dominance of the Parmenidean concept of being, wherein multiplicity is devalued in relationship to the one.

Proceeding from Cusa also allows us to query Hans Blumenberg's thesis that the rehabilitation of curiosity was a reaction to the theological teaching of *deus absconditus*. Already in *De docta ignorantia*, the insight into the limits of human knowledge does not culminate in resigned skepticism but opens up new horizons of thinking, in both theology and cosmology: namely the theory of the *coincidentia oppositorum* and the limitlessness of the universe. In Cusa's late philosophy, the affirmation of a limitless striving for knowledge is further emphasized and enlarged upon—by turning away from negative theology. It is not the hidden or "dead God" but the self-communicating God who paves the way for the limitless curiosity of the world.

Moreover, Cusa's daring speculations on a limitless universe and the creative potency of the human mind exude an ongoing fascination down to the present day; with unbounded curiosity manifesting in a remarkable, if not strange, innocence, the arguments brought forward by power-oriented critics of modern science seem to gain no traction. Cusa radically assigns human reason the capacity to know the world and the self. This does not mean, however, as in

Horkheimer and Adorno's objection to the Enlightenment, that "There shall be neither mystery nor any desire to reveal mystery" (2002: 2). Quite the opposite: progressive knowledge of the world has as its final goal precisely the self-revelation of the divine. It is not demystification but philosophically mediated re-enchantment that sets the process of curiosity in motion. The determinative motivation behind the rational exploration of the world is not, as Horkheimer and Adorno allege of enlightened reason, fear; it is rather astonishment, which for Cusa is sparked not solely by the richness of the unlimited universe but also by the power of the human mind. This means that Cusa's vision of progressive knowledge of the world leads neither to the subjugation of nature by "the standard of calculability and utility" (Horkheimer and Adorno 2002: 3) nor to the destruction of all gods and qualities (Horkheimer and Adorno 2002: 5).

Cusa's idea of limitless curiosity about the world also circumvents Heidegger's critique of modern science. The philosophy of mind that finds its first formulation in *De coniecturis* radically unfurls the representing imagination; as the divine spirit unfolds a de-limited world out of itself, so the human mind conceives an infinite wealth of ideas and language worlds. But a consciousness of the self-empowerment residing in the human mind does not lead—as Heidegger claimed of modern science—to "the presumption of the de-limitation of representation for self-securing certitude" (Heidegger 1982a: 122). Cusa's philosophy of knowledge evades the pincer of the Heideggerian alternative of "dispositive re-presenting versus remembrance of being." While the consciousness of the world-creating power of the human mind is already emerging and taking shape in Cusa's thought, the order of the universe, shrouded in the mystery of the absolute, cannot simply be deduced from things as they are. The human mind is expected to forge order by creating language worlds. And because humans and the world are teleologically correlated to one another through the divine order of creation, the meaning of theoretical curiosity is not exhausted in simply establishing self-security and exercising power over the world, both of which entail turning nature into the projection surface of human re-presentation. Amid the enhanced appreciation of the mind's creative power, it is classical antiquity's astonishment at the beauty and harmony of the universe that remains the fundamental motif of thought.

6

Freedom as self-creation: Pico della Mirandola's *Oratio de hominis dignitate*

Operating within the framework of the Christian teaching of the *imago Dei*, the anthropology of the Renaissance initiates and consummates an epoch-making revaluation of the power of human creativity: "The possibility of human creativity was one of the more original contributions of the Renaissance to western culture …. The distinction of the Renaissance lay in the application of these verses [Gen. 1:26f.] to human creativity; the recognition of the radical creativity of god thus pointed to the almost equally radical creativity of his human creatures" (Bouwsma 1993: 25–6). Working within this perspective, Nicholas of Cusa had already interpreted the human mind in terms of an analogy to divine creative power (as discussed in Chapter 5 of this book). The *vis creativa* manifests itself first and foremost in the forming of conceptual and linguistic worlds (see section 5.2). As Bouwsma has framed it, "the most radical expression of human creativity in the Renaissance was its application to what Stephen Greenblatt has called 'self-fashioning.' This owed something, perhaps, to Petrarch's interest in cultivating, like an actor, the individuality of his own literary style, and to Alberti's insistence on the malleability of children" (1993: 31; Greenblatt 1984). The most famous text on human freedom in the sense of self-fashioning is undoubtedly Pico della Mirandola's *Oratio de hominis dignitate* (1486/7),[1] wherein the human being is addressed as the "molder and maker of thyself [*tui ipsius quasi plastes et fictor*]" (*Oratio*, n.22). It is eminently important here to mark out how, for Pico, this power can be activated "to degenerate into the lower forms of life, which are brutish" or "to be reborn into the higher orders, those that are divine" (*Oratio*, n.23).

Since the eighteenth century, Pico has been considered one of the originators of the modern idea of autonomous freedom and inalienable human dignity. For Jacob Burckhardt, the Renaissance spirit is uniquely manifest in Pico, expressing an affirmation of the world and the individual. Pico's oration devoted to the dignity of humanity is "one of the noblest bequests of that great age" (Burckhardt [1878] 2014: 2.103–4). Ernst Cassirer declares that Pico's idea of human freedom is "more than a mere rhetorical showpiece. Its rhetoric pathos contains a specific modern pathos of thought" (Cassirer [1927] 1963: 84). In fact, for some, Pico's idea of human self-creation sparks associations with the understanding of freedom explicated in German idealism and even in Sartre (Garin 1952: 36f.) In stark contrast, Karl Jaspers criticizes Pico's self-creation as an early expression of the typical modern hubris behind human beings' self-deification (Jaspers 1964: 166; cf. A. Buck 1990: xix–xx).

Studies in the history of philosophy have, though, often rejected this image of Pico as the founder of the modern idea of freedom, considering it an anachronistic projection. And indeed, originally the *Oratio* is not a contribution to Renaissance *dignitas hominis* tractates, but the text of a speech to open a planned congress in Rome for which Pico had prepared 900 theses. With Pope Innocent VIII condemning thirteen of these, the congress had to be cancelled, and so the *Oratio* was never delivered. The text was first published posthumously by Gianfrancesco Pico della Mirandola, Pico's nephew, with the title—*Oratio de hominis dignitate*—added later (De Lubac 1974: 58f.; Euler 1998: 100f.; 122; 155). In the *Oratio*, Pico is thus referring to themes central to his 900 theses, in particular his version of mystical theology, a bridge to connect Christian thought with the Kabbalah. In short, "the speech does not exalt the dignity of man" but "promotes ascetic mysticism" (Copenhaver 2019: 94). As Thomas More's *Life of Pico* makes clear, to his contemporaries Pico was famous not because of his idea of freedom but for his exemplary ascetic life, specifically in showing how humanity strives to attain harmony with the nature of the angels, i.e., a pure, bodiless spiritual being. Pico's anthropology in the *Oratio* is, as Copenhaver puts it, "a theory of the human condition whose corresponding practice is an ascetic and mystical regimen of disembodiment. Such a theory is starkly incompatible with any post-Kantian conception of human freedom and dignity" (Copenhaver 2019: 218).

As Pico prefaces mystical theology with a specific anthropology, the thesis of "man's polymorphous potential for exaltation or abasement" is undoubtedly "a key theme" in Pico's speech, as Copenhaver concedes (2019: 383). Further, Pico's *Oratio* was not first rediscovered in the nineteenth century; numerous Renaissance thinkers, foremost Juan Luis Vives and Charles de Bovillus, took up its themes in diverse ways, and they are even mentioned in speeches by popes (Dougherty 2007: 148f.). Indeed, as my studies on the colonial debate of the early modern period and the philosophies of the seventeenth century will show later in this book, Pico's idea of creative freedom has been diversely modified and transformed into a major motif of modern European thought.

Given this background, I would like to begin by considering Pico's idea of creative freedom as it is developed in the *Oratio de hominis dignitate*. My first step (section 6.1) is devoted to identifying the core anthropological theses of the *Oratio* and explicating them with reference to other works, with special emphasis placed on *Heptalpus*, a philosophical commentary on the book of Genesis that Pico wrote between 1488 and 1489. In laying down anthropological principles as the foundation for mystical theology, Pico attempts to demonstrate the superiority of humankind over pure spirit beings and angels, a thesis that is surprisingly based on the self-fashioning capacity of the human being. The dynamic concept of human freedom, connected to microcosm anthropology, forms the basis for the interpretation of the mystical union with God, i.e., the deification of humans. In both thematic fields mapped out in the *Oratio*, Pico seeks to mark a departure from the classical ancient teaching of a static, pregiven human nature.

In a second step (section 6.2), I then broach the difficult question of where Pico's idea of creative freedom stands between tradition and modernity. Pico's *Oratio* has frequently been associated with modern ideas of freedom, extending right down to Sartre; on the other hand, many historians of philosophy have identified numerous anticipations of this teaching on freedom in classical ancient and medieval thought. According to Dougherty, important motifs of Pico's idea of human freedom are to be already found in Aristotle and Boethius (2002). Since Eugenio Garin, the influence of patristics, especially that of Origen, in Pico's thought has often been underlined (Garin 1938; de Lubac 1974; Kobusch 1985). For Mahoney it is indisputable "that there is a general similarity between Pico's conception of the indeterminacy of humans according to his *Oratio* and Origen's *De principiis*" (1994: 376). And finally, Avery Dulles has placed Pico's conception of freedom in the context of scholasticism: "his anthropology was in all essentials that of the Christian Middle Ages" (Dulles 1941: 127). But despite its connectedness with tradition, Pico's *Oratio* cannot be seamlessly slotted into the lineaments of classical ancient and medieval thought, as I hope to show in a few historical sketches. Instead, as I propose, the innovative point of Pico's anthropology becomes more discernible when placed under a historical spotlight—the affirmative revaluation of the flexibility of human freedom and the chameleon-like nature of the human being.

6.1 Transcending the bounds of human nature: self-fashioning and mystical union with God

In his 900 theses, Pico pays tribute to the philosophies of almost all nations of the *oikumene*, along with Christian and Greek thinkers also acknowledging the teachings of Zoroaster, the druids, and not least the Kabbalah. Imbued with a spirit of sincerity that leaves behind the boundaries separating the religions, and thus seeking to achieve reconciliation among the *oikumene* (Blum 2002a), Pico opens his speech with the following words:

> Most esteemed fathers I have read in the ancient texts of the Arabians that when Abdallah the Saracen was questioned as to what on this world's stage, so to speak, seemed to him most worthy of wonder, he replied that there is nothing to be seen more wonderful than man. This opinion is seconded by Mercury's saying: 'A great miracle, Asclepius, is man [*magnum miraculum est homo*]'.
>
> (*Oratio*, n.1–2)

To corroborate his thesis that humans are the most wondrous beings among the creatures, Pico calls on two witnesses who could not be more different: Abdul, an unknown Saracen and thus, in the fourteenth century, one of the detested enemies of Christendom; and the *Asclepius* of Hermes Trismegisthos, who in the Renaissance was erroneously considered an ancient Egyptian priest and whose wisdom inspired Plato. Thanks to Ficino's translation of the *Corpus hermeticum*, Hermes Trismegisthos was held in the highest regard in fifteenth-century Europe.[2]

For Pico, since Asclepius the "excellence of human nature [*humanae naturae praestantia*]" has been sought in humanity's endowment with reason, the capacity that enables humans to partake in the divine (*Asclepius* 6; see also Cic. *Off.* 1.11–15; 96–8). The human is thus seen as a "messenger between creatures [*creaturarum internuntium*]," "the part in between the standstill of eternity and the flow of time [*stabilis aevi et fluxi temporis interstitium*]," and "a bond tying the world together [*mundi copulam*]" (*Oratio*, n.3). The philosophical determination of humanity's place in the cosmos appears, as Pico emphasizes, to be confirmed by the Bible as well, for "according to David [*Ps* 8, 6] man is only 'a little lower than the angels'" (*Oratio*, n.3.).

If, despite their superiority over the animals, humans are beneath angels in the order of the cosmos, then for Pico the question becomes: "Why should we not wonder more at the angels themselves and at the very blessed heavenly choirs?" (*Oratio*, n.3.) The esteem implied in the introduction, the human as the being "most worthy of wonder [*admirandum maxime spectaretur*]," was obviously not merely decorative rhetorical hyperbole. On the contrary, humanity ranks—and this is the main anthropological thesis Pico puts forward in the *Oratio—above* the angels.³ Significantly, this means that Pico defends the dignity of humanity not only against the Augustinian doctrine of original sin but also against Neoplatonic anthropology, in which angelology is given primacy over anthropology (McEvoy 1973: 342; Turner 1995: 18) because the human, a corporeal being, is beneath the pure spirit beings, i.e., the angels.

For Pico, humans, as the supreme beings among all creatures, are also the recipients of the greatest fortune. The idea that the human being is destined to attain a greater bliss than the angels appears to contradict all traditional notions of the place of humanity in the cosmos, an impression that Pico also concedes in the exclamation that "it is wonderful and beyond belief" (*Oratio*, n.3); and yet despite this brief hesitancy, Pico is firmly convinced that he can reasonably explain his audacious thesis.

> At length, it seemed to me that I had come to understand why man is the most fortunate [*felicissimum*] of beings and therefore worthy of all admiration, and what finally is the condition that befell him in the universal order, a condition to be envied not only by beasts but even by the stars and the intelligences dwelling beyond this world [*ultramundanis mentibus*].
>
> (*Oratio*, n.6)

With this thesis of human superiority over the angels, Pico is by no means breaking new ground. Quite the contrary, in fact: because integrating the Christian teaching of God's incarnation into Neoplatonic thought is anything but unproblematic, the relationship between human and purely spiritual beings had already been a *quaestio disputata* in the theology of the Middle Ages,⁴ with Aquinas and Bonaventura each adopting a mediating position. Because rational nature is more perfectly developed in angels, these pure spirit beings are ranked above humans; however, because the human soul permeates the body and through it rules over the visible world, rational human beings represent the dominion and presence of God in the visible world more fully and completely than incorporeal spirit beings: "For there is no contradiction in saying that though *ontologically* the human exists at a lower point on the scale than do angels, *representationally* the human has the greater power to reflect the divine, since it contains microcosmically, in a way that angels do not, the representational power of the whole universe" (Turner 1995: 124). A similar constellation emerges in the teaching of divine mercy. According to Bonaventura, because of their nature human beings may be positioned beneath the pure spirits; but divine mercy can elevate humans to attain the dignity of the angels or indeed lift them beyond angels (Trinkaus 1970: 1:188).

Against this historical background, Pico proceeds to explicate humanity's superiority over the angels in the *Oratio* through an artful narrative of creation, evoking two anthropological theses: the indeterminacy or intermediate position of human nature and the self-transformative capacity of the human being.

According to Pico, the cosmos is made up of three worlds: the sublunar, the astral, and the *mundus intelligibilis*, the dwelling place of the angels (*Oratio*, n.10f.). The place of humanity in this cosmos is described with the ancient motif of the human being as *contemplator mundi*: "But when the work was finished, the Craftsman still longed for there to be someone to ponder the meaning of such a magnificent achievement, to love its beauty and to marvel at its vastness. So, when everything was done (as Moses and Timaeus testify), He finally thought to bring forth man" (*Oratio*, n.12–13). In bringing forth humans, however, the Creator becomes entangled in an awkward situation: "But there was nothing among His archetypes from which He could mould a new progeny, nor was there anything in his storehouses that He might bestow upon His new son as an inheritance, nor was there among the seats of the world any place for this contemplator of the universe" (*Oratio*, n.14). Pico's reference point here is the myth of Protagoras as related by Plato. Because Epimetheus had distributed all the qualities and capabilities to non-human creatures, there were no more gifts left to be endowed to humans. As a result, the human being is utterly vulnerable, unprotected from the whims of nature (*Prot.* 320c–323a).[5] In Pico's rendering it is not one of the Titans who has plunged unwittingly into the dilemma, but the Creator. God had already used up all the archetypes before bringing forth the human. And to exacerbate the situation, so many beings dwell in the three worlds of the cosmos that there is simply no place left for humans at all: "Every place was by then filled; all things had already been assigned to the highest, the middle, and the lowest orders" (*Oratio*, n.15).

This situation of acute deprivation facing humanity is overcome in two steps in the Protagoras myth. Firstly, Prometheus brings fire and the arts (*technia*), enabling human beings to attain the food needed to survive and ensure protection from hostile nature. Secondly, however, after humans have redressed their vulnerability to savage animals and the rigors of weather, a new malady arises. Without social competence humans become embroiled in conflict and are in danger of self-extermination through violent wars. To avert the self-destruction of humankind, Zeus brings to humanity "justice and shame [*dike kai aidos*]" (*Prot.* 321d), i.e., the indispensable foundations for human coexistence.

While the Protagoras myth emphasizes the conditions necessary for the physical and social self-preservation of humankind, in his creation myth Pico attempts to demonstrate human superiority over all creatures, including angels. Pico therefore describes humans not as weak and deficient but as beings without an archetype to provide orientation and guide human life. In contrast to Aristotle, Pico describes the human as a "creature of indeterminate image [*indiscretae opus imagines*]" (*Oratio*, n.18). This indeterminacy of human nature is not a deficiency, however, for—as Pico emphasizes by invoking microcosm anthropology—it enables humanity to actively share in all natures: "At length, the Master Creator decreed that the creature to whom He had been unable to give anything wholly his own should share in common whatever belonged to every other being [*ut, cui dari nihil proprium poterat, commune esset*]" (*Oratio*, n.17). This openness for all natures is the basis for the ancient idea of the human being as *contemplator mundi*. In addressing humans, the Creator says: "We have set you at the centre of the world so that from there you may more easily gaze [*ut circumspiceres*] upon whatever it contains" (*Oratio*, n.21).

The call for humanity to gaze around at the world and all it contains has been frequently interpreted as an anticipation of the modern urge for knowledge and the modern subject's claim to power over nature (Reinhardt 1989: 23; Gerl 1989: 123). But for Pico, this world is part of a cosmos structured by God and not merely physical raw materials malleable to the human will to power. Pico therefore laments that it no longer seems important "to have the causes of things, the ways of nature, the reason of the universe, the counsels of god, the mysteries of heaven and earth very certain before our eyes and hands" (*Oratio*, n.17). In *Heptaplus* Pico then expressly rejects the Promethean hubris of subjugating nature (5.7). Even more salient is the conclusion Pico draws from the idea that human beings find all possible natures within themselves— to know the world is to know oneself: "For he who knows himself, knows all things in himself" (*Oratio*, n.5). Thus whenever humans make nature into an adversary, ultimately they are damaging themselves (*Heptaplus* 5.7). This means that humans can gaze and consider all that is in the world as it suits, for all natures are already present in them, as Pico alludes to with microcosm anthropology. Ontologically, Pico thus has no qualms about speaking of humans as "intermediary [*interstitium*] and, so to speak, the mixture [*quasi cynnus*]" of different natures (*Oratio*, n.117).

The connection between humanity's intermediary position and microcosm anthropology, merely hinted at in the *Oratio*, is explained in more detail in *Heptaplus*. This late work shifts the emphasis from the indeterminacy of human nature to its sharing of all dimensions of the cosmos. Due to sharing in all three worlds, i.e., the sublunar, the heavenly, and the intelligible worlds, humanity forms a "fourth world" (*Heptaplus* 5.6; G 300) or is virtually "a new creature [*quasi nova aliqua creatura*]" (*Heptaplus Prooemium* 2; G 193; 5.6; G 300).

Microcosm anthropology, the roots of which go back to the pre-Socratics, was controversial in Christian thought due to the danger of cosmological determinism (Gatzemeier and Holzhey 1980). Pico, too, calls the teaching of humanity as a microcosm "trite school learning" (*tritum in scholis*; *Prooemium*, G 192). The mere existence of several natures in an individual is not, however, a unique privilege of humankind, as Pico notes somewhat polemically. Cattle, devoid of intellect but capable of being domesticated by humans, obviously have a share in different natures (*Heptaplus* 5.5; G 300). Pico thus does not simply adopt microcosm anthropology but recasts it in the light of his idea of the creative freedom of humanity (Craven 1981: 29f.).

To this end, there is a need to distinguish between two meanings of "medium." The concept of medium, as Pico elaborates, designates a relationship of affinity or similarity between things or natures. Thus, with respect to the essence of humanity, two types need to be distinguished. Firstly, medium marks an affinity in the essential character between humans. As a lion resembles all other lions due to it being one of the same kind, different humans resemble one another because they share the same human nature (*Heptaplus* 6.4; G 318). Thus, despite the thesis on the indeterminacy of human beings, Pico still adheres to the ontological concept of humans as *animal rationale* (*Heptaplus* 4.1; G 270). Along with this affinity, there is a second kind of medium, one that relates to the extremes—"Est ultima ratio affinitatis quae est mediae naturae ad extrema" (*Heptaplus* 6.4; G 318)—and unites them (ibid.). In this sense, Christ is the unifying medium between human and divine nature (*Heptaplus* 6.7; G 324).

But humanity is not merely static in the middle of the ontological hierarchy; rather, the human being unifies (*univit*), through reason and freedom (*praeditus intelligentia et libertate arbitrii*), all natures of the cosmos (*Heptaplus* 6.7; G 322; *Heptaplus* 7, *Prooemium*; G 328). As God the Creator unifies (*unit*) and colligates (*colligit*) the essence of all things in their absolute perfection, humanity convenes all natures of the universe (*corrogat*) and unifies them with God (*counit*). In this sense, the human being is the unifying medium (*Heptaplus* 5.6; G 302) or as the formulation in *Heptaplus* puts it, "the bond and knot of heavenly and earthly things [*caelestium et terrestrium vinculus et nodus*]" (*Heptaplus* 5.7; G 304). With the interpretation of "medium" as the free unification of distinct natures, Pico as it were breaks open microcosm anthropology from within (Thumfart 1996: 195).

Starting from this dynamic interpretation of humanity's middle position, in the *Oratio* Pico describes freedom as the power humans possess to determine their own natures. In the Creator's words to humans:

> He therefore took man, this creature of indeterminate image, set him in the middle of the world, and said to him: "We have given you, Adam, no fixed seat or form of your own, no talent peculiar to you alone. This we have done so that whatever seat, whatever form, whatever talent you may judge desirable, these same may you have and possess according to your desire and judgment. Once defined, the nature of all other beings is constrained within the laws We have prescribed for them. But you, constrained by no limits, may determine your nature for yourself, according to your own free will, in whose hands We have placed you. We have set you at the centre of the world so that from there you may more easily gaze upon whatever it contains. We have made you neither of heaven nor of earth, neither mortal nor immortal, so that you may, as the free and extraordinary shaper of yourself, fashion yourself in whatever form you prefer. It will be in your power to degenerate into the lower forms of life, which are brutish. Alternatively, you shall have the power, in accordance with the judgment of your soul, to be reborn into the higher orders, those that are divine".
> (*Oratio*, n.19–23)

The movements of non-human creatures follow, as Pico emphasizes in line with Aristotle, the respective laws given to their nature. This is not just the case for heavenly bodies but also animals: "As soon as they are born, brutes bring [their nature] with them from their mother's Womb" (*Oratio*, n.25). Even the pure spiritual beings, originally created by God as free beings, assimilate into the universal order of creation, Pico alluding here to medieval angelology: "The Intelligences have been, either from the beginning or soon thereafter, what they are perpetually going to be throughout eternity" (*Oratio*, n.26).

For Aquinas, the angels have established their status for all time "after" their free decision for or against God, i.e., after the fall of Lucifer (*Summa theologica* I, q. 64, art. 2). Because the angels live an existence that is outside of time from the outset, the question arises in which sense is it possible to speak of a timespan between their creation and their decision for freedom (*Summa theologica* I, q. 63, art. 6). The distinction Aquinas draws between the "now" of creation and the "now" of the fall of the angels is secondary for Pico, however.

Decisive alone is the fact that pure spirit beings no longer possess the free will to choose, whether from the beginning or "after" their decision prior to time. This means that all non-human creatures, including pure spirit beings, enact their being in accordance with their underlying nature.

Against this background, Pico focuses attention on the proprium of the human being: in contrast to *all* other creatures, humans are not immutably limited to *one* specific nature. Quite the contrary—thanks to sharing in all natures, resting in us like seeds, humans have the power to transform: "If he cultivates his vegetative seeds, he will become a plant. If he cultivates his sensitive seeds, he will become a brute animal. If he cultivates his rational seeds, he will become a heavenly being. If he cultivates his intellectual seeds, he will be an angel and a son of God" (*Oratio*, n.29).

To avoid typical neo-Kantian and existentialist misunderstandings of the *Oratio*, it is necessary to clarify two points. Firstly, the essence of human freedom resides in the capacity to transform the self, not in self-creation. This freedom is given with birth: "having been born into this condition; that is, born with the possibility to become what we wish to be [*postquam nati sumus condicione, ut id simus, quod esse volumnus*]" (*Oratio*, n.46). Humans do not create their own natures but, proceeding from the innate, the seeds, the human being "fashions, shapes, and transforms [*effingit, fabricat et transformat*]" their own nature. Secondly, it needs to be emphasized that self-transformation into an animal or angel nature is not in relation to the first nature of the human as an *animal rationale*, and most certainly not animal nature, but to a "second nature," i.e., specific forms of life. Accordingly, in the *Commentary on a Poem of Platonic Love* Pico describes humanity's self-exaltation into an angelic figure in a language resonant with "existentialist" motifs. When the soul intensively engages a specific faculty, other activities weaken or vanish completely. Immersed in thoughts, for example, we no longer hear or see much of what is going on around us. Pico believes that the same phenomenon is observable in the relationship between the intellect and reason:

> Likewise, whoever arrives at the exercise of the intellectual part will lack the acts and operations of both reason and all other lower cognitive powers …. And because … the rational part is peculiar to man and through the intellectual he communicates with the angels, this latter lives a life no more human than angelic and, dead to the sensible world, is reborn to a more perfect life in the intellectual.
> (Pico 1986: 85f.)

Here, a tentative recapitulation is advisable. Pico breaks with the anthropology of Aristotelian-Scholastic metaphysics, where nature or essence is understood as "an intrinsic principle of a thing that establishes its powers, making it be *what* it is and not some other kind of being" (Dougherty 2007: 135). Because *telos* means limit (*peras*) in Aristotle, then "the substantial form of a thing is a restricting principle or principle of limitation that keeps the thing from being the unlimited and unrestricted pure existence who is God" (Dougherty 2007: 135). Thus—and this marks the break—when Pico identifies the human beings' superiority as the capability to adopt *several distinct* natures, sweeping aside the more modest Aristotelian notion of mere rationality, then the power to transcend the limits of human nature means that Pico "removes human beings from the medieval hierarchy of being or places human beings outside the Great Chain of Being" (Dougherty 2008: 135).

In *Heptaplus* Pico compares humanity's position in the cosmos, preponderant over the world, with the statue of a ruler. Like a monarch who has a statue of himself erected in the center of a city, God has placed the human, created in his image, at the center of the world so that he may be seen from the whole world (*Heptaplus* 5.6; G 300–2). Indeed, this means that, endowed with the function of the universal mediator, humanity accrues responsibility for the whole cosmos.

Peace and strife in the world depend on the inner calm of humanity (*Heptaplus*, 5.7; G 304–6). In short, the human being is God's representative in the world, and the representative of the universe in relation to God (Monnerjahn 1960: 25; Euler 1998: 169).

For Pico, the idea of freedom *qua* self-fashioning is the basis for his interpretation of human perfection, described in the terms of mystical theology as unification with God. As Pico indicates at the opening of his oration, with respect to perfection the human surpasses the angels: "I had come to understand why man is the most fortunate [*felicissimum*] of beings and therefore worthy of all admiration" (*Oratio*, n.6). Hence, the greatest happiness a person can enjoy resides in cultivating the best seeds within. Thus, in terms of the relationship to the pure spirits, Pico calls on people to "emulate their [the angels'] dignity and glory, unwilling as we are to yield to them and unable to endure second place" (*Oratio*, n.49).

Pico describes the ascent to the greatest happiness with the traditional imagery of Jacob's ladder. The "tripartite philosophy [*philosophia tripartite*]" (*Oratio*, n.115) guides humanity through the first stages on the way to divine peace, i.e., moral philosophy, dialectics, and the philosophy of nature, which Pico interprets with the theory of angels from Dionysius Areopagite. Moral philosophy cleanses the spirit of the confusions caused by the passions, while dialectics liberates it from the "darkness of reason" (*Oratio*, n.71). With the wonders of the universe, the philosophy of nature demonstrates the power of God (*Oratio*, n.141). But the highest stage of happiness possible to humanity is not yet reached with the philosophical contemplation of nature. Because "nature is the offspring of war, as Heraclitus said … it is said that in philosophy true rest and stable peace cannot reveal themselves to us alone" (*Oratio*, n.92). The highest stage, union with God—which is compared with, among other things, Socratic mania (*Phdr* 244a–245a)—cannot be attained by humans alone; rather, as Pico emphasizes in full agreement with Christian theology, humans need the help of divine mercy. Certainly, Socratic frenzies "will surely lead us away—but only once we ourselves have taken control of what is ours" (*Oratio*, n.111).

In the encounter with God, the human is no longer the active fashioner of their own nature; instead, through divine mercy, a transformation takes place, human metamorphosed into God: "And at last, roused by ineffable love as if by a frenzy, and borne outside ourselves like ardent seraphim, filled with the godhead, we shall no longer be ourselves, but He Himself Who made us" (*Oratio*, n.113). Whoever lets themselves be embraced by and imbued with divine mercy becomes "a guest at the table of the gods while still alive on earth and, inebriated by the nectar of eternity, to receive, though still a mortal creature, the gift of immortality" (*Oratio*, n.108). Thus, with respect to the greatest happiness as well, humanity is no longer beneath the angels.

As Pico explains in *Heptaplus*, the mystical union with God may no longer be described in terms of the Aristotelian concept of *eudaimonia*, i.e., the fulfillment of humanity's highest capacities (*Heptaplus* 7, *Prooemium*; G 330). In a general sense, Pico sees happiness as a return to origin; for the highest good that all aspire to is at the same time the origin of all (*Heptaplus* 7, *Prooemium*; G 326). The greatest happiness can be striven for in two ways, namely "*aut in se ipsis, aut in ipso*" (*Heptaplus* 7, *Prooemium*; G 328). Pico explains the distinction as follows: we seek to reach God either in the creatures to whom he discloses himself, or in himself (*quoniam vel in creaturis, quibus se Deus participat, vel in ipso Deo Deum assequimur*; *Heptaplus* 7, *Prooemium*; G 332). When we seek God in the creatures, then the principle holds that the respective entity finds its goal in fulfilling its natural possibility. This means that, supported by its own strength, an entity cannot attain a perfection greater than what its own nature permits (*utique nihil nitens per se ipsum ad felicitatem maius aliquid vel perfectius sua natura assequi poterit*; *Heptaplus* 7, *Prooemium*; G 330). Pico is thus not simply rejecting the traditional definition of happiness in the sense of realizing innate nature but limiting its scope to the natural happiness of the human being. Ultimately, though, for Pico the Aristotelian definition of happiness, applicable not just to humans but to all realms of being, is problematic. Because the animals and the heavenly bodies, in so far as they are subjected to fixed laws, fulfill their nature out of sheer necessity, they would thus be even happier than humans. And hence freedom would not be a human privilege but the cause of insurmountable misery (*Heptaplus* 7, *Prooemium*; G 332).

In mystical theology it is therefore necessary to overcome the Aristotelian concept of happiness: "That is true bliss, that we are one spirit with God, that we are invested with God himself and not with us, that we recognise how we have been recognised" (*Heptaplus* 7, *Prooemium*; G 336). Ultimately, this differentiation of happiness underpins the main thesis of *Oratio*, namely that the human is the most fortunate being among all creatures. At the same time, however, neither angels nor humans can ascend to the highest union with God on their own: they need to let themselves be infused with and elevated by divine mercy. The hubris of the fallen angels was to rely on themselves when seeking to ascend to God (*Heptaplus* 7, *Prooemium*; G 332).

6.2 The wonder of the chameleon: on the modernity of Pico's idea of self-creation

Since Jacob Burckhardt, Pico's idea of creative freedom has been frequently acclaimed as an early example of the modern subject and its world-creating capability. In contrast, following their own trajectories, historians of philosophy see Pico's philosophy of freedom as a rhetorically brilliant reprise of motifs taken from classical ancient and medieval anthropology, placing far less emphasis on its status as an anticipation of Kant or Sartre. Against this background, I would like to take a closer look—through the prism of a couple of historical sketches—at the difficult question of the modernness of Pico's idea of creative freedom.

Pico himself does not claim to construct a new anthropology in the *Oratio*, placing his thinking instead in the tradition of the *prisca theologia*, founded by Orpheus and Zarathustra and, via Moses and Plato, developed into the foundation of *philosophia perennis* (Sudduth 2007). Pico supports the idea of the power of self-transformation with numerous references from both classical ancient philosophy and Christian theology, for example Pythagorean-Platonic metempsychosis, Enoch's transformation into an angel, and the mythological narratives about Calypso and Proteus (*Oratio*, n.33–4). These references are not to be understood as precise sources; rather, in the spirit of the Aristotelian dialectic, Pico recalls the voices of recognized philosophers and theologians, whose ideas he does not simply adopt but modifies and reinterprets (Dougherty 2008).

The idea of a *prisca theologia* is a historical fiction widely used in the Renaissance. Nonetheless, some motifs of Pico's understanding of freedom can indeed be traced back to the Old Testament. The formula that God has relinquished free will [*liberum arbitrium*] to the human being—"according to your own free will in whose hands We have placed you [*pro tuo arbitrio, in cuius manu te posui*]" (*Oratio*, n.20)—is to be found almost verbatim in the vulgate version of the apocryphal book of Sirach: "From the beginning God appointed man and left him in the hands of his own counsel [*Deus ab initio constituit hominem et reliquit illum in manu consilii sui*]" (*Sir*. 15:14; cf. Wicke-Reuter 2000: 45–50). The motif of the human as a "moulder and maker of thyself [*tui ipsius quasi plastes et fictor*]" (*Oratio*, n.22) also has a biblical background. In the book of Sirach, the relationship between God and the human being is compared with that of the potter to clay: "Like clay in the hand of the potter, to be moulded as he pleases, so are humans in the hand of their Marker, to be given whatever he decides" (*Sir*. 33:13–14). In the vulgate, "to mold" is rendered with the Latin "plasmare": "*quasi lutum figuli in manus ipsius plasmare* [sic!] *illud et disponere, omnes viae eius secundum dispositionem eius sic homo in manu illius qui se fecit reddet illis secundum iudicium suum.*" This means that Pico translates the biblical image of the divine potter to the self-relationship of the human being. Out of the seeds given to them, humans form their own natures like the potter shapes clay. But this translation of the pottery image into the self-relationship of the person is not completely new; it is indicated in the New Testament in *Tim*. 2:20f. and subsequently systematically developed by Origen (Schockenhoff 2012: 53), whose influence on Pico we still need to consider.

The striking thesis of the *Oratio*—that the human being, by virtue of their freedom, can degenerate to an animal or be reborn into the divine—is also not a new idea, as Pico concedes: it was already a widespread motif in classical ancient anthropology. Aristotle, for example, compares the life of the multitude, concerned solely with self-preservation and not the good life, to an animal existence: "Now the mass of mankind are evidently quite slavish in their tastes, preferring a life suitable to beasts, but they get some ground for their view from the fact that many of those in high places shares the tastes of Sardanapullus" (*NE* 1.3.1095b19f.). And like Pico, Aristotle calls on humanity to decide for the divine reason (*nous*) within:

But such a life would be too high for man; for it is not in so far as he is man that he will live so, but in so far as something divine is present in him; and by so much as this is superior to our composite nature is its activity superior to that which is the exercise of the other kind of virtue. If reason is divine, then, in comparison with man, the life according to it is divine in comparison with human life.

(*NE* 10.7.1177b27–32)

The scope for self-determination based on free will is distinctly limited through the natural dispositions in Aristotle, albeit problematically. For example, the barbarians in the northern and southern regions of the inhabitable world, as Aristotle emphasizes with reference to the climate, are denied a rational life because of their natural dispositions (*Pol.* 7.7.1327 b23–33). At the same time, however, the women in Hellas are also denied a full use of reason (*Pol.* 1.5.1254b13–14).

In contrast, with the *prisca theologia*, Pico overcomes the Aristotelian opposition between Greeks and barbarians from the outset. Further, in the *Disputationes adversus astrologos*, also published posthumously in 1496 by Gianfrancesco Pico from existing manuscripts, Pico defends human freedom against both astrology and the theories of climate and instincts (Reinhardt 1987: 388f.; Rabin 2007). Thus, unlike Aristotle, for Pico the path to ascend to the divine or to descend to the beastly is open to *every* human.

However, according to Aristotle, the virtues of human beings in the temperate zone are determined to a specific degree by natural dispositions. In the *Eudemian Ethics* Aristotle names six, in the *Nicomachaen Ethics* only two natural virtues (*physikai aretai*, namely *aidos* and *nemesis*—shame and righteous indignation) (Krämer 1959: 173–5; 240). The proportion of freedom varies depending on the kind of virtue. Whereas rational virtues are acquired through instruction (*didaskalia*), the ethical virtues are forged through habit: "For the things we have to learn before we can do them, we learn by doing them, e.g., men become builders by building and lyre players by playing the lyre; so too we become just by doing just acts, temperate by doing temperate acts, brave by doing brave acts" (*NE* 2.1.1103a 34–b2).

As Aristotle emphasizes, although the ethical virtues are not formed *through* nature, they are also *not against* nature: "rather we are adapted by nature to receive them and are made perfect by habit" (*NE* 2.1.1100b 24–6). For the virtues to become stable, they must therefore be consolidated by education and the state. For this reason, Aristotle compares a person not yet established in virtue with a chameleon: "we should often call the same man happy and again wretched, making the happy man out to be 'a chameleon, and insecurely based'" (*NE* 1.11.1100b6f.). Subsequently in ancient and medieval thought, but also then in the Renaissance, the chameleon is an emblem for the vice of inconstancy (Copenhaver 2019: 363f.).

Against this background, a central aspect of Pico's idea of human freedom becomes discernible. With provocative emphasis, Pico lauds the human being's chameleon-like power to transform: "Who will not wonder at this chameleon of ours? Or rather, who will admire any other being more?" (*Oratio*, n.31). Pico underlines this affirmation of human mutability with a comparison to Proteus: "Not without reason, Asclepius the Athenian said that man was represented in the secret rites by Proteus because of his changing and metamorphous nature" (*Oratio*, n.33). Here, too, Pico counters the ancient tradition. Plato had prohibited poets from mentioning Proteus to preserve the idea of God's immutability (*Rep.* 381d). Moreover, Plato compares the Homerian singer Ion to Proteus, who dodges argumentative justification through rhetorical tricks: "Really, you're just like Proteus, you twist up and down and take many shapes, till finally you've escaped me altogether by turning yourself into a general" (*Ion* 541e). Later, for Erasmus, Proteus is still a symbol for the corruptive inconstancy of humanity.

In contrast to Aristotle, the Stoics had affirmatively underscored the role of freedom in their interpretation of self-care (*epimeleia heautou*). According to Epictetus, while nature has provided animals with all they need, Zeus gave humans the possibility and the duty to care for themselves (*Epict. Diss.* 1.1.4; 2.8.18–23). For Seneca, in turn, the practices of self-care serve to form and elevate the self. "Just now I am still fashioning and moulding myself and trying to lift myself to the height of a lofty ideal [*Cum maxime facio me et formo et ad exemplar ingens attollo*]" (*De vita beata* 24.4).

Cicero goes even further, introducing the concept of *natura altera* or *natura secunda* (*Fin.* 5.25.74; Waszink 1980; Funke 1984) for those attitudes acquired through habit. Nonetheless, the goal of self-formation in Stoic thought remains the stability of virtue, mirrored in *ataraxia*. For Cicero, too, the *natura altera* shares with humans' first nature the character of immutability. Pico, however, conceives the human being primarily as a shaper and not a captive of second nature; a person can freely decide to move in either direction, to become a beast or an angel, or to transform from an angel back into the beast.

Because the idea of freedom presented in the *Oratio* is difficult to integrate into the anthropology of Greek and Roman philosophy, at variance with all theories at some point, the close relationship between Pico and Origen has been pointed out frequently and for some time now (Garin 1938; Mahoney 1994; Kobusch 2015). Pico is undoubtedly an important voice in the broad reception of Origen in the age of humanism (Schnär 1979; Monnerjahn 1960: 185–190). In his 900 theses, Pico defends Origen against the excessive condemnation of the church. Unsurprisingly, the papal commission placed under suspicion of heresy the thesis that "It is more rational to believe that Origen is saved, than to believe that he is damned" (*Theses* 4< >29). Ultimately, in *De salute Origenis disputatio* (1487), Pico explicitly defends his condemned thesis on Origen (Schnär 1979: 126–42).

Origen is also expressly mentioned in the *Oratio*, however (*Oratio* n.235; n.243). Indeed, as more recent studies have discerned, an alternative lineament begins to emerge here, with the Christian metaphysics of freedom—for which Origen laid the foundation—entering modern thinking through Pico, evident most notably in German idealism, Kierkegaard, Sartre, and even Richard Rorty (Schockenhoff 2012; Kobusch 2015).

And in fact, like Pico, Origen draws a strict distinction between the realm constituted by natural laws (*kataskeue*) and the realm of freedom (Kobusch 2015: 146). As Origen explained in his main work *On First Principles*, the "essence" of humanity resides in the faculty of moral self-determination: "there is no rational creature which is not capable both of good and evil" (Origen 2013: 69; chap. 1.8.3). All who invoke external events or natural dispositions as the reason for moral behavior see themselves "like sticks and stones, which are dragged along by agents that move them" (Origen 2013: 162; chap. 3.1.5). Because human beings are themselves the cause of both good and evil, then they also are the cause for their moral state, i.e., their second nature. In short, "to live rightly or otherwise is our task and not a thing that depends on external causes, nor, as some think, on the irresistible pressure of fate" (Origen 2013: 163f.; chap. 3.1.6).

In contrast to Aristotle and the Stoics, Origen, like Pico, accentuates mutability in the concept of "second nature." Origen thus vehemently rejects the maxim of Celsus that "it is very difficult to change a man's nature completely" (Origen 1980: 174; chap. 3.69). Although conceding "that many men have become evil by upbringing and by perversion and by environment, so that in some people evil has even become second nature" (ibid.), no human being lapses irreversibly into evil. And the opposite is also true: anyone supposing that they are assuredly stable in virtue can deviate from the right path in a short time or stolidly remain the same: "the most licentious men frequently becoming better than those who formerly did not seem to be such by nature; and the most savage men passing into such a state of mildness, that those persons who never at any time were so savage as they were, appear savage in comparison, so great a degree of gentleness having been produced within them" (Origen 2013: 162; chap. 3.1.5).

Despite the emphasis on freedom, through which in principle every person is endowed with the faculty to initiate self-change, Origen by no means neglects the natural and cultural conditions and contingencies impinging on human freedom:

> And certain of them, from the hour of their birth, are reduced to humiliation and subjection, and brought up as slaves, being placed under the dominion either of masters, or princes, or tyrants. Others, again, are brought up in a manner more consonant with freedom and reason: some with sound bodies, some with bodies diseased from their early years; some defective in vision, others in hearing and speech; some born in that condition, others deprived of the use of their senses immediately after birth, or at least undergoing such misfortune on reaching manhood. And why should I repeat and enumerate all the horrors of human misery, from which some have been free, and in which others have been involved, when each one can weigh and consider them for himself?
>
> (Origen 2013: 131; chap. 2.9.3)

The fact that some humans are born with disabilities or are hindered in using their freedom from early childhood contradicts the idea of a just creator who has created all to develop towards the good. To preserve the freedom of man as well as the goodness and justness of God, Origen constructs extremely speculative philosophies of nature and history.

In Origen's account, God has created a limited number of rational natures endowed with free will and fully equal with one another (Origen 2013: 129f.; chap. 2.9.1). Because some of these rational beings have renounced their origin, the creator gave them different kinds of matter. The order of the cosmos, including the hierarchy between humans and pure spirit beings (angels, demons, devils), is the result of the freely made decisions of the original spirit beings either for or against God (Daniélou 1948: 207). Because the present "nature" of the pure spirit beings resides in their freedom, even an angel can change into a devil and a devil into an angel.

> From which, I think, this will appear to follow as an inference, that every rational nature may, in passing from one order to another [*ab uno in alterum ordinem transeuntem*], go through each to all, and advance from all to each, while made the subject of various degrees of proficiency and failure according

to its own actions and endeavours, put forth in the enjoyment of its power of freedom of will.

(Origen 2013: 57; chap. 1.6.3)

Nonetheless, creation is not merely the result of the respective decisions based on free will made by pure spirit beings, for God has preserved the harmony of the cosmos since the beginning of creation through Christ, the logos (Hengstermann 2016: 306–21). To disburden God of responsibility for those physically and socially conditioned inequalities among humans which cannot be directly traced back to individual decisions, Origen takes up the Pythagorean-Platonic theory of the transmigration of souls, combining it with the Stoic age of the world (Daniélou 1948: 207–15). Origen rules out the Platonic notion that human souls can incarnate into animals (1980: 20f.; 12f. 194f.) after initially having deliberated its possibility (Origen 2013: 71–5; chap. 1.8.4). The reinterpretation of Platonic transmigration is then taken up by the Neoplatonic school, in particular Porphyry and Aeneas of Gaza (Kobusch 2012: 72). The different talents shown by humans stem from the merit or misconduct of their souls in an earlier life: "This is the reason why some are found right from their earliest years to be of ardent keenness, while others are duller, and some are born extremely dense and altogether unteachable" (Origen 2013: 127; chap. 2.8.4).

Key motifs of Origen and patristics are undoubtedly present in Pico's theory of human freedom, in particular the primacy of freedom over Greek thought on nature and essence. Nonetheless, Pico's anthropology is not simply a "condensed version of the Patristic teaching of freedom" (Kobusch 2015: 142). At this point, a brief look at Aquinas' criticism of Origen may prove worthwhile. If empirical reality is first formed by the original spirit beings renouncing God, then the cosmos and even the creation of humanity cannot arise directly from the wisdom of the Creator (see *De substantiis seperatis seu de angelorum natura*, chap. 12). Indeed, according to Aquinas, the Creator has indued the world with immutable laws which cannot be changed through any decisions of free will made by spirit beings. In addition, from among all the creatures it is solely the human being, by virtue of freedom, who can always be steered toward the good *and* the bad. Non-human spirit beings are, as Aquinas once more emphasizes contrary to Origen, fixed for ever in their essence "after" their original act of freedom: "So it is customary to say that man's free-will is flexible to the opposite both before and after choice; but the angel's free-will is flexible … before the choice, but not after" (*Summa theologica* I, q. 64, art. 2).

Pico clearly takes up both of Aquinas' objections. As he emphasizes in the *Oratio*, the Creator has determined the nature of all things, with humanity the sole exception; and Pico refuses to speculate on any future decisions made by angels in the later eons. The human is—and here Pico and Aquinas are in full accord—the only flexible being in the universe. At a decisive juncture, however, Pico deviates from Aquinas. Following Aristotle, Aquinas sees the perfection of humanity as residing in choosing the goal given by nature, and thus the pure spirit beings, who constantly and thoroughly recognize the good, stand above rational human beings in the hierarchy, as the latter can still be manipulated to either good or evil. For this reason, pure spirit beings, although they can no longer sin, have greater freedom [!] than human beings: "Hence there is greater freedom of will in the angels, who cannot sin, than in us, who can sin [*Unde major libertas arbitrii est in angelis qui peccare non possunt, quam in nobis qui peccare possumus*]" (*Summa theologica* I, q. 62, a.8. ad 3). In contrast, for Pico, flexibility is not a sign of humans' imperfection, but rather proof of their superiority. At this juncture, Pico adopts a position running fundamentally contrary to Aquinas (Reinhardt 1989: 226). Indeed, as already mentioned, Pico accentuates the affirmative recasting of humans' creative ability to transform by invoking their chameleon-like nature, with a verse from the Chaldeans: "'Man is by nature diverse, multiform and inconstant' [*id est homo, variae ac multiformis et desultoriae naturae animal*]" (*Oratio*, n.44).

Origen and the patristics had positively revalued the freedom of humanity in the light of the idea of God's freedom in the Old Testament. It is thus no surprise that parallels to Pico's philosophy of freedom are to be found in Islamic theology, most prominently in the works of al-Ghazali (Truglia 2010). In the *Alchemy of Happiness* al-Ghazali writes: "His spirit is lofty and divine. When in the crucible of abstinence, he is purged from carnal passions to the highest, and in place of being a slave to lust and anger becomes endowed with angelic qualities. Attaining that state, he finds his heaven in the contemplation of Eternal Beauty … The spiritual alchemy … operates this change in him" (chap. 15). Indeed, al-Ghazali proceeds to claim, like Pico, that humans alone possess the freedom for good and evil, a distinction from Origen who assigns this freedom to the angels, including the devil:

> Thus man is capable of existing on several different planes, from the animal to the angelic, and precisely in this lies his danger, i.e., of falling to the very lowest. In the Koran it is written, "We proposed the burden [i.e., responsibility or free will] to the heavens and the earth and the mountains, and they refused to undertake it. But man took it upon himself: Verily he is ignorant." Neither animals nor

angels can change their appointed rank and place. But man may sink to the animal or soar to the angel, and this is the meaning of his undertaking that "burden" of which the Koran speaks.

(al-Ghazali 2005: 37)

Besides the Kabbalah, Pico engages with Islamic theology. In the 900 theses he focuses mainly on Ibn Sina, al-Farabi, and Ibn Rushd (Farmer 2016: 251–63; 269–71). There is no evidence either way that he was familiar with the writings of al-Ghazali. In any case, al-Ghazali seems to interpret human freedom to be a burden and a distinction that elevates human beings over the angels.[6]

To conclude these sketches of the historical contexts of Pico's idea of human freedom, we need to consider its place in the Neoplatonic thought of the Renaissance. Without a doubt, the anthropology of the *Oratio* is closely related to Cusa and Ficino. Like Pico, Cusa interprets microcosm anthropology in the light of his teaching on the creative mind: "Therefore, man can be a human god; and just as he can be a god humanly, so he can be a human angel, a human beast, a human lion, or a human bear, or any other such thing" (*De conjecturis* II.14.n.143; H 1.236). For this reason, Pico's *Oratio* has frequently been seen as a consequential continuation of Cusa's anthropology (Watts 1982: 32; Euler 1998; Schwaetzer 2002). Crucially, however, Cusa—less concerned with the flexibility of human freedom—accentuates how all things are enfolded in the human mind: "just as in the universe all things are unfolded after the fashion of the universe, so in humanity all things are unfolded in a human way, since [man] is a human world. Finally, in humanity all things are *enfolded* in a human way, since [man] is a human god" (*De coniecturis* II.14.n.144). A similar constellation emerges in the relationship between the *Oratio* and Ficino, with whom Pico was close. In *Theologia Platonica* (1482), Ficino describes in striking terms the creative power of human freedom within the framework of microcosm anthropology. According to Kristeller, Pico transformed Ficino's anthropology and posited humanity's creative freedom outside the hierarchy of being (1965). However, if the *Heptaplus* is also taken into account, the differences between Pico and Ficino are not so clear (Euler 1998: 190f.).

In whatever way the historical references are evaluated, Pico certainly assimilates numerous traditional and contemporary motifs into his anthropology. And yet in the *Oratio* Pico describes human freedom in a way that remains—and not just due to its rhetorical flourishes—impressive today. Pico posits the flexibility of human freedom, i.e., the chameleon-like nature of the human being, as the very foundation of human supremacy over all other creatures, including pure spirit beings.

Despite Pico's radical affirmation of the creative power of human freedom, his thought by no means presages the modern hubris that deifies humans or the *homo faber*, who degrades nature as an object of their will to power. In *Heptaplus* the human being is God's representative on earth, without however the divine power of the *creatio ex nihilo* being assigned to humankind. According to Pico, the highest perfection of humanity lies not in the technological manipulation of nature, but elevation to a pure spirit, i.e., angel-like, existence, which ushers in the gracious intuition of the divine. Despite the enthusiastic revaluation of the chameleon-like nature of the human being, the idea of boundless freedom is something unfamiliar to Pico. While humans have the capacity to metamorphose into all natures, the seeds already within them mirror the hierarchical order of the cosmos. The self-transformative power embedded in human freedom thus always remains bound to a stable order of values (Kessler 2005: 62). At the same time, however, the dynamic interpretation of human freedom contains a dangerous ambivalence: whoever destroys their humanness through moral transgressions no longer deserves to be called human.

> If you see someone who is a slave to his belly, crawling along the ground, it is not a man you see, but a plant; if you see someone who is enslaved by his own senses, blinded by the empty hallucinations brought on by fantasy (as if by Calypso herself) and entranced by their bedevilling spells, it is a brute animal you see, not a man.
>
> (*Oratio*, n.38)[7]

While Pico is very much grounded in the ethical universalism of Stoic-Christian thought, the dynamic anthropology of self-formation opens the floodgates for a dubious devaluation of human dignity.

Even if the normative framework of the Neoplatonic hierarchy of being implodes as a result, with the image of the human being as a "free and extraordinary shaper of yourself," able to "fashion yourself in whatever form you prefer" (*Oratio*, n.22), Pico forges a metaphor that, as the following studies on Renaissance and early modern thought will show, exerts a most profound influence on the further development of modern thought across numerous modifications.

7

The conquest of the Americas and the foundations of global cosmopolitanism: Francisco de Vitoria and Juan Ginés de Sepúlveda

The main intellectuals of the European Enlightenment looked back in admiration at the age of discovery. The crossing of the Atlantic and the exploration of the sea route to India represented—as Jean Antoine de Condorcet emphasized—a huge leap forward for humankind: "For the first time man knew the globe that he inhabited, was able to study in all countries the human race as modified by the long influence of natural causes or social institutions, and could observe the products of the earth or of the sea, in all temperatures and all climates" (Condorcet [1795] 1955: 104). At the same time, the European Enlightenment was also aware, at least subliminally, of the dark side of the transoceanic discoveries. Condorcet's shock at the fate of the victims of the Conquista remains palpable: "The bones of five million men covered those unfortunate lands where the Portuguese and the Spaniards brought their greed, their superstitions and their wrath" (Condorcet [1795] 1955: 106).

In Europe, the importance of Columbus for the modern age has been emphasized often and lauded since the Enlightenment. In the philosophical discourse about modernity, however, European expansion has remained in the shadow of the Copernican turn and the rise of the modern natural sciences, a position exemplified in the work of Jürgen Habermas. There is a stark contrast between the European perspective and Latin American philosophy, in which unsurprisingly the conquest and colonialization of the Americas is often the focal point of the discourse of modernity. For Enrique Dussel, the year 1492 marks nothing less than the birth of modernity (see section 3.2 of this book).

To appreciate the significance of the voyages of Columbus for modern philosophy, it is necessary to consider the structural parallel between the cosmological and geographical world conceptions in antiquity. Because Aristotle's cosmology is based on a teleological ontology, which in turn serves as the foundation for anthropology, ethics, and political philosophy, the revision of the ontological fundaments, as exemplified in the thought of Nicholas of Cusa, triggered a series of spectacular innovations in other areas, in particular cosmology and epistemology. Since in antiquity the geographical conceptions of the world were also entwined with anthropological, moral, and political theories, the expansionism of the Iberian powers not only broadened humanity's geographical horizons but initiated far-reaching transformations in other fields, ranging from ethics and politics through to the modern sciences. One of the first—and perhaps the most important—philosophical innovations directly related to the early modern de-limitation of the geographical conception of the world is that of a new global cosmopolitanism.

Against this background, I wish to first address the question as to how the early modern voyages of discovery corrected the geographic worldview of classical ancient and medieval thought (section 7.1). In a second step I will then turn to the debate over the Conquista of the Americas, which, as I propose, laid the foundation for modern cosmopolitanism. Given the enormous number of varying positions on these events, I shall narrow my focus to two thinkers: firstly, Francisco de Vitoria, who, once long celebrated as the founder of modern international law, is currently criticized by post- and decolonial thinkers as the originator of colonial ideology in modernity; and secondly, Ginés de Sepúlveda, who took up the Aristotelian doctrine of the natural slavery of barbarians and, as early as the sixteenth century, was fiercely criticized by Bartolomé de Las Casas and is cast as the very incarnation of Spain's inhumane imperial ideology. Sepúlveda himself, along with some interpreters of the twentieth century, did, however, vehemently reject the claim that he was justifying the enslavement of the Amerindian peoples. From my consideration of these two thinkers, it seems possible to closely analyze the problem of coloniality in the genesis of modern cosmopolitanism. To contour the rational and ideological elements in Vitoria's thinking, I shall draw on a few main characteristics of cosmopolitan thought in antiquity and the Middle Ages (section 7.2). Emerging here is Vitoria's pivotal doctrine of *ius gentium*, the first philosophical theory of international law in Europe (section 7.3). From Vitoria, an arc may be traced to Sepúlveda (section 7.4), guided by the proposition that the two thinkers are by no means antipodes, but indeed that the latter builds on the former. Moreover, Sepúlveda's justification of the Conquista of the Americas is embedded in a specific context: the anthropology of the Renaissance and the debate about the Ottoman Wars.

Despite the undoubted problematic devaluation of Amerindian cultures, Vitoria and Sepúlveda raise a difficult and still pressing issue: how to assert universal ethical norms globally, an issue that even today remains at the center of global political discussion under the banner of human rights. As my concluding summary then argues, the colonialism debates of the sixteenth century reveal breakthroughs of rationality toward a global cosmopolitanism, intimately entwined however with power syndromes and cultural visions (section 7.5).

7.1 The "Age of Discovery" and the rationalization of European geographic worldviews

The voyages of Vasco da Gama and Columbus brought about the most radical change to the geographical conception of the world since antiquity. Legends abound about the "age of discovery." In the nineteenth century, the myth arose that to carry out his plan to reach India by a sea route from the west, Columbus had to first convince the members of the commission convened by the Spanish king that the earth was spherical (Russel 1991). In Christian thinking, however, except for Lactantius and the Alexandrian monk Cosmas, who called himself Indicopleusteus ("Indian voyager"), the disc theory of the earth had ceased to be propounded by the great theologians of the Middle Ages (Brincken 1976; Simek 1992: 37–54). In the fifteenth century it was not the shape of the earth that was contentious, but its dimensions. The main split revolved around whether to believe the calculations of Eratosthenes, which proved to be extremely close to determining the circumference of the earth, or those of Poseidonios, who came to a figure that was one-third less (Stückelberger 1987: 189, n. 2). Of even more importance in our context is that, based on the theory of the spherical shape of the earth, ideas about other continents (*oikumene*) were already circulating in antiquity. Against this background, the contribution of early modern voyages of discovery to rationalizing the geographic conception of the world can only then be precisely determined when consideration is given to geographical thought in antiquity and the Middle Ages.

Early Greek natural philosophy had adopted Homer's image of the earth as a disc encircled by the sea. According to Anaximander, supposedly the first Greek to create a map of the world, the cylindrical earth floats freely in the middle of a spherical cosmos. The top surface of the cylindrical earth forms a perfect circle that is surrounded by the *okeanos* (KRS: fr.122–4; Szabó 1992: 91f.). Anaximander's world map represents an enormous act of abstraction in comparison to an everyday relationship to the world, one that paves the way for a mathematically based geography (Gehrke 1998).

Hecataeus, the second great pre-Socratic geographer, filled the geometric space with historical and ethnographical information (Kahn 1960: 81–3), drawing on two sources: knowledge gathered during his own journeys, which took him to Egypt, the Black Sea coast, the Near East, and Massalia; and Greek and Phoenician descriptions of the coastlines, known as the *Periplus*, a literary genre since the seventh century BCE (Güngerich 1950; Gisinger 1937b). As Herodotus noted, accounts of spectacular expeditions were already circulating in early antiquity, for example the circumnavigation of Africa by Phoenician sailors sponsored by Pharoah Necho or the voyage of Colaeus, who passed through the Strait of Gibraltar as early as the seventh century BCE (Htd. 4.42; 1.152). A fragment has survived of the sea route taken by Euthymenes of Massilia, who in the mid-sixth century BCE journeyed along the west African coast, presumably reaching the mouth of the Senegal or Gambia Rivers (Heilen 2000a: 48). Famous in antiquity was the sea route description by the explorer Skylax of Caryanda. Sent by the Persian emperor Darius to explore the Indus estuary between 518 and 512 BCE, he then sailed around the Arab Peninsula and reached Suez (Hdt. 4.44; Heilen 2000a: 42). These descriptions and accounts explain why Hecataeus' map already covers the geographical space extending from India to the Pillars of Hercules. The earth is divided into two land masses, Asia and Europe, and Asia in turn divided into Libya, Arabia, and India. Hecataeus' view of the world presents a tripartite division of the continents, namely Europe, Asia, and Libya (present-day Africa), which was to remain undisputed for over two millennia in the West. Methodologically, Hecataeus' achievement resides in connecting Anaximander's conception of geometrical space with the *Periplus* literature, which borrows from the lifeworld accounts of these spaces (Gehrke 1998: 36f.)

The rudiments of a scientific geography are not the only innovations in knowledge among the pre-Socratics in antiquity; first beginnings are also evident in medicine. The pseudo-Hippocratic treatise *On Airs, Waters, and Places* examines the influences of habitat (location, climate) on the life and morals of the peoples of the known world. Here the thesis is already formulated that a warm climate promotes the effeminacy of the will, while a harsh climate fuels an urge for freedom (Müller 1980: 1.137–44).

The ethnographic tradition of *Periplus* literature, the Hippocratic doctrine of the influence exerted by place and climate on morals, and the physical geography of the pre-Socratics all merge in Herodotus' histories (Bichler 2000: 15). Given that the assumptions about the shape of the earth and the ratio of land to sea, as well as the historical accounts, all needed to be examined in terms of their truthfulness or feasibility, Herodotus also questions the Homerian idea of the earth as a disc surrounded by the *okeanos*. Due to the lack of reliable sources, Herodotus concludes that neither the idea that the inhabited world is surrounded by the sea, nor the assumption that the earth is circular, are capable of being proven. Indeed, given the state of knowledge, it was not even certain that Europe is surrounded by the sea at all (Hdt. 4.45). These considerations clearly show that the *okeanos* was already demythologized and now served as a hypothesis requiring empirical verification.

In addition, Herodotus introduces the concept of the *oikumene* into scientific geography (Hdt. 17.2.1; Gisinger 1937a: Sp. 2124). Where formerly the earth as a limited terrain (*peras*) encountered the limitless ocean, the idea of an inhabited world connected through human communication is posited, a world that has open ends, empty areas (*eremoi*), and varying climate zones (Romm 1992: 37f.).

The demythologizing of the *okeanos* alters how the limits of the earth or the *oikumene* are conceived. While in the west the *oikumene* is bounded by the sea, for Herodotus it is now conceivable that boundless deserts stretch out in the east, south, and north (Hdt. 3.98; 4.17; 4.185; 5.9). Already in early antiquity the brinks of the known world were populated with all manner of mythical creatures. While examining these stories of marvelous treasures and monstrous creatures at the edge of the world to determine their truth, Herodotus himself provided the imagination with abundant material. His inquiries abound with stereotypes, for instance of the vast sources of gold in India (Hdt. 3.105–6), of humans with canine heads or headless, of mysterious islands in the Atlantic (Hdt. 4.8), etc., all of which remained alive in European consciousness until the age of discovery.

During the transition from the fifth to the fourth century BCE, the doctrine of the earth's spherical shape is developed, presumably in Pythagorean circles (Burkert 1962: 282f.). According to Plato, when viewed from the celestial world, the earth looks like a mottled leather ball (*Phd.* 110b). Aristotle furnishes a proof demonstrating the spherical shape of the earth that still holds today—because the earth casts a spherical shadow during a lunar eclipse, it must be globular in shape (*Cael.* 2.14.297a8; 297b.24–31). The disc theory remains symbolically present in antiquity, however. For Pindar, the Pillars of Hercules are symbolic boundaries that humans should not seek to cross: "What lies beyond [the Pillars of Hercules] neither wise men nor fools can tread. I will not pursue it; I would be foolish" (*O.* 3.44f.).

The doctrine of the earth's spherical shape was not seriously disputed after Aristotle. The sole contentious point was the composition and structure of the globe's surface. Ancient science formulated three theories in dealing with this problem: the zonal theory, the theory of the four landmasses, and Ptolemy's assumption that the earth's larger bodies of water are inland seas.

The zone theory, which according to ancient sources goes back to Parmenides (Abel 1974) but first found its authoritative version in Aristotle, divides the surface of the earth into five zones, whereby the regions in the extreme north and south as well as the torrid zone are uninhabitable for humanity. For Aristotle, human life is only possible in the two temperate zones on the northern and southern hemispheres (*Mete.* 2.5.262a33–62b6). The zone theory thus fosters speculation about human life in the southern hemisphere, already expressed by Plato (*Ti* 63a).

Crates of Mallos extended the scope of the zone theory in the mid-second century BCE, assuming the existence of four landmasses (Mette 1936). The globe is divided into four equally large sectors by two oceans, the polar and equatorial, which intersect at right angles. Because the universe is ordered according to the principles of geometrical harmony, each sector of the surface must have an *oikumene*.

For this reason Crates assumed four continents, the *oikumene* (Europe, Asia, North Africa) and the Perioici on the northern hemisphere, and the Antipodes and the Antioeci in the southern hemisphere. Crates' view was adopted by numerous ancient scholars, among them Dicaearchus, Aristarchus, and Eratosthenes, while his doctrine reached a broader audience through Cicero's *Somnium Scipionis*. According to Cicero, viewing the earth from the heavens would reveal not only the *oikumene*, i.e., Europe, Asia, and Libya, but also other landmasses beyond the oceans: "You see that humans inhabit small and scattered portions of the earth, and that huge emptiness separates the blotches of human habitation" (*Leg.* 6.20.99).

Ptolemy occupies a special place in ancient geography (Dilke 1987; Stückelberger 2000). In contrast to Crates, Ptolemy regards the idea of an *oikumene* surrounded by an *okeanos* to be erroneous; it is not the ocean that surrounds the earth, but the earth the ocean (Figure 1). Because each of the landmasses extends to the poles, the Indian Ocean must be an inland sea. And distinct from the zone theory, Ptolemy believes that all the regions of the earth are habitable, omitting the need to assume the existence of a torrid zone impenetrable to humans.

A discussion emerged in antiquity around the question of whether the boundaries of the *oikumene* were in fact unsurpassable. Because the sea route

Figure 1 Map of the world, according to Ptolemy

Source: *Australia, New Zealand and Oceania in Pictures*, by H. Clive Barnard, M.A., Blitt. (A. & C. Black, Limited, London, 1923). Credit: "Map of the World, According to Ptolemy," 1923. Creator: Agathodaemon of Alexandria. The Print Collector/Alamy Stock Photo.

from Spain to India lies entirely within the temperate zone, according to Aristotle a crossing of the Atlantic must be geographically possible in principle. The difficulty is solely maritime technology, for coastal voyages were the rule in antiquity, thus: "if it were not for the ocean which prevents it, the complete circuit could be made" (*Mete.* 2.5.262b.19–20). Strabo followed a similar logic: "if the immensity of the Atlantic sea did not prevent, we could sail from Iberia to India along and the same parallel over the remainder of the circle" (*Geography* 1.4.6). By contrast, there was considerable skepticism about any possible foray into the southern hemisphere. In the zone theory as well as for Crates, the equatorial zone was an insurmountable barrier for humans. According to Pomponius Mela (author of *De Chorographia*, the first geographical tractate in Latin), the southern hemisphere, where the Antichthones live, is "unknown because of the heat of the intervening expanse" (1998: 34). For Tacitus, who could already look back at Roman expansion into the northern Atlantic, a religious dread once again arises in face of the Pillars of Hercules. After Drusus Germanicus, the first to advance as far as Europe's northern coast between 12 and 9 BCE, there had been no further attempt to explore the Pillars and beyond: "it was voted more religious and more reverent to believe in the works of Deity than to comprehend them" (*Germ.* 34).

The idea of the antipodes was a source of inspiration for the literary imagination in antiquity (Moretti 1993). Lucian of Samosata tells of a voyage to the antipodes where "we saw land and judged it to be the world opposite the one which we inhabit." While the seafarers were embroiled in debate about whether to go ashore or turn back, "a violent storm struck the boat, dashed it ashore and wrecked it" (*Ver. hist.* 2.47). Servius' commentary on the *Aeneid* by Virgil includes an account of a letter that the wind had blown from the antipodes into the *oikumene*. The inhabitants of the antipodes, who believe themselves to be superior (*superi*), bid greeting to the inhabitants of the *oikumene*, the inferior (*inferis*). Thus, in late antiquity, the idea of the antipodes assumes a similar function to early modern speculations on the inhabitants of other planets; they open a space to articulate a perspectival questioning of entrenched notions of self and world (Moretti 1993: 253–5).

The boundaries of the known world were not only questioned in antiquity but, at least partially, also crossed and expanded by expeditions (Schulz 2005). Since the mid-second century BCE, the Ptolemies had been exploring the Red Sea and the east African coast as far as Cape Guardafui. In 120 BCE, Eudoxus of Cyzicus discovered the route from east Africa to India. From Britannia, Pytheas embarked on a six-day voyage to an island he called Thule (Roseman 1994; Heilen 2000b). Seneca tells of an expedition to find the sources of the Nile which presumably got as far as the ninth parallel (*QNat.* 6.8, 3–4), an achievement first repeated in 1839. The extension of geographical knowledge laid the basis for new hypotheses, with many peripheral areas no longer interpreted as the ends of the known world but as the tips of another *oikumene* (*alter orbis*). Pomponius Mela, for example, ventured to propose that Taprobana (Sri Lanka) could be the northern tip of the antipodes (1998: 121f.; *De Chorographia* 3.70). According to Posidonius, who divided the earth into seven zones, with the torrid zone much smaller and relocated in the tropical region, the equator had a temperate climate. An expedition to the southern hemisphere was therefore no longer inconceivable (Aujac 1987: 168f.).

The various expansions of the Roman Empire between 67 BCE and around 85 CE were interpreted as the most significant exceeding of the boundaries of the *oikumene* in antiquity (Schulz 2003: 29). Since Caesar's push into Britain, in Rome, as evidenced by Plutarch, the *okeanos* was no longer considered uncrossable: "For he was the first to launch a fleet upon the western ocean and to sail through the Atlantic sea carrying an army to wage war. The island was of incredible magnitude ... and in his attempt to occupy it he carried the Roman supremacy beyond the confines of the inhabited world" (*Caes.* 23.2). Caesar's

Atlantic expedition turned Britain into an *"alter orbis"* (Romm 1992: 141–3; Schulz 2003: 34). A rush of further expeditions to the north followed: Tiberius reached the Wadden sea, Drusus set out to find the northeast passage to the Black Sea, and Agricola circumnavigated Britain and then sailed to the Orkney Islands (Hennig 1944–56: 1.380–2). Based on calculations made by Posidonius, who estimated the circumference of the earth to be one-third smaller than Eratosthenes' calculation, even an expedition across the Atlantic to India now seemed feasible in the first century CE. Not without a sarcastic undertone, Seneca asked: "For what distance lies between the farthest coasts of Spain and the Indies? An interval of very few days, if a ship is driven by a favourable wind" (*QNat*. Pref. 13). The successful expeditions to the North Sea fueled hopes that lands hitherto unknown could be discovered and conquered, hopes which found literary expression in Seneca's *Medea*: "There will come an age in the far-off years when Ocean shall unloosen the bonds of things, when the whole broad earth shall be revealed, when Tethys shall disclose new worlds and Thule not be the limit of the lands" (*Med*. 375–9).

Amid the euphoria over the imminent conquest of other *oikumene*, concerns were raised in the Late Republic about the danger of overexpansion. In *Somnium Scipionis* Cicero, employing the literary fiction of looking down on earth from the heavens, exposes the minuteness of the Roman Empire and the transitoriness of military fame: "The Antipodes have for Cicero become an exemplary case of lands that can never be conquered, a visible symbol of the limits of Roman expansion" (Romm 1992: 135). Seneca the Elder takes up the motif of Alexander to denounce the immoderateness of the imperial urge for territorial expansion. Alexander's plan to sail beyond Gibraltar is spurned, for it violates holy boundaries:

> In nature everything that has magnitude has limits too: there is nothing boundless except the Ocean. It is commonly said that there lie fertile lands in the Ocean, that beyond the Ocean again other shores, another world arises, and there is no end to created things, but ever a new world begins where the old seems to end. It is easy to invent such tales since one cannot sail the Ocean. Let Alexander be content with having conquered that portion of the world where the sun is content to shine.
>
> (*Suas*. 1.1)

Following the collapse of the western Roman Empire, the ancient geography of Ptolemy and Strabo was forgotten in Latin Christianity. Notwithstanding the loss of mathematical geography, Christian theology did not simply revert to the level of mythical geography. Through Macrobius and Marcianus Capella, the world conception of Crates of Mallus entered Christian thought (Brincken 1992: 27–43). With salvation history the fulcrum of Christian thought, deliberations on geography and maps of the world (*mappae mundi*) are found almost exclusively in history books. Geographical treatises primarily served to identify and describe the most important localities in salvation and church history. In contrast to ancient thought, no causal relationship was posited between the geographical location and the historical event. Moreover, early medieval theology shows no real distinct interest in measuring the world (Brincken 1970: 249–53).

At the same time, the world conception of Crates caused some irritation in Christian thought, if not confusion. Augustine, for example, queries the theory of the antipodes on theological—and not geographical—grounds. Because the oceans, as Augustine assumes in line with Crates, are unsurpassable barriers for humankind, the classical idea of the antipodes contradicts the biblical teaching on the oneness of the human species. Moreover, the existence of humans on unknown landmasses would cast doubt on the universality of Christ's act of redemption (*De civ. D.* 16.7–9; Brincken 1992: 28f.).

A fourth continent south of Africa was a firm component of the geographical world conception of Christian thought since Isidor of Sevilla (Brincken 1992: 84f.). However, because the *oikumene* was the locale where salvation history had played out, there was no pressing need to embark on forays into unknown regions. Early medieval Christianity had even greater difficulty in making sense of *Terrae Incognitae* (Brincken 1998: 565). The edges of medieval *mappae mundi* are not white blank spaces, calling to be filled in through discovery, but depict the Rivers of Paradise and the territory of Gog and Magog.

In contrast, the Arab world had already studied the writings of Ptolemy in the first half of the ninth century CE, spawning a new heyday for scientific geography (Miquel 1967–88). Around 950 CE, the polymath al-Masudi reverently refers to the great philosopher Ptolemy in his work *Murudj al dhaba* (Stückelberger 2000: 206; Pellat 2012). The adoption of mathematical geography into Islam was religiously motivated at first, an aid to identify the necessary orientation of the prayer niches (*quibal*) in the mosques toward Mecca (Scholten 1982: 12; Lindgren 1993: 92). Beginning with al-Muqaddasi (tenth century CE), Arab science then extended the scope of historiographical and ethnographical geography through explorations in Asia and Africa. In the field of cartography, the work of al-Idrisi stands out: commissioned by Roger II, he wrote the *Compendium of the Properties of Diverse Plants and Various Kinds of Simple Drugs*. Al-Idrisi's world map incorporates both Arab learning about Asia, which extended to China and Japan, and considerable knowledge of Europe's northern regions, including Scandinavia and Iceland, which he had collected during his stay in Naples. Al-Idrisi's work thus represents the first comprehensive expansion of the geographic conception of the world since Ptolemy (Maqbul 1992). Although Ibn-Battuta extended ethnographic knowledge once more, the archaic fear of the Atlantic, the "sea of darkness," remained present until the fifteenth century in Arab geography (Hennig 1944–56: 2:422–32). Maritime expeditions along the western periphery of the *oikumene* thus obviously stayed close to the coastline of Africa.

With the adoption of the Aristotelian philosophy of nature, a rationalization of the geographic world emerges in Christian thought in the High Middle Ages. In 1175 Gerard of Cremona translated Ptolemy's *Almagest*, while at the beginning of the fifteenth century, Ptolemy's *Geographia* once again became prevalent in Christian thought thanks to the Latin translation by Jacopo d'Angelo (Stückelberger 2000: 206f.; Randles 1993: 16). Strabo's *Geography* is another work first rediscovered in the fifteenth century.

With the economic boom in the cities, the willingness to embark on new journeys increased. The northern Italian port cities were the foremost starting point of ambitious expeditions. In 1291, the brothers Ugalino and Vadion Vivaldi set out on an expedition to the Atlantic with the aim of reaching India (Rogers 1955). In 1336, a Portuguese expedition under the leadership of the Genovese Lancelotto Malocelli "discovered" the Canary Islands. The Mongolian invasion of 1237–1241 radically broadened the geographical horizon eastwards. Marco Polo provided Latin Christianity with accounts of the cultures of the regions of China and Japan, hitherto unknown to them, although contemporaries doubted their authenticity.[1]

Knowledge of new kingdoms in the east was not enough, however, to significantly shift the geographical horizon of the *oikumene*. On Christian maps of the time, China is presented to the north of India; the fourth continent merges with a somewhat enlarged Africa (Brincken 1989: 5; 30). The failure of the Vivaldi brothers' Atlantic expedition resonated in a prominent work, however: Dante's *Divine Comedy*. In Dante's account, Odysseus does not return to Ithaca but instead sails out with his companions through the Straits of Gibraltar. After five months of voyaging on open seas, land is suddenly in sight, only for the ship to capsize. Dante does not describe Odysseus' failure as punishment for illegitimate transgression; rather, intermingled with the archaic fear of the western ocean is the typical modern passion to discover new worlds. Since leaving Circe, nothing more could hold Odysseus back from the audacious undertaking, "neither the sweetness of a son, nor compassion for my old father, nor the love owed to Penelope, which should have made her glad, could conquer within me the ardor that I had to gain experience of the world" (Dante 1996a: 403; Inferno 26.94–6). Hans Blumenberg was thus moved to claim that Dante's version of the return of Odysseus is early evidence of the awakening of a modern curiosity about the world (Blumenberg 1983: 338–41). In a speech to his companions, Dante indeed emphasizes the motif of discovery: "'O brothers,' I said, 'who through a hundred thousand perils have reached the west, to this so brief vigil of our senses that remains, do not deny the experience, following the sun, of the world without people. Consider your sowing: you were not made to live like brutes, but to follow virtue and knowledge'" (Dante 1996a: 403; Inferno 26.112–20).

The rediscovery of Ptolemy's writings initiated a fundamental shift of geographic ideas in Latin Christianity. Given Ptolemy's view that all the earth was inhabitable, in Christian thought the question began to emerge as to whether the oceans could indeed be sailed and crossed. Moreover, medieval theology had been beset with the problem of how to reconcile the contradictions between the world conception of Crates, the zone theory, and Ptolemy's geography.

With the rediscovery of Ptolemy's mathematical geography—"a gift from the Arabs to the occident" (Brincken 1970: 257)—a rationalization of ideas on geography also began in Latin Christianity. Despite Augustine's reservations about the existence of the antipodes, important theologians adopted and modified Crates' world conception in the High Middle Ages. William of Conches considered all four landmasses to be inhabited; for Albertus Magnus, crossing the equatorial zone was difficult but not impossible (Randles 1993: 32f.); Roger Bacon and Pierre d'Ailly were both familiar with Seneca's thesis that it was possible to cross the Atlantic (Randles 1993: 9; Stückelberger 1987: 338). The revisions of the geographic view of the world in medieval theology found expression in cartography, albeit after a delay. Prominent among the new true-to-scale maps was that of the "geographicus incomparabilis," Fra Mauro (1459), who made important corrections of Ptolemy and came astoundingly close to an accurate determination of Africa's dimensions (Cattaneo 2011).

Against the background of the geographic ideas of the antiquity and the Middle Ages, it is now possible to determine more coherently the significance of the voyages of discovery in the early modern period for the rationalization of geographic models in Europe. Unlike the astronomical revolution of the early modern period, where the geocentric model was replaced by the idea of a boundless universe, the transoceanic expeditions cannot be simply interpreted as a transition from a closed to an open system, for the notion of other *oikumenes* was already a central component in the geographical worldviews of antiquity. Viewed from the standpoint of the ancient world, the voyages of Vasco da Gama and Columbus appear to be nothing other than the belated realization of the expansion plans of Roman emperors. On the theoretical level as well, the early modern discoverers build on the knowledge of the ancients, in particular Ptolemy. And Columbus also knew of the claims made by Aristotle that a voyage from Spain to India was considered possible in principle (Randles 1993: 43–6).

Despite all the links to ancient sources, the early modern voyages of discovery mark an epochal advance in the rationalization of geographical conceptions. It was only with Columbus and Vasco da Gama that doubts about the possibility of crossing the oceans were definitively dispelled in Europe. The Portuguese exploration of the coast of Africa furnished the first secure knowledge about the equatorial zone, which both Aristotle and Crates of Mallus had regarded as uninhabitable because of the great heat. Moreover, remnants of mythical geography were also debunked. The "discovery" of the Americas consigned ancient speculation about wonderous isles in the Atlantic (Atlantis, Insulae fortunatae) to the realm of fantasy. The circumnavigation of Africa deprived the literary fantasies about the antipodes of any foundation. And not least, the voyages of Columbus and Vasco da Gama cast doubt on the authority of Aristotle and indeed also Ptolemy, whose geography had only been recently rediscovered. At the end of the sixteenth century, José de Acosta tried to counter Aristotle's loss of authority in his work *Historia natural y moral de las Indias* (1590). According to Acosta, with respect to the Aristotelian philosophy of nature, distinctions need to be drawn between correct theses, justified assumptions, and excusable misperceptions, for example the notion of an extremely hot equatorial zone where human life is impossible. Contrary to Aristotle's claims, the discoveries have shown that the region around the equator is a "region of all the world the most fruitful of waters and pastures, and very temperate in the greatest part," which means that "wee must beleeve that the burning zone is well inhabited, although the aunciens have held it impossible" (Acosta 2010: 28f.).

At the end of the sixteenth century, the broadening of the geographical horizon leads to a new confidence vis-à-vis the entrenched authority of the ancients.

The Portuguese expeditions to southern Africa revealed the contours of a new scientific spirit. Unlike the voyage of Columbus, the deed of a single adventurer, the exploration of the African coast was a project spanning generations, coordinated by Henry the Navigator, himself never in the southern Atlantic, from Lisbon. Henry not only collected accounts of ancient circumnavigations of Africa but also undertook practical measures, founding his own maritime school, where leading figures in cartography and nautical skills trained seafarers (Hamann 1968: 39–50). This enabled new empirical data and technological innovations to be connected systematically. The Portuguese project to circumnavigate Africa thus heralds the spirit of Francis Bacon's new science.

The voyages of discovery in the early modern period led, finally, to a more cogent understanding of geographical limits and the rationalization of the geographical conception of world that was bound but yet unknown. The *oikumene* was replaced by the idea of a space that, in principle, could be crossed and something new reached. In the mid-fifteenth century, Cusa had translated the Aristotelian concept of potential limitlessness to the cosmos. Just over a century later, José de Acosta, considering the geographical conception of the world, stated "that there is much more land not yet discovered" (Acosta 2010: 29) and drew the conclusion "it is likely, a good parte of the world is not yet discovered" (Acosta 2010: 18).

In theories of modernity oriented on the Enlightenment, the voyages of Columbus and Vasco da Gama are often celebrated as a breakthrough of reason, as a theoretical and practical overcoming of mythical geography. Reflecting on ancient and medieval thought shows, however, that the various notions, conceptions, and models of the world had been demythologized to a high degree already prior to 1492 and, theoretically at least, there was an openness to the possibility of the existence of other continents.

7.2 Retrospect: ethical and political universalism in ancient and medieval thought

The notion of other *oikumene* may have stirred the imagination of poets and ambitious generals in ancient Rome, but it was never a theme for political philosophy. It was only with the transoceanic expansion of the Iberian powers that occidental philosophy was forced to face up to the actual historical challenge of encountering peoples from other inhabited worlds. In the early sixteenth century, the "discovery" and conquest of the Americas set off an intensive debate on the universal political ideas of Latin Christianity and their anthropological, ethical, and theological premises. In this context, Francisco de Vitoria, the main representative of what has come to be known as the Salamanca School, laid a foundation stone of epochal importance for global cosmopolitanism.

In order to appropriately profile what was new in Vitoria's global political thought, but also trace its deep ambivalences, it is necessary to approach his theory of *ius gentium* from the background of cosmopolitan thought in antiquity and Latin Christianity, and not see it exclusively in the light of later theories of international law.

From classical Greek thought to Roman philosophy: the arduous path to an ethical-political universalism

Although the Greek city-states throughout the Mediterranean maintained relations with numerous peoples, the *polis* is the focus of interest in the political philosophy of Plato and Aristotle. Relations to other states are primarily dealt with, if at all, as problems resulting from a disorganized *polis*. According to Plato, a *polis* is compelled to wage war against neighboring peoples when the needs of its citizens increase, for war is the means to securing access to and maintaining the availability of resources (*Rep.* 372c–374d). In contrast, Aristotle sees the greed for power among tyrants to be a major cause for wars between *poleis*. But democracies, wherein the poor rule, also inflict war on other city-states to appropriate the latter's goods and wealth (Bellers 1996). The ideal *polis* of both Plato and Aristotle thus revolves around an ethical and political idea of autarky.

Historically, however, the Greek city-states most certainly developed institutions operating in the sense of international law, for example courts of arbitration, alien laws, trade and shipping contracts, and also truces and peace agreements (Preiser 1978: 30–5). After the treaties between ancient Egypt, the kingdoms in Mesopotamia, and the Hittites between 1450 and 1200 BCE, relationships between the Greek city-states may be seen as the second phase in the practice of international law in antiquity (Preiser 1978: 105–21).

This means that a contradiction emerged in ancient Greece: between a political philosophy that had no place for an international legal order (Höffe 1999: 231) and the practice of the *poleis*, oriented toward what we would today call international law. What is more, Plato and Aristotle may have established the universal claims of philosophical reflection, but in their ethical and political thought they remained caught in a particularism that justified the denigration of women and the institution of slavery (Vlastos 1981: 147–63; Spelman 1994). Not least, Plato and Aristotle reinforced the opposition between Greeks and barbarians, already criticized by the Sophists Alcidamas and Antiphon (Baldry 1965: 80–4; Unruh 2002).

Plato strictly distinguishes conflicts between Greek city-states, seen as quarrels between friends, from wars against barbarians, who may be annihilated to achieve victory (*Rep.* 469b–71c). A universalistic perspective first crystallizes in the *Laws*, where the antithesis shifts from that between Greeks and barbarians to the opposition between the citizens of the ideal *polis* and the rest of the world (Baldry 1965: 80–4). Ultimately, Plato seems to even presume that a latent state of war exists between peoples:

> In this, I think, he [the legislator] censured the stupidity of ordinary men, who do not understand that they are all engaged in a never-ending lifelong war against all other states. So, if you grant the necessity of eating together for self-protection in war-time, and of appointing officers and men in turn to act as guards, the same thing should be done in peace-time too. The legislator's position would be that what most men call "peace" is really only a fiction, and that in cold fact all states are by nature fighting an undeclared war against every other state.
>
> (*Leg.* 625e–626a)

By contrast, like Herodotus and Aeschylus, Aristotle sets the freedom of the Greek *polis* against the barbarism of the oriental empires. Defending the *polis*, Aristotle draws on the fundamental principle of his metaphysics: that every existing thing is striving not merely for self-preservation but for a final state (*telos*), i.e., to attain its limit (*peras*). As Aristotle elaborates in his *eudaimonia* teaching, the perfectness attainable by humans resides in unfolding intellectual capacity, concretely the search for truth, the good, and the just: "And it is the characteristic of man that he alone has any sense of good and evil, of just and unjust" (*Pol.* 1.2. 1253a 16–18). In the family and the village, but also in the mighty empires, humans are imprisoned in a dull mind geared solely to ensuring self-preservation. It is only in the *polis*, i.e., in a surveyable community of free citizens organized into a state, that humans can exercise their faculty of reason through the rights of political participation, in particular their ability to exercise moral judgment: "He who has the power to take part in the deliberative or judicial administration of any state is said by us to be a citizen of that state" (*Pol.* 3.1. 1275a 19–23f.). As the rule of the free and equal, the *polis* thus not only guarantees economic independence but genuine autarky in the sense of the complete development of the mental proficiency of the human being. For this reason, the human wish for community has its limit (*peras*)—in the sense of striving toward what is best—in the *polis* and not in an empire.

> When several villages are united in a single complete community, large enough to be nearly or quite self-sufficing, the state comes into existence. And therefore, if the earlier forms of society are natural, so is the state, for it is the end of them, and the nature of a thing is its end ... Besides, the final cause and end of a thing is the best, and to be self-sufficing is the end and the best.
>
> (*Pol.* 1.2.1252b27–1253a1)

The model of self-government by the citizenship, the foundation for the republican tradition in European political philosophy, is overshadowed by Aristotle's idea of the natural slavery of barbarians. According to this perspective, while the peoples of Asia were highly developed in terms of their civilizations, because of the warm climate they were so feeble and languid that they submissively obeyed the rule of violent despots. Thus, for Aristotle, not only the tribal societies in the extremely torrid or cold climes, but also the peoples of the Near Orient were barbarians, i.e., humans who by their very nature are prevented from fully developing their reason and thus incapable of self-rule. Only the Greeks, because they lived in the temperate zone, possessed the necessary virtues, audacity, and intelligence, and had the disposition to establish and maintain the freedom of the organized *polis* (*Pol.* 7.7. 1327b23–33). The consequence drawn was simple—the Greeks had a natural right to rule over other peoples: "That is why the poets say,—It is meant that Hellenes should rule over the barbarians; as if they thought that the barbarian and the slave were by nature one" (*Pol.* 1.2.1252b7–9). Indeed, waging a war of aggression against barbarians for the sole purpose of supplying the Greek *polis* with slaves was not a contradiction to the principles of justice:

> And so, from one point of view, the art of war is a natural art of acquisition, for the art of acquisition includes hunting, an art which we ought to practice against wild beasts, and against men who, though intended by nature to be governed, will not submit; for war of such a kind is naturally just.
>
> (*Pol.* 1.8.1256b23–6)

This means that the absence of reflections on international law in Plato and Aristotle is not merely a negligent gap in their political thought; it is, rather, the consequence of their ethical particularism with its strict distinction between Greeks and barbarians.

In Hellenistic and Roman philosophy, a radical shift away from the ethical and political thought of Greek antiquity took place. On the one hand, in a move of epochal significance, the Stoics articulated a universalistic ethics; on the other, with Alexander the Great, the oriental idea of empire entered occidental culture. The cosmopolitan thinking of Hellenistic Roman philosophy was thus shaped by three components: the ethical idea of the unity of humankind and the oriental idea of empire, each of which is then connected to specific geographical conceptions of the world. This background enables us to distinguish between basic types of cosmopolitanism in ancient thought.

The historical origins of the ancient idea of a world empire lie in ancient Egypt and Mesopotamia. The rulers of the Sumerian Empire already saw themselves as rulers over the four continents (Holland 2005: 42f.). But it seems that the great Persian kings were the first to pursue the goal of extending their rule to the outermost peripheries of the earth, surrounded by the *okeanos*. Because the Persian idea of world rule still related to the disc theory of the earth, the expansion of the empire aimed to conquer the ocean itself (Miltner 1952: 538).

Alexander the Great brought the expansionist campaigns of the Persian Empire to an abrupt end. It remains contentious whether Alexander himself then adopted the idea of a world empire after his victory over the Persians (Tarn 1951: 378–98). Undisputable, though, is Alexander's own urge for territorial expansion, which saw his military campaigns penetrate into India and reach the Caspian Sea. In antiquity, it is reported that Diodorus passed on Alexander's "last plans," which envisaged the conquest of the western Mediterranean through to the Atlantic and then the circumnavigation of Africa; the authenticity of the ancient sources is disputed, however (Bosworth 1988: 164f.; Geus 2003: 241). Educated by Aristotle, Alexander was familiar with the teaching on the earth's spherical form and the zonal theory. Thus the idea of world dominion, if it were indeed the goal of his conquests, could have encompassed only the habitable world (*oikumene*) of the northern hemisphere, and not the whole earth; for, as Aristotle claimed, humans could not cross the equator (Geus 2003: 232–6).

Plutarch interpreted Alexander's military campaigns to be not only spectacular conquests but also a process civilizing Asia, which for Aristotle was still a zone of barbarism (*De Alex. fort.* 5–10; Tarn 1951: 399–449). Irrespective of the idealizing tendencies in Plutarch's portrait of Alexander, as A. B. Bosworth has forcefully pointed out, the idea of civilizing Asia contradicts the extreme brutality of the conquests: "We have travelled a long way from Plutarch and his rhetorical creation of Alexander the civiliser … That is not to say that there are no positive features to the reign of Alexander … The price of Alexander's sovereignty was killing on a gigantic scale, and killing is unfortunately the backcloth of his regime" (1988: 29f.).

The breakthrough to an ethically substantial cosmopolitanism stems neither from Plato and Aristotle nor rulers such as Alexander—it is the achievement of a new philosophical school. After early formulations in Democritus and the Sophists, the Stoics developed an ethical universalism that, finally and conclusively, overcame the Aristotelian teaching of the natural slavery of barbarians. At the same time, with the rise of Rome to hegemonic power in the Mediterranean, the oriental idea of a world empire took on a new form. The cosmopolite ideas of the Stoics are thus embedded in a tense relationship between ethical universalism and Roman imperialism.

Zenon of Citium, the founder of the Stoic school, boldly envisioned a homogenous world state, which Plutarch claimed could be summarized in one sentence: that "we should no longer live under laws distinct from another, but that we should look upon all people in general to be our fellow countryfolk and citizens, observing one manner of living and one kind of order, like a flock feeding together with equal right in one common pasture." While for Plutarch this gave shape "to a dream or, as it were, a shadowy picture of a well-ordered and philosophic commonwealth," it was Alexander "who gave effect to the idea" (*De Alex. fort.* 6.329A–B). The relationship to Alexander's expansionist politics claimed by Plutarch undoubtedly contradicts Zenon's intentions, however, influenced as he was by the Cynics (Schofield 1991: 104–11). The ideal state can only be established by the wise, among whom friendship and unity is possible, and not by rulers. This means that Zenon was not concerned with an international system of peace, imagining rather an unpolitical community made up of virtuous people, where money and polytheistic cults are abolished, family ties disbanded, and a uniform dress code installed (*Diog. Laert.* 7.33). "What Zenon put forward in the *Politeia* was not a description of a world state or community as some have supposed but a philosophical inquiry. It is an ideal and natural society not located in any particular time or place" (Erskine 1990: 23). Despite overcoming familial and ethnic boundaries, a new gap emerges separating peoples in Zenon's thought, namely that between the wise and the foolish. As Cassius reports, Zeno "applies to all men who are not virtuous the opprobrious epithets of foemen, enemies, slaves, and aliens to one another, parents to children, brothers to brother, friends to friends" (*Diog. Laert.* 7.32–3; Baldry 1965: 160f.).

Chrysippus, the second founder of the Stoic school, adopted Heraclitus' speculation on the logos to argue the unity of humankind. According to Heraclitus, human laws (*nomoi*) are nurtured by the universal logos that permeates all of reality (*KRS* 250; fr. 114; *Diog. Laert.* 7.87–8). For Chrysippus, this order of the cosmos, following discernible patterns, is not merely a paradigm (*paradeigma*), as it was for Plato, for structuring the order of the polis (*Rep*. 500c–501c), but rather a fundament for the unity of all humans prior to politics. Moreover, Chrysippus seems to have understood the law of the cosmos to be the standard for laws governing the state; the *koinos nomos* is the criterion for the just and unjust in different polities (Forschner 1996: 33). Little is known about the concrete ethical demands Chrysippus derived from this idea of the unity of humankind. It is clear, though, that he vehemently rejected the Aristotelian teaching of natural slavery. As Seneca claims, for Chrysippus, the slave is "'a hireling for life' [*perpetuus mercenarius*]" (*Ben*. 3.22.1). An abolishment of the institution of slavery remains, however—as with later Stoics—out of consideration.

To sum up: the first Stoics corrected the ethical particularism of Platonic-Aristotelian philosophy, but neither Zenon nor Chrysippus elaborated their approaches into an ethical universalism through considerations on international law.

The breakup of Alexander's empire and the rise of Rome in the second century BCE scarcely left a mark, at least initially, on the political philosophy of antiquity. The world historical importance of the rise of the Roman Empire is recognized and presented, for instance, by ancient historiography and not by philosophy. Polybius, captured after the Battle of Pydna in 168 BCE and sent to Rome as a hostage, where he then became friends with Cornelius Scipio Aemilianus, interprets the Roman expansion into the eastern Mediterranean as the definitive realization of the oriental idea of the world empire. Previously, the Persian Empire was limited to Asia, the Alexandrian to Asia and Hellas. Rome, with the victory over the Carthaginians and then over the Greeks, created an unprecedented situation in human history, with the fate of Europe, Libya, and Asia now interrelated: "Previously the doings of the world had been, so to say, dispersed, as they were held together by no unity of initiative, results, or locality; but ever since this date history has been an organic whole, and the affairs of Italy and Libya have been interlinked with those of Greece and Asia, all leading up to one end" (*Polyb*. 3. 3–4). Rome thus not established just another empire but in fact "succeeded in subjecting nearly the whole inhabited world to their government" (*Polyb*. 1.1.5). Unlike Herodotus, for whom the goal of history was coexistence between Europe and Asia, Polybius sees history as culminating in the unity of all peoples under Roman rule (Alonso-Núñez 1983: 411–13; Clarke 1999: 114–27).

In the second century BCE, Rome was far from having subjugated all peoples of the *oikumene*. Nonetheless, Polybius is partly justified in speaking of Roman rule. The oriental idea of world rule implies hegemony within the known world and not the outright occupation of all the territory: "It is clear that Polybius—who was aware of the eastern dimensions ... cannot mean that the Romans dominated the entire area of the *Oikoumene*, but rather that they were present in each of its parts and—at this date—had no serious rivals" (Nicolet 1991: 30f.). In distinction from modern nation states with clearly defined boundaries, the world empires of antiquity had open frontier zones where various processes were at work, administrative, military, and mercantile (Cooter 1977; Elton 1996: 113).

Polybius describes the expansion of the Roman Empire primarily as a spectacular turning point in the power-political conflicts being played out in the *oikumene*. Ethical criteria remain largely ignored in his interpretation of history: "Polybius' belief in the unity of history was not accompanied by any egalitarianism, any talk of need for change in the structure of human society. His visions transcend the frontiers, but left the traditional divisions of class and status undisturbed" (Baldry 1965: 176).

In the following centuries, Rome consolidated its power in the Mediterranean. Nonetheless, the idea of a world empire had gradually asserted itself in Rome. The earliest testimonies emerged during the rule of Sulla (Nicolet 1991: 31f.). In this context, at the turn of the eras, new constellations arose in the relationship between the ethical universalism of the Stoics and the idea of world empire.

Under the influence of Crates' speculations about other *oikumene*, an important differentiation in the idea of world dominion emerged in Rome in the first century BCE. Caesar's Britannia campaign raised hopes in Rome that a crossing of the oceans was possible. From that point, the aspiration of world dominion was understandable either as rule over the directly known *oikumene*, i.e., the Near East and the Mediterranean world, or as rule over the whole globe. In Roman times *both* variations were seriously considered, undoubtedly one of the more astonishing developments in antiquity.

The hope for expansion to other *oikumene* is expressed primarily in literary texts, however. In the eulogy to Mesalla Corvinus, Tibullus presents the prospect of not only the conquest of Britannia but also the southern hemisphere: "The Briton whom Roman prowess has not vanquished is reserved for thee, and the other portion of the world, with the Sun's path set between" (*Elegy* 7.149). Thus, after victory Mesalla will be lauded both in the *oikumene* and the antipodes: "So, then, when thy deeds shall be spread by thy glorious triumph, thou only shalt have the name of great in either world [*solus utroque idem diceris magnus in orbe*]" (*Elegy* 7.175f.). And as Virgil put it, the power of Augustus reaches to the stars: "Lo, under his auspices, my son, shall that glorious Rome extend her empire to earth's ends, her ambitions to the skies" (*Aen.* 6.781–3); the gods have promised that the Roman Empire will be an "empire without end [*imperium sine fine*]" (*Aen.* 1.279).

In contrast, Strabo, the most important geographer during the turn of the eras, warns against overextending the empire by incorporating other *oikumene*. Indeed, Rome should remain within the *oikumene* and limit itself to hegemony over the *already civilized* regions of Asia, Africa, and Europe. As long as they pose no danger to the empire, there is no need to conquer the peripheries, only scantily or superficially civilized (Nicolet 1991: 334). Moreover, Strabo combines his geographic work with an ethics and theology informed by the Stoic spirit. With the *Historika Hypomnemata* lost, it is no longer possible to exhaustively reconstruct Strabo's synthesis of Stoic ethics and imperial geography.

A systematic synthesis of ethical universalism and the idea of world empire is therefore first found in the work of Cicero. Through the conquests of Sulla, Caesar, and Pompey, Rome had, as Cicero emphasizes in the spirit of Polybius, overcome the separation of three continents (Vogt 1960: 156). Like Strabo before him, Cicero limits the Roman claim to power to the *oikumene* from the outset. The Romans are the source of world dominion, "our own people … whose rule now controls the whole world" (*Rep.* 3.24). Of course, Cicero was aware that large areas of the *oikumene* were yet to be conquered. The Roman Empire "could be called more accurately a protectorate of the world than a dominion" (*Off.* 2.8.27). But to legitimate the claim to world rule, it was sufficient that the geopolitically important zones were in Roman hands and the still independent peoples were held in check through alliances and friendships. Approached from this perspective, emphatic declarations of Rome's world dominion are expressed in poetry, historiography, and official documents in the imperial era. Livy's *History of Rome* (*Ab urbe condita*) mentions the head of the world ("caput orbis terrarium"; Livy 1919: chap. 1.16); the *Res Gestae* proclaim Roman rule over the whole earth ("toto in orbe terrarium"; Augustus 2009: chap. 3). Rome had achieved what Herodotus claimed the Persians failed in—to rule on land and at sea ("per totum imperium populi Romani terra marique"; chap. 13). And Ovid frankly emphasizes: "The land of other nations has a fixed boundary: the circuit of Rome is the circuit of the world [*gentibus est aliis tellus data limite certo: Romae spatium est Urbis et orbis idem*]" (*Fast.* 2.683). In the *Lex Rhodia* the Roman emperor is openly addressed as the master of the whole globe ("dominus totius orbis"; *Dig.* 14.2.9).

Amid the euphoric paeans to the Roman imperium, Cicero, in a decisive move, develops the ethical universalism of the old Stoics, drawing closely on Panaetius.

In contrast to Zenon's elitist community of the wise, Cicero formulates the idea of a natural community based on language and reason, wherein "the whole human race is bound together" (*Leg.* 1.32). As Cicero explains in the teaching on the law of nature (*lex naturalis*), with reason humans are given a basic ethical orientation: "Those who have been given reason by nature have also been given right reason, and therefore law too, which is right reason in commands and prohibitions; and if they have been given law, then they have been given justice too" (*Leg.* 1.33). And yet—and Cicero is acutely aware of this—humankind is *de facto* anything other than united through universal moral and legal ideas. What humanity is given is the faculty to use reason. Thus, depending on the degree this faculty has been cultivated, false opinions and corruptive customs can develop which endanger the unity of humankind: "reason, the one thing by which we stand above the beasts ... is shared by all, and though it differs in the particulars of knowledge, it is the same in the capacity to learn" (*Leg.* 1.30). But despite the moral errors and confusions, the principal orientation toward the good remains in all persons: "What nation does not scorn and hate people who are proud, or evildoers, or cruel, or ungrateful?" (*Leg.* 1.32) As Cicero, drawing on Panaetius, emphasizes in relation to old Stoic thinking, humankind is, however, united not only through right reason but also by affective bonds (Baldry 1965: 180f.).

Because all humans are born free, for Cicero behavior and attitude toward strangers is the test case for ethical universalism. In effect, this means that those "who say that regard should be had better endure any loss than wrong a fellow man for gain, for the rights of fellow-citizens, but not of foreigners, would destroy the universal brotherhood of mankind" (*Off.* 3.6.28). At this point, Cicero encounters a basic problem besetting every universalistic ethics, namely that of making excessive demands: "But since the resources of individuals are limited and the number of the needy is infinite, this spirit of universal liberality must be regulated according to that test of Ennius—'No less shines his'—in order that we may continue to have the means for being generous to our friends" (*Off.* 1.16.52). Moral obligations are to be gradated depending on, firstly, the closeness of affective ties: "But when with a rational spirit you have surveyed love of country. the whole field, there is no social relation among them all more close, none more dear than that which links each one of us with our country. Parents are dear; dear are children, relatives, friends; but one native land embraces all our loves [*omnes omnium caritates patria*]" (*Off.* 1.16.57). The genuine locus of love (*caritas*) and charity (*beneficium*) are the family and, above all, the fatherland— the Roman Empire. Secondly, Cicero relates the obligation to help foreigners to benefits which do not adversely impact on one's own life and entail painful sacrifices: "to bestow even upon a stranger what it costs us nothing to give" (*Off.* 1.16.51). Cicero names the following examples of sharing "common goods": "'Deny no one the water that flows by'; 'Let anyone who will take fire from our fire'; 'Honest counsel give to one who is in doubt'" (*Off.* 1.16.52). Rigorous restrictions on giving material aid to foreigners cannot be justified solely by referring to the problem of disadvantage and overburdening. The questionable weakening of the scope and force of ethical universalism is the consequence of another factor, "a shared view that derives from Stoicism, concerning the irrelevance of material goods for human flourishing" (Nussbaum 2019: 32).

To avoid detrimental consequences resulting from the idea of universal moral responsibility, Cicero gave precedence to obligations toward the fatherland (*patria*), the *Imperium Romanum*. The initially circumspect alignment between ethical universalism and the idea of a Roman world empire is then strengthened in Cicero's doctrine of just war (*bellum iustum*) (Botermann 1987; Forschner 1988). In this context, Cicero formulates moral preconditions for belligerent action: a war is only then permissible when a resolution through negotiations could not be achieved (*Off.* 1.11.34.); peace must always be the aim of war (*Off.* 1.23.80); and after victory the enemy should be treated mildly, except if they have acted cruelly and inhumanely during the war (*Off.* 1.11.35). In a second step, Cicero then turns to the moral justification of wars, i.e., to the question of just reasons. Just reasons for war are defense against enemies and vengeance of injustices: "Those wars are unjust which are undertaken without cause. For aside from vengeance or for the sake of fighting off enemies no just war can be waged" (*Rep.* 3.35a). Although the doctrine of just war is supposed to serve the purpose of containing outbreaks of belligerent violence, the duty to avenge injustices opens the door for dubious justifications of wars of aggression. Cicero leaves it open whether the vengeance may be exacted only by those who suffered the injustice, or also by third parties, who avenge the injustice on behalf of those directly affected (Forschner 1988: 10). Beyond this, Cicero considers legitimate not only wars to defend a state against enemy attacks, but also military interventions to protect allies (*Rep.* 3.34), an argument that according to Cicero justifies Roman expansion over the whole *oikumene*: "All successful imperial powers, including the Romans themselves who have gained possession of the entire world, if they should wish to be just—that is to say to return property that belongs to others" (*Rep.* 3.21b).

To reconcile ethical universalism with the imperial power claims of Rome, Cicero, as Augustine passes down, eventually takes up the principle of natural rule of the best over the weak, with which Aristotle, among others, had justified the natural slavery of the barbarians (*Pol.* 1.5.1254a15–17b): "that empire is just because slavery is useful for such men and that when it is rightly done, it is done on their behalf, that is, when the right to do injury is taken away from wicked people: the conquered will be better off, because they would be worse off if they had not been conquered." In order to bolster this reasoning, Cicero supplies a noble illustration drawn from nature, and says: "Do we not see that the best people are given the right to rule by nature herself, with the greatest benefit to the weak? Why then does god rule over man, the mind over the body, reason over desire, anger, and the other flawed portions of the mind?" (*Rep.* 3.4.1d.; August. *De civ. D.* 19.21).

Once serving to contain belligerent violence, the doctrine of just war is turned into a justification of the Roman world dominion (Forschner 1988: 12): "the concept of the *orbis terrarium* became in effect an appropriation by the political realm of the Stoic notion of a single human genus" (Pagden 1995: 23). Nonetheless, Stoic cosmopolitanism was not merely an ideological superstructure but in fact a moral corrective to the Roman imperium. The Stoic idea of the equality of all humans furthered in the long term the legal betterment of the slaves, without however calling the institution of slavery into question (Manning 1989). Beyond this, there were at least a few voices that broke the mantle of silence over imperial violence, with Seneca for example acridly denouncing those Roman legions indulging in aimless violence, asking why "attack men you do not even know, to be enraged without having been wronged, to destroy everything you come across, and like wild beasts to kill who you do not hate?" (*QNat.* 5.18.9).

The world dominion claimed by Rome was not only in conflict with the ethical universalism of the Stoics, but it also ran contrary to the actual power-political boundaries of the Roman Imperium. In Persia, first the Parthian and then later the Sasanian Empires challenged Roman hegemony. Because the existence of other empires could not be denied, the justification of imperial claims placed special emphasis on the idea of a superior civilization. For Suetonius, the Roman people represented the human species: "the Roman people, or I may say all of mankind [*populus Romus vel dicam humanum genus*]" (*Calig.* 13; Vogt 1960: 309f.). The Roman claim to be a civilizing force was based primarily on the legal system, seen as creating a domain of peace and prosperity. Law was, in turn, part of urban culture. According to Horace, the cultural substance of the Roman Empire had its foundation in the cities, with Rome the "queen of cities [*princpes urbium*]" (*O.* 4.3.13). In this way, Roman thought establishes a bridge to the Aristotelian defense of the *polis* ideal and the idea of the world empire.

Given the loss of power within the *oikumene*, which was further aggravated by internal conflicts and eventually led to the split of the Empire in 293 CE, Rome began to organize and govern its relations with neighboring peoples through a complicated system of different agreements (Schulz 1993: 17). Without Rome ever rescinding its claim to world dominion, agreements based on the principle of equality were concluded with the Sasanian Empire. As in the time of the Greek city-states, the intensified practice of international law led to the elaboration of a *philosophical* theory of international law. The concept of *ius gentium*, which constituted the relationships—to be regulated by the *praetor peregrinus*—between foreigners or between Romans and foreigners within the Roman Empire, had already been introduced into political philosophy by Cicero, and had been used at times to organize relations with other peoples (*gentes*), in particular with respect to the right to wage a just war (*ius belli*) and the right to protect missions (Steiger 1992: 98; Kaser 1993: 1–8; 14–20). But unlike Grotius, who integrated both rights into a theory of the law of nations in the sixteenth century, Cicero converged the *ius gentium* with the doctrine of *ius naturale* (Steiger 1992: 100f.). In Cicero's formulation, the *ius gentium* is not a right between peoples, but the right that connects all humans (*ius commune omnium hominum*).

Besides the Parthian and Sasanian, knowledge of empires in the Far East also threatened to question Rome's claim to world dominion. There is evidence there was trade between Rome and China in the Augustinian period (Burstein 2017: 109f.). At the end of the first century CE, China sought to establish direct contact with the Mediterranean world. Under the leadership of Ban Chao, a delegation set off for Rome in 97 CE, but after being warned of the dangers of such a mission by the Parthians, they never arrived. As for the other direction, the Han annals report a delegation of the Roman emperor Marcus Aurelius at the Chinese court in 166 CE (Burstein: 116f.). While contact remained sporadic on a diplomatic level, trade relations continued into the late period of the Roman Empire and the T'ang dynasty (621–907 CE).

Against this background, the question arises as to how the Roman Imperium could maintain the claim to world dominion despite knowledge of an empire in the Far East. Strabo's interpretation of Roman imperialism opens an important perspective on this problem. Strabo not only decoupled the idea of world dominion from the aspiration to completely dominate and control all peoples and territories, but, in a further step, he limited the idea to the civilized regions of the *oikumene*, between which a constant flow of communication existed. So, while Rome and China were acquainted with one another, there were hardly any direct relations. Like possible inhabitants of the antipodes, the Chinese empire was not part of the world in the sense of a qualitatively understood *oikumene*: "It was that these other worlds, the Chinese for instance or the inhabitants of the antipodes, had no separate identity as communities—much less as political powers—and that, in the nature of things, they would one day be absorbed into the *imperium, the* world, itself" (Pagden 1995: 23). For this reason, Roman thought simply did not entertain the idea of an order based on international law with peoples outside the *oikumene*.

Ethical universalism and world empire in Latin Christianity until the European expansion

As with the early Stoics, the Judeo-Christian tradition achieved a breakthrough to an ethical universalism. The idea of the equality of all humans is present in the teaching on their Godlikeness (*Gen.* 1:26) and in Christian ethics. According to Paul, the boundaries between people are dissolved in the Christian community: "There is no longer Jew or Greek, there is no longer slave or free, there is no longer male and female; for all of you are one in Christ Jesus" (*Gal.* 3:29). Moreover, it seems that Paul alludes to the Stoic law of nature. The Gentiles "show that what the law requires is written on their hearts, to which their own conscience" (*Rom.* 2:14). Whether Paul is in fact referring to the Stoic doctrine is controversial. It is beyond dispute, however, that the church fathers and medieval Christian theology carried forward the doctrine in different ways.[2] Like that of the Stoics, the ethical universalism of the early Christians resided primarily in an ethical-spiritual attitude and not in a political program. The New Testament texts question the sacralization of the Roman Empire. The idea of world dominion is even branded a temptation of the devil (*Lk.* 4:4–8). No ideas for a new political order were developed, however, because of the expected Second Coming (*parousia*) of Christ. Already in the New Testament, relations to political powers are determined depending on the respective political constellation. Besides the calls for obedience toward state offices (*Rom.* 13:1; *Pet* 2:13f.), the book of Revelation contains a scathing criticism of Roman imperialism (*Rev.* 13). Given the lack of interest in questions concerning the basic elements of a political order, the institution of slavery remained untouched in early Christianity. Like Seneca, Paul calls on masters to treat their slaves leniently (*Phlm.* 15–17; Glancy 2002).

Despite this affinity, Christian theology makes significant modifications to the ethical universalism of the Stoics. Firstly, the depravation of sin discloses a significant problem: is the law of nature recognizable solely through reason, i.e., without the help of Christian revelation, in unadulterated form? Secondly, as evident in Augustine, the hope of resurrection splits the Aristotelian *eudaimonia* teaching into earthly happiness (*felicitas terrena*) and the eternal bliss of beholding God (*beatitudo aeterna*) (*De civ. D.* 19.4). Thirdly, Christian ethics is tied to the biblical mandate to preach the gospel to all nations (*Mt.* 28:19). Originally, the Christian mission was issued to all in the *oikumene*, for divine revelation knows no *terrae incognitae* (Brincken 1998: 561). The rapid spread of the gospel outside the Roman Empire, for example among the Parthians or Marcomanni, considerably bolstered the confidence of early Christianity in the first century CE. According to Tertullian, Christians form a universal community (*gens totius orbis*) that surmounts the boundaries and divisions between peoples and empires from below (*Apol.* 37; Vogt 1960: 169f.).

In the fourth century CE, Christianity's view of relations to the political powerholders changed radically with the conversion of Constantine. The reconciliation of Christian faith with the Roman idea of world dominion, until then completely alien to the Jesuanic message, was justified theologically by Eusebius and then officially confirmed by Pope Leo I. The meaning of the *oikumene* shifted qualitatively as a result: "The *orbis terrarum* thus became, in terms of the translation effected by Leo the Great in the fifth century, the 'orbis Christianus.' A century later, Gregory the Great would translate this into the 'sancta respublica,' a community endowed with the same simultaneous open exclusiveness which had been a feature of the Ciceronian 'respublica totius orbis'" (Pagden 1995: 24). Despite this, the adoption of the Roman idea of world dominion, as testified by Augustine's criticism of the logic of worldly power in *De civitate Dei*, remained controversial in Christian theology. As with the Stoics, the connection to the Roman Imperium led to deformations of ethical universalism in Latin Christianity. For instance, the concept of "barbaros" enters Christian thinking as early as Eusebius (*Praep. evang.* 1.4.9; *Vit. Const.* 4). Like Aristotle, Eusebius calls not only the Scythians barbarians, but also the Persians (*Praep. evang.* 4.5; 4.56). During Gregory the Great's papacy, "barbarus" becomes a synonym for "paganus," non-believers (Pagden 1982: 20).

It was not just the heritage of Roman imperialism that neutralized the social explosiveness of ethical universalism in early Christianity. Augustine had already distilled a theological justification of dominion and servitude from the narrative of the fall of humankind. While all humans are created by God to be free, human nature is corrupted by hereditary sin; humans thus need to be harnessed, even if this means placing them under forms of domination exercised by other humans, including slavery (*De civ. D.* 19.15; Töpfer 1999). Augustine's justification of bondage as the consequence of hereditary sin enters high medieval theology through Bonaventura (Mensching 2005: 125f.). Taking a different approach, although influenced by Aristotle, Thomas Aquinas develops a theology of servitude based on natural law (Mensching 2005: 126-9; Brett 1994: 3-91). As a rational being, no human can be the tool or possession of another. But due to the inequality arising from varying endowments of reason, many persons are—as Aquinas emphasizes, referring to Aristotle—"innately" reliant on the guidance of others. The servants (*servi*) are the charges of the stronger and cleverer. To avoid the blatant contradiction with the ethical universalism of the Christian message, Aquinas compares the relationship between master and servant with intrafamilial relations. The servant is similarly "part" of the master as the son is "part" of the father (*Summa theologica* II-II, q. 54, ad. 4; Brett 1994: 24). Furthermore, in *De regimine principum* (*On Kingship*), a work of Bartholomew of Lucca on the basis of texts of Thomas Aquinas, a reference is asserted between climate and spiritual endowment that recalls Aristotle: "Those who live in hot regions are keen-witted and skilful in the things of the mind but possess little spirit, and so are in continuous subjection and servitude [*sine animositate autem, propter quod subiectae quidem sunt, et subiectae perseverant*]" (Thomas Aquinas 1947: chap. 2.1). This reference is taken up repeatedly in the colonial debates of the sixteenth century (Zavala 1944: 26f.; Pagden 1982: 48f.).

Significantly, this means that while Christian theology discarded the Aristotelian doctrine of the natural slavery of barbarians, new sources of legitimation nonetheless emerged to entrench domination and servitude in the *orbis christianus* with the premise that the human being, naturally sinful, is corrupted and with the adoption of the Aristotelian proposal for the rule of rational over less rational beings. Medieval theology therefore left the institution of feudal serfdom untouched; slaves remained present in the Christian empires of the Middle Ages, both the Carolingian and the Byzantine Empire (Rio 2021; Lenski 2021); and Italian cities were engaged in the Mediterranean slave trade (Fynn-Paul 2021).

In parallel with the splitting of Christianity's ethical universalism into different variants, political powers in the Middle Ages continued, in a variety of ways, to uphold the idea of a Christian world empire. With the Roman Empire continuing to exist in Byzantium, Christian rulers in Latin Europe were not primarily concerned with laying claim to world dominion. On the contrary: Charlemagne, with whom the history of occidental emperorship commences, "did not see himself as a Roman emperor, and he in no way imagined himself to be a successor to or a replacement for the Byzantine emperors" (Nobel 1984: 296). The Ottomans, though, still recognized the Byzantine emperor as the representative of the Roman universal monarchy (Ohnsorge 1983: 15). Open rivalry with Byzantium first began with the Staufers, culminating in the conquering of Constantinople by the crusaders in 1204. Beyond this, structural differences are evident between emperorship in Latin Christianity and the Byzantine Empire: "For the Carolingians, emperor was a title of honour that added nothing to their power or territories. At most, the imperial title provided some responsibilities, such as the protection of the papacy. The empire had no governmental infrastructure. It lacked any real institutional infrastructure to hold it together" (Muldoon 1999: 29). The power of the emperor, whose rule was essentially limited to lands in Germany, Burgundy, and Italy, was thus challenged by the ambitious emerging monarchies of Spain, Britannia, and France. Admittedly, the power of the Byzantine emperor was also limited, ruling over only parts of the former eastern Roman Empire. After 1261, the Byzantine Empire sank in significance to the *de facto* status of a petty state. As in the Late Roman period, the Christian emperor's claim to world dominion was not supported by the exercising of genuine power but resided primarily in the perceived superiority of Christian civilization, now underpinned by the truth claims raised by the Christian faith. As such, the Byzantine Empire was able to maintain its claim to world dominion until the fall of Constantinople in 1453 (Ohnsorge 1983: 27). In Latin Christianity, however, the claim to power made by the popes effectively split the idea of world dominion itself. Unlike the emperor, whose sphere of power was considerably limited, operating on the religious level the pope could lay claim to be the representative of the universal *orbis christianus*. In this sense, the pope attempted to extend the spiritual claim to world dominion beyond the frontiers of the former Roman Empire. Innocent IV dispatched several delegations to the Far East to convert Mongol rulers to Christianity. The head of the most important mission, John of Piano Carpini (Pian di Carpine), provided Latin Christians with valuable insight into the imperial expansions of the Mongols (Jackson 2018: 92–7). As the Mongol Great Khan relocated the seat of government to what is today Beijing in 1260/7, the Christian mission itself advanced into China. Besides Carpini, Benedictus Polonos, Simon of Saint-Quentin, and William of Rubruck all wrote detailed missionary reports, among the most important western sources of information on the Mongols (Brincken 1989: 11). Given the supremacy of the Islamic empires and the emergence of territorial states, the conflict between pope and emperor over the claim to world dominion had at times fictive status (Höffner 1969: 31–41).

The disputes between the Christian universal powers are reflected upon extensively in medieval theology. Over time, three fundamental positions crystallize in the debates on the relationship between *regnum* and *sacerdotium*. One group, the so-called hierocrats, for example Aegidius Romanus or Antoninos of Florence, assign the pope not just authority over the spiritual affairs of the church but also the power to appoint Christian rulers and judge their administration of office. A second group of theologians, however, give spiritual and secular power solely to the emperor. A mediating position draws on Aquinas. With secular rule founded in natural law, the power of the pope extends only to spiritual concerns (*spiritualia*). At the same time, though, the pope may indirectly utilize political power should this be necessary to advance spiritual goals (Höffner 1969: 15–31).

The debates on the relationship between *imperium* and *sacerdotium* in medieval theology result in profound transformations of the cosmopolitanism of antiquity and the ethical universalism of Early Christianity. As in late antiquity, international law is put into practice beyond the ideas of world dominion (Preiser 1978: 45–56). Thus, despite all the rivalry, diplomatic relations existed between Byzantium and the western Empire. Indeed, in the fourteenth and fifteenth centuries, permanent missions were set up, allowing a completely new form of diplomacy to develop. In addition, both the Christian emperor and the Italian maritime powers based their relations with Islamic rulers on numerous agreements. On the theoretical level, medieval theology takes up and continues the ideas of international law dispersed throughout antiquity. Above all through Augustine, Cicero's deliberations on just war enter medieval theology (Mattox 2006). However, unlike Cicero, for Augustine it is inconceivable that a world empire could arise solely by waging just wars. If Rome had indeed only waged war to avenge injustices inflicted on allies, then the Romans should, as Augustine notes with heavy irony, "worship ... Foreign Iniquity as a goddess" (*De civ. D.* 4.15). Augustine thus cautiously frees the doctrine of just war from the restrictive clutch of world dominion (*De civ. D* 5.1). The civilizing achievements of the Roman Empire are therefore given a new justification; no longer moral, they are part of a historical theology, i.e., seen as divine providence at work. Nonetheless, Augustine adds: "if men were always peaceful and just ... all kingdoms would be small ... There would be as many kingdoms among the nations of the world as there are now houses of the critics of a city" (*De civ. D.* 6.15). Augustine refrains, however, from elaborating the vision of peaceful coexistence between independent kingdoms into a theory of international law. Because war is understood *a priori* as a violent conflict between peoples or kingdoms (*gentes, civitates*), relations between such entities are assigned their own sphere of political life (Steiger 1992: 102). A few centuries later, Isidore of Sevilla uses the concept of *ius gentium* to synthesize numerous agendas with an inter-gentile dimension, which are then in turn incorporated into a philosophical theory of the law of nations in the sixteenth century: "The law of nations concerns the occupation of territory, buildings, fortifications, wars, captivities, enslavements, the right of return, treaties of peace, truces, the pledge not to molest ambassadors, the prohibition of marriages between different races. And it is called the 'law of nations' [*ius gentium*] because nearly all nations [*gentes*] use it" (*Etym.* 5, 5).

Aquinas then ultimately combined the dispersed Christian ideas on just war into a new synthesis (Beestermöller 1990). The interpretation of the three conditions constituting just war (*auctoritas, causa iusta, intentio recta*) sparked numerous controversies in the twelfth and thirteenth centuries. Controversial from the outset was which authority may declare war, i.e., solely the pope and the emperor, or, as Aquinas proposed, also kings, princes, and the principals of the city-states. From among the just reasons for war—defending against an attack, reclaiming stolen possessions, revenging acts of injustice—it was above all the third reason, the precise determining of which had remained vague in Cicero, that gave cause for concern. The debate ignited on whether it is legitimate to wage war against infidels. Because secular power is justified through natural law, according to Aquinas even unbelievers possess the right to rule (*dominium*) and jurisdiction (*iurisdictio*). Thus, it is in principle possible for infidels to legitimately exercise rule over believers; and *a fortiori* unbelievers may rule over other unbelievers (*Summa theologica* II–II q. 10, a.10; Gillner 1997: 101). However, drawing on Augustine, if secular rule is considered the consequence of the fall of humankind, then it is possible to fundamentally question the legitimacy of pagan regents, an argument put forward by Henry of Segusio, generally known as Hostiensis. Because the world is *de iure* subordinate to Christian rulers, the kingdoms of pagans may be conquered solely because of their unbelief. Only when pagans acknowledge of their own accord the dominance of the Church is their *dominium* to be tolerated by Christians. According to Hostiensis, the reconquering of former Christian territories is indeed the duty of a Christian ruler (Fisch 1984: 189; Muldoon 2015: 15–19).

The dispute about infidels is not restricted to theological issues, impacting also on papal political aims. Whereas Pope Clement VI followed the position taken by Hostiensis, Pope Innocent IV drew on Aquinas. Innocent IV acknowledged the right to rule (*dominium*) of infidels. But because the conversion of pagans must be completed by the Second Coming, Christians have the right to evangelize.

Should the infidels use force to prevent the Christian mission and continue to venerate their idols, then for Innocent this was a just reason for Christians to wage war (Muldoon 2015: 2; 9–48).

Beyond this, the Christian reinterpretation of Aristotle's philosophy of the *polis* opens the space for dubious justifications of violence. For Aristotle, the purpose of the state resides in supporting the "good life," whereby *eudaimonia* can be achieved through political existence on the one hand, and through the philosophical intuition of the divine on the other. Because philosophy is a matter for the few, the task of the *polis* is to provide individual citizens with the social conditions for a philosophical existence. According to Christian teaching, *all* humans, i.e., not only philosophical natures, are required to partake of the *visio beatifica* for perfect happiness. For this reason, a Christian ruler, entrusted with the task of promoting the good life in terms of Christian teaching, can no longer be content with guaranteeing a small group the social space needed for intuiting the Christian god. Instead, the task of the ruler or the pope is to now provide their subjects with a Christian upbringing. Belief itself and the final intuition of God are gifts of divine mercy and can thus be removed from the incursions of political institutions. But because leading a virtuous life serves to prepare for eternal bliss, according to Aquinas the task of the rulers is to support the individual's path to God (Struve 1978: 162). In this connection, Augustine had already justified the use of force against heretics. In medieval theology, the doctrine of just war thus comes to serve an array of purposes, ranging from the violent imposition of Christianity through to the persecution of infidels and heretics.

In the face of escalating violence within the Christian world and the ongoing threat posed by the Islamic empires, Dante Alighieri develops a philosophical theory of universal peace in *De Monarchia*. Without attacking Aristotle directly, Dante's treatise unsparingly reveals the weaknesses in the Aristotelian philosophy of the *polis*. As the history of the Greeks has shown, small city-states cannot maintain their independence when threatened by the aggression of larger kingdoms or empires, meaning that the ideal of an autarkic *polis* is ultimately an ahistorical chimaera. The only authority capable of creating and maintaining stable peace is the universal monarchy (Struve 1978: 211–22; Grasmück 1999). But Dante invokes not only political security to justify the universal monarchy; he also brings the Aristotelian *eudaimonia* teaching into play. The full development of human reason is not possible in the arena of the *polis*; it is, rather, an undertaking involving the whole of humankind. And because reason can develop only in peace, a universal authority is needed to keep peace and hold rivalries in check.

Contemporaries saw Dante's political treatise as supporting the power claims of the emperor. There can be no doubt that his primary interest was to bring peace to Latin Christianity (Münkler 2005: 129). But his vision of a ruling universal order expressly includes all within the *oikumene*, the Scythes in the far north—"beyond the seventh"—and the Garamantes, who "live in the equatorial zone" (Dante 1996b: chap. 1.14.6): "Therefore mankind [not only Europeans] living under a monarch is in its ideal state; from this it follows that monarchy is necessary for the well-being of the world" (Dante 1996b: chap. 1.12.13). At the same time, the Holy Roman Emperor is for Dante the sole feasible candidate to be world monarch, for the universal monarchy has already existed once before, namely under Augustus (Dante 1996b: chap. 1.16.1). Despite this narrowing of perspective, Dante's treatise on the universal monarchy is of major importance in the history of European political thought—neither in the cosmopolitan thought of antiquity nor in the political theology of the High Middle Ages had a philosophical justification of the idea of a world empire been formulated that even came close to the level achieved by Aristotle. Dante thus fills a gap that had spanned a whole millennium in the political philosophy of the Occident.

7.3 Francisco de Vitoria: a philosophical foundation of the law of nations and global ethics

Since the late nineteenth century Vitoria has often been celebrated as the founder of modern international law (Nys 1894; Scott 1934; Soder 1955); more recently, however, decolonial philosophies have criticized Vitoria's theory of *ius gentium* as furnishing a justification of European colonialism (Anghie 2004; Mignolo 2011: 86). The debate about Vitoria's position on the history of international law and modernity is still going on today (Brieskorn and Tiening 2011; Beneyto Pérez and Corti Varela 2017).

Francisco de Vitoria's engagement with the "New World" reaches back to the 1520s and the early lectures on Aquinas' *Summa theologica*. In the *Relectiones*, central theses distilled from the Thomas commentaries for a public lecture held before the entire university—and thus the title "relectio" or also "repetitio"— Vitoria addresses issues relevant to the colonial debate, for example the scope of papal and imperial power (*Relectio de Potestate civili*, 1528; *Relectio de potestate ecclesiae* I–II, 1532–3). Shocked by the perfidious murder of Atuahalpa in Peru, Vitoria considers the Amerindians with increasing focus in the mid-1530s (Innarone 1967; Pagden 1982: 64f.; Urbaño 1992: 275f.). Vitoria first presents his decisive contribution to the assessment of the Conquista of the Americas in 1539, the *Relectiones de Indis*.[3] *De Indis* revolves around fourteen legal titles which Vitoria claims can be used to legitimize Spanish rule over the Amerindians. With this tableau of potential legitimate and illegitimate legal titles, Vitoria took the debate on the Conquista, which had already begun just a few years after Columbus, to a new level, laying the foundation for further discussions in the sixteenth century, including the debate between Bartolomé de las Casas and Ginés de Sepúlveda (Fisch 1984: 212).

De Indis in the context of the first debates on the transoceanic expansion

The expansionism undertaken by the Portuguese and Spaniards, which reached its first highpoint as early as the fifteenth century with the conquest of the Canary Islands, sparked numerous debates within the Church and among theologians, providing, as it were, a testing ground for the universalist political ideas formulated in medieval Christianity.

After Byzantium was conquered, the idea of Christian world dominion lived on primarily in the papacy. Pope Nicholas V revived the idea of papal world rule after hopes were kindled that, following the Portuguese circumnavigation of Cape Bojador, a sea route to India would break the supremacy of the Islamic empires. The papal bull *Romanus Pontifex* (1455) awards the Portuguese king Alfonso V all lands and kingdoms "as far as through Guinea, and beyond toward that southern shore" (Davenport 1917: 24). Indeed, fully in accord with the hierocratic theology of Hostiensis, Nicholas V denies infidels all rights of rule and ownership. The pagans outside the *oikumene* may even be taken into perpetual slavery (Davenport 1917: 23). A few decades later, in the bull *Inter caetera* (1493), Pope Alexander VI confirms the rights of Spanish sovereignty over all discovered and still to be discovered territories in the Americas. The bull also sets a line of demarcation between the Spanish and Portuguese spheres of influence, which shortly afterward, in 1494, is however then moved to Portugal's advantage in the Treaty of Tordesillas.

A few years after Columbus's voyage, John Mair, a Scottish theologian who taught in Paris, challenged the hierocratic doctrine of papal world dominion, stating that the pope does not have the power to distribute lands overseas to Christian rulers (Leturia 1930-1: 59). At the same time, however, Mair introduces the Aristotelian teaching on natural slavery into the debate on the newly "discovered" peoples, a step with fatal consequences (Hanke 1974: 118),

As a Christian theologian, Mair still proceeds from the assumption of the universal equality of all humans. Hence, returning in Mair's deliberations is the antinomy between the Aristotelian doctrine of natural slavery and the Christian egalitarianism of Paul, a tension that had already shaped the thought of Aquinas (Capizzi 2002: 35–40).

In contrast to Mair, Juan Lopez de Palacios Rubios, the main legal advisor to the Spanish crown from 1504 to 1524, defends hierocratic theology in *Libellus de insulis oceanis quas vulgus indias appelat* (1516). The rule of the king, since transoceanic expansion is no longer limited to the *oikumene*, can only be legitimized by the authority of the pope, who as the representative of Christ possesses the authority of jurisdiction over all humans:

> In the manner of the Pope possessing the highest authority over the whole universe and every creature is subjected to him as the founder of the law and the representative of the Creator, … he consequentially has power and jurisdiction over all, including the most remote and unknown infidels of the world [*super omnes nifeles, etiam a nobis ermotissimos et innotos*].
>
> (Palacios Rubios [1516] 1954: chap. 4.7)

Here Palacios Rubios closely ties the hierocratic doctrine on the universal power of the pope to the idea of Spanish world dominion (Lantigua 2020: 62–7), which indeed is temporarily part of colonial policy. In Palacios Rubios' *Requerimiento* (Requirement) of 1513, the Amerindians, addressed in Spanish, are called to capitulate to the Christian king and warned, should refusal or resistance eventuate, that a just war would be waged.

The expansion of the Iberian powers to Africa and the Americas breathed new life into not only the papal claims to world dominion, but also those of the Holy Roman Emperor. Mercurino Gattinara, the chancellor to Charles V of Spain and an admirer of Dante's *De Monarchia*, considered Charles's election to emperor an opportunity to turn the idea of a Christian universal monarchy into reality. Gattinara's dream of Spanish world dominion revolved around subjugating other Christian princes on the one hand, while repelling the Turks and reconquering former Christian territories in Africa and Asia on the other. If this were successful there would be no rival to fear, and Spain would have then fulfilled the aim of Roman world dominion (Bosbach 1988: 51). It was in the context of this perspective that Miguel de Ulzurrun also revived Dante's idea of a universal monarchy in his work *Catholicum opus imperiale regiminis mundi* (1525), now expressly encompassing the whole population of the earth. As for

Dante, the goal of a universal monarchy was primarily to secure peace. Whereas the spiritual authority of the pope was restricted to Christians, the universal monarch, ruling over Christians and infidels, was in the position to ensure that peace would reign across the globe (Lupher 2002: 46–8). Thus, even before Vitoria, Ulcurrunus recast the Roman concept of *ius gentium* into *ius inter gentes* (Thumfart 2012: 118–20). Because the emperor, as the universal monarch, bore sole responsibility for defining and implementing the *ius inter gentes*, this new concept of a law *between* nations was not one that the nations could actively contribute to.

Although experiences with foreign peoples and cultures in the first phase of European expansion were reflected on intensely in the light of the traditional ideas of Latin Christendom on universal politics, once the extreme acts of violence against the Amerindians began, the antinomies between the spiritual egalitarianism of Stoic-Christian ethics and the Roman idea of world dominion suddenly came to the fore. As early as 1511, the Dominican Antonio de Montesinos publicly condemned the savagery of the colonialists in a sermon: "Tell me by what right or justice do you keep these Indians in such a cruel and horrible servitude? On what authority have you waged a detestable war against these people, who dwelt quietly and peacefully on their own land?" (quoted from Hanke 1949: 17). Montesinos triggered a discussion about Spanish colonialism that would rage for decades, not only in universities but also in political institutions, above all in the Council of the Indies and the bodies advising Charles V. Thus the contradiction between the traditions of early Christianity, critical of imperialism, and the inheritance of the Roman idea of world dominion, present since the fourth century CE, flared up immediately in the very first phase of the debate on the transoceanic expansion of the Iberian power.

When Vitoria began with the *Relectiones de Indis* in 1539, decades had passed since the voyages of Columbus. Despite the debates and criticism, the colonial system was by and large established (Horst 1995: 89). Although "the barbarians in the New World, commonly called Indians ... came under the power of Spaniards some forty years ago" (*De Indis*; LP, 233), Vitoria is not solely concerned with questions of colonial administration. "But when we hear subsequently of bloody massacres and of innocent individuals pillaged of their possessions and dominions" (*De Indis*; LP, 238), then, as Vitoria emphasizes by way of introduction, the question as to the very legitimacy of Spanish rule over the "newly-discovered" peoples must be revisited. Provocatively, Vitoria asks his audience to hypothetically go back to before Columbus's voyage and, from this vantage point, consider the Conquista of the Americas from a *moral* perspective. With this move, Vitoria carefully detaches legal learning from theology (Rovira Gaspar 2004: 115–25). The fictive return to a time when the military expansion was about to get underway sets up a direct confrontation between the universalistic claims of medieval Christianity and the violent atrocities committed during the Conquista. This means that in *De Indis* Vitoria puts both aspects of Stoic-Christian thought on trial, universal ethics versus universal politics.

Clarification of Stoic-Christian ethics: *nullus est servus natura*

Vitoria turns his attention first to the moral and theological legitimations of the Conquista. The decisive point for morally judging the conquests in the "New World" can be summarized in a question: "Whether these barbarians, before [!] the arrival of the Spaniards, had true dominion, public and private?" (*De Indis*; LP 249) In a second step, those arguments are listed which were used in the early decades of the sixteenth century to dispute the dominion rights of the "newly-discovered" peoples, namely the Aristotelian doctrine of the natural slavery of barbarians, Hostiensis's doctrine that denies property and possession rights to mortal sinners and infidels, and the general principle that humans who have lost their faculty of reason must be placed under the rule and in the custody of others.

The Aristotelian doctrine of natural slavery contradicts, as Vitoria notes in advance, the Christian teaching that all humans are made in the image of God, i.e., that they are beings endowed with reason. In principle all humans, including sinners, have the capacity to rule, "for man is the image of God by his inborn nature, that is by rational powers. Hence, he cannot lose his dominion by mortal sin" (*De Indis*; LP, 242). The conclusion of the *Sectio prima* thus states unequivocally: "*nullus est servus natura* [nor can they be counted among the Slaves]" (*De Indis*; LP, 251). Vitoria refrains, however, from directly challenging the authority of Aristotle. With the doctrine of natural slavery, Aristotle was not saying that humans endowed with less reason were to have their possessions taken from them and be forced into slavery; the point to be made is, rather, that humans with greater intellectual capacity and intelligence are to rule over those who are less rationally endowed. Just as it is beneficial for children to obey their parents, it is beneficial for the less rationally endowed to follow the guidance of the wise (*De Indis*; LP, 251). But even the Christian version of natural slavery, less harsh as it is, cannot be applied to the "New World." It would contradict the wisdom of the Creator if a large part of humankind were not endowed with sufficient reason: "Furthermore, God and nature never fail in the things necessary for the majority of the species, and the chief attribute of man is reason" (*De Indis*; LP, 215). The capacity to exercise reason becomes stunted primarily through poor education and not climatic conditions: "THUS if they seem to us insensate and slow-witted, I put it down mainly to their evil and barbarous education [*mala et barbara educatione*]. Even among ourselves we see many peasants [*rustici*] who are little different from brute animals" (*De Indis*; LP, 250). Through the Christian theology of creation, Vitoria therefore frees moral philosophy from the clasp of the political geography of antiquity, which for thousands of years had led to the debilitating distortions of ethical universalism in the Stoic-Christian tradition.

In rejecting "natural" slavery on the basis of natural law, Vitoria also draws on the Stoic teaching of humankind's original common property. According to Cicero, there is no private property in the natural state: "There is, however, no such thing as private ownership established by nature" (*Off*. 1.7.21). And because, as Vitoria states, natural law retains its validity even after the expulsion from paradise, the order of common property in the *status corruptionis* remains principally in place. The transition to private property can thus only be justified through a theory of social contracts, i.e., contrary to Aquinas, who identified it as in accord with the law of nature (Deckers 1991: 183–94). This means that the rights of dominion and property are based in an imagined consensus among all humankind, from which the peoples of the "New World" are not to be excluded. As Vitoria already explains in his commentaries on Aquinas, no people could be as barbaric as not to believe that the appropriation of goods is permissible to preserve the species (Deckers 1991: 173–8). Thus, the compelling conclusion to be drawn from the theory of property is that the barbarians were the rightful masters over their lands.

Vitoria rejects the second argument against the dominion rights of the Amerindian peoples, that they are infidel, by drawing on Aquinas's teaching on the relationship between nature and grace: "We have also a proof based on reason. Aquinas shows that unbelief does not cancel either natural or human law, but all forms of dominion [*dominia*] derive from natural or human law; therefore they cannot be annulled by lack of" (*De Indis*; LP, 244; cf. *De potestate civili*; LP, 17f.). Thus, unbelief must be discarded as a possible reason for the justification of the Conquista.

The third argument—that dominion rights lapse through loss of the capacity of reason—is valid in principle according to Vitoria; anyone no longer in control of themselves because of madness or dementia must be placed in the care of others. The Amerindian peoples cannot be considered maniacal or demented, however, when their civilizations are considered: "They have properly organised cities, proper marriages, magistrates and overlords [*domini*], laws, industries, and commerce, all of which require the use of reason" (*De Indis*; LP, 249).

But even where and if their social organization contravenes the ethical standards of the law of nature, then this does nothing to change the fact that the peoples in the "New World" are beings endowed with reason and their dominion rights are to be respected: "Hence, granting that these barbarians are as foolish and slow-witted as people say they are, it is still wrong to use this as grounds to deny their true dominion; nor can they be counted among the slaves" (Vitoria 1991: 251). Vitoria seems to retract this clear statement at the end of the *Sectio tertia*, where the argument of the indigenous lack of reason is once again broached: "these barbarians, though not totally mad, as explained before [cf. 1.6], are nevertheless so close to being mad, that *they are unsuited to setting up or administering a commonwealth both legitimate and ordered in human and civil terms*" (*De Indis*; LP, 290). Vitoria is by no means revising his original view, however, for the third section is referring to the nomadic peoples who "have neither appropriate laws nor magistrates fitted to the task" because of "their lack of letters, of arts and crafts (not merely liberal, but even mechanical), of systematic agriculture, of manufacture, and of many other things useful, or rather indispensable, for human use." Thus, they "feed on food no more civilized and little better than that of beast" (*De Indis*; LP, 290f.). In this special case, as Vitoria weighs up with great caution—"I myself do not dare either to affirm or condemn it out of hand" (Vitoria 1991: 290)—the argument of mental incapability could furnish a legitimate legal right to conquer the Amerindian tribes; it is conceivable that it would be "for the benefit and good of the barbarian" that they, at least for a time, "be governed partly as slaves [*ex parte gubernari ut servi*]" (*De Indis*; LP, 291). The principle proclaimed at the outset, that nobody is a slave by nature, still holds valid. At any rate, the conquest of the Aztec and Inca realms cannot be justified with the argument presented in *Sectio tertia*.

Destruction of the universal powers of medieval Christianity and the philosophical foundation of the law of nations

In the debate on a Spanish universal monarchy, Vitoria radically rejects the millennium-old idea of world dominion, revived with the ascension of Charles V: "the emperor is not master of the whole World [*Imperator non es dominus totius mundi*]" (*De Indis*; LP, 253). The emperor's claim to world dominion not only violates the natural right to dominion of pagan peoples but also the divine right (*ius divinum*). Although Christ is addressed as the lord of the world in the Bible, in the gospel of John Jesus emphasizes that "my kingdom does not belong to this world" (*John* 18:36). The kingdom of Christ is spiritual, not political: "It is evident, therefore, that to say that there is a single emperor and master of the world by livery of seisin [*traditio*] from Christ is simple twisting of the evidence" (*De Indis*; LP, 256). Furthermore, Vitoria brings into play the power-political limits faced by the emperor in Latin Christianity vis-à-vis the idea of the universal Christian monarchy: "the German emperors never claimed that their title made them lords of Greece. Besides, the emperor of Constantinople John VIII Palaeologus was recognised as the legitimate emperor at the Council of Florence (1439)" (*De Indis*; LP, 257). Not even within Latin Christendom did the German emperor exercise hegemony, a point Vitoria underlines with some irony: "But the kingdoms of Spain and France are not subject to the emperor." And, not least, the papal state itself places an insurmountable limit on imperial power: "the patrimony of the Church is not subject to the emperor" (*De Indis*; LP, 257). This means that the idea of world dominion, which has determined the history of the Near East and Europe since the Persians, must be fully relinquished without any comprises: "So it is obvious that no one before Christ obtained an empire by divine law; and the emperor is not entitled on any such grounds to arrogate to himself the dominion [*dominium*] of the whole world, nor, as a consequence, of these barbarians" (*De Indis*; LP, 255). Vitoria thus destroys the dream of a Spanish universal monarchy claimed by Gattinara and Ulcurrunus.

In a second step, Vitoria rejects the papal claims to world dominion: "The pope is not the civil or temporal master of the whole world [*Papa non est dominus civilis aut temporalis totius orbis*]" (*De Indis*; LP, 260). While limiting the authority of the pope to religious domains (*spiritualia*), Vitoria still supports the doctrine of the pope's indirect power (*potestas indirecta*), so that with respect to achieving spiritual goals, the pope may utilize the worldly power of Christian monarchs and princes. This indirect power spans, for example, the right to suspend laws in Christian realms which flagrantly contradict natural law, as well as the right to depose of kings or pass judgment in a conflict between Christian rulers (*De Indis*; LP, 262; *De potestate ecclesiae I*; LP, 55f.). Further, the indirect power of the pope must be differentiated with respect to the various groups of infidels. Those unbelievers who live *de jure* and *de facto* under Christian rulers, e.g., the Saracens, enjoy the same rights as Christian subjects; while a just war, launched at the behest of the pope, may be waged against pagans living in formerly Christian territories. In contrast, for Vitoria, those unbelievers who live neither under

Christian rulers nor in formerly Christian territories are not subject to papal jurisdiction. Hence, contrary to the hierocratic justification of the Conquista, Vitoria states that because the pope has no right to exercise jurisdiction over pagan monarchs outside the former Imperium Romanum, in the case of the Amerindians unbelief is not a just reason for waging war (*De Indis*; LP, 264).

After his destruction of the idea of a universal monarchy, Vitoria formulates a philosophical theory of the law of nations that governs relations between the peoples who are the legal masters of the respective lands. As shown, practices based on the law of nations are nothing new in European history. In the sixteenth century, European colonial powers used agreements to govern their relations with the rulers of Asia. Vitoria therefore did not simply invent international law. The epochal significance of his thought resides elsewhere—the *philosophical* justification of a *global* order based on law. Although the concept of *ius gentium* is introduced into political philosophy as early as Cicero, neither classical ancient nor medieval thought had developed a systematic *theory* international in scope.

At the same time, Vitoria's doctrine of *ius gentium* is substantially different from the law of nations used to implement the Peace of Westphalia, organized around the sovereignty of territorial states. Vitoria bases the idea of international law, initially following Cicero, on natural law, the norms of which are not just valid for states but generally for all natural communities based on partnership and communication (*naturalis societas et communicatio*): "the law of nations [*ius gentium*], which either is or derives from natural law" (*De Indis*; LP, 278). The relationship between *ius naturale* and *ius gentium* was a *quaestio disputata* in medieval theology, to which Vitoria adopts a mediating position (Deckers 1991: 358–87). For Vitoria, the *ius gentium* encompasses not only natural law norms but also "the consent of the greater part of the world [*consensus maioris partis totius orbis*] is enough to make it binding, especially when it is for the common good of all men" (Vitoria 1991: 281). In short, the *ius gentium* may be closely linked to the *ius naturale*, but with the consensus among humankind it also has an independent source of justification, a source capable of furnishing further norms in the future.

By introducing this consensus element into the doctrine of *ius gentium*, adopting earlier ideas from Bartolus Sassoferrato and William of Ockham (Steiger 1992: 106), Vitoria transforms the Stoic vision of the unity of the human species (*societas humani generis*). Humanity may be subject to natural law (*koinos nomos*), but it also posits its own laws: "The whole world, which is in a sense a commonwealth, has the power to enact laws which are just and convenient to all men; and these make up the law of nations [*Habet enim totus orbis, qui aliquo modo est una res publica, potestatem ferendi leges aequas et convenientes omnibus, quales sunt in iure gentium]*" (*De Indis*; LP, 49; cf. *De potestate civili*; LP, 40). Although Vitoria is here importing the principle of self-rule, he remains within the horizon of the *ius naturales*. The consensual justification of concrete norms in the law of nations must be oriented on a strict standard, the furthering of the "common good of all men [*maxime pro bono communi omnium*]" (*De Indis*; LP, 281). Because the welfare of humankind is the primary principle for judging political actions, the right of the whole of humankind has precedence over the right of individual states (Figueroa 2004: 59; Deckers 1991: 329).

The idea of a self-ruling world community is thus established on an anthropology that understands humans to be *animal sociale* in an emphatic sense. Vitoria had already positioned language and communication at the center of his anthropology in the *Relectio de potestate civili*. Unlike animals, humans live in a state of vulnerability and need: "But to mankind Nature gave 'only reason and virtue', leaving him otherwise frail, weak, helpless, and vulnerable, destitute of all defence and lacking in all things" (*De potestate civili*; LP, 7). In short, nature makes human beings "come out of misery, contrary to her principle" (*De potestate civili*; LP, 7). To counteract the weakness and frailty of human nature, "mankind was obliged to give up the solitary nomadic life of animals, and to live life in partnerships [*societates*], each supporting the other" (*De potestate civili*; LP, 7). As Vitoria states in reference to Aristotle, only gods or wild animals can live without the security afforded by community (*De potestate civili*; LP, 8; cf. Arist. Pol. 1.2.1253a27–9). Indeed, humans can only develop the reason they have been endowed with in relationship to others. Whereas animals recognize what is necessary instinctively, human knowledge is only ever possible and attainable through interaction with others. Language, "the messenger of understanding," is therefore a specific human aptitude through which a human being "excels or surpasses all other animals" (*De potestate civili*; LP, 8). Indeed, community and communication are more than just means to securing survival; they are ends in themselves. For this reason, even an intuition of the cosmic order is ultimately fully mundane if it cannot be shared with a friend (*De potestate civili*; LP, 8).

The political anthropology of *De potestate civili* stands in the tradition of Aristotle. Because the family and the village community primarily serve the purpose of securing survival, it is first the state that creates the adequate framework enabling humans to develop their communal nature: "It follows that the city [*ciuitas*] is, if I may so put it, the most natural community, the one which is most comfortable to nature" (*De potestate civili*; LP, 9). Unlike Aristotle, however, Vitoria connects the social animal theory with the specific idea of a community encompassing *all* humans that is based and organized on both natural and international law, the idea of "natural partnership and communication [*naturalis societatis et communicationis*]" (*De Indis*; LP, 278).

Maintaining this perspective, we can then appreciate how Vitoria deduces the individual norms of international law from the anthropological idea of a universal communicative community: the right of free movement and settlement, the right to trade, the right to use and enjoy common properties, the right of citizenship by naturalization, and the right of diplomatic delegation.

The global right to travel or migrate (*ius peregrinandi*) means that every person has the right to travel in all territories and lands of the earth when this is not detrimental to the local or indigenous population (*De Indis*; LP, 279). Here Vitoria refers first to the traditional guest right and the Christian commandment of love. This, though, only serves to conceal the innovative substance of *ius peregrinandi*. Neither the archaic custom of being hospitable to strangers nor the biblical commandant of charity were understood as giving a *right* to travel in all lands, including other continents. Vitoria thus resorts to deriving this global right to travel from the natural law doctrine of an original common property: "in the beginning of the world, when all things were held in common, everyone was allowed to visit and travel through any land he wished. This right was clearly not taken away by the division of property [*diuisio rerum*]" (*De Indis*; LP, 278). From this Vitoria concludes "that amity [*amicitia*] between men is part of natural law, and that it is against nature to shun the company of harmless men" (*De Indis*; LP, 279). This means that it is only through the right to be able to travel unimpeded through all lands across the globe that the idea of a global communicative community can become reality.

In *De Indis* the right to travel is presented in the context of a possible legitimate legal title for the Conquista. At first this may appear strange, but it is soon explainable by considering Vitoria's method—the fiction of taking the audience of his lectures back to a time before Columbus. When a group of peaceful explorers from Europe embarked for the Americas, then, in Vitoria's hypothetical scenario, the inhabitants of the "New World" would have been obliged to hospitably take them in. To refuse entry would be an act severing communication and thus stunting the development of human aptitudes (Justenhoven 1991: 98). Because norms based on the law of nations are however assigned a damage clause ("so long as they do no harm to the barbarian"), then, when considered in light of the global right to travel, the Conquista can only be condemned. As the siege of Tenochtitlan had demonstrated to Vitoria and his contemporaries, the Spanish were anything but a peaceful touring party—heavily armed soldiers had invaded the lands of the Amerindians.

The second international law norm, the right to trade (*ius negotiandi*), means "that travellers may carry on trade so long as they do no harm to the citizens" (*De Indis*; LP, 279). Already in his Aquinas commentaries Vitoria had, contrary to ancient and scholastic reservations, positively revaluated trade (Deckers 1991: 242–72; Figueroa 2004: 54–8). For Vitoria, trade is useful because, firstly, no society is completely an autarky; secondly, trade serves global communication. Because the provision of goods necessary for securing survival is also possible through local trade relations, the real legitimacy for the global expansion of trade relations lies in the vision of a universal communicative community. Vitoria thus concludes the section on trade with the dictum of Plautus: "man is not a wolf to his fellow man ... but a fellow" (*De Indis*; LP, 280).

Because global travel and trade rights promote contact between peoples, the rights that foreigners are accorded *in* the host land are an important component in Vitoria's theory of the law of nations. Foreigners must not be disadvantaged in using and enjoying common goods and properties. Vitoria fails to distinguish precisely between natural resources, which may be seen as the commons of all humanity, and goods which are the possession or property of a specific state. Rather dubiously, Vitoria justifies the extraction of gold in the "New World," which as early as the sixteenth century had become the symbol of Spanish greed, by referring to the occupation right formulated in antiquity: "If gold in the ground or pearls in the sea or anything else in the rivers has not been appropriated, they will belong by the law of nations to the first taker, just like the little fishes of the sea" (*De Indis*; LP, 280). Of course, natural resources can be seen as belonging to the local native population (Cavallar 2002: 108).

Further, the right of an individual to naturalize is part of the law of nations: "if anyone were willing to take up domicile in one of these barbarian communities, for example because he had taken a wife there or for one of the other reasons by which denizens customarily acquire citizenship, it does not seem to me he could be prohibited from doing so, any more than the other inhabitants" (*De Indis*; LP, 281). This is eminently important for children of migrants born in the host land. Here Vitoria's strategy to globally expand Aristotle's political philosophy is once more discernible: "The confirmation is that man is a civil animal, but a man born in one community is not a citizen of another community; therefore, if he is not a citizen of the first community, he will not be a citizen of any community, and this would be inequitable by the law of nature and of nations [*ius naturale et gentium*]" (*De Indis*; LP, 281).

Because the regulations of the law of nations possess the character of law through the virtual consensus of humanity, for Vitoria any violation of travel, trade, and settlement rights can be responded to with force if necessary. At this point, Vitoria aligns the vision of a communicatively networked global society to the doctrine of just war. With war always the *ultima ratio*, before resorting to violence the Spaniards must first demonstrate, in an argumentatively and constructively peaceful manner, the laws of nations to the Amerindians: "But if the barbarians deny the Spaniards what is theirs by the law of nations, they commit an offence against them. Hence, if war is necessary to obtain their rights [*ius suum*], they may lawfully go to war" (*De Indis*; LP, 282). Against the backdrop of how imperialist violence had escalated, Vitoria's deliberations on the Amerindians denying peaceful Spaniards the right to entry, trade, and settlement have the status of a fiction.

The constellation alters abruptly with Christian right to evangelize, which Vitoria also deduces from the idea of a universal communicative community. Christians are not only duty-bound to "preach and announce" the gospels throughout the globe but have a right to (*De Indis*. LP, 284). Vitoria allies this Christian right to the principle protecting the inviolability of envoys, one of the oldest norms of the law of nations: "The foregoing is confirmed by the fact that ambassadors are inviolable in the law of nations [*ius gentium*]. The Spaniards are the ambassadors of Christendom, and hence the barbarians are obliged at least to give them a fair hearing and not expel them" (*De Indis*; LP, 283). This means that whenever Amerindians use force to prevent Christian evangelizing on their territory, on behalf of the pope the Christian ruler may launch a just war against them (*De Indis*; LP, 285). At this point, Vitoria radically calls into question his own communications theory of international law through this recourse to Christianity's claim of absolute truth. Because the pope, as Vitoria emphasizes drawing on Aquinas, may also intervene in worldly affairs when the salvation of humanity is at stake, then the door is suddenly open for religiously motivated violence. Although the pope is denied jurisdictional authority over the pagans outside the *orbis christianus*, should a pagan ruler force subjects who had converted to Christianity to renounce, then this is sufficient ground for Christian rulers to wage a just war (*De Indis*; LP, 286). Indeed, should a large enough number of Amerindians convert to the Christian faith, the pope even has the right to install a Christian ruler (*De Indis*; LP, 287).

The special rights afforded Christianity in *ius gentium* are not solely the result of a divine right; for Vitoria, they ensue from a concept of commonwealth strongly influenced by Christianity, whereby earthly welfare is extended in scope—worldly conditions are an important factor in preparing for eternal salvation. For this reason, the violent enforcement of the right to evangelize ultimately benefits the barbarians. The removal of pagan rulers who suppress their Christian subjects follows, as Vitoria expressly emphasizes, "not only on grounds of religion, but on grounds of human amity [*amicitia*] and partnership [*societas*]" (*De Indis*; LP, 286). Indeed, utilizing the Christian interpretation of the welfare of humankind enables Vitoria to void the principle of reciprocity in the domain of the law of nations. While Christians are permitted to resort to force in pursuing their right to spread the Christian religion, other religions are forbidden from missionizing on Christian territory. Further, it is inconceivable that Turkish monarchs possess an intervention right should most of the subjects of a Christian ruler convert to Islam. And in a further step in this direction, Vitoria views wars between groups from a biased standpoint, namely not the welfare of humanity but the *Christian* world. Wars between Christian rulers are thus more damaging than a war waged by Christians against Turks (*De potestate civili*; LP, 21f.).

Against this background it is certainly understandable how Vitoria, despite his criticism of the teaching on natural slavery and the dominion claims of Christian universal powers, has been cast in the role of defender of Spanish imperialism.

The idea of global responsibility: humanitarian intervention

For Vitoria, the law of nations covers more than relations between states and kingdoms. The idea of universal communication between all humans implies a moral unity of the human species, from which, in the *Sectio tertia*, a right of intervention is deduced to save innocents from tyrannical rule: "THE NEXT TITLE could be either on account of the personal tyranny of the barbarians' masters toward their subjects, or because of their tyrannical and oppressive laws against the innocent, such as human sacrifice practised on innocent men or the killing of condemned criminals for cannibalism" (*De Indis*; LP, 287f.).

As Vitoria emphasizes, the right to intervene to save innocents is not dependent on papal authority: "I assert that *in lawful defence of the innocent from unjust death, even without the pope's authority, the Spaniards may prohibit the barbarians from practising any nefarious custom or rite*" (*De Indis*; LP, 288). At this point, Vitoria breaks the logic of Christian special rights, for the saving of the innocent is based on natural law and not justified theologically.

The legal title of intervention injects a certain tension in the argumentation of *De Indis*: according to Vitoria, peoples whose customs contravene natural law are nonetheless legitimate rulers of their lands (*De Indis*; LP, 274f.). As Vitoria notes in a *Relectio* from 1537, even cannibalism and human sacrifice are no reason to deprive barbarians of their lands and possessions (*De temperantia*; LP, 225). Because the pope has no jurisdictional authority over pagans outside the former Christian territories, "Christian princes, even on the authority of the pope, may not compel the barbarians to give up their sins against the law of nature, nor punish them for such sins" (*De Indis*; LP, 273). Now, suddenly without papal authority, the Spaniards are permitted to wage war against peoples perceived as violating natural law. Vitoria is noticeably at pains to dissolve any possible contradictions to earlier statements. The right of intervention to save the innocent represents an exception, and by no means retracts the distinction drawn vis-à-vis hierocratic theology: "In this case [sic], there is truth in the opinion held by Innocent IV and Antoninos of Florence, that sinners against nature may be punished" (*De Indis*; LP, 288). Violent intervention must pursue a sole goal—to save people from an unjust death; it is not a punitive measure against perpetrators.[4]

In antiquity, Cicero considered extending the duty to assist to all the needy of the world; faced with the reality of the overwhelming demands of such a task, he then limited moral responsibility of the individual to family and fatherland. Vitoria, too, has an eye on the problem of overexerting resources when presenting his daring idea of saving the innocent far away. Firstly, the intervention to save the innocent is not among the absolute moral obligations. The Spaniards could ("*possunt*") attempt to save victims of tyrannical violence or ritual practices in other lands, but there is no compelling obligation. Secondly, the cases where intervention holds are limited to the core dimension of morality, namely the prohibition on killing. Violent interventions are, consequently, only permissible when there is a mass killing of innocents.

This means that with the legal title to save the innocent, Vitoria radically broadens the horizon of moral responsibility, the archaic dichotomy between the close and the distant dissolved. Wherever humans are grievously wronged, even if it is on another continent, then the individual is called to save the lives of the victims.

Although the idea of humanitarian intervention transcends the horizon of ancient cosmopolitanism, in justifying the fifth legal title Vitoria calls on tradition, first the Christian teaching of charity and two places in the Bible: "The proof is that God gave commandment to each man concerning his neighbour

(*Ecclus.* 17:14). The barbarians are all our neighbours, and therefore anyone, and especially princes, may defend them from such tyranny and oppression" (*De Indis*; LP, 288). The second source of authority is from the book of Proverbs: "A further proof is the saying: 'deliver them that are drawn unto death, and forbear not to deliver those that are ready to be slain' (*Prov.* 24:11)" (*De Indis*; LP, 288).

But with this recourse to the Bible, Vitoria is only obscuring the revolutionary substance of his idea of humanitarian intervention. The Israelites were by no means called to moral action through a state-sanctioned injustice taking place far away. Precisely in the *Book of Sirach*, which Vitoria quotes, the concern about humanity as a whole is left to God, while the responsibility of the individual is limited to fellow humans: "The compassion of human beings is for their neighbours, but the compassion of the Lord is for every living thing" (*Sir.* 18:13). In the Bible, morally repugnant practices of other peoples are more a sign of godlessness than an occasion for launching rescue missions and, if need be, resorting to violence. There is thus no evidence that the early Christian communities protested against the massacres of the Roman legions on the peripheries of the *oikumene*, e.g. in Britannia.

An objectively verifiable starting point for a link to the idea of humanitarian intervention is present, however, in the ancient doctrine of just war. Besides defending against an aggressor and regaining robbed possessions, Cicero also included vengeance and the prevention of injustice among the reasons for just war: " but he who does not prevent or oppose wrong, if he can, is just as guilty of wrong as if he deserted his parents or his friends or his country" (*Off.* 1.7.23). Because the duty to prevent injustice refers to the whole of humankind (Forschner 1988: 14), the idea of humanitarian intervention is already inherent in Cicero. Because Cicero's doctrine of *bellum iustum* entered medieval theology via Augustine, Aquinas also seems to continue the idea of humanitarian intervention with the psalm verse: "Rescue the weak and the needy; deliver them from the hand of the wicked" (*Ps* 82:4) (*Summa theologica* II–II, q. 40, a.1; Beestermöller 2012: 71; Schüssler 2002).

There is no doubt that Cicero's doctrine of just war holds a motif that Vitoria could use as foundation for humanitarian intervention. At the same time, the differences cannot be ignored. Cicero identifies the Roman Empire with the *oikumene*. An intervention to rescue innocents outside the Imperium Romanum lies beyond his horizon. The same constellation pertains to Aquinas, for whom the right of intervention serves primarily to protect Christians living under pagan rulers (Beestermöller 2012: 94f.; Schüssler 2002: 209).

Despite ancient and medieval thought anticipating much of it, Vitoria's ethic of humanitarian intervention marks a caesura in the history of occidental moral philosophy. Never before in European philosophy had the suffering of innocent persons *outside* the immediate world or society, indeed outside the *oikumene*, been seen as a call to assume moral responsibility and demand action.

7.4 Ginés de Sepúlveda: the violent humanization of the barbarians

By the end of the sixteenth century, Vitoria's vision of a global community of communication appears to have fallen by the wayside. The Spanish monarchy had prohibited Jews, Moriscos, Lutherans, and foreigners from emigrating to the "New World" (Delgado 1994: 50, n. 31). In *Città del Sole* (1602), Tommaso Campanella revives the idea of world dominion, albeit now studded with utopian elements such as the abolishment of private property or the establishment of a women's community (Blum 2002b: 203–21). Giordano Bruno effectively turns Vitoria's cosmopolitanism on its head. Trade and commerce serve, as Bruno emphasizes in *The Ash Wednesday Supper*, not the spread of peace but of stupidities and vices:

> The Typhons have found the way of disturbing the peace of others, of violating the patron spirits of homesteads, of confusing that which provident nature keeps separate, by doubling the defects of man through commerce, by adding vice to vice from one generation to another, by propagating with violence new follies, and by planting unheard-of stupidities where none was, concluding in the end that the stronger is the wiser, by showing new studies, instruments, and skills to let people tyrannize and assassinate one another; because of such feats the time will come when those who have learned at their own expense, through the force of the vicissitude of things, will have the know-how and will be able to produce similar and even worse fruits of such pernicious inventions.
>
> (Bruno 1975: 59f.)

Criticism of Vitoria had begun though in the Spanish colonial debate itself. For Luis Molina, every nation has the right to restrict migration and trade relations with foreigners, or indeed to prohibit them, independently of the question of whether this would be disadvantageous or beneficial (Höffner 1969: 325; Brieskorn 2000). Fray Alonso de la Vera Cruz, a pupil of Vitoria who studied at Alcalá and Salamanca, but was in Mexico from 1536, reinterpreted Vitoria's *ius gentium* in the light of his experiences there. Moctezuma was not, in his view, a tyrant who had to be eliminated in a just war. And neither did the violent resistance to evangelization justify the Christian rulers waging war. If, however, the Amerindians rejected the gospels after a peaceful sermon, then, as de la Vera Cruz again emphasizes contrary to Vitoria, an indirect compulsion to baptize is legitimate (Beuchot 1991; Aspe Armella 2021).

Juan Ginés de Sepúlveda appears to not just adapt and correct aspects of Vitoria's theory on the law of nations but indeed articulate a radical counter position. In his work *Democrates alter, sive de iustis belli causis apud Indos*[5] Sepúlveda justifies the conquest of the Amerindians, drawing on the Aristotelian doctrine of the natural slavery of barbarians, which was categorically rejected by Vitoria. Today, Sepúlveda is still considered the author of the prototype colonialist ideology and the violent universalism of European modernity (Dussel 1995: 63–70; Wallerstein 2006: 1–29; Todorov 1984: 151–7).

Up until his response to the Conquista, Sepúlveda was primarily known for his humanist studies. After studying in Alcalá, Sepúlveda moved to Italy for two decades and spent time in Bologna, which through the influence of Pomponazzi had become an important center of legal philosophy. After returning to Spain, Sepúlveda was appointed court chronicler by Charles V in 1536 and teacher of the future king Philip II in 1542. Sepúlveda's work is accordingly broad, covering writings on theology and metaphysics, legal and political philosophy, historiography, and translations of ancient texts into Latin, most notably the *Politics* of Aristotle (Losada 1949: 1–134; 331–402).

Sepúlveda's reputation as an important humanist who corresponded with Erasmus was damaged in his lifetime because of his legitimation of the Conquista. Faced with the acrid criticism of Bartolómé de las Casas in the famous Valladolid disputation of 1551, Sepúlveda saw himself compelled to refute the reproach that he had justified the enslavement of the Indians and the pillaging of their possessions, as evidenced by his penning of an *Apologia* (1550) to *Democrates secundus* and a letter to Francisco de Argote (1552).[6]

Against this background, it is no surprise that views of Sepúlveda have remained divided down to the present day. On the one hand, he is considered a proponent of the neopagan teaching of natural slavery, retrospectively somewhat understated or partially amended (Hanke 1959: 44–61; Hanke 1974: 117; Schäfer 2002: 363); on the other hand, some interpreters have been vehement in their defense of him against claims of racism (Bell 1925; Losada 1971; Fernández-Santamaría 1977; Pietschmann 1987).

Any pertinent interpretation of Sepúlveda's justification of Spanish colonialism must first consider the broad lineaments of developments in his ethical and political thought. After all, in *Democrates secundus* Sepúlveda is reworking an earlier treatise on just war, written as part of the debates on the Ottoman Wars of the early fifteenth century. Moreover, in his late work, in particular *De regno* (1571), Sepúlveda addressed and enlarged upon some of the questions of the Valladolid dispute.

Ottoman imperialism: defending freedom against new Asian barbarity

Sepúlveda's early ethical-political thought was primarily concerned with the expansion of the Ottoman Empire in southeast Europe. As Ottoman forces besieged Vienna in 1529, in *Cohortatio ad Carolum V. ut bellum suscipiat in Turcas* Sepúlveda publicly called on Charles V to conclude peace with Christian rulers and wage war against the Islamic threat. A few years later, the voluminous dialogue *De convenientia militaris disciplinae cum christianae religione dialogus, qui inscribitur Democrates* (1535) was published, Sepúlveda's interpretation of the traditional doctrine of just war.

The expansion of the Ottoman Empire led to a deep division among intellectuals of Latin Christendom. On the one hand, numerous scholars called for Christian unity and war against the Turks. This did not prevent Christian regents from entering alliances with Ottoman rulers if it served to strengthen their power within the Christian world. On the other hand, the wars between the Christian powers in the first decades of the sixteenth century in Europe were accompanied by the rise of a radical pacifism. Invoking the Sermon on the Mount, the pacifist movement had the support of important humanists, in particular Erasmus and Juan Luis Vives (Muñoz Machado 2012: 186–92). While rejecting the doctrine of just war, Erasmus endorsed Christian powers waging war against the barbaric Turks as a lesser evil. Thanks to translations, Erasmus's peace treatises enjoyed such widespread support among students that Losada has named him the "Marcuse of the sixteenth century" (1978: 556).

Against this background, Sepúlveda considers in detail the relationship between Christian ethics and the profession of the soldier in *Democrates primus*.[7] Because Christian pacificism invokes the Sermon on the Mount, Sepúlveda feels compelled to address the question of the legitimacy of a defensive war as part of fundamental reflections on the relationship between the law of nature and the ethos of the New Testament. Recalling his earlier position in *Democrates secundus*, natural law comprises just a few basic norms, specifically the Ten Commandments, and from those primarily the prohibitions on killing, on theft, and on lying (*DS* 1.2.2–3). The purpose of basic moral laws resides in "preserving human community in this life [*conservandum societatem humanam in hac vita*]," the basis for which is "mutual love and benevolence [*mutua caritate et benevolentia*]" (*DS* 1.2.3). The law of nature thus demands not some act of heroic sacrifice but complying with a morality resting on the principle of mutuality, i.e., the golden rule (*DS* 1.2.2). Human welfare, fostered by the law of nature, is identical with public welfare (*salus et commoditas publica*) (*DS* 1.2.2). As Sepúlveda then emphasizes, drawing on Augustine, peace, the highest good on earth, is merely the anticipation of the perfect happiness secured through the eternal intuition of God (*DS* 1.1.2; 1.2.2–3).

For Sepúlveda, invoking Aquinas, divine grace does not suspend the law of nature (*DS* 1.2.1). A war of self-defense is therefore morally legitimate. The biblical commandment to love one's enemies is, like the ideal of poverty, part of a supererogatory moral, which may be demanded of Christians but not all humans. The blessings of the Sermon on the Mount are admonitions referring to apostolic perfection (*apostolicam perfectionem*) and not how to organize social life (*vitam commune*) (*DS* 1.2.2). As praiseworthy as the poverty ideal of mendicants may be, communal life would break down if all members of a society were to cease working and wander about like preachers (*DP* 3.17). Priests and members of religious orders are to refrain from inflicting violence; but the regents must hold on to power for the common good, for it is the means to enforce the law (*DP* 3.15).

While the specifics of natural law remain largely oriented on Aquinas, with respect to the question as to how natural laws are even recognizable, Sepúlveda undertakes a cautious shift. The law of nature is known by all humans, i.e., by pagans as well. But at the same time, insight into the *lex naturae* can be corrupted to a large degree, on both individual and group levels (*DS* 1.3.1–2). The correct interpretation of the law of nature is retained however by the moral sensibility of civilized peoples (*gentes humaniores*), which Sepúlveda, in the spirit of humanism, identifies with the Greeks and Romans, i.e., not only through Christian revelation (*DP* 1.10–11). In this way, the philosophy of classical antiquity is elevated to the main authority for determining the *lex naturae*. From this vantage point, Sepúlveda justifies not only the virtues of the soldier but also the Aristotelian ideal of aristocratic magnanimity and the striving for glory, which, as Erasmus and other Christian thinkers noted, contradicts the Christian morality of humility.

Sepúlveda is firmly planted—and this may serve as a provisional marker in our considerations—on the ground of the Thomasian reconciliation of reason and faith. In refuting Christian pacifism, however, which derives its moral norms for political ethics directly from the Bible, Sepúlveda distinguishes morals based on natural law from the Christian ethos of love with a decisiveness that goes beyond both Aquinas and Vitoria: "Never is this separation [between the secular and transcendental order] better recorded ... in carrying out his proposed task in terms far more secular than were possible to those theologians of the School of Salamanca ... gives the true measure of Sepúvelda's contribution" (Fernández-Santamaría 1977: 174; 172). Nonetheless, Sepúlveda is not gravitating toward Machiavelli's interpretation of politics as an instrument of power, a claim often raised (Méchoulan 1974). Certainly, Sepúlveda is calling for a realistic view of politics, and in this point is in full accordance with Machiavelli; in contrast, however, war and violence are never merely instruments of politics for Sepúlveda (Muñoz Machado 2012: 210–16). As an Aristotelian humanist, Sepúlveda adheres to a doctrine of just war that aims to limit but not abolish military force (*DP* 1.18f.; 1.4.1). The dawning awareness of the epistemological problems plaguing ethics based on natural law is compensated by enhancing the authority of classical ancient philosophy.

In the war against the Ottomans, Sepúlveda is not merely concerned with the right of self-defense; at stake here is nothing less than victory in an either-or struggle, "freedom or barbarity." Like many humanists of the day, Sepúlveda interprets the Ottoman Wars in the light of the Greek struggle for freedom from the Persians. While acutely aware that the unscrupulous power politics of Christian princes are no less abhorrent than the imperialism of the Ottoman rulers, and in effect for the common people it seems almost irrelevant if they live in Christian or Ottoman servitude, the harsh yoke of a Christian prince is preferable to Turkish rule (*Cohortatio* 3.2).

Comparing the struggle against the Ottomans with the Greek struggle for freedom seems to entangle Sepúlveda in grave contradictions, however. The cultural superiority of Hellas vis-à-vis the Near Eastern empires stemmed, according to Aristotle, from the culture of freedom practiced in the *polis*. But the adversaries in the Ottoman Wars are powerful monarchies looking to establish hegemony throughout the *oikumene*. Indeed, only recently in Spain the Comunidades uprisings, seeking to establish republican ideals, had been brutally suppressed (Maravall 1984).

Sepúlveda fails to address these contradictions arising from the historical comparison in the *Cohortatio*. Thus, now unbalanced, his criticism of the

Ottoman Empire, cast as the new embodiment of Asian despotism, is even more vehement. The Ottoman Empire is a tyranny, which, unlike a monarchy based on laws, is subject to the arbitrary whims of its ruler. Even its highest administrators are defenseless vis-à-vis the absolute power enjoyed by the sultan. Moreover, as Sepúlveda depicts it, the subjects of the Ottoman Empire have no rights of possession and property. The sole owner of the land, the sultan is joint heir not only when subjects die without having left a will and have no descendants, but also for deceased with well-regulated affairs, enjoying the same status as the sons (*Cohortatio* 5.1; cf. Faroqhi 2000: 47). Besides the lack of public laws, the suppression of philosophy and the liberal arts is a grave shortcoming. Upon the Ottomans occupying Greece, the learned fled westward. While a king consults scholars and advisors for the common good, the tyrannical character of the Ottoman Empire is manifest in the disdain the sultan displays toward philosophers, treating them as enemies because philosophy is the means to fomenting aversion toward slavery, to fostering a love of freedom, and to cultivating a contempt of death (*De regno* 1.10.5–6).

Sepúlveda is certainly aware that humanist studies are also suppressed in Christian kingdoms; just a few years later he himself will be a victim of censorship, denied permission to publish his *Democrates secundus* (Castilla Urbaño 2020: 223–5). Despite all the difficulties, the spirit of philosophy was institutionally anchored in the universities throughout the Christian kingdoms. At least in Christian lands there is hope that, following a tyrant, a monarchy would be reinstalled based on the rule of law. Because in the Ottoman Empire there is no possibility to forge a link to an ancient tradition of freedom, oppression becomes unbearable: "With which hope can the present misery be endured without the supreme pain after not only freedom but also the hope for freedom has been lost?" (*Cohortatio* 3.5).

Numerous stereotypes about the Islamic world long circulating in Latin Christendom are undoubtedly manifest in Sepúlveda's criticism of the Ottoman Empire (Schwoebel 1967: 147–75; Tolan 1996; Lawrence 2001). The descriptions of ferocious Saracens slaughtering noble men and children, raping women, and demolishing churches, were projected on to the Turks in the fifteenth century. Before Sepúlveda, humanist circles compared the Ottoman Empire with the despotic empire of the Persians. The expulsion of the sciences was another widespread bias (Bisaha 2010: 43–93). In the mid-fifteenth century, the *Cohortatio ad bellum contra turcos* formed a literary genre and numerous humanists tuned their rhetorical skills (Schwoebel 1967: 153). The sharply contoured and exaggerated picture of Turkish tyranny ultimately distracted contemporaries from the Habsburgian expansion of power, which the French kings took to be nothing other than an attempt to erect tyrannical rule within Europe (Bosbach 1988: 57–63).

There can be no doubt today that the humanists' view of the Ottoman Empire needs to be corrected. The sciences by no means came to a standstill. Quite the opposite in fact: as early as the fourteenth century, the *medrese*, originally adjoined to dervish monasteries, were turned into independent educational institutions, although only religious and legal studies were practiced. After conquering Constantinople, Mehmet II founded a comprehensive education center, the Fatih *küllïyesi* (Fatih complex), comprising a mosque, numerous *medreses*, a public kitchen, etc.: "With the foundation of the Fatih *medreses*, the Islamic world experienced an unprecedented wave of scientific progress. This was due in part to broadening the scope of *medrese* education, opening the door to rational sciences, including subjects such as logic, mathematics, astronomy, and the natural sciences, in addition to continued instruction in religious sciences" (İhsanoğlu 2004: 16). Thus by the sixteenth century the sciences were actually blossoming in the Ottoman Empire, with scholars bringing together and continuing Arab, Persian, and Western traditions. Above all, astronomy boomed spectacularly thanks to a series of technological innovations, bringing it on a par with the achievements of Copernicus and Brahe (Lohlker 2019). And like the Iberian powers, the Ottoman Empire launched its own age of discovery (Casale 2010) that enabled the already highly developed Islamic geography to progress even further. Against this background, Alan Mikhail has recently argued that the Ottoman Empire was a main player in the birth of the modern world (2020).

In the middle of all these ideological fallacies Sepúlveda introduces a rational element to his criticism of the Ottoman Empire: the idea of civil freedom. For Sepúlveda, one of the most serious weaknesses of the Ottoman Empire was its lawlessness, i.e., the lack of a legislative based on the law of nature (Castilla Urbaño 2013: 88). Except for the legal scholars and religious leaders, even the administrative elite were subject to the caprice of the sultan and at the mercy of his despotism. Certainly, Sepúlveda's appeal to Aristotelian republicanism is overshadowed by the flight of Jews from Spain to the Ottoman Empire. Nonetheless, the idea of a legal order guaranteeing freedoms remains an important measure for judging empires. In the nineteenth century, though, the Ottoman Empire introduced reforms (*tanzimat*) to correct some of the institutional weaknesses criticized by Sepúlveda. The Edict of Gülhane of 1839 initiated a far-reaching restructuring of the relationship between the sultan and his subjects. For the first time, Muslims and non-Muslims were granted fundamental legal guarantees, the security of life, honor, and property. In effect, the slave-like status of all subjects, having emerged in the sixteenth century and impacting even on Ottoman high officials, was abolished (Faroqhi 2000: 94). The codification of state property (*miri*) in 1858 protected the property rights of small farmers (Findley 2009: 20). In short, the criticism of the orientalism displayed by Western historians should not simply be reversed into an idealization of the Ottoman Empire (Faroqhi 1999: 24, n. 7).

The conquest of the Americas: the humanization of the barbarians

Sepúlveda had made a name for himself as an expert on natural law and an open-minded humanist with his *Democrates primus*. It is thus no surprise that he, together with Bartolomé de las Casas, was commissioned by the Council of the Indies to make a representation on the war in the "New World" in 1550. He had however already formulated his justification of the Conquista in 1545 in *Democrates secundus*, a work that had remained unpublished following negative evaluations by the universities of Alcalá and Salamanca. Transcriptions of the dialogue circulated in the scholarly world. Sepúvelda thus felt compelled to write a few apologetics prior to the Valladolid dispute, among them the *Apologia pro libro de iustis belli causis* (Rome, 1550), which was, though, banned in Spain. It is conjectured that Las Casas was familiar with a copy of the *Apologia* but not *Democrates secundus* (Hanke 1974: 63).

Although *Democrates secundus* is conceived as a continuation of earlier dialogues on a just war (*DS*, Prologus), it by no means merely utilizes already known principles. Instead, Sepúvelda takes up and elaborates the innovative ideas of Vitoria's *Relectiones de Indis*, which had left an indelible impression on his thinking (Andrés Marcos 1947: 99–112).

Because the Spaniards were not conducting a defensive war in the "New World," Sepúlveda claims that the scope of the traditional doctrine of the just war needs to be broadened. In agreement with Vitoria, for Sepúlveda the expansion of the imperium is not a just reason for war (*DS* 1.4.4–5; Andrés Marcos 1947: 107–12). Thus, four further reasons are cited for a just war against the Amerindians, reasons which, as he concedes, "are less clear and less frequently occur, but are considered just" (*DS* 1.4.9): the inferiority of the Indians, sins against nature, rescuing innocents from cannibalism and human sacrifice, and the rapid spread of Christianity. Some of the new reasons for war were also discussed by Vitoria in *De Indis*. Crucially, this means that Sepúlveda and his *Democrates secundus* are very much steeped in Vitoria's global cosmopolitanism.

First reason justifying war: the inferiority of the Indians

The first reason for waging a just war that best applies to the barbarians of the "New World" (*quae maxime convenit in istos barbarous, Indos vulgo dictos*) is "the conquest by arms [*imperium*] if no other way is possible, of those who by natural condition [*conditio naturalis*] must obey others and refuse to do so" (*DS* 1.4.10). Here Sepúlveda takes up the Aristotelian principle of the natural rule of the perfect over the imperfect, with which Panaitios had justified the dominion of the Roman Empire over the barbarians (see section 7.2). The rule of the rationally intelligent over the less intelligent was also a fundamental principle for organizing society in the political theology of the Middle Ages, in particular when determining the power wielded by a king. Sepúlveda once more confirms this organological theory of the state in his later work *De regno* (1.2–3). Indeed, this principle of rule exercised by the intelligent over the less intelligent had found resonance in the colonial debate before Sepúlveda. Vitoria had considered the temporary sovereignty of Christians over the primitive tribal societies (*De Indis* 1.3.17). However, whereas Vitoria ascribes the harsh mores and customs of some Amerindians to their poor education, at this juncture Sepúlveda surprisingly invokes the notorious doctrine of Aristotle on the natural slavery of barbarians, which Vitoria had firmly rejected (*DS* 1.5.4–5). It is difficult not to have the impression that Sepúlveda, blinded by a humanist adoration of Aristotle (Schäfer 2002: 263), regresses to a position not only prior to Vitoria but even to the Stoic-Christian doctrine of the freedom and equality of all humans. Even Pope Paul III had condemned the enslavement of the Amerindians in the bull *Sublimis Deus* from 1537. Sepúlveda openly acknowledges the indignation that the Aristotelian doctrine of natural slavery must have ignited in his own time after the clarifications formulated by Vitoria, with the figure of Leopold expressing dismay: "And who is born under such an unlucky star that nature condemned him to servitude [*ut servitute fuerit a natura damnatus*]?" Democrates, i.e., the voice of Sepúlveda, has with this teaching, as Leopold points out, greatly distanced himself from the prevailing view (*DS* 1.5.1). Bewilderment then sets in as Sepúlveda, without retracting the dictum of Aristotle on natural slavery, refers affirmatively to Cicero's idea of a natural community between all humans: "*universam hominum rempublicam et humanam societatem*" (*DS* 2.3.2; cf. 1.15.6). Therefore, according to Sepúlveda, it is only naturally right that each person enjoys their "natural freedom [*libertate naturali*]" (*DS* 2.2.4). From this background, we may assume that Sepúlveda has adopted the doctrine of natural slavery but *not* in the sense meant by Aristotle.

The first shift in accentuation vis-à-vis Aristotle emerges in the distinction between the juristic concept of slavery as the consequence of defeat in a war and the philosophical idea of servitude, according to Sepúlveda characterized by "inferior intelligence along with inhuman and barbarous customs [*philosophi tarditatem insitam et mores inhumanos ac barbaros nomine servitutis appellant*]" (*DS* 1.5.2). While natural factors are to be considered in the cultivation of customs and mores, they are not to be overestimated. Nature sets certain conditions, and the virtues themselves are primarily formed through repeating good works and the exercise of reason. Economic factors appear to play a role in the concept of natural slavery. The poor—not only in the "New World" but also in Spain—are forced by sheer distress to treat their sons almost like slaves (!) ("*filiis quasi servis uti*"); due to the lack of ease and leisure, they hardly have an opportunity to develop their capabilities (*De regno* 1.25.1).[8]

This means that with the revaluation of human freedom in the doctrine of natural slavery, the Aristotelian justification of a just war against the barbarians, who may be hunted and enslaved like animals, loses all factual foundation. Instead, Sepúlveda takes his orientation from Vitoria's idea of a temporary subjugation of nomadic tribal societies. In this special case, the goal of sovereignty is not to subjugate or enslave the barbarians but to educate them to conduct a civilized life. The Spaniards may therefore rule over the barbarians for the period in which they are in primitive stages of civilization ("*quamdiu essent in tali statu*"; *De Indis* 1.3.7; LP, 290).

The idea of a temporary guardianship over primitive tribal societies is no basis for justifying the conquest of the Aztec Empire, however. Las Casas therefore reproached Sepúlveda with ignoring the achievements of Mesoamerican civilizations or devaluing them in boundless arrogance. As Las Casas shows, offering an abundance of material, the Amerindians have formed and developed all forms of human rationality, beginning with monastic prudence, i.e., the competence of rational self-determination, and economic intelligence, manifested in the institutions of marriage and family and the running of a household, through to political sagacity (1988: 500–3). Certainly, Las Casas could draw on his own experiences when describing the Amerindians, whereas Sepúlveda relied mainly on information from Fernández de Oviedo's *Historia general y natural de las Indias* (1537).[9] This is one reason why there are numerous derogatory remarks about people in the "New World" in Sepúvelda's work. Along with all the moral and cultural deficiencies claimed, Sepúlveda, in the spirit of humanism, deplores the lack of writing and literacy, the barbarians possessing neither genuine science, documentation about their history nor, not least, any public laws (*DS* 1.10.1).

Despite this, Sepúlveda by no means ignores the achievements of Mesoamerica's advanced civilizations. Tenochtitlán, the Aztec capital, is so splendid that, as Cortés noted, the only other comparable city is Venice (*DS* 1.10.2). The elective monarchy and extensive trade relations of the Aztecs (*DS* 1.10.3) are described approvingly. However, in a frightful twist to his polemic, Sepúlveda denies that such cultural achievements are an argument against barbarism, rhetorically asking: "the fact of their having houses and some rational way of public life and the trading [*aliquam in commune vivendi rationem et commercia*] to which natural necessity induces, what does it prove but that they are not bears or monkeys completely devoid of reason?" (*DS* 1.10.3). The polemical tone should not conceal the point being made, however. Sepúlveda is not claiming that the Amerindians are bears or monkeys but rather that all attempts, in particular those of Las Casas, to primarily locate their humanness in the achievements of their civilization, necessarily assume the contrary absurd notion, namely that the Aztecs are devoid of all reason and hence, biologically, are not even members of the human species.

What crystallizes here is the same argumentative contour as in the criticism of the Ottoman Empire: on the one hand, the Aristotelian ideal of civil freedom is posited as the norm to judge the barbarism of the Aztecs, whereby this presupposes a culture of writing and literacy and property relations; on the other hand, the ethical criterion of the Christian view of the law of nature is invoked.

For Sepúlveda, the barbarism of the Amerindians is manifest in the mixture of a repressive system of rule and a servile population, whereby—as in the criticism of the Ottoman Empire—the organization of property ownership is assigned a key role. Because only a third of landholdings are in the hands of families, the majority is forced to work on royal estates. Indeed, Sepúlveda claims that people born into a despotic society no longer have the energy and vigor to rise up and free themselves in the spirit of rational self-determination. A menial disposition has taken hold and become second nature, meaning that they are natural slaves. For this reason, the Aztecs, although finding themselves in a power vacuum after the death of their ruler, had not risen and replaced the tyranny with a state based on liberty:

> And if this type of servile and barbarous nation had not been to their liking and nature, it would have been easy for them, as it was not a hereditary monarchy, to take advantage of the death of a king in order to obtain a freer state and one

more favorable to their interests; by not doing so, they have stated quite clearly that they have been born to slavery and not to civic and liberal life [*vitam civium et liberalem*].

(*DS* 1.10.3; Codices VTM)

The civilizing ideals of Renaissance humanism are unmistakably central to Sepúlveda's criticism of the tyrannical imperium of the Aztecs, as they were already determining factors in the debate on the Ottoman Wars. Accordingly, two questions need attention. Firstly, how legitimate is it with respect to civil freedom, in Aristotle's theory solely possible in the *polis*, for Sepúlveda to assign, *a priori*, the Spanish imperium a civilization superior to the Aztec Empire, a precedence already virulent in his criticism of despotism in the Ottoman Empire? Secondly, is it legitimate to adapt the principle of the rule of the more rationally intelligent over the less intelligent, used by Sepúlveda—following Panaitios—to justify the conquest of the Aztec Empire, to relations between states and empires?

Sepúlveda returns to the first problem, which we may formulate as *"polis versus empire,"* in his late work *De regno*. As is typical in medieval theology, the monarchy is defended vis-à-vis the Aristotelian ideal of the rule of the free and equal as the most perfect form of the state (Struve 1978: 157f.). For Sepúlveda, there are several telling reasons. Firstly, the monarchy is the oldest of all social orders, developing directly out of the household community (*De regno* 2.3). Secondly, the monarchy guarantees greater stability in comparison to other forms of government, which ultimately tend toward civil conflict and wars (*De regno* 2.12). Therefore Rome, after the Republic was subverted by conspiracies, returned to the monarchy (*De regno* 2.13). For Aristotle—and Sepúlveda is acutely aware of this as a translator of the *Politika*—the rights of political participation are the decisive criterion for determining the perfect state. Sepúlveda expressly takes up Aristotle's definition of the citizen as someone who "shares in the administration of justice, and in the offices" (*Pol.* 3.1.1275a22–3): "*Nam proprie civis in sua quisque civitate seu republica intelligitur qui iudicandi aut deliberandi particeps est*" (*De regno* 1.7.2). Because governmental authority in a monarchy is concentrated in the hands of the king, Sepúlveda formulates an alternative to replace the participatory rights of a *polis* citizen—a broad spectrum of advisory boards at court, which in turn are to maintain close ties with universities. The permanent discussion process between monarchical rule and the universities replaces the public discussions among citizens in the Aristotelian *polis*. A monarchy supported by institutionally anchored communication with universities was not an abstract ideal but in fact already, partially at least, a firm reality in early-sixteenth-century Spain (Losada 1978: 555). Indeed, the debates and disputations on the "New World," taking place on the highest political level, in the Council of the Indies and at the Spanish court, as well as various universities, are proof of Sepúlveda's ideal of an enlightened monarchy oriented on Christianity.

As with the Ottoman Empire, in the debate on the Conquista Sepúlveda underestimates the culture of consultation and deliberation among the Amerindians. The Aztec rulers were educated by the wise (*tlamatinime*) in special schools (*calmecac*) (León-Portilla 1963: 3–24). Moctezuma was thus supported by a council of the wise, especially during the conflict with Cortés (Dussel 1995: 97–151).

With respect to the second problem, namely transferring the principle of the rule of the rationally superior over the less intelligent to relationships between nations or peoples, Las Casas had already articulated a clear-sighted criticism. Because so-called "inferior" peoples eventually take a stand against their subservience, offensive wars in the name of a higher civilization unleash belligerent violence (1988: 660–3; cf. Gillner 1997: 210f.). The rule of the more rational can thus be the basis for creating order within a state at the very most but has no part to play in the doctrine of just war (Las Casas 1992: 534).

Sepúlveda shows no interest, however, in addressing the awkward question of whether a war waged for the purpose of civilizing a group or nation leads to an escalation in violence; instead, under the influence of the chronicle of Oviedo, he gives a dismal portrayal of the peoples of the "New World," whose customs (cannibalism, human sacrifice, clan feuds, the so-called flower or ritual wars) "exceed human depravity [*cum omnem humanam pravitatem excedant*]" (*DS* 1.11.1). From here, three further reasons for war emerge, with Sepúlveda considering them objectively interwoven: violation of natural law, the protection of the innocent from cannibalism and human sacrifice, and the efficient spread of Christianity.

Second reason justifying war: sins against nature

As Sepúlveda emphasizes, in accord with Vitoria, the pagans are the legitimate masters over their own lands (*DS* 1.20.5) and they are not to be challenged simply because of their disbelief (*DS* 1.12.2). Like the Christian pacificists before him, Sepúlveda clearly rejects hierocratic warmongering. At the same time and in contrast to Vitoria, Sepúlveda incorporates "violations of nature" into the reasons for just war. This concession to hierocratic theology was fiercely criticized by Las Casas. Because the Amerindians do not live on formerly Christian territories, they are not under the jurisdictional authority of the Church and cannot be punished by Christians for violating natural law (1988: 126–41). But for Sepúlveda this is not the issue: the second reason for waging war is not based on Church authority but stems, first and foremost, from the Stoic-Christian idea of a universal community between humans. Sepúlveda underlines his affirmative belief in the unity of humankind by referring to the dictum of Terence: "I am human, and I think nothing human is alien to me [*Homo sum, nihil humanum a me alienum puto*]" (*DS* 1.15.6). Thus, Sepúlveda remains very much on the terrain of Vitoria's cosmopolitan ethics.

Because the principle of waging war against other peoples due to their public immorality amounts to a license to use unlimited force, Sepúlveda can no longer step around the problem of international anarchy, already present and virulent in the first cause of war. As Leopold interjects, he has difficulty understanding how Democrates is using natural law, "unless you say that it is observed by those who abstain from mortal sin and other like infamies, no matter how many other grave crimes they may commit. Even in this form you will find very few people who observe natural law" (*DS* 1.151). Theft, adultery, murder, and other grave offences against the law of nature are, as Leopold notes, part of everyday life among Christians (*DS* 1.15.2). In response, Sepúlveda offers an important clarification of the second cause for war. Initially once again close to the position of Vitoria, Sepúlveda states that individual violations of natural law cannot justify the use of force against an entire nation, for this is no reason for saying that this nation does not observe natural law, because the public cause is to be considered not individually in each person but in public customs and institutions (*DS* 1.15.4). *Casus belli* then exists when a people would be so barbaric and inhuman as to fail to count crimes as reprehensible acts and punishes them neither on the basis of their mores and customs nor of their laws (*DS* 1.153). Violations of nature are only then a legitimate reason for a just war under two conditions: firstly, they must be particularly grave incidents or practices, for example ritual human sacrifice and cannibalism (*DS* 1.21.3); and secondly, the violation must be sanctioned by public morality and laws, or at least be tolerated to a high degree. Only when both conditions are met may a state or a nation be punished for violations against the law of nature (*DS* 1.15.5). Such a war, as Sepúlveda expressly states, is to deter barbaric peoples from committing crimes and infamies (*possunt tamen a flagitiis prohibere*; DS 1.15.7) but is by no means to be used to annihilate or enslave them.[10]

At this juncture it is possible to define more closely how Sepúlveda understands the natural slavery of barbarians. If the laws and institutions of a state violate the basic norms of natural law, then the population's moral consciousness is inevitably dimmed. Thus, it is possible for entire peoples to become prisoners of their own barbaric customs and practices, which Sepúlveda expresses in the phrasing, "by nature slaves." Sepúlveda is not simply repeating the Aristotelian doctrine of natural slavery, for the barbaric nature of the Amerindians is not to be explained by their physical nature—it is the result of their public mores and morals, i.e., their "second nature."[11]

The concept of a "natural" slavery in the sense of a collective moral delusion runs contrary to Sepúlveda's understanding of natural law, however, according to which it is in principle possible for all humans to gain insight into fundamental moral laws without the guidance of revelation. The latent contradiction between an innate aptitude for grasping the *lex naturae* and the factual obscuration of a moral sense can be resolved, as Fernández-Santamaría has noted, through consideration of Renaissance anthropology, specifically the idea that a human can adopt several natures: "The explanation lies with Sepúlveda's understanding of the word 'nature'" (1977: 193f.; cf. Gillner 1997: 51).

However, in his political writings Sepúlveda never refers to the *Oratio de hominis dignitate*, although he knew Alberto Pio, Pico's nephew. Nonetheless, the idea that humans can take on different natures is present in the Aristotelian humanism of Bologna, as Pomponazzi's work *On the Immortality of the Soul* shows:

> Now, I hold that the beginning of our consideration should be made at this point. Man is clearly not of simple but multiple, not of certain but of ambiguous nature, and he is to be placed as a mean between mortal and immortal things ... And to man, who thus exists as a mean between the two, power is given to assume whichever nature he wishes.
>
> (Pomponazzi 1948: 282)

Significantly, this means that Sepúlveda applies to entire peoples Pico's idea that an individual can assume an animal, human, and angelic nature. Human nature, i.e., *humanitas* in the qualitative sense, arises from a life led in line with the law of nature. Endowed with reason, all humans are fundamentally capable of knowing and understanding natural law, but Amerindians have debased themselves to an animalistic way of life through their barbaric mores and customs, a life that—in terms no less drastic than the extreme rhetoric of Pico—has hardly any "vestiges of humanity [*humanitatis vestige*]" (*DS* 1.10.1). As the notorious dictum claims, in this state they are "*homunculi*" (*DS* 1.10.1).

Because the barbarism of the Amerindians is not innate but the result of a collective practice spanning generations, Sepúlveda asserts—in contrast to Aristotle—that no peoples are condemned to eternal barbarism. For Pico, the individual possesses the power to rise from an animal to a higher nature. According to Sepúlveda, however, if entire peoples have debased themselves to the animalistic level, the possibility for an individual to ascend to a human nature through their own exertions, i.e., to gain and lead a life conforming to natural law, is non-existent. Overcoming barbaric customs and mores demands a violent intervention from an outside force, an intervention that—and this is Sepúlveda's core thesis—eliminates the despotic regimen and establishes a new legal order consistent with the law of nature: through admonitions, laws, and habits Sepúlveda hopes that the barbarians can be returned to sanity, humanness, and piety (*monitis ac legibus et consuetudine ad sanitatem humanitatem pietatemque* reducerentur; *DS* 1.15.5; emphasis mine). In short, the goal of military intervention is to *restore* the *humanity* of the Amerindians.

Third reason justifying war: protect the innocent from cannibalism and sacrifice

With the third reason Sepúlveda takes up Vitoria's doctrine of humanitarian intervention (*DS* 1.15.8; 1.21.3), arguing that all humans are obliged by divine and natural law to prevent innocents from dying ignobly in slaughter if this is possible without themselves suffering too great a harm or disadvantage (*Apologia* 8.1). Military force is no longer justified through the necessity of enforcing punitive measures but solely serves the purpose of preventing any further grave injustices being committed against scores of innocent humans who the barbarians sacrifice annually (*DS* 1.21.3).

Like Vitoria, for Sepúlveda it is not just the princes who are obligated to launch a humanitarian intervention; in principle, this applies to anyone capable of doing so (*DS* 1.21.3). More markedly than Vitoria, however, Sepúlveda accentuates the mass killing of innocents. He estimates that 20,000 are killed annually in officially organized ritual sacrifices in the Aztec Empire. If killing innocents is integral to the ritual practices implemented by the ruling authority, then, as Sepúlveda envisions the situation, any isolated campaign or rescue mission comes to nothing—once the foreign forces leave, the practice of ritual human sacrifice will simply resume. Thus, Sepúlveda sees no other option but for the Spanish to conquer and occupy the Aztec Empire. Indeed, establishing a legal system consistent with natural law principles, capable of effectively preventing the violent excesses of inhumanity and facilitating the internalization of a corresponding morality, requires that the intervening power remain for an extended period.

The demand to rescue the innocent from cannibalistic practices and ritual sacrifice was Sepúlveda's strongest argument in Valladolid, and its validity was not queried by Las Casas (Las Casas 1988: 360–75). Las Casas interpreted the ritual practice of human sacrifice differently, however, considering it an expression of religious consciousness, albeit in perverted form (Las Casas 1988: 422–51; Gillner 1997: 229–32). For this reason, he staunchly rejected violent intervention.

Fourth reason justifying war: the efficiency of Christian evangelization

The fourth just cause for war ensues not from natural law but from the Christian imperative to evangelize, which, as Sepúlveda describes it, demands leading, on the most direct and quickest path, an endless multitude of errant human beings out of the ruinous darkness to the light of truth (*exequendum et infinitam hominem multitudinem in perniciosis tenebris errantem ad lucem veritatis proxima et compendiaria via reducendum*; DS 1.15.11). Although it is striking that the efficiency of the evangelization is accentuated, Sepúlveda is not simply advocating a use of force. A conversion of the individual—and this is beyond doubt for Sepúlveda—cannot be achieved through violence inflicted from outside sources (*DS* 1.16,1–2; *Apologia* 5.7). As for Vitoria, the only question to be considered is which means may be employed to remove external hindrances for preaching the gospels.

In contrast to Las Casas, Sepúlveda calls on the Amerindians to submit *before* the peaceful evangelizing begins. The moral and political conditions, he argues, conducive for peaceful evangelizing are not present in a despotic society in which the people are held in servile subordination and public morals are perverted by practices contrary to natural law. Firstly, the Christian preachers in the Amerindian societies would be inevitably exposed to mortal danger; and secondly, the Christian message can hardly be heard in a society that undercuts natural law. Sepúlveda therefore again demands the institutionalizing of morals based on natural law, in this case as the prerequisite for an efficient evangelizing.

The goal of history: the coexistence of Christian empires

For Sepúlveda, the goal of the war against the barbarians is to establish, as the finale of the *Democrates secundus* emphasizes, a rule serving the salvation of the subjugated and the freedom that corresponds to their nature and situation (*"aptam libertatem accommodatum"*; *DS* 2.8.4). Spanish rule must accommodate progress in establishing a new legal system and public morals: "When in the course of time they have become more human and the uprightness of their customs and the Christian religion have been strengthened under domination, the servants may be treated more liberally and generously [*liberius erunt liberaliusque tractandi*]" (*DS* 2.8.1). This begs the question, however: which freedoms are the Amerindians entitled to enjoy at the end of the civilizing process? If natural law has been internalized again as the measure for moral consciousness, the Amerindians must at least have the right, as Sepúlveda deliberates through the voice of Leopold, to live in the Spanish empire as citizens with equal rights (*DS* 2.8.1). Here, again, this is in line with Vitoria's thinking, who saw the necessity of temporary domination if civilizing had to be imposed violently.

Surprisingly, Sepúlveda brusquely brushes aside Leopold's proposal. The lasting rule of Spain over the Amerindians is not only justified by how the barbarians are yet to be sufficiently pacified (*nonundum bene pacatis barbaris*), but also because of their physical nature, conditioned by living a life in specific regions and latitudes (*in regionibus quibusdam ac mundi declinationibus*; *DS* 2.8.1). At this point, Sepúlveda is at least partially conforming to the Aristotelian doctrine of the natural slavery of barbarians. Later in *De regno*, along with freedom and reason, natural conditions are also seen as important for forming and developing virtues (*De regno* 3.4). In this context, Sepúlveda states more precisely his justification of the Conquista. Due to their natural limitations, the Amerindians are prevented from advancing to the highest stage of humanity. In contrast, between the lower strata of the respective populations no essential differences exist between Spaniards and the Amerindians in the "New World" (Fernández-Santamaría 1977: 231–5). Without a nobility that comes close to the level of the Spanish elite, Spanish rule over the "New World" needs to remain ongoing. Nonetheless, as Sepúlveda emphasizes again, the Amerindians are not to be handled like slaves but to be governed like free servants in a household (*tamquam ministros, sed liberos*), i.e., by exercising a mixture of despotic and fatherly power (*quodam ex herili et paterno temperato imperio*; *DS* 2.8.1). On the communal level, however, the Amerindians, like the Spanish population, are to be conceded certain rights of participation, for example the election of mayors (*DS* 2.8.2).

Although the new doctrine of a just war legitimized Spanish rule over the "New World" for an unforeseen period and a war of aggression against despotism in the Near East (*De regno* 3.15), Sepúlveda is not advocating a universal monarchy. The idea of world dominion is expressly refuted with reference to the dialogue, related by Cicero, between Alexander the Great and a pirate: "For when he was asked what crime drove him to ravage the seas with one galley, he [the pirate] replied, 'the same one that drove you to ravage the whole world'" (*Rep.* 3.14.24; *DS* 2.8.3). Indeed, because the pagans are legitimate rulers over their lands, Sepúlveda—with even more logical consequence than Vitoria— acknowledges that the barbarians have the right to keep strangers from panning for gold and silver in their mountains or diving for pearls in their rivers (*DS* 1.20.6). However, as we have seen in detail above, pagan peoples can lose their autarky due to their barbaric mores and customs. Should the barbarians prohibit human sacrifice and institutionalize natural law like the Greeks and Romans before them, i.e., based on a philosophical monotheism, then the autonomy of their empires is sacrosanct. Without orientation on the law of nature, however, all empires, as Sepúlveda emphasizes with reference to Augustine, decay into brutal robber bands (*DS* 2.8.3; *De civ. D.* 4.1), a fate that had even befallen the Roman Empire, in its glorious period the most perfect monarchy to have ever existed (*De regno* 1.4.2). As Fernández-Santamaría puts it, "because he accepts the existence of autonomous states Sepúlveda's 'Stoicism' will be consciously modified by Aristotelian and civic humanistic influences" (1977: 171). At the same time, however, pagan empires where natural law is already institutionalized still require Christian evangelizing to reach their full potential. Thus, for Sepúlveda—as for Vitoria and Las Casas—the goal of history resides in creating peaceful coexistence between Christian empires.

7.5 A critical review: colonial ideology or a breakthrough to a global cosmopolitanism?

The colonialism debate of the sixteenth century can be understood as an early contribution to the ethical and political philosophy of modernity. Despite all the references to classical ancient and medieval thought, the Salamanca School faces up to the challenges of Europe's transoceanic expansion, a reckoning that was essential to advancing the development of a modern global society. In which sense, however, the global political ideas of sixteenth-century Spanish philosophy open the door to modernity has become the focal point of fierce controversy. In Western thought, from the nineteenth century onwards Francisco de Vitoria has often been praised, along with Grotius, as one of the founders of modern international law, a discipline that since Kant has been one of the political ideals of the Enlightenment. In contrast, Ginés de Sepúlveda was regarded as an anachronistic defender of the Aristotelian doctrine of the natural slavery of barbarians. In the critical view of post- and decolonial thinkers, in which "the relationship between the origins of international law and the colonial encounter" (Anghie 2004: 15) is unsparingly analyzed, the divide between Vitoria and Sepúlveda is for the most part dissolved. In the footsteps of Carl Schmitt, Walter Mignolo has criticized Vitoria as the founder of coloniality in which the Tawantinsuyu and Anáhuac peoples, gauged in terms of a rational epistemic hierarchy, are depreciated as inferior (Mignolo 2011: 86f.). As for Sepúlveda, Enrique Dussel has claimed that the idea of a violent civilizing of allegedly inferior peoples laid the foundation stone for the sacrifice myth of modernity, which justifies the innocence of its concomitant violence (1995: 137).

Without denying the connection between modernity and colonialism, I hope to have shown that Vitoria and Sepúlveda cannot be fully integrated into either the Enlightenment-inspired interpretation or the post- and decolonial criticism of the Salamanca School. Rather, different paradigms of modern global political thought based on ethics are developed, each of which uniquely interweaves various elements, foremost conceptions of rationality and intelligence, theories of power, and particularistic cultural interests.

In the *Relectiones de Indis* Vitoria lays the foundation for a modern, i.e., global, cosmopolitanism. Compared to classical ancient and medieval thought, Vitoria's law of nations marks a rational advance in the ethical consciousness of the West in three aspects. Firstly, Vitoria detaches the ethical universalism of Stoic-Christian thought from its problematic synthesis with the oriental idea of the world empire. Secondly, Vitoria is the first thinker to integrate the practices of the law of nations, reaching back a millennium, into a philosophically founded cosmopolitanism. Vitoria's doctrine of *ius gentium* fills a gap in European political philosophy, which since antiquity had been fixated on the *polis* and the idea of a global empire. Thirdly, Vitoria broadens the horizon of moral responsibility to apply to the whole of humanity, out of which the idea of humanitarian intervention to save the innocent emerges. All three innovations share a foundation: Vitoria's idea of a global society based on and linked by partnership and communication (*naturalis societatis et communicationis*), at the time undoubtedly a utopian vision (Redondo 1992). The significance of this constellation is enormous, for it means that while the cosmopolitanism of antiquity was primarily an ethical-spiritual attitude, and thus impacted only indirectly on legal and political systems, Vitoria's thought reveals the contours of an order between states based on the law of nations and a cosmopolitan ethics, which transcends the boundaries of state sovereignty.

Despite all its rational advances, Vitoria's theory is still interwoven with problematic colonialist ideas. The decisive question is where the ideology of coloniality may be diagnosed in Vitoria's thought. According to Anghie, despite the idea of a society of universal communication, Vitoria denies some non-Christian groups the status of subjects participating in international law, in particular the Saracens and the Amerindians. In effect, this means "*that the Saracens are inherently incapable of waging a just war*. The initial exclusion of the Saracens—and, in this case, by extension, the Indians—then, is fundamental to Vitoria's argument. In essence, only the Christians may engage in a just war" (Anghie 2004: 26). This criticism misses the point, however. Based on his doctrine of just war, Vitoria sees the Ottomans as entitled to capture and even enslave Christians who invade Turkish regions: "*si christiani turcarum terras invaderent, turcae possent iure belli subdere christianos suae poetstati et facere quod christiani essent servi*" (*De Indis* 3.3.2; Vitoria 1967: 133; Thumfart 2012: 248). Moreover, Vitoria expressly adds a provision to the right of global trade: "so long as they do no harm to their homeland." Thus Anghie's summation that Vitoria's *ius gentium* "naturalizes and legitimates a system of commerce and Spanish penetration" (Anghie 2004: 21) is quite misleading.

As noted, Vitoria's list of specific norms for organizing the law of nations undoubtedly has a connection to colonial violence, which can, though, be questioned by his own theory. The norms to be applied in international law require the consensus of all humanity. Vitoria seems to have understood the idea of a *consensus totius orbis* in a more refined way than merely tacit consensus, i.e., in the sense of a factual agreement between nations, moving toward an interpretative consensus based on strict reciprocity (Thumfahrt 2012: 264f.). Vitoria's norms, developed without dialogue with other peoples, thus have the status of tentatively anticipating a universal consensus of humanity. This hypothetical status of his *ius gentium* theory seems to have eluded him, however. Given that he was deluded by the seemingly unquestionable superiority of Christianity over all other religions, this is hardly surprising, for there is no doubt in his mind that humankind will ultimately be made up of Christian empires. Based on a concept of the common good (*bonum commune*) of humanity heavily influenced by Christian teachings, connected in turn to specific Christian controversies such as the relationship between natural and divine law, the role of the pope, etc., Vitoria rigorously places the cultural traditions of other peoples in the constrictive framework of a specifically Christian world order. Indeed, because any defying of the norms of international law are to be avenged through just wars, Vitoria's theory threatens to furnish a justification of imperial violence. The right to evangelize, to which solely Christians are entitled, is nothing other than a permit to wage "just" wars against Amerindian peoples.

The colonial and imperial biases of the law of nations can be righted, at least partially, with the help of the idea of a consensus among humanity, using, as it were, the implications of Vitoria's theory against his own explicit formulations. A template for this correction already exists in late Spanish Scholasticism, where specific aspects of Vitoria's *ius gentium* were criticized. For example, Las Casas and De Soto make it clear that the rights to travel and use natural resources cannot be claimed without gaining prior agreement from the Amerindian peoples (Cavallar 2002: 111f.). Moreover, Las Casas also strictly rejected the violent imposition of the right to evangelize, basing his argument on Christian theology.

A special case is Vitoria's idea of humanitarian intervention to save potential victims of human sacrifice, taken up and elaborated on by Sepúlveda. On this point, Vitoria is also vehemently criticized by post- and decolonial thinkers. The criticism is twofold. Firstly, the empirical basis for Vitoria's and Sepúvelda's justifications of humanitarian intervention is questioned. Sepúlveda claims that some 20,000 human sacrifices were taking place among the Aztecs annually, a number that is clearly exaggerated. The precise number of ritual sacrifices remains extremely controversial, as the disputes about the Templo show. According to David Carrasco, the Templo Mayor was "the scene of elaborate human sacrifices, which increased to incredible numbers during the last eighty years of Aztec rule" (1999: 81). On the basis of strictly archeological data, recent researchers assume "that Spanish accounts were heavily exaggerated and that the Mexica sacrificed hundreds, not tens of thousands, of victims" (Martin 2022: 7).

Secondly, the problems of carrying out humanitarian intervention were already under discussion in the sixteenth century. Notably Las Casas, who was not fully averse to intervention to save the innocent, vehemently demanded that the possibilities for launching a peaceful rescue of potential victims needed to be exhausted. Because every belligerent intervention sets off spiraling violence, the reasonableness of the means employed must be weighed up. Because, as a rule, it is not individuals but only political powers who are able to liberate persons from subjugation under despotic regimes, the idea of humanitarian intervention, as history and contemporary politics all too clearly show, is extremely susceptible to exploitation and abuse by imperial interests.

Beyond the problems besetting the application of humanitarian intervention, both post- and decolonial criticism query the idea as such. As Robert Williams has put it, "Vitoria's Law of Nations provided Western legal discourse with its first secularly oriented, systematized elaboration of the superior rights of civilized Europeans to invade and conquer normatively divergent peoples" (1990: 106). For Anghie, humanitarian intervention is nothing other than a manifestation of Western cultural imperialism, for on its basis "the Spanish acquire an extraordinarily powerful right of intervention and may act on behalf of the people seen as victims of Indian rituals ... Thus Spanish identity or, more broadly, an idealised Western identity, is projected as universal" (2004: 22f.; see also Wallerstein 2006: 5f.).

Without doubt, humanitarian interventions are suspected of universalizing particularistic cultural norms through illegitimate means. And Vitoria himself confirms this suspicion through his defense of the Christian prerogative to proselytize. For modern scholars, therefore, the differences between humanitarian intervention and a Christian imperialism are hardly discernible (Muldoon 2006). At the same time, a strict rejection of the validity claims of universal ethics comes at a high price. Without the possibility of a liberating intervention, the potential victims of despotic and totalitarian systems are at the mercy of their tormentors. A radical ethical culturalism therefore bears a high burden of reason. A simple ethical relativism seems to encounter its limits precisely in the case of the Aztec human sacrifices. It seems to be—at the very least—questionable that, as Anghie assumes with other decolonial thinkers, the calls made by Vitoria and Sepúlveda to save potential victims of human sacrifice through violent intervention do in fact ensue from a projection of Spanish or Western identity on to Amerindian cultures. According to Leon-Portilla, however, the human sacrifices were themselves criticized in the Aztec imperium before the arrival of the Spanish. The Toltecs, the precursor culture of the Aztecs on the Mexican high plateau, had already practiced human sacrifice as a state cult, but the ethno-historical sources also indicate trends toward reducing the frequency of human sacrifice through an ethicizing of polytheism and the initiating of a metaphysical cosmology, which was then continued by the Aztec wisdom teachers. At the same time, though, Tlacaélel, an advisor to two Aztec rulers, had overseen the implementation of a radical reform of cult practices in the fifteenth century, re-establishing Huitzilopochtli, the Aztec tribal deity, as the sacral authority of a new imperial mythology. Under

Tlacaélel, the practice of human sacrifice seems to have massively expanded again, leading to the notorious flower wars against neighboring peoples. This reform was resisted by the Aztec wisdom teachers and a few princes, including Nezahualcóyotl. The alliances that many neighboring peoples forged with the Spaniards during the Conquista were a critical response to the flower wars and the human sacrifices of the Aztecs (León-Portilla 1963: 129–78).

This background sheds new light on Sepúlveda's contribution to the sixteenth-century colonial debate. Admittedly, Sepúlveda developed probably the most comprehensive exemplar of colonial ideology, elevating the hegemony of Europe into a normative foundation for the burgeoning global society by fusing it with the ontological principle of the rule of the rationally intelligent over the less rational, first articulated by Aristotle and transposed by Panaitios to relations between nations. On the other hand, obviously shocked by the Aztec human sacrifices, Sepúlveda also made use of Vitoria's idea of humanitarian intervention. Accentuating a suggestion in Vitoria, for Sepúlveda, in order to prevent violence again taking hold after the intervention was ended, the cultic practices fostered by the state must be abolished and a new legal system established. Thus, the conquest and at least temporary occupation of the Aztec Empire was imperative.

Sepúlveda's political philosophy is therefore not solely concerned with justifying colonialist ideology. The demand to permanently abolish the Aztec practice of human sacrifice points to a grave problem of international politics still prevalent today, namely the question of using violence to implement universal ethical norms on a global scale. From this perspective, Losada has even included Sepúlveda among the founders of modern international law (Losada 1978: 555).

To sum up: despite the constraints of Christianity, Vitoria, Sepúlveda, and Las Casas developed paradigmatic conceptions of global cosmopolitanism which recur, transformed, in the secular debates on an ethical-political order for a global society. With the founding of the United Nations, an institution ensuring a consensus-based definition of norms for international law, hinted at but not explicated by Vitoria, was created in the twentieth century. Indeed, what is even more significant is how, in recent times, the principle of state sovereignty has been relativized by the idea of human rights. For this reason, humanitarian interventions have become an integral part of international law when human rights are violated on a massive scale and these violations are sanctioned by a state. Beyond this, the UN Security Council has extended the mandate of humanitarian interventions to include measures for building coherent and stable democratic structures. The limits to the implementation of human rights and democracy through outside powers have become blatantly obvious in events taking place in the Near East and Africa. A military intervention by outside forces all too easily sets off spiraling violence, as Las Casas warned in the sixteenth century. And as Las Casas saw human sacrifice as an expression of a religious consciousness, today post- and decolonial movements criticize every kind of humanitarian intervention as an instance of aggressive cultural imperialism. In this scenario, the Gulf War, i.e., the West's invasion of Iraq, is merely a contemporary version of the idea of humanitarian intervention developed by Vitoria and Sepúlveda (Dussel 1995: 62; Anghie 2004: 320).

In the discussion about humanitarian interventions and civilizing strategies employing force, it seems imperative to avoid limiting considerations to the Global South. In the mid-twentieth century Europe itself became the object of a violent civilizing process in the wake of fascism and National Socialism. Without the military elimination of the Nazi regime by the Allies, the extermination of the Jews and other "sub-humans" could not have been stopped. Of course, the Allies were primarily fighting off an aggressive war launched by Hitler. However, striving to prevent regression to fascist terror in the long term, the Allies could not be content with the capitulation of the Nazi regime and had to occupy Germany and Austria for years, during which they instigated and supported the establishment of democracies based on the rule of law by conducting re-education programs and reforming institutions. Inspired by Pico della Mirandola, Sepúlveda described the transition from collective barbarism to a life led in accordance with basic moral norms as the adoption of different human natures. In an objective convergence with Sepúlveda, in the post-war years Karl Jaspers called Germany's lapse into barbarism an "*Umschmelzung unseres Wesens* [recasting of our nature]" (Jaspers 1965: 32). Thus, for Jaspers, the transition to a democratic order demanded a profound turnaround, a reversal requiring re-education by the Allies (Jaspers 1965: 47–52). To overcome the fascist nature, the intellectual sources nourishing racist and totalitarian politics in German cultural history need to be detected and unsparingly disclosed; at the same time, the Germans were able to draw on other influences, for example the traditions of freedom and liberty emerging out of the Enlightenment, most notably represented by Kant. The situation was similar in the Aztec Empire of the sixteenth century, where there were both defenders and critics of human sacrifice, whom both Vitoria and Sepúlveda, blinded by Eurocentrism, simply failed to notice.

This means that every conception of an ethical universalism runs the risk of becoming a vehicle of cultural imperialism and a means to impose particularistic norms. Conversely, ethical relativism threatens to become an accomplice of power syndromes between allegedly incommensurable cultures. The dilemmas of global ethics cannot be resolved all at once, but require a gradual approach, broadening step by step the scope of those processes that facilitate understanding—or in other words, what is needed is a framework like Vitoria's vision of a global community based on partnership and communication. In this sense, the Spanish colonial debate is a striking example of how the horizon of moral responsibility is broadened, i.e., the previous limits abolished, and new boundaries are drawn, which in turn become the target of new critical impulses. This perspective sheds new light on the age of Enlightenment, where Christian natural law, based upon which Vitoria and Sepúlveda had justified humanitarian intervention in the Aztec Empire, was superseded by a secular ethics based on human rights. And from the nineteenth century, the racist and patriarchal elements sedimented in declarations of human rights drawing on the heritage of the Enlightenment became in turn the focal point of new social criticism.

The colonial debate thus also sheds light on how discourse ethics justifies and argues the case for an ethical universalism. Discourse ethics takes up, *de facto*, Vitoria's idea of a global communication community. At the same time, however, the sixteenth-century colonial debate shows that the internal norms of such a global communication community do not simply concur with moral norms. Aside from the empirical limits to real practical discourses, where not all potential discourse partners can take part, within the framework of a global communication community two different moral conceptions have been developed since the sixteenth century: Christian natural law and secular human rights, both of which continue to be critically reinterpreted by non-European philosophies down to the present day.

8

Experimental self-fashioning in an unlimited world: Michel de Montaigne

8.1 To a philosophical hermeneutics of the *Essais*

Michel de Montaigne's *Essais*[1] are widely considered to mark the end of Renaissance thought. In fact, Montaigne's thought brings together numerous threads of philosophy present since the fourteenth century. Because the *Essais* distance themselves not only from scholasticism but from any form of systematic thought, Montaigne still has no self-evident place in the history of European philosophy (Marchi 1994; Carraud 1999). Although Hegel admitted that he found "highly spiritual thought about human life" in the *Essais*, for him they "do not properly belong to the history of philosophy" because "they have not reasoned from thought as such" ([1825–26] 2009: 74f.). In contrast, Nietzsche felt a deep intellectual affinity, in particular with Montaigne's unwavering honesty: "That such a man wrote has truly augmented the joy of living on this earth. … If I were set the task, I could endure to make myself at home with him" (Nietzsche 1997: 135). In the twentieth century, a variety of thinkers, from Cassirer (1999: 144–63) and then Horkheimer (1993b) through to Brunschvicg (1945) and Popkin (2003), positioned Montaigne's skepticism as the negative foil to Descartes' program of establishing a self-foundation for reason, an interpretation schema radically challenged by Stephen Toulmin's *Cosmopolis: The Hidden Agenda of Modernity* (1990). According to Toulmin, Cartesianism represents a problematic counter-Renaissance that, by striving for indubitable certainty, ultimately perpetuates the dogmatism of the religious wars. Philosophical postmodernism has also discovered Montaigne, with Lyotard succinctly claiming that "the essay (Montaigne) is postmodern, and the fragment (the *Athenaeum*) modern" (Lyotard 1992: 15). Meanwhile a range of different authors have interpreted Montaigne's thought as a genuine alternative—and not merely as a negative contrastive foil—to Cartesian subject philosophy (Taylor 1989: 143–84; Bürger 1998: 29–51; Navarro Reyes 2007: 36–7).

Aligning with this perspective, I also interpret Montaigne as the founder of the modern idea of a finite, bodily and historically situated subject, an idea continued by the moralists and then moved, since the nineteenth century, to the center of philosophy by post-idealist thought. Without seeking to offer an overall interpretation of the *Essais*, I will mainly situate Montaigne's self-reflections on the subject in the broad context of the de-limitations of the Renaissance: the evaluation of insatiable curiosity (section 8.2 of this chapter), the anthropological idea of self-fashioning (section 8.3), and the colonial expansion of European powers (section 8.4).

At first glance, Montaigne seems to be the very embodiment of a radical counter position to the de-limitation of the *oikumene* and human nature through the *vis creativa*. His retreat to the paternal chateau sharply contrasts with the voyages of Columbus, and while Vitoria radically extends the scope of human moral responsibility, Montaigne takes leave of political offices and withdraws from public life: "Now I do indeed stay at home most of the time" (*E* 3.9; 726). Like Augustine, Montaigne sees the seemingly unquenchable curiosity about the world to be a flight away from the intimacy of oneself: "Every man rushes elsewhere and into the future, because no man has arrived at himself" (*E* 3.12; 799). In his *Apologia for Raymond Sebond* (*E* 2.12), Montaigne vehemently attacks the elevation of humanity's position in Renaissance philosophy. The human being is not the crown of creation, but the "most vulnerable and frail of all creatures ... and at the same time the most arrogant" (*E* 2.12; 330). And yet numerous passages in the *Essais* point in the opposite direction. Montaigne not only criticizes the exaggerated elevation of the status of humans in Renaissance philosophy, but also any contrary tendency to human self-abasement: "As for the opinion that disdains our life, it is ridiculous." And noting this ridiculousness leads to an ever deeper probing: "it is against nature that we despise ourselves and care nothing about ourselves. It is a malady peculiar to man, and not seen in any other creature, to hate and disdain himself" (*E* 2.3; 254). Peter Burke has rightly warned against any facile simplifying of Montaigne's examination of Renaissance *dignitas hominis* literature. "As for the dignity of man, it would be a mistake to draw too strong a contrast between Pico della Mirandola's *Oration on the Dignity of Man* and Montaigne's puncturing of human pretensions in his 'Apologia for Raymond Sebond' (2.12)" (Burke 1981: 11).

A similar constellation emerges with Montaigne's attitude toward curiosity about the world. While warning of the dangers capable of flourishing under the thrall of *curiositas*, at the same time, in *Education of Children* (*E* 1.26), Montaigne recommends against constraining and impeding the curious minds of children. "Put into his head an honest curiosity to inquire into all things; whatever is unusual around him he will see: a building, a fountain, a man, the field of an ancient battle, the place where Caesar or Charlemagne passed" (*E* 2.26; 15). Moreover, by no means does Montaigne judge early modern cosmopolitanism merely negatively. While cherishing the value of a reclusive private life, the major political upheavals are constantly "present" in the study in the chateau tower, and so too, as underscored by the essay *Of Cannibals*, the Conquista of the Americas.

The diverging and at times contradictory views Montaigne presents in the *Essais* pose serious problems for every interpretation. For this reason, it seems necessary to preface any considerations on Montaigne with cogent hermeneutical reflections. The hermeneutical problems encountered when reading the *Essais*, which first became acutely obvious in the early twentieth century, crystallize around the question of the physical text. Montaigne published several editions during his lifetime. The first edition of 1570, containing books 1 and 2, were published twice more in the immediately following years with minor changes. A fifth edition appeared in 1588 that includes a third book with new chapters and the first two parts augmented with around 600 additions (Maskell 1982). On the title leaf Montaigne points out that additions have been made but they are not noted in the text itself. In his copy of the 1588 edition, known as the "Bordeaux copy," there are a significant number of handwritten additions made during his final years (Desan 2001). The plan to publish a sixth edition failed to materialize before Montaigne's death in 1592. Marie de Gournay, Montaigne's confidante for the last years of his life, eventually brought out a new edition of the *Essais* in 1595 that contains many but not all of the marginalia from the Bordeaux copy. Ultimately, this means that there is no definitive edition of the *Essais*. For as long as he could, right up to just before his death, Montaigne was constantly augmenting and reworking the *Essais*.

On a second level, hermeneutical problems emerge from the self-understanding of the *Essais*. In the introductory address *To the Reader*, Montaigne presents his book as a personal portrait.

> This book was written in good faith, reader. It warns you from the outset that in it I have set myself no goal but a domestic and private one. I have had no thought of serving either you or my own glory. My powers are inadequate for such a purpose. I have dedicated it to the private convenience of my relatives and friends, so that when they have lost me (as soon they must), they may recover

here some features of my habits and temperament, and by this means keep the knowledge they have had of me more complete and alive.

If I had written to seek the world's favour, I should have bedecked myself better, and should present myself in a studied posture. I want to be seen here in my simple, natural, ordinary fashion, without straining or artifice; for it is myself that I portray. My defects will here be read to the life, and also my natural form, as far as respect for the public has allowed. Had I been placed among those nations which are said to live still in the sweet freedom of nature's first laws, I assure you I should very gladly have portrayed myself here entire and wholly naked.

Thus, reader, I am myself the matter of my book; you would be unreasonable to spend your leisure on so frivolous and vain a subject.

So farewell. Montaigne, this first day of March, fifteen hundred and eighty

(*E* To the Reader; 2)

These words addressed to the reader obviously left behind an indelible impression—for centuries, arguments about and disputes over Montaigne's *Essais* were conducted as arguments and disputes about Montaigne the person. Following Pascal's critique, interest long revolved around Montaigne's stance on religion and the church. Despite the pronouncement that the *Essais* are a personal portrait, the first book contains scarcely any noteworthy personal revelations, offering rather a wealth of comments on classical ancient texts. Moreover, at numerous places throughout the text Montaigne mentions, in various ways, the purpose of the *Essais*. At first, he speaks about the *Essais* in terms of keeping an account of his capricious mind (*E* 1.8); elsewhere he sees the purpose to be examining his cognitive faculties (*E* 1.26; 107); and finally, the idea of the self-portrait presented in the preface is once again taken up and modified (*E* 2.17; 496). And yet, in contrast, Montaigne mentions that his book has grown out of the sadness he felt at the death of his friend La Boétie (*E* 1.28): the *Essais* are grotesques, serving the purpose of framing a picture of La Boétie and above all his treatise *De la servitude volontaire* (Starobinski 1985: 36–53).

At the beginning of the twentieth century, Pierre Villey attempted to resolve the contradictions in the multifaceted subject matter and the problem of diverging self-interpretations through a reading that plotted a developmental history (Villey 1933). Villey discerned variously a Stoic early phase, primarily evident in the first book of the *Essais*; a phase of skeptical crisis that reached its peak in the *Apologia for Raymond Sebond*; and an Epicurean late phase, predominant in the third book. Despite critical voices, Villey's reading served as the foundation for Montaigne studies for decades, until at the end of the 1960s it was supplanted by a postmodern approach (Defaux 1983; McKinley 2001). According to Yves Pouilloux, the *Essais* cannot be read as if they were a stone quarry, the various cuttings in the face revealing the "development" or indeed even the "wisdom" of Montaigne and his thought. Instead, the goal of the text resides precisely in throwing everything into a state of disarray ("désordre"). The reflexivity of the text whips up a whirlwind of perspectives, with the self-commentaries on every statement made on the content level laying down new levels of signification (Pouilloux 1969: 41).

Because the *Essais* set off a firework display of different perspectives, with the different fuses lit by new reflections on specific themes and new interpretations as to what the project of the *Essais* is to be, from the scarcely comprehensible plethora of perspectives I would like to filter out and trace a *few* "attempts" Montaigne offers on the three central motifs of the Renaissance: that were analyzed in the writings of Nicholas of Cusa, Pico, and Vitoria.

The whirlwind whipped up by permanently questioning one's own positions is already stirring in Montaigne's address "to the reader." Just a few lines after his avowal of the truthfulness of his self-portrait—"This book was written in good faith"—Montaigne points out that unequivocal truthfulness is now only possible among "those nations which are said to live still in the sweet freedom of nature's first laws." And thus, at the opening of the *Essais*, a discourse begins to take shape on the problem of authentic self-presentation and -expression. Whether, and if so in which sense, humanity is actually capable of "truthfulness" is not merely mentioned as a premise for the whole undertaking but is a theme of the *Essais* that is examined again and again from various perspectives. In the chapter *Of Giving the Lie*, Montaigne even names "dissimilation" to be one of "the most notable qualities of this century" (*E* 2.18; 505). Even more significant for our considerations is how the doubt as to the very possibility of truthful self-portrait arises in a contrastive relationship to the naturalness of Amerindian peoples, and so the problem of truthfulness—of eminent importance for the following examination of Montaigne's thought— is linked to the discovery of the Americas from the outset.

8.2 The unfathomableness of the "natural" human and curiosity

Like the Hellenistic schools of philosophy that were forced to come to terms with the loss of importance of the *polis*, Montaigne's withdrawal to the seclusion of the chateau and its tower is a reaction to far-reaching sociocultural upheavals.

Again and again, Montaigne characterizes the age as "licentious and sick" (*E* 2.7; 277), lamenting that there is no true philosophy, no reliable science, and no virtue: "It is a strange fact that things should be in such a pass in our century that philosophy, even with people of understanding, should be an empty and fantastic name, a thing of no use and no value, both in common opinion and in fact" (*E* 1.26; 118). The plague, which had significantly decimated the population in his region (*E* 3.12; 802), and the turmoil of civil war have not only paralyzed intellectual life but also undermined moral standards. The solitude of the tower is therefore not an idyll for introspection, but a place haunted by the spirit of the age, the constant fear of death: "I have gone to bed a thousand times in my own home, imagining that someone would betray me and slaughter me that very night" (*E* 3.9; 741). Embroiled in the chaos of social upheaval in which "every Frenchman, whether as an individual or as a member of the community, sees himself at every moment on the verge of the total overthrow of his fortune," Montaigne claims that "we must keep our courage supplied with stronger and more vigorous provisions" (*E* 3.12; 800). Consequently, philosophy can no longer pretend to offer a universal interpretation of the world; it now carries weight only if it provides guidance in the art of living, drawing its inspiration from ancient thinkers such as Seneca, Plutarch, and Pyrrho of Elis: "My trade and my art is living" (*E* 2.6; 274).[2]

Montaigne's return to the philosophy of late antiquity takes place at a time when the *studia humanitatis* had already plunged into deep crisis (A. Buck 1987). Humanist studies had not only broadened knowledge about antiquity but also brought to light the contradictions of classical ancient thought, for example the countless theories on the highest good (*E* 1.53; 224f.). Moreover, the erudition of humanist learning had long since deteriorated into the mindless repetition of the views of ancient authors: "We know how to say: 'Cicero says thus; such are the morals of Plato; these are the very words of Aristotle.' But what do we say ourselves? What do we judge? What do we do? A parrot could well say as much" (*E* 1.25; 100). The maxims of moral theories are thus not simply adopted but examined in the light of personal experience. Upon retreating to his chateau, Montaigne's contemplative journey inward brings him anything but tranquillity, the *ataraxia* promised by ancient philosophical schools. The mind is actually a tormentor:

> like a runaway horse, it gives itself a hundred times more trouble than it took for others, and gives birth to so many chimeras and fantastic monsters, one after another, without order or purpose, that in order to contemplate their ineptitude

and strangeness at my pleasure, I have begun to put them in writing, hoping in time to make my mind ashamed of itself.

(*E* 1.8; 21)

The experience of inner turmoil and disunity was well known to the Hellenist philosophers, a fact Montaigne himself attests to with numerous quotes. Ancient theories on morals and ethics therefore placed all their emphasis on understanding the highest good, for "the soul that has no fixed goal loses itself" (*E* 1.8; 21). But precisely because ancient philosophy was fixated on identifying the highest good, new theories accumulated, and the humanist turn to antiquity inevitably fails to provide any credible orientation. Montaigne draws a surprising conclusion from this uncertainty about the ultimate goal of humankind, namely the need to explore the "natural," i.e., the mutable and everyday human being, including the chimeras and fantastic monstrosities spawned by the imagination. This resolution to keep an account of the chaotic and monstrous life of his mind represents a cautious break with both classical ancient and Christian ideals of existence, as a comparison with Plutarch and Augustine shows.

As Plutarch emphasizes with reference to Plato, the presence of the eternal and immutable God is a mirror of self-knowledge for human beings. Once in the presence of the divine, however, the self-experience of human individuals can only be that of a mutable creature subjected to countless changes: "and if you apply the whole force of your mind in your desire to apprehend it, it is like unto the violent grasping of water, which, by squeezing and compression, loses the handful enclosed, as it spurts through the fingers." Orientating on the mutability of human nature would make it simply impossible "to apprehend a single thing that is abiding or really existent" (Plutarch 1936: 241; *De E apud Delphos* 18). Due to their participation in the divine spirit, humans are able to gain firm ground amid all the whirling change by leading a life under the guidance of reason, this stable position then mirrored in a person's tranquillity. Although profoundly influenced by Plutarch's biographies, Montaigne dares a radical break with Plutarch by turning attention to humanity's mutable nature, making it, rather than the "better self," the subject of self-exploration.

A similar constellation emerges with respect to Montaigne's relationship to Augustine. Like Montaigne, Augustine mercilessly reveals the weaknesses of his individual nature; in Book X of the *Confessiones* Augustine touches upon the seemingly endless stream of ideas produced by the human mind. This depiction of human flightiness, unsteadinesss, and fragility serves solely to demonstrate the impotence of the sinful human and reliance on divine grace. As an ideal type, the autobiography therefore plots for the readers their own path of conversion. The *Essais* are replete with motifs drawn from the *Confessiones*, and Montaigne openly hopes, in a pronounced allusion to Augustine, "to make my mind ashamed of itself" (*E* 1.8; 21), a shaming that shall move him to cast off his pride (*superbia*). The contemplative retreat inward is no longer, though, as it had been for Augustine, a stage on the pathway of ascent to God. On the contrary, probing into his mutable nature will gradually become the dominant maxim of his thought (Bürger 1998: 32; Schärf 1999: 55). While Augustine moves from the images of sensual things through immutable ideas to finally ascend to God, Montaigne surrenders to the plethora of phantasms produced by the imagination and volatile thinking. The anthropological observation that "truly man is a marvellously vain, diverse, and undulating object" (*E* 1.1; 5) has an ontological foundation, for "variety is the most general fashion that nature has followed" (*E* 2.37; 598).

Now that the subject under consideration is no longer the ideal but humankind's mutable existence, then it is only consequential that the *Essais* remain uncompleted; they "must" be continually reworked, compiled in new editions, and augmented with additional insertions: "Who does not see that I have a road along which I shall go, without stopping and without effort, as long as there is ink and paper in the world?" (*E* 3. 9: 721). In a sense, the *Essais* merge with their author, with the gestation of the self; as Montaigne puts it, they are "a book consubstantial with its author, concerned with my own self, an integral part of my life; not concerned with some third-hand, extraneous purpose, like all other books" (*E* 2.18; 504).

At this point, the question emerges: what prompted this irrepressible will to explore the ever-changing worlds of the imagination? As Montaigne concedes, his urge to explore his inner world and present his observations is not driven by a longing for fame, which he says he scarcely notices, but by a passion, seemingly insatiable: "I am hungry to make myself known" (*E* 3.5; 643). A note in the Bordeaux copy reads: "je me deschiffre moy-mesme … curieusement" (*E* 3.9). Montaigne later deleted this addition (Frame 1982: 6f.); naturally enough, however, the curiosity mentioned provides a significant pointer. As a skeptic, Montaigne is extremely reserved about all forms of intemperate striving for knowledge. At the same time, though, as he gradually realizes, in exploring the inner turmoil of his character he is borne along by a boundless curiosity. A problematizing of *curiositas* thus runs through the *Essais* like a thread, constantly reappearing here and there (Charpentier 1986; 2004) and casting light on the overall project of a written self-exploration.

In the first step of this problematizing, Montaigne addresses the discrepancy between the immense diversity of the universe and the limitedness of human cognitive faculties. Referring to the Americas, Montaigne notes that the earth itself reveals "an infinite difference and variety due solely to distance in place. Neither wheat nor wine is seen, nor any of our animals, in these new lands that our fathers have discovered" (*E* 2.12; 390). And hence in the universe, infinite variety and permanent change are so predominant that any claim to gain comprehensive knowledge of the world is doomed to failure from the outset: "The world is but a perennial movement. All things in it are in constant motion—the earth, the rocks of the Caucasus, the pyramids of Egypt—both with the common motion and with their own. Stability itself is nothing but a more languid motion" (*E* 3.2; 610). In the final chapter, Montaigne's emphasis has a programmatic note: "there is no quality so universal in this aspect of things as diversity and variety" (*E* 3.13; 815). The contradictions between the cosmological systems—the Ptolemaic and the ancient plurality of worlds (Sayce 1972: 78–82)—are ultimately the result of "the mobility and incomprehensibility of all matters" (*E* 2.12; 378).

Besides cosmological considerations, Montaigne also takes up theological reflections to demonstrate the limits of the human striving for knowledge. Revealing a close affinity to Nicholas of Cusa, from the recognition of God's unknowability Montaigne concludes that it is impossible to gain comprehensive knowledge of the world,[3] for "the knowledge of causes belongs only to Him who has the guidance of things, not to us" (*E* 3.11; 785). The sole possibility open to humanity is to come to an approximate knowledge of the truth of things through conjecture and comparisons. But in distinction from Cusa, who conceives any series of conjectures to be stages in an infinite *approach* toward understanding things, Montaigne accentuates the remainder, the inadequacy of all comparisons. Ultimately, specificity or uniqueness evade all comparisons, as a consideration of the relationship between humans and animals reveals: "by comparison we can draw some conjecture; but as for what is peculiar to them, what do we know about it?" (*E* 2.12; 343). Similarly on the knowledge of the social world of humans: "The inference that we try to draw from the resemblance of events is uncertain, because they are always dissimilar" (*E* 3.13; 815). Cusa's philosophical theology softens the discordant sharpness of the contradictions emerging out of the relationship between the limitless universe and the finiteness of human knowledge. God has aligned the realms of being to human cognitive faculties so that the investigation of *all* things is open to humanity. Montaigne however has to explain the problem of human knowledge without the support of a philosophical theology. The notion that the human mind possesses the power to grasp the immanent infinity of the world is therefore repudiated as an immodest overestimation of humanity's place in the cosmos.

Despite skepticism about the scope of human cognitive faculties, it is, according to Montaigne, undeniable *that* a boundless will to know *everything* has been implanted in us. The thirst for knowledge is akin to a fever, one that, like the striving for power and pleasure, threatens to consume us and transport us into a state of frenzy: "In nothing does man know how to stop at the limit of his need; of pleasure, riches, power, he embraces more than he can hold; his greed is incapable of moderation. I find that it is the same with the curiosity for knowledge … *In learning, as in all other things, we suffer from intemperance*" (*E* 3.12; 794). The *conditio humana* is therefore characterized by a fundamental dichotomy between an innate urge for knowledge that knows no limits and the limited capacity of our cognitive faculties: "I am afraid we have eyes bigger than our stomachs, and more curiosity than capacity. We embrace everything, but we clasp only wind" (*E* 1.31; 150). The obvious question is then: how should humanity deal with this tension between an intemperate urge for knowledge and the limited nature of the cognitive faculties? Despite his orientation on pyrrhic skepticism, Montaigne by no means fully rejects the boundlessness of curiosity, the insatiability of the thirst for knowledge. He sternly warns against the unrestrained encroachments of the urge for knowledge, which seduces reason into hastily subjugating the specificity of individual cases under the yoke of generalizing concepts (types, genera) and causes: "They leave aside the cases and amuse themselves treating the causes. Comical prattlers!" (*E* 3.11; 785). And indeed, philosophy itself nurtures curiosity with all manner of speculation about material, formal, and final causes (MacLean 1996: 30–2). But the popular wisdom encapsulated by proverbs and adages, which Montaigne often contrasts with the ivory-tower theories of the philosophers, is also not free of this pathological invention of ever-new causes. Nor are the theologians, who all too easily assume supernatural causes, immune from the vice of inventing new causes, for example in miracles or the demonizing of women in the witches' trials (*E* 3.11; 709), which, in contrast to Bodin, Montaigne sharply criticizes (Meijer 1983).

The insight into the flaws of the human striving for knowledge must be prevented, however, from reverting to its opposite, a disdain and contempt for reason *per se*. The categorical denial of any possibility of knowledge is no less intemperate than the claim for comprehensive knowledge: "The pride of those who attributed to the human mind a capacity for all things produced in others, through spite and emulation, the opinion that it is capable of nothing.

These men maintain the same extreme in ignorance that the others maintain in knowledge" (*E* 3.11; 792).

What is therefore legitimate is the *search* for *provisional* general concepts and causes. In this sense, Copernicus' theory must also be assumed to be provisional, for it will be superseded in the future by new knowledge, just as it had supplanted the Ptolemaic system (*E* 2.12; 429f.; Gessmann 1997: 57–61). For Montaigne, science is a matter for strong, resolute natures, which however are extremely rare (*E* 3.8; 711). And because of his own laziness and poor memory, he himself does not belong to this esteemed circle of true scientists and scholars (*E* 1.26; 106f.; 2.24; 492f.).

The struggle between the insatiability of the thirst for knowledge and the limitedness of cognitive faculties is not however to be misconstrued as a sign of the absurdity of human existence; it is, in fact, a gift of nature. The experience of the limits of our cognitive powers makes human beings acutely aware that the highest good cannot reside in gaining comprehensive knowledge of the universe. For the main concerns of human existence—securing survival and finding happiness—it is unnecessary to explore the causes of things; on the contrary, nature has equipped humans so that a life worth living, precisely under humane conditions, is possible with a limited knowledge of nature: "As she [Nature] has furnished us with feet to walk with, so she has given us wisdom to guide us in life" (*E* 3.13; 822); and because "there is nothing useless in nature, not even uselessness itself" (*E* 3.1; 599), no desire is "more natural than the desire for knowledge" (*E* 3.13; 815).

This means that "The knowledge of causes belongs only to Him [God] who has the guidance of things, not to us who have only the enduring of them, and who have the perfectly full use of them according to our nature, without penetrating to their origin and essence. Nor is wine pleasanter to the man who knows its primary properties" (*E* 3.11; 785).

At this point, Montaigne brings into play the traditional reservations against curiosity about the world, namely loss of self, pride, and immoderateness, formulated in both classical ancient thought and Christian theology: "Christians have a particular knowledge of the extent to which curiosity is a natural and original evil in man. The urge to increase in wisdom and knowledge was the first downfall of the human race; it was the way by which man hurled himself into eternal damnation. Pride is his ruin and his corruption" (*E* 2.12; 368). As Montaigne sees it, the Stoics warn urgently against immoderate indulgence in intellectual pleasures, for "studying being in itself a pleasant occupation, so pleasant that among other pleasures the Stoics forbid also that which comes from the exercise of the mind"; they thus "want a curb on it, and find intemperance in knowing too much" (*E* 2.12; 378). Within the self-exploration of natural existence, the danger of losing oneself looms for Montaigne in excessive curiosity, and indeed unbridled curiosity imperils the whole undertaking of the *Essais*: "We entangle our thoughts in generalities, and the causes and conduct of the universe, which conduct themselves very well without us, and we leave behind our own affairs and Michel, who concerns us even more closely than man in general" (*E* 3.9; 726; cf. 2.17; 499). Here Montaigne relates the anecdote about Thales of Miletus, who stumbled into a well while observing the stars. The Milesian old woman gave Thales the "good counsel to look rather to himself than to the sky" (*E* 2.12; 402; cf. Blumenberg 2015: 54; Gessmann 1997: 63–72). Moreover, the unbridled urge for knowledge runs contrary to the skeptical attitude, which is constitutive for the project of the self-exploration of the natural human being. It is only when we suspend judgment in the sense of the *epoché* of the ancient skeptics that the diverse aspects of our individuality actually open up. "Vainglory and curiosity are," as Montaigne emphasizes, "the two scourges of our soul. The latter leads us to thrust our noses into everything, and the former forbids us to leave anything unresolved and undecided" (*E* 1.27; 135).

In terms of historical considerations on curiosity, Montaigne takes up a middle position between the Augustinian criticism of *curiositas* and its rehabilitation by Cusa. In contrast to the latter, who integrates insatiable curiosity into humanity's ascent toward knowledge of the absolute, Montaigne, drawing on Augustine, demarcates curiosity from the question of human happiness. But in turn, unlike Augustine, Montaigne's path inward no longer leads from the self to a knowledge of God. Turning inward, for Montaigne, means turning to the complexity and changeability of existence, now the dominating subject of his thinking: "I, who make no other profession, find in me such infinite depth and variety, that what I have learned bears no other fruit than to make me realize how much I still have to learn" (*E* 3.13; 823). Corresponding to the infinity of the universe for Cusa, the unfathomability of his natural existence becomes the correlate for a rehabilitation of insatiable curiosity in Montaigne's conception. Since antiquity, monsters and miracles have been the preferred subjects of *curiositas*. And here Montaigne admits that "I have seen no more evident monstrosity and miracle in the world than myself. We become habituated to anything strange by use and time; but the more I frequent myself and know myself, the more my deformity astonishes me, and the less I understand myself" (*E* 3.11; 787). The immoderate urge for knowledge finds a legitimate object to explore after all—man, or more precisely the immanent infinity of the human self-relationship (Charpentier

1986: 119): "I study myself more than any other subject. That is my metaphysics, that is my physics" (*E* 3.13; 821).

Due to the inexhaustible multifaceted complexity of human existence, the problems accrued when striving to gain comprehensive knowledge of the world return on a new level in self-exploration. Like external nature, one's own existence can be tapped into and extrapolated only through perspectival approaches: "I present myself standing and lying down, front and rear, on the right and the left, and in all my natural postures" (*E* 3.8; 721). The assumption that we know ourselves better than we do the world proves to be a deceptive prejudice. Indeed, as Montaigne now firmly demands, curiosity has to be directed not just inwardly but also outwardly. It is only through opening to the world that humans can know themselves: "This great world, which some multiply further as being only a species under one genus, is the mirror in which we must look at ourselves to recognise ourselves from the proper angle" (*E* 1.26; 116).

In the third book of the *Essais*, which Montaigne wrote in the years following his travels through Germany, Switzerland, and Italy, the enhanced status given to curiosity reaches its climax. Already in antiquity the desire to travel, a wanderlust, was a symbol of curiosity. In this context Montaigne openly admits to having a "greedy appetite for new and unknown things," the source of his motivation to travel (*E* 3.9; 723). What is more, Montaigne claims that humanity *should* travel *only out of curiosity* and not because of some necessity related to occupation or a private obligation. Traveling is something that has to be learned, for many people, he surmises, remain trapped in their own world although they are in foreign countries. For example, when abroad, the French wish to dine solely *à la française* and avoid any direct contact with the native inhabitants of a place: "They travel covered and wrapped in a taciturn and incommunicative prudence, defending themselves from the contagion of an unknown atmosphere" (*E* 3.9; 754). In stark contrast, to travel motivated by a desire to experience the unknown requires a willingness to be open to getting to know and trying out other mores, customs, languages, foods, etc. Montaigne thus intentionally sits at the table of the locals when in a foreign land; or in Italy he writes his journal in broken Italian. He has no firm itinerary, but keeps his plans open for any new and unexpected opportunities which may arise. It is in this sense that for Montaigne travel represents a genuine model for the art of living, which itself becomes a journey: "My plan is everywhere divisible; it is not based on great hopes; each day's journey forms an end. And the journey of my life is conducted in the same way" (*E* 3.9; 747).

In justifying the lust to travel, Montaigne is forced to specifically repudiate the traditional reservations brought against curiosity, fleeing from oneself and neglecting moral duties. We can flee ourselves not only when traveling, he points out, but just as easily when in solitude at home. Moreover, domestic worries often threaten to preoccupy us to the extent that there is no room left for contemplative inner reflection. In contrast to Cicero's qualms, for Montaigne it is not the case that curiosity prevents a person from fulfilling their social or marital duties *per se*. In fact, it is likely to be other way around: the alternation between intimacy and distance enlivens the relationship between married couples, elevating it out of a shared life bogged down in the daily grind (III, 9; 745). The duties toward the fatherland, which Cicero had evoked to set a clear limit on the insatiability of curiosity, are important, concedes Montaigne, who held the office of mayor on several occasions. When a society such as France at the end of the sixteenth century descends into anarchy and violence, however, then it is no longer apposite to mobilize duties of this kind as an argument against curiosity. Indeed, quite the opposite: in certain situations, traveling opens up the possibility of fulfilling specific duties of natural law, for example ensuring one's own survival. At this point, Montaigne distances himself, ever so cautiously, from Socrates, the overpowering exemplar for the *Essais*:

> What Socrates did near the end of his life, in considering a sentence of exile against him worse than a sentence of death, I shall never, I think, be so broken or so strictly attached to my own country as to do. … That was a very fastidious attitude for a man who considered the world his city. It is true that he disdained peregrination and had scarcely set foot outside the territory of Attica.
>
> (*E* 2.9; 743f.)

Montaigne realizes that his retreat to the chateau and tower does not automatically mean embarking on an exploration of the self. On the contrary: because we can only recognize ourselves in the mirror of the boundless world, traveling opens up diverse possibilities for self-exploration: "travel seems to me a profitable exercise. The mind is continually exercised in observing new and unknown things; and I know no better school, as I have often said, for forming one's life" (*E* 3.9; 744). With this depiction of traveling for the sake of traveling, Montaigne ultimately detaches curiosity from the purpose of self-exploration: "I undertake it [a journey] neither to return from it nor to complete it; I undertake only to move about while I like moving" (*E* 3.9; 747). Experiencing new worlds no longer merely serves as a mirror for gaining self-knowledge, but steps forward to become an end in itself. In the concluding chapter of the *Essais*, Montaigne casts aside circumspection and euphorically praises curiosity:

There is no end to our researches; our end is in the other world. It is a sign of contraction of the mind when it is content, or of weariness. A spirited mind never stops within itself; it is always aspiring and going beyond its strength; it has impulses beyond its powers of achievement. If it does not advance and press forward and stand at bay and clash, it is only half a life. Its pursuits are boundless and without form; its food is wonder, the chase, ambiguity.

(*E* 3.13; 817f.)

Through this enhancing of curiosity Montaigne becomes entangled in an increasingly rigid opposition to the ideal of *ataraxia*. As he now emphasizes, however, the restlessness that curiosity generates merges into the universal variety and mutability of being, and humans are not excluded: "I know well that if you take it literally, this pleasure in traveling is a testimony of restlessness and irresolution. And indeed these are our ruling and predominant qualities" (*E* 3.9; 756). In classical ancient and Christian moral theories, traveling motivated by the *sheer* desire to experience the new is the very symbol of humanity's succumbing and bondage to the frivolity of the ever-changing world. Against this background it is not surprising that in the essay *On Vanity* Montaigne undertakes nothing less than the revaluation of the spiritual core principle of ancient philosophies of life, namely the *tranquilitas animi*. The vanity of human life has no basis in the world's ceaseless changing and proliferating diversity; rather, it is futile and ridiculous to attempt to escape the mutability of all earthly existence by positing what is ultimately a hubristic ideal: to lead a life determined by reason. "The admonition of Ennius—'*There is no peace and quiet except that which reason has contrived*'—can be expressed more briefly in a word: 'Be wise'. This resolution is [however] beyond wisdom; [because] it is wisdom's work and product. The physician does thus who keeps shouting at a poor languishing patient to be cheerful" (*E* 3.9; 755).

The lofty ideals of existence proclaimed in ancient moral theories are, as Montaigne emphasizes not without a hint of irony, only suitable for strong characters; for run-of-the-mill people, rigorous ethics lead merely to hypocrisy: "I have not attained that disdainful vigour which finds fortitude in itself, which nothing can neither aid or disturb; I am a peg lower" (*E* 3.9; 748). Montaigne would like to maintain the perplexity of human life even in the face of death: "death is the same to me anywhere. However, if I had the choice, it would be, I think rather on horseback than in a bed, and out of my house, away from my people" (*E* 3.9; 747). At this point, Montaigne definitively leaves behind the classical ancient ideal of *ataraxia*, which had been always compared to a calm and still sea.

However, the insatiable striving for knowledge, as Montaigne demonstrates in another shift of perspective, presupposes a specific form of calm and composure. Only those who have freed themselves from the vices of pursuing glory, of greed and pride can open up to the new candidly; and only those who have found and practiced equanimity are in a position to consider a problem from a variety of perspectives. And thus, via detours, Montaigne arrives back at a positive view of tranquillity, but crucially now no longer as a superhuman ideal; rather, it is now itself the very prerequisite for the curious exploration of self and world. The Bordeaux copy features the following entry. "All the glory that I aspire to in my life is to have lived it tranquilly—tranquilly not according to Metrodorus or Arcesilaus or Aristippus, but according to me. Since philosophy has not been able to find a way to tranquillity that is suitable for all, let everyone seek it individually" (*E* 2.16; 471).

Since the *tranquilitas animi* was intimately tied to the virtues of self-control, any affirmation of insatiable curiosity unavoidably questions the ethical fundaments of ancient philosophies of life, especially the virtue of moderation. As with curiosity, Montaigne's examination of the virtue of temperance initially recalls the traditional critique of the intemperance of human desires: "And the greatest defect they [the ancient philosophers] observe in our nature is that our desires incessantly renew their youth ... We have one foot in the grave, and our appetites and pursuits are just being born" (*E* 2.28; 531). Because the insatiability of desires is not seated in the body, for its needs are always limited, but rather in the mind, Montaigne sees an internal connection between the insatiability of the urge to know and boundless needs. Although frequently bewailing that "the excess and unruliness of our appetite" outstrips "all the inventions with which we seek to satisfy it" (*E* 2.12; 335), it cannot be denied that the insatiability of desires is itself a gift of nature, and in recognition of this Montaigne thus explores the possibilities of finding an affirmative way of dealing with the unleashed dynamism of human needs. To this end, Montaigne begins by problematizing the animosity toward desire and lust inherent to the classical ancient ideal of rational self-control. Because reason cannot conceal its own weaknesses in harnessing desire and craving, then it is continuously forced into inventing new rules of mortification. Ultimately, reason destroys every kind of enjoyment in sensory pleasures. Humans seem a morbid species, condemned to suppressing sensual desires: "Hardly is it in his power, by his natural condition, to taste a single pleasure pure and entire, and still he is at pains to curtail that pleasure by his reason: he is not wretched enough unless by art and study he augments his misery" (*E* 1.30; 148). In the third book of the *Essais*, Montaigne therefore recommends a composed approach to the pleasures of the senses, a maxim that Villey assigns to the Epicurean phase of his thought. But Montaigne alters the Epicurean teaching on happiness. Whereas Epicurus defines pleasure defensively in the sense of an absence of pain, Montaigne considers not only a reconciliation between reason and pleasure, but indeed an intensifying of sensual pleasures. "I do not go about wishing that it [life] should lack the need to eat and drink, and it would seem to me no less excusable a failing to wish that need to be doubled" (*E* 3.13; 854).

Far greater problems are encountered when seeking a more relaxed way of dealing with the drives and desires of the soul, for the dynamic of perpetual intensification is inherent to them: "Whereas the passions that are all in the soul, such as ambition and avarice, give the reason much more to do, for it can find no help for them except in its own resources; nor are these appetites capable of satiety, but rather they grow sharper and increase by enjoyment" (*E* 2.33; 551). The excessive power of these desires is also evident in how they even keep the abandonment to sensual pleasures under control. Ambition and honor preserved Caesar from succumbing fully to love; at the same time, they drove Caesar to extend his power limitlessly and to be venerated like a god, which ultimately led to his downfall (*E* 2.33; 551–3). Utmost care is therefore needed when dealing with the passionate desires of the soul.

To sum up: Despite all skeptical caution, based on the examination of curiosity Montaigne paves the way for an epochal shift in occidental moral philosophy, marginalizing the classical ancient virtue of temperance common to Aristotelian, Stoic, and even Epicurean ethics (Friedrich 1993: 164).

8.3 Problematizations of the *dignitas hominis*: self-fashioning through writing

With the project of a self-exploration of mutable human nature, Montaigne initiates a profound transformation of Renaissance anthropology. Although there are no direct references to Manetti or Pico to be found in the *Essais* (Villey 1933: 266), central themes of Renaissance anthropology flow into Montaigne's thinking through the *Theologia naturalis* (1434-6) of the Spanish theologian Raimundus Sabundus, a work Montaigne translated into French at the wish of his father, publishing his translation in 1569. The study and analysis of Sabundus therefore offers a first inlet to Montaigne's position on the *dignitas hominis* literature of Renaissance philosophy.

In *Theologia naturalis* Sabundus asserts that Christian belief can be demonstrated infallibly solely by studying humanity, i.e., without recourse to the authority of the Bible (Sabundus 1966: Prol., 28*; 35*). Self-knowledge, or more precisely self-experience (*experientia*), opens up to a realm of maximal certainty (*maxime certum*), from which all sciences have to start (Sabundus 1966: Prol. 42*), clearly a manifestation of the anthropological turn initiated by the humanist movement (Bippus 2000: 192). Self-knowledge, however, is not a Cartesian result of the self-reflection of reason, but is attained through comparisons (*comparationes*) with nonhuman nature (Sabundus 1966: Prol. 47*). By reading the "book of nature" humans recognize that they are unique and superior to all other creatures because of self-reflective reasoning (Sabundus 1966: Prol. 36*).

Human free will faces a decision: to love the good or the bad. Because love grips and fills the whole being, when sheltering in the domain (*dominium*) of the beloved the lover merges, as it were, with the beloved. For this reason, love that loves the unalive, the creaturely, the human, or the divine is correspondingly called dead, creaturely, human, and divine love. And crucially: through love an individual can transform and metamorphose into a higher or lower entity—"Et ita homo potest per amorem mutari, transformari, et converti in aliam rem nobiliorem vel turpiorem libere et sponte"; Sabundus 1966: Tit. 131). Through this understanding of love, Sabundus gravitates close to the human power of self-transformation elaborated by Pico.

Sabundus's *Theologia naturalis* furnishes an initial insight into Montaigne's relationship to the *dignitas hominis* anthropology of the Renaissance. Like Sabundus, Montaigne identifies self-knowledge as the key to knowledge of the world. But unlike Sabundus, in his exploration Montaigne fails to find a secure foundation capable of supporting an edifice for the sciences; instead, all he sees is the changeability of human existence. This encounter with the unfathomable in human nature shakes his faith not only in the sciences but also in the traditional teaching that humans are made in the image of God (Martinet 1998: 251–83). Thus, in the *Apologia for Raymond Sebond*, Montaigne insists: "Let us consider for the moment man alone, without outside assistance, armed solely with his own weapons, and deprived of divine grace and knowledge, which is his whole honour, his strength, and the foundation of his being" (*E* 2.12; 328).

While Montaigne concords with Pico that humans can be "reborn" (*regenerari*) into the divine with the help of grace, once so elevated they must serve God not only in thought but also through action. Experience tellingly reveals, however, that Christians are no less at the mercy of their passions than other persons.

Indeed, even more poignantly, despite the Bible's exhortation to love one's enemy, Christian powers surpass, as Montaigne critically notes, all other peoples in their hatred and their use of violence (*E* 2.12; 322–4). Obviously, only very few humans are capable of accepting divine grace. It is against this backdrop of the disillusioning insight into the weakness of human nature that the true significance of pyrrhic skepticism is thrown into relief: "There is nothing in man's invention that has so much verisimilitude and usefulness [as Pyrrhonism]. It presents man naked and empty, acknowledging his natural weakness, fit to receive from above some outside power" (*E* 2.12; 375).

Although in the *Apologia*, by far the longest piece in the *Essais*, the exaggerated notions of humanity's place in the cosmos are vehemently opposed and dismantled, Montaigne does not simply return to the medieval theology of the *miseria hominis*. The exploration of his own changeable nature serves to expose both the Stoic-Christian image of humanityand the dynamic anthropology of the Renaissance to a veritable whirlwind of problematizing (Friedrich 1993: 114–18; Martinet 1998).

Pico opens the *Oratio* with the dictum of Hermes Trismegisthos: "homo miraculum est." For Montaigne, however, this dictum seems a highly questionable self-deification of humanity: "Listen to Trismegisthos praising our capacity: 'Of all wonderful things, thus has surpassed wonder, that man has been able to discover the divine nature and to make it, too'" (*E* 2.12; 395). But because God eludes human knowledge, all comparisons between God and humans are doomed to fail. The "essence" of humanity can only be determined through comparisons drawn from within the bounds of earthly reality. Classical ancient notions of human self-divination, for example Seneca's dictum "that the sage has courage like unto God" (*E* 2.12; 361), spring from vanity and the thirst for glory. And as if this were not a questionable enough source and motivation, Montaigne admonishingly elaborates its folly: "whereof to make gods of ourselves, like antiquity, passes the utmost bounds of feeblemindedness" (*E* 2.12; 383). Because God evades all comparisons, any attempt to determine human nature in the light of divine perfection loses its bearings, perpetually erring in the mist of human projections: "In short, the construction and the destruction of the deity, and its conditions, are wrought by man, on the basis of a relationship to himself. What a pattern and what a model! Let us stretch, exalt, and magnify human qualities all we please; inflate yourself, poor man, and more, and more, and more" (*E* 2.12; 396). In contrast to Pico, for the *Apologia* Montaigne thus aims to identify the illusory claims rooted in Christian teachings that the human is made in God's image, and then to "sharply and boldly shake the ridiculous foundations on which these false opinions are built" (*E* 2.12; 361). This critique of human hubris in self-deification is the reverse side of the apparent main thrust of Montaigne's *Essais* project: the plotting and presenting of his natural and everyday nature.

Unlike Pico, who calls humanity to self-transform into the angelic, Montaigne warns us to remain dispassionate and prosaic: "we have more need, for the most part, of lead than of wings, of coolness and repose than of ardour and agitation" (*E* 3.3; 624). In *De la vanité* he advocates a contrary trajectory of the mind: "Others study how to elevate their minds and hoist them up tight; I, how to humble mine and lay it to rest. It is defective only when it reaches out" (*E* 3.3; 623).

Self-deification leads to a distorted view of humanity's position in the cosmos. Blinded by the illusion of sharing in divine nature, the human being inevitably imagines that their place is in the midst of the world. In classical ancient cosmology, however, the earth is in the middle of the cosmos, but ranking below the celestial spheres. Montaigne, following Cusa, uses the premodern idea of the cosmos to dismantle the human overestimation of oneself. "Man, however, feels and sees himself lodged here, amid the mire and dung of the world, nailed and riveted to the worst, the deadest, and the most stagnant part of the universe, on the lowest story of the house and the farthest from the vault of heaven" (*E* 2.12; 330). If humanity's domicile is the lowest recess of the cosmos, then the ancient notion of the human as *contemplator mundi* literally has no solid ground. God has not placed human beings at the center of the world so that they can comfortably survey all things. For Montaigne, the claim raised by humanity "to recognize its beauty and its parts, the only one who can give thanks for it to the architect" (*E* 2.12; 329), is mere hubristic pretension without the slightest basis in experience. Whoever asserts this should "show us his letters patent for this great and splendid charge" (*E* 2.12; 329).

But the strategy laid out by Protagoras, to present human beings as deficient creatures only to then, in a second step, elevate them above the animals, also leads to distorting notions of human nature. With the ultimate result, the superiority of humans over the animal world, already achieved, comparisons are inevitably biased and yield only lopsided judgments. The starting assumption of such comparisons is already questionable, namely the idea that human beings' animal nature is inferior. As Montaigne recalls, like animals, humans can ensure that they have what they need to survive thanks to their physical capabilities. And the parallels continue: human skin, for example, provides sufficient protection from the rigors of the weather and exposure to the elements. Montaigne refers specifically to the native peoples of the Americas as evidence, for they still live naked, subsist on the fruits of the earth, and manage to maintain their ground vis-à-vis animals through the use of simple technology (*E* 2.12; 334f.). This rebuts the myth of Protagoras: "Nature has universally embraced all her creatures; and there is none that she has not very amply furnished with all powers necessary for the preservation of its being" (*E* 2.12; 333).

No less problematic for Montaigne is the distinction between human freedom and animal subjection to instincts. The dichotomy of "freedom versus subjugation under natural laws," which had become the centerpiece of Pico's anthropology, builds on a biased judgment. Already the assumption that animal behavior is completely determined by instincts is based on vague conjecture, because we have no insight into the inner impulses of animals. It is in this context that Montaigne formulated his query: "When I play with my cat, who knows if I am not a pastime to her more than she is to me?" (*E* 2.12; 331). And pondering this, then:

> So I say ... that there is no apparent reason to judge that the beasts do by natural and obligatory instinct the same things that we do by our choice and cleverness. We must infer from like results like faculties, and consequently confess that this same reason, this same method that we have for working, is also that of the animals.
>
> (*E* 2.12; 336f.)

Conversely, Montaigne adds for consideration that modes of behavior seen as typically human are quite possibly not the decisions of a free will, but stem from innate reactions and capabilities. The human being is also "fettered and bound, he is subjected to the same obligation as the other creatures of his class" (*E* 2.12; 336). It is only the "vanity of our presumption" that allows us to see our ability as the result of our powers in preference over "nature's liberality" (*E* 2.12; 337).

Ever since Cicero, the superiority of humanity over the animals had been explained through the dual gifts of reason and language, and in principle Montaigne upholds the uniqueness of human nature. What seems problematic to him is the exaggerated worth ascribed to human rational abilities. In agreement with Cusa, Montaigne accepts that humanity extrapolates the world through the creative production of language worlds in which sensory data are processed. However, because not only things but humans themselves are permanently subjected to change, then the idea of truth in the sense of an *adaequatio rei et intellectus* threatens to turn into a chimera. In this context Montaigne now refines the thesis on the unbridgeable gap between the cognitive faculties of humanity and the universe, which had already guided his problematizing of curiosity.

The dichotomy between the limitless universe and limited cognitive faculties is already discernible in the analysis of sensory perception. Whereas the intellect reveals a fickleness, the senses are "the base and the principles of the whole edifice of our knowledge" (*E* 2.12; 444). Nevertheless, for Montaigne it is beyond dispute that we perceive things not in themselves, but solely in accordance with our sensory organs. And elaborating on this, because the number of our sense organs is limited, then sensory perception inevitably reduces the infinite diversity of the universe. It seems that "mankind is doing something equally foolish for lack of some sense," and following on from this observation, then the question arises "whether by this lack the greater part of the face of things is hidden from us?" (*E* 2.12; 445). And indeed, it may be surmised that things can only be adequately known through an expanded spectrum of sense organs: "We have formed a truth by the consultation and concurrence of our five senses; but perhaps we needed the agreement of eight or ten senses, and their contribution, to perceive it certainly and in its essence" (*E* 2.12; 446).

The intellect arranges sensory data according to the idea of truth, but "it has no way to distinguish them or to pick out truth from falsehood" (*E* 2.12; 280; 421). Unlike Cusa, Montaigne does not distinguish between *ratio* and *intellectus*. The intellect is identical with human reason; true reason resides solely with God, and we therefore cannot lay claim to it (*E* 2.12; 405). Without the compass of innate ideas, human reason perceives things in the light of the constitutive state of each individual person: "Things in themselves may have their own weights and measures and qualities; but once inside, within us, she [the soul] allots them their qualities as she sees fit. Death is frightful to Cicero, desirable to Cato, a matter of indifference to Socrates" (*E* 1.50; 220). As the disputations among the philosophers shows, any random question evinces a tangled jumble of opinions (*E* 2.12; 421f.). But humans, as Montaigne observes with respect to himself, are also constantly changing their views, and not just about the external world but about themselves: "My footing is so unsteady and so insecure, I find it so vacillating and ready to slip, and my sight is so unreliable, that on an empty stomach I feel myself another man than after a meal" (*E* 2.12; 425). Applying human reason resembles a ship pitched and tossed by stormy seas: "My judgement does not always go forward; its floats, it strays, *Like a tiny boat, caught by a raging wind on the vast sea* [Catullus]" (*E* 2.12; 426). Against this background, for Montaigne even the voyage of Columbus turns into a symbol for the erring of human reason. The modern cosmographer's sense of superiority, pouring scorn over the classical ancient philosophers of nature, is queried in turn by Montaigne: "'What?' I said to him, 'Then did those who navigated under the laws of Theophrastus go west when they headed east? Did they go sideways, or backward?'" (*E* 2.12; 430). This means that "reason, of which, by its condition, there can be a hundred contradictory ones about one and the same subject, is an instrument of lead and wax, stretchable, pliable, and adaptable to all biases and all measures" (*E* 2.12; 425). For this reason, Montaigne rejects vehemently the *homo mensura* of Protagoras:

> Truly Protagoras was telling us some good ones, making man the measure of all things, who never even knew his own. If it is not he, his dignity will not permit another creature to have this advantage. Now, he being in himself so contradictory, and one judgement incessantly subverting another, that favourable proposition was just a joke which led us necessarily to conclude the nullity of the compass and the compasser.
>
> (*E* 2.12; 418)

In contrast to Montaigne's disbelief, Cusa had understood the principle of Protagoras positively: vis-à-vis the senses, the human intellect possesses the capability to map, like a "living compass," the immanent infinity of the world (cf. chap. 5.2); Montaigne reads it very differently, seeing the creative agility of reason more as a symptom of the pliancy and fickleness of the human mind. Because philosophical theology, which had founded and sustained the cohesion between reason and reality in Cusa's thought, has become questionable, interpretations based on language threaten to become indistinguishable from phantoms conjured by the imagination. Hence, people are in danger of becoming merely entangled in chimeras of their own making: "Men do not know the natural infirmity of their mind: it does nothing but ferret and quest, and keeps incessantly whirling around, building up and becoming entangled in its own work, like our silkworms, and is suffocated in it. *A mouse in a pitch barrel* [Erasmus]" (*E* 3.13; 817). Given the dizzying groundlessness of reason, humanity's deficiency resides less in instinctive animal nature than in reason and how imagination reacts to the maladies of life: "And if it is true that he alone of all the animals has this freedom of imagination and this unruliness in thought ... it is an advantage that is sold him very dear ... for from it springs the principal source of the ills that oppress him: sin, disease, irresolution, confusion, despair" (*E* 2.12; 336).

Despite the blunt unmasking of the weaknesses of the rational mind, Montaigne does not sink into an epistemological pessimism. While the gulf between reason and being may be unbridgeable, it also opens into a space for experiential and experimental thinking. In contrast to Aristotle's teleological concept of knowledge, Montaigne explores an "epistemology that is not one" (Kritzman 2009: 161).[4] Relieved of the burden of having to fulfill the exaggerated expectations of delivering truth, Montaigne argues the case for a new way of approaching the world with curiosity: a playful use of human cognitive faculties. Because any hope of attaining complete accordance with reality has evaporated, then the crucial point when exercising the intellect is now the how and not the what, the skillful craft of a composed argumentation weighing up factors rather than producing specific knowledge: "It is enough that my judgement is not unshod, of which these are the essays" (*E* 2.17; 495). The daily examination of cognitive faculties may not liberate humankind from the shrouds of mist produced by the myriad interpretations of the world, but nature does provide a certain orientation; for Montaigne, the voice of nature asserts itself behind humankind's back, as it were, i.e., through the tangle of human opinions. Despite this epistemological modesty, Montaigne by no means adopts a fully negative stance toward the idea of progress in the sciences; if the exaggerated ideal of complete knowledge is discarded, then in retrospect the tangled confusion of accumulated opinions can be understood as a process of experimenting with different perspectives. Montaigne thus sees his own "attempts" as possessing some significance for future generations: "I open up to whoever follows me some facility to enjoy it more at his ease, and make it more supple and manageable for him" (*E* 2.12; 421).

Along with this rehabilitation of the intellect, Montaigne cautiously re-evaluates the imagination positively (McFarlane 1968; Westerwelle 2002: 189–249; 438–44; Kritzman 2009: 29–50). Because no gift of nature is useless, then even an imagination that almost inevitably takes on a life of its own can be recast to have a positive function. Firstly, for Montaigne—in contrast to Descartes—the faculty of the imagination, as the connective link between the senses and the intellect, is indispensable for the cognitive process despite all its weaknesses. Moreover, it appears that nature, as Montaigne suspects, has bestowed humans with an imagination "for the consolation of our miserable and puny condition" (*E* 2.12; 360). The fantasy worlds produced by the imagination divert human attention not just from physical pain but also from emotional suffering: "For time, which she has given us as the sovereign physician of our passions, gains its effect principally in this way: furnishing our imagination with other and ever other business, it dissolves and breaks up that first sensation, however strong it may be" (*E* 3.4; 635).

This soothing function of the imagination sheds new light on the *Essais* overall, which Montaigne presents as a logbook of the phantasms produced by his imagination and the chimeras arising from flights of fancy. Resolving to keep an account of the daydreams spawned by his imagination, Montaigne is in effect also drawing on a gift of nature, utilizing it to soothe the sufferings of human life: "Though I tickle myself, I can scarcely wring a poor laugh out of this wretched body any more. I am merry only in fancy and in dreams, to divert by trickery the gloom of old age" (*E* 3.5; 639). The *Essais* thus serve not merely as a forum for self-exploration and scrutinizing the power of human judgment; rather, as Montaigne clarifies with increasing candor in the third book, they are also a source of amusement, or more precisely a distraction from the tribulations of old age: "In my youth I studied for ostentation; later, a little to gain wisdom; now, for recreation" (*E* 3.3; 629).

After reason and imagination, Montaigne finally examines creative freedom (*vis creativa*), where Renaissance anthropology had located the dignity of humanity. Considered in the framework of experimental self-examination, the hymns of praise for humanity's power to creatively transform overestimate the actual scope for action available to human freedom. Each and every person is already born with an individual nature, which can only be partially changed through upbringing: "Just consider the evidence of this in our own experience. There is no one who, if he listens to himself, does not discover in himself a pattern all his own, a ruling pattern [*une forme maistresse*], which struggles against education and against the tempest of the passions that oppose it" (*E* 3.2; 615). The scope to activate change is moreover severely restricted by education and morals: "Most of my actions are conducted by example, not by choice" (*E* 3.5; 648). The imprints of early childhood and adolescence, akin to a second nature, prove to be shackles as resistant to the freedom to creatively change as the bonds of first nature (*E* 3.2; 616; 3.10; 772). Moreover, as we age, the energy and will to once again give life a new orientation dwindles: "I am no longer headed for any great change or inclined to plunge into a new and untried way of life, not even a better one. It is too late to become other than I am" (*E* 3.10; 772).

Besides the conditionality resulting from natural and social factors, human freedom is also subjected to diverse restrictions from within. Bodily impulses evade the control of the mind (*E* 1.21; 72f.). As each one of us can observe and confirm, reason can do little when the power of passion is at work. And not least, the will becomes transfixed by the figments of imagination: "I am one of those who are very much influenced by the imagination. Everyone feels its impact, but some are overthrown by it. Its impression on me is piercing. And my art is to escape it, not to resist it" (*E* 1.21; 68). In short, the human being is not the sovereign master over their thoughts and actions but resembles a battlefield, with different impulses and passions locked in combat to gain ascendancy. And indeed, even more refined are moods, which are capable of turning into their opposite unexpectedly and suddenly: "No quality embraces us purely and universally" (*E* 1.38; 173). Our lives are characterized by inner contradictions: "But we are, I know not how, double within ourselves, with the result that we do not believe what we believe, and we cannot rid ourselves of what we condemn" (*E* 2.16; 469).

This insight into the apparent inherency of ambiguity in our inwardness casts, once again, a new light on the project of the *Essais*. The undistorted presentation of his inner self is not only endangered by outward conventions, a factor indicated in the preface to the reader, but moreover it is in itself compromised by human nature. Montaigne refuses, though, to abandon the project, for the blunt disclosure of the inner contradictions in human existence can give rise to a higher degree of truthfulness:

> Bashful, insolent; chaste, lascivious; talkative, taciturn; tough, delicate; clever, stupid; surly, affable; lying, truthful; learned, ignorant; liberal, miserly, and prodigal: all this I see in myself to some extent according to how I turn; and whoever studies himself really attentively finds in himself, yes, even in his judgment, this gyration and discord. I have nothing to say about myself absolutely, simply, and solidly, without confusion and without mixture, or in one word. *Distinguo* is the most universal member of my logic.
>
> (*E* 2.1; 242)

Without a firmly unified subject, the idea of the *self*-transformation of the human into the divine or the creaturely is a chimera. Montaigne thus pours scorn on the aggrandizing of humanity's chameleon-like changeability: "The chameleon takes the colour of the place where he is set; but the octopus himself assumes the colour he likes, according to the occasion ... We have some changes of colour in fear, anger, shame, and other passions that alter our complexion, but it is a passive effect, as with the chameleon" (*E* 2.12; 344). With this demonstration of the changeability and immanent discord of human nature, Montaigne stands undoubtedly in stark contrast to Pico's idea of creative self-fashioning, which was explicitly compared with the chameleon. The heterogeneous forces within us strain to move in different directions: "And for this reason we are wrong to try to compose a continuous body out of all this succession of feelings" (*E* 1.38; 174). Precisely the capacity to at least harness these forces means that humanity can attain a loose formation, but we can never unify them into a proper artwork: "We are all patchwork, and so shapeless and diverse in composition that each bit, each moment, plays its own game. And there is as much difference between us and ourselves as between us and others" (*E* 2.1; 244).

Against this background, Montaigne sharpens his criticism of the idea of human self-deification, which runs through the *Essais* from the outset. The ideal of perfected self-mastering and spiritualization, whereby humanity partakes in a divine or angelic nature, stands in stark contrast to human changeability. It is alleged that even Pyrrhus, whose equanimity was admired throughout antiquity, once lost his temper when a dog unexpectedly leaped on him. Drawing on this example, Montaigne quotes Pyrrhus' defense of his behavior: "'It is very difficult entirely to strip off the man'" (*E* 2.29; 533). But for Montaigne, the ideal of overcoming one's own human nature is askew for a variety of reasons. Besides the fact that humans are simply incapable of perfect self-control, a dangerous dynamic resides in any striving for superhuman ideals. As Montaigne clear-sightedly diagnoses, suppressing human nature only increases aggression and violence, and ultimately humanity sinks to an animal form of existence: "They [some philosophers] want to get out of themselves and escape from the man. That is madness: instead of changing into angels, they change into beasts; instead of raising themselves, they lower themselves. These transcendental humours frighten me, like lofty and inaccessible places" (*E* 2.13; 856).

According to Pico, humanity faces the decision to either degrade to the animal or to become reborn into the divine. In contrast, Montaigne calls on us to work up to the level of the human once again from animal existence, into which, in a paradoxical outcome, we have debased ourselves through the self-aggrandizing attempt to become angels. Because human reason obscures the orientation provided by nature through a myriad of opinions and phantasms, Montaigne comes up with a surprising change of perspective—man needs to orientate on animals: "and we must seek in the animals evidence of her [nature] that is not subject to favour, corruption, or diversity of opinion" (III, 12; 803). And "it is … a fine thing that our sapience learns from the very animals the most useful teachings for the greatest and most necessary parts of our life: how we should live and die, husband our possessions, love and bring up our children, maintain justice—a singular testimony of human infirmity" (*E* 3.12; 803).

The opposition between the volatility of the human mind and the naturalness of the animal world, which also encompasses the intimate relationship to nature displayed by simple farmers, forms only *one* sequence in Montaigne's perspectival problematizing of Renaissance anthropology. For animals, as Montaigne concedes, do not always precisely follow the path of nature (*E* 3.12; 803). With the *Essais* accumulating a flood of opinions scarcely imaginable in scope, ultimately Montaigne himself has long deviated from the unaltered voice of nature as seen in the life of animals. Consequently, Montaigne sees that the only alternative is to accept the mutable nature of humanity, which means vehemently rejecting Seneca's dictum that a human is "a vile and abject thing ... if he does not raise himself above humanity" [*QNat.* Praef 3]:

> That is a good statement and a useful desire, but equally absurd. For to make the handful bigger than the hand, the armful bigger than the arm, and to hope to straddle more than the reach of our legs, is impossible and unnatural. Nor can man raise himself above himself and humanity; for he can see only with his own eyes, and seize only with his own grasp.
>
> (*E* 2.12; 457)

Montaigne's criticism of human self-deification shares with Pico however the proviso of a divine act of grace. A human being can only overcome their mutable and contradictory nature "if God by exception lends him a hand." This means that it "is for our Christian faith, not for his Stoical virtue, to aspire to that divine and miraculous metamorphosis" (*E* 2.12; 457). Unless we are empowered by a divine power to attain a completely virtuous life, we need to remain faithful to human nature with all its contradictions.

This vision of a calm and simultaneously pleasurable relationship to the contradictions of human nature gives a new meaning to the "dignity" of humanity (Martinet 1998: 346–55). Here Montaigne even positively invokes the Christian metaphor of humanity's divine likeness: "It is an absolute perfection and virtually divine to know how to enjoy our being rightfully. We seek other conditions because we do not understand the use of our own, and go outside of ourselves because we do not know what it is like inside" (*E* 3.13; 857). Montaigne's penetrating examination of the *dignitas hominis* literature thus finds its succinct expression in the dictum that "'You are as much a god as you will own/That you are nothing but a man alone [Amyot's Plutarch]'" (*E* 3.13; 857).

The dialectic between the deconstruction and reconstruction of traditional notions of the dignity of humankind may also be exemplified by considering the creative power of human freedom, the centerpiece of Renaissance thought. Through his descriptions of the outer and inner compulsions constraining a natural human being, Montaigne demystifies the exalted ideas about the creative power of human freedom, and so the contrast to Pico's image of the human being as "molder and maker of thyself [*tui ipsius quasi plastes et fictor*]" (*Oratio*, 22) could scarcely be greater. At the same time, however, the idea of creative self-formation returns in the *Essais* as part of the reflections on the difficulties encountered when exploring and portraying the self, this time on an altogether different level. Montaigne's self-exploration is not merely descriptive, as he emphasizes when presenting the nominalist premises of the *Essais*, but a practice that brings forth order.

> In modelling this figure upon myself, I have had to fashion and compose myself so often to bring myself out, that the model itself has to some extent grown firm and taken shape. Painting myself for others, I have painted my inward self with colours clearer than my original ones. I have no more made my book than my book has made me—a book consubstantial with its author, concerned with my own self, an integral part of my life; not concerned with some third-hand, extraneous purpose, like all other books.
>
> (*E* 2.18; 504)

This means that despite the criticism of the idea of the human capacity to transform, Pico's image of the human as *plastes et fictor sui ipsius* returns on a new level. Nonetheless, the skepticism toward an overestimation of human creative power remains present in the *Essais*. The scope for forming the self through writing is, as Montaigne observes of himself, quite severely restricted by the burden of age: "Others form man; I tell of him, and portray a particular one, very ill-formed, whom I should really make very different from what he is if I had to fashion him over again. But now it is done" (III, 2; 610). Notwithstanding the resigned remark—"But now it is done"—there is a strong yearning for limitless self-formation: "If it were up to me to train myself in my own fashion, there is no way so good that I should want to be fixed in it and unable to break loose" (*E* 3.3; 621). Montaigne's call to us to reconcile with our mutable nature is thus simultaneously sustained by a fascination with the human capacity for self-transformation. Indeed, he goes even further. In Pico's conception the possibilities of self-formation are fixed from the outset by a hierarchy of values. Despite all the paeans to the chameleon-like essence of human beings, it is beyond question that the goal of human endeavor is to ascend to the divine. In contrast, for Montaigne both the cosmic hierarchical structure and the classical ancient ideals of deifying humanity have become dubious. Despite his sobering consideration of the limits of human freedom, Montaigne actually enhances the status afforded humanity's power of self-formation, in one respect even surpassing Pico. Montaigne encourages us to not be content with just seeking a better form of life conformable to reason but to move beyond any rational weighing up and to simply test out *other* forms of life. The typical early modern vision of an experimental approach to human capabilities resonates here: "Our principal talent is the ability to apply ourselves to various practices. It is existing, but not living, to keep ourselves bound and obliged by necessity to a single course. The fairest souls are those that have the most variety and adaptability" (*E* 3.3; 621).

8.4 What is civilization? The Americas in the mirror of "our" projections

Already in the address *To the Reader*, Montaigne refers to the peoples of the "New World," "which are said to live still in the sweet freedom of nature's first laws" (*E* To the Reader; 2). Thus, from the outset self-exploration moves within a mirror relationship to the New World. Montaigne even addresses this directly in the chapter *Of Cannibals* (*E* 1.31).[5] Like Las Casas, Montaigne vehemently denounces the violent excesses perpetrated by the Europeans in the New World. Given the unbridled destruction wreaked by the conquistadors, any talk of the "peoples of the New World" is nothing but a euphemism, "for the desolation of their conquest—a monstrous and unheard-of case—has extended even to the entire abolition of the names and former knowledge of the places" (*E* 2.18; 505f.).

In contrast to Las Casas or Sepúlveda, Montaigne shows no zeal to proselytize or civilize. Faced with the religiously motivated civil wars raging in Europe and aware of the advanced civilizations in the Far East, the claims to a superior European civilization have become questionable. For Montaigne, China's civilization is at least on a par with Europe: "We exclaim at the miracle of the invention of our artillery, of our printing; other men in another corner of the world, in China, enjoyed these a thousand years earlier" (*E* 3.6; 693). Against this background, the boundaries marking the difference between civilization and barbarism in the *Essais* begin to shift. Because Christianity has now also been sucked into the vortex of skeptical questionability, the idea of peaceful proselytization, as proposed by Las Casas, is no longer an option. Whereas Vitoria moved the listeners of his *Relectio de Indis* to a time before Europeans arrived on American soil, Montaigne reverses the encounter, the *Cannibals* essay ending with three Brazilian kings in Europe. Asked what has struck them the most about European life, they answer "that in the first place they thought it very strange that so many grown men, bearded, strong, and armed, who were around the king (it is likely that they were talking about the Swiss of his guard) should submit to obey a child, and that one of them was not chosen to command instead." Secondly, they were amazed "that there were among us men full and gorged with all sorts of good things, and that their other halves were beggars at their doors, emaciated with hunger and poverty"; and therefore, thirdly, "they thought it strange that these needy halves could endure such an injustice, and did not take the others by the throat, or set fire to their houses" (*E* 1.31; 159).

While Montaigne is articulating his own criticism of circumstances in Europe in the answers given by the Brazilians, the fictive judgment of European civilization through the Indians marks, as Hinrich Fink-Eitel has correctly emphasized, nothing less than an epochal reversal of the ethnological gaze, with Montaigne and Europe viewed from the outside (1994: 125; 129). Because, in the *Cannibals* essay, Montaigne admires the peoples of the Americas for their "original naturalness" (*E* 1.31; 153), unspoiled by harmful influences, he is still considered the founder of the modern myth of the "noble savage" (Kohl 1986: 21–32; Castany Prado 2016). This interpretation underestimates the complexity of Montaigne's considerations on the New World, however, which also problematize the stereotypes circulating about the peoples of the Americas, including the image of the "noble savage." As with the *dignitas hominis* thematic, Montaigne scrutinizes "our" ideas about the indigenous peoples of the Americas from different perspectives. The obstinacy that ethnocentric prejudices reveal in defying philosophical therapy is pointedly noted by Montaigne at the conclusion of the essay. Not without irony, yet another mark of condescending distinction is found: "All this is not too bad—but what's the use? They don't wear breeches" (*E* 1.31; 159).

To disengage from the prevailing opinions about the peoples of the New World, it is first necessary to examine the sources of information. In the early decades of the sixteenth century, as Montaigne critically notes, the New World was perceived in the light of the fantastical ideas of classical antiquity, for instance the Platonic legend of Atlantis. Montaigne's disengagement strategy thus juxtaposes the projections of humanist scholars to the accounts of a simple seafarer who, unfamiliar with the ancient classical world, had spent a number of years in the Americas.[6] The hope that accounts of unpretentious persons are more reliable than those of "scientific" geography is itself immediately called into question. Like everyone else, simple sailors also tend to fabricate and embellish legends: "But because they [topographers] have over us the advantage of having seen Palestine, they want to enjoy the privilege of telling us news about all the rest of the world" (*E* 1.31; 152). For Montaigne, the production of fantastical worlds is anchored in the *conditio humana*, and hence any hopes of gaining objective reports about the peoples of the New World have to be relinquished. The confusion deliberately sown about the sources is obviously staged to shake and unsettle the authority of evidence, creating an open space to think freely (Tournon 2000: 220f.). The *Of Cannibals* essay is not all that concerned with exactly describing the lives of the peoples of the Americas; its real thrust is to examine "our" notions *about* the "barbarians."

To this end, Montaigne distinguishes between the various meanings of "barbarian." Firstly, "we" call everything "barbarian" that deviates from our mores and customs. In this case, the voice of reason is fully drowned out by the habits of the respective land. Secondly, peoples are counted among the barbarians who do not cultivate the sciences and the arts, who live without laws and morality, or even more simply who are far removed from Christian religion. For Montaigne, however, a lack of civilization is not necessarily a deficiency; the peoples who had still lived in the original order of creation during the earliest periods of humankind were of course unfamiliar with our civilizing achievements. Thus, the "barbarism" of the peoples of the Americas can be recast: "These nations, then, seem to me barbarous in this sense, that they have been fashioned very little by the human mind" (*E* 1.31; 153). Their natural purity, Montaigne emphasizes, surpasses even the classical ancient ideas of the peoples of the Golden Age or the legendary island of Atlantis.

> This is a nation, I should say to Plato, in which there is no sort of traffic, no knowledge of letters, no science of numbers, no name for a magistrate or for political superiority, no custom of servitude, no riches or poverty, no contracts, no successions, no partitions, no occupations but leisure ones, no care for any but common kinship, no clothes, no agriculture, no metal, no use of wine or wheat.
>
> (*E* 1.31; 153)

Amply supplied with the gifts of nature, there are no divisive struggles for survival among the peoples of the Americas. Indeed, as Montaigne notes, they have yet to have the need to invent the relevant language: "The very words that signify lying, treachery, dissimulation, avarice, envy, belittling, pardon—unheard of" (*E* 1.31; 153).

Montaigne abruptly breaks off the description of the natural simplicity of the peoples of the Americas, however. Instead of describing a naturally peaceful disposition, which is the finishing touch in Las Casas's image of the "noble savage," Montaigne suddenly changes tack and depicts the savageries of tribal wars, polygamy, and cannibalism. In contrast to Sepúlveda, who took all this to be proof of the inhuman barbarism of the Amerindian peoples, Montaigne practices here the art of differentiation. On the one hand, he depicts, without playing it down, the violence unleashed in tribal conflicts, "which never end but in slaughter and bloodshed" (*E* 1.13; 155). But unlike the Europeans, who wage war against other nations solely because of the immoderateness of their needs, Montaigne emphasizes that these peoples live "still in that happy state of desiring only as much as their natural needs demand" (*E* 1.31; 156). Thus, for Montaigne, the Indians go to war not because of economic interests but like Leonidas as a demonstration of bravery. In a similar way, Montaigne then addresses cannibalism, the main characteristic in the image of the "savage beast." On the one hand, the moral reprehensibility of cannibalistic practices is beyond dispute; on the other, Montaigne criticizes the self-righteousness of the Europeans, who have plenty of blood on their hands.

> I am not sorry that we notice the barbarous horror of such acts, but I am heartily sorry that, judging their faults rightly, we should be so blind to our own. I think there is more barbarity in eating a man alive than in eating him dead; and in tearing by tortures and the rack a body still full of feeling, in roasting a man bit by bit, in having him bitten and mangled by dogs and swine (as we have not only read but seen within fresh memory, not among ancient enemies, but among neighbours and fellow citizens, and what is worse, on the pretext of piety and religion), than in roasting and eating him after he is dead.
>
> (*E* 1.31; 155)

The actual point of Montaigne's criticism of the ethnocentric delusion of European reason is first revealed when compared in retrospect to the single steps of the argumentation in the *Cannibals* essay. Through the juxtaposition of the images of the "noble savage" and the "savage beast," the formative influences on the European idea of the Amerindian peoples since Columbus, locking them as it were in a binary opposition, they are exposed *as* projections of our mind. In a second step, Montaigne attacks the self-righteousness of Europeans directly. The violent excesses and moral brutalization stirred up in the turmoil of the civil wars, the indiscriminate tyranny of rulers, the widespread practice of torture, and last but not least the trials against witches—all these are striking testimony of the moral decay of European culture. In the *Apologia for Raymond Sebond*, Montaigne sarcastically notes: "It is credible that there are natural laws, as may be seen in other creatures; but in us they are lost; that fine human reason butts in everywhere, domineering and commanding, muddling and confusing the face of things in accordance with its vanity and inconsistency" (*E* 2.12; 438). Montaigne is thus reversing Sepúlveda's view of the New World: it is not the Amerindians but the Europeans who have sunk into the subhuman through barbaric morals. Because the voice of nature is drowned out by a reason that has lost its bearings, Montaigne considers it necessary to first contrast European culture with the unadulterated naturalness of the Amerindians. In the image of the "noble savage," those characteristics return, now positively connoted, with which Sepúlveda had identified the inhuman barbarism of the Amerindians: the peoples of the New World live "without letters, without law, without king, without religion of any kind" (*E* 2.12; 362). In short, Europe, itself deeply mired in incomprehensible barbarism, needs to emulate the naturalness of the Indians and in this way elevate itself to an existence worthy of humans. The dichotomy between the naturalness of the Indians and the barbaric civilization of Europe is scaled back, however, in the next step: Montaigne suddenly inscribes the idyllic image of the noble savage with gruesome tribal wars and cannibalistic practices. Once the Amerindian cultures have again lost their exemplary function for Europe, a new constellation arises—barbarism obviously exists in both Europe and the New World.

With the confusing interplay between the imagery of the "noble savage" and "savage beast" Montaigne attempts to prize open the rigidified ideas about the New World. To this end, he overwhelms his readers with countless accounts of the customs and habits of foreign peoples: "The murder of infants, the murder of fathers, sharing of wives, traffic in robberies, license for all sorts of sensual pleasures, nothing in short is so extreme that it is not accepted by the usage of some nation" (*E* 2.12; 437). Due to this presentation of the diversity of moral ideas, Montaigne has always been seen as a "pioneer of 'cultural relativism'" (Duval 1983: 95). But by no means do the *Essais* steer the reader into a moral no-man's-land. On the contrary, Montaigne is unequivocal in the *Cannibals* essay: "So we may well call these people barbarians, in respect to the rules of reason [!], but not in respect to ourselves, who surpass them in every kind of barbarity" (*E* 1.31; 156). The "rules of reason" obviously revolve around a universally valid nucleus of morality, including most prominently the prohibition on killing but also the principle of truthfulness, the source from which Montaigne criticizes not only the cannibalism of the Amerindians but also the violent atrocities in Europe, in particular the practice of torture: "Very inhumanly, however, and very uselessly, in my opinion. Many nations, less barbarous in this respect than the Greeks and Romans who call them barbarians, consider it horrible and cruel to torture and break in pieces a man of whose guilt you are still in doubt" (*E* 2.5; 266). As Montaigne admonishes with respect to the witchcraft trials, dubious religious reasons may not be permitted to suspend the prohibition on killing: "To kill men, we should have sharp and luminous evidence; and our life is too real and essential to vouch for these supernatural and fantastic accidents" (*E* 3.11; 789). At this juncture, Montaigne's skepticism is not concerned with dissolving all core moral values but in fact serves to preserve their integrity.

In stark contrast to his initial depiction of the unspoiled naturalness of the Indians, Montaigne suddenly shifts tack in the second section of the *Cannibals* essay and points out their civilizing accomplishments, most predominantly their technical manual skills, the imposing buildings accommodating several hundred persons, and tools and weapons, highly effective although not made of iron but carved from particularly hard wood. After describing their religious institutions, Montaigne finally turns to their artistic achievements: "not only is there nothing barbarous in this fancy, but it is altogether Anacreontic. Their language, moreover, is a soft language, with an agreeable sound, somewhat like Greek in its endings" (*E* 1.31; 158). The piece *Of Coaches* (*E* 3.6) continues the depiction of their civilizing achievements, Montaigne praising above all the masterly technological innovations of the Aztecs and Incas (cf. Hampton 1997). The road from Quito to Cuzco, three hundred miles long and twenty-five paces wide, paved and lined on both sides with walls and trees, is a true marvel of the art of engineering: "neither Greece nor Rome nor Egypt can compare any of its works, whether in utility or difficulty or nobility" (*E* 3.6; 698).

The dichotomy between nature and culture, employed to initially delineate the relationships between Europe and the Amerindian peoples, is thus dismantled by Montaigne in the second section of the *Cannibals* essay (Duval 1983). This departure from the idea of primitive peoples devoid of culture means however that the foundation laid to support the imagery of the "noble savage" and the "savage beast" collapses. And moreover, after a century of colonial domination and violently imposed "civilization," the whole idea of a "*New* World" is dragged into the maelstrom of collapse triggered by skeptical scrutiny. At the very moment that Montaigne acknowledges, in the *Cannibals* essay, independent civilization in the Americas, he begins to question the romanticizing notion of a "New World." Criticizing the idealization of the "otherness" of the American peoples is presaged, paradoxically, in the discourse with the three Brazilians:

> Three of these men, ignorant of the price they will pay some day, in loss of repose and happiness, for gaining knowledge of the corruptions of this side of the ocean; ignorant also of the fact that of this intercourse will come their ruin (which I suppose is already well advanced: poor wretches, to let themselves be tricked by the desire for new things, and to have left the serenity of their own sky to come and see ours!).
>
> (*E* 1.31; 158f.)

While Montaigne once again takes up the opposition between the naturalness of the Indians and depraved European civilization, here the boundaries between nature and culture are now permeable. For example: reproaching the Brazilians for letting their curiosity spur them to travel to Europe contradicts Montaigne's general recommendation to visit foreign lands in order "to bring back knowledge of the characters and ways of those nations, and to rub and polish our brains by contact with those of others" (*E* 1.26; 112). By departing for Europe, the Brazilians have followed a maxim Montaigne considers essential for educating young men and which he, as has been shown, lets himself be guided by in the *Essais*. Just as Montaigne detached himself from the ancient ideal of *ataraxia* by pursuing the path of inquisitiveness and self-exploration, with their journey to Europe the Brazilians also forsook the calm happiness of their customs and morals. For this reason, Montaigne definitively dissolves the dichotomy between the Old and New Worlds at the end *Of Cannibals*. After a century of transatlantic relations, the indigenous peoples of the Americas are infected with the same immoderateness as Europeans.

At this point, the question emerges as to the criterion with which to judge Europe's immoderateness, this seemingly irrepressible drive toward excess, which is beginning to spread across the globe. Having succumbed to one of the immoderate indulgences of Renaissance culture by pursuing the inquisitive self-exploration of his changeable being, Montaigne further elaborates this question—for him potentially explosive—in *Of Coaches* (*E* 3.6). To critically examine the immoderateness of his own century, Montaigne evokes the temperate order of Greco-Roman culture. The humanist veneration of antiquity comes into play again, this time as a mirror: our habitual and rigid notions about the connections between the Americas and Europe are to be revived. From the perspective of the Old World, the Amerindian peoples appear to be at the dawn of an aspiring cultural development. As Montaigne attempts to show by referring to the architectural achievements of the Incas and Aztecs, some of the civilizing accomplishments are already comparable to those of ancient Western cultures. In contrast, modern European societies, as reflected in the mirror of antiquity, appear to be in a state of irreversible disintegration and on the verge of completely falling apart. Moreover, the unleashing of economic forces and the ongoing politico-religious divisiveness means that Europe is not only plunging itself into ruin but impelling the New World to follow suit:

> we took advantage of their ignorance and inexperience to incline them the more easily toward treachery, lewdness, avarice, and every sort of inhumanity and cruelty, after the example and pattern of our ways. Who ever set the utility of commerce and trading at such a price? So many cities razed, so many nations exterminated, so many millions of people put to the sword, and the richest and most beautiful part of the world turned upside down, for the traffic in pearls and pepper! Base and mechanical victories! Never did ambition, never did public enmities, drive men against one another to such horrible hostilities and such miserable calamities.
>
> (*E* 2.6; 695)

Unlike *Of Cannibals*, Montaigne's *Of Coaches* highlights the brutality of the conquistadors. The Amerindian cultures have been either obliterated by European colonial powers or irreversibly deformed through the immoderate currents in European culture. At this point, where any hope for a positive future threatens to vanish, Montaigne presents a surprising fiction. Because contemporary Europe has disqualified itself as a cultural model, antiquity is suddenly installed as the hope for civilized development. The inspiring figures of antiquity

> would have gently polished and cleared away whatever was barbarous in them [the Amerindians], and would have strengthened and fostered the good seeds that nature had produced in them, not only adding to the cultivation of the earth and the adornment of cities the arts of our side of the ocean, in so far as they would have been necessary, but also adding the Greek and Roman virtues to those originally in that region.
>
> (*E* 3.6; 694f.)

Imploringly he asks: "Why did not such a noble conquest fall to Alexander or to those ancient Greeks and Romans?" (*E* 3.6; 694f.).

The historical fiction of a cultural synthesis between Amerindians and Greco-Roman antiquity primarily serves the purpose of prizing open the rigidified imagery and ideas about the connections between Europe and the Americas. As previously with the stereotypes of the "noble savage" and the "savage beast," Montaigne puts into perspective his own utopia of an integration of the Amerindian peoples into the *Imperium Romanum*: "Finding myself useless for this age, I throw myself back upon that other, and am so bewitched by it that the state of that ancient Rome, free, just, and flourishing (for I love neither her birth nor her old age), interests me passionately" (*E* 3.9; 763). The idealization of the Roman empire springs from a personal inclination: "Likewise this is generally true of me, that of all the opinions antiquity has held of man as a whole, the ones I embrace most willingly and adhere to most firmly are those that despise, humiliate, and nullify us most" (*E* 2.17; 480). Nonetheless, Montaigne once more takes up the fiction of the Romans crossing the Atlantic, which in fact had been considered in ancient times, and employs it as the starting point for a vision of a peaceful encounter between Europe and the Amerindian peoples.

> What an improvement that would have been, and what an amelioration for the entire globe, if the first examples of our conduct that were offered over there had called those peoples to the admiration and imitation of virtue and had set up between them and us a brotherly fellowship and understanding! How easy it would have been to make good use of souls so fresh, so famished to learn, and having, for the most part, such fine natural beginnings!
>
> (*E* 3.6; 695)

In his search for a positive vision of relations between Europe and the peoples of the Americas, Montaigne tones down markedly both the idealization of the Indians and the strident self-criticism of European civilization. Although betrayed in the conquest of the Americas by the Europeans themselves, the moral traditions of Europe can still be commended for emulation to the peoples of the New World. Any form of civilization that is violent or forcibly imposed remains categorically precluded, however.

Even if Montaigne presents no considerations on the law of nations in the narrower sense, his image of a peaceful encounter between Europe and the Americas comes close to Vitoria's cosmopolitanism. As if it were self-evident, Montaigne presupposes Vitoria's *ius peregrinandi*: "I am so sick for freedom, that if anyone should forbid me access to some corner of the Indies, I should live distinctly less comfortably. And as long as I find earth or air open elsewhere, I shall not lurk in any place where I have to hide" (*E* 3.13; 820). Sympathy for other peoples, at times effusive, replaces the Christian zeal to proselytize: "Not because Socrates said it, but because it is really my feeling, and perhaps excessively so, I consider all men my compatriots, and embrace a Pole as I do a Frenchman, setting this national bond after the universal and common one" (*E* 3.9; 743). Thus, strewn through the *Essais* are the traces of a utopia—universal fraternity. Montaigne is enough of a skeptic however to simultaneously recognize that the idea of embracing all people springs from an exuberance of feeling.

This means that aspects of a Christian world society have largely vanished in Montaigne's cosmopolitanism. Because the very sense and spirit of "civilization" have become highly questionable, and need to be cleared of rash prejudices, Montaigne disavows any right to a civilizing mission, but also the obligation of humanitarian intervention to save innocent people. In effect, "Montaigne forces his sixteenth-century readers to revise their preconceptions. Before appropriating to 'civilize' other peoples, we must ask: 'What is civilization?'" (Rigolot 1992: 21).

Part III

Foundations of modern science, politics, and economy in the philosophy of the seventeenth century

The seventeenth century is considered the period when the founding thinkers of modernity emerged. The central debates of Euro-American philosophy continue to move within the horizon of the problems set by Bacon, Galileo, Descartes, and Hobbes. As I wish to show in the following studies on Francis Bacon, Thomas Hobbes, and John Locke, the laying of the first theoretical foundations for the main subsystems of modern societies can be analyzed in the philosophy of the seventeenth century. With his *Instauratio magna* Francis Bacon lays an important foundation for modern science; Thomas Hobbes considers himself the founder of a new political philosophy; and in his *Second Treatise on Government* John Locke formulates, in the midst of a theory of the state, a philosophical justification for a modern market economy. Science, the state, and the market economy crystallize in Bacon, Hobbes, and Locke as independent social realities driven forward by an immanent logic. At the same time, however, merged into these guiding ideas of modern science, the modern territorial state, and a market economy are, suitably modified, numerous motifs from the Renaissance. Francis Bacon connects the program of an experimental science with the vision of an unlimited unleashing of the productive forces of humans and nature; Thomas Hobbes constructs the modern state on the basis of the extreme scenario of a universal unfettering of power, the *bellum omnium contra omnes*; and with his justification of a money economy, John Locke lays an important foundation for the idea of limitless economic growth.

9

Francis Bacon's vision of modern science and limitless technological progress

In the eighteenth century, Francis Bacon, along with Galileo and Descartes, was still celebrated as a founder of the modern natural sciences.[1] As Bacon's vision of a union between science and technology finally materialized on a large scale in the industrial age, his star was paradoxically on the wane. Justus von Liebig questioned Bacon's competence as a scientist. In the twentieth century, Karl Popper rejected Bacon's inductive method: "his myth of scientific method that starts from observation and experiment and then proceeds to theory" has next to nothing to do with the real practice of modern science. For Popper, in fact, the path of science runs the other way around, science proceeding from theories, which are then verified in experiments: "Bold ideas, unjustified anticipations and speculative thought, are our only means for interpreting nature: our only organon, our only instrument, for grasping her" (Popper 2002: 279f.). Even though Popper's criticism of the *Novum organum* misses the point (Urbach 1987), it is undeniable that Bacon, who held numerous political offices, including that of Lord Chancellor, produced hardly any scientific findings. Eduard J. Dijksterhuis contends that the history of scientific knowledge can be written without even mentioning Bacon: "if Bacon with all his writings were to be removed from history, not a single scientific concept, not a single scientific result would be lost" (1961: IV.183; 387).

Bacon's rehabilitation as the founder of modern science was initiated at the end of the nineteenth century by James Ellis, one of the compilers of the edition of his writings still standard today. According to Ellis, the importance of Bacon "is neither to the technical part of his method nor to the details of his view of nature and progress of science that his fame is justly owing. His merits are of another kind. They belong to the spirit rather than to the positive precepts of his philosophy" (1963: 64). Despite his critique, Dijksterhuis also concedes that "Bacon had an extremely stimulating influence on scientific research in England, while owing to his pregnant formulations he was also a herald of the modern era for many continental scholars" (Dijksterhuis 1961: IV.192). It is in this sense that Wolfgang Krohn has appreciatively called Francis Bacon's contribution to modern science a "philosophy of scientific research" (1987: 13).

Nevertheless, reservations about Bacon have not ceased. The line of thought in the twentieth century that was critical of progress took aim at precisely the "spirit" of Baconian science. If shortly after the Second World War Farrington was still celebrating Bacon as a "philosopher of industrial science," Max Horkheimer and Theodor W. Adorno criticized his thinking as the very origin of the power syndrome driving modern reason. This criticism of Bacon focusing on power has enjoyed a renaissance among feminist philosophers and ecological thinkers. According to Evelyn Fox Keller, the repressive spirit of Baconian science is revealed by the sexual metaphors mirroring the patriarchal power relations of the early modern period.[2] Carolyn Merchant has seen analogies to the torture practices used in the witch trials in the method of the experimental interrogation of nature.[3] These two radical critiques of Bacon have however triggered controversy within feminist philosophy. Herta Nagl-Docekal has warned strongly against sweepingly discrediting the program of a scientific mastering of nature on the basis of a justified criticism of Bacon's patriarchal idea of marriage.[4] For Uta von Winterfeld, Bacon's interpretation of the human–nature relationship is ambivalent. Even if humans "can become mighty manipulators" through science, still shimmering through in his thinking is the "attentive observer who beholds and reveres the forms and workings of a spawning nature" (Winterfeld 2006: 164).

The main thrust of the following studies on Bacon can be sketched against this background. Interest centers around the fundamental objectives of the new science, not the details of the method, which, as Bacon himself noted, can be merely provisional in character. It only stands to reason that methodological questions need to be continually reset as science progresses. Bacon explains the tasks of the new science in very distinct discourses, ranging from the interpretation of biblical and mythical texts, through philosophical reflections on history and nature, through to moral and political considerations. Accordingly, I believe it necessary to approach Bacon's vision of a new science from various angles. The first step, a sketch of the contours of the vision of a new science in conjunction with the idols of the mind, is to set the theological framework, or more precisely to present the idea of a "restoration of paradise" and the "historical-philosophical" place of science in the age of discoveries (section 9.1 of this chapter). A reconstruction of the philosophical foundations of the new science looks at the philosophical premises regarding productive nature, the much-criticized connection between science and power (section 9.2), and the incipient steps toward a moral-philosophical grounding (section 9.3). To conclude, I will also consider the anthropological and cosmopolitan dimensions of the new science, which Bacon explicates mainly in *New Atlantis* (section 9.4). Despite the ambition to place science on a new footing, Bacon remains deeply influenced by the spirit and scientific awakenings of the Renaissance (Jardine 1974; Schmidt-Biggemann 1983: 213–25), and this even percolates down into the forms of his literary style (Vickers 1968). This is why the de-limitations of Renaissance philosophy recur, in surprising modifications, in his vision of a new science, whether as the ideas of a limitless universe, of *curiositas*, or of a world society.

9.1 *The Great Instauration*: the partial restoration of paradise in the age of Columbus

As the title of his main work *Instauratio magna imperii humani in universum* announces, in his conception of a new science Bacon is pursuing no less a goal than the restoration of the original power that humanity had over the universe. Bacon's assuredness of proclaiming a new epoch of humankind springs from a blunt analysis of the human mind on the one hand, which is combined with a radical critique of the science of the classical ancient world, and from theological and "historic-philosophical" reflections on the other, which promise the restoration of paradise and the constant discovery of new continents of knowledge.

Already in the early fragment *The Masculine Birth of Time* (1603), Bacon polemically aims a sweeping blow at the philosophical tradition. Aristotle is berated as the "worst of sophists" (Farrington 1964: 63), Plato as a "welling poet" and "deluded theologian" (Farrington 1964: 64). Cicero, Seneca, Galen, and indeed also Plutarch, all held in particularly great regard in the Renaissance, are condemned as unoriginal followers of Plato (Farrington 1964: 64). Although sweeping, the blow is not aimed at the philosophical tradition *in toto*. Along with the pre-Socratics (Pythagoras, Heraclitus, Democritus), Epicurus, Pyrrhus, and above all Democritus receive special approval: "Democritus attributed to nature immense variety and infinite succession, thus setting himself apart from all other philosophers, who were prisoners of their times and slaves of fashion" (Farrington 1964: 71).

Faced with the incalculable diversity and changeability of the world, Michel de Montaigne had already called for skeptical modesty. While Bacon sets the goal of overcoming Montaigne's skepticism, in the theory of the idols, which forms the negative starting point for founding a new science, Bacon takes up Montaigne's observations on the weaknesses of human reason. In *Novum organum* Bacon famously distinguishes four kinds of idols of the human mind, which are to be strictly kept apart from the divine ideas, i.e., the structures ordering the universe. The "Idols of the Theatre" are the wrong paths taken by the philosophical schools, concretely the rationalism founded by Aristotle, alchemy, and the commingling of theology into philosophy, established by Pythagoras and Plato, a trait that has held the human spirit captive for millennia (Farrington 1964: 71). The "Idols of the Marketplace" refer to bedevilment of human reason through vulgar everyday language (*N.O.* 1.59–60). Everyday language, but indeed also the philosophical language anchored in it, contains the names of non-existent things, e.g., fate, prime mover, etc. But so too the names of existing things are "confused and ill-defined, and hastily and irregularly derived from realities" (*N.O.* 1.60; works 4.61). This is why the confusion caused by language cannot be overcome through definitions, "since the definitions themselves consist of words, and the words beget others" (*N.O.* 1.59; works 4.61). The "Idols of the Cave" encompass the individual conditionality of human reason, such as natural dispositions, upbringing, habits, and the specific circumstances of one's life. "The Idols of the Tribe," however, "have their foundation in human nature itself, and in the tribe or race of men" (*N.O.* 1.41 and 45; works 4.54). According to Bacon, among the regrettable peculiarities of the intellect is the disposition to frivolously see more order in things than actually exists (*N.O.* 1.45; works 4.56). Moreover, the human intellect tends to be taken in by immediately given things, fails to examine remote things because of indolence, and follows authorities out of gullibility *(N.O.* 1.47–9). Not least, the human mind gravitates to biasedness and partisanship: "For what a man had rather were true he more readily believes" (*N.O.* 1.49; works 4.57).

Montaigne had already ridiculed the *homo mensura* proposition of Protagoras because of "the nullity of the compass and the compasser" (*E* 2.12; 418), i.e., that of human reason. For Bacon, too, the human mind is "like a false mirror, which, receiving rays irregularly, distorts and discolours the nature of things by mingling its own nature with it" (*N.O.* 1.41; works 4.54).

With notion of the "Idols of the Tribe," however, Bacon himself threatens the project of renewing the sciences. If these "Idols of the Tribe" are grounded in human nature itself, then Bacon must show how the human mind can escape the universal nexus of delusion. Descartes and later Kant responded to the challenge of radical skepticism with a rigorous reflection on the limits of human reason. Bacon, though, refrains from undertaking a strict self-reflection of reason (Krohn 1987: 98). Instead, in the footsteps of Montaigne, Bacon looks for a pragmatic alternative. By instigating a skeptical play of perspectives, Montaigne attempted to examine how the human mind—through interpretations of the world—has entangled itself in a spiderweb of its own creation. In contrast, Bacon replaces the restless wandering curiosity of Montaigne with a methodologically disciplined experimental science, which overcomes, at least partially, the weaknesses of the human mind and is thus capable of changing the *conditio humana*.

Theological framework: the restoration of paradise

Because the new science aims at changing the position of humanity in relation to the world overall, Bacon places his idea of a new science in a theological framework. The term *instauratio* alludes to a theological motif, namely the Jewish hope that Solomon's temple be rebuilt (Whitney 1986: 23–5; McKnight 2006: 45–71). Moreover, Bacon defends the new science against theological reservations by providing an independent interpretation of the biblical narrative of creation and the fall of humankind.

For a long time, Bacon's religious vindication of the new science was dismissed as merely an embellishment typical of the age. The secularized portrayal of Bacon's thought has been meanwhile corrected: "Bacon's politicotheology is not an easy part in Bacon's thought, but it is crucial for an understanding of his natural philosophy" (Gaukroger 2001: 76). Bacon's theory of the idols, starting from the assumption that the human mind has become fully corrupted, cannot be understood without reference to the biblical narrative of the fall of humankind (Sessions 1996: 29). Conversely, the twentieth-century critics of progress have presented Bacon's idea of recreating paradise to be the centerpiece of his thought. Faced with the ecological crisis and the totalitarian temptations of political philosophy in modernity, such critics have come to consider the *Instauratio magna* as the very symbol of the hubris of secular modernity. Given this background, it seems necessary to look back at some of the basic lineaments that Bacon maps out in his theological vindication of modern science.

As Bacon emphasizes with respect to the biblical account of creation in Genesis 2, the human being is created to contemplate and master the world: "After the creation was finished, it is set down unto us that man was placed in the garden to work therein; which work so appointed to him could be no other than work of contemplation" (*Adv. Learn.* 1; works 3.296). In his admiration of the world, Adam is emulating God, who rested on the seventh day of creation and contemplated his work: "we see the day wherein God did rest and contemplate his own works, was blessed above all the days" (*Adv. Learn.* 1; works 3.296). In paradise, human dominion over the world rests on the act, carried out without force, "to give every living creature a name according to his propriety" (*Val. Term.*; works 3.219). This original union of contemplation, naming, and dominion over nature was lost irreversibly as a result of Adam's fall. The misdeed stemmed not from striving for a knowledge of nature, but from yearning for a tree giving a definitive knowledge of good and evil, "for behold it was not that pure light of natural knowledge, whereby man in paradise was able to give unto every living creature a name according to his propriety, which gave occasion to fall; but it was an aspiring desire to attain to that part of moral knowledge which defineth of good and evil" (*Val. Term.*; works 3.219).

Because the fall is limited to the realm of morality—symbolized by the tree of knowledge of good and evil—Hans Blumenberg has critically noted that Bacon basically bisects the Enlightenment. Humans gain "the license to be or become a being empowered to exercise dominion over nature while remaining subservient to the divine will, that is, morality" (2022: 72).

But according to Bacon, it was not the search for what is morally correct that led to the fall, but "the ambitious and proud desire of moral knowledge [*ambitiosa illa et imperativa* [sic!] *scientia moralis*] to judge good and evil" (*Instauratio magna*, Praef., works 1.132; 4.20); or, in another formulation, "the proud knowledge of good and evil, with an intent to give law unto himself and to depend no more upon god's commandments" (*Adv. Learn.* 1; works 3.265). As witnessed by his own contributions to moral philosophy, Bacon by no means abandons morality simply to revelation theology. It is solely the obligatory character of fundamental moral norms that reason cannot completely explain and justify.

In contrast, knowledge of nature is evident in the fall narrative without any qualification. As Bacon emphasizes in accord with Augustine, the human striving for knowledge can only be allayed when the divine fullness of being is known, and hence no danger arises out of the quantitative expansion of humanity's knowledge of nature (*Adv. Learn.* 1; works 3.265f.). Nevertheless, expulsion from paradise still has consequences for the relationship between humans and nature. After the fall, humankind is not only subject to mortality, but moreover the original unity of *contemplatio* and *actio* is lost forever: "in the first event or occurrence after the fall of man, we see … an image of the two states, the contemplative state and the active state, figured in the two Persons of Abel and Cain" (*Adv. Learn.*1; works 3.297). Once in the *status corruptionis*, the human striving for knowledge always has to struggle against hurdles, in particular against the "shortness of life, ill conjunction of labours, ill tradition of knowledge over from hand to hand, and many other inconveniences whereunto the condition of man is subject" (*Adv. Learn.* 1; works 3.265). Mortality and the travail lying over all human activities are insurmountable consequences of the fall:

> It is true, that in two points the curse is peremptory and not to be removed [!]; the one that vanity must be the end in all human affects, eternity being resumed [!], though the revolutions and periods may be delayed. The other that the consent of the creature being now turned into reluctation, this power cannot otherwise be exercised and administered but with labour, as well in inventing as in executing; yet nevertheless chiefly that labour and travel which is described by the sweat of the brows more than of the body.
>
> (*Val. Term.*; works 3.222f.)

But humanity has lost more than Adam's nonviolent power over things. After expulsion from paradise, humankind has sunk into a permanent state of violence and injustice; as a result of the flood, God has also brought confusion to human language: "In the age of the flood, the first great judgement of God upon the ambition of man was the confusion of tongues; whereby the open trade and intercourse of learning and knowledge was chiefly imbarred" (*Adv. Learn.* 1; works 3.297). Here Bacon initiates a remarkable deviation from the biblical story, where, in the book of Genesis, the confusion of languages comes about not because of the flood (Gen. 6) but because of the building of the tower of Babel (Gen. 11). With the original union of *contemplatio* and *actio*—the ability to master things without exercising force by merely naming them—irreversibly lost after the fall of humanity, the new science can thus only restore paradise "in the great part" (*Val. Term.*; works 3.222). The *Great Instauration* is by no means driven by the hubristic aim to fully restore creation in the original state.

In light of the biblical fall narrative, Bacon explicates some of the fundamental reforms characterizing the new science: firstly, the Adamic unity of *contemplatio* and *actio* is to be restored on a new level, achievable by systematically relating a theoretical philosophy of nature to the mechanical arts; and secondly, the division among humankind resulting from the diversity of languages is to be overcome, at least in the area of the sciences, by establishing channels of communication, temporally and spatially unlimited, between scientists. Thus, important impulses in the new science are grammar and the development of the various vulgates into erudite languages of learning (*Adv. Learn.* 2; works 3.400f.).

With the envisioned coupling to the mechanical arts, Bacon formulates the conception for a science that is no longer limited to identifying the essential structures of the world. Now science is to penetrate to the very secrets of nature to unleash, as far as possible—as already proclaimed in *Valerius Terminus*—the productive power of human beings: "And to speak plainly and clearly, it is a discovery of all operations and possibilities of operation from immortality (if it were possible) to the meanest mechanical practice" (*Val. Term.*; works 3.222). Such an unleashing of humankind's productive power is stigmatized in the Bible, however, as godless hubris, epitomized by the tower of Babel (Gen. 11). Considered from this background, it is now understandable why Bacon deviates from the biblical model and transplants the confusion of languages to the flood narrative. Before its elaboration, the new science needs to be exonerated from any suspicion of hubris.

In defending the new science against the critical reservations of theology, Bacon resorts to other biblical motifs alongside the paradise narrative. The pillars of the new science are preordained in the wisdom of Solomon. Not only moral maxims, laid down in the Bible in wise judgments and sayings, are traced back to Solomon, but he is also said to have written a natural history that encapsulated the richness of the animate world, "from the cedar upon the mountain to the moss upon the wall … and also of all things that breathe or move" (*Adv. Learn.* 1; works 3.299). Moreover, Solomon furthered the use of the mechanical arts by building palaces and houses and by supporting shipping and navigation, not motivated, as Bacon emphasizes, by the objective of increasing material prosperity but "only to the glory of inquisition of truth" (*Adv. Learn.* 1; works 3.299). Finally, Bacon even attempts to provide a Christological argument for justifying the new science. The central tenets for the upcoming reform of the sciences are already prefigured in the ministry of Jesus, namely the purification of the idols, sovereignty over nature, and a use of language able to communicate beyond limits and boundaries. Aged twelve, Christ had fought ignorance in his encounter with the priests; his miracles had proven his power over nature; and resurrected, he overcame the confusion of languages through the Holy Spirit: "And the coming of the Holy Spirit was chiefly figured and expressed in the similitude and gift of tongues, which are but *vehicula scientiae*" (*Adv. Learn.* 1; works 3.299).

The goal of this allegorical interpretation of biblical texts is to defend the insatiability of inquisitiveness and the unleashing of the mechanical arts, which forge an inseparable union in the new science, against theological doubts. At the same time, Bacon's idea of a new science undoubtedly moves beyond the horizon of meaning posited in the Bible's worldview. As the example of Cusa has shown, boundless curiosity about the world was positively reappraised in Christian thought only a few centuries before Bacon; and the utilization of the mechanical arts for scientific experiments had begun in the philosophy of nature of the Late Middle Ages, above all in the ideas of Robert Grosseteste and Roger Bacon, and not in ancient Israel (Crombie 1953; Gaukroger 2001: 74f.). Although a new meaning is assigned to the biblical sources, Bacon does not succumb to boundless hubris when proclaiming a restoration of paradise. The goal of the *Instauratio magna* is not to build a "tower with its top in the heavens" (Gen. 11:4). Humanity's power over nature has two insurmountable limits—human mortality and the toils of human life:

> whence there cannot but follow an improvement in man's estate, and an enlargement of his power over nature. For man by the fall fell at the same time from his state of innocency and from his dominion over creation. Both of these losses however can even in this life be in some part repaired; the former by religion and faith, the latter by arts and sciences. For creation was not by the curse made altogether and for ever a rebel, but in virtue of that charter.
>
> (*N.O.* 2.52; works 3.247f.)

This means that the new science is to extend humanity's power as far as possible, i.e., as far as the conditions of humanity's fallen nature allows (*status corruptionis*): "so may I succeed in my only earthly wish, namely to stretch the deplorably narrow limits of man's dominion over the universe to their promised bounds" (*The Masculine Birth of Time*; Farrington 1964: 62). Thus, Bacon's vision of restoring paradise is not a sacralization of modern science and technology; rather, as the emphasis on humanity's lapsing into a corrupted state through the fall makes clear, the new science actually gravitates toward Dante's purgatory (Höffe 1993: 70f.).

The signs of history: Columbus and the age of discovery

With this vision of an *Instauratio magna* Bacon interprets the present as a transition to a new epoch of humanity, establishing an epochal consciousness, one of the key characteristics of modernity, if not the most telling: "Bacon's stance ... is essentially modern because of its acute historical self-consciousness" (Whitney 1986: 99). The doctrine of the idols begs the question, however, as to why humankind should suddenly now be able to extricate itself from a millennia-old nexus of delusion. To address this, Bacon develops not just a theological but also a historical justification of the new science. At this point, Europe's transoceanic expansion becomes significant; in the frontispiece of *Instauratio magna* Bacon guides the reader's gaze in this direction, namely through the Pillars of Hercules to the open seas (Figure 2).

The voyage of Columbus is a historical sign marking the project of a new science in several respects. Firstly, Columbus is a symbol for the vanquishing of faintheartedness. Because the fear of entering unknown territory is one of the greatest obstacles to achieving a fundamental reorientation of the sciences, one of the main tasks of the *Instauratio magna* is to kindle hope. In this aspect, Bacon sees himself as taking on the role of Columbus:

> And therefore it is fit that I publish and set forth those conjectures of mine which make hope in this matter reasonable; just as Columbus did, before that wonderful voyage of his across the Atlantic, when he gave the reasons for his conviction that new lands and continents might be discovered besides those which were known before; which reasons, though rejected at first, were afterwards made good by experience, and were the causes and beginnings of great events.
>
> (*N.O.* 1. 92; works 4.91)

The lack of courage to seek out and achieve new knowledge arises from a twofold self-blockage of the spirit, namely an overestimation of the current store of knowledge and an underestimation of present capabilities. These two misjudgments are for Bacon like "pillars of fate," and like the Pillars of Hercules, they confront the human urge for knowledge with a seemingly insurmountable barrier:

> It seems to me that men do not rightly understand either their store or their strength, but overrate the one and underrate the other. Hence it follows, that either from an extravagant estimate of the value of the arts which they possess, they seek no further; or else from too mean an estimate of their own powers, they spend their strength in small matters and never put it fairly to the trial in those which go to the main.
>
> (*Instauratio magna*, Praef.; works 4.13)

The overestimation of previous achievements afflicts both the mechanical arts and philosophy. Until now, the mechanical arts have been content with accidental discoveries, for inventions have come about "without any regular system of operations." Mechanics have taken it to be a "great matter to work out some single

Figure 2 Frontispiece of Francis Bacon's *Instauratio magna* (1620)

Source: illustration from *A Short History of the English People*, by John Richard Green, illustrated edition, Volume II, Macmillan and Co., London, New York, 1893. Photo by Ann Ronan Pictures/Print Collector/Getty Images.

discovery" (*Instauratio magna*, Praef.; works 4.17); moreover, the experiments and inventions were geared toward achieving specific outcomes. In short, the ancients were merely searching through "experiments of Fruit, not experiments of Light" (*Instauratio magna*, Praef.; works 4.17), which expand the knowledge of nature. A lack of methodology and utilitarian purpose conglomerate into a sheer cliff against which the ship of the *Instauratio* is in danger of being smashed (Krohn 1987: 66). The other cliff, blocking an embarking of the new sciences, is the widespread deference toward the philosophies of classical antiquity: "Philosophy and the intellectual sciences ... stand like statues, worshipped and celebrated, but not moved or advanced" (*Instauratio magna*, Praef.; works 4.14). Scholars comment on the texts of ancient authors as if they were holy books, unmotivated to pose the question of truth.

Bacon's second perspective on the voyage of Columbus is as a historical sign pointing toward the future, in that the future of the sciences lies in combining the philosophy of nature with the mechanical arts. The devaluing of the mechanical arts by classical ancient philosophy has not only blocked any further evolution of humanity's productive powers but also led to an enormous narrowing of the horizon of human experience. In contrast, Columbus has shown how technological innovations, specifically the improvements in shipbuilding and the invention of the compass, are capable of broadening the horizons of knowledge to a hitherto unimaginable degree:

> But as in former ages when men sailed only by observation of the stars, they could indeed coast along the shores of the old continent or cross a few small and mediterranean seas; but before the ocean could be traversed and the new world discovered, the use of the mariner's needle, as a more faithful and certain guide, had to be found out; in like manner the discoveries which have been hitherto made in the arts and sciences are such as might be made by practice, meditation, observation, argumentation,—for they lay near to the senses, and immediately beneath common notions; but before we can reach the remoter and more hidden parts of nature, it is necessary that a more perfect use and application of the human mind and intellect be introduced.
> (*Instauratio magna*, Praef.; works 4.18)

The discovery of the Americas is therefore a sign that new worlds can be made accessible through the minutest technological aids. Moreover, the invention of the compass shows that important secrets of nature are often hidden in the most unremarkable things, like that of an iron needle: "So we see how that secret of nature, of the turning of iron touched with the loadstone toward the north, was found out in needles of iron, not in bars of iron" (*Adv. Learn.* 2; works 3.332). As Bacon sees it, ever since Thales ancient philosophy had invariably nothing but disdain for the near and obvious. If he had kept an eye out for what was right in front of him, Thales would not only have avoided his fall into the well but also been able to observe the faraway, the stars, in the water's reflection (*De augmentis* 2.2; works 1.499; cf. Blumenberg 2015: 62f.).

With the discovery of the Americas—and herein lies the third historical watershed of Columbus's voyage—present historical time is definitively extricated from the overwhelming influence of antiquity: "For at that period there was but a narrow and meagre knowledge either of time or place" (*N.O.* 1.72; works 4.73). Instead of a historical science worthy of the name, the ancients had

> only fables and rumours of Antiquity. And of the regions and districts of the world they knew but a small portion; giving indiscriminately the name of Scythians to all in the North, of Celts to all in the West; knowing nothing of Africa beyond the hither side of Æthiopia, of Asia beyond the Ganges; much less were they acquainted with the provinces of the New World.
> (*N.O.* 1.72; works 4.73)

Compared to the Spanish and Portuguese voyages of discovery, the often admired and renowned travels of Democritus, Plato, and Pythagoras were "rather suburban excursions". In short: "In our times on the other hand both many parts of the New World and the limits on every side of the Old World are known, and our stock of experience has increased to an infinite amount" (*N.O.* 1.72; works 4.73). The early modern voyages of discovery have given rise to historical consciousness, and along with it a sense of confidence, for antiquity suddenly seems to be nothing but the infancy of human development. And not least, transoceanic seafaring initiates spatially limitless communication between the sciences. Supported by the no less significant invention of printing, seafaring enables the confusion caused by different languages to be overcome, at least partially:

> So that if the invention of the ship was thought so noble, which carrieth riches and commodities from place to place, and consociateth the most remote regions in participation of their fruits, how much more are the letters to be magnified, which as ships pass through the vast seas of time, and make ages so distant to participate of the wisdom, illuminations, and inventions, the one of the other?
> (*Adv. Learn.* 1; works 3.318)

As Bacon already heralds in the frontispiece of the *Instauratio magna* (Figure 2) with the saying from the book of Daniel, "Multi pertransibunt & augebitur scientia [Many shall go and fro, and knowledge shall be increased; Dan. 12:4]," the voyage of Columbus is the most significant historical sign of the possibility of a new science, "clearly intimating that the thorough passage of the world (which now by so many distant voyages seems to be accomplished, or in course of accomplishments), and the advancement of the sciences, are destined by fate, that is, by Divine Providence, to meet in the same age" (*N.O.* 1.93; works 4.92). The thoughts may be new; their meaning and significance arise not merely from ahistorical individual inspiration, but as an expression of the powers at work at the historical juncture of the time. For this reason, Bacon regards the Great Instauration "as a child of time rather than of wit [*magis pro partu temporis quam ingenii*]" (*Instauratio magna*, Praef.; works 1.123; 4.11). The close relationship between early modern voyages of discovery and the vision of a new science is again underlined in *Novum organum*:

> Nor must it go for nothing that by the distant voyages and travels which have become frequent in our times, many things in nature have been laid open and discovered which may let in new light upon philosophy. And surely it would be disgraceful if, while the regions of the material globe,—that is, of the earth, of the sea, and of the stars,—have been in our times laid widely open and revealed, the intellectual globe should remain shut up within the narrow limits of old discoveries.
>
> (*N.O.* 1.84; works 4.82)

9.2 Productive nature, science, and power

As Bacon explains through theological and historical reflections, the *Instauratio magna* is to place humankind in a new relationship to nature. Restoring humanity's sovereignty over things presupposes, however, an understanding of nature that differs from Platonic-Aristotelian metaphysics. And immediately at this point Bacon faces a methodological dilemma: a specific idea of nature must be introduced if the new science is be given a solid foundation; but it is the investigation of nature that is the very goal of the new science. Thus, anyone seeking to position science on the path of discovery and new knowledge needs to realize that their own contributions are highly likely to be revised or even rebuked in future. For this reason, Bacon expressly presents the principles and methods of his new science as revisable proposals for future research and not as dogmatic precepts: "Nor again do I mean to say that no improvement can be made upon these. On the contrary, I that regard the mind not only in its own faculties, but in its connection with things, must needs hold that the art of discovery may advance as discoveries advance" (*N.O.* 1.130; works 4.115; Box 1989: 45–7). Moreover, Bacon sees himself unable to complete the planned main sections of the *Instauratio magna*, presented individually after the preface. Even the first section, the division of the sciences, remains incomplete; sections III–VI are described only briefly. From the main sections only the second one, the *Novum organum*, is elaborated, albeit "not however in the form of a regular Treatise, but only a Summary digested into Aphorisms" (*Instauratio magna*, Distributio operis, works 4.22). Perhaps never before in the history of philosophy has the fragmentariness of a work been so readily admitted.

For Bacon, then, a provisional description of its methods suffices to set the new science in motion, an approach that Bacon once again justifies by referring to Columbus's voyage. The *Novum organum* is to prepare the human mind for a voyage across the open seas (*Instauratio magna*, Distributio operis, works 4.22).

Because ascertaining the current state of knowledge should "take into account not only things already invented and known, but likewise things omitted which ought to be there" (*Instauratio magna*, Distributio operis, works 4.22f.), the division of the sciences is in any case provisional in character. The areas of knowledge that have lain dormant will only emerge gradually, i.e., in the light of future discoveries: "For in adding to the total you necessarily alter the parts and sections" (*Instauratio magna*, Distributio operis, works 4.23). Thus, while the absence of the first main section leaves a lacuna, it is by no means enough to jeopardize the overall undertaking of *The Great Instauration*.

The heart of *The Great Instauration*, the *Novum organum*, is no exception to the caveat of future discoveries. Bacon thus deliberately presents the *Novum organum* in the form of aphorisms: "Aphorisms, representing a knowledge broken, do invite men to inquire further; whereas Methods, carrying the shew of a total, do secure men, as if they were at furthest" (*Adv. Learn.* 2; works 3.405; cf. Vickers 1968: 60–2). Bacon understands his task as akin to that of a reconnoitering guide, accompanying the process without dogmatically expecting a specific outcome: "For I do not propose merely to survey these regions in my mind, like an augur taking auspices, but to enter them like a general who means to take possession" (*Instauratio magna*, Distributio operis; works 4.23). It is in this spirit that Bacon then presents the other sections of *The Great Instauration*.

It is only in the third section, the *Historia naturalis et experimentalis*, in which Bacon suggests that all knowledge about nature and the technologies developed by humankind is to be collected, that we first really enter the terrain of a new science. Knowing a method is no substitute for the scientific work on real objects, "for it is in vain that you polish the mirror if there are no images to be reflected" (*Instauratio magna*, Distributio operis; works 4.28). Thus the third section is only a preparatory text. The fourth section, the *Scala intellectus*, presents "actual types and models, by which the entire process of the mind and the whole fabric and order of invention from the beginning to the end, in certain subjects, and those various and remarkable, should be set as it were before the eyes" (*Instauratio magna*, Distributio operis; works 4.31). The fifth section describes those discoveries and inventions which need to be acquired prior to setting out the grounds of the "second philosophy," then to be presented in the final section; maintaining the imagery, the inventions "will serve in the meantime for wayside inns, in which the mind may rest and refresh itself on its journey to more certain conclusions" (*Instauratio magna*, Distributio operis; works 4.32). This section can be aligned to Bacon's work *De fluxu et refluxu maris* (Krohn 1987: 63). The sixth section, "New Philosophy; or Active Science" (*Instauratio magna*, Distributio operis; works 4. 22), is, as Bacon concedes, beyond the scope of his powers, indeed his imagination:

> The completion however of this last part is a thing both above my strength and beyond my hopes [!]. I have made a beginning of the work—a beginning, as I hope, not unimportant:—the fortune of the human race will give the issue;—such an issue, it may be, as in the present condition of things and men's minds cannot easily be conceived or imagined. For the matter in hand is no mere felicity of speculation, but the real business and fortunes of the human race, and all power of operation.
>
> (*Instauratio magna*, Distributio operis; works 4.32)

With this background it is now possible to give a more precise description of the goal Bacon is aiming for with the new science. The new science is a project serving and involving humanity, one not pursued by individual thinkers but only realizable through cooperation between scientists in all lands. This vision of a planetarily-organized research project spanning generations allows Bacon to resolve the contradiction between limitless curiosity and the limitedness of individual cognitive faculties, a theme constantly broached since classical ancient philosophy. For this reason, Bacon presents merely a provisional concept of "nature," one at least capable of supporting an experimental method and the universal goal of the new science, namely, to produce all possible works ("all power of operation"). To achieve this, Bacon takes up the idea of the infinite diversity of the universe, already emerging in Renaissance philosophy, and expands on it in two directions. Firstly, the immanent infinity of the world arises out the subtlety of nature. Although the "subtlety of nature is greater many times over than the subtlety of the senses and understanding" (*N.O.* 1.10; works 4.48), this is no reason for skeptical resignation. The frailty of the senses can be compensated for by using technical aids, for example the telescope or microscope (*N.O.* 2.39). Thus, while Bacon mistrusts direct sense perceptions because they are inadequate and deceive us continually, in so far as experiments enable sense perceptions, Bacon can call himself "a true priest of the sense (from which all knowledge in nature must be sought, unless men mean to go mad)" (*Instauratio magna*, Distributio operis; works 4.26). Secondly, Bacon utilizes the idea of an experimenting nature to expand the scope of the de-limited universe. Nature is like a workshop in which new things are being continuously produced. The immeasurable diversity of things can be further increased through human interventions. This means that the experimental inquiry into nature not only sets up a vantage point to look into the hidden structures of the universe but also compels nature into producing new manifestations.

Bacon's concept of nature thus spans three levels: free nature, i.e., nature left to follow its own laws; the aberrations of nature; and lastly, nature altered through human skill (*Instauratio magna*, Distributio operis; works 4.28f.). In distinction from classical ancient philosophy, which had almost exclusively approached free nature and its immutable types and species, Bacon shifts the human mind to the irregular phenomena of nature artificially produced by humans; thus, it is indispensable for the new science to gather "a collection … of everything in short that is in nature new, rare, and unusual" (*N.O.* 2.29; works 4.169). Indeed, Bacon shows no interest in reducing nature to a substrate of human power, as Horkheimer and Adorno would critically suggest (see Chapter 2, section 2.1 of this book), but speaks of nature's inherent activation, of its liberty: "so the passages and variations of nature cannot appear so fully in the liberty of nature, as in the trials and vexations of art" (*Adv. Learn.* 2; works 3.333).

With the vision of a limitless liberation of natural forces, Bacon overcomes the millennia-old distinction between higher and lower: "philosophy has been hindered by nothing more than this,—that things of familiar and frequent occurrence do not arrest and detain the thoughts of men, but are received in passing without any inquiry into their causes" (*N.O.* 1.119; works 4.106). The revaluation of the base and low stems from a theological interpretation of creation: "And for things that are mean or even filthy,—things which (as Pliny says) must be introduced with an apology,—such things, no less than the most splendid and costly, must be admitted into natural history ... For whatever deserves to exist deserves also to be known, for knowledge is the image of existence" (*N.O.* 1.120; works 4.120f.). Hidden treasures lie dormant even in things usually held in contempt, treasures which reveal unimagined possibilities for science and human ingenuity: "Moreover as from certain putrid substances—musk, for instance, and civet—the sweetest odours are sometimes generated, so too from mean and sordid instances there sometimes emanates excellent light and information" (*N.O.* 1.120; works 4.107). Against this background it becomes understandable why Bacon turns attention not only to traditional handicrafts but also to the spectacles of performing traveling artists (minstrels, jugglers, acrobats, etc.) and the extravagance of alchemists, both of whom, for all their tricks and superstitions, provide valuable insights into the workings of nature (*N.O.* 2.31; works 4.172f.).

In laying a philosophical foundation for the *scientia activa*, Bacon revises the Aristotelian theory of causes, placing more emphasis on the material and efficient cause vis-à-vis the final cause, and reinterpreting the metaphysical tradition's notion of the formal cause. Because neither the Platonic doctrine of forms nor Aristotelian substance ontology are capable of describing the mechanisms of action in single bodies, it is necessary to redefine the concept of formal cause. According to Bacon, "form" is neither an element of an intelligible world—"For though in nature nothing really exists beside individual bodies" (*N.O.* 2.2; works 4.120)—nor a universal essence of entities; it is rather the regular effect of the various qualities or "natures" of a body. Thus, the deducible principle is that a form is in existence when a specific quality is observable: "Lastly, the true Form is such that it deduces the given nature from some source of being which is inherent in more natures, and which is better known in the natural order of things than the Form itself" (*N.O.* 2.4; works 4.121). Bodies are therefore "a troop or collection of simple natures" (*N.O.* 2.5; works 4.122). The infinite diversity of nature is comprised out of a limited reservoir of simple natures; to investigate their modes of operation is the primary task of the new science: "the nearer it approaches to simple natures, the easier and plainer will everything become" (*N.O.* 2.8; works 4.126). Indeed, if the forms of simple natures were known, for example weight, extensibility, solidity, fusibility, solubility, etc., then it must be possible to transfer the various qualities into random bodies. Human artistry is not limited to merely correcting or completing nature; rather, the new science assigns human beings the power to produce things which have never existed before (*N.O.* 2.5). Insight into the efficacy of first natures, out of which all things are formed, would open up unimagined possibilities to produce new things, for it is "the force implanted by God in these first particles, from the multiplication whereof all the variety of things proceeds and is made up" (*De principiis atque originibus*; works 5.463). Even the dream of the alchemists, to transmute base metals into gold, can no longer be banished to the realm of fantasy (Rossi 1968). In Bacon's thought, the *vis creativa* of the human spirit, already elaborated by Cusa with the example of the spoon carvers, gains in importance.

With the idea of the unleashing of human technology, the relationship between science, truth, and power now takes center stage in Bacon's justification of the new science. One question in particular becomes preponderant: whether, and if so in which sense, can the power to produce new things still be considered "science," i.e., be part of the search for truth.

In the general definition of the tasks facing natural philosophy, Bacon notes, along with the investigation of causes, the production of effects: "I divided Natural Philosophy into the Inquiry of Causes and the Production of Effects" (*De augmentis* 3.4; works 5.346). The first part of the definition basically reiterates the traditional purpose of natural philosophy, namely the search for the causes of movement of natural bodies. The second task, however—the production of effects—marks a clear break with tradition. Since the nineteenth century Bacon's insistence on the production of effects has been consistently understood as the making of useful artifacts. However, as Bacon himself emphasizes in the preface to *The Great Instauration*, the reason for striving toward a new science is "not either for pleasure of the mind, or for contention, or for superiority to others, or for profit, or fame, or power, or any of these inferior things; but for the benefit and use of life" (*Instauratio magna*, Praef.; works 4.21). From this background it becomes easier to understand the special meaning Bacon affords medicine in his tableau of the sciences (*Adv. Learn.* 2; works 3.370–7). This would mean that with the second part of the natural philosophy Bacon abandons the ancient idea of the autotelic of knowledge and delegates science to serve an extraneous purpose—to advance the welfare of humanity. Otfried Höffe has thus recast the opposition between Bacon and Aristotle, encapsulating it in the phrase "medicine instead of metaphysics" (1993: 64). The production of new effects is to primarily serve the investigation of causes: "works themselves are of greater value as pledges of truth than as contributing to the comforts of life" (*N.O.* 1.124; works 4.110).

On the one hand, then, Bacon resolutely rejects subjugating science to the advancement of material prosperity (Zagorin 1998: 60f.); on the other, however, technical intrusions serve more than the experimental inquiry into nature. The task of the new science resides in not merely using technical aids to isolate specific elements in things and from there to analyze their effects; in addition, it must be possible to transpose specific qualities to other substances: "For instance, if a man wishes to superinduce upon silver the yellow colour of gold or an increase of weight (observing the laws of matter), or transparency on an opaque stone, or tenacity on glass" (*N.O.* 2.4; works 4.121). The influence of alchemy on Bacon's thought is obvious in this idea of transposing specific qualities into different bodies (Rossi 1968; Krohn 1987: 117); the basic idea, however, as Pérez-Ramos has shown, need not be traced to alchemy to be understood. An alternative is the *verum-factum* principle, although here, too, Bacon offers a rather specific interpretation. In contrast to Descartes, Bacon is not solely concerned with the technical imitation of natural objects in order to better understand how nature functions through machines; Bacon's principal aim is the production of new things (Pérez-Ramos 1988: 152). Moreover, the technical manipulation of things is always reliant on the immanent forces of nature: "Towards the effecting of works, all that man can do is to put together or put asunder natural bodies. The rest is done by nature working within" (*N.O.* 1.4; works 4.47). The new arises not only through human ingenuity but also out of the interaction between human creativity and the workshop of nature. Given the fact that up to this point in history technological inventions had resulted from accidental observations, Bacon sees "much ground for hoping that there are still laid up in the womb of nature many secrets of excellent use, having no affinity or parallelism with any thing that is now known, but lying entirely out of the beat of the imagination, which have not yet been found out" (*N.O.* 1.109; works 4.100).

As Bacon quite clearly states at the beginning of the second book of *Novum organum*, the production of new effects is an autonomous goal of the new science alongside the experimental investigation into causes. This means that science (*scientia*) and human power (*potentia*) are geared toward different ends (*fines*):

> On a given body to generate and superinduce a new nature or new natures, is the work and aim of Human Power. Of a given nature to discover the form, or true specific difference, or nature-engendering nature, or source of emanation (for these are the terms which come nearest to a description of the thing), is the work and aim of Human Knowledge.
>
> (*N.O.* 2.1; works 4.119)

The goal of science resides in gaining a knowledge of truth, as Bacon emphasizes in line with the tradition, i.e., in discovering the form of a given quality. While Bacon bemoans that classical ancient philosophy had scorned the mechanical arts and technological inventions in the name of *theoria*, i.e., the purposeless knowledge of truth, its basic idea, to strive for knowledge for its own purpose, holds valid: "so assuredly the very contemplation of things, as they are, without superstition or imposture, error or confusion, is in itself more worthy than all the fruit of inventions" (*N.O.* 1.129; works 4.115). The *telos* of human power lies in generating new qualities in different bodies. New inventions are also to provide humans with new comforts. But the goal of human power transcends the horizon of utility; the goal of the new science is, as Bacon clearly states in *New Atlantis*, "the effecting of all [!] things possible" (works 3.156).

Despite their distinctive goals, science and human power are parts of one natural philosophy. It is therefore crucial to precisely determine the relationship between science and power. In philosophies critical of progress, Bacon's thought is often reduced to the famous phrase "knowledge is power." In *Novum organum*, however, knowledge and power are not simply identical, but placed in a relationship of reciprocal conditionality. On the one hand, science relies on the works of *potentia* for its experiments; on the other, the production of works presupposes science, i.e., the knowledge of causes, "for where the cause is not known the effect cannot be produced" (*N.O.* 1.3; works 4.47).

Knowledge and power thus remain distinct, for "that which in contemplation is as the cause is in operation as the rule" (*N.O.* 1.3; works 4.47). Thus, instead of the formula "knowledge is power," in the *Novum organum* the formulation reads: "Human knowledge and human power meet in one [*Scientia et potentia humana in idem coincidunt*]" (*N.O.* 1.3; works 1.157; 4.47). The pivotal question is, however, wherein knowledge and power, despite their distinct ends (*fines*), coincide. The answer is to be found in the reciprocal conditionality of knowledge and power. New knowledge into causes broadens the scope of potential; and conversely, new inventions open up the possibility to penetrate deeper into the secrets of nature. *Scientia* and *potentia* are thus related to one another in a way that facilitates "works and experiments to extract causes and axioms, and again from those causes and axioms new works and experiments," resulting in "a legitimate interpreter of nature" (*N.O.* 1.117; works 4.104). As long as *scientia* inquires merely into the material and efficient cause of similar things in their natural course, then the scope for *potentia* is limited. A spectacular extension of human power first emerges through a knowledge of the forms of the simplest natures, which are to be found in distinct bodies as particles. It is following this procedure that the constrictive horizon of effects between similar things can be transcended. Because the human mind as a rule is oriented on the normal course of natural phenomena, such inventions have been hitherto exceptional and only came about through chance observations. Bacon illustrates this through the example of silk: because the mind usually looks at what is obvious and similar, in the search for a textile fiber finer than wool people have instinctively searched for solutions in what is similar, e.g. plant fibers or fine animal hair—"but of a web woven by a tiny worm, and that in such abundance, and renewing itself yearly, they would assuredly never have thought" (*N.O.* 1.109; works 4.99f.). The same is true for the compass. If not for chance, then when searching for an instrument to exactly determine the cardinal points of geographic direction, "men would have been carried by their imagination to a variety of conjectures concerning the more exquisite construction of astronomical instruments; but that anything could be discovered agreeing so well in its movements with the heavenly bodies, and yet not a heavenly body itself, but simply a substance of metal or stone, would have been judged altogether incredible" (*N.O.* 1.109; works 4.100).

Against this background, a double trajectory emerges for Baconian science: through insight into and knowledge of the form of the simplest natures, a process through which *scientia* is brought to completion, humans would be equipped with an unimaginable power (*potentia*) to produce new works.

> But whosoever is acquainted with Forms, embraces the unity of nature in substances the most unlike; and is able therefore to detect and bring to light things never yet done, and such as neither the vicissitudes of nature, nor industry in experimenting, nor accident itself, would ever have brought into act, and which would never have occurred to the thought of man. From the discovery of Forms therefore results truth in speculation (*Contemplatio vera*) and freedom in operation (*Operatio libera*).
>
> (*N.O.* 2.3; works 1.229; 4.120)

This means that the point where science and power converge—the enigmatic *idem* in aphorism 3—lies in the realization of all possible works on the basis of complete knowledge of the simplest forms (Krohn 1987). Because the knowledge of the forces at work in the simplest basic components of the universe is denied to humanity, the coincidence of science and power is utopian in character. At the same time, even at the utopian endpoint of their spiral interplay there remains a certain difference between *scientia* and *potentia*. At least ideally *scientia* has an endpoint, in as far as investigating the causes comes to rest with the insight into the effecting mechanisms of the simplest natures. As Bacon emphasizes, the *telos* of science resides in the *contemplatio vera*. In contrast, no rest point can be designated for *potentia*: on the one hand, there are no limits to human imagination and creativity; on the other, nature itself is in perpetual motion, whether in regenerative or experimental form. The trajectory of *potentia* lies therefore not in calm contemplation but *operatio libera*.

These differing goals of *scientia* and *potentia* can be elaborated through the imagery of the alphabet. For Bacon, it is up to *scientia* to know the limited number of letters; the task of *potentia*, though, is to form potentially endless words out of the limited number of letters (*Adv. Learn.* 2; works 3.355f.) This means that "Although the roads to human power and to human knowledge lie close together" they are not identical but only "nearly the same" (*N.O.* 2.4; works 4.120). From the standpoint of science there is no inner necessity to use knowledge of the causes for the production of *all possible* works. While the production of new things may be useful for discovering hidden causes, it is not an end in itself for science. The excessive production of effects, which surpass the interests of scientific knowledge, can thus only be rendered comprehensible from the goal of *potentia*, which Bacon understands as a constitutive part of the *philosophy* of nature.

9.3 Toward a moral orientation of science: boundless charity

With the union of knowledge and power, which connects insatiable inquisitiveness to the idea of a radical unleashing of the productive forces of nature and humanity, Bacon's natural philosophy finds itself pitted against traditional moral philosophy. To resolve the conflict, *The Great Instauration* requires not only a theological justification but also a moral orientation. While Bacon can resort to specific strands of Renaissance philosophy for his positive valuation of curiosity, fully new ground must be sought to justify the power to produce all works (*omnis operum potentia*).

In defending worldly inquisitiveness, Bacon first addresses the classical ancient objections to *curiositas*, namely restlessness and the inversion of the hierarchical order of being:

> Again, it will be thought, no doubt, that the goal and mark of knowledge which I myself set up ... is not the true or the best; for that the contemplation of truth is a thing worthier and loftier than all utility and magnitude of works; and that this long and anxious dwelling with experience and matter and the fluctuations of individual things, drags down the mind to earth, or rather sinks it to a very Tartarus of turmoil and confusion; removing and withdrawing it from the serene tranquillity of abstract wisdom, a condition far more heavenly.
>
> (*N.O.* 1.124; works 4.110)

Bacon resolutely rejects the rebuke that the *scientia activa* plunges humanity into a state of utter turmoil. In fact, he asserts the opposite: it is not the new science but classical ancient *theoria* that is unable to point us in the direction of a calm contemplation of truth. Because natural philosophy as conceived by the ancients, deluded by their contempt toward the simple and common, proceeded all too hastily from sense perception to groundless speculations on eternal causes, the classical contemplation of the cosmos exudes a misleading calm. Without access to the true causes of nature, ancient wisdom ultimately remains entangled in its own ideas, caught in a spiderweb of its own making. In contrast, experimental science paves the way, albeit arduously but for all that reliably, toward an intuition of the final causes of the universe. The restlessness inherent to curiosity passes into contemplation only when the utopian endpoint of the *scientia activa* is reached, a transition Bacon illustrates with the image of a composed onlooker:

> *It is a pleasure to stand upon the shore, and to see ships tossed upon the sea; a pleasure to stand in the window of a castle, and to see a battle and the adventures thereof below: but no pleasure is comparable to the standing upon the vantage ground of Truth,* (a hill not to be commanded, and where the air is always clear and serene,) *and to see the errors, and wanderings, and mists, and tempests, in the vale below.*
>
> (*Essays* 1; works 6.378)

Because there is no prospect of ever scaling the impassable heights of infallible knowledge, where the restlessness of the search for truth could come to an end, Bacon undertakes a second step in justifying the new science, the *scientia activa*—he questions the ideal of *ataraxia* itself. As the joys of the passions surpass the pleasures of the senses, the joys of the spirit exceed those of the affects. The higher degree of intellectual joys ensues, as Bacon emphasizes vis-à-vis the ancient ideals of tranquillity and the ethics of moderation, precisely from their insatiability.

> We see in all other pleasures there is satiety, and after they be used, their verdure departeth ... But of knowledge there is no satiety, but satisfaction and appetite are perpetually interchangeable, and therefore appeareth to be good in itself simply, without fallacy or accident. Neither is that pleasure of small efficacy and contentment to the mind of man.
>
> (*Adv. Learn.* 1; works 3.317)

However, not every form of insatiable curiosity is useful in meeting the tasks demanded by the new science. Bacon thus develops a typology of curiosity.

Natural curiosity is completely untenable, for it presses ahead without taking the goal into account (*Val. Term.*; works 3.232). Tedious curiosity observes things closely but to the point that it becomes engrossed solely in the effect and its accompanying circumstances; it thus never attains the knowledge of causes necessary for examining the effects across different cases. Trapped in its own amazement of things, tedious curiosity has no prospect of ever extricating itself and moving on to knowledge (*Val. Term.*; works 3.246). In contrast, the curiosity of craftsmen produces—and herein resides its superiority over the *theoria* of the ancients—useful things; the joy felt at the discovery made is so great, however, that any further investigation into causes is prematurely terminated. Genuine curiosity is driven by a twofold motivation: firstly, a restless mind impels the investigation of causes through to the simple natures; and secondly, a powerful will is at work, one that is not content with inventing useful things but strives to produce all possible works: "I do not mean, when I speak of use and action, that end before mentioned of the applying knowledge to lucre and profession" (*Adv. Learn.* 1; works 3.294). And in telling imagery: keen attention is needed to ensure "that knowledge may be not as a courtesan, for pleasure and vanity only, or as a bondwoman, to acquire and gain to her master's use; but as a spouse, for generation, fruit, and comfort" (*Adv. Learn.* 1; works 3.295). The interplay between *scientia* and *potentia* admits no contentment, no fulfillment, let alone a sedate and comfortable life "as if there were sought in knowledge a couch, whereupon to rest a searching and restless spirit; or a terrace, for a wandering and variable mind to walk up and sown with a fair prospect ... or a shop, for profit or sale" (*Adv. Learn.* 1; works 3.295).

Because science moves beyond the walls of the university by producing new works and changes the living conditions of humans, Bacon considers it necessary to morally justify the *scientia activa*. In this context Bacon first clarifies the question whether the new science, aiming to unleash the productive power of humanity and nature, is subjected to any limits. From this perspective, he names three fundamental limits on the *scientia activa*:

> The first, *that we do not so place our felicity in knowledge, as we forget our mortality*. The second, *that we make application of our knowledge to give ourselves repose and contentment, and not distaste or repining*. The third, *that we do not presume by the contemplation of nature to attain to the mysteries of God.*
> (*Adv. Learn.* 1; works 3.266)

Nature's abundant wealth, identified and exploited by science and technology, may provide humans with repose and contentment as Bacon mentions in the second limitation, but it cannot still the human desire for happiness: "For mere

Power and mere Knowledge exalt human nature, but do not bless it [*Etenim ipsum Posse et ipsum Scire naturam humanam amplificant, non beant*]" (*N.O.* 2.49; works 1.349; 3.232). Because the new science cannot overcome mortality, we remain dependent on divine salvation. With the first and third limits of science Bacon is thus reconfirming the distinction between natural philosophy and theology.

Overall, however, Stoic-Christian morality recommends an attitude of self-limitation or moderation when dealing with goods. Both virtues are incompatible with the project of an unfettered production of endlessly more goods. Bacon is therefore looking for a virtue that steers the unleashed power of science and technology in a direction beneficial to humankind without stifling its innovative dynamic. In this context Bacon makes a surprising move and decides to take up the Christian ethic of charity. According to Bacon, two reasons justify establishing a connection between the new science and Christian charity. Firstly, quite simply, "of charity there can be no excess" (*Instauratio magna*, Praef.; works 3.21). Because love knows no measure, it is the only virtue that can at once absorb the exorbitance of the new science and still provide the orientation necessary for maintaining human welfare. Secondly, in line with scholastic teaching, the love of God, orienting all virtues toward the final goal, is obviously not one virtue among others, but the very form and consummation of all virtues. Thomas Aquinas called love the inner law of virtue because it pervades all virtues (*Summa theologica* II–II, q. 32, art. 8 resp. dic.). It is in this sense that Bacon sees charity as pervading knowledge and power from within and directing them to serve the wellbeing of humankind: "Charity, which is excellently called the bond of Perfection, because it comprehendeth and fasteneth all virtues together" (*Adv. Learn.* 2; works 3.442). Love does not impose external limits on the unfettered dynamic of the new science but purifies it from within by excising those motives directing science into unmoral channels (*Adv. Learn.*; works 3.265f.).

Love protects the new science from going astray morally in two respects. Firstly, love protects the investigators from "swelling" with pride, which Christian thought since Augustine has seen as the main threat posed by curiosity (*Adv. Learn.* 1; works 3.268). Secondly, love steers the production of new works in the direction of human benefit, without limiting the unleashed dynamic through the imposition of a rigid hierarchy of the good. Conversely, Bacon characterizes knowledge without love as malign and snakelike: "all manner of knowledge becometh malign and serpentine, and therefore as carrying the quality of the serpent's sting and malice it maketh the mind of man to swell" (*Val. Term.*; works 3.221f.). By converting a part of the countless works produced by the *scientia activa* into benefits for humankind, love delegates an additional purpose to science, namely, to further the welfare of humankind. Nevertheless, and this needs reiterating, Bacon does not subjugate science to the purpose of increasing material prosperity. Along with investigating causes, the goal of the new science is the production of all possible works. Indeed, as Bacon notes, multiplying the wealth of creation possesses value in itself. In this sense, the new science serves not only to benefit humankind but to demonstrate the glory of God. In short, the new science has a dual purpose: it is "for the glory of the Creator and the relief of man's estate" (*Adv. Learn.* 1; works 3.294). For this reason, "Bacon did not look upon knowledge from a narrowly utilitarian standpoint. The end to which he dedicated the achievements of the human intellect was also moral insofar as it served religion and the welfare of mankind by showing through discoveries in natural philosophy the greatness of god's Works" (Zagorin 1998: 61).

The complicated interplay between science, power, and charity (*scientia, potentia, caritas*) finds vivid expression in *New Atlantis*. At the center of Bacon's utopia is "Solomon's House," the scientific hub of the island Bensalem. As the "Father" of the House explains to the arriving Europeans, the laboratories serve the two goals pursued by the new science, "the knowledge of Causes, and secret motions of things; and the enlarging of the bounds of the Human Empire, to the effecting of all things possible" (*New Atlantis*; works 3.156). Numerous experiments are also conducted in Solomon's House to advance the welfare of humankind, foremost among them medical investigations, while technological developments are also prominent, for they can protect humanity from the threats of nature. Solomon's House has its own "Chambers of Health" where an extremely effective cure is available, known as the "Water of Paradise." More astoundingly, Solomon's House is capable of predicting dangers in advance, producing "natural divinations of diseases, plagues, swarms of hurtful creatures, scarcity, tempests, earthquakes, great inundations, comets, temperature for the year, and divers other things" and able to give "counsel thereupon what the people shall do for the prevention and remedy of them" (*New Atlantis*; works 3.166). The activities of the House are not exhausted by producing useful works, such as the cultivation and crossbreeding of plants in the botanic gardens to produce medicine (*New Atlantis*; works 3.158); there are experiments which have no immediately discernible input to furthering the welfare of humankind, for example changing natural sizes, colors, forms, and scents of plants; the production of completely new plants; or transforming one plant species into another (*New Atlantis*; works 3.158). It is no different in the production of technological devices, described enthusiastically as "fireworks of all variety" produced "both for pleasure [!] and use" (*New Atlantis*; works 3.163). In short, the experiments conducted in Solomon's House cannot be fully explained with reference to the goal of discovering the truth or the purpose of increasing prosperity. What strikingly emerges in Bacon's utopia is rather a passion to produce the new.

The moral philosophical justification of Baconian science does not therefore result in a materialist utilitarianism but leads to a modern form of the Christian ethic of love, with the positive humanist revaluation of the *vita activa* allied to the virtue of mercy (Vickers 1984). Indeed, as Bacon details in *De augmentis* and the *Essays*, science and technology enable considerably more than effectively helping the needy; in the end, they can change the very living conditions of all of humankind for the better.

According to Bacon, moral philosophy has two main tasks: explicating the purport of what is morally good and explaining the virtues (*De augmentis* 7.1; works 1.715). The morally good resides in an orientation on the wellbeing of others: "I TAKE Goodness in this sense, the affecting of the weal of men, which is that the Grecians call *Philanthropia* ... and without it man is a busy, mischievous, wretched thing; no better than a kind of vermin" (*Essays* 13; works 6.403). The philanthropic sense of morality has a natural philosophy foundation. The good toward which all beings strive spans two dimensions, namely unity with itself (*Bonum Individuale*) and the connection with a large whole (*Bonum Cummunionis*) (*De augmentis* 7.1; works 1.717). Because individual improvement toward self-perfection, i.e., *bonum individuale*, is given a dubious preponderance in the ancient idea of virtue, for Bacon it is necessary that morality, which is to now primarily focus on the *bonum communionis*, take the idea of duty (*officium*) as its starting point: "let us resume the good of communion, which respects and beholds society, which we may term Duty: because the term of duty is more proper to a mind well framed and disposed toward others, as the term of virtue is applied to a mind well formed and composed in itself" (*De augmentis* 7.2; works 5.14f.).

Oriented on the original sense of morality, Bacon maintains that it is possible to end the centuries-old controversy over the primacy of *contemplatio* or *actio*. The primacy of the *vita activa* directly ensues from the duty to ensure the wellbeing of humans. The privileged role of the spectator in the theater of life is reserved solely for God and the angels (*De augmentis* 7.1; works 5.8). Bacon resolves a further controversy through the *bonum communionis*, namely that between the Stoics and Epicures as to whether happiness resides solely in virtue or conversely virtue is a factor in the hedonistic understanding of happiness. Here, once more, Bacon criticizes the ancient ideal of *ataraxia*. Because in love a person is unavoidably exposed to the freedom of others to make decisions, then the ideal of tranquillity—indeed even Epictetus' maxim, to seek happiness in only what is in our power—is problematic: "as if it were not a thing much more happy to fail in good and virtuous ends for the public, than to obtain all that we can wish to ourselves in our private fortune" (*De augmentis* 7.1; works 5.9). It would be wrong, however, to deduce a contradiction between happiness and morality simply from the contingencies that moral action is exposed to. Quite the contrary; if one is aware of having conscientiously striven for the good with all one's energy, a greater satisfaction emerges than that generated by defensive strategies for preserving tranquillity: "the conscience of good intentions however failing in success imparts a joy truer, surer, and more agreeable to nature, than all the provision which a man can make either for satisfying of his desires or for the repose of his mind" (*De augmentis* 7.1; works 5.9).

Bacon questions the ancient ideal of *ataraxia* not only in terms of moral duty but also in the idea of individual and collective perfection. Once again, an argument from natural philosophy forms the starting point: there are only two tendencies in nature, namely "the one, to preserve or continue themselves; and the other, to multiply and propagate themselves" (*De augmentis* 7.2; works 5.10f.). The tendency to multiplication exists in human life in the innate "love of novelty and variety" (*De augmentis* 7.2; works 5.11), albeit narrow limits are imposed upon it because of the sheer necessities and hardships of everyday life. Moreover, as Bacon describes it, the monotonous cycle of eating, drinking, and sleeping threatens to crush the vitality of the curious spirit. To escape the drab monotony of satisfying sensual needs, people, even those living in luxury, seek out spectacular adventure. Nero and Commodus plunged into reckless and morally reprehensible undertakings such as gladiatorial fights and chariot races (*De augmentis* 7.2; works 5.12).

From this twofold meaning of the good, the possibility now opens to anchor insatiable curiosity and unleashed human power in the realm of morality. The moral significance of the new sciences lies, firstly, in overcoming the physical misery of humankind, specifically helping to tackle hunger and disease. Medicine is thus assigned a key role in *The Great Instauration*: "Medicine is a most noble art" (*De augmentis* 4.2; works 4.379). Secondly, in so far as the new science produces not only technologies sustaining life but also a vast multiplicity of works, it serves to alleviate boredom. Bacon explains the dual use of science through the example of botany. Studying and cultivating new plant species serves the discovery of medicinal herbs while, with a reference to horticulture, also reinvigorating the human spirit: "GOD ALMIGHTY first planted a Garden. And indeed it is the purest of human pleasures. It is the greatest refreshement of the spirits of man; without which buildings and palaces are but gross handyworks" (*Essays* 46; works 6.485). The new science therefore secures and advances the earthly welfare of humankind in two ways: providing what is needed for securing human survival and satisfying the unquenchable desire for the new.

In his attempt to merge the unleashed dynamic of science and technology with moral ends, Bacon questions fundamental criteria of traditional ethics, namely the ideas of moderation and self-control. At the same time, however, he very rarely directly addresses the fault lines of separation from traditional morality, one exception being a brief commentary on the dispute between Socrates and Callicles (*De augmentis* 7.2; works 5.13f.). In Plato's dialogue *Gorgias*, Callicles states the provocative thesis that people should not curb their passions but actually allow them rein to increase. The maxim of self-control drains the very life out of existence, so that in the end we exist much like a stone or piece of wood (*Gorg.* 491e). In contrast, Socrates sees a person who lets their passions increase as a bottomless barrel into which new water has to be constantly poured (*Gorg.* 493a). In a clear distinction from the moral philosophy tradition, which had always seen Callicles as a symbol for the immoderateness of the principle of pleasure, Bacon attempts to mediate between the Socratic ethics of moderation and the Sophistic maxim of intensifying pleasure (Hamilton 2016: 138f.). For Bacon, the dispute between Socrates and Callicles revolves around the question of whether human nature is able to strive for *ataraxia* while preserving, or indeed increasing, the vitality of life—a question, Bacon emphasizes, that moral philosophy has never (!) addressed adequately (*De augmentis* 7.1; works 5.725). The moral philosophers of antiquity have coaxed humans into "pusillanimous life forms" with the ideals of self-control and *ataraxia*, in which, as Callicles laments, great passions and feelings are repressed. The overvaluation afforded to self-control, which according to Bacon presupposes the maxim "enjoy not, that you may not desire; desire not, that you may not fear," stifles vitality and then strangulates human life itself (*De augmentis* 7.2; works 5.14). The consequence is the creation of a frightfully dubious uniformity of ways of life, a contradicting of the principle of multiplication that is also part of natural and moral philosophy: "So have philosophers sought in all things to make men's minds too uniform and harmonical, not breaking them to contrary motions and extremes" (*De augmentis* 7.2; works 5.14). Any future ethics worthy of the name must therefore not solely focus on the concerns securing common welfare, but must also give rein to the cultivation of *magnanimitas*, i.e., a nobility of mind and a generous spirit (*De augmentis* 7.2; works 5.14).

Bacon's justification of the new science leads ultimately to anthropology. Although Bacon cautiously prizes open the millennia-old criteria of classical ancient ethics, his view of humankind has been repeatedly seen set against the anthropology of the Renaissance. With respect to the idols, a blunt catalogue of the weaknesses of the human mind, William A. Sessions has even interpreted Bacon's anthropology as a counterpoint to Renaissance *dignitas hominis* literature, specifically "the polar opposite from that of Pico della Mirandola's Platonic anthropology" (1996: 26). For Paolo Rossi, Pico's idea of human creative freedom is completely alien to Bacon:

> One of the basic theories of Renaissance philosophy was the absence of a specific nature in man and his ability to acquire the nature of his choice ... yet it never took a substantial hold on Bacon. For him man's powers were not infinite but always subject to the laws of nature (*obsessus legibus naturae*), and he cannot break or loosen the causal ties that govern it.
>
> (Rossi 1968: 18)

As already shown, however, the *vis creativa* in Pico's conception is concerned not with physical but with second nature, i.e., the habits people cultivate. While Bacon has reservations about the idea that human beings can shape different natures, like Montaigne he nevertheless takes up Pico's understanding of freedom and modifies it.

So as to depict not just sublime images of virtue but to effectively support moral practice, Bacon—here in agreement with Machiavelli—is convinced that it is necessary to address real human beings and eschew an idealized notion of human nature. In the essay presenting love as the very epitome of the morally good, it comes as no surprise that Bacon points out how some people have a natural disposition to act morally while others reveal a "natural malignity": "For there be that in their nature do not affect the good of others" (*Essays* 13; works 6.404). While "unmoral" people are "errors of human nature," in the spirit of Machiavelli Bacon adds that they are also "the fittest timber to make great politiques of" (*Essays* 13; works 6.404f.). Innate natures may determine human beings throughout their lives, but to a certain if by no means haphazard degree, they are rendered immutable through education and habit (*Essays* 38 and 39; works 6.469–72). The distance from Pico becomes clear on the symbolic level in Bacon's interpretation of Proteus. His Proteus no longer symbolizes human beings' chameleon-like capacity to metamorphose, but stands for the very malleability of material, which under the force applied by human technology assumes ever new forms (*Parasceve* 5; works 1.399; cf. Box 1989: 47f.).

The question as to which factors of human nature are changeable and which are naturally given cannot be answered through metaphysical speculations but only through experiments. To expand the scope of human freedom, Bacon proposes for example the experiment of comparing various inclinations, bringing nature into play against nature, as it were (*De augmentis* 7.2; works 1.173). In short: "Experiment is a profounder habituation than the ancient training because it can actualise the full range of the wand's metamorphic potential, thereby discovering a more basic nature in it" (Briggs 1989: 37). Moreover, Bacon applies the experimental investigation of nature to another dimension, using it to analyze interpersonal relations. Through simulation and dissimulation, for example, others may be impelled to reveal their true natures (*Essays* 6; works 6.387–9). In political history, however, external circumstances have forced kings and others in power to turn their essential characteristics inside out: "The conversion of human beings on the basis of these Proteus-inspired principles discounts the integrity of characters not yet vexed and reduced. The true student of nature is encouraged to use simulation … to 'lay asleep' and 'surprise' others in order to 'discover the mind' of man" (Briggs 1989: 37f.). This means that Bacon augments the ancient tradition of the *cultura animi* with the idea of an experimental forming of the human mind, encapsulating the complex relationship between freedom and natural dispositions in a succinct formulation: "NATURE is often hidden; sometimes overcome; seldom extinguished" (*Essays* 38; works 6.469).

Pico's idea of creative freedom is thus not simply supplanted by a mechanistic anthropology; on the contrary, Bacon expressly bemoans "the predominancy of custom" that is turning humans into "dead images, and engines moved only by the wheels of custom" (*Essays* 39; works 6.471). Pico's idea of creative self-fashioning remains present in Bacon's thinking, at least indirectly.

9.4 An ambivalent utopian outlook: unleashing the productivity of nature and human creativity

Baconian science aims to restore humanity's original dominion over nature under the conditions of the *status corruptionis*. *The Great Instauration* thus features a utopian vision of the transformation of humankind as a whole. For this reason, the justification of the new science is inseparably tied to questions concerning a global order. After more than a century of violent expansion, Vitoria's question as to whether the Conquista of the Americas can be morally justified is for Bacon no longer relevant. Although peaceful settlement of uninhabited regions is preferable to violent conquest (*Essays* 33; works 6.457–9), Europe's colonialist expansion is basically no longer questioned. With the hope of qualitatively advancing the sciences, both Montaigne's doubts about Europe's superior civilization and the images of the "noble savage" and the "wild beast" wane. For Bacon, the inferiority of the Amerindian peoples is not due to barbaric morals and customs but stems from the primitive state of their technology. And yet, when describing the civilization gap between Europe and the Amerindian peoples, the rhetoric of Renaissance anthropology returns, with humanity either brutal or divine:

> Again, let a man only consider what a difference there is between the life of men in the most civilised province of Europe, and in the wildest and most barbarous districts of New India; he will feel it to be great enough to justify the saying that "man is a god to man", not only in regard of aid and benefit, but also by a comparison of condition. And this difference comes not from soil, not from climate, not from race, but from the arts.
> (*N.O.* 1.129; works 4.114)

Nonetheless, Bacon is not simply an apologist for colonialist politics. On the contrary, from *The Great Instauration* perspectives emerge for a new cosmopolitan thinking, whereby its focal point is no longer international law but the nonviolent spreading of scientific and technological innovations, which for Bacon advances the civilizing of humankind far more effectively than political or military measures:

> For the benefits of discoveries may extend to the whole race of man, civil benefits only to particular places; the latter last not beyond a few ages, the former through all time. Moreover the reformation of a state in civil matters is seldom brought in without violence and confusion; but discoveries carry blessings with them, and confer benefits without causing harm or sorrow to any.
> (*N.O.* 1.129; works 4.113)

In the long run, a nonviolent spreading of new scientific discoveries and inventions elevates the whole of humanity into a qualitatively new state. The hope of civilizing all peoples no longer rests on the ambitions of fickle imperial powers. Here Bacon transfers Pico's idea of self-creation not to nations, as Sepúlveda had, but to humanity itself. With this extension Bacon can avoid becoming embroiled in the controversies of the sixteenth-century colonial debate, in particular the difficult questions surrounding the doctrine of a just war. Despite this, the problems of international law or of cosmopolitan ethics cannot be fully dismissed. Above all else, Bacon encounters the problem of how peaceful communication between scientists of all the regions of the world is to remain possible amid imperial rivalry and violent conflict. Bacon never systematically addressed the practical issues of establishing a global order of peace; rather, these unresolved aspects are taken up in a literary form, namely in *New Atlantis*,[5] where Bacon presents the utopia of a knowledge society.

New Atlantis, alongside Thomas More's *Utopia* and Campanella's *La cittá del Sole* one of the most important utopian works at the advent of the modern age, is perhaps Bacon's most puzzling text. The first point of contention is whether the text's fragmentary form was intentional or, if not, whether a complementary section on the state was to follow.[6] The actual subject matter itself has evoked very diverging interpretations (White 1968; Weinberger 1985; Price 2002). Specifically, with the exception of the House of Solomon, Bacon proposes no spectacular changes to the political and economic order, which has repeatedly led to criticism that a genuinely powerful utopian vision is lacking. At the same time, however, the plans for future research institutions, ranging from subterranean laboratories in caves 600 fathoms beneath the surface through to a laboratory producing deceits and fallacies, must have seemed much like a wonder world of the impossible to his contemporaries (*New Atlantis* 6.137f.; Krohn 1987: 162).

The isolationism in *New Atlantis* certainly provoked consternation and criticism, with Bensalem—as the inhabitants call their island (*New Atlantis*; works 3.136)—dispatching expedition corps to all lands of the earth to collect scientific knowledge and inventions. These "merchants of Light" live unknown in their guest lands, a ploy to ensure that no one finds out about the island's existence. Conversely, all travelers accidentally landing in Bensalem are forbidden from ever making its existence known in their homelands. Bensalem thus knows in precise detail much about other lands of this earth, but itself remains unknown to the rest of the world. Charles Whitney has thus called the inhabitants of Bensalem "intellectual imperialists" whose relationships to other countries follow the motto: "We know, and are ourselves unknown" (Whitney 1986: 198). Bensalem's relationship to other nations of the world fatally recalls the panopticon, which according to Michel Foucault embodies the power syndrome of the modern state (Foucault 1977: 195–228). For Whitney, Bensalem's way of dealing with knowledge casts a harsh light on our contemporary global society, characterized by extreme inequality: "If a measure of a classic is that it continues to be timely, Bensalem's modernity, its resistance to historical process partly through its one-way commerce in ideas, also offers parallel, if not precedent, for neo-colonial industrial development today" (Whitney 1986: 198). In addition, Bacon supported the rise of England/Britain and its expansion as a colonial power and was himself involved in both the Virginia Company and the Newfoundland Company (Irving 2006: 252).

On the other hand, because Bacon describes Bensalem as an island without any colonial possessions outside its territory, his utopia could be interpreted as "pre-colonial" text (Serjeantson 2002). However, the colonial world of the early modern period is omnipresent, at least indirectly, in *New Atlantis*. Bacon even addresses the violence of colonialism in cryptic allusions. In distinction from *Novum organum*, where the frontispiece directs the reader's gaze through the Pillars of Hercules to the open seas, in *New Atlantis* the Europeans depart from Peru in the direction of Japan and China. The ship encounters distress at sea and the Europeans attempt to reach the harbor of an unknown island. Before they can go ashore, eight men in a small boat come toward them and prevent their landing. They unroll a scroll, displaying a text in ancient Hebraic, ancient Greek, Latin, and Spanish that demands shipwrecked parties not to land and to take to sea again within sixteen days. During this time, they are guaranteed provisions and medical help. Only after each European individually swears they are not a pirate and have not spilled human blood in the last forty days is permission granted to enter the "Strangers' House," the guesthouse. There is no trace of colonialist arrogance in the opening narrative sequences of *New Atlantis*. Quite the opposite: Bacon depicts the Europeans in need of help and protection but also as potential aggressors. The atmosphere during the first contact bristles with a deep mistrust that, as later conversations with the island's head reveal, stems from the historical experience of the conquest of the Americas. As the governor explains to the Europeans, the lawmaker king of Bensalem issued various "interdicts and prohibitions which we have touching entrance of strangers; which at that time (though it was after the calamity of America) was frequent" (*New Atlantis*; works 3.144).

As Bacon signals with numerous allusions to the annihilation of the Amerindians, the encounter between the Europeans and the Bensalem inhabitants takes place in the shadow of the Conquista of the Americas. Bensalem's negotiators protect themselves from infectious diseases whenever there is contact with the Europeans. The notary boards the ship of the Europeans "holding in his hand a fruit of that country, like an orange, but of colour between orange tawney and scarlet, which cast a most excellent odour. He used it (as it seemeth) for a preservative against infection" (*New Atlantis*; works 3.132). The Europeans are then placed under medical observation in the guesthouse. Here Bacon is obviously referring to the decimation of the Amerindians in the sixteenth century through the introduction of diseases by Europeans. The seal of the scroll used to welcome and instruct the shipwrecked Europeans features cherubim wings and a cross. The inhabitants of Bensalem are "angels" (*New Atlantis*; works 3.136; 140), i.e., in Bacon's view a people capable of merging high scientific and technological standards with the practice of benevolence and goodwill. The cross indicates that they are already Christians. As the superior later explains, through a divine miracle they received a casket containing writings from the Old and New Testaments (*New Atlantis*; works 3.136–9).

Against the grim background of the violent European conquests, the opening scene of *New Atlantis* presents the utopia of a nonviolent encounter between Europe and non-European cultures. The two main reasons invoked to justify the Conquista in the sixteenth century, namely the missions of civilization and Christianization, are no longer relevant for Bensalem. Like Montaigne before him, Bacon prizes open numerous stereotypes of colonialist thinking. Countering the stereotype of wild naturalness, in terms of civilization the island's inhabitants are clearly superior to the Europeans in all areas of life. It is not they who are representative of the "other" but the Europeans, and it is no coincidence that the Europeans are lodged in the "Strangers' House." As Kate Aughterson has shown, *New Atlantis* inverts the colonial stereotype:

> It is not-Europe and not-the-New-world. Thus, this space does not participate in the imperial construction of "otherness" as foreign, dangerous and feminised. The destabilising of settled and Western identity continues in the subsequent inversions ... These inversions reconfigure emergent early modern Western assumptions and discourses about territory, economics, identity, Christian history, the natural world, and practical science.
>
> (2002: 161)

Finally, the backdrop of the Conquista reveals the significance of Bensalem's isolationist strategy. The aim behind their practice of dispatching two ships to various countries across the globe every twelve years is "to give us knowledge of the affairs and state of those countries to which they were designed, and especially of the sciences, arts, manufactures, and inventions of all the world" (*New Atlantis*; works 3.146). This is not to be read as an anticipation of the neo-colonial dominance of the West, but understood in terms of its function, i.e., as a fiction illustrating the contradiction between the idea of a peaceful, globally networked community of scientists and the violent nature of international relationships. As long as international anarchy prevents free exchange between scientists and a peaceful application of their inventions, then Bensalem must remain unknown to the rest of the world. The concentration of knowledge does not serve to extend the island's power, for unlike the European colonial powers Bensalem has no intention to conquer and colonize the countries it has spied on. But nor are the expeditions launched to plunder material wealth, "not for gold, silver, or jewels; not for silks; nor for spices; nor any other commodity of matter" (*New Atlantis*; works 3.146f.). All the "Merchants of Light" have on board when they return are "books, instruments, and patterns in every kind" (*New Atlantis*; works 3.146). The accumulation of knowledge brings with it a strategic advantage, however. Thanks to its technological superiority, Bensalem is impregnable.

Instead of justifying imperialism, in *New Atlantis* Bacon, employing a fictive retrospective to the early years of humankind, takes up key elements from Vitoria's idea of a world society. The governor tells the stranded Europeans "that about three thousand years ago, or somewhat more, the navigation of the world, (specially for remote voyages), was greater than at this day" (*New Atlantis*; works 3.141). Back then there was brisk trade between Asia, Europe, Africa, and the Americas: "China also, and the great Atlantis (that you call America), which have now but junks and canoes, abounded then in tall ships"; Bensalem's own ships at this time voyaged to all coasts "as well to your Straits, which you call the Pillars of Hercules" (*New Atlantis*; works 3.141). Like Montaigne, through a radical shift in perspective Bacon dislodges firmly entrenched notions about non-European peoples and the accompanying imagery. While the voyage of Columbus was a symbol for the advent of the new age in the *Instauratio magna*, this initial euphoria has meanwhile dampened, *New Atlantis* offering a broader, and hence more somber, historical context. As the governor relates to the unknowing Europeans, the peoples of the Americas and Asia had sailed to the harbors of the Mediterranean thousands of years before. The expansionist aims of Old Atlantis, the contemporary Americas, brought the peaceful era of worldwide trade to an abrupt end, however. All of the expeditions of Old Atlantis failed; no one ever returned from the military campaign against Egypt, and even Bensalem had to repel an attack. Ultimately, God punished Old Atlantis because of its imperialist campaigns, unleashing a flood that just a few mountain settlers survived. The cultural backwardness that Europeans perceived in the Americas is thus explainable through their civilizations' shorter history in comparison to other cultures:

> So as marvel you not at the thin population of America, nor at the rudeness and ignorance of the people; for you must account your inhabitants of America as a young people; younger a thousand years, at the least, than the rest of the world; for that there was so much time between the universal flood and their particular inundation.
>
> (*New Atlantis*; works 3.143)

Bensalem was therefore not isolated from the beginning, but part of the peaceful relations and commerce between all nations in the early period of humanity. Global trade, however, has broken down completely due to the belligerent conflicts and their repercussions: "As for the other parts of the world, it is most manifest that in the ages following (whether it were in respect of wars, or by a natural revolution of time) navigation did everywhere greatly decay" (*New Atlantis*; works 3.143). In short, the isolationism practiced by Bensalem is not an ideal but a necessary, if unwanted and pernicious, response to a situation, and thus one that may be relinquished. As Bacon emphasizes, the regents of Bensalem, "still desiring to join humanity and policy together" (*New Atlantis*; works 3.144), have installed specific measures for dealings with strangers. For example, strangers are not to be detained forcibly against their will; rather, as Bacon states again in sober concordance with Vitoria, all strangers arriving at the island are to be offered a right to stay. Because of the advantages enjoyed by living in Bensalem, only a few have decided to leave the island and return home. And because their accounts of the wondrous island of Bensalem were given little credence, the island has remained unknown (*New Atlantis*; works 3.144f.). Considering these aspects, Whitney's criticism that the imperialism of the great European powers is reflected in Bacon's ideal state clearly misses the point of *New Atlantis*.[7] Moreover, any centralizing of knowledge contradicts Bacon's idea of a globally networked community of researchers and scientists, whereby their concerted efforts prove capable of overcoming the barrier of confusion resulting from language differences.

These intimations on Bensalem's relationships to other countries form, as it were, the foreign policy framework of Bacon's utopia of a knowledge society. At the center of *New Atlantis* is the depiction of the "House of Solomon." As already shown, Bacon plots the interaction between *scientia*, *potentia*, and *caritas* in the activities undertaken by the research community. Beyond this, Bacon treats the precarious problem of the new science's relationships to politics and society. Although the king has installed the research center, the scientists decide autonomously on their respective projects. Indeed, the scientists are responsible for the decision as to which discoveries and technologies are to be made available to the public:

> And this we do also: we have consultations, which of the inventions and experiences which we have discovered shall be published, and which not: and take all an oath of secrecy, for the concealing of those which we think fit to keep secret: though some of those we do reveal sometimes to the state, and some not.
>
> (*New Atlantis*; works 3.165)

In the oath to keep secret the projects and the knowledge of the House of Solomon, Bacon illustrates the relationship between the new science and the moral principle of charity, a relationship that, selectively drawing on the abundance of knowledge and inventions, is to foster those works serving the overall welfare of humankind. To ensure that the dynamic between *scientia* and *potentia* is not unnecessarily constrained by the aims of philanthropy, the decision as to which areas of knowledge are to be made accessible for the benefits of society, and which are to be held back, remains exclusively with the scientists because they are the only ones to possess an overview and understanding of the current potentialities of science and technology: "'Lastly, we have circuits or visits of divers principal cities of the kingdom; where, as it cometh to pass, we do publish such new profitable inventions as we think good'" (*New Atlantis*; works 3.166).

In contrast, the relationship between the new science and political power remains open. There are no clear guidelines in *New Atlantis* as to how the tensions between *scientia*, *potentia*, *caritas*, and political power are to be balanced out. Rather, at the text's conclusion, Bacon points out the limitedness of the utopian horizon. The "Father" of the House of Solomon grants the Europeans permission "to publish it [a report about Bensalem] for the good of other nations" (*New Atlantis*; works 3.166). The island's isolation has long been breached in any case, for "we," i.e., the readers of *New Atlantis*, know about Bensalem. With the text itself dissolving its own literary fiction of the "unknown place," Bacon directs our attention back to the current political situation. The depiction of the laboratories and projects of the House of Solomon will stimulate scientific and technological curiosity in numerous countries. The political and institutional conditions necessary for mediating between the unfettered dynamic of scientific progress and the moral goals of humanity are something that "we" ourselves need to determine, giving appropriate consideration to the state of scientific and technological possibilities and political power relationships. Perhaps this is why Bacon forgoes elaborating a political theory and leaves *New Atlantis* as a fragment. Faced with the danger that the absolutist monarchies of Europe would exploit the new science for their power interests, Bacon considered the secrecy of knowledge to be the sole reasonable path for a responsible steering of scientific and technological progress—not only for Bensalem but also for seventeenth-century English society.

To sum up: in the *Instauratio magna* Bacon establishes modern science as an independent institution with its own goals. The differentiation of modern science ensues from its detachment from fulfilling the requirements of religious, metaphysical, and political objectives. In distinction from the metaphysics of antiquity and Christianity, both of which sought to determine the final causes of things, Baconian science is limited to investigating material and efficient causes. While politics is assigned the task of establishing and supporting science as a social institution, as far as the actual scientific research is concerned—which extends to determining what is be researched and technologically tested—ideally it remains autonomous, as illustrated by Bacon in the House of Solomon.

The differentiation of modern science does not imply, however, a rigorous demoralization of scientific research; rather, science is connected to a new morality, one that integrates and modifies two ethics, the moderation of antiquity and Christian love. Bacon's science is thus not subjugated to the dictate of a materialist utilitarianism. Establishing modern science as an autonomous subsystem of society is not based on a simple logic of secularization (McKnight 2006). The new science does not supplant religious salvation. Instead, Bacon justifies the new position of humankind in the cosmos, itself determined by modern science, through an innovative reinterpretation of theological motifs, concretely the partial restoration of paradise and the rebuilding of the temple of Solomon. There is, however, a dangerous ambivalence discernible at the center of Baconian science. It crystallizes out of the dual goal Bacon sets science: the search for truth, i.e., the investigation of the causes in natural events, and the production of all possible works. Assuming that nature is ever alive and productive, the production of new works is not necessarily contradictory to striving for truth. The hidden forces generating effects in nature can only be identified when they are unlocked by technological interventions. The idea of the production of all possible works acts as a fulcrum, connecting modern science to a utopia that can no longer be justified on purely epistemological grounds.

The idea of unleashing the productive forces of humanity and nature implies, in the long run, a radical reorganization of the living circumstances of all humankind, an implication that Bacon is fully aware of. Because the dynamic of the new science inevitably reaches into the realm of moral-practical reason, Bacon augments the interplay between knowledge and human power with charity, which however is not akin to setting boundaries to the new science; rather, from the wealth of works produced, those are to be selected which serve the welfare of humanity.

Since, along with the search for truth, the production of ever new works is an end in itself for modern science, a purpose only partially justifiable through moral philosophy, Bacon again brings into play a theological argument: that the reproduction of the world's immanent wealth through science and technology serves to glorify the divine creator.

With the option to "effect all things possible," Bacon however connects modern science to a vision, albeit one no longer oriented on rational objectives: the very reorganizing of reality. This trajectory has led to Brian Vickers even radically querying the rationality of Bacon's idea of science: "Indeed the whole end of his philosophy is a non-rational vision of man's unlimited capacity to dominate the universe" (Vickers 1968: 5). Given the distinct goals of *scientia* and *potentia*, however, Vickers' blanket verdict needs to be corrected with respect to the *Instauratio magna*. Baconian science indeed possesses a rational component, namely the experimental exploration of nature. Beyond the moral benefit, the rational achievement of Baconian science is connected with the irrational vision of producing all possible works. These three factors are closely entwined in Bacon's idea of a new science; but they remain distinct.

For Horkheimer and Adorno, Bacon develops an idea of knowledge through which the human is elevated to the position of a dictator over things, degrading nature to a mere substrate for an unbridled will to power (see Chapter 1, section 1.2 of this book). The critique of power disregards pivotal dimensions of Baconian science, however. What manifests in increasing human power is the productive power of nature, without which humanity is simply incapable of creating anything. In the sense of the *verum-factum* principle, the true is not reduced to that produced in the new science. The goal of *potentia* resides thus not in the artificial reproduction of already known things, but precisely in the production of new works through an unleashing of the productive powers of nature. In short, the fascination, pervading Renaissance thought since Cusa, with the endless wealth of the limitless universe remains alive in Baconian science.

Despite Bacon's profound admiration for the immanent potentiality of nature, the insight into how the effects emanating from corpuscles operate, forming the very basis for the existence of things, opens up unimagined possibilities to manipulate nature in the new science. In the laboratories of the

House of Solomon, the growth, magnitude, and qualities of plants and animals are altered. Even the winds are at the disposal of human power. The wonder at the workshop of nature and the excessive vision of reorganizing natural events and processes enter a dubious union. Ultimately, Baconian science amalgamates rational ideas, power theory, and an extreme utopia of the production of all possible works.

10

Thomas Hobbes: The foundation of modern politics amid escalating social conflicts

Thomas Hobbes saw himself as the founder of a new political philosophy. The philosophy of the state was, he claimed, "no older ... then my own book *De cive*" (*De corpore*, Ep. ded.; *EW* 1.ix).[1] For some time now, research into Hobbes has generally followed this self-appraisal. The political philosophy of Hobbes is, as Leo Strauss frames it, "specifically modern. One is inclined to say that it is the deepest stratum of the modern mind" (1952: 5; cf. Willms 1987: 22). Opinions vary widely, however, as to wherein the specific modernity of Hobbes's political philosophy exactly resides. One the one hand, Hobbes is considered, along with Descartes, to be a founder of the Enlightenment. Indeed, the stringently rational theory of the state of nature, indebted to a geometrical method, and the construction of the state based on it, remain impressive today. On the other hand, the imagery of the war of all against all has long been a target of critiques of modernity focusing on the dynamics of power.

According to Macpherson, the early capitalist economy, seen as fierce, remorseless competition between isolated individuals, is mirrored in Hobbes's theory of the state of nature (1962: 9–106). As Carl Schmitt saw it, at the basis of Hobbes's political philosophy is a colonialist worldview, wherein Europe is defined as a sphere of law (*status civilis*), while contrastingly the non-European world is in a natural condition, i.e., lawless (2003: 97f.). Although Enrique Dussel considers the foundations of modern political philosophy to have been laid by Sepúlveda, and thus before Hobbes, he has identified Hobbes as a cornerstone in the colonialist ideology of modernity. Hobbes's famous dictum of *Homo homini lupus* "is the real—that is, political—definition of the *ego cogito*," which in turn builds on the "*ego conquiro*" (Dussel 2003: 9; cf. Chapter 3, section 3.2 in this book). Hannah Arendt and Jürgen Habermas take a different approach, criticizing Hobbes in the light of communicative reason. Under the spell of the mechanistic philosophy of nature predominant in the early modern period, Hobbes reduces moral reason to instrumental rationality; the Aristotelian concept of *praxis* is supplanted by *poiesis* (Arendt 1998: 294–304). For Habermas, "Hobbes investigates the mechanics of social relations in the same way as Galileo investigates that of motion in nature," thus transforming classical political philosophy for the first time into a "physics of sociation" (Habermas 1973: 86; 84). Against the interpretation of a mechanistic theory of power relations stands the fact that all of Hobbes's three major works on political philosophy—*Elements of Law Natural and Politic* (1640), *De cive* (1642; 2nd edn 1647), and *Leviathan* (1651; Latin version 1668)—contain detailed considerations on natural law or the *leges naturales*. This is why, beyond the interpretations geared to revealing and criticizing ideology, the debate on Hobbes's moral philosophy continues unabated.

Beyond dispute is, however, that Hobbes analyzed the state as an autonomous system of human actions, in which, as with Machiavelli, the logic of power in social relationships comes into focus. Under the indelible influence of the English Civil War, with the image of the war of all against all Hobbes shifts the unleashing of power and violence, morally disqualified in the thought of classical antiquity and the Middle Ages, to the very center of political theory.

At this point, I would like to build a bridge from Hobbes's political philosophy to Renaissance thought, which has come increasingly into focus in recent times (Skinner 1978; 2002; 2018; Tuck 1979; Thierney 1982; Koch 2005). In the following I hope to show that all of the de-limitations of Renaissance philosophy are still present, though specifically modified, in Hobbes's political philosophy. This thesis may seem surprising at first. The mechanistic philosophy of nature, also integrated into anthropology, seems to be an unsurmountable contradiction to Pico's idea of creative freedom; and Hobbes's focusing on the internal conflicts ravaging European societies would seem to narrow the cosmopolitan horizon of Spanish late scholasticism. But this first impression is misleading. Through the influence of Bacon, the motifs of insatiable curiosity and the idea of self-fashioning flow into Hobbes's thinking. And as in Montaigne, the "New World" is present at key places in his work. The figure of *Libertas* on the frontispiece of *De cive* is an Amerindian chief with a spear in his hand, behind whom two men are attacking another person with just such a spear; and in *Leviathan*, too, Hobbes refers at a prominent juncture to "America," where so many peoples still live in the state of nature. "In this respect," comments Schmitt, "Hobbes obviously was influenced not only by the creedal civil wars in Europe, but also by the New World" (2003: 96).

In the context of the de-limitations proclaimed by Renaissance thought, Hobbes's political philosophy can be interpreted as a theory on unleashing and limiting human power relations. My first step in this undertaking is to present Hobbes's project of laying a new foundation for political philosophy (section 10.1 of this chapter). The starting point here is the English Civil War, which Hobbes, in a reversal of the Eurocentric perspective, considers to be a regression to the barbarity of inner societal violence. The cause for this social deterioration lies not just in the moral failings of the social actors, but in the deficiencies of the tradition of moral philosophy, which are so far-reaching that they encompass both the philosophy of classical antiquity and Christian theology. Confronted with this failure of traditional moral philosophy, Hobbes attempts to lay a new foundation *more geometrico* for ethics and political philosophy. His philosophy is therefore not concerned with delineating a thoroughgoing philosophy of extreme power, but rather with establishing a science of justice (*scientia iustitiae*).

In the anthropological founding of the geometrical method, Hobbes elevates the passion of insatiable curiosity into a distinctive human characteristic, marking a difference with animals. Simultaneously, this bursts the constrictive corset of materialistic body ontology. Because Christian groups are embroiled in hostilities against one another in the European civil wars, Hobbes considers it necessary to take the ground from under the religious legitimations of violence already in his preliminary considerations on the philosophy of the state. To this end, Hobbes restricts the field of morality to worldly peace.

Section 10.2 of this chapter then offers a sketch of the theorem of the natural condition and the theory of the state that is based on it. With the help of the methodological fiction of the natural state, Hobbes attempts to uncover the logic behind violence in real historical situations on the one hand, while on the other discerning *more geometrico* those elements inherent to a theoretical construction of the state. In the description of the dialectic between *status naturalis* and *status civilis*, motifs central to Renaissance anthropology return on a new level. As in Pico, for Hobbes the human being cannot be assigned a specific nature; unlike Pico, however, for Hobbes social constellations primarily determine if a person is to be a wolf or a God to their fellow humans. In the establishing of a state, understood as an act of collective self-civilizing, creative freedom returns in a positive sense (section 10.3). To conclude, I will consider both the rational achievements and the ambivalences in Hobbes's *scientia iustitiae* (section 10.4).

10.1 The project: *scientia iustitiae*, a bulwark against the regression to barbarism

The diagnosis: regression to barbarism

Despite his focus on the civil wars raging within Europe, the broad horizon of sixteenth-century cosmopolitan thinking by no means vanishes from Hobbes's view. As the conclusion of *Leviathan* makes clear, Hobbes considers the calamity of a civil war from the perspective of an inhabitant of the New World:

> *adeo ut si quis ex mundi partibus remotioribus huc appulsus, eorum, quae tunc perpetrabantur; falgitiorum spectator fuisset, justitiae divinae sensum in his locis nullum omnino tunc fuisse pro certo habuisse* (that anyone brought here from the remoter parts of the world who had witnessed the outrages perpetrated at that time would have been convinced that there was at that time absolutely no sense of divine justice here.
>
> (*Lev.* 47; 1127–9; addition to the Latin edition)

On the one hand, the gloomy view of his own country recalls the Brazilians in Montaigne's essay *Of Cannibals*, who express their amazement at the unjust social conditions in Europe (*E* 1.31; 158f.); on the other hand, reversing the ethnological gaze, Hobbes takes up a key element of Sepúlveda's critique of the barbarity of the Amerindian peoples. Sepúlveda had reproached the Indians of having lost an awareness for fundamental moral norms. Sepúlveda's strategy of civilizing by force is not an option for Hobbes, however. England cannot be civilized by another power. But Montaigne's hope that the remnants of the existing order could at least stem the spread of social anarchy is also no longer convincing. Hobbes believes that the solution is to be found in Bacon's idea of a new science, whereby investigating the causes serves to produce new works. In this sense, as Hobbes conceives it, any political philosophy looking to lay out plans for stable and lasting peace has to build on a blunt analysis of the causes of violence.

Like Bacon's new science, Hobbes's political philosophy is based on a scathing criticism of the tradition: "that what hath hitherto been written by Morall Philosophers, hath not made any progress in the knowledge of Truth" (*De cive*, Ep. ded.; 26). For both Hobbes and Bacon, the turn away from classical ancient philosophy entails a fictive alliance with archaic traditions of knowledge. According to Hobbes, the birthplace of philosophy is not Greece but the empires of the Orient, for "*Leasure* is the mother of *Philosophy*" (*Lev.* 46.6; 1054). This leisure necessary requires, in turn, a stable political order. For this reason, the

"*Gymnosophists* of *India*, the *Magi* of *Persia*, and the *Priests* of *Chaldaea* and *Egypt*" must be counted as "the most ancient Philosophers; and those Countreys were the most ancient of Kingdoms" (*Lev.* 46.6; 1054). Conversely, the rivalry and turmoil between the city-states in Greece prevented the development of a solid philosophy, i.e., one founded on geometry: "*Philosophy* was not yet risen to the *Graecians*, and other people of the West, whose *Commonwealths* (no greater that *Lucca*, or *Geneva*) had never *Peace*, but when their fears of one another were equall; nor the *Leasure* to observe any thing but one another" (*Lev.* 46.6; 1054). For the same reason, the "Savages of America, are not without some good Morall Sentences, also they have a little Arithmetick ... but they are not therefore Philosophers" (*Lev.* 46.6; 1054).

Moreover—and this was of eminent importance for Hobbes—the original idea of justice as the protection of the weak was forged and developed in these archaic monarchies. In implementing justice, however, as Hobbes emphasizes, these archaic kingdoms started from the premise that any dissonance in questions of morality would destroy the foundations of human coexistence:

> *I suppose those antients foresaw this, who rather chose to have the Science of Justice* [Justitiae scientia] *wrapt up in fables, then openly exposed to disputations: for before such questions began to be moved, Princes did not sue для, but already exercised the supreme power. They kept their Empire entire, not by arguments, but by punishing the wicked, and protecting the good* [proborum vero defensione]; *likewise Subjects did not measure what was just by the sayings and judgements of private men, but by the Lawes of the Realme; nor were they kept in peace by disputations, but by power and authority: yea they reverenced the supreme power, whether residing in one man or in a councell, as a certain visible divinity.*
>
> (*De cive*, Pref., 6)

Hobbes's view of these archaic kingdoms has since been confirmed by historical research. Contrary to the Hegelian stereotype of oriental despotism, justice—and not arbitrary power—was the normative basis of the pre-axial monarchies in Egypt, Mesopotamia, and even China and India (Bellah 2011: 210–64). Above all, the reign of the pharaohs was legitimized by the *ma'at* (order, justice, truth), which encompassed both cosmic and societal order. Thus, the "Egyptian state is the implementation of a legal order that precludes the natural supremacy of the strong and opens up prospects for the weak (the 'widows and orphans') that otherwise would not exist. The political hierarchy of the state is the means by which the ruler 'saves the weak from the hand of the strong'" (Assmann 2003: 155). As Hobbes emphasizes, however, the legal protection of the weak or the righteous (*proborum vero defensione*) can only be asserted when questions of justice are withdrawn from the private judgment of individuals. In the archaic monarchies, decisional power resided solely with the king, whose authority was then idealized in myths. According to Hobbes, this is why the people revered the ruler "as a certain visible divinity" and "Wherefore it was peace, and a golden age" (*De cive*, Pref., 6).

For Hobbes, however, this archaic knowledge of justice has been dangerously undermined in European history, firstly by Greek philosophy and then by Latin Christianity (Kraynak 1990: 7–68). Only the Seven Sages, who had learned astronomy and geometry from the Chaldeans and Egyptians, had kept the original idea of justice alive. And in this period "we hear not yet of any *Schools* of *Philosophy*" (*Lev*. 46.6; 1054). In the classical era, though, a moral pluralism takes hold in Greek society thanks to Socratic philosophy, which radically calls into question the authority of the state order. This is exacerbated by countless wars between the Greek city-states, leading to far-reaching disruptions of social life. In contrast to Hegel, Hobbes, who had translated Thucydides' *History of the Peloponnesian War* in 1629, does not consider the Greek democracies to represent "progress in the consciousness of freedom" (Hegel), but a time of permanent violence and civil wars (Evrigenis 2014: 135–43). Later, as the Roman Empire expands, the forces of order regain the upper hand to an extent. Nonetheless, the Christian emperor could not restore the archaic authority of the divine king. Indeed, a rivalry then erupts between the pope and the emperor in Latin Christianity, the cause of countless conflicts. The reception of Greek philosophy leads to the formation of theological schools within the Church, which further decomposes the normative foundations of society.

> The first doctors of the Church, next the Apostles, born in those times, whilst they endeavoured to defend the Christian faith against the Gentiles by natural reason, began also to make use of philosophy ... From that time, instead of the worship of God, there entered a thing called *school divinity* ... For it has raised an infinite number of controversies in the Christian world concerning religion, and from those controversies, wars.
>
> (*De corpore*, Ep. ded.; *EW* 1.x)

This broad retrospective view of the weakening of state authority through Greek philosophy and Latin Christianity forms the background to Hobbes's analysis of the civil wars in Europe, so that in effect "Hobbes investigated the condition of civil society from the time of ancient Egypt to seventeenth-century England" (Kraynak 1990: 11).

According to Hobbes, the conflict potential residing in the processes of enlightenment, which had undermined state authority since antiquity, was erupting in the religious civil wars in contemporary Europe. In *Behemoth or the Long Parlament* (1668), Hobbes laments for example how Protestant groups, acting in the name of their own specific interpretation of the gospels, refuse obedience to the king; for their part, the scholars and London merchants, appealing to Greek democracy, question the monarchy (Hobbes 2010: 109–11). In short, a fundamental crisis is manifesting in the English Civil War, one not limited to Britain but gripping all Western culture (Kraynak 1990: 37; 60f.)

Although the stability of the sacral monarchies is evoked in the historical retrospective, for Hobbes there is no way back to archaic times. The breakthrough of philosophy—and Hobbes is adamant here—cannot be reversed. Attempts to re-sacralize political power, for example James I's defense of the divine right of kings, are condemned to failure. Political philosophy now faces an epochal challenge—to replace the sacral sources of state rule with rational foundations. In short, the divine king has to be replaced by a *"Mortall God,"* as Hobbes calls Leviathan (*Lev.* 17.13; 260). At the same time, however, after his retrospective view into the history of moral philosophy, Hobbes faces an aporia. On the one hand, the breakthrough of reason is irreversible, but on the other, philosophy, or more precisely the formation of schools of philosophy, is itself part of the problem. It is at this point that Hobbes resorts to geometry's ideal of exactness. The geometrical method is to lift moral and state philosophy out of the mire of endless disputes among schools and place them on secure footing.

First principles: geometrical method and curiosity

In the spirit of Bacon, Hobbes declares the task of science to be the exercising of power over nature for the benefit of humankind (*De homine* 11.13; *De corpore* 1.6). In contrast to Bacon, however, Hobbes sees the key to constructing a new science not just in pursuing an experimental philosophy of nature, but above all in geometry. The advantage of geometry lies in the apodictic evidence of its axioms and deductions on the one hand, and in its utility on the other. In both respects geometry is the methodological model for moral philosophy:

> And truly the Geometricians have very admirably perform'd their part. For whatsoever assistance doth accrew to the life of man, whether from

the observation of the Heavens, or from the description of the Earth, from the notation of Times, or from the remotest Experiments of Navigation. Finally, whatsoever things they are in which this present Age doth differ from the rude simplenesse of Antiquity, we must acknowledge to be a debt which we owe meerly to Geometry. If the Morall Philosophers had as happily discharg'd their duty, I know not what could have been added by humane Industry to the completion of that happinesse, which is consistent with humane life.

(*De cive*, Pref. 5–6; cf. *De corpore* 1.7)

Like Bacon, Hobbes interprets the new science in the light of the early modern voyages of discovery. However, for Hobbes it is no longer the embarking on a voyage into the unknown, the open sea of the Atlantic, but the view *over* the various seas that serves as a symbol for the new science.

And from the diversity of the matter about which they are conversant, there hath been given to those branches a diversity of Names too: For treating of Figures, tis call'd Geometry; of motion, Physick; of naturall right, Moralls; put all together, and they make up Philosophy. Just as the British, the Atlantick, and the Indian Seas, being diversly christen'd from the diversity of their shoares, doe notwithstanding all together make up The Ocean.

(*De cive*, Pref. 5)

In contrast to Bacon, Hobbes no longer considers himself to be merely a prophet heralding a new science to be achieved by future explorers. This distinction from Bacon is not the result of arrogance but based on objective reasons. Moral philosophy cannot afford the luxury of countless experiments, whereby the results eventually converge into a process of knowledge spanning generations. Confronted with the destructive violence of the civil wars, authoritative and binding orientation has to be found here and now to prevent any further bloodshed. This is another reason why the geometrical method is of pivotal significance for Hobbes; it furnishes universally valid knowledge and not just suppositions (*coniecturae*).

In the realm of political philosophy, however, Hobbes initially starts from a materialist ontology of the body, which is then connected with the geometrical method in a second step: "The *subject* of philosophy, or the matter it treats of, is every body of which we can conceive any generation, and which we may, by any consideration thereof, compare with other bodies, of which is capable of composition and resolution" (*De corpore* 1.8; *EW* 1.10). The bridge to political philosophy is created through the concept of the artificial body, which includes not only artifacts but also states. Philosophy is therefore divided into two parts: the philosophy of nature is concerned with bodies pieced together by nature, while the philosophy of the state deals with a body which "is called a *commonwealth*, and which is made by the wills and agreement of men" (*De corpore* 1.9; *EW* 1.11). And this civil philosophy has to be divided again, "into two parts, whereof one, which treats of men's dispositions and manners, is called ethics; and the other, which takes cognizance of their civil duties, is called *politics* or simply *civil philosophy*" (*De corpore* 1.9; *EW* 1.11).

With ethics, coextensive with anthropology, the philosophy of the state also contains a part devoted to the philosophy of nature. Although bodies are perceived from the outset in the horizon of their reproduction, Hobbes, unlike Bacon, no longer sees the task of science to be the transference of specific properties to *any arbitrary* body; rather, the goal of philosophy "is to search out the properties of bodies from their generation or their generation from their properties" (*De corpore* 1.8; *EW* 1.10; cf. *Lev.* 46.1: 1053). Because figures and lines are constructed by humans, exact knowledge is possible in geometry in accordance with the *verum-factum* principle: "Therefore science is allowed to men through the former kind of *a priori* demonstration only of those things whose generation depends on the will of men themselves" (*De homine* 10.4; 41f.). Studying natural things, however, as Hobbes presumes in an objective convergence with Nicholas of Cusa, moves within the field of conjecture, i.e., in assuming *possible* causes and modes of generation (*De homine* 1.5).

The importance of geometry for universal science stems from its grounding in a nominalist philosophy of language (Isermann 1991). According to Hobbes, philosophy is to provide clarifying definitions from everyday language. Scientific concepts are added together to form sentences, sentences in turn syllogisms. But it is also possible to deduct from a conclusion another statement again and to arrive at a different conclusion. For Hobbes, the geometricians proceed no differently, adding and deducting figures and angles, etc.; and so too political philosophy, which adds together contracts to justify obligations (*Lev.* 5.1-2; 64-6). In short, geometry is "with a most perfect pattern of the logic by which they were enabled to find out and demonstrate such excellent theorems as they have done" (*De corpore*, Ep. ded.; *EW* 1.vii.). Nonetheless, philosophy is not to be reduced merely to a critical scrutiny of language usage. As Hobbes notes, the best method of defining was discovered by the practical geometricians, for their definitions also contain knowledge on how a thing is generated. Whoever knows the definition of the circle, for example, can draw a circle at any time, even if the instrument, namely the compass, is not at hand (*De corpore* 1.5; *EW* 1.6). Moreover, the practical geometricians are concerned with material things and their qualities are taken into account when constructing. Both of these aspects are relevant for applying the geometrical method to political philosophy. Besides *a priori* deductions from evident axioms, a philosophy of the state must also take into consideration the empirical data of human life, in particular the effects generated by the passions (Tricaud 1988: 140).

In the analysis of human nature, however, Hobbes initially arrives at an extreme determinism on the basis of the materialist ontology of the body. The stimuli aroused by contact with things are reproduced via the nervous system within humans, whereby different ideas about the things perceived are generated in the brain, whereas in the heart feelings of attraction and aversion arise (*Lev.* 6.9; 82). In short, the intellectual life of a human being is nothing more than a reflex triggered by external influences. At this point, a pressing question emerges: how can a new foundation for a science of justice be laid within the framework of a mechanistic philosophy of nature in which freedom, in the sense of accountability and self-determination based on reason, is excluded by definition? And what is more, without a discerning concept of human freedom, Hobbes's *scientia iustitiae*—like the geometric method itself, which presupposes the capacity of *free* construction—threatens to peter out and vanish in the causal mechanisms animating bodily motions.

But Hobbes avoids the obvious contradiction between a mechanistic philosophy of nature and the project of a new moral philosophy. In the middle of the empiricist analysis of human nature, at certain points at least, the deterministic schema is pierced. While not possessing innate ideas, humans do have innate drives, according to Hobbes, and moreover, these do not fully fit into the simple stimulus-reaction schema: "Of appetites, and Aversions, some are born with men; as appetite of food, Appetite of excretion, and exoneration … and some other Appetites, not many" (*Lev.* 6.4; 80). The innate dispositions are moments of the elementary drive to self-preservation, through which a human does not merely react to external stimuli but evaluates if the things encountered in the external world are beneficial for preserving human life or a hindrance (Esfeld 1995: 192–4; 212). The pre-reflexive evaluation of external things causes either "appetite" or "aversion," and these feelings determine human action directly. As Hobbes emphasizes, human beings do not have the power and will to act otherwise at all: "for every man is desirous of what is good for him, and shuns what is evil, but chiefly the chiefest of natural evils, which is Death" (*De cive* 1.7). It is therefore from the self-preservation drive that the first foundational concepts of morality, in classical terms the pleasantly good, agreeable, and useful (*bonum delectabile, bonum iucundum, utile*), are derived: "But whatsever is the object of any man's Appetite or Desire; that is it, which he for his part called *Good*: and the object of Hate, and Aversion, *Evill*; And of his Contempt, *Vile* and *Inconsiderable*" (*Lev.* 6.7; 80). At this level of analysis, the *bonum honestum*, i.e., the good for its own sake, in which since the Stoics the real meaning of morality had been seen, is obviously excluded.

Nonetheless, not all things we are attracted to through our elementary drives serve the preservation and furthering of our lives. Whether an object is indeed "good," i.e., beneficial for our vital motions, is only evaluable by proceeding "from Experience, and triall of their effects upon themselves, or other men" (*Lev.* 6.4; 80). Experience, though, presupposes the capacity to remember. In this way Hobbes goes beyond the simple stimulus-reaction schema and toward an appraising and deliberative orientation on life. Both humans and animals are capable of remembering and experiencing. Because the memory capacity of animals is weak, their self-preservation drive is directed toward immediately satisfying elementary needs. In contrast, human beings possess the ability to look at and account for life as a whole. With consciousness extending into a future, humans are superior to animals; albeit this advantage is the cause of a particular misfortune, for "whereas there is no other Felicity of Beasts, but the enjoying of their quotidien Food, Ease, and Lusts," due to the de-limited temporal horizon humans necessarily live "in a perpetuall solicitude for the time to come" (*Lev.* 12.4–5; 167).

Hobbes thus strongly contradicts classical ancient anthropology, especially that of Xenophon, where foresight was considered a privilege of humans that ensures their good fortune and happiness: "In the first place, the human is the only living creature that they have made to stand upright; and the upright position gives him a wider range of vision in front and a better view of things above, and exposes him less to injury" (*Mem.* 1.4.11). Provocatively, Hobbes sees Prometheus, traditionally venerated as a cultural hero, as symbolizing the fall into profound misfortune because of this capacity to think ahead (*promethein*):

> For as *Prometheus*, (which interpreted, is, *The prudent man*,) was bound to the hill *Caucasus*, a place of large prospect, where an Eagle feeding on his liver, devoured in the day, as much as he was repayred in the night: So that man, which looks too far before him, in the care of future time, hath his heart all the day long, gnawed on by feare of death, poverty, or other calamity; and has no repose nor pause of his anxiety, but in sleep.
>
> (*Lev.* 12.5; 164–6)

In the light of the materialistic ontology of bodies, Hobbes sees the difference between humans and animals as one of gradation and not qualitative. Only through discipline and diligence can a human *become* a prudent being and thus superior to animals. This means that Hobbes transforms the Renaissance idea of creative freedom; no longer—as was still the case for Pico—relating solely to the decision pro or contra different forms of life, it now also encompasses the gradual process of becoming human, i.e., an *animal rationale* (Isermann 1991: 38).

Despite this, and without questioning materialistic monism, Hobbes acknowledges a certain ontological difference between humans and animals. The decisive distinction resides not in the endowment of reason but in the passion of curiosity. Whereas the desire of an animal is primarily activated through external things and the unknown hence has no allure, humans possess "a desire to experience the unknown. Whence it is that the infants desire few things, while youths try many new things, and with increasing age mature men, especially educated ones, experiment with innumerable things even with those that are unnecessary" (*De homine* 11.3). And where does this desire come from? "For nature hath made man an admirer of all new things" (*De homine* 11.9). Thus, "Hobbes does not give a causal explanation of curiosity's specificity to man, and does not go further into the definition of the 'organs' that make it possible" (Paganini 2012: 249). Unlike the unbounded future-oriented consciousness, which plunges humans into fear and worry, curiosity is a source of joy: "Admiration is the passion of joy in novelty ... This passion is almost peculiar to man" (*De homine* 12.12).

Herein lies the difference between humans and animals. Whenever other animals "behold something new or unusual, admire it as far as they are able whether it be harmful or harmless to them; men, when they see something new, seek to know whence it came and to what use they can put it. And so they rejoice in novelty as an occasion for learning about causes and effects" (*De homine* 12.12). Curiosity is therefore not limited to simply moving humans to admire things; instead, it kindles an interest to find out the causes behind them: "*Desire* to know why, and how, CURIOSITY; such as in no living creature but Man" (*Lev.* 6.35; 86). On the one hand, curiosity is an insatiable desire, "a Lust of the mind, that by a perseverance of delight in the continuall and indefatigable generation of Knowledge, exceedeth the short vehement of any carnall Pleasure" (*Lev.* 6.35; 86); on the other, it also possesses an innovative power. Since earliest times, humans have produced things securing survival, but also broadened the horizon of their physical and intellectual motions. As Hobbes specifies,

"But the most noble and profitable invention of all other, was that of SPEECH, consisting of *Names* or *Appellations*, and their Connexion" (*Lev.* 4.1; 48). While in the animal kingdom and early humankind various language tools were in use, such as signals produced through movements of the tongue, palate, and lips, it was first with the invention of signs and their systematization that humans were able to conceive of the causes and effects of *all* things. For Hobbes, curiosity and language thus rely on one another circularly (G. Buck 1976: 241).

Like all passions, curiosity harbors numerous dangers. While curiosity saves people from dogmatism and pride because the curious still search for truth, it can, as Hobbes points out in agreement with Augustine, also activate ambition and pride, i.e., a sense of superiority over others. In turn, pride is one of the main causes of human conflict and violates the moral law of equality (*Lev.* 15.21; 123; Lloyd 2018: 369f.). Above all else, however, curiosity seduces us into inventing all sorts of reasons and causes, a concern Hobbes shares with Montaigne. When seeking to allay difficult questions of morality or to find happiness, a human will mostly imagine and readily adopt "causes" which, like ghosts and heathen gods, "his own fancy suggesteth" (*Lev.* 12.4; 87). And philosophy is by no means immune to the danger of abnormally inventing new causes. The invention of the formal cause is a dangerous product of a fanciful imagination because it nurtures the assumption of independent spiritual entities and thus misleads to a belief in ghosts or higher powers. To forestall this danger, curiosity requires methodological discipline, i.e., it needs to be oriented on a regulated line of thinking (*discursus ordinatus*), for which Hobbes deems it necessary to draw a distinction between two types. The first form of ordered thought is "when of an effect imagined, wee seek the causes, or means that produce it" (*Lev.* 3.5; 40). Because prudence and primitive forms of purpose-bound rationality are to be found in animals, the first form of regulated thinking is "common to Man and Beast" (ibid.). With the second form of the *discursus ordinatus*, namely "imagining any thing whatsoever, we seek all the possible effects [!], that can by it be produced" (ibid.), something that only humans are capable of, Hobbes comes close to Bacon's idea of a new science based on a "creative curiosity" (Lloyd 2018: 367f.).

Despite his orientation on the evidence of geometry, in which a certain distance from Bacon is discernible, Hobbes's philosophy remains within the vision of "effecting all things possible" and relates the creative power of science primarily to human life:

By PHILOSOPHY, is understood *the Knowledge acquired by Reasoning from the Manner of the Generation of any thing, to the Properties; or from the properties,*

to some possible Way of Generation of the same; to the end to bee able to produce, as far as matter, and humane force permit, such effects, as humane life requireth.
(*Lev.* 46.1; 1052)

Although the boundary between humans and animals has become fluid, for Hobbes the idea of manipulating the biological nature of humans still remains beyond his intellectual horizon. As for Montaigne, the medium of self-creation for humans remains language: "For as when one paints a man, he paints the image of some man; so he, that defines the name man, makes a representation of some man to the mind" (*De corpore* 1.6.15; *EW* 1.84).

To sum up: Through a de-limited consciousness of the future, aligned with curiosity and a focus on the invention of language, Hobbes prizes open the mechanistic determinism of materialistic ontology. "Man is … the linguistic, curious, forward-looking being, and all that flows from that" (Kavka 1986: 30). By identifying curiosity as the passion driving humans' development into rational beings, Hobbes overcomes the metaphysical dualism of nature and mind that had again become virulent with Descartes. "The idea of 'passionate thought' is a real novelty in Hobbes's philosophy" (Paganini 2012: 279). Nonetheless, the gap between nature and mind is not completely bridged by materialistic monism because "Hobbes does not give a causal explanation of curiosity's specificity to man" (Paganini 2012: 249). Not least, based on Renaissance thought from Nicholas of Cusa through to Montaigne and Bacon, Hobbes articulates an outstanding contribution to the revaluation of insatiable curiosity in modern philosophy (Daston and Park 1998: 304–7). Moreover, Hobbes describes curiosity, in accord with Montaigne, as a passion characteristic of human beings, while connecting it, unlike Montaigne, to modern science. As Paganini acknowledges, within this constellation Hobbes occupies a "key position in the development of modern thinking" on curiosity (2018: 30).

The subject matter of morality: peace on earth as the greatest of all goods

Although all humans are driven by the passion of curiosity, according to Hobbes only a small minority have applied themselves to a methodologically disciplined search for causes and effects. Not only the peoples of the Americas, who possess "some good Morall Sentences" and "a little Arithmethik," lacked science because "there was no Method, that is to say, no Sowing, nor Planting of Knowledge by it self, apart from the Weeds, and common Plants of Errour and Conjecture" (*Lev.* 46.6; 1054); Europeans have also remained stuck on the level of mere empirical knowledge: "men that know not what it is that we call causing, (that is, almost all men) have no other rule to guesse by, but by observing" (*Lev.* 12.8; 89). This is why people are caught in a quandary about civil war. While rejecting it as an evil, because they do not look for the causes of the conflicts, an end of the violence is not foreseeable (*De corpore* 1.1.7; *EW* 1.8). Ultimately, civil wars arise out of and are perpetuated by a lack of curiosity.

For Hobbes, one of the principal causes of wars is a false understanding of what makes up morality. Hobbes therefore prepends his theory of the state not only with the natural condition, in which the mechanisms escalating violence are examined, but also a definition of fundamental moral concepts, which in keeping with the critical linguistic method builds on the intuition of everyday moral consciousness: "For Moral Philosophy is nothing else but Science of what is *Good*, and *Evill*, in the conversation, and Society of man-kind" (*Lev.* 15.40; 242). Considering the sacral kingship of oriental empires, Hobbes had identified the subject matter of morality through the idea of justice in the sense of protecting the weak from the despotism of the strong; on the basis of empirical anthropology, however, until now it was possible to elaborate merely a subjectivist definition of good and bad as an object of our likes and dislikes. To bridge the gap between the sensualistic concept of morality and the archaic idea of justice in the sense of legal protection for the weak, Hobbes surprisingly resorts to the Christian teaching on natural law: "naturall [Law] is that which God hath declared to all men by his eternall word borne with them, to wit, their naturall Reason" (*De cive* 14.4). But because there is no consensus in moral philosophy on the significance or the foundations of "natural law," the law of nature is obviously not present in the human mind as an infallible rational intuition. In contrast to humanist thinkers such as Sepúlveda, Hobbes rejects all attempts to base the laws of nature on "the generall Agreement of all the most wise, and learned Nations" or on the "the Generall consent of all Man-kind." With the former it remains unclear "who shall be the judge of the wisdome and learning of all Nations"; while with respect to the latter, it is "in truth unreasonable … to receive the Lawes of Nature from the Consents of them, who oftner Break, then Observe them" (*De cive* 2.1). Thus, Hobbes avoids the Eurocentric trap that the humanistic doctrine on natural law fell into, understanding and deriving, as became evident in Sepúlveda, the content of *lex naturae* exclusively from Greco-Roman philosophy (cf. Chapter 7, section 7.4 in this book). The disagreement about natural law can only be overcome when the fundamental norms are derived *more geometrico* from self-evident principles. Therefore "we ought to judge those Actions onely *wrong*, which are repugnant to right Reason, (*i.e.*) which contradict some certaine Truth collected by right reasoning from true Principles" (*De cive* 2.1).

Like the Stoics, Hobbes assumes that the first principle of morality is self-preservation: "A LAW OF NATURE, (*Lex Naturalis,*) is a Precept, or generall Rule, found out by Reason, by which a man is forbidden to do, that, which is destructive of his life, or taketh it may be best preserved" (*Lev.* 14.3; 64). Pursuing things necessary for sustaining life is not just a natural desire but also a moral obligation and indeed a right. However, the transition from the empirical concept of natural striving for self-preservation to the normative concept of "moral or natural right" remains unexplained (Habermas 1973: 79; Geismann and Herb 1988: Scholie 190).

The crucial and still controversial question is whether Hobbes's natural right justifies only instructions promoting the self-preservation of individual agents (Kavka 1986: 360; Hampton 1986) or includes the common good, i.e., the good of humanity (Lloyd 2019: 97–150).

There is no doubt that Hobbes's principle of self-preservation embraces both individual and socio-ethical dimensions. Thus, "Drunkeness, and all other parts of Intemperance" (*Lev.* 15.34; 238) contradict the imperative to preserve one's own life. But the main concern of Hobbes's theory of natural law relates to the socio-ethical domain. For this reason, the idea of peace is the first conclusion to be drawn from the self-evident principle of self-preservation: "For it can never be that Warre shall preserve life, and Peace destroy it" (*Lev.* 15.38; 240). Hobbes focuses his analysis of the *lex naturalis* to those "Laws of Nature, dictating Peace, for means of the conservation *of men in multitudes*" (*Lev.* 15.34; 238; emphasis added). The first law of nature inseparably tied to the self-preservation principle is: "*That every man, ought to endeavour Peace, as farre as he has hope of obtaining it*" (*Lev.* 14.4; 200). In this respect—and not because of a divine decree—the laws of nature are "Immutable and Eternall; For Injustice, Ingratitude, Arrogance, Pride, Iniquity, Acception of persons, and the rest, can never be lawful" (*Lev.* 15.38; 240).

However, even the duty to seek peace can still be interpreted from the perspective of individual self-preservation. Thus, natural laws are not intrinsically binding but "only prudential reasons governing the dispositions and actions that are the relevant means for peaceful social interaction" (Abizadeh 2018: 223). In the further analysis of both the state of nature and the *status civilis*, however, it will become apparent that Hobbes's law of nature transcends the narrow horizon of mere individual self-interest.

In the demand that everything be done to establish peace, Hobbes knows he is in agreement with traditional moral philosophy. And indeed, in the history of ethics, as Hobbes concedes, there was never any dispute that "*Justice*,

Gratitude, Modesty, Equity, Mercy" (*Lev.* 15.40; 242) belong to the moral virtues and their opposites to the vices. The deficiency plaguing moral philosophy up until now was thus not a false catalogue of virtues but distortions of the guiding preconception of morality.

> But the Writers of Morall Philosophie, though they acknowledge the same Vertues and Vices [!]; Yet not seeing wherein consisted their Goodnesse; nor that they come to be praised, as the means of peaceable, sociable, and comfortable living; place them in a mediocrity of passions: as if not the Cause, but the Degree of daring, made Fortitude; or not the Cause, but the Quantity of a gift, made Liberality.
>
> (*Lev.* 15.40; 242)

The moral quality of virtues ("their goodness") no longer resides in a "mean" (*mesotes*) between extremes but in how they foster peaceful, sociable, and congenial coexistence. For this reason, the willingness to help the needy and fit in with others is at the very heart of morality: "*That every man do help and endeavour to accommodate each other, as far as may be without danger of their persons, and loss of their means, to maintain and defend themselves*" (*Elem.* 1.16.8). Since self-preservation is possible only in and through the community, Hobbes's morality is in a natural way altruistic (Ludwig 1998: 374). Hobbes therefore derives from the first law of nature duties that promote community, such as the willingness to forgive, or not to offend anyone by an act, a word, an expression, or a gesture (*Lev.* 15.18–20; 232–4). In contrast, what does not belong to the inner domain of morality is the Christian demand to love one's enemies. Whoever fulfills moral obligations unilaterally makes themselves prey for others and therefore violates the moral principle of self-preservation (*Lev.* 15.36; 240).

Pivotal motifs from traditional ethics flow into Hobbes's thinking through this inclusion of natural law, in particular the idea of peace, which Augustine had already moved to the center of moral philosophy. But the distinction between fundamental norms of natural law and the Christian ethos of self-sacrifice is by no means unfamiliar to traditional moral theology, as Sepúlveda's critique of Christian pacifism revealed. Against this background, Hobbes's verdict on the tradition appears to be an exaggeration. Nonetheless, the aspiration to save the original sense of morality from the moral philosophy tradition is not baseless. Christian theology always defined the common good (*bonum commune*) as a union of earthly and heavenly peace, meaning that the concept of morality was always defined from the standard of the highest good, i.e., the otherworldly vision of God. The natural laws therefore not only served to promote peace on earth, but also prepared the way for eternal salvation. This is where Hobbes's criticism of Christian morality begins. Heavenly peace has to be eliminated from the concept of morality for two reasons. Firstly, eternal felicity is no longer a good because "there would be nothing to long for, nothing to desire" (*De homine* 11.15; cf. *Lev.* 6.58; 96); and secondly, limiting the concept of morality to earthly peace is the only way to ensure that fundamental moral norms, the obligation of *pacta sunt servanda* for example, are not relativized or indeed overridden in the name of eternal felicity. In this context Hobbes refers to the Christian justification of breaching fidelity with respect to heretics: "Others, that allow for a Law of Nature, the keeping of Faith, do nevertheless make exception of certain persons; as Heretiques, and such as use not to performe the Covenant to others: And this also is against reason" (*Lev.* 15.9; 226).

The sense of morality must be explicated from the fundamental good of self-preservation. Hobbes thus criticizes Christian theology "that proceed further; and will not have the Law of nature, to be those Rules which conduce to the preservation of mans Life on earth; but to the attaining of an eternall felicity after death; to which they think the breach of Covenant may conduce; and consequently be just and reasonable" (*Lev.* 15.8; 226).

By limiting the realm of morality to the promotion of earthly peace, Hobbes removes in a single blow one of the most important reasons employed to legitimate the escalation of violence in medieval society. But also in the colonial debates of the early modern period, as became discernible in Vitoria, the union of earthly and eternal felicity led to dubious perversions of ethical universalism, in particular the justification of the violent imposition of Christian mission law (see Chapter 7, section 7.3). Unlike Sepúlveda, who valorizes the autonomy of natural law over *ius divinum* without dissolving their unity, Hobbes decouples morality from its religious context.

Along with separating morality from the *visio beatifica*, Hobbes undertakes a second significant correction of traditional moral philosophy. Peace on earth is inseparably tied to the idea of justice, specifically protecting the weak from the despotism of the strong. Since Aristotle, however, moral philosophy has distinguished between *iustitia commutativa* and *iustitia distributiva*. Whereas the equality of all humans is presupposed in commutative justice, in distributive justice, wherein each person is allocated what they deserve, the dignity of a person is taken into account. The distinction between the two concepts of justice is thus based on the principle of the natural rule of persons exercising their reason over those less able. The Aristotelian doctrine that some are naturally suited to rule thanks to their capacity of reason, while for others it is best to obey, contradicts the original equality of human beings according to Hobbes: "for neither almost is any man so dull of understanding as not to judge it better to be ruled by himselfe, then to yield himselfe to the government of another" (*De cive* 3.13). For this reason, the Aristotelian distinction between commutative and distributive justice "is not well made, inasmuch as injury, which is the injustice of action, consisteth not in the inequality of things changed, or distributed, but in the inequality that men (contrary to nature and reason) assume unto themselves above their fellows" (*Elem.* 1.16.5).

The right of self-determination is closely associated with the principle of self-preservation. A conscientious decision about the means most suitable for ensuring self-preservation, and above all for defending one's own life, cannot be left to someone else. This means that "every man by right of nature is judge himself of the necessity of the means, and the greatness of danger" (*Elem.* 1.14.8). In other words, all humans are "masters of their lives" (*Lev.* 21.6; 328). Even if some are superior to others in their intellectual abilities, in the domain of morality the consciousness of one's freedom, articulated in the will to "govern" oneself, must be respected. For Hobbes, the law of nature thus prescribes "that every man acknowledge the other for his Equall by Nature. The breach of this Precept is *Pride*" (*Lev.* 15.21; 123).

The laws of nature are subject to a dual condition of rationality. The *lex naturae* must not only be evident and comprehensible for all rational beings beyond doubt (*Lev.* 26.13; 215), but moreover it has to contain the principle of recognizing the rational autonomy of every individual. For Hobbes, the heart of morality is expressed in the Golden Rule directly understandable for all: "*Do not that to another, which thou wouldest not have done to thy selfe*" (*Lev.* 15.35; 234). Certainly, the Golden Rule can also still be interpreted in the logic of self-interest. However, since Hobbes, contrary to Aristotle, demands respect for the autonomy of reason of every human being, his moral philosophy is ultimately based on the idea of a common good.

10.2 The "state of nature": the "war of all against all" as a methodical fiction and its applications to historical reality

Hobbes places the postulate that each person has to endeavor to create peace under the proviso "as farr as he has hope of obtaining it" (*Lev.* 14.4; 105). On the level of abstract reflection, the principle that solely peace and never war secures the self-preservation of the individual is intuitively evident. In the historical world, however, characterized as it is by violence and war, the unilateral adherence to the peace imperative means gambling with one's life. The first law of nature therefore contains the problem of how to meet the demand of peace without renouncing self-preservation. In order to demonstrate coherently and rigorously, i.e., *more geometrico*, the relationship between the peace postulate and self-preservation, Hobbes sees it necessary to first identify the causes of violence. This is the topic of the famous doctrine on the state of nature (*Elem.* 1.14; *De cive* 1; *Lev.* 13).[2]

To gain a perspective on the logic behind escalations of violence, Hobbes designs a fictitious laboratory situation in which human interaction is analyzed under the methodological exclusion of a state power exercising authority and, at least in *De cive*, of familial and cultural ties ("consider men as if but even now sprung out of the earth ... without all kind of engagement to each other"; *De cive* 8.1; *EW* 2.108–9). In as far as relationships between adult individuals are modeled in a pure natural condition, starting from their natural dispositions and natural reason, then what the *status naturalis* articulates is an ahistorical truth that necessarily emerges from the main features of human nature.

Hobbes's theory of the state of nature has long been a focal point of extremely controversial interpretations. Already at the time of writing, Hobbes was confronted with the accusation that he was basing political philosophy on a negative anthropology, reducing human beings and their actions to a striving for power. Down to the present day, this strand of criticism has pointed to the dictum on the nature of the wolf (*De cive*, Ep. ded. 1–2) and humankind's insatiable striving for power: "I put for a generall inclination of all mankind, a perepetuall and restlesse desire of Power after power, that ceaseth onely in Death" (*Lev.* 11.2; 150; cf. *Lev.* 8.15; 110). Thus it would seem that Hobbes, diametrically opposed to Pico, assigns humankind an evil nature. But Hobbes explicitly rejects this thesis:

> Some object that this principle being admitted, it would needs follow, not onely that all men were wicked (which perhaps though it seeme hard, yet we must yeeld to, since it is so clearly declar'd by holy writ) but also wicked by nature (which cannot be granted without impiety). But this, that men are evill by nature, followes not from this principle.
>
> (*De cive*, Pref. 12)

Modern interpreters have deciphered Hobbes's theory of the natural state as reflecting a historical reality. According to Macpherson, the figure manifesting in the Hobbesian natural state is nothing other than the *homo oeconomicus* of early capitalist competitive society. In contrast to Macpherson, Francis Cheneval has explained the ahistorical natural state in terms of the power struggles between the territorial states of the early modern period, because only states can be fully separate, independent, and autarkic natural-state subjects capable of surviving (2002: 221). Referring to the extensive considerations on natural law, Leo Strauss has noted the presence of Stoic-Christian ethics in Hobbes's thought, an aspect that morally characterizes the striving for power as "vanity." Starting from the materialist ontology, the moral qualities of human nature are however increasingly relegated in importance. As Strauss puts it: "In laying the foundations of his political philosophy, Hobbes puts vanity more and more into the background in favour of innocent competition, innocent striving after power, innocent animal appetite, because the definition of man's natural appetite in terms of vanity is intended as a moral judgement" (Strauss 1952: 14). The Stoic-Christian elements flimsily conceal "Hobbes's characteristic theories—the denial that 'altruism' is natural, the theses of man's rapacious nature, of the war of every one against every one as the natural condition of mankind, of the essential impotence of reason" (Strauss 1952: 3). Without a nostalgic retrospective on classical ancient ethics, Hobbes's doctrine of the state of nature has been interpreted as a pre-societal condition of isolated self-interested individuals (Hampton 1986: 7–11) or as a prisoner's dilemma based on the rational choice theory (Hoekstra 2007).

In the following I would like to approach Hobbes's mature version of the natural condition, as explicated in *Leviathan* (Eggers 2008), from the context of the *scientia iustitia*. In a first step Hobbes examines the mechanisms of interaction between individuals who are guided solely by the natural striving for self-preservation and pleasure (*Lev.* 13.3; 190). In the second step, however, Hobbes complements this description of the state of nature in the light of his concept of natural laws.

Insofar as the natural laws are methodologically suspended, the natural condition is conceived as an "Inference made from the Passions" (*Lev.* 13.10; 194). The striving for self-preservation is at the same time a pursuit of power: "The POWER of a Man, (to take it Universally) is his present means, to obtain some future apparent Good" (*Lev.* 10.1; 132). Within the morally neutral concept of power, Hobbes distinguishes between Natural Power, for example "the eminence of the Faculties of Body, of Mind: as extraordinary Strength, Forme, Prudence, Arts, Eloquence, Liberality, Nobility," and instrumental powers, "which are acquired by these, or by fortune, are means and instruments to acquire more" (*Lev.* 10.2; 132). The often criticized thesis of the restlessness seemingly innate to the striving for power emerges for Hobbes initially out of the neediness of human existence, which forces all humans to strive for life-sustaining goods day in, day out, just to ensure their physical existence, i.e., power (McNeilly 1968: 144f.; Geismann and Herb 1988: Scholie 166). This broad concept of power encompasses social power as well: "Also, what quality soever maketh a man believed of many; or the reputation of such quality, is Power; because it is a means to have the assistance, and service of many" (*Lev.* 10.6; 134).

To analyze the destructive dynamic of the striving for power, according to Hobbes two further anthropological factors need to be considered, namely the unlimited future-oriented trajectory of the human mind and the instability of social relations. In contrast to the self-preservation drives of animals, limited to the immediate satisfaction of elementary needs, human desire, when animated by language and imagination, can be augmented and broadened at will, knowing no limits. As Hobbes puts it, for this reason "man surpasseth in rapacity and cruelty the wolves, bears, and snakes that are not rapacious unless hungry and not cruel unless provoked, whereas man is famished even by future hunger" (*De homine* 10.3). Human striving is not merely for a single moment, "to enjoy one onely, and for one instant of time, but to assure for ever, the way of his future desire" (*Lev.* 11.1; 150). The broader consciousness of a future corresponds to a heightened need for security, and this need in turn triggers a striving for ever more power: "but because he cannot assure the power and means to live well, which he hath present, without the acquisition of more" (*Lev.* 11.2; 150).

Nonetheless, Hobbes's theory of the state of nature is not simply based on the uncritical affirmation of a limitless extension for power. Due to the main purpose of self-preservation, the restlessness of the striving for power is, as Hobbes expressly states, "not always" (!) because "a man hopes for a more intensive delight, that he has already attained to; or that he cannot be content with a moderate power" (*Lev.* 11.2; 150).

However, as Hobbes emphasizes in the spirit of Montaigne, because people not only appreciate the same things differently, but moreover every single individual, in some cases quite frequently, is bound to change their opinion as to what is good and comfortable, a rational consensus is simply impossible on the level of the *bonum iucundum*, irrespective of whether the person concerned is content with modest power or not (*Lev.* 15.40; 242). Like Montaigne, Hobbes attributes the fickleness of the human mind to the influences of the body, which, however, are no longer analyzed by introspection but by natural science: "And because the constitution of a mans Body, is in continual mutation; it is impossible that all the same things should always cause in him the same Appetites, and

Aversions. Much lesse can all men consent, in the Desire of almost any one and the same Object" (*Lev.* 6.6; 80). Unlike Montaigne, however, Hobbes does not see the fickleness of human inclinations as merely reflecting the unsteadiness of human nature; rather, he probes further and identifies it as a breeding ground for the escalation of violence. Two factors transform varying opinions as to what is good and bad into the potential for dangerous conflict: the physical and the psychological vulnerability of humans.

Despite differences in physical or mental strength, for Hobbes humans are universally equal due to their vulnerability: "For as to the strength of body, the weakest has strength enough to kill the strongest, either by secret machination, or by confederacy with others, that are in the same danger with himselfe" (*Lev.* 13.1; 188). Not only physically, but in their need for recognition and appreciation, all humans are vulnerable in the same way: "For such is the nature of men, that howsoever they may acknowledge many others to be more witty, or more eloquent, or more learned; Yet they will hardly believe there be many so wise as themselves. For they see their own wit at hand, and other means at a distance" (*Lev.* 13.2; 188). Because each person, no matter whether scholar or simple citizen, tends to overvalue oneself, then a sense of being insulted and suffering emotional injury are *de facto* inevitable in interpersonal relationships.

Disagreement about the good in the sense of what is comfortable, in conjunction with the double vulnerability of human life, lays a breeding ground out of which ever new conflicts arise. The countless reasons able to set in motion the dynamic of conflict can be traced back to three causes: "First, Competition; Secondly, Diffidence; Thirdly, Glory." (*Lev.* 13.6; 192).

According to Hobbes, rivalry is ignited "if any two men desire the same thing, which nevertheless they cannot both enjoy" (*Lev.* 13.3; 190). Because the good is indivisible, the two become rivals "and in the way to their End, (which is principally their owne conservation, and sometimes their delectation only), endeavour to destroy, or subdue one an other" (*Lev.* 13.3; 190). Hobbes offers an example:

> And from hence it comes to passe, that where an Invader hath no more to feare, than an other mans single power; if one plant, sow, build, or possesse a convenient Seat, others may probably be expected to come prepared with forces united, to dispossesse, and deprive him, not only of the fruit of his labour but also of his life, or liberty.
>
> (Lev. 13.3; 190)

The struggle to gain scarce resources has repeatedly been interpreted as the first cause of the war of all against all, a problem that Locke however alleviated somewhat, perhaps even solved, with the idea of increasing productivity (Eggers 2008: 102–4). In *Leviathan* at least, Hobbes does not appear to assume a scarcity of goods. Assuming that all humans strive for nothing else than self-preservation and pleasure, then for the aggressor it would also make more sense to occupy another piece of land rather than get involved in a dangerous struggle with others. Only in a case of extreme overpopulation, when there is not enough arable land to support everyone, would the striving for self-preservation as such be a sufficient reason for engaging in a conflict to gain more resources or goods which could not be consumed and enjoyed by all. Hobbes discusses this problem elsewhere, namely when analyzing the tasks incumbent on the sovereign for looking after the poor capable of work, who, once state employment measures no longer suffice, need to be transferred to unsettled regions (*Lev.* 30.19; 540). War triggered by scarcity will come about only when the world's population has grown to such an extent that the earth can no longer support everyone: "And when all the world is overcharged with Inhabitants, then the last remedy of all is ware, which is provideth for every man, by Victory, or Death" (ibid.). The scenario of overpopulation does not underlie the depiction of the natural condition, however. The assumption of a scarcity of goods and land can be supported by drawing on Hobbes's anthropological thesis on the limitless striving for more and more power. This means that assuming a stable production level, when *all* humans limitlessly pursue their needs, then scarcity will arise and inevitably lead to conflicts (Nonnenmacher 1989: 24–7; Münkler 2001: 101f.). This reconstruction of the *status naturalis* is contradictory however to the Hobbesian assumption that people are "not always" striving for more and more pleasure. Moreover, in the example Hobbes gives for the rising tensions of a competitive situation, not all the parties are driven by an insatiable will to power. Quite the contrary: Hobbes depicts a situation in which a solitary farmer, wanting to live a modest life on a small piece of land, is attacked by an aggressor. Considering this background, the reasons why a conflict situation arises remain initially obscure.

It is only the second cause of conflict, diffidence, which creates an inlet to understanding the competitive situation prevailing in the state of nature: "Also because there be some that taking pleasure in contemplating their own power in the acts of conquest, which they pursue farther than their security requires" (*Lev.* 13.4; 190). As Hobbes emphasizes, the peaceful farmer becomes a victim of violence because *a few*, i.e., by no means all, exercise and extend their power immoderately, attacking "for Gain" (*Lev.* 13.7; 192).

Questions remain despite this important clarification. Without an objective measure, each human uses their own reason to decide what is necessary to ensure self-preservation and gain enjoyment. Thus it is impossible to precisely determine the dividing line between those who "would be glad to be at ease within modest bounds" (*Lev.* 13.4; 100) and those boundlessly expanding their power. This means that even if all humans always act on the basis of moral motives, the war of all against all can still not be redressed because each person subordinates the natural laws to their own judgment. In contrast to this line of interpretation, Hobbes himself maintains the distinction between the moderate and the immoderate in all three descriptions of the natural state. And Hobbes seems to confirm this view in the Latin version of *Leviathan* when the motif of the limitless expansion of power is defined more closely through the idea of world dominion: "*Quoniam enim sunt animi et gloriae causa universum terrarum* [!] *orbem supere vellent* [for reasons of pride and glory would wish to conquer the whole world]" (*Lev.* 13.4; 191; cf. Esfeld 1995: 234). Whenever hegemony is striven for across the globe, instead of remaining within the *oikumene*, then the conflict situation sketched by Hobbes is indeed universal, as was already the case historically with ancient Rome and the Spanish empire in the sixteenth century. Even if the modest withdraw to the peripheral zones of the inhabitable world, they are still not safe from the imperators, driven on to extend their power to the *very ends* of the earth: "if others, that otherwise would be glad to be at ease within modest bounds, should not by invasion increase their power, they would not be able, long time, by standing only on their defence, to subsist" (*Lev.* 13.4; 190).

Since it is impossible to know who will look to limitlessly extend their power in the future, "For though the wicked were fewer then the righteous, yet because we cannot distinguish them" (*De cive*, Pref. 12), then those content to otherwise remain in "modest bounds" have to expand the realm of their power to avoid being taken by surprise and attacked by the power-hungry without any preceding dispute. Moreover, to secure their permanent survival, ultimately the modest are forced to extend and augment their power to the point where no serious rival exists who poses a threat: "And from this diffidence of one another, there is no way for any man to secure himselfe, so reasonable, as Anticipation; that is, by force, or wiles, to master the persons of all men he can, so long, till he see no other power great enough to endanger him" (*Lev.* 13.4; 190). In other words, the principle of self-preservation implies that claim be laid to world dominion.

Consequently, the first two causes of conflict in the natural state arise out of the same scenario, the attempt to violently dominate peaceful farmers, which is analyzed from two perspectives: "The first use Violence, to make themselves Masters of other mens persons, wives, children, and cattell; the second, to defend them" (*Lev.* 13.7; 192). The aggression stems from the passionate drive to gain world dominion, while the peaceful and moderate farmer resorts to violence motivated by the moral reason of self-defense. In the Latin version, therefore, Hobbes calls the second cause of conflict "*Defensio*" (*Lev.* 13.6; 193) and not merely diffidence. Hobbes obviously maintains the *moral* difference between the power-hungry and those content to live modestly when describing the natural state. The legitimacy of the peaceful farmer's exercising and augmenting of power resides, as Hobbes emphasizes, in the *moral* right to ensure self-preservation: "And by consequence, such augmentation of dominion over men, being necessary to a mans conservation, it ought to be allowed him" (*Lev.* 13.4; 190). At this point, the description of the state of nature as "Inference, made from the Passions" changes into a moral analysis based on the doctrine of natural law. Moreover, the choice of the means for ensuring self-preservation stems from the autonomy of an individual's reason, as Hobbes underlines by appealing to natural law:

> The Right Of Nature, which Writers commonly call *Jus Naturale*, is the Liberty each man hath, to use his own power, as he will himselfe, for the preservation of his own Nature; that is to say, of his own Life; and consequently, of doing any thing, which in his own Judgement, and Reason, hee shall conceive to be the aptest means thereunto.
>
> (*Lev.* 14.1; 198)

Because the universal augmentation of power is the sole means available to secure the preservation of one's own life, each human has a right of dominion over everyone else: "It followeth, that in such a condition, every man has a Right to every thing; even to one anothers body" (*Lev.* 14.4; 198). This means that the preventive augmentation of power is not only an "Inference, made from the Passions" (*Lev.* 13.10; 194), but at the same time a demand of natural law. The exhaustive formulation for the first law of nature therefore is: "*That every man, ought to endeavour Peace, as farre as he has hope of obtaining it; and when he cannot obtain it, that he may seek, and use, all helps, and advantages of Warre*" (*Lev.* 14.4; 200).

The third cause of conflict, the striving to attain glory, refers to the vulnerability in interpersonal relations. Because all humans have a need to be recognized and acknowledged, while at the same time tending to overvalue themselves, social life is a productive breeding ground for having one's sense of honor violated. The struggle to gain recognition is no less intense than the struggle to procure material goods: "For every man looketh that his companion should value him, at the same rate he sets upon himselfe: And upon all signes of contempt, or undervaluing, naturally endeavours, as far as he dares ... to extort a greater value from his contemners, by dommage; and from others, by the example" (*Lev.* 13.5; 190). The struggle for recognition can be set off by the smallest gesture showing disregard, "a word, a smile, a different opinion, and any other signe of undervalue, either direct in their Persons, or by reflexion in their Kindred, their Friends, their Nation, their Profession, or their Name" (*Lev.* 13.7; 192). Like the claim to world dominion, the injuring of honor and worth sets in motion an endless spiral of violence. This is because the idea of honor eludes the measure of justice; thus efforts to restore honor unfailingly bring with them a boundless escalation of violence.[3]

Hobbes's theory of the natural state thus describes a scenario in which humans are exposed to a situation of extreme insecurity in a number of aspects. Firstly, the human in the natural condition is in a situation of permanent threat. Even if violence is not employed incessantly in the *status naturalis*—for "the nature of War, consisteth not in actual fighting; but in the known disposition thereto, during all the time there is no assurance to the contrary, All other time is PEACE"—then "continuall feare, and danger of violent death" (*Lev.* 13.8; 192) dominate due to mutual mistrust. Secondly, in a situation "wherein men live without other security, than what their own strength, and their own invention shall furnish them withall" (*Lev.* 13.9; 192), then the civilizing achievements of a society crumble and decay. As Hobbes's famous dictum expresses it, life in the natural condition is "the same is consequent to the time ... And the life of man, solitary, poore, nasty, brutish, and short" (*Lev.* 13.9; 192). Because the modest are also forced to resort to violence in the natural condition, then—thirdly—a dangerous corrosion of morality takes hold. According to Hobbes, in a situation where all are striving to limitlessly augment their power, basic moral principles evaporate, or indeed reverse into their opposite: "The notions of Right and Wrong, Justice and Injustice have there no place ... Force, and Fraud, are in warre the two Cardinall vertues" (*Lev.* 13.13; 196).

At this point it is possible to detail Hobbes's reversal of the ethnological perspective, which, as noted in the beginning, connects motifs from Montaigne and Sepúlveda. Hobbes also uses the theory of the state of nature to elaborate on how a foreigner stepping on European soil for the first time and surveying the carnage of raging civil wars must have the impression that any sense of morality and justice has gone missing in this corner of the world. From the observer perspective, it is indeed impossible to distinguish the upright and honest from the power-hungry. As Hobbes sees it, though, by no means can the conclusion be drawn that in the natural condition the *sense* of what is morally good and just has evaporated completely. In contrast to the power-hungry, the modest augment their power for the moral reason of self-defense and not out of the lust for conquest or acquisitiveness. Moral consciousness has not simply vanished in the natural condition but has been banished to the realm of inwardness: "The Lawes of Nature oblige *in foro interno*; that is to say, they bind to a desire they should take place: but *in foro externo*; that is, to the putting them in act, not alwayes" (*Lev.* 15.36; 240).

At this point the suspicion arises again that Hobbes ultimately strips human interactions of their moral dimension with his theory of the natural condition. In the theoretical construction of the natural state, the actors seem to be completely freed of moral consideration through the *ius ad omnia et omnes*. However, the right of self-defense, including the deployment of *all* means necessary, was already justified in classical ancient and medieval theories of natural law. Thus Cicero affirms the law "that, should our life have fallen into any snare, into the violence and the weapons of robbers or foes, every method of winning a way to safety would be morally justifiable" (*Pro Milone* 4; cf. *Summa theologica* II, q. 94, art. 2; Ludwig 1998: 424). What the tradition had never done prior to Hobbes was to interpret the right of self-defense in a preventive sense. Moreover, Hobbes does not dissolve moral consciousness in the state of nature because, at least *in foro interno*, a qualitative difference remains between moral and egoistic actors. The moderate individuals extend their power from the moral motive of self-defense, the aggressors from the immoral motive of "taking pleasure in contemplating their own power in the acts of conquest, which they pursue farther than their security requires" (*Lev.* 13.4; 100). With the differentiation between *foro interno* and *externo* Hobbes obviously confirms the independent normative authority of the law of nature against the logic of self-interest.

The theory of the natural condition is a methodological fiction and thus does not describe a real historical situation: "But though there had never been any time, wherein particular men [!] were in a condition of warre one against another" (*Lev.* 13.11; 103). Nonetheless, the pure state of nature examined in the laboratory setting provides an inlet to the internal dynamics of real societal conflicts. In this sense, Hobbes applies the logic of the pure natural condition to three historical scenarios, namely tribal wars, civil wars within territorial states, and wars between states. As Lloyd has rightly emphasized, "the state of nature is actually a continuum concept that allows not only for conditions that are 'more or less' states of nature outside commonwealths, but also for incomplete removals from the state of nature within established commonwealths" (2021: 156).

In his analysis of conflicts between tribal societies, Hobbes, in a passage that has become famous, refers to the peoples of the Americas. The wars between the Amerindian peoples differ from the pure state of nature because it is not individuals but clans or tribes, unified by familial, cultural, and religious ties, who are in situation of mutual mistrust: "but there are many places, where they live so now. For the savage people in many places of *America*, except the government of small Families, the concord whereof dependeth on naturall lust, have no government at all; and live at this day in that brutish manner, as I said before" (*Lev.* 13.11; 194). This reference by no means emanates from a colonialist arrogance; rather, the image of the "savage beast," which had shaped sixteenth-century colonial debates, is replaced by a structural analysis of social interactions. According to Hobbes, the reason for the tribal wars resides not in innate savageness or the moral brutalization, but simply in the lack of an overriding state power; without the protection it provides, even peaceable tribes wishing to live a modest life are forced to augment their power and preventively force back any potential enemies. In many regions of the Americas, however, some peoples have succeeded in overcoming the anarchy between the tribal societies by establishing a religiously legitimated empire. Like the sacral kingships of the ancient Orient, the empires of the Aztecs and Incas have adorned their systems of rule with numerous myths, foremost the sun cult: "and the first King and founder of the Kingdome of *Peru*, pretended himselfe and his wife to be the children of the Sunne" (*Lev.* 12.20; 176–8).

The primary field in which the theory of the natural condition is applied is that of the civil wars in the emerging European territorial states, conflicts fought out by interest groups and religious communities, not tribes. If during tribal or clan feuds the solidarity and coherence of a society remains intact within the individual group, civil wars trigger a dramatic dissolution of all social ties and consequently lead to a collapse of the achieved level of civilization. According to Hobbes, civil wars represent the worst form of empirical versions of the natural state.

Last but not least, Hobbes analyzes the relationships between states and empires in the light of the pure natural condition. The history of humankind reveals in drastic terms how "yet in all times, Kings, and Persons of Soveraigne authority, because of their Independency, are ... in the state and posture of Gladiators; having their weapons pointing, and their eyes fixed on one another; that is, their Forts, Garrisons, and Guns upon the Frontiers of their Kingdomes; and continuall Spyes upon their neighbours; which is a posture of War" (*Lev.* 13.12; 103). Because the inner coherency is reinforced by the friend-versus-enemy dichotomy, and the competition to attain a military advantage with better weapons fosters technological innovation, conflicts between states have less destructive potential than civil wars: "But because they uphold thereby, the Industry of their Subjects, there does not follow from it, that misery, which accompanies the Liberty of particular men" (*Lev.* 13.12; 196). Without doubt, Hobbes trivializes the violent excesses of imperial wars that had already been criticized by Erasmus more than a century before. Given the devastating capacity of modern weapons of mass destruction, Hobbes's analysis on the destructive potential of wars between states is certainly outdated.

And indeed, ultimately for Hobbes, between states this conflictive natural condition is insurmountable (*Lev.* 13.12; 196; 17.2; 254–6; 30.30; 552; *De cive* 10.17; 13.7–8; *Elem.* 2.10.10). Hobbes therefore replaces Vitoria's utopia of a global order of peace with the scenario of a state of permanent war on an international scale. Hobbes levers the dialectical reversal of Vitoria's cosmopolitanism precisely through the concept with which Vitoria had envisaged universal communication between peoples a century before, namely the law of nations: "Concerning the Offices of one Sovereign to another, which are comprehended in that Law, which is commonly called the *Law of Nations*, I need not say any thing in this place; because the Law of Nations, and the Law of Nature, is the same thing" (*Lev.* 30.30; 552).

Hobbes's acceptance of the permanent conflicts between states has been generally interpreted as one of the main foundations of the so-called realistic theory of international relations in the tradition of Thucydides and Machiavelli (Beitz 1979: 27–59). This view is too simple, however (Malcolm 2002: 432–56; Williams 2009: 19–50). Even in the pure natural condition of humankind, the law of nature is still valid *in foro interno*. For this reason, the moral laws and duties are in principle valid also in the international version of the state of nature, albeit though not fixed by covenant and a supranational authority. Moreover, Hobbes applies the analysis of the causes of the state of nature to international relations. Especially the vainglorious striving of kings, sharply criticized by Erasmus, threatens the sovereignty of the states by implicating them in high-risk wars: "For the Militia in order to profit, is like a Dye wherewith many lose their estates, but few improve them" (*De cive* 13.14).

Thus, despite the radical reinterpretation of the law of nations into the law of a war of all against all, Hobbes's view of international relations retains some elements of Vitoria's cosmopolitanism, at least in reduced form. Because the state of war is often only latent, and there are no open clashes or hostilities, there is room to maneuver for negotiating peaceful relations on the international level, in particular with respect to trade relations, voyages of exploration, or the exchange of scientific and technological knowledge. Even the spread of religious teachings is not completely halted by international anarchy. In distinction from Vitoria, for Hobbes the spread of Christianity is not an official church undertaking or indeed a matter of state, but exclusively an individual decision, and therefore in no need of a mandate from the pope or any other church authority (*Lev.* 46.39; 1098).

10.3 The social contract: collective self-civilization through creative freedom

According to Sepúlveda, a people that has fallen into barbarism can only be led back to the path of civilization through a violent intervention by external powers. The strategy of forced civilization of "barbarian" peoples was built, in the sixteenth century, on the idea of the superiority of Christian Europe. Both Montaigne and Hobbes are shocked and appalled, however, at the escalating violence triggered by the civil wars in Europe itself, and with the European powers entangled in seemingly endless state-of-nature conflicts among themselves, forced civilization imposed by outside powers is currently out of the question. Against this background Hobbes has to confront the question as to how the Europeans can overcome their own barbarism.

The principles enabling the establishment of a civilized and ordered polity can be explicated, once again, by observing the laboratory situation of the state of nature. Just as the war of all against all arises out of the interplay between the passions and a reason based on natural law, the possibilities of overcoming violence also reside "partly in the Passions, partly in his Reason" (*Lev.* 13.13; 196). The state cannot therefore be founded exclusively on reason but must also likewise have a grounding in specific passions: "The Passions that encline men to Peace, are Feare of Death; Desire of such things as are necessary to commodious living; and a Hope by their Industry to obtain them" (*Lev.* 13.14; 196). As varying as opinions are on what is good and useful, according to Hobbes all humans have an aversion to a state of permanent threat: "And consequently all men agree on this, that Peace is Good" (*Lev.* 15.40; 242). The task of reason, on the other hand, is to set out the "*Articles of Peace*" (ibid.). In the rational construction of a stable peaceful order, the *ius in omnia et omnes*, to which the argumentation or the arithmetic operation had led in the context of the natural condition, has to now be "subtracted." But because the natural condition rests heavily on the natural law principle of self-preservation, Hobbes faces a problem: How can relinquishing the right of all to everything be justified without once again calling into question the legitimate striving for self-preservation?

In order to avoid the renunciation of the *ius in omnes et omnia* resulting in an altruistic self-sacrifice, Hobbes introduces the formal principles of natural law, namely the principles of reciprocity and impartiality, which are general principles of reason as such, into the line of argumentation (Lloyd 2019: 123–8). The second law of nature thus reads: "*That a man be willing, when others are so too, as farre-forth, as for Peace, and defence of himselfe he shall think it necessary, to lay down this right to all things; and be contented with so much liberty against other men, as he would allow other men against himselfe*" (*Lev.* 14.5; 200). The second law of nature is therefore connected with the Golden Rule (ibid.), itself based on the common good.

As a further clarification for renouncing this right, Hobbes appeals to the idea of individual voluntary obligation: "[T]here being no Obligation on any man, which ariseth not from some Act of his own; for all men equally, are by Nature Free" (*Lev.* 21.10; 336). Hobbes compares the binding character of such an obligation to the indisputability of the principle of contradiction. Just as the principle of contradiction cannot be doubted without simultaneously making use of it, not complying with a promise also implies a self-contradiction, for every promise is grounded in a voluntary decision made by the individual: "For as it is there called an Absurdity, to contradict what one maintained in the Beginning: so in the world, it is called Injustice, and Injury, voluntarily to undo that, which from the beginning he had voluntarily done" (*Lev.* 14.7; 202). According to Hobbes, the idea of a contractual self-obligation therefore makes it possible to move beyond the level of fluctuating opinions on the good and the bad, including subjective interpretations of the laws of nature. Promises and contracts are the most important "Bonds, by which men are bound, and obliged" (*Lev.* 14.7; 202).

At this point, Hobbes's position on traditional moral philosophy can be further clarified. His moral theory contains not just two dimensions, namely the prudential idea of the good and the rightness created by covenants (Abizadeh 2018), but three levels: the good in the sense of the *bonum iucundum* and *utile*, natural law, and the contractual self-obligation (Malcolm 2002: 436). These three levels are not separated but intertwined. The law of nature justifies the vital striving for self-preservation and commodious life; and the covenants are not totally arbitrary but constrained by the natural laws, above all the principles of self-preservation, impartiality, and reciprocity. For this reason, there are to "be some Rights, which no man can be understood by any words, or other signes, to have abandoned, or transferred. As first a man cannot lay down the right of resisting them, that assault him by force, to take away his life … The same may be sayd of Wounds, and Chayns, and Imprisonment" (*Lev.* 14.8; 202). In contrast, those promises have validity in which it has been agreed that one of the contractual partners will fulfill the obligation at a later time: "and then the Contract on his part, is called PACT, or COVENANT" (*Lev.* 14.11; 204). In this context Hobbes distinguishes between "*Simply* Renouncing," where one does not concern oneself with who gains advantage, and "TRANSFERRING," "when he cares not to whom the benefit thereof redounded" (*Lev.* 14.7; 200).

While the idea of contractual self-obligation enables the "subtraction" of the *ius in omnia et omnes* from the natural law principle of self-preservation to be conceptually understood as the renouncing of a right, just as the *leges naturales* does not guarantee general observance, a pledge cannot compel a fulfillment of the duty of loyalty, on which Hobbes soberly notes: "And Covenants, without the Sword, are but Words, and of no strength to secure a man at all" (*Lev.* 17.2; 254). As long as there is no superior power to enforce observance under the threat of penalties, then pledges and natural laws oblige merely *foro interno*. At this point, Hobbes makes the decisive step in the direction of overcoming the state of nature. Renouncing the right to the universal augmentation of power is not to be thought of as a "simple renunciation" but as a "transference," whereby those concerned cede their right to decide for themselves what is good and just, as well as the means for ensuring self-preservation, to a third instance, an overriding authority, "to conferre all their power and strength upon one Man, or upon one Assembly of men" (*Lev.* 17.13; 260). The overcoming of the natural condition, conceived *more geometrico*, in which the use of force or the unleashing of violence is effectively and sufficiently curbed by a stable social order, thus requires a fictive act of collective self-commitment, or more precisely a "Covenant of every man with every man," in which each says to the other: "*I Authorise and give up my Right of Governing my selfe, to this Man, or to this Assembly of men, on this condition, that thou give up thy Right to him, and Authorise all his Actions in like manner*" (*Lev.* 17.13; 260).

With the social contract Hobbes achieves his goal of placing moral and political philosophy on a new foundation. The fictive establishment of a state authority restores, under enlightened conditions, i.e., the individual's autonomous use of reason, the archaic idea of justice as the protecting of the weak and honest. The Leviathan is thus the modern equivalent to the God-King. The authorization of state authority and the use of force are no longer put into effect from above, by the sun god, but from below, by the individual citizen. Or "to speak more reverently": Leviathan is "that *Mortall* God" to which "wee owe under the *Immortall* God, our peace and defence" (*Lev.* 17.13; 260).

In terms of argumentation, Hobbes resorts to three levels in his theory of the state: evaluative ethics, which is based on the passions; natural law, belonging to the realm of reason; and conceptions of obligation, whereby Hobbes, attuned to language, again brings into play the creative power of the human mind. Pivotal is the recognition that, in distinction to the natural laws, the validity of which reason can always ascertain, pledges produce a *new* reality between humans. As Hobbes sees it, in contractual self-commitment humans are imitating nothing less than the divine power expressed in creation: "Lastly, the Pacts and Covenants, by which the parts of this Body Politique were at first made, set together, and united, resemble that Fiat, or the Let us make man, pronounced by God in the Creation" (*Lev.* Introd.; 16).

Hobbes therefore interprets the contractual model of morality and justice, developed in antiquity by the Sophists and above all by Epicurus, through the prism of the Renaissance idea of creative freedom. Moreover, the deterministic body ontology does not hinder Hobbes from further enhancing the *vis creativa* compared to Pico and Bacon. Human creative power is not limited to making decisions on specific ways of how to organize life, nor the production of new works, but culminates in the constitution of a "COMMONWEALTH (in Latin CIVITAS) which is but an Artificiall Man" (*Lev.* Introd.; 16; Ludwig 1998: 226). With the idea of creative freedom, Pico's motif of self-transformation nonetheless finds its way into Hobbes's thinking, albeit in a modified form. *De cive* opens: "To speak impartially, both sayings are very true; That Man to Man is a kind of God; and that Man to Man is an arrant Wolfe; The first is true, if we compare Citizens amongst themselves; and the second, if we compare Cities" (*De cive*, Ep. ded. 1–2). While Hobbes shares with Pico the assumption that no human has a fixed nature, and thus there is also no natural malevolence, in contrast to Pico Hobbes believes it is not an individual decision if a person degenerates into the creaturely or ascends to the divine, but this depends rather on social constellations. Without a state order, as had become discernible in the laboratory of the natural condition, *all* humans are forced to boundlessly augment their power. This means that "Good men must defend themselves by taking to them for a Sanctuary the two daughters of War, Deceipt and Violence: that is in plaine termes a meer brutall Rapacity" (*De cive*, Ep. ded. 2). Like Pico, Hobbes describes the regression to a creaturely way of life as "degeneration"—"by the manner of life, which men that have formerly lived under a peacefull government, use to degenerate [!] into, in a civill Warre" (*Lev.* 13.11; 194). With the theory of the state of nature, Hobbes demystifies Pico's idea of freedom, wherein a human, "without any limits," creates their own nature. Like the regression into barbarism, the ascent into a divine nature does not lie in the power of individual freedom; the "natures" humans adopt depend upon social constellations. In an ordered state, people encounter one another like gods; should social anarchy prevail, then humans are like wolves to each other. Emphasizing the continuation of Bacon's philanthropic morality, humans move toward divine nature solely through the virtues of peace, namely "Justice and Charity, the twin-sisters of peace" (*De cive*, Ep. ded.)—and not, as Pico had claimed, through the contemplation of the divine.

To avoid disempowerment into a brutish creaturely existence, humans have to renounce, at least partially, the autonomous use of their reason. The Hobbesian construction of the state aims—to express it in Pico's metaphor—at self-divinization by way of a partial self-deprivation of the right of reason. Hobbes thus ends the republican tradition in Renaissance political philosophy. As Skinner notes: "His theory of covenant collapses any distinction between subjects and citizens. His claim that in covenanting we specifically give up our right to govern ourselves undermines the need for an active and virtuous citizenship" (2002: 2.9). Completely renouncing the use of reason is avoided in two ways. Firstly, the state rules over only external conduct. Where the laws fall silent is where the individual still has the freedom to organize and lead a life at one's own discretion (*Lev.* 21.18; 340). Secondly, the dignity of humans as a rational species is retained in so far as state authority is authorized through the individual. For this reason, the state does not confront the individual as some alien body but as their own will. Nevertheless, the weak point of the Hobbesian social contract is unmistakable, namely the paradoxical idea of a partial self-incapacitation of reason in the name of reason. Hobbes's social contract is a founding treaty of domination, but not a treaty limiting domination (Kersting 1996: 226). This is why limiting the power of the Leviathan emerges as one of the main tasks of political philosophy in the modern era.

10.4 Critical review: the dialectic of enlightenment amid early modern de-limitations

Although the theory of the state of nature is supposed to point a way out of the logic of power, already during his lifetime Hobbes attracted a barrage of criticism with the imagery of the war of all against all. The extreme scenario of a universal unleashing of power builds, according to the usual line of criticism, on extremely questionable premises, whether it be atomistic individualism or the boundless will to power manifesting in the *ius in omnia et omnes*. Since Macpherson, Hobbes's state of nature has become nothing less than a symbol for capitalist modernity. In contrast, postcolonial criticism sees in Hobbes, as Dussel has shown, the prefiguring of the power syndrome of colonialist modernity.

Despite the deep ambivalences which undoubtedly permeate Hobbes's political philosophy, the interpretations put forward by ideological criticism miss the main achievements of his thinking. Some objections are obviously based on misunderstandings. Hobbes does not trace the escalation of violence in the natural condition back to the problem of scarce resources in early capitalist competitive society, at least not in *Leviathan*, but to the expansionism of imperators who boundlessly extend their power for the sheer enjoyment of it. Hobbes resolutely counters the idealizations of Roman imperialism in Renaissance humanism: "But what a Beast of Prey was the Roman people, whilst with its conquering Eagles it erected its proud Trophees so far and wide over the world, bringing the Africans, the Asiaticks, the Macedonians, and the Archæns, with many other despoiled Nations, into a specious bondage, with the pretence of preferring them to be Denizons of Rome?" (*De cive*, Ep. ded., 1). Hobbes's theory of the state of nature thus in fact contains a criticism of imperial violence, not a justification.

Not least, the assumption that only adult individuals interact in the natural condition is part of the methodological fiction, mainly introduced in *De cive*, and not an anthropological thesis. Hobbes does not reduce society to interactions between atomic individuals. He explicitly affirms that every child "oweth its life to the Mother and is therefore obliged to obey her rather than any other" (*Lev.* 20.5; 310). And yet, with the idea of a war of all against all Hobbes places the conflictive and adversarial at the very center of political thinking with a radicalness unprecedented in occidental philosophy. As mentioned at the outset, this is why Hobbes is frequently acclaimed to be the founder of modern political philosophy. Despite his rhetoric claiming a break with tradition,

Hobbes's thought is intimately related to classical ancient philosophy and above all to Renaissance humanism. Seen against this background, the modernity of Hobbes's political philosophy must be defined more closely in comparison with these traditions.

For determining the relationship between his thought and the philosophical tradition, Hobbes himself gives a consequential hint. In *De cive* Hobbes draws a stark contrast between *scientia iustitiae* and the Aristotelian doctrine of the *zoon politikon*: "We doe not therefore by nature seek Society for its own sake, but that we may receive some Honour or Profit from it" (*De cive* 1.2). This is however a false lead, for his criticism of the theory of the natural sociality of humans is based on a set of misunderstandings about Aristotle. By no means does Aristotle, as Hobbes implies, start from the assumption of a peaceful nature, wherein "by nature one Man should Love another (that is) as Man" (*De cive* 1.2). Nor does the Aristotelian idea of the *zoon politikon* claim that humans possess all the abilities necessary for leading a life in a state *from birth* ("born fit for society"; ibid., Annotation). For Aristotle, education and consolidating the virtues are a *conditio sine qua non* for any form of human coexistence. Hobbes's objection that children and the ignorant are not yet capable of society because they have no knowledge of loyalty and agreements therefore misses the point. Hobbes's own proposition—"wherefore Man is made fit for Society not by Nature, but by Education" (ibid.)—is thus not a contradiction of Aristotle. Hobbes's misunderstanding of the *zoon politikon* arises out of a shift in the concept of nature (Wolfers 1991: 70). Aristotle underpins political philosophy with a teleological concept of nature that undermines the modern opposition between "natural" and "artificial" reality: "A social instinct is implanted in all men by nature, and yet who first founded [!] the state was the greatest of benefactors" (*Pol.* 1.2.1253b27–9). For this reason, the *polis* is an artificial entity because it is erected by humans, but at the same time it is a materialization of human "nature" in so far as the individual can develop their natural aptitude of reason solely in the *polis*: "And therefore, if the earlier forms of society are natural, so is the state, for it is the end of them, and the nature of a thing is its end" (*Politics* 1.2.1252b31f.). Conversely, because Hobbes does not trace the escalating violence to an innate power drive, the difference between Aristotle and Hobbes cannot be construed as an opposition between a social and an adversarial nature of human beings.

Furthermore, it needs to be kept in mind that the thinking of antiquity by no means turned a blind eye to social anarchy and violence. Above all the myth of Protagoras, wherein the scenario of humankind's looming self-destruction crystallizes, evokes associations with the Hobbesian state of nature (Pl. *Prot.* 320c–322d). But Aristoteles, too, insists that the human being, although superior to animals, is the cruelest species when there is no state ensuring law and order: "For man, when perfected, is the best of animals, but, when separated from law, and justice, he is the worst of all; since armed injustice is the more dangerous … That is why, if he has not excellence, he is the most unholy and the most savage of animals" (*Pol.* 1.3.1253b31–7). As Aristotle, in agreement with Hobbes, emphasizes, justice can only be genuinely manifested in a state community: "But justice is the bond of men in states; for the administration of justice, which is the determination of what is just, is the principle of order in political society" (*Pol.* 1.2,1253b37–9). Like Hobbes, in its interpretation of the development of humankind, the Epicurean tradition proceeds from an assumption of an amoral primal condition. According to Lucretius, the first humans lived in the forests without morality or laws (*Lucr.* 5.958–70). A similar scenario is evident, as Roetz has shown for example, in ancient Chinese philosophy. Mengzi's maxim directed at Yang Zhu, "'to know neither ruler nor father is the state of beasts,' [Mengzi 3B9] can claim the consent of all Confucians" (Roetz 1993: 67). Xunxi, Mengzi's opponent, traces the conflicts of the stateless condition of humans back to a scarcity of goods and resources:

> Without a ruler to control the subjects, and without superiors to control the subordinates, the world would be harmed because everybody would give rein to his desires. Men's desires and dislikes are directed towards the same things. But desires are many, and things are few. Because of the scarcity of things, there will inevitably be strife. The products of a hundred crafts are necessary to support a single individual. Even an able person could never be skilled in all of them together. One man, moreover, cannot occupy several.
>
> (cited from Roetz 1993: 67)

Not least, it should be recalled that a passage in Seneca, writing in the context of Roman imperialism, expresses an awareness of the permanent threat posed by potential aggressors that strikingly resembles the situation of the peaceful farmer in the Hobbesian state of nature:

> No land is so far removed from neighbours that it cannot send forth in some direction its evil propensities. How do I know but that some ruler of a great nation meantime concealed from view, swollen by fortune's kindness, may choose not to confine his arms within the boundaries of his own realm, but with

secret design may even now be fitting out his fleet against us? How can I tell whether this wind or that shall convey war to me?

(QNat. 5.18.12)

A recognition of how humankind descends into social anarchy without the support of law and order was very prevalent in classical ancient political philosophy. And yet neither Aristotle, Lucretius, nor Seneca present their argument for a state order as the conclusion to be drawn from an analysis of social anarchy. Solely the myth of Protagoras reveals a certain parallel to the Hobbesian construction of the state. Because humans lack the "civic art," Zeus sends Hermes to spread "justice and a sense of shame [*dike kai aidos*]" (Pl. *Prot.* 322b–c) as a way of establishing peaceful coexistence.

From this background, we can determine more closely the specifically modern gain in rationality in Hobbes's political philosophy. Hobbes replaces the *politiké téchne* of Protagoras with his *scientia iustitiae*. Peace and justice are thus no longer gifts from Zeus, but the benefit stemming from the authority of the state endorsed by humans. Indeed, Hobbes undertakes a twofold corrective of the political philosophy of antiquity. Firstly, under the influence of the civil wars of the early modern period, Hobbes places the question of legitimating political rule as such at the center of attention; and secondly, Hobbes bases the analysis of dissent fissuring a society internally on the idea of human equality.

In the tradition of political philosophy founded by Plato and Aristotle, the explosive force of intra-social violence appears to be at least defused by the idea of a normative order sufficiently coherent to be understandable for all members of the society. For this reason, Aristotle's political philosophy does not revolve around the issue of the legitimation of state rule as such, but rather focuses on the *quality* of societal orders. Aristotle turns against the widespread opinion "that the qualification of a statesman [*politikon*], king [*basilikon*], householder [*oikonomikon*], and master [*despotikon*] are the same, and that they differ, nor in kind, but only in the number of their subjects" (*Pol.* 1.1.1252a7–10). Because every community pursues a good, in which specific abilities of humans come to the fore, the quality of the different forms of community can only be determined with recourse to a normatively substantial anthropology. The distinctive feature of a *polis* therefore arises from how it is only in a community of free citizens, limited in number but enjoying the benefits of being organized into a state, that a sense for "good and evil, for the just and the unjust," communicable through language and reason, can be realized to its full potential. Moreover, from the very outset Aristotle alleviates the danger of intra-social dissent by claiming the necessary rule of the reasonable over the less reasonable.

Because the appreciation for what is good and just has become caught up in the maelstrom of fractious argument between the schools, of which the frightful unleashing of uninhibited violence in the civil wars is a continuation, Hobbes can no longer restrict his considerations to the question of the qualitative distinctions between societal orders. Under the shock of the prevailing social anarchy, the focus shifts fundamentally: how a state order can even be formed at all becomes the new *causa prima* of political philosophy. At this point, Hobbes deviates not only from the line of Aristotle, but also from that of classical ancient theories on the social contract. Neither Carneades, who had criticized the Stoics' theory on natural law by pointing out the plurality of moral ideas (Tuschling 2005: 118–24), nor the Epicurean tradition developed a systematic reflection on how social anarchy can be subdued and overcome through an organized state.

Moreover, because the enlightenment processes in the early modern period are no longer limited to small elites, as in antiquity, but thanks to printing increasingly involved a broader mass of the population, for Hobbes the Aristotelian principle of the rule of the perfect over the imperfect has completely lost its meaning. The universal use of reason—Hobbes refers here to Protestant groups who use their own reason to interpret the Bible and London merchants who invoke the Republican ideals of antiquity—does not advance peace but social anarchy.

In the methodological fiction of the natural condition, the spiral of violence is initiated by the individual use of reason on the one hand, leading as it does to disagreements and social anarchy; on the other, it gains momentum through the indisputable fact that when undertaking action it is never the case that all people take their orientation from moral laws, but rather they succumb to at least some of their passions and expand and augment their power without heeding limits. According to Hobbes, when people anticipate both of these factors and connect them with the moral right of self-preservation, then the scenario of the war of all against all is the only logical consequence.

This means that the foundations of the Hobbesian theory of the state of nature is not so much imbued with the mercantile spirit of the early modern period, which leads to a dismantling of natural law; instead, it is informed by the poignant problematic of the processes of human enlightenment, namely the conflict potential residing in the individual use of reason. Hobbes's political philosophy is therefore an early lesson in the dialectic of enlightenment. At the same time, Hobbes overcomes the elitism of ancient philosophies by postulating the idea of equality. In Aristotle, the equality between the *polis* citizens relies on the inequality of women, slaves, and *metics*. Ancient Confucianism places its trust in the authority of rulers of moral integrity: "It is the guarantor of order, because the mass of the people, this is the common conviction of all Confucians, does not by itself find the right course. 'The people can be made to follow something, but not to understand it,' [Analects/ Lunyu 8,9] says Confucius" (Roetz 1993: 67). In contrast, Hobbes constructs the state on the principle of equality. The imaginary social contract is based on the consensual agreement of all citizens. In this sense, Hobbes's political philosophy signifies a certain progress in political thought, offering a solution to a problem left unconsidered in the political philosophy of antiquity (Tuschling 2005: 123). Incidentally, parallels can also be found in Hobbes's idea of overcoming social anarchy in non-European cultures. Similarly to Hobbes, Han Feizi sees social order as being grounded in the sovereignty of state which is above the laws (Martinich 2011).

Nonetheless, the advances in rationality evident in Hobbes's political philosophy have their weak spots, and these are subsequently worked on in the political philosophy of the early modern period. Here I would like to point out just two problems, namely the overbearing superiority of the Leviathan and the question of whether Hobbes's political theory can indeed solve the disagreements between philosophies, or if it is not just another voice in the ongoing quarrels between schools. At the same time, as we have seen, Hobbes's political philosophy is closely interwoven with the thought of the Renaissance and its spectacular innovations. Present in new modifications are the geographical-political de-limitations of the *oikumene*, the positive revaluating of the *curiositas* and the *vis creativa*, and, albeit in the *modus negationis*, the idea of the law of nations. In this context, along with the advancements in rationality over ancient moral philosophy, moments emerge in Hobbes's theory of the state which fit in with the cultural upheaval of the early modern period. This thesis may initially seem surprising, for in Hobbes's thinking the purpose of the state no longer resides in fostering the "good life" in the Aristotelean sense. On the contrary, the Hobbesian state is an emergency order. If all humans could observe the law of nature, then there would be no need for a state. Nevertheless, the Leviathan is not there solely to secure bare survival. The "inversion of teleology" does not elevate self-preservation to the highest and only good, as suggested by Spaemann (1996: 80). Hobbes may place all the importance on safety when defining peace on earth—"Peace was sought after for safeties sake" (*De cive* 13.2)—but "safety" is "not the sole preservation of life in what condition soever, but in order to its happiness [!]" (*De cive* 13.4).

Hobbes therefore principally adheres to the traditional maxim that "the welfare of the people shall be the supreme law [*salus publica suprema* lex]." Unlike classical ancient philosophies, however, Hobbes quite clearly distinguishes between public welfare and individual happiness. The task of the state is no longer to guide individuals to the highest goodness and virtue through education, "for the Ruler (as such) provides no otherwise for the safety of his people, then by his Lawes, which are universall" (*De cive* 13.3). But the Hobbesian state is not simply neutral with respect to the happiness of its citizens. At this point, the question arises as to precisely what kind of "happiness" the state should support and encourage through general laws. Because social order is based on the partial self-curtailing of the citizen's capacities, there is little room in Hobbes's thinking for the Aristotelian *eudaimonia* in the sense of exercising the right of political participation. Moreover, inspired already by Bacon, Hobbes dismisses the fundamental principle of classical ancient theories of happiness, namely the ideal of the tranquillity of the soul: "Felicity is a continuall progresse of the desire, from one object to another; the attaining of the former, being still but the way to the later" (*Lev.* 11.1; 150; cf. Hamilton 139–47). Despite this, Hobbes by no means turns vices into virtues. Although it is recommended to the regent to support trade and crafts by creating conducive conditions through legislation, Hobbes, fully in line with traditional moral philosophy, condemns every form of excessive striving for wealth, a pursuit that is just as dangerous for peace as the insatiable quest for recognition: "The love of money, if it exceeds moderation, is called covetousness; love of political power, inmoderate, ambition; for this perturb and pervert the mind" (*De homine* 12.8). *Pleonexia*, "the desire of more than theire share" (*Lev.* 15.22; 236), has a pejorative meaning in the thought of Hobbes. And even more forcefully: The "love of money is *turpe*, it is a sign of one that can be led anywhere by bribe. Furthermore, it is a sign of need, even in wealthy men" (*De homine* 11.13). The criterion for moderation with respect to wealth is no longer the "mean" (*mesotes*) between thriftiness and extravagance, as in Aristotle, but the principle of self-preservation: "but moderation, both in the desire of fame and in the desire for other external things, is useful; certainly insofar as it can offer protection" (*De homine* 12.8). Like Aristotle, however, the Hobbesian state, albeit following different criteria than Aristotle, is not aiming to completely overcome the love of money and fame, but to moderate and limit it to the point where "the strength of Avarice and Ambition ... would presently faint and languish" (*De cive*, Ep. ded., 6).

In short, Hobbes rejects the classical ancient idea of the tranquillity of the soul on ontological and moral grounds, but without thus reducing happiness to some restless pursuit of material goods. Moreover, Hobbes adheres to his program of a *scientia iustitiae* serving to protect the weak. The principle of self-preservation obliges the state to provide public charity securing the subsistence of all citizens:

> And whereas many men, by accident unevitable, become unable to maintain themselves by their labour; they ought not to be left to the Charity of private persons; but to be provided for (so far-forth as the necessities of Nature acquire). For Uncharitablenesse in any man, to neglect the impotent; so it is in the Soveraign of the Common-wealth, to expose them to the hazard of such uncertain Charity.
>
> (*Lev.* 30.18; 538)

When compared to the alms practice of the Middle Ages, where providing for the poor was always somewhat precarious, the right of subsistence, guaranteed by the state, undoubtedly marks moral progress. The surplus from which the poor were given voluntarily was determined on the basis of a generously assessed *necessarium*, which included for example maintaining a life befitting one's social status (Priddat 1988: 106–10; *Sth* II–II, q. 32). For Hobbes, however, the poor capable of work could be forced into working. At the very least, the state must ensure greater employment through laws promoting the main branches of the economy (*Lev.* 30.19; 273). Certainly, Hobbes justifies public welfare policy on strategic grounds as well. For a large number of poor would threaten peace because "needy men, and hardy, not contented with their present condition ... are enclined to continue the causes of warre" (*Lev.* 11.4). But the welfare policy is also grounded in the laws of nature, especially the ninth law on the equality of all humans and the fifth law to the effect that "a man that by asperity of Nature, will strive to retain those things which to himselfe are superfluous, and to others necessary and for the stubbornness of his Passions, cannot be corrected, is to be left, or cast out of society, as cumbersome thereunto" (*Lev.* 11.17; 323; cf. Seaman 1990).

Furthermore, when describing public welfare, Hobbes assigns curiosity greater importance. This can be deduced from the list of deficiencies of the *status naturalis*, where, *ex negativo* as it were, aspects of public welfare are marked which the state is to support indirectly:

> In such condition, there is no place for Industry; because the fruit thereof is uncertain; and consequently no Culture of the Earth; no Navigation, nor use of the commodities that many be imported by Sea; no commodious Building; no Instruments of moving, and removing such things as require much force; no Knowledge of the face of Earth; no account of Time; no Arts; no Letters; no

Society; and which is worst of all, continuall feare, and danger of vielent death; And the life of man, solitary, poore, nasty, brutish, and short.

(*Lev.* 13.9; 192)

Firstly, because agriculture comes to a halt without the protection of peace provided by the state, the very material survival of humans is endangered in the natural state. The second aspect in the list of deficiencies of a life in the *status naturalis* are the perils facing shipping and trade, which Aristotle includes among the institutions of the *polis* only with provisos because of their corrupting influence on civic virtues (*Pol.* 5.7). According to Hobbes, however, navigation is not merely the import and export of goods but broadens our geographical knowledge of the earth. This means that, as Hobbes emphasizes in the context of the transoceanic expansion of Europe since the fifteenth century, part of the misery of the natural state is the limitation of the scope of human action to the immediate sphere of life. In addition to this limitation, trade is by no means assigned a model function for happiness in the sense of striving for ever new goals; for the greatest joy humans can experience arises from insatiable curiosity.

With the close relationship between the state and trade, Hobbes undertakes more than just a superficial external alteration vis-à-vis the political philosophy of Aristotle. In contrast to the latter, in the Hobbesian state the happiness of the individual and the common good no longer coincide, insofar as the institution of the market economy is integrated into the construction of the state. Viewed from the perspective of classical ancient philosophy, then, this state cannot be neutral toward the different ways of life. For Aristotle, economic practices such as trade change the moral ideas of humans. To avert the logic of the market ending up "colonializing the lifeworld" of the citizens in a *polis*, Aristotle shields it from the influences of trade. This means, however, that by affirming the market economy, Hobbes ties the philosophy of the state to a specific cultural project, and indeed one that simply cannot be deduced *more geometrico* from self-evident premises. Ultimately, however, the union of the state and the market economy remains unfounded in Hobbes's thinking—a lacuna that John Locke attempts to fill a few decades later, as I will discuss in Chapter 11.

11

John Locke: The justification of an unlimited market economy

Along with Bacon, Descartes, and Hobbes, John Locke[1] was long considered one of the leading figures of the European Enlightenment. His *Essay Concerning Human Understanding* (1689) laid the foundation stone for the sensualist epistemology of the modern age. This was followed by the *Two Treatises on Government* (1690), a work that paved the way for the rise of liberal democracy resting on secular morality, religious tolerance, individual human rights—in particular the right to private property—and a market economy. Since the nineteenth century, however, Locke has been the target of (neo-)Marxist critiques of capitalism. In more recent times, postcolonial thought has exposed Locke's colonial involvements, both in his biography and in his political philosophy, with protagonists of modern human rights and tolerance meanwhile casting Locke as the ideologue of racist colonial capitalism.

Against this background I wish to trace the complex relationships between reason, power, and coloniality in Locke's thought. My analysis will not focus on Locke's political philosophy, however, but will shift the perspective to his reflections on the economy. This may seem surprising, not least because Locke's reputation as an economist has been often questioned. As Joseph A. Schumpeter noted, while as an economist Locke "made significant contributions," they "stand in no relation to either his philosophy or his political theory" (1954: 117). Schumpeter's verdict primarily refers to how Locke intervened in the coinage crisis in England, however (1954: 117: 298f.), an extremely narrow consideration of Locke's economic views. Similarly to how Bacon developed a philosophy of modern science still influential today, although in comparison to Copernicus or Galileo he presented no new scientific knowledge, Locke's thought contains a philosophical theory on the basic orientation and goals of modern market economics which, contrary to Schumpeter's claim, is closely tied to his moral and political philosophy. Indeed, I would contend that Locke, tacitly confronting

Aristotle, articulates a comprehensive justification of a limitless money economy that remains relevant today in debates on modernity and capitalism.

Of course, the benefits of a market economy had already been rehabilitated centuries before Locke. Medieval Christian theology called into question the prohibition on interest in the Bible. The Renaissance humanist Leonardo Bruni justified the striving for limitless wealth by evoking the virtue of magnanimity (Busche 2004: 463). For Francisco de Vitoria, international trade was a major component in his theory on the law of nations (see Chapter 7, section 7.3 in this book). Despite these prominent predecessors, Locke's defense of a market economy marks a caesura in the economic thinking of the early modern period. Firstly, Locke analyzes the systemic dynamic of a market economy, which becomes an autonomous subject matter of scientific study (Nonnenmacher 1989: 87). Secondly, justifying the money economy, Locke implicitly affirms the idea of limitless economic growth. In contrast, Aristotle had criticized the unlimited making of money (*chremastike*) as unnatural, i.e., irrational, because the blind accumulation of money absolutizes the means used to gain it. Moreover, chrematistics is a form of greed (*pleonexia*) that is irreconcilable with the virtues of a good citizen in the *polis*. In the twentieth century, Crawford B. Macpherson and Leo Strauss took up Aristotle's criticism of the market economy and turned it against Locke's economics (Macpherson 1962: 194–262; Strauss 1965: 202–51). The criticism of an amoralized affirmation of limitless capital accumulation has since prompted intensive debate on both the ethical and the theological foundations of Locke's theories of the state and the economy (Dunn 1969; Colman 1983; Schneewind 1994; Marshall 1994; Waldron 2002).

Against this background I will analyze Locke's idea of an unlimited economy within the broad horizon of the de-limitations of early European modernity. In diverse aspects, Locke examines the typical modern ideas of insatiable curiosity, experimental self-fashioning, Bacon's unleashing of science and technology, and the challenges of global cosmopolitanism. Thus, in a first step, I shall sketch the moral foundations of Locke's economics (section 11.1 of this chapter). The key points to clarify here are the relationship between natural law and a hedonistic concept of morality that introduces the idea of an increase of pleasures against all ancient ethical traditions, including Epicureanism. Moreover, by redefining natural law in the theory of the state of nature, Locke develops a criticism of the Hobbesian fiction of a de-limitation of power relations between humans, e.g., the scenario of a war of all against all. In a second step, I examine Locke's reconstruction of the socio-economic evolution of humankind, which starts with an analysis of a pre-monetary economy based on the labor theory of property (section 11.2) and culminates in a justification of a limitless money economy (section 11.3). Drawing on the Aristotelian *oikonomia*, e.g., the limited administration of a household, to conclude I analyze the deep ambivalences of Locke's justification of a money economy (section 11.4.).

11.1 In search of moral foundations

Between natural law and hedonism: the increase of pleasure

Locke's moral philosophy links extremely heterogeneous approaches. The early *Essays on the Law of Nature* (1664), published posthumously, contain a comprehensive examination of the natural law in confrontation with Grotius and Pufendorf (Zuckert 1994: 187–215). Locke also invokes "the Law of Nature" in the *Two Treatises of Government*, claiming that as a "Law of Reason" it is "plain and intelligible to all rational Creatures" (*TTG* 2.124). The epistemological problems of the theory of natural law are mainly treated in the *Essay Concerning Human Understanding*, where the doctrine of innate moral ideas are rejected (1.2–3). Since we ourselves spawn moral ideas as we do mathematics, then it is possible to establish moral principles by furnishing irrefutable proof (*Essay* 4.3.18). But aside from smaller sketches in which Locke draws a number of conclusions from the ideas of God and human beings endowed with reason, the envisioned program of a moral philosophy *more geometrico* was never elaborated. Instead, within the framework of a sensualist epistemology, Locke develops a hedonistic concept of happiness that starkly contrasts to conceptions of natural law. And, with the trust in a rational justification of morality seemingly waning, the later theological treatises reveal yet another picture. In contrast to earlier claims, Locke emphasizes in *Reasonableness of Christianity* "that human reason unassisted, failed Men in its great and Proper business of Morality. It never from unquestionable Principles, by clear deductions, made out an entire Body of the Law of Nature" (Locke [1695] 1999: 149f.). Even if it proved possible to conceptualize an axiomatic system, for Locke not much would be gained for morality because a science-based ethics would fail to reach the uneducated masses (Locke [1695] 1999: 157).

Locke's political philosophy—and the justification of a money economy developed within it—thus rests on divergent moral philosophical theories, whereby the coherency of their connection has remained contentious down to the present day. Without analyzing the divergent strands in detail, the following considerations aim to identify and briefly sketch the salient motifs in Locke's moral philosophy which are then utilized to justify a money economy, namely the teaching on natural law, the assumption of *ius creationis*, and the hedonistic idea of happiness.

The early *Essays on the Law of Nature* (1664) provide a vital insight into Locke's moral philosophy, with the law of nature anchored, as in Thomas Aquinas, in the *lex aeterna* with which God governs the world. For this reason, the creator prescribes a law or purpose to every being ([1664] 1988: 117). This means that, in contrast to Pico della Mirandola, the early Locke proceeds from a human nature antecedent to human freedom. Moreover, as Locke emphasizes in a direct reversal of Pico's *Oratio*,

> it does not seem to fit in with the wisdom of the Creator to form an animal that is most perfect and ever active, and to endow it abundantly above all others with mind, intellect, reason, and all the requisites for working, and yet not assign to it any work, or again to make man alone susceptible of law precisely in order that he may submit to none.
>
> ([1664] 1988: 117)

As beings with sense organs, reason, and language, humans have a threefold determination: self-preservation, striving to know God, and leading life in a community ([1664] 1988: 157–9; Marshall 1994: 169f.). Because man is an *animal sociale* by nature, natural law cannot be justified on the basis of self-interest, "and thus the rightness of an action does not depend on its utility; on the contrary, its utility is a result of its rightness." The proper sense of morality emerges first in actions, specifically "that we do good to others at our own loss" (Locke [1664] 1988: 215; 207). The right to self-preservation is anchored in the order of creation, in the sense that the whole wealth of nature is there to serve humans in their efforts to maintain life. In his early writings, however, Locke still proceeds from the assumption that the resources of the earth are limited. For this reason, all those who limitlessly expand the scope of their needs necessarily endanger the right of self-preservation of others. In short, the wealth of individuals always grows at the cost of the rest of humankind ([1664] 1988: 211). Under the influence of Bacon's philosophy of science, Locke will abandon this conviction from the early 1660s. One motif from the *Essays* remains prevalent throughout the transformations of Locke's natural law theory, however, namely that of *ius creationis*.

According to Locke, the law of nature is a decree of divine will. Evoking William of Ockham, Locke emphasizes that God could have created a different human nature, out of which then other duties and obligations would have ensued ([1664] 1988: 200). Locke is wrestling here with the problems of theological absolutism, which according to Hans Blumenberg necessitated the self-assertion of reason specific to the early modern period. Locke, though, neutralizes the distortion of a despotic God from the outset. Because God's omnipotence is inseparable from his wisdom, the order of creation posited by human reason offers a solid foundation for an orientation as to how to live life (Buckle 1991: 128f.). Instead of speculating on creating other worlds, from the voluntarist conception Locke derives God's universal dominion over nature as creation, which is then split into two rights, namely the right to subjugate the created to divine purposes and the right to annihilation (Locke [1664] 1988: 185).

By the time he turns to Bacon's science, Locke interprets human freedom in terms of an analogy to God's creative power, emphasizing however the dissimilarity between human and divine creative power. Whereas God summons living creatures into existence out of nothingness and prescribes them their law, humans may be capable of passing on life through the act of procreation, but they do so *without* any knowledge of the building plan: "If any one thinks himself an Artist at this, let him number up the parts of his child's Body which he hath made, tell me their uses and Operations, and when living and rational Soul began to inhabit this curious Structure, when Sens began, and how this Engine which he has framed Thinks and Reasons" (*TTG* 1.53). From the insight that, in an ontological sense, human beings cannot have possibly created themselves, but owe their existence to God, Locke forges two fundamental principles: firstly, the prohibition on killing, including suicide, results from the divine *ius creationis*, for human beings "are his Property, whose Workmanship they are, made to last during his, not one anothers Pleasure" (*Treatises* 2.6); and secondly, contrary not only to medieval theology but also to Sir Robert Filmer, where the doctrine of creation serves as a legitimation for a hierarchical social order in both cases, Locke derives from the *ius creationis* the freedom and equality of all: "And being furnished with like Faculties, sharing all in one community of Nature, there cannot be supposed any such *Subordination* among us, that may Authorize us to destroy one another, as if we were made for one another's uses, as the inferior ranks of Creatures are for ours" (*TTG* 2.6; cf. *Essay* 4.3.18). God's act of creation entails for Locke the duty to contribute to the "Preservation of all the Mankind" (*TTG* 2.7). Moreover, the right of self-preservation is not to be reduced to egoistic self-interest. On the contrary: "when his own Preservation comes not in competition, ought he, as much as he can, *to preserve the rest of Mankind*" (*TTG* 2.6).

Even if the equality of all humans is vehemently defended against Filmer, by invoking Christian creation theology Locke risks, like the Salamanca School before him, becoming entangled in the snares of coloniality. In his early *Essays on the Law of Nature*, "Locke insists that God is simply indispensable to the law of nature ... Locke thus emphatically rejects the Grotian *etiamsi*. For Locke, no God, no natural law" (Zuckert 1994: 188). As Locke explicitly points out, the transoceanic expansion of European powers discovered nations, "amongst whom there was to be found no notion of a God ... These are instances of nations where uncultivated nature has been left to itself, without the help of letters and discipline, and the improvements of arts and sciences" (*Essay* 4.4.8; cf. Hindess 2007: 10f.). In order to overcome the deficiencies of the knowledge of natural laws, Sepúlveda introduced the idea of a violent civilizing of the barbarians. At this crucial point, the question arises as to how Locke explains both insight into and the failure of natural law.

In the *Essay Concerning Human Understanding* Locke critically examines the early modern idea of a limitless curiosity about the world. According to Locke, God has not endowed humans with infallible knowledge but with faculties of knowledge (*facultates*), namely sense and reason, and these "lead us to the Knowledge of the Creator, and the Knowledge of our Duty; and we are fitted well enough with Abilities, to provide for the Conveniences of living: These are our Business in this World" (*Essay* 2.23.12). Thus, Locke starts his epistemological reflections with the famous criticism of the *ideae innatae*, already initiated by travel literature, which told of the different views on nature and moral duties of peoples in Asia, Africa, and the Americas (Armitage 2021: 93f.). Moreover, Locke prefaces his comprehensive work on sensualist epistemology with some general theses on the extent to which a human being is capable of gaining knowledge of nature and moral duties.

In the area of the philosophy of nature, Locke surprisingly rejects the idea of limitless curiosity, defended from Nicholas of Cusa through to Francis Bacon. The idea of an all-encompassing knowledge of nature exceeds in every respect the limits of the human faculties for knowledge. Moreover, because the attempt to know the universe as a whole is necessarily condemned to failure, the danger of a sudden slip into a resigned skepticism looms large. In turn, this would mean that the possibilities actually open to humans are left unutilized. According to Locke, the sceptic is like someone refusing to work by candlelight because there is no sunlight. Thus, humans should not "throw away the Blessings their Hands are fill'd with, because they are not big enough to grasp every thing" (*Essay*, Introd. 5). A proper philosophy of knowledge needs to follow the example of the seafarer, for whom it is important "to know the length of his Line, though he cannot with it fathom all the depths of the Ocean" (*Essay*, Introd. 6).

Although it is possible to extend the range of human cognitive faculties—and in this point Locke still concurs with Bacon—through the means of technology and a strict methodology, this does nothing to alter the fact that an all-embracing knowledge of the world necessarily eludes humans. For Locke, the insurmountable limits of human cognitive faculties are no reason for resignation, however. God has given humankind all it needs, namely reason: "Whatsoever is necessary for the Conveniences of Life, and Information of Vertue; and has put within the reach of their Discovery the comfortable Provision for this Life and the Way that leads to a better" (*Essay*, Introd. 5). According to Locke, human cognitive faculties suffice in the area of moral philosophy to identify and formulate fundamental principles for regulating human coexistence. But because the majority of humankind has failed to adequately develop the faculty of reason, morality has in fact fragmented into a variety of moral doctrines. In the spirit of Montaigne, Locke describes the dissent between peoples about even the most basic moral norms (*Essay* 1.3.10; cf. Locke ([1664] 1988: 160–79).

In the context of moral pluralism, doubts about the possibility of furnishing a rational foundation of morality are already creeping into Locke's early considerations on natural law. In the *Essay* and the *Treatises*, reason and revelation are still bracketed together as complementary; this shifts in the theological late works however, with revelation at times accorded predominance: "The Experience shews," writes Locke at the end of his life, "that the knowledge of Morality, by meer natural light, (how agreeable soever it be to it) makes but slow progress, and little advance in the World" (Locke [1695] 1999: 50). Wherever reason and revelation are interrelated, any knowledge of the natural law is a matter of historical exploration, found in and explicated by outstanding thinkers on the one hand and the practice of moral heroes on the other (Buckle 1991: 147). Locke sees his own conception of natural law to be also subjected to the historical restrictions of moral knowledge; therefore, the labour theory of property is presented as "my Hypothesis" (*TTG* Pref.).

In the *Essay* Locke raises the question of *how* reason, without the guiding orientation of innate ideas, can access and develop a moral orientation by searching through history. It is here that Locke, proceeding from a sensualist epistemology, introduces a hedonistic notion of happiness into his moral philosophy: "That we call *Good*, which *is apt to cause or increase Pleasure, or diminish Pain in us* ... And on the contrary we name that *Evil*, which *is apt to produce or increase any Pain, or diminish any Pleasure in us; or else to procure us any Evil, or deprive us of any Good"* (*Essay* 2.20.2). As Locke emphasizes, what constitutes the pleasurable and what the painful is always a subjective experience (*Essay* 2.21.43).

The subjectivation of the Aristotelian *eudaimonia* is without doubt one of the main issues in early modern moral philosophy. With the idea of an increase of pleasure, however, Locke makes a second epochal break with classical ancient hedonism, which, like other philosophical schools, adhered to the ethics of moderation. Because pleasure and pain form the poles of a continuum, and hence entail neither limit or boundary identifying, for example, where pleasure ends and pain begins, Plato had assigned the *hedone* ontologically to the principle of the "infinite dyad [*aoristos dyas*]" (*Phlb.* 23c–25b). In this perspective, Locke also describes pleasure and pain as extremes eluding any precise cognitive knowledge: "Happiness and Misery are the names of two extremes, the utmost bounds whereof we know not … But of some degrees of both, we have very liveley impressions" (*Essay* 2.21.41). Ignoring Callicles for the moment, ancient hedonism was always committed to the ideal of imperturbability (*ataraxia*) and an ethics of moderation. Therefore, neither Epicurus nor his ancient followers recommend the strategy of maximizing pleasures but rather, carefully surveying existing ones, ask if most of them are not in fact meaningless. Because pleasure and pain reside in a domain of the limitless, Epicurus faces the problem of how to define a limit for a hedonistic ethics. Thus, the main teachings, the *kyriai doxai*, state: "The magnitude of pleasure reaches its limit (*horos*) in the removal of all pain" (*Diog. Laert.* 10.39). This means that, as the liberation from pain, pleasure reaches an absolute limit, beyond which any further increase is simply impossible, so that any desire to exceed it would be empty (Hossenfelder 1991: 60).

In contrast to Plato and all Hellenistic and Roman philosophies of life, including the Epicurean school, Locke defends the pursuit of greater sensual happiness, although the horizon of potentially infinite stages of happiness undermine any notion of what is good in itself (*bonum honsteum*) inherent to the doctrine of natural law: "Farther, though what is apt to produce any degree of Pleasure, be in it self good … yet it often happens, that we do not call it so, when it comes in competition with a greater of its sort" (*Essay* 2.21.42). Accordingly, evaluations of happiness and misery are always the result of a comparison: "For the cause of every less degree of Pain, as well as every greater degree of Pleasure has the nature of good, and vice versa" (*Essay* 2.21.42). Thus, Locke defines happiness in terms of the superlative, as "the utmost Pleasure we are capable of" (*Essay* 2.21.42).

Since the idea of a limitless increase in pleasures implies distinct tensions for the theory of natural law, Locke tries to bridge the gap between these contrarian moral philosophies by his sensualistic epistemology. As sensation and reflection provide the data for gaining knowledge of nature, the experiences of pleasure and pain yield the data necessary for moral-practical reason to proceed on its path to the law of nature. Sensual experiences direct humans to a dual obligation, namely that of self-preservation and that of respecting the freedom and lives of others. Disregarding moral obligations toward others inevitably causes pain and suffering. Translated into the theological language game of Lockean natural law, this means that joy and pain are the reward or the punishment stemming from the moral law God has endowed the world: "For God, having, by an inseparable connexion, joined *Virtue* and publick *Happiness* together" (*Essay* 1.3.6; cf. 2.28.5). For Locke, instead of contradicting morality based on natural law, the hedonistic understanding of happiness enables and directs its very discovery (Aarsleff 1969). This model recurs in the *Treatises of Government*. On the one hand, in terms of natural law, the subject matter of morality is recast with "the great Maxims of Justice and Charity" (*TTG* 2.5): the "Law of Nature" demands "the Peace and Preservation of all Mankind" (*TTG* 2.7). On the other hand, the purpose of human existence, as enacted by God, is defined as the utmost possible increase of happiness in the hedonist sense. According to Locke, God has bestowed humankind with the wealth of nature not merely for the purpose of preserving existence, nor merely for ensuring a peaceful and comfortable life, "but since he [God] gave it them for their benefit, and *the greatest Conveniences of Life they were capable to draw from it*" (*TTG* 2.34; emphasis added).

Nevertheless, unsolved problems remain in the synthesis of a natural law ethics and a hedonistic idea of happiness. The logic of pleasure and pain can explain, at best, the obligation to individual self-preservation but not an altruistic preconception of morality (Colman 1983: 203).

Revising Hobbes: moral standards in the state of nature

Like Hobbes, Locke develops the normative foundations of a social and political philosophy based on the state of nature: "To understand Political Power right, and derive from its Original, we must consider what State all men are naturally in" (*Treatises* 2.4). Even if any direct discussion with Hobbes is questionable historically, Locke's theory of the *status naturalis* nonetheless represents a significant revision of the scenario of a war of all against all. Locke does not simply, however, as has been contended at times, counter Hobbes with the idyll of a peaceful original state of humankind; instead, varying descriptions of the state of nature are offered depending on the specific questions and aims of the justification. On the one hand, Locke uses the doctrine of the state of nature to explain some topics of his moral and political philosophy, especially for criticizing Filmer's theocratic absolutism; on the other hand, it is deployed in the theory of property and the plotting of the economic development of humankind, with the modern European states and market system as its *telos* (Hindess 2007: 4–6).

In the first part of the *Second Treatise of Government*, Locke refers to the state of nature in order to clarify the moral principles of his political philosophy. Already in his first approach to the natural state, Locke evokes three scenarios. Firstly, Locke portrays a fully peaceful natural state of humankind: "The State of perfect Freedom to order their Actions, and dispose of their Possessions, and Persons as they think fit" (*TTG* 2.4). This rests on the ahistorical assumption that all humans are not only aware of the moral law but follow it unfailingly and without exception (Colman 1983: 181–6). In other words, human beings perform their freedom "within the bounds of the Law of Nature" (*Treatises* 2.4), i.e., the requirement of self-preservation, the preservation of the rest of humankind, and the principle of equality (*TTG* 2.4–5). The obligation to respect others as free and equal prohibits depriving them of the goods they have acquired for the purpose of survival, more concretely whatever "tends to the Preservation of Life, the Liberty, Health, Limb or Goods [!] of another" (*TTG* 2.7). While according to Hobbes it is only in the *status civilis* that a distinction can be made between mine and yours, Locke already asserts the claim to goods in the state of nature, which removes them from any use by others. The justification for this assumption is not given here; Locke furnishes it later, namely in the labor theory of property.

Intentionally factoring out the historical experience that some individuals boundlessly exert and exercise their power, the construction of the perfect state of nature allows Locke to circumvent the Hobbesian paradox of a self-contradicting reason. The fiction of peaceful coexistence enables Locke to implement the foundational principle of morality in the natural state, namely the principle of respecting the "property" of others, embracing both the freedom and physical integrity of all humans[2] as well as the possession of goods necessary for securing existence: "By Property I must be understood here, as in other places, to mean that Property which Men have in their Persons as well as Goods" (*TTG* 2.173).

It is only in a second scenario of the *status naturalis* that Locke turns to the problem that some individuals, despite knowing the law of nature, disregard heeding its practical requirements (*TTG* 2.16). In this situation, those virtuously adhering to the law have the right "to punish the transgressors of that Law to such a Degree, as may hinder its Violation" (*TTG* 2.7). This is why in a "State of War" (*TTG* 2.16), which is to be strictly distinguished from the "*properly State of Nature*" i.e., a "State of Peace, Good will, Mutual Assistance and Preservation" (*TTG* 2.19), the law of nature principally retains its validity. In conflict situations, however, protecting the innocent takes priority over the aggressor's right to exist. According to Locke, it is permitted "to destroy a Man who makes War upon him, or has discovered an Enmity to his being, for the same Reason, that he may kill a Wolf or a Lyon" (*TTG* 2.16). Since natural law enables a sufficiently clear distinction between victims and aggressors, Locke's state of war is not simply another version of a *bellum omnium in omnes* in which the moral orientation of the virtuous is present only *in foro interno*. Moreover, the natural law sets limits to the punishment meted out to the culprits. Vengeance is to be exacted only "as calm reason and conscience dictates, what is proportionate to his Transgression, which is so much as may serve for *Reparation* and *Restraint*" (*TTG* 2.8).

Both of the first two scenarios of the natural state rest on the premise that the moral law is known to all. In the third variant, Locke addresses the problem that "men interpreting the Law of Nature are biased by their Interest, as well as ignorant for want of study of it" (*TTG* I2.124). The subjective distortion of the natural law blurs any clear distinction between aggressors and victims. Moreover, the uncertainty about moral orientation turns into a breeding ground for spiraling violence. The resultant state is one "full of fears and continual dangers," where everyone is "constantly exposed to the Invasion of others" (*Treatises* 2.123). The belligerent state of nature is the outcome of a threefold deficiency: firstly, there is no generally acknowledged explication of the natural law; secondly, there is no judge to impartially interpret and apply the law; and thirdly, there is no one with enough power to enforce judicial decisions (*TTG* 2.124–6). At this point, Locke comes extremely close to the Hobbesian theory on the state of nature (cf. chap. 10.2).

For Locke, the principles underpinning political philosophy address the deficiencies revealed in the natural state. Of the two powers every person possesses in the natural state, namely free self-determination within the bounds of the law of nature and the right to impose punishment, only the executive power needs to be fully renounced in the *status civilis*. The first power, "viz. *of doing whatsoever he thought fit for the Preservation of himself*, and the rest of Mankind," is to be delegated only partially to the state "so far forth as the preservation of himself, and the rest of that Society shall require" (*TTG* 2.129).

In contrast to Hobbes, Locke can construct a state without resorting to the paradoxical idea of a self-incapacitation in the name of reason. Because the requirements of the natural law are only distorted and not rendered invalid in the state of nature, at no point is the construction of the state left stranded in a normative no-man's-land. The government authority thus has a single task, the clarification and enforcement of the natural law: "The Obligations of the Law of Nature, cease not in Society, but only in many Cases are drawn closer" (*TTG* 2.135). As distinct from Hobbes, the power of the government does not first encounter its limit in the individual's right of self-preservation. A government is not only prohibited "to destroy, enslave, or designedly to impoverish the Subjects" (*TTG* 2.135); rather, the state power is to refrain from random despotic action and govern strictly on the basis of publicly announced and acknowledged laws (*TTG* 2.137). If stipulated limits are transgressed by the state, then the people are entitled to revolt (*TTG* 2.210f; 2.243f.). Thus, Locke's theory of the state of nature aims at limiting Hobbes's logic of unleashed power relations. "Hobbes wants to show why we have to obey. Locke also wants this, but he wants as well to show why and when we have to disobey. Leviathan is to be controlled; these natural law and social contract materials have also to provide grounds for the limits of Government" (Harrison 2003: 191).

11.2 The pre-monetary economy: the labor theory of property and its colonial applications

Unlike Hobbes, who examines various forms of society in light of the fiction of the state of nature, Locke supplements the different scenarios of the state of nature with a description of "several stages of economic and social development" (Ashcraft 1968: 908f.). Moreover, Locke sketches a comprehensive reconstruction of the socioeconomic evolution of humanity from nomadic tribal societies symbolized by the Amerindian peoples—"World was *America*, and more so than it is now" (*TTG* 2.49)—through to the territorial market states of Western Europe as its *telos*.

On the political level, Locke traces the evolution of families and clans into monarchies, from whose crises there then emerged political societies built on the explicit consensus of its members. In contrast to Filmer's biblical fiction of Adam as universal monarch, Locke presents a more historical view of the early stages of humankind. Although the origins of human evolution are obscure, according to Locke there is good reason to assume that the patriarchal family marked the beginning of social development and that, out of these, small monarchies then arose over time. Because the "equality of a simple poor way of liveing confineing their desires within the narrow bounds of each mans small propertie made few controversies" (*TTG* 2.107), the main task of the father or king was to protect the society from external enemies. The principle of consensus initially took on simple forms in these patriarchal societies. The implicit obedience with which sons bow to the authority of the father is a form of *tacit consent*. Furthermore, in exceptional situations, for example when the patriarch or his heir are incapable of rule, the members of a clan chose "the wisest and bravest Man to conduct them in their Wars, and lead them out against their Enemies" (*TTG* 2.107). At this point, Locke already situates the tribal peoples of the Americas into his theory of the economic evolution of humankind. Thus "we see, that the Kings of the Indians in America, which is still a pattern of the first Ages in *Asia* and *Europe* ... are little more than *Generals of their Armies*" (*TTG* 2.108). The emergence of stationary cultures based on agriculture fundamentally changes social relations. Because social differentiation and a rise in production bring about an increase in boundary disputes and property conflicts, legislative authority gains in prominence in agrarian societies. As long as the rulers reigned in keeping with established morality, Locke regards it as an epoch generally characterized by peace. Moreover, despite only modest prosperity, this phase of human history can indeed be considered "the Golden Age," for it possessed "more Virtue, and consequently better Governours, as well as less vicious Subjects" (*TTG* 2.111) than later times. However, with agrarian surplus production stimulating "Ambition and Luxury" (ibid.), the gap between the rulers and the people began to widen. And as abuses of power took hold and became entrenched, the people were ultimately forced "to examine more carefully *the Original* and Rights of *Government*, and to find out a way to *restrain the Exorbitances*, and *prevent the Abuses* of that Power, which they having intrusted on another's hands only for their own good" (*TTG* 2.111).

In connection with the history of socio-political orders, Locke proposes a comprehensive reconstruction of the economic development of humankind, which starts with hunter-gatherer societies and ends with the limitless money economy. The turning point of history is the introduction of money. History can therefore be divided into a time *prior to* and a time *after* the invention of money. Nonetheless, Locke's economics must not be hastily dismissed as an ideology promoting the blind accumulation of capital. On the contrary, the reconstruction of the economic evolution of humankind is guided by a tripartite normative fundament: the labor theory of property with two provisos, natural law and the hedonistic concept of happiness as an increase in pleasure.

The starting point of Lockean economics is the Stoic-Christian doctrine of the common property of humankind: "God gave the World to Men in common" (*TTG* 2.34). However, the traditional idea of common property no longer serves as an ahistorical ideal, a foil for criticizing historical configurations of property relations; rather, it functions merely as a logical premise for the natural law obligation of self-preservation: "natural *Reason* ... tells us, that men, being once born, have a right to their Preservation, and consequently to Meat and Drink, and such other things, as nature affords for their Subsistence" (*TTG* 2.25). For Locke, this obligation of self-preservation implies a right to use natural resources and their products. Wild-growing fruits and free-roaming animals are at the disposal of all, for "they are produced by the spontaneous hand of Nature": "nobody has originally a private Dominion, exclusive the rest of Mankind, in any of them" (*TTG* 2.26). Because humans can only preserve their lives by consuming, i.e., by annihilating natural goods, the idea of common property is ultimately a chimera, as Locke illustrates by drawing on the example of the indigenous inhabitants of the Americas: "The Fruit, or Venison, which nourishes the wild Indian, who knows no inclosure and is still a Tenent in common, must be his, and so his, i.e. a part of him, that another can no longer have any right to it" (*TTG* 2.26). The decisive question for Locke is therefore not *if* but *how* the unavoidable private appropriation of the products available in the natural state can be justified: "it seems to some a very great difficulty, how any one should ever come to have a *Property* in any thing" (*TTG* 2.25).

In antiquity, Cicero had traced the legitimacy of private property back to the act of the first occupier (*occupatio*) (Pierson 2013: 45–52; Chiusi 2005). In contrast, early Christian thought justified the institution of private property as a concession to the corrupt natural state of human beings after original sin (Pierson 2013: 53–76). Thomas Aquinas supplants the element of force in Cicero's theory of original appropriation, already discovered by the Church fathers, through the principle of a general consensus. Therefore, property theory cannot be part of natural law but merely appended to it (Brocker 1992: 58). Hugo Grotius and Samuel Pufendorf then placed the principle of consensus at the center of their theories of private property. However, the consensual justification of private property, as Filmer had emphatically pointed out, is vulnerable in two respects: firstly, unanimous consensus is highly improbable as a historical event and *de facto* not producible; and secondly, should a consensus ever be achieved, then it can only ever hold for those involved and is not obligatory for following generations (Buckle 1991: 161f.).

While Locke rejects Filmer's justification of monarchical power, which declares the king, as Adam's descendant, to be the sole owner of property and land, he adopts the criticism leveled against the consensual legitimation of property. Although Locke attaches great importance to the principle of consensus in his political philosophy, the theory of private property is guided by the question "how Men might come to have a *property* … without any express Compact of all the Commoners" (*TTG* 2.25).

Already in his early lectures on natural law Locke had rejected the attempt to justify moral norms through a consensus of humankind ([1664] 1988: 5). The right to subsistence anchored in the *ius creationis* is also the decisive argument Locke uses to dislodge, at a single stroke, the consensual elements in the justification of property: "And will any one say he had no right to those Acorns or Apples he thus appropriated, because he had not the consent of all Mankind to make them his? Was it a robbery thus to assume as that was necessary, Man had starved, notwithstanding the Plenty of god given him" (*TTG* 2.28).

The moral right to secure subsistence abrogates, in cases of conflict, the general demand to solve moral controversies through consensual deliberation. At this point Locke introduces the labor theory of property with a twofold argument:

> Though the Earth, and all inferior Creatures be common to all Men, yet every Man has a *Property* in his own *Person*. This no Body has any right to but himself. The *Labour* of his Body, and the *Work* of his Hands, we may say, are properly his. Whatsoever then he removes out of the State that Nature hath provided, and left it in, he hath mixed his *Labour* with, and joyned of it something that is his own, and thereby makes it his *Property*.
>
> (*TTG* 2.27)

The first part of the argument—"every man has a Property in his own Person"— expresses, despite the unusual phrasing, the fundamental premise of property theory, namely self-consciousness, reason, and freedom. Otherwise, one would have to assume that animals would acquire a right to property in acts of feeding (Brocker 1992: 355). Moreover, in contrast to his early essays on natural law, in which God still prescribes humans their essence, Locke now clearly valorizes human freedom as self-fashioning. Self-ownership implies a *"Right of Freedom to his Person, which no other Man has a Power over, but the free Disposal of it lies in himself"* (*TTG* 1.190). Since humans are at the same time the property of the divine creator, the human freedom to dispose of themselves is limited, as the prohibition of suicide shows (Olsthoorn 2019). Therefore, Locke unfolds the creative power of self-fashioning with his concept of "person" as diachronic self-consciousness: "as far as consciousness can be extended backwards to any past Action or thought, so far reaches the Identity of that *Person*" (*Essay* 2.27.4). In contrast to the biological substance of human life that is created by God, personhood consists in the self-constitution of human consciousness: "For it being the same consciousness that makes a Man be himself to himself, personal Identity depends on that only" (*Essay* 2.27.10; Seagrave 2016: 284–6). Thus, Locke reformulates the Renaissance idea of creative freedom within the new framework of the philosophy of consciousness.

The second part of the argument—things "he hath mixed his *Labour* with, and joyned of it something that is his own, and thereby makes it his *Property*"— is somewhat puzzling. The so-called *mixing* argument has elicited at least three interpretations in Locke scholarship. The idea that humans can "mix" their work with natural goods can be understood, firstly, as *incorporation*, an interpretation that can call on Locke's example of eating fruit. But Locke also refers the labor theory of property to complex activities, for example the cultivation of land and the employment of servants (*TTG* 2.28). Thus, secondly, the mixing argument is also expounded as an extension of the sphere of human self-relations on to nature (Olivecrona 1974: 226). Because we identify with the things we work on or have others work on, renouncing those things appropriated through labor would mean a violation of the sphere of our conscious freedom. Whether Locke indeed wished to base the right of property on the mere consciousness of an identification with things seems to be questionable, however. In a third interpretation, James Tully has examined the metaphor of mixing in the light of the "right of creation [*ius creationis*]" Locke "sees the labourer as making an object out of material provided by God and so having a property in this product, in a manner similar to the way in which God makes the world out of the prior material He created" (Tully 1980: 116f.). Tully's interpretation has evoked numerous objections (Colman 1983: 186–90; Ashcraft 1986: 58). And indeed, the gathering of fruit is difficult to construe as an act of creative human power. Moreover, the *ius creationis* would mean that humans gain not only a right to property but also a right to annihilation, which Locke rejects on moral grounds. In addition, Waldron has pointed out that, in a strict sense, creation as the production of new objects is according to Locke reserved solely for God: "when he uses this description [of the *imago Dei*], Locke is referring to man's intellectual nature not of man as *homo faber* or *homo laborans*. He never connects man's God-likeness with his productive capacity" (Waldron 1988: 199).

While human beings are not the creators of natural things, for Locke they are undeniably creators and thus owners of their ideas, actions, and labor. Although skeptical of inflating the creative powers of human beings, the anthropology of the Renaissance remains present in Locke's thinking, human freedom interpreted in analogy to the divine creative power. Against this background, the labor theory of property can be explained in more detail in two ways. Because human beings are creators of their ideas and it is through ideas that things are transposed into the horizon of what is useful to humankind, the human and natural spheres "commingle." Elaborating on the interpretation of the mixing argument presented by the philosophy of consciousness, some authors have suggested shifting away from understanding Locke's concept of labor as a process of production and approaching it instead primarily as a legal act of appropriation: "What I 'add' to the thing on which I labour (II, 28) is its role in my purposive activities and the consequent right over it that I acquire" (Simmons 1992: 274; cf. Priddat 1988: 84; Tully 1980: 117). In this broader sense, Locke's concept of labor also encompasses the activities of gathering and hunting, which do not produce new objects. For Locke, however, the creative power of humans is not exhausted simply in producing ideas, but—in the spirit of Baconian science—entails the alternation of nature. Like Bacon, Locke emphasizes that human "Power, however managed by Art and Skill, reaches no farther, than to compound and divide the Materials, that are made to his Hand; but can do nothing towards the making the least Particle of new Matter, or destroying one Atom of what is already Being" (*Essay* 2.2.2).[3] In the labor theory of property Locke draws on *both* dimensions of creative human power, i.e., the placement of things within the horizon of the purpose of human action as well as the scientific-technological processing of nature. Which of these aspects of labor is given preeminence depends on the stage of development a society has attained, i.e., a hunter-gatherer society, an agricultural society, or a developed market economy, the latter making use of the results of Baconian science.

At the same time, Locke situates the labor theory of property in a normative framework. One of the first fundamental limitations Locke places on property rights is directly derived from the analogy between divine and human creative power underpinning the concept of labor. Because humans do not create natural things but merely produce new objects from already-existing things by separation or composition, human property rights are qualified with reference to divine proprietorship. This means that humans are not entitled to an absolute property right, which would also include the right to annihilation. Moreover, Locke regulates the appropriation of property through two provisos: firstly, only such an amount of goods can be appropriated whereby it is certain that nothing spoils due to being left unused (*TTG* 2.31); the second proviso is that human property rights must ensure that enough goods of the same quality are left for others (*TTG* 2.27; 2.33). The spoilage proviso preserves the theological doctrine that only God has the right to annihilate. While Locke permits humans to consume the fruits of the earth for the purpose of self-preservation, and hence grants a human right to annihilation, a wanton annihilation of goods is prohibited because God is the sole proprietor of nature. In contrast, the sufficiency proviso brings to bear the natural law principle of the equality of all humans, expressed here in the sense of everyone enjoying a fair share of natural resources.

In his theory of economic evolution Locke analyzes various modes of production in the light of the labor theory of property. Depending on the production mode, both the concept of human labor and the respective moral provisos need to be specified. This is why the precise meaning of the labor theory of property, respectively the mixing argument, cannot be determined through *one* interpretative approach, but requires a consideration of its applications for various types of society.

In hunter-gatherer societies the concept of labor barely developed. While gathering fruits and hunting animals required experience and skill, no scientific knowledge of the laws of nature was necessary. Nonetheless, for Locke, living in hunter-gatherer societies was not just about securing subsistence. In line with natural law, the fruits of the earth are not given to humans simply for maintaining life but are a source of enjoyment: "*God has given us all things richly*, 1 Tim. vi.17 is the Voice Reason confirmed by Inspiration. But how far has he given it to us? To enjoy" (*TTG* 2.31). And for hunter-gatherer societies the spoilage proviso can be set out as follows: "one may *ingross* as much as he will … to *any advantage* of life before it spoils; so much he may by his labour fix a Property" (*TTG* 2.31). In short, everyone may appropriate as many goods of nature as they can consume for themselves. The sufficiency proviso is also valid but has little or no application among nomadic tribal societies. Due to the low density of the world population and the meagre level of needs among hunter-gatherer societies, there was always more than enough fruits and animals, similar in quality, throughout the early period of humankind, and hence there was "little room for Quarrels or Contentions about Property so establish'd" (*TTG* 2.31).

A completely new situation arises with the transition to agricultural societies. These societies are no longer solely concerned with collecting plants and pursuing wild animals, but the land itself comes to the fore, i.e., the very source of the natural goods. Legitimizing the appropriation of land is thus the most pressing problem facing all property theories: "But the *chief matter of Property* being now not the Fruits of the Earth, and the Beasts that subsist on it, but the *Earth it self*" (*TTG* 2.32). Despite the new problematic situation, in Locke's view the labor theory of property, although initially formulated with respect to hunter-gatherer societies, may be applied to the contentious issue of land rights: "I think it is plain, that Property in that [the Earth] too is acquired as the former" (*TTG* 2.32). To ensure this, however, the concept of labor needs to be expanded. The right to own property is not given, as Cicero had assumed, simply by occupying and enclosing it off; it is only through the cultivation and development of a specific territory that this right is constituted: "And hence subduing or cultivating the Earth, and having Dominion, we see joyned together" (*TTG* 2.35). The legitimation of rights to land rests on a notion of labor that, along with physical activities such as sowing seeds and harvesting, encompasses the organizing and conducting of a production process entailing several working steps. Because not everyone is prepared to organize and take on the toils of agricultural labor, from enclosing and developing through to exchanging the surpluses produced, social differentiations emerge. For Locke, the distinction between master and servant is thus "as old as History" (*TTG* 2.85). And moreover, without any further elaboration, the work performed by the servants can be ascribed to the property of the master: "Thus the Grass my Horse has bit; the Turfs my Servant has cut; and the ore I have digg'd in any place where I have a right to them in common with others, become my Property, without the assignation or consent of any body" (*TTG* 2.28).

In agricultural societies, as the concept of labor alters so too does the scope of the spoilage proviso. The rule not to allow gathered plants or fruits to spoil now needs to be supplemented with respect to owning property: "*As much Land* as a Man Tills, Plants, Improves, Cultivates, and can use the Product of, so much is his *Property*" (*TTG* 2.32). Everyone may appropriate only as much land as they themselves can develop and make use of what it yields: "Whatsever he tilled and reaped, laid up and made use of, before it spoiled, that was his peculiar Right" (*TTG* 2.38). Conversely, this means any enclosed land that remains undeveloped is to be considered ownerless and may not only be used by others but also appropriated: "But if either the Grass of his Inclosure rotted on the Ground, or the Fruit of his planting perished without gathering, and laying up, this part of the Earth, notwithstanding his Inclosure, was still to be looked on as Waste, and might be the Possession of any other" (*TTG* 2.38).

The application of the sufficiency proviso to agricultural societies can no longer be expressed in a simple rule but demands a differentiation between various social constellations. In the early stage of humankind, the sufficiency proviso could be maintained in its original sense, for marking off specific areas did not disadvantage others because of the low population density. As the population grows, however, and land becomes scarce, to ensure that equally good and enough land remains left for everyone Locke deems it necessary to modify the sufficiency proviso. When this case eventuates, then two scenarios need to be distinguished, namely the transition from tribal agricultural societies to territorial states and the clash between agricultural and nomad hunter-gatherer societies.

Because increases in productivity enable a growth in the population, which in turn forces ever larger areas of land to be used for farming, an expansive dynamic is inherent to agricultural societies. For this reason, clashes between expanding agricultural societies already occurred at an early stage in human development in some regions, resulting in territories being defined and marked out through warfare or treaties:

> But as Families increased, and Industry inlarged their Stocks, their *Possessions inlarged* with the need of them; but yet it was commonly *without any fixed property in the ground* they made use of, till they incorporated, settled themselves together, and built Cities, and then, by consent, they came in time, to set out the *bounds of their distinct Territories*, and on limits between them and their Neighbours, and by Laws within themselves, settled the properties of those of the same Society.
>
> (*TTG* 2.38)

With the transition to territorial states, the labor theory of property loses its field of possible applications. Just as the boundaries between cities or kingdoms are fixed by explicit or tacit consent, so the property claims of citizens are regulated by legislation (*TTG* 2.45). Thus, the sufficiency proviso also lapses, namely, to leave for others the same amount of land of the same quality. As will be shown below, the substance of this proviso is incorporated into the right to subsistence guaranteed by the state.

With this analysis of the first scenario, the transition from agricultural societies to territorial states, Locke enters the contemporary debate on the power of a king. In *Patriarcha: or the Natural Rights of Kings* (1680), Sir Robert Filmer had traced the absolute power of the monarchy back to Adam. Kings, so is the claim, are thus the sole owners of the territory over which they reign. Besides refuting Filmer's interpretations of the Bible in the *First Treatise*, Locke counterposes the absolute power of the king with the property rights of citizens, legitimated originally through labor. Upon the transition into the *status civilis*, the individual retains the property rights acquired prior to the formation of the state (*TTG* 2.138), and these can now only be changed on the basis of consensus. If the state violates this mode of organizing property, then citizens have the right to revolt (*TTG* 2.222).

The second scenario to which the labor theory of property can be applied refers to the relations between agricultural and hunter-gatherer societies. At this point, Locke again seems to draw on a conflict of his time, namely that between English settlers and the indigenous peoples of North America. The colonial context of the labor theory of property has become a highly controversial focal point of scholarly research on Locke in recent decades.

Beyond dispute is Locke's personal involvement in British colonialism. Locke was Secretary to the Lords Proprietors of Carolina from 1669 to 1675 and became a landgrave of Carolina; he also profited financially from the slave trade through his investments in the Royal African Company and trade in the Bahamas (Farr 1986: 367; 2008: 497). In his function as Secretary, Locke was involved in drafting *The Fundamental Constitutions of Carolina* (1669) and its later revisions, which granted English settlers "absolute power and Authority over his Negro slaves" (Locke [1669] 1997: 180). As a member of the Council of Trade and Plantations between 1673 and 1675 and then secretary of William III's Board of Trade and Foreign Plantations from 1696 to 1700, Locke influenced the colonial politics of the British Empire. For this reason, Locke has been criticized as a defender of racist colonialism and modern slavery (Tully 1993: 137–76; Arneil 1996; Armitage 2004). However, the degree of this involvement in British colonialism has also been questioned. It appears to be contentious whether Locke's own views found expression in the constitution of Carolina or if, in his role as secretary, he was merely revising and editing a text reflecting the views of the settlers (Brewer 2017: 1052). After all, the *Two Treatises of Government* rigorously reject the idea of an absolute power; moreover, slavery is only justified as the consequence of a just war, whereby slavery itself is not hereditary (*TTG* 2.176; 189). It is also pointed out that Locke vehemently condemns slavery and the horrific violence against the indigenous and African populations, firstly in a draft of the Temporary Law for Carolina from 1671 and, shortly before his death, in a set of instructions for the Governor of Virginia in 1698 (Farr 1986: 286; 2008: 508).

One focal point of debates on Locke's racist colonialism is the issue of the property rights of English settlers in North America. Like Vitoria and Sepúlveda before, Locke categorically rejects idolatry and conquest as justification for appropriating the lands of indigenous peoples (*TTG* 2.182; 191; Armitage

2012: 105). The problem posed by state-sanctioned transgressions of natural law—specifically the human sacrifices of the Aztecs, which was in the sixteenth century still at the center of the debate between Sepúlveda and Las Casas—no longer plays a role for Locke. Indeed, Locke appears to have been scarcely affected by the virus of coloniality, which even his decolonial critics concede: "Locke's theory was nonhierarchical and inclusive to the extent that all adult humans possessed the same rationality because reason is likewise equal 'both in *America* and *Europe*' (and China, for example)" (Armitage 2012: 109).

However, Locke seems to justify the property rights of the English settlers with the labor theory of property. In the wide expanses where only nomads live, the labor theory of property claims that it is permissible to appropriate land without gaining the consent of the nomadic tribes *if* the land is then developed and farmed. And because agricultural utilization raises the yield of the land, the unilateral appropriation of land does not lead to a constraint on the subsistence rights of nomadic hunter-gatherer societies. Nor are the settlers, according to Locke, infringing the sufficiency proviso, although its purport needs to be adjusted to fit the new situation. The requirement that the rest of humankind is left an equal share of equally good land cannot simply be maintained without considering the question as to *how* the land is used. Because farming cultures require less land to satisfy their elementary needs than nomads, the strain on those areas that are still the common property of humankind is reduced. Thus, the colonists do not merely meet the requirement of the sufficiency proviso but in fact exceed it. "And therefore He, that incloses Land and has a greater plenty of the conveniencys of life from ten acres, than he could have from an hundred left to Nature, may truly be said, to give ninety acres to Mankind" (*TTG* 2.37).

At this point, serious objections emerge as to Locke's justification of English colonialism. From the indisputable fact that farming and planting increase the yield of the earth—"he who appropriates land to himself by his labour, does not lessen but increase the common stock of mankind" (*TTG* 2.37)—it by no means stringently follows that there is a right to *private* property. "Locke has here not considered the possibility that a piece of land may be both common and cultivated; nor has he considered the possibility that the 'Industrious and Rational' cultivators may be whole communities working together rather than individuals working on their own initiative" (Waldron 1988: 171).

In his effort to defend the claims of the English settlers, Locke dubiously undermines the original meaning of the sufficiency proviso. The settlers "give" a part of their claim to the common property of humanity only to those societies which *want to remain* on the stage of hunters and gatherers, and not the rest of "humankind." Should nomads decide to switch to agriculture at a later point, then there is no guarantee that they will ever find enough and, above all else, equally good land. The argument that agriculture increases the wealth of humankind may not negate the subsistence rights of nomads, in as far as they have access to agricultural surpluses through bartering, but it does not accommodate their rights to an equitable claim to land. With the principle that "property is acquired by those who cultivate the land *first*," Locke gravitates dangerously close to the position of the criticized occupation theory.

Moreover, because property questions in state societies are now resolved more on the level of political processes of consensus, the colonial situation in North America becomes a model case for the application of the labor theory of property. The world is divided into two spheres. While in European state societies appropriation of land is subject to the principle of consensus, in the Americas the European settlers are permitted to appropriate land without the consent of the indigenous peoples who live in the state of nature. Thus Locke "justifies European settlement in America without the consent of the native people, one of the most contentious and important events of the seventeenth century and one of the formative events of the modern world" (Tully 1993: 145f.). This means that Locke acknowledges, in accord with Vitoria, the sovereignty (*imperium*) of the indigenous peoples of the Americas but, contrary to Vitoria, negates their rights of property (*dominium*) (Armitage 2012: 105). The agricultural argument is then subsequently taken up by the physiocrats and, via Emer de Vattel, integrated into European versions of international law (Armitage 2012: 101).

The application of this theory to the territorial claims of the English settlers raises further questions, however. For the indigenous peoples of North America were not all nomadic, but also practiced agriculture, which was mentioned, admired, and used by European colonists from the very beginning. The English settlers even negotiated with the indigenous peoples for the purchase of land. Moreover, the main indigenous tribes united as the Five (later Six) Nation Confederacy founded by the Iroquois in the fifteenth century (Bishop 1997: 317–19). In this case, even according to Locke himself, the labor theory of property should not be applied to the territories of North America. At this point, the question arises whether Locke had a false or incomplete picture of the indigenous peoples (Tully 1993: 163f.). However, the constitution of Carolina explicitly mentions treaties between the settlers and the indigenous peoples. And Locke was familiar with reports on colonial publications and peoples outside Europe; his library contained 195 books on the "New World" (Corcoran 2018: 230–4). Against this background, Locke's labor theory of property does not seem to be applicable to the English settlers in North America without causing certain problems (Corcoran 2018: 241). The colonial slant of Locke's thought may therefore not stem solely from the labor theory of property, but from his ideal of a civilized society, which presupposes the invention of money.

11.3 The introduction of "money" and the emergence of a global market system

The natural law principle that one can only appropriate as much land as they are able to cultivate and consume the produce yielded would still appertain in the seventeenth century, according to Locke—"since there is Land enough in the world to suffice double the Inhabitants" (*TTG* 2.36)—if the money economy had not fundamentally changed economic relations. Why and in which sense money could propel the development of human society into a completely new direction demands cogent analysis.

As Locke sees it, the invention of money can be explained as resulting from the problems caused by simple bartering. To facilitate the exchange of natural goods, humans, almost on a whim, assigned a special value to certain metals: "Gold, Silver, and Diamonds, are things, that Fancy or Agreement hath put the Value on, more than real use" (*TTG* 2.46). Despite their fictive value, as universal mediums of exchange gold and silver can be traded for useful goods at all times: "And thus *came in the use of Money*, some lasting thing that Men might keep without spoiling, and that by mutual consent Men would take in exchange for the truly useful, but perishable supports of Life" (*TTG* 2.47). But money not only facilitates the exchange of surpluses, but also contains an incentive, namely, to enlarge the store of possessions: "so this *Invention of Money* gave them the opportunity [sic!] to continue and enlarge them" (*TTG* 2.48). Somewhat cautiously at first, Locke mentions the *opportunity* arising from the invention of money, by no means a compelling necessity to expand ownership of property and possessions. Nomads, for example, traded with furs and salt, which served as universal mediums of exchange, without fundamentally changing the level of their needs or production. Locke does not elaborate on the simple, money-mediated exchange of commodity-money-commodity (C-M-C), however; his interest is focused exclusively on the logic of accumulating money, i.e., the exchange of money-commodity-money (M-C-M′) (Peters 1997: 31). The incentive to accumulate implicated with money is so irresistible it must be assumed that a compulsion to enlarge ownership is at work, and not some mere passing opportunity: "Find out something that hath the *Use and Value of Money* amongst his Neighbours, you shall see the same Man will begin presently [sic!] to *enlarge* his Possessions" (*TTG* 2.48). The incentive stimulated by money to accumulate presupposes, however, the possibility of entering into cross-border relationships with other groups or peoples. Without the hope of trade relations unrestricted by boundaries, there is, as Locke illustrates through the example of a village on a lonely island, no incentive to appropriate and cultivate land to any extent exceeding one's own needs (*TTG* 2.48).

However, Locke explains his theory of money not only with a fictional example, but also with the concrete situation of the English colonists in North America, who are locked into a subsistence economy due to trade barriers:

> For I ask, What would a Man value Ten Thousand, or an Hundred Thousand Acres of excellent *Land*, ready cultivated, and well stocked too with Cattle, in the middle of the in-land Parts of *America*, where he had no hopes of Commerce with other Parts of the World, to draw Money to him by the Sale of the product? It would not be worth the inclosing.
>
> (*TTG* 2.48)

This means that Locke focuses less on the general function of money as a means to facilitate exchange between useful and necessary commodities, but rather on its specific function as an incentive to extend the appropriation of land. More concretely, the scope of the labor theory of property is not limited to merely justifying the appropriation of land in the Americas by European settlers for expanding their subsistence farming but is in fact geared to the large-scale development of land through commercial agriculture, with goods to be produced for the world market. The restructuring involved in establishing a market-oriented agricultural economy dramatically exacerbates the conflict between the English settlers and the native peoples in North America. As Locke himself concedes, an idyllic coexistence between European farmers and the native American peoples would still exist today if were not for "the Invention of Money, and the tacit Agreement of Men to put a value on it, introduced (by consent) larger Possessions, and the Right to them" (*TTG* 2.36). Money does not merely serve the exchanging of surpluses but is a means to purchase land and other resources, and once transformed into monetary value or capital, they are sources out of which a monetary gain can be generated (Binswanger 1991: 133).

To justify the money-based expansion of land possession, Locke is forced to modify the moral provisos of the labor theory property. No changes are needed in the spoilage limitation because gold, silver, or diamonds—"*a little yellow Metal*, which would keep without wasting or decay" (*TTG* 2.37)—are unperishable goods. In contrast, serious problems emerge when the sufficiency proviso is applied to the commercially based agricultural economy. Because the accumulation of unperishable money is unlimited, the continuous expansion of land ownership is an inevitable consequence. And if the accumulated money is used to employ additional servants who farm these new areas of land, then the basic requirement of the labor theory of property, namely, to appropriate only as much land as can be cultivated, is also fulfilled. In the long run, however, the continuous expansion of land ownership gives rise to a situation in which the requirement to leave others just as much and just as good land cannot be fulfilled. Indeed, a commercial agricultural economy undermines the very means of existence of nomadic societies. With a view to the conflict in North America, this means that the indigenous peoples must expect that all of their living spaces will eventually be occupied by the colonists. To justify the expansive dynamic of a money economy, Locke is compelled to ultimately abandon the sufficiency proviso in its original usage. If they wish to maintain their way of life, the indigenous peoples are thus confronted in Locke's schema with the alternative to either withdraw to regions with poorer quality land or integrate into the settler societies as servants. And indeed, because this expansive dynamic has no inherent boundaries and escalates limitlessly, all nomadic tribal societies on the planet are ultimately threatened with the same fate.

Because the commercial agricultural economy ignites a dynamic that, when thought through to its conclusion, leads to the complete repression of pre-monetary societies, Locke has to resort to two further arguments in support of the transition to a money economy. For the first argument strand, Locke returns to the consensual figuration of his rationale. As money was introduced, humankind had tacitly consented to even the long-term consequences of a money-based economy, in particular the widening of social divides:

> But since Gold and Silver ... has its value only from the consent of Men ... it is plain, that Men have agreed to disproportionate and unequal Possession of the Earth ... This partage of things, in an inequality of private possessions, men have made practicable out of the bounds of Societie, and without compact, only by putting a value on gold and silver and tacitly agreeing in the use of Money.
> (*TTG* 2.50)

It certainly cannot be assumed that the peoples of America had tacitly consented to the introduction of money, which implies the appropriation and loss of their living space. As Locke himself admits, it is only a "part of Mankind that have consented Use of Money" (*TTG* 2.45). Given the rational weakness of this tacit consent, Locke attempts to mitigate the damage done by the conflict situation by mobilizing empirical arguments; although "the human race has spread itself to all corners of the world, and infinitely outnumbers those who were here at the beginning," for Locke sufficient free land remains available, both in the Americas and even in some regions in Europe, for instance in Spain (*TTG* 2.36). This argument trivializes the problematic, however. Once a money economy is established, then, as Locke himself emphasizes, a limitless economic expansion gathers momentum that in the long run will completely transform the common property of humankind into private ownership. Conflicts are therefore inevitable and foreseeable in the domain of actual history. At this point, we need to note that, as a change of direction fundamentally impacting on the whole of humankind, the introduction of a profit-oriented money economy cannot be justified by the paltry argumentative instrument of tacit consent.

In a second strand of argument, Locke attempts to justify the money economy by referring to the hedonist theory of eudemonism. In a developed money economy, where producers are in a state of global competition, "Invention and Arts" (*TTG* 2.44) assume a key role. Here the creative dimension of labor, having remained dormant in the hunter-gatherer stage, emerges as the focal point of Locke's theory. Given the increases in productivity made possible by the expansion of trade and the technological inventions of Baconian science in the early modern era, Locke develops a moral justification of the expansive appropriation of land and the concomitant squeezing out of nomadic peoples. While monetary agrarian societies no longer leave the nomads any free land, they increase the prosperity of humankind on a scale inconceivable and unprecedented for earlier ages. Monetary societies bestow the rest of humankind with a twofold advantage. Firstly, they transform the "waste land" (*TTG* 2.42) inhabited by indigenous peoples into "valuable" land, i.e., agrarian croplands; and secondly, thanks to their innovations, profit-based agrarian societies present humankind with a continuously growing amount of goods, and hence make life more comfortable: "And that which made up the great part of what he applied to the Support or Comfort of his being, when Invention and Arts had improved the conveniences of Life, was perfectly his own and did not belong on common to others" (*TTG* 2.44). Although the expansion of profit-based agrarian societies leads to an ousting of non-monetary societies, when the indigenous peoples integrate into the European settler communities as farm servants, they can now go beyond merely securing a subsistence existence and share in the comforts and conveniences produced by a money economy. The restrictions placed on self-determination that an existence as a day laborer entails are compensated by material advantages. As Locke put it, it is because native Americans do not improve the soil by labor that "they have not one hundredth part of the Conveniences we enjoy: And a King of a large and fruitful Territory there feeds, lodges, and is clad worse than a day Labourer in *England*" (*TTG* 2.41).

To sum up, the Lockean economy aims at a forced enlargement of land ownership through ever-advancing appropriation, whose final consequence consists in colonization on a global scale (Priddat 1988: 78). The suppression of nomadic peoples through expansive monetary societies is justified by two arguments: the introduction of money by tacit consent and the hedonistic idea of happiness. Given the paltriness of the tacit consent argument, the burden of justification falls principally on the idea of a potentially limitless increase of conveniences making human life more comfortable (Tully 1980: 160). Thus the civilized status of societies is measured primarily on the degree of material prosperity. This begs the question whether the chief of an indigenous tribe, who despite material hardships enjoys great social recognition within the group, would not in fact have a "better" life than an English day laborer, surrounded by conveniences unknown to the native Americans but forced to endure a large degree of social contempt (Ryan 1984: 41f.). Locke however omits such comparisons, for the socio-cultural achievements of non-profit societies are almost fully neglected. The Americas merely serve as "a Pattern of the first Ages in Asia and Europe" (*TTG* 2.108). Nonetheless, Locke's idea of social progress is not seamless, as the comparison between the early monarchies and the "Golden Age" shows (*TTG* 2.111; cf. Tully 1980: 147–51).

11.4 Embedding the market system: political economy and social policy

Once states become established, then the borders between them as well as domestic property relations have to be fixed by contracts. From now on, the appropriation of land can no longer be justified by its cultivation through labor. In the pre-monetary kingdoms, however, "a great part of the Land lay in common; that the Inhabitants valued it not, nor claimed Property in any more than they made use of" (*TTG* 2.38). Therefore, nomads were able to move around freely on these unfarmed areas but only with the consent of the respective rulers, as Locke illustrates with an example from the Bible. Abraham was able to settle in Gerar, "a Country where he was a Stranger," with the permission of King Abimelech (*TTG* 2.38). Moreover, as long as there is no incentive to extend production, and so the uncultivated land does not possess an exchange value, then strangers may take possession of land given the consent of the ruler and abiding by the spoilage proviso. In contrast, in monetary societies every stretch of "waste land" is now a potential object facilitating the expansion of economic activities: "in some parts of the World, (where the Increase of People and Stock, *with the use of Money*) had made Land scarce, and so of some Value [sic!]" (*TTG* 2.45). Because money can be increased at will, the appropriation and cultivation of land now takes place within the horizon of potentially limitless economic expansion. For this reason, the rulers of monetary societies may no longer gift "waste land" to nomads or settlers but have to sell it at the current market price.

Here it once again becomes apparent how Locke dovetails the justification of the money economy with the interests of English colonialism. In contrast to territories of North America, where based on the labor theory of property English settlers could appropriate land without the consent of the nomadic peoples, with respect to the empires of the Incas and Aztecs the Europeans would have had to gain consent from the local ruler for the right to settle and take possession of land. Because these empires no longer exist, and Locke obviously does not recognize the confederacies of the Iroquois or Hurons, this rule can no longer be applied. In statal societies, however, applying the labor theory of property is precluded in principle.

Nonetheless, the labor theory of property is not simply rendered meaningless for monetary European societies. Based on the unequal appropriation of land in the natural state, the legal system has only one task: to regulate property relations (*TTG* 2.45). But because changes to how property is organized in the *status civilis* cannot be made without the consent of those affected, concretely the owners—"The *Supream Power cannot take* away Man any part of his *Property* without his own consent" (*TTG* 2.138)—redistribution of property is difficult to enforce. Regardless of whether redistributions are possible (Tully 1980: 163–5) or not (Waldron 1988: 137–56), Locke is faced with the question of how the monetary economy in the *status civilis* can be reconciled with the natural law, in particular with every individual's right of subsistence. For this purpose, Locke conceives a political economy resting on two pillars: a state politics for the poor and a politics promoting economic growth.

Locke presented his basic ideas concerning the poverty problem in *An Essay on the Poor Law* (1697) (Goldie 1997: 182–98) and, in part at least, in writings on interest policy. For Locke, poverty stems not from the inequality of property relations; poverty is primarily the result of laziness: "virtue and industry being as constant on the one side as vice and idleness are on the others"

(Goldie 1997: 182). This criticism is leveled not only at the idle poor but also the lazy rich who fail to ensure that their land is efficiently worked, succumbing instead to luxury.

Because the state is denied any substantial intervention in existing property relations, the poor can secure their subsistence only by leasing land or borrowing money to set up a business of some sort (Vaughn 1980: 51f.). The poor are thus forced to be particularly industrious. Through their labor and industry, they generate, beyond their own means of subsistence, an idle income for all those who—thanks to preceding appropriation and inheritance—possess more goods than they themselves can utilize. Since it can be assumed that the wealthy have an intrinsic interest in leasing land and lending money, in Locke's scenario an economic cycle arises that in principle secures the subsistence of everyone.

Although Locke accepts deep social inequalities, the poor are not simply abandoned to their fate. Every person who can no longer earn a living through their labor because of illness, or some other external emergency situation, has a right to partake in the surpluses generated by others:

> But we know God hath not left one Man so to the mercy of another, that he may starve him if he please ... As Justice gives every Man a Title to the product of his honest Industry, and the fair Acquisition of his Ancestors descended to him; so Charity gives every Man a title to so much out of another's Plenty, as will keep him from extream want.
>
> (*TTG* 1.42)

Like Hobbes, in his intervention against a governmental regulation of interest rates, Locke demands that the right of subsistence inhering to every individual must be guaranteed and safeguarded by state social policy: "only common Charity teaches, that those should be most taken care by the Law, who are least capable of taking care for themselves" ([1692] 1991: 220). However, if a larger number of the poor fail to shoulder the "double" burden of industry, which is connected with the leasing of land, borrowing money, and indentured labor, then the system of state welfare for the poor, financed by taxes, threatens to collapse: "The multiplying of the poor, and the increase of the tax for their maintenance, is so general on observation and complaint, that it cannot be doubted" (Locke [1697] 1997: 183). The problem of growing poverty can only be solved when the state provides work for the poor capable of it. In the *Essay on the Poor Law*, Locke thus proposes "some proper methods for setting on work and employing the poor of this kingdom, and making them useful to the public thereby easing others of that burden" (Locke [1697] 1997: 183).

Locke divides the poor capable of work into two groups: beggars and families with many children. Beggars capable of work aged between 14 and 50 are to be placed in "houses of correction" where they may be forced into work for three years, receiving board, lodgings, and a low wage. Maritime powers can also force beggars to work on a ship for three years. Whoever refuses this enforced work is to be punished like a deserter, the penalties ranging from floggings to cutting off ears. For families with many children, Locke proposes a whole bundle of measures. First, once they have completed their third year, the children are to be sent to "working-schools," where they receive the training necessary for performing menial labor. The wages they earn can be used to meet the costs for their keep, ensuring that they do not become a burden to the state. At Sunday school they are given a rudimentary education. Introducing working-schools has the added benefit of enabling the wives of day laborers to work. This also contributes to eradicating the problem of children begging (Locke [1697] 1997: 185–8).

These draconian measures for combating poverty have attracted much criticism. The proposal to dump the children of the poor in working-schools while developing sophisticated "ideas for the education" of the sons (not the daughters!) of the aristocracy and bourgeois establishment is clearly offensive to modern sensibilities about equal opportunity. Nonetheless, Macpherson's reproach to the effect that Locke assumed "that the members of the labouring class do not or cannot live a fully rational life" (1962: 222) misses the mark. According to Locke, the children of the poor, should they receive a good education, are capable of developing the same capabilities as the children of the upper classes. This idea, anchored objectively in the *tabula rasa* conception of reason, did not inspire Locke to come up with any proposals for social reform. However, in a manuscript entitled "Labour" from 1693 there is the vision of a utopian society where social barriers are overcome and *all* members have the same opportunity to cultivate and develop their physical *and* intellectual abilities. Scholars, as Locke further elaborates, devote their energies not just to intellectual pursuits but would also perform six hours of physical labor each day (Locke [1693] 1997b: 326–8; Dunn 1969: 231f.).

Combating poverty through policy is by no means the only instrument Locke draws on to reconcile the monetary economy with natural law. Because any genuinely effective support for the poor unable to work requires the production of surpluses, poverty policy needs to be embedded in a comprehensive economic policy. The task of a government is thus not limited to merely protecting civil liberties and property but must also include initiating an active economic policy in which, if possible, all members of society are motivated and given the support to engage in productive activities increasing wealth and prosperity: "the increase of lands and the right imploying of them is the great art of government" (*TTG* 2.42).

Besides the legislative codification of property rights, among the most important regulatory elements of an economy are taxation and interest policies, the basic lineaments of which are sketched in the treatise "Some Considerations of the Consequences of the Lowering of Interest, and Raising the Value of Money" (Locke [1692] 1991), later complemented by "Further Considerations of the Lowering of Interest, and Raising the Value of Money" (Locke [1696] 1991). The historical background to this essay is a long-standing dispute in English domestic politics: should the state lower interest from six percent to four percent? The proponents of lowering had hoped that this measure would vitalize the economy; its opponents saw it as nothing but an instrument to cut the king's debt. Locke elevates the debate as to the sense—or otherwise—behind a state interest policy on to a scholarly and moral level.

Because the prices of all goods, including money, are subject to the law of supply and demand, it is *de facto* impossible to reduce the interest rate through state regulation. If market-based prices and interest rates continue to be paid under the hand, though, then all hitherto attempts to fix the prices of staples or the interest rate level through a state decree have failed. Furthermore, the enforced lowering of the interest rate by the state would have counterproductive consequences, a view Locke makes clear with an example. If interest rates are kept artificially low, owners of money have no incentive to offer loans. Domestic commerce would be gripped by paralysis. Beneficiaries of the resultant weakening of the national economy would then be the banks, who would lend the surplus money at the real interest rate to foreign borrowers. In this case, the English population would effectively be subsidizing foreign loans and the outflow of money from the national economy ([1692] 1991: 224).

Moreover, for a country like England, such a state lowering of interest rates would have fatal consequences for foreign trade, an area where higher interest rates are the norm because of the greater risks. And the slackening of foreign trade threatens in turn the very existence of England, which has neither gold or silver mines and therefore can only acquire money through commercial trade with manufactured goods. When a country's own products are no longer competitive on the world market because of a misguided interest policy, its society threatens to become impoverished and "quickly leave us Poor, and exposed. Gold and

Silver though they serve for few yet command all the conveniences of life; and therefore in a plenty of them consists Riches" (Locke [1692] 1991: 221).

Nevertheless, access to precious metals is no guaranteed safeguard against poverty and economic decline. On the contrary, because the mining of precious metals is an extremely complex and costly undertaking, countries such as Spain, despite having exploited the rich gold and silver mines, have dropped behind economically in a short space of time. Trade is the better instrument to attract more money from other nations. For, as a comparison between Spain and the Netherlands shows, money flows spontaneously of itself into those countries which can sell great amounts of goods on the world market. Thus, in the unpublished *For a General Naturalization* (1693), Locke refers to "the Comparison of Holland and Spain: The later having all the advantages of situation and the yearly aflux of wealth out of its owne dominions yet so for want of hands the poorest country in Europe. The other ill situate but being cramed with people abounding in riches" (Locke [1696] 1991: 487). It is not therefore the interest rate that it is decisive but "our Importation or Exportation of consumable Commodities" (Locke [1692] 1991: 225).

In short, the prosperity or misery of a society depends on the competitiveness of its products on the international markets. Therefore, according to Locke, the valid principle to be followed is: "Riches do not consist in having more Gold and Silver, but in having more in proportion, than the rest of the World, or than our Neighbours" ([1692] 1991: 222). Because the inflow of additional money would lead to inflation, production and trade must expand. The expansive dynamic of the market economy thus rests on two pillars, trade, which encompasses the production and distribution of goods, and a certain amount of money (Pridatt 1988: 194): "Trade then is necessary of the producing of Riches, and Money necessary to the carrying on of Trade" (Locke [1692] 1991: 223f.).

Locke's description of economic cycles is undoubtedly flawed in many respects (Vaughn 1980; Priddat 1988: 111–231). For example, the insight of Philippe de Cantillon into the cyclical movement between imports and exports is neglected (Foucault 2002: 202–6). For this reason, low domestic prices are not seen as a chance for additional exports which bring money into the country. Locke is, rather, fixated on the secondary effect of the limitations placed on imports by the high price levels overseas. Nonetheless, Locke already perceives the systemic dynamics of the market economy at an early stage. And the systemic approach toward the economy decouples economic interactions from moral constraints, especially on the level of individual ethics. But Locke's justification of a market economy system does not lead to a full de-moralization of the economic sphere.

On the institutional level, Locke's economy remains embedded in the moral framework of natural law. For this reason, economic policy measures are not only examined with respect to their economic efficiency, but also, as the analyses on interest policy testify, in terms of their consequential moral costs. A state lowering of interest rates would, as Locke has us consider, hit the widows and orphans particularly hard because securing their future depends on stable monetary value. Moreover, a state lowering of interest leads to a disadvantage for those who have saved money and, according to Locke, have the right to draw the same amount of interest on their savings as owners of land: "give to *Richard* what is *Peter's*. Due, for no other Reason, but because one was Borrower, and the other Lender" ([1692] 1991: 219). It is also morally dubious when a state lowering of interest intervenes into existing contracts and agreements. Because the prescribed interest rates are ignored in practice, the state interest policy fosters a collective perjury which in the long term has disastrous consequences for social cohesion: "it will be impossible for the society (these Bonds being dissolved) to subsist: All must break in Pieces, and run to confusion" (Locke [1692] 1991: 1.213).

Moreover, Locke justifies moral norms for interactions even within the market economy. In principle, the market price and the just price coincide because the needy would also immediately sell on any cheaper goods they acquired at the prevailing market price. In emergency situations, however—as Locke illustrates in the unpublished *Venditio* (1695) with the example of a famine—the laws of the market, following the charity rule, are curtailed through special norms of ethical economics. If an English ship goes ashore in Dünkirchen, where the population is currently suffering a famine, the traders should not transport the urgently needed food to another location to benefit from higher prices:

> yet if he carry it away unless they will give him more than they are able, or extorts so much from their present necessity as not to leave them the means of subsistence afterwards he offends against the common rule of charity as a man and if they perish any of them by reason of his extortion is no doubt guilty of murder.
>
> (Locke [1695] 1997: 342)

Locke proposes a double rule: any knowledge about the plight of the buyer is not to be used to increase profit margins; and goods are only to be offered for sale at local customary prices.

11.5 Critical review: unlimited money economy versus Aristotelian *oikonomia*?

Aristotle distinguishes between an economy that serves the good life of the *polis* (*oikonomiké*) and an unnatural art of limitlessly accumulating money (*kapeliké o chremastiké*) (*Pol.* 1.9–11). The Aristotelian economy is grounded in the ontological structure of the cosmos. As nature sets a limit (*telos*) to all existing things, the desire for material goods has to be limited in the light of the *bios politicos*, which is one realization of the *eudaimonia*. Since the pre-monetary natural state is almost identical with the Aristotelian economy (Priddat 1998: 34), Locke's justification of a monetary economy appears to be nothing short of an inversion of the condemned chrematistics (Schütrumpf 1991: 354). The contrast between Aristotelean and Lockean economics has been seized upon by different critics of modernity. According to Leo Strauss, Locke's defense of a money economy reveals the moral perversion of modernity, namely a revaluing of avarice, the *amor sceleratus habendi*, into a virtue, a revaluing that Locke's invocation of natural law merely conceals: "Since the burden of his theory of property is that covetousness and concupiscence channelled, eminently beneficial and reasonable, much more so than 'exemplary charity.' By building civil society on 'the low but solid ground' of selfishness or of certain 'private vices', one will achieve much greater 'public benefits'" (Strauss 1965: 247). For Hannah Arendt, Locke's labor theory of property promotes the rise of the *homo laborans* in the modern age, the far-reaching consequence of which is the supplanting of the Aristotelian concept of politics, e.g., the good life guaranteed by the self-government of citizens. The endless reproduction of biological life was seen in classical ancient philosophy as a pre-political activity, however: "since labour actually is the most natural and least worldly of man's activities" (1998: 31; cf. 28–37; 109–25; 320–6). Locke is thus seen as having paved the way for modern "worldlessness," in which the preservation and enhancement of life is elevated to the highest goal of politics. However, "when man no longer acts as an individual, concerned only with his own survival, but as a 'member of the species', a *Gattungswesen* as Marx used to say," then the process of accumulation "can be as infinite as the life process of the species" (Arendt 1998: 116).

From a more analytical perspective, Max Weber positioned Aristotle's concept of the household economy as the background foil for explicating his theory of the de-moralized modern economy. The Aristotelian economy is still based on the principle of "material rationality"; economic activities are oriented on substantive values, irrespective of whether "ethics, politics, utilitarianism, hedonism, social rank, egalitarianism, or whatever else, introduce some other requirements" (Weber [1921–2] 2019: 172). In contrast, modern economic systems are determined by a "formal rationality" that subsumes economic activity exclusively under the logic of a cost–yield calculation. In short, the economy no longer has its measure in the "good life" of the *polis* but instead in the standards set by the laws of the market for generating profit.

As the juxtaposing of Aristotle and Locke frequently serves as a historical basis for comprehensive interpretations of modernity on the whole, I wish to conclude this study of Locke with a comparison between both theories of the economy, focusing on correcting some of the schematic opposites which have become entrenched. In the light of our previous interpretation, we can already reject one critical portrayal of Locke: rather than recasting the vice of avarice as a virtue, Locke, like Aristotle, embeds the economy in a moral horizon and offers evaluative criteria. The simplifying schema of the "household economy limited by morality versus a limitless money economy stripped of moral principles" must be corrected. For this reason, the deficiencies as well as the achievements of the economic theories of both Aristotle and Locke require more differentiated analysis.

Numerous parallels are initially discernible between Aristotle and Locke in their respective reconstructions of human economic development. In a first step, Aristotle synthesizes hunter-gatherer and agricultural societies into a single stage. Nomads and settled farmers secure survival not "by exchange and trade" but through "natural labor [*autóphyton ergasían*]" (*Pol.* 1.8.1256a40–1256 b1). The concept of "natural labor" covers two forms of acquisition, namely agriculture and warfare, to which various forms of hunting belong, including the hunting for slaves (*Pol.* 1.8.1256b22–7; Schütrumpf 1991: 310; Pellegrin 2001: 44). At the same time, though, like Locke, Aristotle gives pre-eminence to the farmers' way of life over that of work-shy nomads (*Pol.* 1.8.1256a31). That the description of pre-monetary economies also underpins Locke's provisos, as has been suggested (Peters 1997: 25–9), seems a questionable claim. Although Aristotle emphasizes that the *oikonomia* makes available the goods essential for life which could be stored (*Pol.* 1.8.1258b31), the moral rule to only store as many goods as one consumes oneself is never mentioned. The limits on natural forms of acquisition are defined rather by the *telos* of the community (Schütrumpf 1991: 317). It also seems doubtful that the sufficiency proviso is genuinely contained in a law mentioned by Aristotle, namely "that no one should possess more than a certain quantity of land" (*Pol.* 6.4.1319a7f.). But the sufficiency proviso presupposes the idea, alien to Aristotle, of an original common property among humanity.

In the next step of the description of the economic evolution, Aristotle turns attention to exchange relations. As communities became larger and families branched out, the need arose to exchange utility goods. The natural exchange, "giving and receiving wine, for example in exchange for corn, and the like … is not part of the wealth-getting art and is not contrary to nature, but is needed for the satisfaction of men's natural wants" (*Pol.* 1.8.1257a 29–30). Money ultimately resulted out of the needs of bartering, according to Aristotle, which, as for Locke, has its basis in human agreement (*Pol.* 1.8.1257a 35–8). At least looking back historically, Aristotle firmly mentions the possibility of a "natural" exchange mediated through money that, like the natural exchange itself, serves to provide goods essential for life (*Pol.* 1.8.1257a 35f.). "The use of currency is natural insofar as it allows exchange to develop to a sufficient extent to be effective in protecting the household from severe deficiencies" (Lewis 1978: 82).

Over the course of time, however, the art of making money (*chrematistike*) developed out of the simple exchange or the C-M-C cycle, a development that, as Aristotle emphasizes, caused a fundamental change in the economic relationship. For chrematistics, wealth no longer resides in having essential goods at one's disposal but in accumulating money: "Originating in the use of coin, the art of getting wealth is generally thought to be chiefly concerned with it, and to be the art which produces riches and wealth, having to consider how they may be accumulated" (*Pol.* 1.8.1257b 5–10).

Aristotle and Locke are largely in agreement as to the description of the historical development of economic systems. For Locke, as well, it is not the introduction of money as an exchange medium that initiates the decisive turning point in the socio-economic evolution of humankind, but what is connected with money—the incentive to limitless accumulation. In *evaluating* the limitless money economy, however, deep divisions emerge between Aristotle and Locke. While Locke focuses on the growth in productivity generated by a money economy, Aristotle directs attention to the negative consequences for the moral consciousness of a society. With the institutionalizing of chrematistics, a perverted idea of wealth pervades society. And what is more, striving for more and more money ultimately threatens to deform all areas of human life so that, as Aristotle laments, even physicians and generals are primarily concerned with augmenting their wealth instead of ensuring the health of patients or the security of the *polis*. As Aristotle emphasizes with respect to the Sophists, philosophy is also not immune to chrematistics *per se* (Meikle 1995: 70f.). In short, "some men turn every quality or art into means of getting wealth; this they conceive to be the end, and the promotion of the end they think all things must contribute" (*Pol.* 1.9.1258a 13-15). Nonetheless, unlike Plato, Aristotle does not focus solely on a moral criticism, claiming "that human wickedness begets the idea that wealth is unlimited, and that people then abuse money by making it into a means of pursuing unlimited wealth … He thinks that vicious end is inherent in the institution itself" (Meikle 1995: 60; 76). This means that chrematistics is not a morally neutral art, but—to draw on Jürgen Habermas's formulation—it leads to a "colonization of the lifeworld."

The criticism leveled at chrematistics is based on a distinction between use and exchange value, first introduced into Western philosophy by Aristotle (*Pol.* 1.8.1257a 8-9). What is contrary to nature is not *that* we exchange goods of use, but *how* we no longer use them for the purpose of satisfying justifiable needs. Exchange no longer serves to balance abundance and deprivation in chrematistics, where goods are not sold occasionally but always and completely (Binswanger 1991: 117). Thus, the appropriate relationship between ends and means is reversed. Since, according to Aristotle, all actions aim at some goal (*telos*), the question emerges as to what end does the absolutizing of the means serve? At this point, only two possible ends are thinkable for Aristotle: the striving for more and more money serves either the preservation of life (*Pol.* 1.9.1257b41-1258a2) or a hedonistic idea of perfect life. "For, as their enjoyment is in excess, they seek an art which produces the excess of enjoyment" (*Pol.* 1.9.1258 a7-8). In both cases, the good life in the sense of *eudaimonia* is missed.

Because chrematistics has developed unintended by social actors out of natural exchange, a moral critic of the merchants, as for example Plato's call for traders to be educated to moderate their striving for profit (*Leg.* 918c–d), comes too late. In view of the dynamics inherent in a money-based exchange economy and its destructive effects on social life, Aristotle demands institutional control and containment of chrematistics. Although chrematistics is not completely rejected because of its limited importance in providing the material basis of the *polis* (*EN* 5.8.1133b15ff; Meikle 1995: 49f.), this is the point where Aristotle and Locke part company in their historical reconstruction of economies. At the same time, however, Locke's economics cannot be simply reduced to an uncritical affirmation of Aristotelian chrematistics, a view that radical critics of European modernity assumed in the twentieth century. Here, two questions need to be clarified. Firstly, with respect to Locke, it needs to be seen whether the main objections against chrematistics put forward by Aristotle, namely the absolutizing of means and the option for hedonistic ways of life, actually pertain to his economics. Secondly, a question can be posed back to Aristotle: how can the material basis of the *polis* be secured and maintained without any developed trade linked to chrematistics?

To begin, I shall address the second question. The ideal of the perfect *polis* itself demands—even if this term may appear to be utterly un-Aristotelian—a "political economy" that identifies those forms of production and acquisition which can economically sustain the religious, cultural, and political institutions of the *polis*. At this point, a peculiar lacuna becomes discernible in Aristotle's thinking. Although sections of the first book of *Politics* dedicated to economics deal with the negative consequences of chrematistics in great detail, a constructive perspective for a political economy is missing. Even the very basic issue of how to prevent other members of the *polis* from going hungry finds no consideration (Schütrumpf 1991: 319–21). The situation is very different in the theory on the forms of the state, however, with Aristotle expressly tackling the problem of how to secure the economic foundations of the *polis*. The approaches to solving the problem vary, as two examples show, depending on the social and political constitution of the *polis*.

Politics and economics are strictly separated in the ideal *polis*: the head of the household meets the costs arising from the exercise of political offices and the conducting of belligerent undertakings (*Pol.* 7.8.1328b10; 4.4.1291a33–40). The prosperity of an ideal citizen stems primarily from agriculture, operated with the help of slaves. Then there is the wealth generated by trade, which however remains restricted to the import of essential goods. Public festivals, feasts, and religious cults are paid in part from the proceeds given off by state common property, which is worked by state slaves (*Pol.* 7.10). While no citizen should lack food (*Pol.* 7.19.1330a3), for securing subsistence no assistance is provided by the state, let alone a redistribution of property and assets. Because the household heads are not compensated for exercising political offices and artisans and day laborers are in any case excluded from taking part in political life, there is no need to even discuss or consider state financial resources or revenues in the ideal *polis* (Schütrumpf 1982: 42, note 4).

A different situation prevails in democracies, however, where besides the head of an *oikos*, small farmers and artisans participate in political life and have to be compensated for these activities from public funds. Since Cleisthenes, the raising and distributing of public funds was a *quaestio disputata* of public life in Athens, as witnessed by Xenophon's work on problems of state economy *Ways and Means* (*De vectalibus*). To be able to pay poor citizens a basic income of three obols a day, Xenophon proposes a whole cluster of measures to increase state revenues. These range from expanding harbor facilities for bringing in regular rents through to intensifying silver mining by using private and state slaves (*Vect.* 4.1–5). Aristotle also inevitably encounters the problem of political economy in the context of his considerations on democracy. While Aristotle sees the remuneration of the *demoi* for public activities as the cause for the rise of the extreme form of democracy, like Xenophon he nevertheless makes the case for providing needy citizens with lasting security of subsistence: "The true friend of the people should see that they are not too poor, for extreme poverty lowers the character of the democracy; measures therefore should be taken which will give them lasting prosperity; and as this is equally the interest of all classes." This goal can only be achieved, as Aristotle elaborates, when the poor are not only paid for their public activities but also receive from state revenues enough money "as may enable them to purchase a little farm or, at any rate, make a beginning in trade or farming" (*Pol.* 6.5.1320a32–b1). All proposals for solving the problem of poverty—and herein Aristotle and Xenophon are in accord—serve solely the purpose of preventing the poor from rising up in protest (preserving *stasis*). As distinct from Locke, securing the subsistence of the needy is not a moral issue but a question of political foresight and wisdom.

As for the first question, a number of terms need to be clarified before we can determine whether the Aristotelian objections to chrematistics, namely the absolutizing of the means and the reduction of morality to hedonism, also pertain to Locke's justification of a money economy. Aristotle understands the money economy primarily as profit-oriented trade with *existing* goods. For this reason, Aristotle can illustrate how chrematistics function with an anecdote about the business acumen shown by Thales of Miletus. As legend has it, Thales took advantage of astronomy observations predicting that the coming year would yield a particularly bountiful olive harvest, purchasing all the olive presses in Miletus and Chios in good time so as to lease them for the harvest at a high profit (*Pol.* 1.11.1259a9–17). Aristotle comments: "his scheme for getting wealth is of universal application, and is nothing but the creation of a monopoly" (*Pol.* 1.11.1259a20f.). In contrast, as Locke explains in the unpublished *Notes on Trade* (1674), trade includes not only exchange but also the production of goods:

> Trade is twofold. 1. Domestick manufacture, whereby is to be understood all labour emploid by your people in preparing commodities for the consumption, either of your owne people (where it exclude foreigne importation) or of foreigners. 2. Carriage, i.e. Navigation and Merchandise.
>
> (Locke [1674] 1997: 222)

Trade accelerates a process already observable in the pre-monetary agriculture societies, namely the appropriation, production, and technological enhancement of goods. Of course, gold and silver enter a land through overseas trade, but the accumulation of money is not to be an end in itself for economic reasons, as Locke emphasizes with respect to the mercantilists, but must always serve the purpose of expanding production (Vaughn 1980: 69). Because increasing production requires not only technological innovations but also a growing workforce, along with employment schemes for the poor, the immigration of foreign workers needs to be encouraged, a measure that positions Locke contrary to not only the Aristotelian *polis* ideal but also contemporary public opinion in England. Due to this call for naturalizing foreign workers, Locke sees himself compelled to counter fears of an influx of foreigners. As Locke emphasizes in the unpublished manuscript *For a General Naturalization* (1693), the foreigners are not a threat to the subsistence of England's citizens, but in fact increase their prosperity. And in any case, the pressure to assimilate to the ways of the host country would turn the second generation of these foreigners into "perfect Englishmen, as those that have been here ever since William the Conquerers days and came over with him. For this hardly to be doubted but that most of even our Ancest(o)rs were Forainers" ([1696] 1991: 491).

Moreover, Locke places economics in the framework of natural law. While the insight into the inherent dynamic of the market economy is already discernible, the justification of the money economy by no means leads to a de-moralizing of the economy. On the contrary, it is precisely the inherent dynamic of the market economy that demands a moral justification. The reproach of absolutizing the means therefore misses the point. Moreover, because a tendency to global expansion is inherent to trade, the market economy has to be embedded in a universal *telos*, i.e., one encompassing the whole of humanity. At this point, Locke once again refers to the commandment of the divine creator: "Be fruitful, and multiply, and replenish the earth, and subdue it" (Gen. 1:28). The mission to subjugate nature is fulfilled by Baconian science according to Locke; the call of God to populate the earth, which contains "the main intention of Nature" (*TTG* 1.59), can only be met by a developed market economy. The close connection between labor and begetting ensues from a specific interpretation of the mission proclaimed in the Bible's creation story. The "intention of Nature" aims not just at humankind spreading through all inhabitable regions of the earth, but also at the formation of populous states. This goal can only be achieved through a market economy organized on a global scale. When determining the quality of political systems, Locke therefore has to move beyond the narrower standard of the rule of law and consider population density. Seen in this light, not only are nomadic tribal societies criticized as inefficient forms of society, but many monarchies, for example the Ottoman Empire, also fail to develop the capacity for realizing the goal:

> and indeed his [Filmer's] way of Government is not the way to People the World. For how much Absolute Monarchy helps to fulfil his great and primary Blessing of God Almighty, *Be fruitful, and multiply, and replenish the Earth*, which contains in it the improvements too of Arts and Sciences, and the conveniences of Life, may be seen in those large and rich Countries, which are happy under the *Turkish* Government, where are not now to be found 1/3, nay in many, if not most part of them 1/30, perhaps I might say not 1/100 of the People, that were formerly, as will easily appear to any one, who will compare the Accounts we have of it at this time, with Antient history.
>
> (TTG 1.33)

Humankind is by no means set adrift in an aimless accumulation process with the transition to a money economy; rather, as Locke sees it, the extensive expansion of trade and production enables the fulfilment of God's plan of creation (Priddat 1998: 39). For Locke, however, the divine plan of creation not only encompasses "the increase of Mankind" but also "the continuation of the Species in the highest perfection" (*TTG* 2.59), including "the greatest conveniences of Life" (*TTG* 2.34.). Locke is inspired by the hope to advance the happiness of all humankind through the systematic coupling of the market economy with Bacon's "dream of creating a world of plenty through the application of systematically gathered knowledge" ([1696] 1991: 100).

The effectivity of economic and political systems is to be judged not solely on population density but also on the material standard of life. Here Aristotle's critical objection, that chrematistics ethically presupposes the principle of enhancing sense pleasure, hits the target. Because the idea of a limitless increase of pleasure is still connected with the original moral purposes, however, in particular the securing of subsistence and the charity rule, the second objection put forward by Aristotle is only partially valid.

Against the background of Locke's description of the state of nature and the socio-economic evolution of humankind, in conjunction with the comparative views on Aristotle, both the rational contents and the power syndromes of Locke's political economy can be determined more precisely. Locke's justification of a limitless monetary economy cannot simply be equated with a defense of Aristotelian chrematistics. Locke neither elevates the accumulation of money into an end in itself, nor does he recast avarice into a virtue. While incorporating hedonistic elements into the rationale underpinning economics, the principle of increasing pleasure remains securely embedded within the broader principles of natural law. Moreover, through the requirement that every person is obliged to work and the call to allow foreign workers to enter the country and become naturalized citizens, Locke corrects painful shortcomings in Aristotle's economics, namely the acceptance of slave labor and the exclusion of the *metics* from all civic rights. In addition, Locke furnishes a realistic alternative to the autarky model of Aristotle, which had already become an unattainable ideal for the Greek city-states.

Locke's vindication of a market economy—and we may keep this in mind as a preliminary summarization at this point—by no means leads to an uncritical affirmation of limitless economic growth. While a money economy follows its own rules, it remains entrenched in the framework of an ethics of natural law. Macpherson's criticism that "unlimited accumulation is the essence of rationality" (Macpherson 1962: 237) misses the point of Lockean economics. The opposite is in fact the case: the supreme implementation of reason is the state steering the inherent dynamic of the market economy with a view to adhering to the moral prescriptions of natural law. At this point, even Pico della Mirandola's motif of human self-divinization and self-degeneration shines through. Unlike Pico's scenario, however, the human resemblance to God no longer manifests in the mystic but in the wisdom displayed by the ruler, who not only guarantees freedom and security but also advances the prosperity of a society by implementing state laws encouraging people to act diligently and work. In short, the supreme implementation of reason finds expression in a prince "who shall be so wise and godlike [!] as by established laws of liberty to secure protection and incouragement to honest industry of Mankind against oppression of power and narrowness or Party" (*TTG* 2.42). Conversely, without the right use of reason a human drowns in an "ocean" of fanciful thoughts, and hence degenerates into a "Brutality, below the level of Beasts" (*TTG* 2.58).

Whereas the innovations of Baconian science are beneficial to the whole of humankind, the blessings emanating from the acumen and prudence of Locke's prince primarily serves the economy of a county. Indeed, the godlike prince who steers the system of the market economy for the benefit of the people "will quickly be too hard for his neighbours" (*TTG* 2.42). This is because states practicing a money economy are embroiled in a relentless struggle for ascendancy. Francisco de Vitoria had considered trade primarily as an instrument for fostering understanding among peoples. For Locke, too, the positive aspects of a globally linked economy enjoy priority; but the dangers ensuing from the inherent dynamic of a market economy are beginning to emerge and come into focus. Thomas Hobbes had supplanted Vitoria's vision of a peaceful community of nations with the sober thesis of a set of impregnable power relations between states. Locke expands on the Hobbesian analysis of international anarchy, as it were, adding the economic dimension. Not just locked into a latent state of war, the states of this earth are moreover patently entangled in a relentless economic struggle for gaining their share on the world market, a struggle that determines the prosperity and misery of entire nations.

Thus, in so far as the inherent dynamic of market-driven processes is not merely accepted but integrated into a political framework based on the principles of natural law, then Locke's justification of a monetary economy contains remarkable rational gains when compared to classical ancient and medieval thought. At the same time, however, with the idea of the global expansion of populous societies enlarging and diversifying their needs, not only culturally specific factors but also ideological tendencies influence Lockean economics. The vision of using all land for private commercial means to provide a growing world population with ever more conveniences implies the systematic demise of societies organized around a subsistence economy, and hence threatening not just the economic basis but also the cultural identity of numerous peoples.

Locke's vision of a global market society rests on highly questionable arguments. The tacit consent to the consequences of the invention of money by all of humankind is a unilateral anticipation of a real consensus-building process, comparable to Vitoria's setting of the norms of international law without the participation of those concerned. And the idea of a potentially limitless increase of conveniences in human life represents a break with millennia-old standards of morality. In addition, the labor theory of property is subtly adjusted to support the interests of the English settlers in North America. Thus the contradiction between ethical universalism and the colonial subjugation of the non-European world, having shadowed the history of early modern thought since the sixteenth century, returns in a new variation. Locke broadly replaces the ideas of Spanish Late Scholasticism on a Christian world civilization with the vision of a global expansion of nation states based on a market economy, although the idea of a Christian mission is not completely abandoned. On the contrary, Locke advocates the nonviolent Christian missionizing of the indigenous peoples and African slaves in the Americas. Moreover, for Locke mission has not only spiritual but also geopolitical goals. To push back the influence of New France in North America, Locke called for an alliance of Protestant settlers with the Five Nations Confederacy (Turner 2011).

Besides colonial entanglements, Locke's economics reveal a highly problematic change in the interpretation of the relationship between humans and nature. The epochal shifts Locke sees as occurring in how humans relate to nature are best approached from the background of Bacon's *Instauratio magna*. As we have seen, Bacon's vision of a new science is sustained by fascination with the endless wealth of nature and its immanent productivity. Although nature has to be forced into new channels, for Bacon humans are ultimately the servants of nature. Moreover, Bacon compels scientists to direct their attention to the creative force of nature: "he could not be content with beholding the rude materials of the art, and then the completed works; but would rather wish to be present while the artificer was at his labours and carrying his work on" (*N.O.* 2.41; works 4.201). In distinction from Bacon, in Locke's property theory nature degenerates more and more into a mere raw material for human labor. Land not used for private commercial means is nothing other than land wasted, "waste" land (*TTG* 2.42); the value of a piece of land is thus tied to human labor and accordingly increases with the degree it has been worked on: "And let anyone consider, what the difference is between an Acre of Land planted with Tobacco, or Sugar, sown with Wheat or Barley; and an Acre of the same Land lying in common, without Husbandry upon it, and he will find, that the improvements of labour makes the far greater part of the value" (*TTG* 2.40).

This devaluing of the productivity of nature results most likely from the necessities demanded by a cogent labour theory of property. Locke "uses it to bolster the claim that appropriation by labour is a legitimate way of excluding the common rights of the rest of mankind. If the usefulness of appropriated resources derived mainly form the spontaneous hand of Nature that would be a difficult task" (Waldron 1988: 192). Locke obviously sees himself forced to set the necessary proportion of human labour as high as possible. Even the goods of daily need like bread, wine, or clothing are "wholly *owing to labour* and industry"; and "for whatever Bread is more worth than Acorns, *Wine* than Water, and *Cloth* or *Silk* than Leaves, Skins, or Moss" (*TTG* 2.42). The example of silk, which Locke here juxtaposes to valueless leaves of nature, tellingly reveals the difference from the Baconian understanding of nature. For Bacon, the production of silk exemplifies the hidden treasures of nature, capable of surpassing even the most audacious ideas of the human imagination, while Locke identifies silk as an example of the creative power inherent to human work, for "Nature and the Earth furnished only the almost worthless Materials" (*TTG* 2.43). Locke initially estimates the share of human work in producing useful goods to be 9/10, then 99/100, and finally 999/1,000 (*TTG* 2.40; 43), a scaling that formulates the devaluing of nature's productivity in mathematical language.

Once exchange value displaces use value in a money economy, then even the creative power of labor is sucked into the fatal maelstrom of devaluing. While two pieces of equally fertile land in North America and England may have "the same natural intrinsick Value," "the Benefit Mankind receives from the one, in a Year, is worth 5 Pounds, and from the other possibly not worth a Penny, if all the Profit an *Indian* received from it were to be valued, and sold here; at least, I may truly say, not 1/1000" (*TTG* 2.43). The difference in the yields stems from the labor invested, or more precisely in the distinct technological levels at the disposal of the English and native American farmers. Ultimately, though, the value of yields is not to be measured on the amount and quality of the harvested fruits or the processed productions, but on the market price. At this point, Locke's justification of the money economy regresses, its level of reflection lagging behind that of Aristotelian economics, where, as a means for securing a good life, "true wealth" is defended against its evaporation through exchange value. Of course, Aristotle focuses his attention so uncompromisingly on the criticism of the chrematistic idea of wealth as the limitless accumulation of money that key economic issues, for example clarifying the suitable modes of production or how to provide for the hungry, all but disappear from view. While Locke addresses this haunting lacuna in Aristotelian economics by positing the subsistence right of each and every individual, the boundaries between use and exchange value become blurred: "Possessions and Commodities are valuable by Money" (*TTG* 1.90). Given that Western societies continue to measure their "wealth" on the basis of gross national product, i.e., in monetary terms, when compared with Aristotle, Locke—despite the undeniable gains in rationality in his idea of economics—ushers in an epochal loss of economic rationality with the monetary reinterpretation of "social wealth."

12

Epilogue: The future of modernity and the search for new self-limitations

Reason, power, and coloniality are constituent and yet entangled principles of European modernity. Reason cannot be fully reduced to power, while coloniality is certainly the dark underside but not the whole essence of modernity. At the same time, however—and this is the thesis of the studies collected here—there is no doubt that the significant epochal enlightenment processes of European modernity are amalgamated in central areas with new power syndromes, in particular with a transcontinental colonialism, and with cultural innovations. This is where the deep—and thus all the more difficult to interpret—ambivalence of European modernity resides. To precisely determine and differentiate the amalgamations between gains in rationality, power syndromes, and cultural components, I have introduced the meta-category of "de-limitation" (*Entgrenzung*), whereby its first application is to describe two heterogenous developments: the overcoming of the teleological worldview, laid out primarily by Aristotle in antiquity, and the transoceanic expansion of Europe that gathered pace in the fifteenth century. Since their initial emergence in the fourteenth century, these two de-limitations each precipitated a profound cultural upheaval.

12.1 From the dialectic of enlightenment to the dialectic of de-limitations

According to Aristotle, every entity strives toward its ultimate end (*telos*) in the sense of unsurpassable perfection, which is identified with the concept of its limit (*peras*). Because ontology is the foundation for all areas of philosophy, as Aristotle explicates in his works, overcoming the teleological conception of the world in early modern thought set off, much like a domino effect, a series of de-limitations in cosmology, epistemology, anthropology, ethics, political philosophy, and even economics.

In the fifteenth century Nicholas of Cusa, working within the framework of a Neoplatonic-inspired philosophy of the absolute and in the process leaving behind the Aristotelian synthesis of *telos* and limit, constructed the idea of a limitless universe. In turn, the idea of an immanent limitlessness to the world becomes a reference point for an epochal affirmation of insatiable curiosity, previously problematized in both classical ancient and Christian thought. Concurrently, an anthropological revolution was taking place in the philosophy of the Renaissance. The revaluation of the creative power of human freedom, which reached at least its rhetorical peak in Pico's idea of the self-fashioning of human nature, then definitively—following the preparative developments in Christian Neoplatonism—burst the boundaries of teleological anthropology.

A no less far-reaching cultural upheaval was triggered by the geographic and political de-limitation of the *oikumene* through the transoceanic expansion of Europe. Because geography was intimately connected to anthropological, ethical, and political ideas, the voyages of Vasco da Gama and Columbus initiated radical cultural transformations in the area of philosophy. After the "discovery" of the Americas, the political philosophy of Europe was suddenly confronted with the existence of peoples from another *oikumene*, about whom only fantasies had circulated since antiquity. For the Amerindians, however, the de-limitation of the *oikumene* by the Iberian powers was not a broadening of horizons but the abrupt end of their cultural development through an orgy of violence, followed by a demographic catastrophe and the beginning of centuries-long colonial rule. With the conquering of the Amerindian empires, colonialism and coloniality become a constitutive factor of modernity, a fact Latin American philosophers have long pointed out.

The excesses of violence unleashed against the Amerindian peoples were not ignored by European thinkers. On the contrary: as early as the sixteenth century a debate on colonialism began in the universities and centers of power that would last for decades, a debate wherein the Conquista was both justified and called fundamentally into question. Indeed, in the midst of the excesses of imperial and colonial violence Francisco de Vitoria laid the foundation for global cosmopolitanism, i.e., for the idea of international law and a global ethics, both of which overcome the limits of the ancient *polis* and the idea of the Roman world empire.

The cultural innovations sparked by the bypassing of teleological ontology and the transcending of the boundaries of the *oikumene* merged into a multifaceted complex of motifs by the end of the sixteenth century. In Montaigne's *Essais* the de-limitations recur in the medium of experimental self-exploration. For Bacon, Columbus's daring voyage out into the open seas is the apposite symbol for a new science, one based on the idea of a limitless and simultaneously productive nature and driven by an insatiable curiosity. Since Bacon, the idea of a dual de-limitation of the classical ancient and medieval world is no longer just a meta-category for reconstructing early modern developments—in a certain respect it is a central motif complex that itself is present in modern European philosophy.

Every transcending of limits unavoidably posits new limits. This is not only the case for colonial expansion. Early modern thought thus reveals a remarkable dialectic between an accelerated dynamic of ever-newer de-limitations in tandem with a search for new limits. At least three focal points of this typical early modern dialectic are discernible: curiosity and its insatiability, the creative power of human freedom, and global cosmopolitanism.

The idea of a limitless universe in Cusa's thought led to an enhanced view of insatiable curiosity. The initial euphoria that followed the unleashing of the urge to seek knowledge of the limitless universe soon encounters the limits of human cognitive faculties, an experience that threatens to trigger a sudden retreat into a resigned skepticism or a religious flight from the world. Cusa had coupled the limitless striving for knowledge of the world with the theory of the self-revelation of the absolute in the world, an idea that was crumbling at the end of the sixteenth century. Because the correspondence between the human mind and the world could no longer be supported by God's power, Michel de Montaigne suddenly faced a problem: conceptually only ever capable of approximate knowledge of things, humanity remains entangled in language worlds of its own creation, much like someone trying to find their way through swirling mists. Montaigne therefore realigns the trajectory of *curiositas* from the infinite universe to the internal multiplicity and changeability of human individuals. In contrast, Francis Bacon reaffirms the idea of comprehensive knowledge of the world. The limits of our human or individual cognitive faculties can be overcome, at least partially, by technological aids and experiments on the one hand, and a globally networked republic of scholars and scientists on the other. Thomas Hobbes then elevates the passion driving curiosity, of great moral concern in antiquity, to the essential characteristic of the human being. In turn, John Locke, despite his affirmation of Baconian science, rejects its excessive pretensions. For Locke, it is precisely the limitedness of our cognitive faculties, which may not provide knowledge of the universe but most definitely enables the insights necessary for a morally proper and comfortable life, the decisive sign for the place God has accorded humanity in the cosmos. While curiosity was frequently and variously problematized in antiquity, the dialectic of limitless curiosity about the world, emerging in Europe in Renaissance thought and continuing into the present through the philosophy of the Enlightenment, ultimately remained alien to classical ancient thought.

A second focal point of the dialectic between transcending and positing limits is the idea of the creative power of the human mind, a subject of diverse and fierce controversy in the early modern period. Despite the spectacular positive revaluation of the *vis creativa* in Renaissance philosophy, the scope for self-creation is initially limited in the thought of Cusa and Pico. For Cusa, the language worlds and concepts that the human reason creatively forges are under the directive of the innate ideas of the intellect. In contrast, human self-fashioning in Pico always moves within the normative framework of the Neoplatonic levels of the cosmos, which sets a purely spiritual life as the orientation for humanity. A century later, the normative horizons of Cusa and Pico are caught up in the maelstrom of radical skepticism. Transforming Pico's idea of self-elevation toward an angelic nature into a practice of experimental self-exploration, Montaigne combines the Socratic maxim of self-knowledge with the aesthetic utopia of exploring new ways of life, which partially suspends the millennia-old criteria of rationally examining the conduct of life, for example the ideal of *ataraxia* or the restraint of the passions.

The modern obsession with creating new—but not necessarily better—ways of life probably attained its most powerful expression in Nietzsche. In *Morgenröthe* ("Daybreak") Nietzsche contends that "we live an existence which is either a *prelude* or a *postlude*, and the best we can do in this *interregnum* is to be as far as possible our own *reges* [kings] and found little *experimental states*. We are experiments: let us also want to be them!" (1985: 190f.). Via Nietzsche the idea of self-creation resonates in various twentieth-century philosophies. Pico's idea of self-creation recurs almost verbatim in Sartre's definition of existentialism and is prominent in the thought of Richard Rorty (1989: 23–42).

Indeed, Pico's idea of self-creation was qualitatively altered even during the Enlightenment by La Mettrie. From Pico through to Nietzsche and Sartre, the power of self-creation is always related to humanity's second nature, i.e., ways of life. In contrast, within his materialist philosophy La Mettrie speculates on manipulating the very physical nature of living creatures, and thus paves the way for modern human genetics. Because there is no qualitative difference between animals and humans, it cannot even be ruled out that in future the nature of apes may be altered into a human nature through technological manipulation and thus trained to be humans.

> Let us not limit nature's resources; they are infinite, particularly when assisted by great skill. Surely the same mechanism which opens the Eustachian tube in the deaf could unblock it in monkeys? Surely a beneficial desire to imitate their master's pronunciation could free the organs of speech in animals ... I hardly doubt at all that if this animal were perfectly trained, we would succeed in teaching him to utter sounds and consequently to learn a language. Then he would no longer be a wild man, nor an imperfect man, but a perfect man, a little man of the town, with as much substance or muscle for thinking and taking advantage of his education as we have.
>
> (La Mettrie 2012: 12)

A third focal point in the specifically modern dialectic of de-limitations is global cosmopolitanism. With the vision of a transcontinental legal order between nations and a morality of global responsibility, Vitoria overcomes the limits of classical ancient and medieval conceptions on universal ethics and the ideas of world empires. A philosophical law of nations had never before been developed in Europe. But like the ideas of insatiable curiosity and creative self-fashioning, Vitoria's idea of global cosmopolitanism was problematized and indeed negated in early modern thought. Hobbes dismantles Vitoria's utopia of a world society and is thoroughly dialectical in exposing its weaknesses. International politics is not based on the rules of free communication but follows the logic of the state of nature, and thus all peoples across the globe are caught in a latent state of war. Later, however, the idea of international law was critically adopted and continued by Grotius, Pufendorf, and most prominently Kant. Indeed, in the eighteenth and nineteenth centuries, single aspects of Vitoria's utopia, namely international trade, cultural intermingling, or the moral unity of the human species, were developed into independent cosmopolitan visions (Kleingeld 1999). After the nineteenth century, however, global cosmopolitanism once again came under fire in Europe, the target of fierce criticism by conservative, nationalist, and (neo-)fascist movements. Most recently, decolonial philosophies have deconstructed cosmopolitan ideas as part of their sweeping criticism of the logics of power at work in European modernity.

There is no doubt that the unleashing of power became a central theme for political philosophy in the wake of the civil wars ravaging Europe and transoceanic colonial expansion, with Ginés de Sepúlveda and Thomas Hobbes still regarded as the intellectual symbols for modern power politics. Although

European modernity is inseparable from colonialism, the political philosophy of the modern age is by no means limited to propounding colonialist ideology. Rather, in European modernity colonialism has been both legitimated and criticized. Even in his justification for conquering the Aztec Empire, Sepúlveda raised a question still prevalent today in debates on cosmopolitanism: how can universal ethical principles, i.e., human rights in contemporary terms, be implemented globally? And so, too, Hobbes, whose political philosophy is not simply a mirror of early capitalism but, despite all its ambivalences, aims to enclose the logic of conflictive power relations within a conception of morality and a legal order, a problematic underestimated in classical ancient and medieval thought.

This means that in modernity, as evident in the philosophy of the Renaissance and the early modern period, the "dialectic of enlightenment" is intertwined with a dialectic of transcending and positing limits.

12.2 Universal claims of European modernity? Some clarifications

The theories of progress in the eighteenth and nineteenth centuries celebrated European civilization as the dawn of an age of reason. Since the critiques of reason articulated in twentieth-century philosophy and the emergence of decolonial thought, the universal claims of European modernity are now irrevocably suspected of being vehicles of cultural imperialism. Conversely, culturalist theories interpreting European modernity as a particular civilization alongside others risk underestimating the gains it has made in rationality. Indeed, a culturalist criticism of *all* figures of reason presupposes its own universal claims to validity. Beyond this, criticism of any hierarchy discernible in forms of knowledge claims for itself to be superior knowledge, namely the knowledge that *all* forms of knowledge are of *equal value*.

The thorny issue of the universal claims of European modernity is thus by no means settled. To find a way out of the problematic alternative of "catch-up enlightenment versus cultural imperialism," it is first necessary to clarify the equivocal concept of "enlightenment."

To avoid Eurocentric dogmatisms as much as possible, enlightenment has to be kept free of the burden of identification with specific claims and meanings. Thus, a modest model of "enlightenment"—in my view a major achievement of the Frankfurt discourse theory of Apel and Habermas—needs to initially restrict itself to the elementary medium of discursive reasoning, i.e., the unforced force of the better argument. Admittedly, the purport of the dialogical search for truth itself requires explanatory interpretation. Nonetheless, meeting the validity claims of argument-based discourse requires respecting and heeding fundamental norms such as impartiality, nonviolence, and equality. As the debate on discourse ethics showed, however (as discussed in Chapter 2, section 2.2), the norms immanent to argumentative dialogue prescribe even moral philosophy merely a bare minimum of normatively substantial standards, and not concrete or specific criteria, indeed not even a general concept of morality, let alone addressing the delicate question of who is a rational being and thus to be acknowledged as a suitable discourse partner. The normative matrix of argumentative reason may refer independently to a political order, one that can be described broadly as deliberative democracy. And yet it remains impossible to derive directly from argumentative reason, as such, concrete models for a political system or indeed even codes for subsystems.

Secondly, processes of enlightenment are not a monopoly of European culture. As Karl Jaspers has shown in his theory of the axial age, radical breakthroughs toward rationality are evident in ancient times, in particular in India and China (1953: 1–21). Indeed, processes of enlightenment open a universal space for communication based on argumentation and discussion. Thus intercultural relationships and dialogical processes of exchange between the philosophies and religions emerged from the outset in this epochal shift.

Thirdly, radical processes of enlightenment—and this pertains to the axial age as well—may create new perspectives through their critique of prevailing interpretations of world and self, but at the same time valuable aspects of the criticized threaten to be lost. Against this a corrective countermovement stirs, the most prominent example of which is how the radical critique of mythology in the classical ancient philosophy of the Hellenist and Roman periods was complemented by a philosophical reinterpretation of mythical traditions. In short, epistemic injustices accompany processes of enlightenment like a shadow.

From this background and expanding on the thesis that the genesis of European modernity bears within it rational processes, power-syndromes, and particularistic cultural factors in all its main areas, it is now possible to roughly outline prospects for a differentiated view of the manifold relations between peoples and cultures in global modernity.

Through the expansion of Europe, but also of China and Russia, a global world society arose between the sixteenth and eighteenth centuries, one that despite all the imperialist violence was a sphere of universal communication and understanding. Thus universalist claims of gains in rationality and the concomitant civilizing achievements, whether raised by European modernity or other cultures or civilizations, can only be justified in a global discourse. Given the long colonial past, this postulate should today be self-evident for European philosophy, a point meanwhile conceded and acknowledged by Habermas (2019: 1.111). Precisely because Europe has no monopoly on enlightenment, potential gains in rationality evident in European modernity and drawn from other cultures cannot be flippantly dismissed—rather, they must be subject to the critical scrutiny of an enlightenment process.

With rational critique invariably threatening to create epistemic injustices, decolonial philosophies have rightly focused attention on the knowledge traditions of indigenous peoples, disdainfully devalued and marginalized by modern science. All the same, as justified as the decolonial criticism of the epistemic injustices of Western scientific culture may be, indigenous forms of knowledge must remain open to critical scrutiny. Moreover, any wholesale rejection of modern science is itself suspicious. No less a figure than Francis Bacon, infamously targeted by Critical Theory and decolonial thought, had insisted, displaying astonishing vehemence, on the validity of marginalized forms of knowledge such as those of simple craftspeople and even magicians at fairs, and integrated them into his idea of a new science. Indeed, Bacon forged the idea of a globally networked community of scientists, responsible for collecting and examining all bodies of knowledge. Thus, the decolonial defense of indigenous knowledge against modern science moves within an institutional framework that itself stems in part from Bacon.

Considering the unsurpassable boundaries limiting argumentative practice, whereby all the arguments of all potential discourse participants can never be exhausted, critical perspectives emerge on the power syndromes and colonial patterns embedded in some European enlightenment processes. Although Vitoria explicates the universality of reason—described as a communion between gods and humans by the Stoics—in terms of a universal community of communication, the specific norms of international law are then determined unilaterally, i.e., without communicating with other peoples or nations. Similarly, Locke rashly blocks any possible consensual justification with his labor theory of property. In both cases, the limitations imposed on building consensus through discourse and exchange of arguments open the door to establishing colonial ideologies.

From this perspective, the founding of the United Nations and the preparation of the Universal Declaration of Human Rights can be understood as the realization and, simultaneously, the correction of Vitoria's ideas. Despite its limits, the UN Declaration is the product of an intercultural dialogue, whereby the characteristic European arguments justifying the freedom and dignity of all humans, which primarily assume their endowment with reason, were critically analyzed by representatives of other cultures and accordingly modified with reference to their own universalist ethical traditions. For example, China's delegate, Peng-Chun Cheng, who had studied under John Dewey, corrected the Western justification of human dignity based on the faculty of reason by drawing on Mencius' teaching of the "heart." Article 1 of the Declaration thus reads: all human beings "are endowed with reason *and conscience*" (my emphasis; cf. Roth 2016). Because every factual discourse is limited, the intercultural discourse of the Declaration was no exception. There were notable exclusions, with no delegates from Africa involved. Moreover, European signatories such as Britain and France, in flagrant contradiction to the Declaration, displayed no intention to forgo their colonies. The UN Declaration was thus only *one*—but for all that an eminently important—stage on the long road to a moral and political order for all of humankind, a road that will presumably never reach a definitive conclusion.

12.3 The question of multiple modernities

In sociology, the unity of modernity is defended mostly by modernization and secularization theories, both building on the social differentiation of subsystems. But the genesis of European modernity fails to fit in with the simple view of a transition from religion to secular reason. So, too, does the social differentiation of subsystems, which simply do not coincide with the uncoupling of moral claims from the different domains of society, a fact highlighted by studies of seventeenth-century philosophy.

While Bacon detaches science from the direct grip of theology, in place since Plato, science is not to replace theology or moral philosophy. On the contrary, with the *Instauratio magna* Bacon places modern science in a new theological framework; the principle of charity is to lend science a moral orientation. Similarly, Hobbes decouples the traditional concept of freedom from theological elements; the task of the state is solely to secure earthly peace. Despite a mechanistic body ontology, though, Hobbes does not reduce political philosophy to analytics of power. A philosophy of the state is rather a *scientia iustitiae*. Although Locke partially relieves economic interactions from moral prescriptions, the market economy system as such is embedded in the broader contexts of moral philosophy and Christian belief.

Habermas interprets the social differentiation of subsystems as the institutionalization of different types of rationality that has spread globally. Nonetheless, our contemporary world society can no longer be described as the globalization of the West's path of development using the tools of modernization theory. Contemporary world society may have gained a global infrastructure through the systems of modern science, the administrative state, and the market economy, but this infrastructure is diversely reinterpreted and implemented in the various major cultural regions (Habermas 2019: 1.119f.). Civilization theory has challenged the binary figure of the integration of universal subsystems by axial cultures. Above all, Árnason has countered Habermas by pointing out the possible existence of cultural patterns in the subsystems (2003: 42f.). The philosophical reconstruction of the genesis of European modernity that I have presented in these studies can thus be understood as a concrete contribution supporting Árnason's clear-sighted identification of the cultural patterns of modernity. The social differentiation of modern subsystems is part of a sweeping and profound cultural upheaval reverberating through Europe since the fourteenth century. Indeed, along with rationality types, the guiding ideas of modern subsystems also contain cultural elements. To take a few examples from the studies presented: Bacon combines the idea of experimental science with the vision of producing all possible works; Vitoria entwines the theory of international law with the utopia of a global civilization under Christian guidance; in Montaigne, the idea of unsparing self-exploration feeds into the aesthetic vision of experimentally creating new forms of living; in turn, John Locke links the positive reassessment of labor in economics to the idea of limitless economic growth. Both the idea of experimenting with forms of living and Hobbes's definition of happiness as the ongoing striving for new goals represent a break with European thought's millennia-old criteria for how to lead a rational and moral life. Bacon's vision of producing all possible works and Locke's justification of the limitless accumulation of money have fallen under suspicion of irrationality in European philosophy itself.

This means that what took place with the spreading of European modernity was *at once* a legitimate diffusion of gains in rationality *and* a problematic transmission of power syndromes, in particular those intertwined with colonial power and particularistic cultural projects.

For this reason, social movements critical of modernity, repeatedly forming both outside and inside Europe, are not to be sweepingly accused of a fundamentalist-like anti-modernism that seeks to evade the demands and obligations of reason. Their protest can actually grow out of a legitimate critique of the particularistic cultural projects of modernity. One classic example here is the struggles undertaken by indigenous peoples or "pueblos originarios" (Mignolo) to assert their interests and gain recognition. In so far as their resistance follows from a critical reflection on indigenous traditions as well as European modernity, then indigenous groups are operating on the basis of enlightenment in the sense of an argumentative practice. Given that limitless economic growth is one of the guiding ideas of the market economy system, the decision of some indigenous groups to continue their nomadic or primarily subsistence existence is not *per se* a repudiation of the rational principle of modernity, namely the primacy of reason. In defending their ways of life, numerous indigenous movements not only use modern technology and market-based economic flows, but indeed actively contribute to the dialogue forums of global civil society, since Vitoria one of the enlightened ideas of European modernity.

Another key and obvious factor to consider is the shift in the geopolitical constellation in the twenty-first century. With the rise of China, India, and other regional powers, the hegemony of the West has given way to a polycentric world society, which Dussel had once called for under the term "transmodernity." At the same time, the factual establishing of several power centers is not *per se* an indicator of moral and political progress. Contemporary world society is characterized by the identity politics of authoritarian movements and regimes, both inside and outside Europe or the West, which openly reject the ideas of human rights and international law, demonizing them as expressions of Western cultural imperialism. Democratic movements in the Global South are thus forced to face up to opposition on two fronts, not only the imperial interests of the West but increasingly oppressive regional powers.

Finally, the particularistic cultural dimensions of European modernity, most notably the idea of freedom as unharnessed self-creation, possess a fascination that has meanwhile gripped numerous cutures far beyond Europe. Non-European cultures transform not only the rational but also the cultural potentials of European modernity, integrating them into their own traditions. This too is part of the diversity of modernity. Accordingly, the excesses of European modernity are also present and absorbed into other cultures, for example Bacon's vision of producing all possible works. Today's hotspots of human genetics are no longer to be found only in the laboratories of Western states. In 2018 the first genome-edited babies are reported to have been born in China.

12.4 Beyond unlimited economic growth: the search for new self-limitations

Despite all the achievements gained through rationality and liberating cultural innovations, an irrational dynamic resides in European modernity, namely the idea of limitless economic growth, which indeed threatens to drive humankind into apocalyptic disaster, evident everywhere today in the dramatic effects of climate change. As Heidegger, Horkheimer, and Adorno incisively and unsparingly showed in the middle of the past century, European modernity has qualitatively altered the relationship between humans and nature. The profound change in the human–nature relationship initiated in the early modern period becomes apparent through a comparison of Aristotle, Bacon, and Locke. For Aristotle, economics is embedded in a teleological cosmology. Supplying humankind with the goods essential for survival rests on nature, with human labor supporting or complementing its productivity. Thus, natural work or any skill involved in natural acquisition are given priority over a money economy. The yields of chrematistics, i.e., the accumulation of money for its own sake, are not produced from humanity's relationship to nature but are gained solely from advantages on the marketplace or monopolies. In contrast, Bacon approaches nature as a workshop where an endless abundance and variety of productive forces await their activation. The goal of science is thus to unleash and exploit the immanent productivity of nature through the creative power of humanity. Although science and technology yield new products, the primacy of nature remains intact. New works can only be produced through altered combinations of the already existing corpuscles of nature. Although Locke takes up the same ground as Bacon, he makes two crucial changes when interpreting the human relationship to nature. Because human labor is seen as the sole production factor creating value, Locke basically relegates the immanent potency of nature to an irrelevance. Land neither cultivated nor built on is now nothing but "waste land." Secondly, Locke's justification of a limitless money economy paves the way for the modern myth of limitless economic growth.

Without Bacon's conception of productive nature, the idea of a limitless economy would have been dismissed as an irrational fiction in the modern period as well. Thus it is all the more paradoxical that modern economics has increasingly ignored—a fatal legacy of Lockean economics—the productivity of nature that Bacon had so exuberantly praised as a production factor. The literal automatization of finance-driven economics, which in 2008 almost brought about the collapse of the entire economic system, reveals the contradiction between a limitless money economy and the limits of natural resources. While money as a virtual reality can be limitlessly increased, nature is principally limited despite all its hidden riches. When nature is integrated into the logic of limitless multiplication of money, then, as Binswanger has astutely explained, an alchemical transmutation process ("*ein alchimistischer Transmutationsprozeß*") takes place, turning nature into money, which—ostensibly—enables humans to lay claim to nature while avoiding the limitedness of nature and expanding the economy into "infinity" ("*der Endlichkeit der Natur auszuweichen und die Ökonomie 'ins Unendliche' auszuweiten*"; 1991: 186f.).

Industrial societies have avoided the contradiction between the limitlessness of money growth and the limitedness of nature by placing a wager, as it were. The substantial destruction of nature is accepted in the hope that the direct consequences and side-effects can at least be mitigated in the future by scientific and technological innovations, up until now used to unleash and harness the hidden riches of nature. As Pascal once wagered on the happiness of a life after death, secular modernity tacitly gambles on Bacon's idea of productive nature in a highly risky wager.

Meanwhile, however, the global process of industrialization is threatening the whole biosphere. The logic of limitless economic growth has plunged humankind into an epochal experiment with unpredictable risks that is taking on apocalyptic dimensions. The constantly accelerating climate catastrophe has exposed the consoling secular promise of technological solutions in a never-determined future as an illusion. For example, energy and resource consumption must be reduced with the technical possibilities available here and now.

With the reorientation toward an economy of sustainability, the search for limits is suddenly at the center of the discourse on the future of modernity. As this study has shown, because since its genesis European modernity has remained formatively influenced by the obsession with transgressing boundaries, not just in economics but also science, anthropology, moral philosophy, and political philosophy, the enormous obstacles confronting a politics of sustainability are unsurprising, obstacles evident not just in the economy but also in the culture of modernity, including the forms and ways of life it has spawned. After all, inseparable from sustainability is the idea of limit, albeit here not in the sense of an obstacle to be overcome but of an unsurpassable barrier. In short, any politics of sustainability, to which the idea of self-limitation is inherent, is diametrically opposed to the signature of a modernity that since its very beginnings is driven by a dialectic of transcending ever newer boundaries.

As we face the urgency of completing an ecological turn, debates on the future of humanity have revitalized the attraction of premodern cultures of self-limitation, foremost the classical ancient ethics of moderation and the spiritual traditions of indigenous peoples, which cultivate a careful and attentive interaction with nature. In searching for possibilities to limit the unleashed dynamics of modernity, peoples from across the world are called on to contribute their cultural assets and resources to an ecological turn while operating within a global discourse.

Nonetheless, the future of humankind cannot be ensured by simply exiting modernity. Leaving the fossil fuel age cannot succeed without modern science and technology. The development of alternative sources of energy, reducing the use of resources through new production methods, even the very means to model and predict climate change and its ecological effects—these are all only possible on the basis of Baconian experimental science. Curiously, Bacon mentions solar energy as an example of the *scientia activa*.

In this perspective the pioneers of sustainable economics have creatively combined the de-limitation dynamic of modernity with strategies of self-limitation. Nicholas Georgescu-Roegen returned to the basic idea of Aristotelian economics, namely the autarkic household economy, but reconfigured the framework of the *oikos* economy, shifting it from Aristotle's patriarchal household of the *polis* to the household of the earth's biosphere (1976). Inspired by John Stuart Mill's idea of an economy without growth, Herman Daly claimed that a sustainable economy by no means implies the standstill of social dynamics. In a steady-state economy, the unleashing of theoretical curiosity and the development of ecologically meaningful technologies must not—and should not—be limited *per se* (Daly 1991; 1996).

Even before the economic debates on sustainability began, Albert Camus called for a new sensibility of limits in his philosophical essay *The Rebel: An Essay on Man in Revolt*, a clear-sighted diagnosis of modernity that eschews questioning the value of insatiable curiosity and self-creative freedom: "This limit was symbolized by Nemesis, the goddess of moderation and the implacable enemy of the immoderate. A process of thought which wanted to take into account the contemporary contradictions of rebellion should seek its inspiration from this goddess" (Camus 1956: 291).

Notes

Chapter 1

1   Heidegger's repressive interpretation of the "will to power" has been criticized as a lopsided reading of Nietzsche's philosophy of life, for example by Thomä (2006), who points to Nietzsche's non-egoistical ethics. Nonetheless, there are a number of passages in Nietzsche supporting Heidegger's interpretation, for example §259 of *Beyond Good and Evil*: "life itself in its essence means appropriating, injuring, overpowering those who are foreign and weaker; oppression, harshness, forcing one's own forms on others, incorporation, and at the very least, at the very mildest, exploitation … [each body] will have to be the will to power incarnate, it will want to grow, to reach out around itself, pull towards itself, gain the upper hand—not out of some morality or immorality, but because it is alive, and because life simply is the will to power … 'Exploitation' is not part of a decadent or imperfect, primitive society: it is part of the fundamental nature of living things, as its fundamental organic function; it is a consequence of the true will to power, which is simply the will to life" (Nietzsche 1998: 152f.).

Chapter 3

1   Dussel established the ethics of liberation in the 1970s in a five-volume work (1973; 1977; 1979; 1980; see Schelkshorn 1992). After the dialogue with Karl-Otto Apel from 1989 to 1997 (see Schelkshorn 1997) and comprehensive studies on Marx (1990; 2001) Dussel extensively reformulated his ethics of liberation (2013 [1998]). The sketch I present here is limited to a few key aspects of Dussel's philosophical theory of modernity.

Chapter 5

1   My references and citations from the works of Nicholas of Cusa are taken from the Heidelberg Academy edition of the *Opera omnia* (1932–). I cite accordingly by Latin title of work, book (if applicable in Roman numerals), chapter number

(if applicable), and section or paragraph number ("n." if applicable) in Arabic numerals. The volumes of the cited works are separately listed in the reference list. The English translations are taken from the translation and edition prepared by Jasper Hopkins (Nicholas of Cusa 2001), cited as H with volume and page number.

2   Blumenberg's interpretation of this passage therefore seems to miss Cicero's intention: "Although Odysseus does not succumb to their enticements, it is suggested by the length of his wanderings alone that knowledge was more important to him than his native country" (Blumenberg 1983: 282). Cicero, however, does not accuse Odysseus of neglecting his native country; on the contrary, it is for Cicero only natural that quenching the thirst for knowledge was more important than the homeland. The opposition between theoretical curiosity and the homeland is already attenuated in the lure of the Sirens; the promise held out to those whose urge to know is then finally satiated and he "went on his homeward way a wiser man [*Doctior ad patrias lapsus pervenerit oras*]" (*De fin.* 5.49; cf. Hom. *Od.* 12.188).

Chapter 6

1   Pico's *Oratio de hominis dignitate* (abbreviated *Oratio*) is quoted according to the Latin text and the new translation edited by Francesco Borghesi, Michael Papio, and Massimo Riva (Cambridge University Press, 2012); the Arabic numerals (cited with "n") refer to the paragraphs that the text is divided into in this edition. References to *Heptaplus* are taken from Pico della Mirandola, *De hominis dignitate; Heptaplus; De ente et uno e scritti vari*, ed. and trans. E. Garin (Florence: Vallecchi, 1942), abbreviated as G, citing book, chapter of the work, and page number of Garin's edition. Other works by Pico are quoted according to the reference list.

2   Modern research has dated the *Corpus hermeticum*, written by several authors, to the period between the first and third centuries CE (Copenhaver 1992b: xliii–xlv). In the introduction to the *Oratio*, Pico refers to *Asclepius* 6: "Propter haec, o Asclepi, magnum miraculum est homo, animal adorandum atque honorandum" (Hermes 1960: 301f.).

3   The historical roots of the philosophical theory on angels go back to Plato, who filled the space between the divine and men with different intermediary beings, which Philo of Alexandria linked with the biblical accounts of angels. On this basis, Neoplatonic philosophies and Christian theologies developed complex theories about the hierarchy of angels, each bridging the gap between the divine One and human beings; cf. Casas (2018).

4   The classical example of this question is in Peter Lombard, Book II, *Distinctiones* XVI; see Trinkaus (1970: 1.188–92).
5   Between 1466 and 1468, besides other Platonic dialogues, Ficino had translated the Protagoras into Latin; see Trinkaus (1976: 194). A direct allusion by Pico to the creation myth of Protagoras is thus historically possible.
6   I agree with Truglia that the astonishing parallels to al-Ghazali deserve far greater attention when interpreting Pico's *Oratio*. The arguments for a direct influence appear somewhat weak. In addition, Truglia accentuates a literally understood transformation of human nature in unification with God, which breaks the chain of being.
7   As Dougherty (2002: 223) has pointed out, Boethius had already considered the possibility that humans can lose their human nature through immoral behaviour:

> wherefore evil men cease to be what they were—but that they were men till now their still surviving form of the human body shows—and therefore by turning to wickedness they have by the same act lost their human nature [*amisere naturam*]. But since only goodness can raise anyone above mankind, it follows necessarily that wickedness thrusts down beneath deserving the name of men those whom it has cast down from the human condition. So it follows that you cannot adjudge him a man whom you see transformed by vices [*hominem estimare non possis*].
>
> (*De consolatione philosophiae* 4.3)

Chapter 7

1   The doubt, still expressed today, that Marco Polo was never in China at all is answered by Vogel (2013).
2   For the influence of the Stoics on Paul, see Forschner (1996: 35–7). Theobald (2000: 145–7) emphasizes in contrast that, according to Paul, the pagans are fulfilling the will of the Creator when they obey a law, and not some anonymous law of nature. For the Christian reception of the ancient theories on natural law in Tertullian, Hieronymus, Origen, Lactantius, Ambrosius, and Augustine, see Reibstein (1958: 24–49).
3   The English translations of the works of Vitoria are taken from Pagden's edition of his political writings (Vitoria 1991; abbreviated LP with page number). The Latin quotations of *De Indis* are taken from the critical edition by L. Pereña and J. M. Perez Prendes, which includes also the third part (Vitoria 1967); Latin texts of the other works are cited according to the edition by T. Urdañoz (Vitoria 1960).
4   In *De temperantia* Vitoria had the punishment of barbaric peoples in mind and probably for this reason refused to broach the question of violent intervention. The distinction between the right to provide protection and the punishment of grave

crimes against humanity plays an important role in the further development of international law. Whereas Grotius considers a punitive war against lawbreakers to be legitimate, Pufendorf regards this with unconcealed skepticism (Pauer 1985: 26f.).

5   Sepúlveda was unable to publish *Democrates alter* (abbreviated DS), completed in 1545, during his lifetime. It was not until 1892 that the text was first published by Marcelino Menéndez Pelayo in *Boletín de la Real Academia de la Historia*. Angel Losada then discovered the original manuscript, publishing it in 1951. In this book, all citations are based on the historical-critical edition of the Latin text with Spanish translation of *Juan Ginés de Sepúlveda. Obras completas* (Pozoblanco: Ayuntamiento, 1995–2015); the Latin title of the work is followed by the chapters and paragraphs denoted by Arabic numerals. The titles of some works are abbreviated: *Democrates sive de convenientia militiae cum Christiana religio dialogus* (*DP*); *Democrates alter* (*DS*); *Cohortatio ad Carolum V. ut bellum suscipiat in Turca* (*Cohortatio*).

6   See *Apologia* 2.4 and the astonishing letter to Francisco de Argote in Sepúlveda (2007: 296; *Ep.* 101) cited by Andrés Marcos (1947: 184) and translated by Fernández-Santamaría (1977: 227, note 94): "I do not maintain that the barbarians should be reduced to slavery, but merely that they must be subjected to our dominion; I do not propose that we deprive them of their goods ... I do not say that we should hold herile empire over them, but regal and civil rule for their benefit."

7   *Democrates primus* is not a scholastic treatise, but a dialogue based on the Platonic model. The dialogue is between Leopold, who comes from Lutheran Germany but frequently argues in the spirit of Erasmus; Alfonso, a general; and Democrates, Sepúlveda's mouthpiece. *Democrates secundus* is a continuation of the earlier dialogue, but now without the involvement of Alfonso. The sketch here of Sepúlveda's natural law theory also draws on passages from *Democrates secundus*.

8   In *DP* 3.22.25 Sepúlveda had still attached *all* importance to freedom with respect to the question of whether the virtues stem from nature or from freedom. In *De regno* 3.24 the virtues are then traced back to several factors—nature, customs and mores, rational intelligence. In this sense, natural conditions are also acknowledged in *DS* as having a certain influence on the morals of a people.

9   In *Apologia* 4.2 Sepúlveda expressly refers to Oviedo. Las Casas therefore saw himself forced to offer an exhaustive refutation of Oviedo in the disputation with Sepúlveda; see Las Casas (1988: 630–42). For Oviedo's portrayal of the Americas, see Myers (2007).

10 Sepúlveda distorted the purpose of a punitive war himself, however, by referring to the Deuteronomistic right to wage war, where God abandons whole peoples to annihilation for their idolatry. Las Casas thus develops a detailed refutation of the

right to wage war, as it is presented in the book of Deuteronomy, in his criticism of Sepúlveda; see Las Casas (1988: 216–29).

11 Numerous interpreters of Sepúlveda have emphasized this. See Andrés Marcos (1947: 220f.): "Sepúlveda, pues, no sostiene la existencia de razas humanas cuyo ser es *esencialmente* superior al de los demás en cuanto a posibilidades culturales … Sepúlveda supone la *transmisibilidad* de la cultura, pues coloca el objeto del dominio sobre las razas inferiores por las superiores, en que estas hagan a aquellas partícipes de su cristiandad y civilidad, sin marcar limite a la participación." Similarly, Losada (1971: 286): "For Sepúlveda, 'natural condition' did not signify the essential quality of their nature, so that one could not say the Indians were composed of animality, rationality, *and* the quality of subjection or submissiveness as the three constituent elements of their humanitas. It signified, rather, a mental and volitive development so rudimentary at the time of the Conquest as to constitute, in Sepúlveda's judgment, a kind of second—but not essential—nature (as charged by Las Casas), but improvable by culture, as Sepúlveda plainly affirms in the second part of Democrates II." Fernández-Santamaría also argues in this sense (1977: 227): "the American natives are *servi natura* but not natural slaves. It follows that as it applies in practice the expression *servi natura* must be attributed a meaning different from the one heretofore given by some historians."

Chapter 8

1 References to Montaigne's *Essais* (abbreviated *E*) are by book and essay numbers, complemented by the page number of the translation by D. F. Frame (Montaigne 1958). French quotations are taken from the edition by von P. Villey and V.-L. Saulnier (Montaigne 1965).
2 On Socrates see *Essais* 3.13; 855. For the appreciation of Seneca and Plutarch see *E* 126; 106f.; *E* 2.10; 296f. Pyrrho is the center of interest in the *Apologia*. Montaigne remains loyal to Pyrrhonic skepticism in the third book of the *Essais*. Thus, Villey's assumption of a skeptical crisis, overcome then by the Epicureanism of his late phase, is misguided; see Tournon (2000: 257–86).
3 A direct influence of Cusa on Montaigne is not expressly evident. Although Montaigne mentions in the *Journal du Voyage* that he had purchased the works of Nicholas of Cusa while in Venice, Cusa is not mentioned once in the *Essais*. For Villey however, analogies are conspicuous: "Par le *De docta ignorantia,* Nicolas de Cusa apparait comme un des précurseurs de Montaigne" (Villey 1933: 121f.).
4 The main epistemological terms in Montaigne are "jugement" (La Charité 1970) and "expérience"; for the important final chapter *De l'expérience* (*E* 3.13) cf. Baraz (1968: 192–7), Starobinski (1985: 159–84), and Kritzman (2009: 154–92).

5   From 1588 onwards, Montaigne turned with increasing intensity to travel literature about the New World (Friedrich 1993: 192f.). Lopéz de Gomara's *Historia general des las Indias* (1552; French translation 1584) had a strong influence on Montaigne. In addition, Montaigne drew on the works of André Thevet and Jean de Léry as well as the 1595 edition of writings by the bishop Jerónimo Osorio; cf. Villey (1933: 1.80; 152f.; 204) and Enders (1993: 199–206).

6   In a similar way Montaigne also relativizes the dialogue with the three Brazilians that supposedly took place at the court of Charles IX in Rouen in 1562. As Enders has shown (1993: 199–203), Montaigne gives no less than three different accounts of this meeting: firstly, he mentions the conversation between Charles IX and the three Brazilians in Rouen; he then refers to a conversation with anonymous discussion partners, of which he himself knows only through hearsay, whereby in response to the question of what they had found noteworthy about Europe, the Indians had given three answers, the third of which Montaigne admits to having forgotten (!); and finally, Montaigne mentions a personal dialogue that was however cumbersome and scarcely comprehensible because of the stupidity of the interpreters (!). See *E* 1.31; 158f.

Chapter 9

1   References to Bacon are based on the edition of his works by J. Spedding, R. L. Ellis, and D. D. Heath: Bacon ([1857–74] 1963), abbreviated "works." I cite by title of work, some of them abbreviated (see the list of abbreviations at the start of this book), book (if applicable), chapter number (if applicable), section or paragraph number complemented by volume and page number of the works, all in Arabic numerals. The English translations of some early texts are taken from Farrington 1964.

2   See Keller (1985: 33–42). Keller refers to two places in *Tempus partus masculus*, a work Bacon himself did not publish. An English translation is to be found in Farrington (1964: 61–72). The first brings the imagery of marriage into play without any detailed explication: "Ego (fili suavissime) tibi sanctum, castum, et legitimum connubium cum rebus ipsis firmabo" (works 3.538f.). Zagorin (1998: 228) has compiled further instances of the metaphor of matrimony and the nuptial chamber. As for the second, Keller is referring to a passage in the first chapter of *Tempus partus masculus*, "sed revera naturam cum fetibus suis tibi addicturus et mancipaturus" (works 3.528), which Farrington has translated as follows: "I come in very truth leading to you Nature with all her children to bind her to your service and make her your slave" (1964: 62). It is however doubtful that Bacon meant the enslaving of nature with "mancipaturus."

3   See Merchant (1982: 172): "The interrogation of witches as symbol for the interrogation of nature, the courtroom as model for its inquisition, and torture through mechanical devices as a tool for the subjugation of disorder were fundamental to the scientific method as power." Merchant focuses on Bacon's telling remarks on the force used in experiments intervening in nature. One example is *Instauratio magna*, Distr. op.: "I mean it to be a history not only of nature free and at large (when she is left to her own course and does her work her own way)—such as that of the heavenly bodies, meteors, earth and sea, minerals, plants, animals—but much more of nature under constraint and vexed; that is to say, when by art and the hand of man she is forced out of her natural state, and squeezed and moulded" (works 4.29). Merchant furnishes no convincing evidence for the thesis that statements like these are referencing the torture practices of the witches' trials. See Winterfeld (2006: 168).

4   Nagl-Docekal (2004: 112): "Though Keller's claim to discern explicitly patriarchal thoughts in Bacon's work is justified, her critique loses plausibility when she considers the detected patriarchal traits a sufficient reason for charging Bacon's entire conception of the sciences with masculine bias." Nagl-Docekal also problematizes Keller's intention to overcome through "love" the subject–object relationship not only in gender relations but the human relation to the world in general: "A problem arises as Keller rejects not only the object status of women but object status as a rule" (2004: 115). A detailed consideration of Bacon's understanding of nature from a feminist point of view is presented by Winterfeld (2006: 111–71), who critically analyzes the controversies within feminist philosophy as to the "masculine" character of Baconian science. In contrast to Nagl-Docekal, however, Winterfeld predominantly refers to Carolyn Merchant.

5   Bacon wrote the last draft of *New Atlantis* in 1624–5. A first draft was quite possibly finished as early as 1614 (Box 1989: 126). William Rawley, Bacon's secretary, published *New Atlantis* posthumously together with *Sylva sylvarum* in 1627; this text was purportedly written by Bacon in 1624.

6   According to Rawley, Bacon intended to devote a special section to law-making and the best constitution for a state; this did not materialize because shortly before his death Bacon had directed his attention to questions of natural history (*New Atlantis*; works 3.127). Some interpreters consider the fragmentary character of *New Atlantis* to be a stylistic device, with Bacon again wishing to underline the open logic of investigation presented in the *Instauratio magna* (Krohn 1987: 156–8; Faulkner 1993: 234). For Davis (1981: 120–4), *New Atlantis* remained incomplete because the idea of an infinitely ongoing perfection of the human species has no place for the completed state of a utopia. For my part, I suspect that Bacon, as Rawley intimates, was aware of the shortcomings of his political philosophy and left the work incomplete.

7   Jowitt also opposes a colonialist interpretation of *New Atlantis*: "This would seem to mean that *New Atlantis* was putting forward an anti-colonial argument in attempting to foster a policy against aggressive empire-building" (2002: 138).

Chapter 10

1   The works of Hobbes are cited according to the following abbreviations and editions: *EW*, the English works edited by W. Molesworth (Hobbes 1962), with references to volume and page number; *Lev.* (*Leviathan*), the edition by N. Malcolm which includes the English and Latin texts (Hobbes 2012), with references to chapter, paragraph, and page number; *De cive*, both Latin and English citations from the critical editions by H. Warrender (Hobbes 1983a; 1983b), with references to chapter and paragraph; *De corpore*, cited from *EW*, with references to part, chapter, and paragraph; *De homine*, English translation from the edition by B. Gert (Hobbes 1972), with references to chapter and paragraph; *Elem.* (*The Elements of Law, Natural and Politic*), from the edition of G. S. A. Gaskin (Hobbes 1994), with references to book, chapter, and paragraph.
2   For comparisons between the versions of the doctrine of the state of nature, cf. McNeilly (1968: 157–64); Tricaud (1988); Esfeld (1995: 253–66); Eggers (2008).
3   For this point, see also Hegel (1998: 1:560f.):
    Now since honour is not only a shining in myself, but must also be envisaged and recognized by others who again on their side may demand equal recognition for their honour, honour is something purely vulnerable. For how far I will extend my demand, and in relation to what, is something dependent entirely on my caprice ... Even in the case of the injury, as of honour in general, the thing in which I must feel myself injured does not matter; for what is negated affects the personality which has made such a thing its own and now considers that what is attacked is itself, this ideal infinite point.

Chapter 11

1   Works of Locke are cited according to the following abbreviations and editions: *TTG*: *Two Treatises of Government*, edition by P. Laslett (Locke [1690] 1970), with treatise and paragraph in Arabic numerals; *Essay*: *Essay Concerning Human Understanding*, edition by P. H. Nidditch (Locke [1700] 1990), with book, chapter, and paragraphs in Arabic numerals.
2   According to Olivecrona, the term "property" can be traced back to *suum* in Grotius. Hobbes had already translated *suum* as "propriety", and in turn Locke

replaced this with "property" (1975: 113). In Grotius, *suum* designates the sphere unique to humans and distinguishes between the *suum internum*, covering life, the body, the limbs, and public reputation, and the *suum externum*, i.e., the possession of external goods (Brocker 1992: 159).

3   Locke distinguishes among three types of human intervention in nature: "generation," "making," and "alternation." In "generation" an already existing internal activity of a substance is actuated by an external cause. "Making" constitutes the world of artificial things, whereby parts of different substances are either separated from or connected to one another. In contrast, "alternation" produces a quality that was hitherto not present in a specific substance. See *Essay* 2.26.2.

References

RE refers to Pauly et al. (eds), *Realencyclopädie der classischen Altertumswissenschaft*.

Aarsleff, H. (1969), "The State of Nature and the Nature of Man in Locke," in J. W. Yolton (ed.), *John Locke: Problems and Perspectives*, 99–136, Cambridge: Cambridge University Press.

Abel, K. (1974), "Zone," *RE*, Suppl. 14, 989–1188, Stuttgart: J. B. Metzler.

Abizadeh, A. (2018), *Hobbes and the Two Faces of Ethics*, Cambridge: Cambridge University Press.

Acosta, J. de (2010), *The Natural and Moral History of the Indies*, ed. C. R. Markham, trans. E. Grimston, Cambridge: Cambridge University Press.

Alcoff, L. (2021), "The Hegel of Coyoacán," in A. Allen and E. Mendieta (eds), *Decolonizing Ethics: The Critical Theory of Enrique Dussel*, 42–63, University Park, PA: Penn State University Press.

Al-Ghazali (2005), *The Alchemy of Happiness*, trans. C. Field, New York: Cosimo Classics.

Alonso-Núñez, J.-M. (1983), "Die Abfolge der Weltreiche bei Polybios und Dionysios von Halikarnass," *Historia*, 32: 411–26.

Alvarez-Goméz, M. (1978), "Der Mensch als Schöpfer seiner Welt: Überlegungen zu De coniecturis," *Mitteilungen und Forschungsbeiträge der Cusanus-Gesellschaft*, 13: 160–6.

Andrés Marcos, T. (1947), *Los imperialismos de Juan Ginés de Sepúlveda en su "Democrates Alter"*, Madrid: Instituto de Estudios Politicos.

Anghie, A. (2004), *Imperialism, Sovereignty and the Making of International Law*, Cambridge: Cambridge University Press.

Apel, K.-O. (1987), "Fallibilismus, Konsenstheorie der Wahrheit und Letztbegründung," in Forum für Philosophie Bad Homburg (ed.), *Philosophie und Begründung*, 116–211, Frankfurt am Main: Suhrkamp.

Apel, K.-O. (1989), "Das sokratische Gespräch und die gegenwärtige Transformation der Philosophie," in D. Krohn, B. Neisser, and N. Walter (eds), *Das sokratische Gespräch—ein Symposion*, 55–78, Hamburg: Junius.

Apel, K.-O. (1992), "Normatively Grounding 'Critical Theory' through Recourse to the Lifeworld? A Transcendental Pragmatic Attempt to Think with Habermas against Habermas," in A. Honneth, T. McCarthy, C. Offe, and A. Wellmer (eds), *Philosophical Interventions in the Unfinished Project of Enlightenment*, trans. W. Rehg, 15–65, Cambridge, MA: MIT Press.

Apel, K.-O. (1996a), "The a Priori of the Communicative Community and the Foundation of Ethics in the Scientific Age," in E. Mendieta (ed.), *Karl-Otto Apel, Selected Essays*, vol. 2: *Ethics and the Theory of Rationality*, ed. and trans. E. Mendieta, 1–67, Atlantic Highlands, NJ: Humanities.

Apel, K.-O. (1996b), "The Challenge of a Totalizing Critique of Reason and the Program of a Philosophical Theory of Rationality Types," in E. Mendieta (ed.), *Karl-Otto Apel, Selected Essays*, vol. 2: *Ethics and the Theory of Rationality*, ed. and trans. E. Mendieta, 250–74, Atlantic Highlands, NJ: Humanities.

Apel, K.-O. (1998), "Auflösung der Diskursethik? Zur Architektonik der Differenzierung in Habermas' Faktizität und Geltung. Dritter, transzendentalpragmatisch orientierter Versuch, mit Habermas gegen Habermas zu denken," in K.-O. Apel, *Auseinandersetzungen in Erprobung des transzendentalpragmatischen Ansatzes*, 701–837, Frankfurt am Main: Suhrkamp.

Apel, K.-O. (2001), *The Response of Discourse Ethics to the Moral Challenge of the Human Situation as Such and Especially Today*, Leuven: Peeters.

Arendt, H. (1998), *The Human Condition*, 2nd edn, Chicago: University of Chicago Press.

Aristotle (1934), *Physics*, vol. 2, books 5–8, trans. P. H. Wicksteed and F. M. Cornford, Cambridge, MA: Harvard University Press.

Aristotle (1939), *On the Heavens*, trans. W. K. C. Guthrie, Cambridge, MA: Harvard University Press.

Aristotle (1957a), *Physics*, vol. 1, books 1–4, trans. P. H. Wicksteed and F. M. Cornford, rev. and repr., Cambridge, MA: Harvard University Press.

Aristotle (1957b), *Politica*, ed. W. D. Ross, Oxford: Clarendon.

Aristotle (1962), *Metereologica*, trans. H. D. P. Lee, Cambridge, MA: Harvard University Press.

Aristotle (1966), *The Politics and the Constitution of Athens*, trans. and ed. S. Everson, Cambridge: Cambridge University Press.

Aristotle (1982), *De generatione et corruptione*, ed. C. J. F. Williams, Oxford: Oxford University Press.

Aristotle (2009), *Nicomachean Ethics*, trans. D. Ross, rev. L. Brown, Oxford: Oxford University Press.

Aristotle (2016), *Metaphysics*, trans. C. D. C. Reve, Indianapolis: Hackett.

Armitage, D. J. (2004), "Locke, Carolina, and the Two Treatises of Government," *Political Theory*, 32 (5): 602–7.

Armitage, D. J. (2021), "John Locke: Theorist of Empire?" in S. Muthu (ed.), *Empire and Modern Political Thought*, 84–111, Cambridge: Cambridge University Press.

Árnason, J. P. (2003), *Civilizations in Dispute: Historical Questions and Theoretical Traditions*, Leiden: Brill.

Arneil, B. (1996), *John Locke and America: The Defence of English Colonialism*, Oxford: Oxford University Press.

Ashcraft, R. (1968), "Locke's State of Nature: Historical Fact or Moral Fiction?" *American Political Science Review*, 62 (3): 898–915.

Ashcraft, R. (1986), *Revolutionary Politics and Locke's "Two Treatises of Government"*, Princeton: Princeton University Press.

Aspe Armella, V. (2021), "The Influence of the School of Salamanca in Alonso de la Vera Cruz's *De dominio infidelium et iusto bello*: First *relectio* in America," in T. Duve, J. L. Egío, and C. Birr (eds), *The School of Salamanca: A Case of Global Knowledge Production*, 294–334, Leiden: Brill.

Assmann, J. (2003), *The Mind of Egypt: History and Meaning in the Time of the Pharaohs*, trans. A. Jenkins, New York: Metropolitan Books.

Aughterson, K. (2002), "Strange Things So Probably Told: Gender, Sexual Difference and Knowledge in Bacon's New Atlantis," in B. Price (ed.), *Francis Bacon's New Atlantis: New Interdisciplinary Essays*, 156–79, Manchester and New York: Manchester University Press.

Augustine, M. A. (1998), *The City of God Against the Pagans*, trans. R. W. Dyson, New York: Cambridge University Press.

Augustine, M. A. (2002), "The Literal Meaning of Genesis," in M. A. Augustine, *On Genesis: A Refutation of the Manichees. Unfinished Literal Commentary on Genesis. The Literal Meaning of Genesis*, 155–506, New York: New City.

Augustine, M. A. (2014–16), *Confessions*, 2 vols., trans. C. J.-B. Hammond, Cambridge, MA: Harvard University Press.

Augustus (2009), *Res Gestae Divi Augusti*, ed. and trans. A. Cooley, Cambridge: Cambridge University Press.

Aujac, G. (1987), "The Foundations of Theoretical Cartography in Archaic and Classical Greece," in J. B. Harley and D. Woodward (eds), *The History of Cartography*, vol. 1: *Cartography in Prehistoric, Ancient and Medieval Europe and Mediterranean*, 130–76, Chicago: University of Chicago Press.

Bacon, F. ([1857–74] 1963), *The Works of Francis Bacon*, 15 vols, ed. J. Spedding, R. L. Ellis, and D. D. Heath, Stuttgart-Bad Cannstatt: Frommann.

Baldry, H. C. (1965), *The Unity of Mankind in Greek Thought*, Cambridge: Cambridge University Press.

Barasch, M. (1998), "Creatio ex nihilo: Renaissance Concepts of Artistic Creation. A Minor Mistranslation," in E. Rudolph (ed.), *Die Renaissance als erste Aufklärung*, vol. 3: *Die Renaissance und ihr Bild in der Geschichte*, 37–58, Tübingen: Mohr Siebeck.

Baraz, M. (1968), *L'être et la connaissance chez Montaigne*, Paris: Corti.

Bayly, C. (2004), *The Birth of the Modern World: Global Connections and Comparisons, 1780–1914*, Oxford: Blackwell.

Beestermöller, G. (1990), *Thomas von Aquin und der gerechte Krieg: Friedensethik im theologischen Kontext der Summa Theologica*, Cologne: Bachem.

Beestermöller, G. (2012), "Thomas Aquinas and Humanitarian Intervention," in H.-G. Justenhoven and W. A. Barbieri (eds), *From Just War to Modern Peace Ethics*, 71–98, Berlin: de Gruyter.

Beierwaltes, W. (1980), *Identität und Differenz*, Frankfurt am Main: Klostermann.

Beitz, C. (1979), *Political Theory and International Relations*, Princeton: Princeton University Press.
Bell, A. F. G. (1925), *Juan Ginés de Sepúlveda*, Oxford: Oxford University Press.
Bellah, R. (2011), *Religion in Human Evolution: From the Paleolithic to the Axial Age*, Cambridge, MA: Harvard University Press.
Bellers, J. (1996), "Aristoteles: Die polis zwischen Aussenpolitik und deren Negierung," in J. Bellers (ed.), *Klassische Staatsentwürfe: Aussenpolitisches Denken von Aristoteles bis heute*, 11–20, Darmstadt: Wissenschaftliche Buchgesellschaft.
Benhabib, S. (1986), *Critique, Norm and Utopia*, New York: Columbia University Press.
Beneyto Pérez, J. M. and J. Corti Varela, eds (2017), *At the Origins of Modernity. Francisco de Vitoria and the Discovery of International Law*, Cham: Springer.
Beorlegui, C. (2004), *Historia del pensamiento filosófico latinoamericana: Una búsqueda incesante de la identitad*, Bilbao: Universidad de Deusto.
Berlinger, R. (1994), "Philosophie der Kunst: Zum Homo-Creator-Motiv des Nikolaus von Kues," *Perspektiven der Philosophie*, 20: 13–30.
Beuchot, M. (1991), "Filósofos humanistas novohispanos," in I. O. Romero (ed.), *La tradición clásica en México*, 109–48, Mexico City: UNAM.
Beuchot, M. (1996), *Historia de la filosofia en México colonial*, Barcelona: Herder.
Bianchi, L. (1997), "Der Bischof und die Philosophen: Die Pariser Verurteilung vom 7. März 1277," in K. Flasch and U. R. Jeck (eds), *Das Licht der Vernunft: Die Anfänge der Aufklärung im Mittelalter*, 70–83, Munich: Beck.
The Bible (1989), New Revised Standard Version (NRSV), https://www.biblegateway.com/versions/New-Revised-Standard-Version-Updated-Edition-NRSVue-Bible/.
Biblia sacra, iuxta vulgatam versionem (1994), ed. R. Weber, 4th edn, Stuttgart: Deutsche Bibelgesellschaft.
Bichler, R. (2000), *Herodots Welt: Der Aufbau der Historie am Bild der fremden Länder und Völker, ihrer Zivilisation und ihrer Geschichte*, Berlin: Akademie-Verlag.
Binswanger, H. C. (1982), *Studien zur Entwicklung der ökonomischen Theorie*, vol. 2, Berlin: Duncker & Humblot.
Binswanger, H. C. (1991), *Geld und Natur: Das wirtschaftliche Wachstum im Spannungsfeld zwischen Ökonomie und Ökologie*, Stuttgart and Vienna: Edition Weitbrecht.
Bippus, H.-P. (2000), *In der Theologie nicht bewandert? Montaigne und die Theologie*, Tübingen: Francke.
Bisaha, N. (2010), *Creating East and West: Renaissance Humanists and the Ottoman Turks*, Philadelphia: University of Pennsylvania Press.
Bishop, J. D. (1997), "Locke's Theory of Original Appropriation and the Right of Settlement in Iroquois Territory," *Canadian Journal of Philosophy*, 27 (3): 311–37.
Blum, P. R. (2002a), "Eintracht und Religion bei Giovanni Pico della Mirandola," in N. Brieskorn and M. Riedenauer (eds), *Suche nach Frieden: Politische Ethik in der frühen Neuzeit*, vol. 3, 29–46, Cologne: Kohlhammer.

Blum, P. R. (2002b), "'Einheit verhindert Krieg': Zur Soziologie einer Universalmonarchie in Tommaso Campanellas 'Sonnenstadt,'" in N. Brieskorn and M. Riedenauer (eds), *Suche nach Frieden: Politische Ethik in der frühen Neuzeit III*, 153–72, Cologne: Kohlhammer.

Blum, P. R. (2010), *Philosophy of Religion in the Renaissance*, Farnham-Burlington, VT: Ashgate.

Blumenberg, H. (1983), *The Legitimacy of the Modern Age*, trans. R. M. Wallace, Cambridge, MA, and London: MIT Press.

Blumenberg, H. (2015), *The Laughter of the Thracian Woman: A Protohistory of Theory*, trans. S. Hawkins, London: Bloomsbury.

Blumenberg, H. (2022), *The Readability of the World*, trans. R. Savage and D. Roberts, Ithaca: Cornell University Press.

Boethius, A. M. S. (1926), *The Theological Tractates and the Consolation of Philosophy*, trans. H. F. Stewart, E. K. Rand, and S. J. Tester, Cambridge, MA: Harvard University Press.

Bordat, J. (2006), *Gerechtigkeit und Wohlwollen: Das Völkerrechtskonzept des Bartolomé de Las Casas*, Aachen: Shaker Verlag.

Bormann, K. (1975), "Koordinierung der Erkenntnisstufen (descensus und ascensus) bei Nikolaus von Kues," *Mitteilungen und Forschungsbeiträge der Cusanus-Gesellschaft*, 11: 62–85.

Bös, G. (1995), *Curiositas: Die Rezeption eines antiken Begriffs durch christliche Autoren bis Thomas von Aquin*, Paderborn: Schöningh.

Bosbach, F. (1988), *Monarchia Universalis: Ein politischer Leitbegriff der frühen Neuzeit*, Göttingen: Vandenhoeck & Ruprecht.

Bosworth, A. B. (1988), *Conquest and Empire: The Reign of Alexander the Great*, Cambridge: Cambridge University Press.

Botermann, H. (1987), "Ciceros Gedanken zum 'gerechten Krieg' in de officiis 1,34-40," *Archiv für Kulturgeschichte*, 69: 1–29.

Bouwsma, W. J. (1993), "The Renaissance Discovery of Human Creativity," in J. W. O'Malley, Th. M. Izbicki and G. Christianson (eds), *Humanity and Divinity in Renaissance and Reformation*, 17–34, Leiden, New York, Cologne: Brill.

Box, I. (1989), *The Social Thought of Francis Bacon*, Lewiston, New York: Mellen.

Brandt, R. (1974), *Eigentumstheorien von Grotius bis Kant*, Stuttgart-Bad Cannstatt: Frommann-Holzboog.

Bredow, G. von (1967), "Der Sinn der Formel meliori modo quo," *Mitteilungen und Forschungsbeiträge der Cusanus-Gesellschaft*, 6: 21–30.

Brett, S. F. (1994), *Slavery and the Catholic Tradition: Rights in the Balance*, New York: Peter Lang.

Brewer, H. (2017), "Slavery, Sovreignty, and 'Inheritable Blood': Reconsidering John Locke and the Origins of American Slavery," *American Historical Review*, 122 (4): 1038–78.

Brieskorn, N. (2000), "Luis de Molinas Weiterentwicklung der Kriegsethik des Kriegsrechts der Scholastik," in N. Brieskorn and M. Riedenauer (eds), *Suche nach Frieden: Politische Ethik in der Frühen Neuzeit I*, 167–90, Stuttgart: Kohlhammer.

Brieskorn, N. and G. Stiening, eds (2011), *Francisco de Vitorias "De Indis" in interdisziplinärer Perspektive*, Stuttgart-Bad Cannstatt: Frommann-Holzboog.

Briggs, J. C. (1989), *Francis Bacon and the Rhetoric of Nature*, Cambridge, MA: Harvard University Press.

Brincken, A-D. von den (1970), " … 'Ut describeretur universus orbis'. Zur Universalkartographie des Mittelalters," in A. Zimmermann (ed.), *Methoden in Wissenschaft und Kunst des Mittealters*, 249–78, Berlin: de Gruyter.

Brincken, A-D. von den (1976), "Die Kugelgestalt der Erde in der Kartographie des Mittelalters," *Archiv für Kulturgeschichte*, 58: 77–95.

Brincken, A-D. von den (1989), "Das geographische Weltbild um 1300," in P. Moraw (ed.), *Das geographische Weltbild um 1300: Politik im Spannungsfeld von Wissen, Mythos und Fiktion*, 9–32, Berlin: Duncker & Humblot.

Brincken, A-D. von den (1992), *Fines Terrae. Die Enden der Erde und der vierte Kontinent auf mittelalterlichen Weltkarten*, Hannover: Hahnsche Buchhandlung.

Brincken, A-D. von den (1998), "Terrae Incognitae. Zur Umschreibung empirisch noch unerschlossener Räume in lateinischen Quellen des Mittelalters bis in die Entdeckungszeit," in J. A. Aertsen (ed.), *Raum und Raumvorstellungen im Mittelalter*, 557–72, Berlin, New York: de Gruyter.

Brocker, M. (1992), *Arbeit und Eigentum: Der Paradigmenwechsel in der neuzeitlichen Eigentumstheorie*, Darmstadt: Wissenschaftliche Buchgesellschaft.

Broderson, K. (1995), *Terra cognita: Studien zur römischen Raumerfassung*, Hildesheim: Olms.

Bruno, G. (1975), *The Ash Wednesday Supper*, trans. J. Stanley, The Hague: Mouton.

Brunschvicg, L. (1945), *Descartes et Pascal, lecteurs de Montaigne*, Neuchâtel: Édition de la Baconnière.

Buchheim, T. (1999), *Aristoteles*, Freiburg im Breisgau, Basel, and Vienna: Herder.

Buck, A. (1987), "Montaigne und die Krise des Humanismus," in A. Buck and T. Klaniczay (eds), *Das Ende der Renaissance: Europäische Kultur um 1600*, 7–21, Wiesbaden: Harassowitz.

Buck, A. (1990), "Einleitung. Giovanni Pico della Mirandola und seine 'Rede über die Würde des Menschen,'" in A. Buck (ed.), *Giovanni Pico della Mirandola: De hominis dignitate/Über die Würde des Menschen*, trans. N. Baumgarten, vii–xxvii, Hamburg: Meiner.

Buck, G. (1976), "Selbsterhaltung und Historizität," in H. Ebeling (ed.), *Subjektivität und Selbsterhaltung: Beiträge zur Diagnose der Moderne*, 208–302, Frankfurt am Main: Suhrkamp.

Buckle, S. (1991), *Natural Law and the Theory of Property: Grotius to Hume*, Oxford: Clarendon.

Burckhardt, J. ([1878] 2014), *The Civilisation of the Period of the Renaissance in Italy*, 2 vols., trans. S. G. C. Middlemore, Cambridge: Cambridge University Press.

Bürger, P. (1998), *Das Verschwinden des Subjekts: eine Geschichte der Subjektivität von Montaigne bis Barthes*, Frankfurt am Main: Suhrkamp.

Burke, P. (1981), *Montaigne*, Oxford: Oxford University Press.
Burke, P. (1987), *The Italian Renaissance: Culture and Society in Italy*, Cambridge: Polity.
Burkert, W. (1962), *Weisheit und Wissenschaft: Studien zu Pythagoras, Philolaos und Platon*, Nürnberg: Carl.
Burstein, S. M. (2017), *The World from 1000 BCE to 300 CE*, Oxford: Oxford University Press.
Busche, H. (2004), "Die moralische Entgrenzung der Ökonomie in der Frührenaissance," in W. Hogrebe and J. Bromand (eds), *Grenzen und Grenzüberschreitungen: XIX Deutscher Kongress für Philosophie, Vorträge und Kolloquien*, 462–77, Berlin: Akademie Verlag.
Camus, A. (1956), *The Rebel: An Essay on Man in Revolt*, trans. A. Bower, New York: Vintage Books.
Capizzi, J. E. (2002), "The Children of God. Natural Slavery in the Thought of Aquinas and Vitoria," *Theological Studies* (Baltimore), 63 (1): 31–52.
Carrasco, D. (1999), *City of Sacrifice: The Aztec Empire and the Role of Violence in Civilization*, Boston: Beacon.
Carraud, V. (1999), "L'Imaginer Inimiginable: Le Dieu de Montaigne," in E. Faye (ed.), *Descartes et la Renaissance: Actes du Colloque international de Tours des 22–24 mars 1996*, 117–44, Paris: Champion.
Casale, G. (2010), *The Ottoman Age of Exploration*, Oxford: Oxford University Press.
Casarella, P. (2013), "Nicholas of Cusa and the Ends of Medieval Mysticism," in J. Lamm (ed.), *The Wiley-Blackwell Companion to Christian Mysticism*, 388–403, Chichester: Wiley-Blackwell.
Casas, G. (2018), "Ontology, Henadology, Angelology. The Neoplatonic Roots of Angelic Hierarchy," in L. Brisson, S. O'Neill and A. Timotin (eds), *Neoplatonic Demons and Angels*, 231–68, Leiden: Brill.
Cassirer, E. ([1927] 1963), *Individual and Cosmos in Renaissance Philosophy*, trans. Mario Domandi, Oxford: Basil Blackwell.
Cassirer, E. (1999), "Das Erkenntnisproblem in der Philosophie der Renaissance," in E. Cassirer, *Gesammelte Werke: Hamburger Ausgabe*, vol. 14, ed. B. Rekki, Darmstadt: Wissenschaftliche Buchgesellschaft.
Castany Prado, B. (2016), "Asnos en el paraíso: la influencia de la filosofía escéptica en la creación del mito del buen salvaje," *Hipogrifo* (New York), 4 (2): 149–68.
Castilla Urbaño, F. (1992), *El pensamiento de Francisco de Vitoria: Filosofía política e Indio americano*, Barcelona: Anthropos.
Castilla Urbaño, F. (2013), *El pensamiento de Juan Ginés de Sepúlveda: Vida activa, humanismo y guerra en el Renacimiento*, Madrid: Centro de Estudios Políticos y Constitucionales.
Castilla Urbaño, F. (2020), "The Debate of Valladolid (1550–1551)," in J. Tellkamp and J. Alejandro (eds), *A Companion to Early Modern Spanish Imperial Political and Social Thought*, 222–51, Leiden, Boston: Brill.
Cattaneo, A. (2011), *Fra Mauro's Mappa Mundi and Fifteenth-Century Venice*, Turnhout: Brepols.

Cavallar, G. (2002), *The Right of Strangers: Theories of International Hospitality, the Global Community, and Political Justice since Vitoria*, Aldershot: Ashgate.

Cerutti Guldberg, H. (2006), *Filosofía de la Liberación latinoamericana*, México: Fondo de Cultura Económica.

Charité, R. C. (1968), *The Concept of Judgement in Montaigne*, The Hague: Nijhoff.

Charpentier, F. (1986), "Les Essais de Montaigne. Curiosité/Incuriosité," in J. Céard (ed.), *La Curiosité à la Renaissance*, 111–21, Paris: Société d'Édition d'Enseignement Supérieur.

Charpentier, F. (2004), "Curiosité," in P. Desan (ed.), *Dictionnaire de Michel de Montaigne*, 238–9, Paris: Champion.

Cheneval, F. (2002), *Philosophie in weltbürgerlicher Bedeutung: Über die Entstehung und die philosophischen Grundlagen des supranationalen und kosmopolitischen Denkens der Moderne*, Basel: Schwabe.

Chiusi, T. (2005), "Strukturen des römischen Eigentums im Spiegel rhetorisch-philosophischer Texte Ciceros," in A. Eckl and D. Ludwig (eds), *Was ist Eigentum? Philosophische Positionen von Platon bis Habermas*, 59–72, Munich: Beck.

Cicero, M. T. (1913), *On Duties*, trans. W. Miller, Cambridge, MA: Harvard University Press.

Cicero, M. T. (1931), *On Ends*, trans. H. Rackham, 2nd edn, Cambridge, MA: Harvard University Press.

Cicero, M. T. (1933), *On the Nature of the Gods: Academics*, trans. H. Rackham, Cambridge, MA: Harvard University Press.

Cicero, M. T. (1953), *Pro Milone; In Pisonem; Pro Scauro; Pro Fonteio; Pro Rabirio postumo; Pro Marcello; Pro Ligario; Pro Rege; Deiotaro*, trans. N. H. Watts, rev. and repr., Cambridge, MA: Harvard University Press.

Cicero, M. T. (1999), *On the Commonwealth and On the Laws*, ed. and trans. J. E. G. Zetzel, Cambridge: Cambridge University Press.

Clarke, K. (1999), *Between Geography and History: Hellenistic Constructions of the Roman World*, Oxford: Clarendon.

Clavijero, F. J. ([1781] 1991), *Historia antigua de México*, México: Editorial Porrua.

Colman, J. (1983), *John Locke's Moral Philosophy*, Edinburgh: Edinburgh University Press.

Colomer, E. (1978), "Das Menschenbild des Nikolaus von Kues in der Geschichte des christlichen Humanismus," *Mitteilungen und Forschungsbeiträge der Cusanus-Gesellschaft*, 13: 117–43.

Condorcet, J. A. N. de Caritat de ([1795] 1955), *Sketch for a Historical Picture of the Progress of the Human Mind*, Westport, ed. S. Hampshire, trans. Barraclough, London: Weidenfeld and Nicolson.

Cooter, W. S. (1977), "Preindustrial Frontiers and Interaction Spheres. Prolegomena to a Study of Roman Frontiers," in D. H. Miller and J. O. Steffen (eds), *The Frontier: Comparative Studies*, 81–107, Norman: University of Oklahoma Press.

Copenhaver, B. P. (1992a), *Hermetica: The Greek Corpus Hermeticum and the Latin Asclepius in a New English Translation with Notes and Introduction*, Cambridge: Cambridge University Press.

Copenhaver, B. P. (1992b), "Introduction," in B. P. Copenhaver, *Hermetica: The Greek Corpus Hermeticum and the Latin Asclepius in a New English Translation with Notes and Introduction*, xiii–lxi, Cambridge: Cambridge University Press.

Copenhaver, B. P. (2002), "The Secret of Pico's 'Oration': Kabala and Renaissance Philosophy", *Midwest Studies in Philosophy*, 26: 56–81.

Copenhaver, B. P. (2019), *Magic and the Dignity of Man: Pico della Mirandola and His Oration in Modern Memory*, Cambridge, MA: Harvard University Press.

Corcoran, P. (2018), "John Locke on Native Right, Colonial Possession, and the Concept of Vacuumdomicilium," *The European Legacy*, 23 (3): 225–50.

Craven, W. G. (1981), *Giovanni Pico della Mirandola: Symbol of his Age: Modern Interpretations of a Renaissance Philosopher*, Genf: Liberairie Droz.

Crombie, A. C. (1953), *Robert Grosseteste and the Origins of Experimental Science 1100–1700*, Oxford: Clarendon.

Daly, H. E. (1991), *Steady-State Economics*, 2nd edn, Washington, DC: Island.

Daly, H. E. (1996), *Beyond Growth*, Boston: Beacon.

Daniélou, J. (1948), *Origène: Le Génie du Christianisme*, Paris: La Table Ronde.

Dante Alighieri (1996a), *The Divine Comedy of Dante Alighieri*, trans. R. M. Durling, vol. 1: *Inferno*, Oxford: Oxford University Press.

Dante Alighieri (1996b), *Monarchy*, ed. and trans. P. Shaw, Cambridge: Cambridge University Press.

Daston, L. and K. Park (1998), *Wonders and the Order of Nature, 1150–1750*, New York: Zone Books.

Davenport, F. G. (1917), *European Treaties Bearing on the History of United States and its Dependencies to 1648*, Washington: The Carnegie Institution.

Davis, J. C. (1981), *Utopia and the Ideal Society: A Study in English Utopian Writing 1516–1700*, Cambridge: Cambridge University Press.

Deckers, D. (1991), *Gerechtigkeit und Recht: eine historisch-kritische Untersuchung der Gerechtigkeitsidee von Francisco de Vitoria (1483–1546)*, Freiburg im Breisgau: Universitätsverlag.

Defaux, G. (1983), "Readings of Montaigne," *Yale French Studies*, 64: 73–92.

Delgado, M. (1994), "Kolonialismus und Menschenwürde. Die Ethikdiskussion des 16. Jahrhunderts im Zusammenhang mit der spanischen Expansion," in T. Brose and M. Lutz-Bachmann (eds), *Umstrittene Menschenwürde: Beiträge zur ethischen Debatte der Gegenwart*, 35–67, Hildesheim: Morus.

De Lubac, H. (1974), *Pic de la Mirandole: Études et Discussions*, Paris: Montaigne.

Derrida, J. (1978), *Writing and Difference*, trans. A. Bass, Chicago: University of Chicago.

Desan, P. (2001), "De l'Exemplar et l'exemplaire," in N. Peacock and J. J. Supple (eds), *Lire les "Essais" de Montaigne: Acte du Colloque de Glasgow 1997*, 247–79, Paris: Edition Champion.

Dijksterhuis, E. J. (1961), *The Mechanization of The World Picture*, Oxford: Oxford University Press.

Dilke, O. W. A. (1987), "The Culmination of Greek Cartography in Ptolemy," in J. B. Harley and D. Woodward (eds), *The History of Cartography*, vol. 1: *Cartography in Prehistory, Ancient, and Medieval Europe and the Mediterranean*, 177–200, Chicago, London: University of Chicago Press.

Diogenes Laertius (1925), *Lives of the Eminent Philosophers*, 2 vols., trans. R. D. Hicks, Cambridge, MA: Harvard University Press.

Dougherty, M. V. (2002), "Two Possible Sources of Pico's Oratio," *Vivarium*, 40 (2): 219–40.

Dougherty, M. V. (2008), "Three Precurses," in M. V. Dougherty (ed.), *Pico della Mirandola: New Essays*, 114–51, Cambridge: Cambridge University Press.

Dougherty, M. V. (2014), "Giovanni Pico della Mirandola, Concordia, and the Canon Law Tradition: On the Habits and Dispositions of Renaissance Exegetes," *Proceedings of the American Catholic Philosophical Association*, 88: 181–96.

Dulles, A. (1941), *Princeps concordiae: Pico della Mirandola and the Scholastic Tradition*, Cambridge, MA: Harvard University Press.

Dunn, J. (1969), *The Political Thought of John Locke: An Historical Account of the Argument of the "Two Treatises of Government"*, New York: Cambridge University Press.

Dussel, E. (1973), *Para una ética de la liberación latinoamericana*, 2 vols., Buenos Aires: Siglo XXI.

Dussel, E. (1977), *Filosofía ética latinoamericana*, vol. 3: *De la erótica a la pedagógica*, Mexico City: Editorial EdicolEditorial.

Dussel, E. (1979), *Filosofía ética latinoamericana*, vol. 4: *La política latinoamericana*, Bogota: Universidad Santo Tomas.

Dussel, E. (1980), *Filosofía ética latinoamericana*, vol. 5: *Arqueología latinoamericana: Una filosofía de la religión antifetichista*, Bogota: Universidad Santo Tomas.

Dussel, E. (1990), *El último Marx (1863) y la liberación latinoamericana: Un comentário de la tercera y cuarta redacción de "El Capital"*, Mexico City: Siglo XXI.

Dussel, E. (1995), *The Invention of America: Eclipse of the "Other" and the Myth of Modernity*, New York: Continuum.

Dussel, E. (2001), *Towards an Unknown Marx: A Commentary on the Manuscripts of 1861–63*, ed. F. Moseley, trans. Y. Angulo, London: Routledge.

Dussel, E. (2003), *Philosophy of Liberation*, trans. A. Martinez, Eugene, OR: Wipf & Stock.

Dussel, E. (2011), *Politics of Liberation: A Critical World History*, trans. T. Cooper, London: SCM.

Dussel, E. (2013), *Ethics of Liberation: In the Age of Globalization and Exclusion*, trans. Y. Angulo, B. Camilo Pérez, N. Maldonado-Torres, E. Mendieta, and A. A. Vallega, Durham, NC: Duke University Press.

Dussel, E. (2015), *Filosofías del Sur: Descolonización y transmodernidad*, Mexico City: Ediciónes AkalMexico.

Dussel, E. (2018), *Anti-Cartesian Meditations and Transmodernity: From the Perspective of Philosophy of Liberation*, ed. A. A. Vallega and R. Grosfoguel, The Hague: Amrit.

Dussel, E., E. Mendieta, and C. Bohórques, eds (2009), *El pensamiento filosófico latinoamericano, del Caribe y "latino," 1300–2000: Historia, corrientes, temas filosófos*, Pátzcuaro: CREFAL/Siglo XXI.

Duval, E. M. (1983), "Lessons of the New World: Design and Meaning in Montaigne's 'Des Cannibales' (I:31) and 'Des Coches' (III:6)," *Yale French Studies*, 64: 95–112.

Eggers, D. (2008), *Die Naturzustandstheorie des Thomas Hobbes: Eine vergleichende Analyse von The Elements of Law, De Cive, und den englischen und lateinischen Fassungen des Leviathan*, Berlin and New York: de Gruyter.

Eisenstadt, S. N. (2000a), "Multiple Modernities," *Daedalus*, 129 (1): 1–29.

Eisenstadt, S. N. (2000b), *Die Vielfalt der Moderne*, Weilerswist: Velbrück Wissenschaft.

Ellington, T. J. (2001), *The Myth of the Noble Savage*, Berkeley: University of California Press.

Ellis, R. L. (1963), "General Preface to Bacon's Philosophical Works," in R. L. Ellis, J. Spedding, and D. D. Heath (eds), *The Works of Francis Bacon*, vol. 1, 21–67, Stuttgart-Bad Cannstatt: Frommann.

Elton, H. (1996), *The Frontiers of Roman Empire*, Bloomington: Indiana University Press.

Enders, A. (1993), *Die Legende von der "Neuen Welt": Montaigne und die "littérature géographique" im Frankreich des 16. Jahrhunderts*, Tübingen: Niemeyer.

Enders, M. (2002), "Unendlichkeit und All-Einheit: Zum Unendlichkeitsgedanken in der philosophischen Theologie des Cusanus," in M. Thurner (ed.), *Nicolaus Cusanus zwischen Deutschland und Italien*, 384–441, Berlin: Akademie-Verlag.

Engels, J. (1999), *Augusteische Oikumenegeographie und Universalhistorie im Werk Strabons von Amaseia*, Stuttgart: Steiner.

Erskine, A. (1990), *The Hellenistic Stoa: Political Thought and Action*, London: Duckworth.

Esfeld, M. (1995), *Mechanismus und Subjektivität in der Philosophie von Thomas Hobbes*, Stuttgart-Bad Cannstatt: Frommann-Holzboog.

Euler, W. A. (1998), *"Pia Philosophia" und "docta religio": Theologie und Religion bei Marsilio Ficino und Giovanni Pico della Mirandola*, Munich: Fink.

Eusebius (1982–3), *Praeparatio evangelica*, 2 vols., ed. E. Des Places, 2nd edn, Berlin: Akademie-Verlag.

Eusebius (1999), *Life of Constantine*, trans. A. Cameron and G. Hall, Oxford: Clarendon.

Evrigenis, I. D. (2014), *Images of Anarchy: The Rhetoric and Science in Hobbes's State of Nature*, Cambridge: Cambridge University Press.

Farmer, S. A. (2016), *Syncretism in the West: Pico's 900 Theses (1486)—The Evolution of Traditional Religious and Philosophical Systems*, Tempe: Arizona Center for Medieval and Renaissance Studies.

Faroqhi, S. (1999), *Approaching Ottoman History: An Introduction to the Sources*, Cambridge: Cambridge University Press.

Faroqhi, S. (2000), *Geschichte des Osmanischen Reiches*, Munich: Beck.

Farr, J. (1986), "'So Vile and Miserable an Estate': The Problem of Slavery in Locke's Political Thought," *Political Theory*, 14 (2): 263–89.

Farr, J. (2008), "Locke, Natural Law, and New World Slavery," *Political Theory*, 36 (4): 495–522.

Farrington, B. (1951), *Francis Bacon: A Philosopher of Industrial Science*, London: Lawrence & Wishart.

Farrington, B. (1964), *The Philosophy of Francis Bacon: An Essay on its Development from 1603–1609, With new Translations of Fundamental Texts*, Liverpool: Liverpool University Press.

Faulkner, R. K. (1993), *Francis Bacon and the Project of Progress*, Lanham, MD: Rowman and Littlefield.

Feldmann, E. (1989), "Unverschämt genug vermass er sich, astronomische Anschauungen zu lehren": Augustins Polemik gegen Mani in "conf. 5,3ff.," in A. Zumkeller (ed.), *Signum Pietatis*, 105–20, Würzburg: Augustinus-Verlag.

Fernández-Santamaría, J. A. (1977), *The State, War and Peace: Spanish Political Thought in the Renaissance 1516–1559*, Cambridge: Cambridge University Press.

Figueroa, D. (2004), *Philosophie und Globalisierung*, Würzburg: Königshausen & Neumann.

Findley, C. V. (2009), "The Tanzimat," in R. Kasaba (ed.), *The Cambridge History of Turkey*, vol. 4: *Turkey in the Modern World*, 11–37, Cambridge: Cambridge University Press.

Fink-Eitel, H. (1994), *Die Philosophie und die Wilden: Über die Bedeutung des Fremden in der europäischen Geistesgeschichte*, Hamburg: Junius.

Fisch, J. (1984), *Die europäische Expansion und das Völkerrecht*, Stuttgart: Steiner.

Flasch, K. (1998), *Nikolaus von Kues: Geschichte einer Entwicklung—Vorlesungen zur Einführung in seine Philosophie*, Tübingen: Klostermann.

Flasch, K. (2001), *Nikolaus Cusanus*, Munich: Beck.

Flasch, K. (2003), *Historische Philosophie: Beschreibung einer Denkart*, Frankfurt am Main: Klostermann.

Fornet-Betancourt, R. (1994), *Hacía una filosofia intercultural*, San José, Costa Rica: Departamento Ecumenico de Investigaciones.

Forschner, M. (1988), *Stoa und Cicero über Krieg und Frieden*, Stuttgart: Kohlhammer.

Forschner, M. (1996), "'Koinos nomos—lex naturalis': Stoisches und christliches Naturgesetz," in T. Grethlein and H. Leitner (eds), *Inmitten der Zeit: Beiträge zur europäischen Gegenwartsphilosophie; Festschrift für Manfred Riedel*, 25–46, Würzburg: Königshausen & Neumann.

Foucault, M. (1977), *Discipline and Punish: The Birth of the Prison*, trans. A. Sheridan, New York: Pantheon.

Foucault, M. (1984), "What is Enlightenment?" in P. Rabinov (ed.), *The Foucault Reader*, 32–50, New York: Pantheon Books.
Foucault, M. (1988), "The Political Technology of the Individuals," in M. Foucault, H. Luther, H. Martin, H. Gutman, and P. H. Hutton (eds), *Technologies of the Self: A Seminar with Michel Foucault*, 145–62, Amherst: University of Massachusetts Press.
Foucault, M. (2002), *The Order of Things: Archeology of Human Sciences*, trans. A. Sheridan, London and New York: Routledge.
Frame, D. M. (1982), "Considerations on the Genesis of Montaigne's Essais," in I. D. McFarlane and I. Maclean (eds), *Montaigne: Essays in Memory of Richard Sayce*, 1–11, Oxford: Clarendon.
Friedrich, H. (1993), *Montaigne*, 3rd edn, Tübingen and Basel: Francke.
Funke, G. (1984), "Natur, zweite," in J. Ritter and K. Gründer (eds), *Historisches Wörterbuch der Philosophie*, vol. 6, 484–9, Darmstadt: Wissenschaftliche Buchgesellschaft.
Fynn-Paul, J. (2021), "The Greater Mediterranean Slave Trade," in P. Craig, D. Eltis, S. L. Engerman, and D. Richardson (eds), *The Cambridge World History of Slavery*, vol. 2: *AD 500–AD 1420*, 27–52, Cambridge: Cambridge University Press.
Garin, E. (1938), "La 'dignitas hominis' e la letteratura patristica," *Rinascita* (Firenze), 1: 102–46.
Garin, E. (1952), "Giovanni Pico della Mirandola," *L'Approdo: Rivista Trimestrale di Letter ed Arti*, 1: 34–8.
Garin, E. (1965), *Italian Humanism: Philosophy and Civic Life in the Renaissance*, trans. P. Munz, Oxford: Basil Blackwell.
Gatzemeier, M. and H. Holzhey (1980), "Makrokosmos/Mikrokosmos," in J. Ritter and K. Gründer (eds), *Historisches Wörterbuch der Philosophie*, vol. 5, 640–9, Darmstadt: Wissenschaftliche Buchgesellschaft.
Gaukroger, S. (2001), *Francis Bacon and the Transformation of Early Modern Philosophy*, Cambridge: Cambridge University Press.
Gauthier, D. (1969), *The Logic of Leviathan: The Moral and Political Theory of Thomas Hobbes*, Oxford: Clarendon.
Gehrke, H.-J. (1998), "Raumbilder in der griechischen Geographie," in T. Hantos (ed.), *Althistorisches Kolloquium aus Anlass des 70. Geburtstages von Jochen Bleicken*, 20–341, Stuttgart: Steiner.
Geismann, G. and K. Herb (1988), *Hobbes über die Freiheit: Widmungsschreiben, Vorwort an die Leser und Kapitel I–II aus "De Cive" (lat.-dt.)*, introduction with scholia, Würzburg: Königshausen & Neumann.
Georgescu-Roegen, N. (1976), *Energy and Economic Myths: Institutional and Analytical Economic Essays*, New York: Pergamon.
Gerl, H. B. (1989), *Einführung in die Philosophie der Renaissance*, Darmstadt: Wissenschaftliche Buchgesellschaft.
Gessmann, M. (1997), *Montaigne und die Moderne: Zu den philosophischen Grundlagen einer Epochenwende*, Hamburg: Meiner.

Geus, K. (2003), "Space and Geography," in A. Erskine (ed.), *A Companion to the Hellenistic World*, 323–45, Oxford: Blackwell.
Gillner, M. (1997), *Bartolomé de las Casas und die Eroberung des indianischen Kontinents: Das friedensethische Profil eines weltgeschichtlichen Umbruchs aus der Perspektive eines Anwalts der Unterdrückten*, Stuttgart: Kohlhammer.
Gisinger, F. (1937a), "Oikumene," *RE*, 17 (2): 2123–74.
Gisinger, F. (1937b), "Periplus," *RE*, 19 (1): 841–2174.
Glancy, J. A. (2002), *Slavery in Early Christianity*, Oxford: Oxford University Press.
Goldie, M. (1997), *John Locke: Political Essays*, Cambridge: Cambridge University Press.
Gottschalk-Mazouz, G. (2000), *Diskursethik: Theorien, Entwicklungen, Perspektiven*, Göttingen: de Gruyter.
Gottschalk-Mazouz, G. (2004), "Gründe, gute Gründe und Moralphilosophie," in G. Gottschalk-Mazouz (ed.), *Perspektiven der Diskursethik*, 175–201, Würzburg: Königshausen & Neumann.
Gracia, J. J. E. (1992), *Philosophy and Its History: Issues in Philosophical Historiography*, Albany: SUNY Press.
Grant, E. (1994), *Planets, Stars, and Orbs: The Medieval Cosmos, 1200–1687*, Cambridge: Cambridge University Press.
Grasmück, E. L. (1999), "Dante Alighieri: De monarchia—Zur politischen Idee vom Kaiser als Garanten des Friedens," in G. Beestermöller and H.-G. Justenhoven (eds), *Friedensethik im Mittelalter: Theologie im Ringen um die gottgegebene Ordnung*, 64–8, Stuttgart: Kohlhammer.
Greenblatt, S. (1984), *Renaissance Self-Fashioning from More to Shakespeare*, Chicago: University of Chicago Press.
Güngerich, R. (1950), *Die Küstenbeschreibung in der griechischen Literatur*, Münster: Aschendorff.
Habermas, J. (1973), *Theory and Practice*, trans. J. Viertel, Boston: Beacon.
Habermas, J. (1984), *Theory of Communicative Action*, vol. 1: *Reason and the Rationalization of Society*, trans. T. A. McCarthy, Boston: Beacon.
Habermas, J. (1987), *Theory of Communicative Action*, vol. 2: *Lifeworld and System: A Critique of Functionalist Reason*, trans. T. A. McCarthy, Boston: Beacon.
Habermas, J. (1990a), "Discourse Ethics—Notes on a Program of Philosophical Justification," in J. Habermas, *Moral Consciousness and Communicative Action*, trans. C. Lenhardt and S. W. Nicholsen, 43–115, Cambridge, MA: MIT Press.
Habermas, J. (1990b), *The Philosophical Discourse of Modernity: Twelve Lectures*, trans. F. G. Lawrence, Cambridge, MA: MIT Press.
Habermas, J. (1991), "A Reply," in A. Honneth and H. Joas (eds), *Communicative Action*, trans. J. Gaines and D. L. Jones, 214–64, Cambridge: Polity.
Habermas, J. (1996), *Between Facts and Norms: Contributions to a Discourse Theory of Law and Democracy*, trans. W. Rehg, Cambridge, MA: MIT Press.

Habermas, J. (1997), "Modernity: An Unfinished Project," in M. Passerin d'Entrèves and S. Benhabib (eds), *Habermas and the Unfinished Project of Modernity: Critical Essays on The Philosophical Discourse of Modernity*, 38–55, Cambridge, MA: MIT Press.

Habermas, J. (2019), *Auch eine Geschichte der Philosophie*, 2 vols., Berlin: Suhrkamp.

Hall, E. (1989), *Inventing the Barbarian: Greek Self-Definition through Tragedy*, Oxford: Clarendon.

Hamann, G. (1968), *Der Eintritt der südlichen Hemisphäre in die europäische Geschichte: Die Erschliessung des Afrikaweges nach Asien vom Zeitalter Heinrichs des Seefahrers bis zu Vasco da Gama*, Vienna: Böhlau.

Hamilton, J. J. (2016), "Hobbes on Felicity: Aristotle, Bacon and Eudaimonia," *Hobbes Studies*, 29: 129–47.

Hampton, J. (1986), *Hobbes and the Social Contract Tradition*, Cambridge: Cambridge University Press.

Hampton, T. (1997), "The Subject of America: History and Alterity in Montaigne's Des Coches," in E. Fowler and R. Greene (eds), *The Project of Prose in Early Modern Europe and the New World*, 80–103, Cambridge: Cambridge University Press.

Hanke, L. (1949), *The Spanish Struggle for Justice in the Conquest of America*, Philadelphia: University of Pennsylvania Press.

Hanke, L. (1959), *Aristotle and the American Indians: A Study of Race Prejudice in the Modern World*, London: Hollis & Carter.

Hanke, L. (1974), *All Mankind is One: A Study of the Disputation between Bartolomé de Las Casas and Juan Ginés de Sepúlveda in 1550 on the Intellectual and Religious Capacity of the America Indians*, De Kalb: Northern Illinois University Press.

Harley, J. B., D. Woodward, and G. Aujac (1987), "Greek Cartography in the Early Roman World," in J. B. Harley and D. Woodward (eds), *The History of Cartography*, vol. 1: *Cartography in Prehistory, Ancient, and Medieval Europe and the Mediterranean*, 161–76, Chicago and London: University of Chicago Press.

Harries, K. (2001), *Infinity and Perspective*, Cambridge, MA: MIT Press.

Harrison, R. (2003), *Hobbes, Locke, and Confusion's Masterpiece: An Examination of Seventeenth-Century Political Philosophy*, Cambridge: Cambridge University Press.

Hegel, G. F. W. (1956), *The Philosophy of History*, trans. J. Sibree, rev. J. Friedrich, New York: Dover.

Hegel, G. F. W. (1998), *Lectures on Fine Art*, 2 vols., trans. T. M. Knox, Oxford: Clarendon.

Hegel, G. F. W. (2008), *Outlines of the Philosophy of Right*, trans. T. M. Knox, rev. and ed. S. Houlgate, Oxford and New York: Oxford University Press.

Hegel, G. F W. ([1825–6] 2009), *Lectures on the History of Philosophy 1825–6*, vol. 3: *Medieval and Modern Philosophy*, ed. and trans. R. F. Brown, Oxford: Oxford University Press.

Heidegger, M. (1968), *What is Called Thinking?* trans. F. D. Wieck and J. G. Gray, New York: Harper & Row.

Heidegger, M. (1979), *Nietzsche*, vol. 1: *The Will to Power as Art*, trans. D. F. Krell, New York: Harper & Row.

Heidegger, M. (1982a), *Nietzsche*, vol. 4: *Nihilism*, trans. D. F. Krell, New York: Harper & Row.

Heidegger, M. (1982b), *The Question Concerning Technology and Other Essays*, trans. W. Lovitt, New York: Harper & Row.

Heidegger, M. (1996), *Being and Time: A Translation of "Sein und Zeit"*, trans. J. Stambaugh, 7th edn, Albany: SUNY Press.

Heidegger, M. (2002), *Off the Beaten Track*, trans. J. Young and K. Haynes, New York: Cambridge University Press.

Heidegger, M. (2003), "Overcoming Metaphysics," in *The End of Philosophy*, ed. J. Stambaugh, 84–110, Chicago: University of Chicago Press.

Heidegger, M. (2010), *Being and Time: A Translation of "Sein und Zeit"*, trans. J Stambaugh, revised D. J. Schmidt, Albany: SUNY Press.

Heidegger, M. (2012), *Contributions to Philosophy: Of the Event*, trans. R. Rojcewicz and D. Vallega-Neu, Bloomington: Indiana University Press.

Heilen, S. (2000a), "Die Anfänge der wissenschaftlichen Geographie: Anaximander und Hekataios," in W. Hübner (ed.), *Geschichte der Mathematik und der Naturwissenschaften in der Antike*, vol. 2: *Geographie und verwandte Wissenschaften*, 33–54, Wiesbaden: Steiner.

Heilen, S. (2000b), "Eudoxos von Knidos und Pytheas von Massalia," in W. Hübner (ed.), *Geschichte der Mathematik und der Naturwissenschaften in der Antike*, vol. 2: *Geographie und verwandte Wissenschaften*, 55–74, Wiesbaden: Steiner.

Hengstermann, C. (2016), *Origenes und der Ursprung der Freiheitsmetaphysik*, Münster: Aschendorff.

Hennig, R. (1944–54), *Terrae Incognitae: Eine Zusammenstellung und kritische Bewertung der wichtigsten Entdeckungsreisen an Hand der darüber vorliegenden Originalberichte*, 4 vols, 2nd edn, Leiden: Brill.

Hermes Trismegisthos (1960), *Corpus Hermeticum*, vol. 1: *Traités 1–11*, ed. A. D. Nock, trans. A.-F. Festugière, Paris: Les Belles Lettres.

Herodotus (1920), *Histories*, trans. A. D. Godley, Cambridge, MA: Harvard University Press.

Herold, N. (1975), *Menschliche Perspektive und Wahrheit: Zur Deutung der Subjektivität in den philosophischen Schriften des Nikolaus von Kues*, Münster: Aschendorff.

Herold, N. (1980), "'Subjektivität' als Problem der Cusanus-Interpretation," *Mitteilungen und Forschungsbeiträge der Cusanus-Gesellschaft*, 14: 146–66.

Hill, J. S. (1997), *Infinity, Faith, and Time: Christian Humanism and Renaissance Literature*, Montreal and London: McGill-Queens University Press.

Hindess, B. (2007), "Locke's State of Nature," *History of the Human Sciences*, 20 (3): 1–20.

Hobbes, T. (1962), *The English Works of Thomas Hobbes of Malmesbury*, 11 vols., ed. W. Molesworth, repr., Aalen: Scientia Verlag.

Hobbes, T. (1972), *De homine*, in B. Gert (ed.), *Man and Citizen*, 33–86, Garden City, NY: Doubleday and Company.

Hobbes, T. (1983a), *De cive: The Latin Version Entitled in the First Edition "Elementorum philosophiae section tertia de cive" and in Later Editions "Elementa philosophica de cive"*, ed. H. Warrender, Oxford: Clarendon.

Hobbes, T. (1983b), *De cive: The English Version Entitled in the First Edition "Philosophical Rudiments Concerning Government and Society"*, ed. H. Warrender, Oxford: Clarendon.

Hobbes, T. (1994), *The Elements of Law, Natural and Politic*, ed. J. C. A. Gaskin, Oxford: Oxford University Press.

Hobbes, T. (2010), *Behemoth or the Long Parliament*, ed. P. Seaword, Cambridge: Cambridge University Press.

Hobbes, T. (2012), *Leviathan*, ed. N. Malcolm, Oxford: Oxford University Press.

Hoekstra, K. (2007), "Hobbes on the Natural Condition of Mankind," in P. Springborg (ed.), *The Cambridge Companion to Hobbes's Leviathan*, 109–27, Cambridge: Cambridge University Press.

Hoff, J. (2013), *The Analogical Turn: Rethinking Modernity with Nicholas of Cusa*, Grand Rapids, MI: Wm. B. Eerdmans.

Höffe, O. (1993), *Moral als Preis der Moderne: Ein Versuch über Wissenschaft, Technik und Umwelt*, Frankfurt am Main: Suhrkamp.

Höffe, O. (1999), *Demokratie im Zeitalter der Globalisierung*, Munich: Beck.

Höffner, J. (1969), *Kolonialismus und Evangelium: Spanische Kolonialethik im Goldenen Zeitalter*, 2nd edn, Trier: Paulinus-Verlag.

Holland, T. (2005), *Persian Fire: The First Wold Empire and the Battle for the West*, London: Abacus.

Hopkins, J., ed. (2001), *Complete Philosophical and Theological Treatises of Nicholas of Cusa*, 2 vols., trans. J. Hopkins, Minneapolis: AJ Banning.

Horace (2004), *Odes and Epodes*, trans. and ed. N. Rudd, Cambridge, MA: Harvard University Press.

Horkheimer, M. (1978), "The Authoritarian State," in A. Arato and E. Gebhardt (eds), *The Essential Frankfurt School Reader*, 95–117, New York: Urizen.

Horkheimer, M. (1989), "Notes on Crisis and Science," in S. E. Bronner and D. M. Kellner (eds), *Critical Theory and Society: A Reader*, 52–7, London: Routledge.

Horkheimer, M. (1993a), "Materialism and Morality," in M. Horkheimer, *Between Philosophy and Social Science: Selected Early Writings*, trans. G. F. Hunter, M. S. Kramer, and J. Torpey, 15–47, Cambridge, MA: MIT Press.

Horkheimer, M. (1993b), "Montaigne and the Function of Skepticism," in M. Horkheimer, *Between Philosophy and Social Science: Selected Early Writings*, trans. G. F. Hunter, M. S. Kramer, and J. Torpey, 265–311, Cambridge, MA: MIT Press.

Horkheimer, M. and T. W. Adorno ([1947] 2002), *Dialectic of Enlightenment*, trans. E. Jephcott, Stanford: Stanford University Press.

Horst, U. (1995), "Einleitung: Leben und Werk von Francisco de Vitoria," in U. Horst and H.-G. Justenhoven (eds), *Vitoria: Vorlesungen (Relectiones)*, vol. 1, 7–99, Stuttgart: Kohlhammer.

Hossenfelder, M. (1991), *Epikur*, Munich: Beck.

Hoyer, U. (2003), "Die Stellung des Nikolaus von Kues in der Geschichte der neueren Naturwissenschaft," in K. Reinhardt and H. Schwaetzer (eds), *Nikolaus von Kues— Vordenker moderner Naturwissenschaft*, 25–43, Regensburg: Roderer.

Husserl, E. (1989), *The Crisis of European Sciences and Transcendental Phenomenology: An Introduction to Phenomenological Philosophy*, trans. D. Carr, Evanston: Northwestern University Press.

İhsanoğlu, E. (2004), "Ottoman Science: The Last Episode in Islamic Scientific Tradition and the Beginning of European Scientific Tradition," in E. İhsanoğlu (ed.), *Science, Technology and Learning in the Ottoman Empire: Western Influence, Local Institutions, and the Transfer of Knowledge*, 1–44, Aldershot, Hampshire: Ashgate Variorum.

Innarone, A. (1967), "Genesis del pensamiento colonial en Francisco de Vitoria," in L. Pereña and J. M. Perez Brendes (eds), *Francisco de Vitoria: Relectio de Indis o libertad de los indios—Edición crítica bilingüe*, xxxi–xli, Madrid: Consejo superior de investigaciónes científicas.

Irving, S. (2006), "'In a pure soil': Colonial Anxieties in the Work of Francis Bacon," *History of European Ideas*, 32: 249–62.

Isermann, M. (1991), *Die Sprachtheorie im Werk von Thomas Hobbes*, Münster: Nodus.

Isidore of Sevilla (2006), *The Etymologies of Isidore of Sevilla*, trans. and ed. St. A. Barney, W. J. Lewis, J. A. Beach, and O. Berghof, Cambridge: Cambridge University Press.

Israel, J. (2009), *A Revolution of the Mind: Radical Enlightenment and the Intellectual Origins of Modern Democracy*, Princeton: Princeton University Press.

Jackson, P. (2018), *The Mongols and the West: 1221–1410*, 2nd edn, New York: Routledge.

Jaeger, F. (2009), "Neuzeit," in F. Jaeger, *Enzyklopädie der Neuzeit*, vol. 9, columns 158–81, Stuttgart, Weimar: Metzler.

Jamme, C. (1991), *Einführung in die Philosophie des Mythos*, vol. 2: *Neuzeit und Gegenwart*, Darmstadt: Wissenschaftliche Buchgesellschaft.

Jardine, L. (1974), *Francis Bacon: Discovery and the Art of Discourse*, Cambridge: Cambridge University Press.

Jaspers, K. (1953), *The Origin and Goal of History*, trans. M. Bullock, New Haven, CT: Yale University Press.

Jaspers, K. (1964), *Nikolaus Cusanus*, Munich: Piper.

Jaspers, K. (1965), *Hoffnung und Sorge: Schriften zur deutschen Politik 1945–65*, Munich: Piper.

Jowitt, C. (2002), "'Books Will Speak Plain?' Colonialism, Jewishness and Politics in Bacon's New Atlantis," in B. Price (ed.), *Francis Bacon's New Atlantis: New*

Interdisciplinary Essays, 129–55, Manchester and New York: Manchester University Press.
Justenhoven, H.-G. (1991), *Francisco de Vitoria zu Krieg und Frieden*, Cologne: J. P. Bachem Verlag.
Jütte, R. (2004), *A History of the Senses: From Antiquity to Cyberspace*, trans. L. Lynn, Cambridge: Polity.
Kadafar, C. (1995), *Between Two Worlds: The Construction of the Ottoman State*, Berkeley: University of California Press.
Kaerst, J. (1903), *Die antike Idee der Oekumene in ihrer politischen und kulturellen Bedeutung*, Leipzig: Teubner.
Kahn, C. H. (1960), *Anaximander and the Origins of Greek Cosmology*, New York: Columbia University Press.
Kant, I. (1999), *Critique of Pure Reason*, trans. P. Guyer and A. W. Wood, Cambridge: Cambridge University Press.
Kaser, M. (1993), *Ius Gentium*, Cologne, Weimar, and Vienna: Böhlau.
Kavka, G. S. (1986), *Hobbesian Moral and Political Theory*, Princeton: Princeton University Press.
Keller, E. F. (1985), *Reflections on Gender and Science*, New Haven, CT: Yale University Press.
Kelly, P. H. (1991a), *Locke on Money*, 2 vols, Oxford: Clarendon.
Kelly, P. H. (1991b), "General Introduction: Locke on Money," in P. H. Kelly (ed.), *Locke on Money*, vol. 1, 1–121, Oxford: Clarendon.
Kersting, W. (1996), "Vertrag, Souveränität, Repräsentation: Zu den Kapiteln 17 bis 22 des 'Leviathan,'" in W. Kersting (ed.), *Thomas Hobbes: Leviathan oder Stoff, Form und Gewalt eines bürgerlichen und kirchlichen Staates*, 211–33, Berlin: Akademie-Verlag.
Kessler, E. (2005), "Menschenwürde in der Renaissance," in A. Siegetsleitner and N. Knoepffler (eds), *Menschenwürde im interkulturellen Dialog*, 41–66, Freiburg im Breisgau: Alber.
Kettner, M. (1995), "Habermas über die Einheit der praktischen Vernunft: Eine Kritik," in A. Wüstehube (ed.), *Pragmatische Rationalitätstheorien*, 5–11, Würzburg: Königshausen & Neumann.
Kirk, G. S., J. E. Raven, and M. Schofield, eds (1983), *The Presocratic Philosophers: A Critical History with a Selection of Texts*, 2nd edn, Cambridge: Cambridge University Press.
Kleingeld, P. (1999), "Six Varieties of Cosmopolitanism in Late Eighteenth-Century Germany," *Journal of the History of Ideas*, 60: 503–24.
Klempt, A. (1960), *Die Säkularisierung der universalhistorischen Auffassung: Zum Wandel des Geschichtsdenkens im 16. und 17. Jahrhundert*, Göttingen: Musterschmidt.
Kobusch, T. (1985), "Die philosophische Bedeutung des Kirchenvaters Origenes: Zur christlichen Kritik an der Einseitigkeit der griechischen Wesensphilosophie," *Theologische Quartalschrift*, 165: 94–105.

Kobusch, T. (2012), "Die Idee der Freiheit: Origenes und der neuzeitliche Freiheitsgedanke," in A. Fürst and C. Hengstermann (eds), *Autonomie und Menschenwürde: Origenes in der Philosophie der Neuzeit*, 67–80, Münster: Aschendorff.

Kobusch, T. (2015), "Origenes und Pico: Picos Oratio im Licht der spätantiken Philosophie," in A. Fürst and C. Hengstermann (eds), *Origenes humanista: Pico della Mirandolas Traktat De salute Origenis disputatio*, 141–60, Münster: Aschendorff.

Koch, B. (2005), *Zur Dis-/Kontinuität mittelalterlichen politischen Denkens in der neuzeitlichen politischen Theorie: Marsilius von Padua, Johannes Althusius und Thomas Hobbes im Vergleich*, Berlin: Duncker & Humblot.

Koch, J. (1956), *Die Ars coniecturalis des Nikolaus von Kues*, Cologne and Opladen: Westdeutscher Verlag.

Kohl, K.-H. (1986), *Entzauberter Blick: Das Bild vom Guten Wilden und die Erfahrung der Zivilisation*, Frankfurt am Main: Suhrkamp.

Koselleck, R. (2004), *Futures Past: On the Semantics of Historical Time*, trans. K. Tribe, New York: Columbia University Press.

Koslowski, P. (1993), *Politik und Ökonomie bei Aristoteles*, 3rd edn, Tübingen: Mohr.

Koyré, A. (1958), *From the Closed World to the Infinite Universe*, New York: Harper.

Krämer, H. J. (1959), *Arete bei Platon und Aristoteles: Zum Wesen und zur Geschichte der platonischen Ontologie*, Heidelberg: Winter.

Kraynak, R. P. (1990), *History and Modernity in the Thought of Thomas Hobbes*, Ithaca and London: Cornell University Press.

Kremer, K. (1998), "Die Einheit des menschlichen Geistes (der Seele) und die Vielheit seiner (ihrer) Kräfte bei Nikolaus von Kues," in M. Thurner (ed.), *Die Einheit der Person: Beiträge zur Anthropologie des Mittelalters*, 357–72, Stuttgart: Kohlhammer.

Kristeller, O. (1965), "Giovanni Pico della Mirandola and his Sources," in *L'opera e il pensiero di Giovanni Pico della Mirandola nella storia dell' umanesimo: Convegno internazionale* (Mirandola, 15–18 September 1963), vol. 1: *Relazioni*, 35–142, Florence: Istituto Nazionale di Studi sul Rinascimento.

Kritzman, L. D. (2009), *The Fabulous Imagination: On Montaigne's Essays*, New York: Columbia University Press.

Krohn, W. (1987), *Francis Bacon*, Munich: Beck.

Labhardt, A. (1960), "Curiositas: Notes sur l'histoire d'un mot et d'une notion," *Museum Helveticum*, 17: 206–24.

La Charité, R. (1970), "The Relationship of Judgement and Experience in the Essais of Montaigne," *Studies in Philology*, 61 (1): 31–40.

Lai, T. (1973), "Nicholas of Cusa and the Finite Universe," *Journal of the History of Philosophy*, 11: 161–7.

La Mettrie, J. O. de (2012), *Machine Man and Other Writings*, ed. and trans. A. Thomson, Cambridge: Cambridge University Press.

Lantigua, D. M. (2020), *Infidels and Empires in a New World Order: Early Modern Spanish Contributions to International Legal Thought*, Cambridge: Cambridge University Press.

Las Casas, F. B. de (1988), *Obras completas*, vol. 9: *Apología*, ed. A. Losada, Madrid: Alianza.
Las Casas, F. B. de (1992), *Obras completas*, vol. 10: *Tratados 1552*, ed. R. Hernández and L. Galmés, Madrid: Alianza.
Lawrence, J. N. H. (2001), "Europe and the Turks in Spanish Literature of the Renaissance and Early Modern Period," in N. Griffiths (ed.), *Culture and Society in Habsburg Spain*, 17–33, London: Tamesis.
Leinkauf, T. (2006), *Nicolaus Cusanus: Eine Einführung*, Münster: Aschendorff.
Lenski, N. (2021), "Slavery in the Byzantine Empire," in P. Craig, D. Eltis, S. L. Engerman, and D. Richardson (eds), *The Cambridge World History of Slavery*, vol. 2: *AD 500–AD 1420*, 453–81, Cambridge: Cambridge University Press.
León-Portilla, M. (1963), *Aztec Thought and Culture: A Study of the Ancient Nahuatl Mind*, trans. J. E. Davies, Norman: University of Oklahoma Press.
Leturia, P. (1930–1), "Maior y Vitoria ante la conquista de America," *Anuario de la Asociación Francisco de Vitoria*, 3: 43–83.
Lewis, T. J. (1978), "Acquisition and Anxiety: Aristotle's Case Against the Market," *Canadian Journal of Economics*, 11: 69–90.
Lindgren, U. (1993), "Von Ptolemäus zu Kolumbus: Das Problem der Zeit- und Ortsbestimmung," in K. Döring and G. Wörle (eds), *Antike Naturwissenschaft und ihre Rezeption*, vol. 3, 90–113, Bamberg: Collibri.
Livy (1919), *History of Rome*, vol. 1, books 1–2, trans. O. Foster, Cambridge, MA: Harvard University Press.
Lloyd, S. A. (2018), "The Moral Assessment of Human Curiosity in Hobbes' Leviathan," in G. Paganini (ed.), *Curiosity and the Passions of Knowledge from Montaigne to Hobbes*, 353–74, Rome: Bardi Edizioni.
Lloyd, S. A. (2019), *Interpreting Hobbes' Political Philosophy*, Cambridge: Cambridge University Press.
Lloyd, S. A. (2021), "The State of Nature as a Continuum Concept," in M. P. Adams (ed.), *A Companion to Hobbes*, 156–79, Hoboken, NJ: Wiley Blackwell.
Locke, J. ([1664] 1988), *Essays on the Law of Nature and Associated Writings*, ed. W. V. Leyden, 2nd edn, Oxford: Clarendon.
Locke, J. ([1669] 1997), "The Fundamental Constitutions of Carolina," in M. Goldie (ed.), *John Locke: Political Essays*, 160–81, Cambridge: Cambridge University Press.
Locke, J. ([1674] 1997), "Trade," in M. Goldie (ed.), *John Locke: Political Essays*, 221–2, Cambridge: Cambridge University Press.
Locke, J. ([1690] 1970), *Two Treatises of Government*, ed. P. Laslett, 2nd edn, Cambridge: Cambridge University Press.
Locke, J. ([1692] 1991), "Some Considerations of the Consequences of the Lowering of Interest, and Raising the Value of Money," in P. H. Kelly (ed.), *Locke on Money*, vol. 1, 203–342, Oxford: Clarendon.
Locke, J. ([1693] 1997a), "For a General Naturalisation," in M. Goldie (ed.), *John Locke: Political Essays*, 322–5, Cambridge: Cambridge University Press.

Locke, J. ([1693] 1997b), "Labour," in M. Goldie (ed.), *John Locke: Political Essays*, 326–8, Cambridge: Cambridge University Press.
Locke, J. ([1695] 1997), "Venditio," in M. Goldie (ed.), *John Locke: Political Essays*, 339–42, Cambridge: Cambridge University Press.
Locke, J. ([1695] 1999), *The Reasonableness of Christianity as Delivered in the Scriptures*, ed. J. C. Higgins-Biddle, Oxford: Clarendon.
Locke, J. ([1696] 1991), "Further Considerations of the Lowering of Interest, and Raising the Value of Money," in P. H. Kelly (ed.), *Locke on Money*, vol. 2, 399–482, Oxford: Clarendon.
Locke, J. ([1697] 1997), "An Essay on the Poor Law," in M. Goldie (ed.), *John Locke: Political Essays*, 182–98, Cambridge: Cambridge University Press.
Locke, J. ([1700] 1990), *Essay Concerning Human Understanding*, ed. P. H. Nidditch, Oxford: Clarendon.
Lohlker, R. (2019), "Global History: Understanding Islamic Astronomy," *ACTA VIA SERICA*, 4 (2): 97–118.
Losada, A. (1949), *Juan Ginés de Sepúlveda a través de su "Epistolario" y nuevos documentos*, Madrid: Consejo Superior de Investigaciónes Científicas.
Losada, A. (1971), "The Controversy between Sepúlveda and Las Casas in the Junta of Valladolid," in J. Friede and B. Keen (eds), *Bartolomé de las Casas: Toward an Understanding of the Man und His Work*, 279–307, De Kalb: Northern Illinois University Press.
Losada, A. (1978), "La polémica entre Sepúlveda y Las Casas: La 'Junta de Valladolid' (1550–1551)," *Cuadernos de Investigaciónes Históricas*, 2: 552–89.
Lubac, H. (1974), *Pic de la Mirandole: Études et Discussions*, Paris: Montaigne.
Lucian of Samosata (2000), "*Alethon diegematon [verae historiae]*," in *Lucian in Eight Volumes*, vol. 1, ed. and trans. A. M. Harmon, 248–357, Cambridge, MA: Harvard University Press.
Lucretius (1924), *On the Nature of Things*, trans. W. H. D. Rouse, rev. M. F. Smith, Cambridge, MA: Harvard University Press.
Ludwig, B. (1998), *Die Wiederentdeckung des Epikureischen Naturrechts: Zu Thomas Hobbes' philosophischen Entwicklung vom De Cive zum Leviathan im Pariser Exil 1640–1651*, Frankfurt am Main: Klostermann.
Lupher, D. A. (2002), *Romans in a New World: Classical Models in Sixteenth-Century Spanish America*, Ann Arbor: University of Michigan Press.
Lyotard, J.-F. (1991), *The Inhuman: Reflections on Time*, trans. G. Bennington and R. Balby, Cambridge: Polity.
Lyotard, J.-F. (1992), *The Postmodern Explained: Correspondence 1982–1985*, trans. D. Barry, B. Maher, J. Petanis, V. Spate, and M. Thomas, Minneapolis: University of Minnesota Press.
MacLean, I. (1996), *Montaigne Philosophe*, Paris: Press Université de France.
Macpherson, C. B. (1962), *The Political Theory of Possessive Individualism: Hobbes to Locke*, Oxford: Oxford University Press.

Maffie, J. (2014), *Aztec Philosophy: Understanding a World in Motion*, Boulder: University Press of Colorado.
Mahoney, E. P. (1994), "Giovanni Pico della Mirandola and Origen on Humans, Choice and Hierarchy," *Vivens Homo: Revista Teologica Fiorentina*, 5: 359–76.
Maior Ioannes (1519), *In secundum librum sententiarum*, 2nd edn, Paris: J. Granjon.
Malcolm, N. (2002), *Aspects of Hobbes*, Oxford: Clarendon.
Mall, R. A. (2000), *Intercultural Philosophy*, Lanham: Rowman & Littlefield.
Manning, C. E. (1989), "Stoicism and Slavery in the Roman Empire," *ANRW*, 36 (3): 1518–43.
Maqbul, A. S. (1992), "Cartography of al Sharif al-Idrisi," in J. B. Harley and D. Woodward (eds), *The History of Cartography*, vol. 2.1, 156–74, Chicago: University of Chicago Press.
Maravall, J. A. (1984), *Las comunidades de Castilla: Una primera revolución moderna*, 4th edn, Madrid: Alianza.
Marchi, D. M. (1994), *Montaigne among the Moderns: Receptions of the "Essais"*, Oxford: Berhahn Books.
Marshall, J. (1994), *John Locke: Resistance, Religion and Responsibility*, Cambridge: Cambridge University Press.
Martí, J. ([1891] 2002), "Our America," in J. Martí, *Selected Writings*, ed. and trans. E. Allen, New York: Penguin.
Martin, R. W. (2022), "A Reevaluation of the Role of War Captives in the Aztec Empire," *Latin American Antiquity*, 33 (1): 1–15.
Martinet, J.-L. (1998), *La notion de "dignitas hominis" dans les "Essais" de Montaigne*, Bordeaux: Presses Universitaires du Septentrion.
Martinich, A. P. (2011), "The Sovereign in the Political Thought of Hanfeizi and Thomas Hobbes," *Journal of Chinese Philosophy*, 38 (1): 64–72.
Maskell, D. (1982), "The Evolution of the Essais," in I. D. McFarlane and I. MacLean (eds), *Montaigne: Essays in Memory of Richard Sayce*, 13–34, Oxford: Clarendon.
Mattox, J. M. (2006), *Saint Augustine and the Theory of Just War*, London: Continuum.
McEvoy, J. (1973), "Microcosm and Macrocosm in the Writings of St. Bonaventure," in J. G. Bougerol (ed.), *S. Bonaventura II*, 309–43, Grottaferrata: Colegio S. Bonaventura.
McFarlane, I. D. (1968), "Montaigne and the Concept of Imagination," in D. R Haggis (ed.), *The French Renaissance and its Heritage*, 117–37, London: Methuen.
McKinley, M. B. (2001), "Lire les 'Essais': 1969-1997—Lecture de la lecture," in N. Peacock and J. J. Supple (eds), *Lire les "Essais" de Montaigne: Acte du Colloque de Glasgow 1997*, 15–26, Paris: Éditions Champion.
McKnight, S. (2006), *The Religious Foundations of Francis Bacon's Thought*, Columbia and London: University of Missouri Press.
McNeilly, F. S. (1968), *The Anatomy of Leviathan*, London, Melbourne, and Toronto: Macmillan.
Méchoulan, H. (1974), *L'Antihumanisme de J. G. de Sepúlveda: Étude Critique du "Democrates Primus"*, Paris: Mouton.

Meier-Oeser, S. (1989), *Die Präsenz des Vergessenen: Zur Rezeption der Philosophie des Nicolaus Cusanus vom 15. bis zum 18. Jahrhundert*, Münster: Aschendorff.

Meijer, M. S. (1983), "Guesswork or Facts: Connections between Montaigne's Last Three Chapters (III: 11, 12 and 13)," *Yale French Studies*, 64: 167–87.

Meikle, S. (1995), *Aristotle's Economic Thought*, Oxford: Clarendon.

Mendieta, E. (2003), "Introduction," in E. Mendieta (ed.), *Latin American Philosophy: Currents, Issues, Debates*, 1–8, Bloomington: Indiana University Press.

Mendieta, E. (2020), "Critique of Decolonial Reason: On the Philosophy of the Calibans," *Graduate Faculty Philosophy Journal*, 41 (1): 1–27.

Mensching, G. (2005), "Die Rechtfertigung von Unfreiheit im Denken des Hochmittelalters," in E. Hermann-Otto (ed.), *Unfreie Arbeits- und Lebensverhältnisse von der Antike bis in die Gegenwart*, 117–29, Hildesheim: Olms.

Merchant, C. (1982), *The Death of Nature: Women, Ecology and the Scientific Revolution*, London: Wildwood House.

Mette, H. J. (1936), *Sphairopoiia: Untersuchungen zur Kosmologie des Krates von Pergamon*, Munich: Beck.

Mignolo, W. (2003), *The Darker Side of the Renaissance: Literacy, Territoriality, & Colonization*, 2nd edn, Ann Arbor: University of Michigan Press.

Mignolo, W. (2005), *The Idea of Latin America*, Oxford: Wiley-Blackwell.

Mignolo, W. (2011), *The Darker Side of Western Modernity: Global Futures, Decolonial Options (Latin America Otherwise)*, Durham, NC: Duke University Press.

Mikhail, A. (2020), *God's Shadow: Sultan Selim, His Ottoman Empire, and the Making of the Modern World*, New York: Liveright Publishing.

Miller, C. L. (2003), *Reading Cusanus: Metaphor and Dialectic in a Conjectural Universe*, Washington, DC: Catholic University of America Press.

Miltner, F. (1952), "Der Okeanos in der persischen Weltreichsidee," *Saeculum*, 3: 522–55.

Miquel, A. (1967–88), *La géographie humaine du monde musulman jusqu'au milieu du 11 siècle*, 4 vols., Paris: Mouton.

Monnerjahn, E. (1960), *Giovanni Pico della Mirandola: Ein Beitrag zur philosophischen Theologie des italienischen Humanismus*, Wiesbaden: Franz Steiner Verlag.

Montaigne, M. de (1958), *The Complete Essays*, trans. D. M. Frame, Stanford: Stanford University Press.

Montaigne, M. de (1965), *Essais*, ed. P. Villey, rev. V.-L. Saulnier, Paris: Presses Universitaires de France.

Moretti, G. (1993), "The Other World and the 'Antipodes': The Myth of the Unknown Countries between Antiquity and the Renaissance," in W. Haase and R. Meyer (eds), *The Classical Tradition and the Americas*, vol. 1, 241–84, Berlin and New York: de Gruyter.

Muldoon, J. (1994), *The Americas in the Spanish World Order: The Justification for Conquest in the Seventeenth Century*, Philadelphia: University of Pennsylvania Press.

Muldoon, J. (1999), *Empire and Order: The Concept of Empire, 800–1800*, London: Macmillan.

Muldoon, J. (2006), "Francisco De Vitoria and Humanitarian Intervention," *Journal of Military Ethics*, 5 (2): 128–43.

Muldoon, J. (2015), *Popes, Lawyers, and Infidels: The Church and the Non-Christian World, 1250–1550*, Philadelphia: University of Pennsylvania Press.

Müller, K. E. (1980), *Geschichte der antiken Ethnographie und ethnologischen Theoriebildung*, 2 vols., Wiesbaden: Steiner.

Münkler, H. (2001), *Thomas Hobbes*, Frankfurt am Main: Campus.

Münkler, H. (2005), *Imperien: Die Logik der Weltherrschaft—vom Alten Rom bis zu den Vereinigten Staaten*, Berlin: Rowohlt.

Muñoz Machado, S. (2012), *Biografía de Juan Ginés de Sepúlveda*, in *Juan Ginés de Sepúlveda: Obras completas*, vol. 17, Pozoblanco: Ayuntamiento.

Myers, K. A. (2007), *Fernández de Oviedo's Chronicle of America: A New History for a New World*, Austin: University of Texas Press.

Myrdal, G. (1944), *An American Dilemma: The Negro Problem and Modern Democracy*, New York: Harper & Brothers.

Nagel, F. (1984), *Nicolaus Cusanus und die Entstehung der exakten Wissenschaften*, Münster: Aschendorff.

Nagel, F. (1986), "Nicolaus Cusanus zwischen Ptolemäus und Kepler," *Mitteilungen und Forschungsbeiträge der Cusanus-Gesellschaft*, 17: 235–50.

Nagl-Docekal, H. (2004), *Feminist Philosophy*, trans. K. Vester, Boulder, CO: Westview.

Navarro Reyes, J. (2007), *Pensar sin certezas: Montaigne y el arte de conversar*, Madrid: Fondo de Cultura Económica.

Nicholas of Cusa (1932), *De docta ignorantia*, trans. and ed. E. Hoffmann and R. Klibansky, Leipzig: Meiner.

Nicholas of Cusa (1944), *Directio speculantis seu de non aliud*, trans. and ed. L. Baur and P. Wilpert, Hamburg: Meiner.

Nicholas of Cusa (1959), *Opuscula I: De deo abscondito; De quaerendo Deum; De filiatione Dei; De dato patris luminum; Coniectura de ultimis diebus; De genesi*, trans. and ed. P. Wilpert, Hamburg: Meiner.

Nicholas of Cusa (1964), *Compendium*, ed. and trans. B. Decker and K. Bormann, Hamburg: Meiner.

Nicholas of Cusa (1970), *De pace fidei*, trans. and ed. R. Klibansky and H. Bascour, Hamburg: Meiner.

Nicholas of Cusa (1972), *De coniecturis*, trans. and ed. J. Koch and K. Bormann, Hamburg: Meiner.

Nicholas of Cusa (1973), *Trialogus de possest*, trans. and ed. R. Steiger, Hamburg: Meiner.

Nicholas of Cusa (1982), *De venatione sapientiae, De apice theoriae*, trans. and ed. R. Klibansky and H. G. Senger, Hamburg: Meiner.

Nicholas of Cusa (1983), *Idiota de sapientia; Idiota de mente; De staticis experimentis*, trans. and ed. R. Steiger, L. Baur, and H. G. Senger, Hamburg: Meiner.

Nicholas of Cusa (1988), *De beryllo*, trans. and ed. H. G. Senger and K. Bormann, Hamburg: Meiner.

Nicholas of Cusa (1994), *Opuscula II, 2, Fasc. 2: De theologicis complementis*, trans. and ed. A. D. Riemann and K. Bormann, Hamburg: Meiner.

Nicholas of Cusa (2000), *De visione Dei*, trans. and ed. A. D. Riemann, Hamburg: Meiner.

Nicholas of Cusa (2001), *Complete Philosophical and Theological Treatises of Nicholas of Cusa*, 2 vols, ed. and trans. J. Hopkins, Minneapolis: AJ Banning.

Nicolet, C. (1991), *Space, Geography, and Politics in the Early Roman Empire*, Ann Arbor: University of Michigan Press.

Nietzsche, F. (1985), *Daybreak: Thoughts on the Prejudices of Morality*, trans. R. J. Hollingdale, Cambridge: Cambridge University Press.

Nietzsche, F. (1997), "Schopenhauer as Educator," in F. Nietzsche, *Untimely Meditations*, ed. D. Breazeale, trans. R. J. Hollingdale, 125–94, Cambridge: Cambridge University Press.

Nietzsche, F. (1998), *Beyond Good and Evil: Prelude to a Philosophy of the Future*, trans. and ed. M. Faber, Oxford: Oxford University Press.

Niquet, M. (2002), *Moralität und Befolgungsgültigkeit: Prolegomena zu einer realistischen Diskurstheorie der Moral*, Würzburg: Königshausen & Neumann.

Nobel, T. F. X. (1984), *The Republic of St. Peter*, Philadelphia: University of Pennsylvania Press.

Nonnenmacher, G. (1989), *Die Ordnung der Gesellschaft: Mangel und Herrschaft in der politischen Philosophie der Neuzeit—Hobbes, Locke, Rousseau, Smith*, Weinheim: VCH-Verlagsgesellschaft, Acta Humaniora.

Norman, Y. A. (2011), "Disputing the 'Iron Circle': Renan, Afghani and Kemal on Islam, Science and Modernity," *Journal of World History*, 22 (4): 693–714.

Nussbaum, M. C. (2019), *The Cosmopolitan Tradition: A Noble but Flawed Ideal*, Cambridge, MA: Harvard University Press.

Nys, E. (1894), *Les Origines du Droit International*, Brussels: Cartaigne.

Offermann, U. (1991), *Christus—Wahrheit des Denkens: Eine Untersuchung zur Schrift "De docta ignorantia" des Nikolaus von Kues*, Münster: Aschendorff.

Ohnsorge, W. (1983), *Ost-Rom und der Westen: Gesammelte Aufsätze zur Geschichte der byzantinisch-abendländischen Beziehungen und des Kaisertums*, Darmstadt: Wissenschaftliche Buchgesellschaft.

Olivecrona, K. (1974), "Locke's Theory of Appropriation," *Philosophical Quarterly*, 24: 220–34.

Olivecrona, K. (1975), "The Term 'Property' in Locke's Two Treatises," *Archiv für Rechts- und Sozialphilosophie*, 61: 109–15.

Olsthoorn, J. (2019), "Self-Ownership and Despotism: Locke on Property in the Person, Divine Dominium of Human Life, and Rights-Forfeiture," *Social Philosophy & Policy*, 36 (2): 242–63.

Origen (1980), *Contra Celsum*, trans. H. Chadwick, Cambridge: Cambridge University Press.

Origen (2013), *On First Principles*, trans. G. W. Butterworth, Notre Dame, IN: Ave Maria Press.

Ovid, P. O. N. (1931), *Fasti*, trans. J. G. Frazer, rev. G. P. Goold, Cambridge, MA: Harvard University Press.

Owen, D. S. (2002), "Habermas' Developmental Logic Thesis: Universal or Eurocentric?" in D. Rasmussen and J. Swindal (eds), *Sage Masters of Modern Thought: Jürgen Habermas*, vol. 4, 239–48, London: Sage.

Paganini, G. (2012), "Passionate Thought: Reason and the Passion of Curiosity in Thomas Hobbes," in S. Ebbersmeyer (ed.), *Emotional Minds. The Passions and the Limits of Pure Inquiry in Early Modern Philosophy*, 227–56, Berlin: de Gruyter.

Paganini, G. (2018), "Introduction: Hobbes Philosopher of Curiosity," in G. Paganini (ed.), *Curiosity and the Passions of Knowledge from Montaigne to Hobbes*, 9–35, Rome: Bardi Edizioni.

Pagden, A. (1982), *The Fall of Natural Man: The American Indian and the Origins of Comparative Ethnology*, Cambridge: Cambridge University Press.

Pagden, A. (1995), *Lords of All the Worlds: Ideologies of Empire in Spain, Britain and France c. 1500–c. 1800*, New Haven, CT: Yale University Press.

Palacios Rubios, J. L. de ([1516] 1954), *De las islas del mar océano: Del dominio de los reyes de España sobre los indios*, ed. S. Zavala, trans. A. M. Carlo, Mexico City and Buenos Aires: Fondo de Cultura Económica.

Pauer, A. (1985), *Die humanitäre Intervention: Militärische und wirtschaftliche Zwangsmassnahmen zur Gewährleistung der Menschenrechte*, Basel: Helbing-Lichterhahn.

Pauly, A., G. Wissowa, W. Kroll, K. Witte, K. Mittelhaus, and K. Ziegler (eds), *Realencyclopädie der classischen Altertumswissenschaft* (Stuttgart: J. B. Metzler, 1894–1980) [*RE*].

Pečar, A. and A. Tricoire (2015), *Falsche Freunde: War die Aufklärung wirklich die Geburtsstunde der Moderne?* Frankfurt am Main: Campus.

Pellat, C. (2012), "al-Masʿūdī," in P. Bearman, T. Bianquis, C. E. Bosworth, E. van Donzel, and W. P. Heinrichs, eds, *Encyclopaedia of Islam*, 2nd edn, https://archive.org/details/in.ernet.dli.2015.529972.

Pellegrin, P. (2001), "Hausverwaltung und Sklaverei (I, 3–13)," in O. Höffe (ed.), *Aristoteles: Politik*, 37–57, Berlin: Akademie-Verlag.

Pérez-Ramos, A. (1988), *Francis Bacon's Idea of Science and the Maker's Knowledge Tradition*, Oxford: Clarendon.

Peters, J. T. (1997), *Der Arbeitsbegriff bei John Locke: Im Anhang—Lockes Plan zur Bekämpfung der Arbeitslosigkeit von 1697*, Münster: LIT-Verlag.

Pico della Mirandola, G. (1942), *De hominis dignitate; Heptaplus: De ente et uno e scritti vari*, ed. and trans. E. Garin, Florence: Vallechi.

Pico della Mirandola, G. (1986), *Commentary on a Poem of Platonic Love*, trans. D. Carmichael, Lanham, MD: University Press of America.

Pico della Mirandola, G. (2012), *Oration on the Dignity of Man: A New Translation and Commentary*, ed. and trans. F. Borghesi, M. Papio, and M. Riva, Cambridge: Cambridge University Press.

Pierson, C. (2013), *Just Property: A History in the Latin West*, vol. 1: *Wealth, Virtue, and the Law*, Oxford: Oxford University Press.

Pietschmann, H. (1987), "Aristotelischer Humanismus und Inhumanität: Sepúlveda und die amerikanischen Ureinwohner," in W. Reinhard (ed.), *Humanismus und Neue Welt*, 143–66, Weinheim: VCH-Verlagsgesellschaft, Acta Humaniora.

Pindar (1997), *Olympian Odes; Pythian Odes*, ed. and trans. W. H. Race, Cambridge, MA: Harvard University Press.

Plato (1989), *Opera*, ed. I. Burnet, 5 vols, Oxford: Clarendon.

Plato (1997), *Complete Works*, ed. J. M. Cooper and D. S. Hutcheson, Indianapolis: Hackluyt.

Plutarch (1936), *De E apud Delphos*, in *Plutarch: Moralia*, vol. 5., trans. F. C. Babbitt, 201–53, Cambridge, MA: Harvard University Press.

Plutarch (2004), *Plutarch's Lives in Eleven Volumes*, vol. 7: *Demosthenes and Cicero, Alexander and Caesar*, trans. B. Perrin, repr., Cambridge, MA: Harvard University Press.

Polybius (2010), *The Histories*, trans. W. R. Paton, rev. F. W. Walbank and C. Habicht, Cambridge, MA: Harvard University Press.

Pomponazzi, P. (1948), "On the Immortality of the Soul," in E. Cassirer, P. O. Kristeller, and J. H. Randall, Jr. (eds), *The Renaissance Philosophy of Man: Petrarca, Valla, Ficino, Pico, Pomponazzi, Vives—Selections in Translation*, 280–381, Chicago and London: University of Chicago Press.

Pomponius Mela (1998), *Description of the World*, trans. F. E. Romer, Ann Arbor: University of Michigan Press.

Popkin, R. H. (2003), *The History of Scepticism: From Savonarola to Bayle*, rev. and expanded edn, Oxford: Oxford University Press.

Popper, K. (2002), *The Logic of Scientific Discovery*, London and New York: Routledge.

Porter, R. (2000), *Enlightenment: Britain and the Creation of the Modern World*, London: Lane.

Pouilloux, J.-Y. (1969), *Lire les "Essais" de Montaigne*, Paris: Maspero.

Preiser, W. (1978), *Macht und Norm in der Völkerrechtsgeschichte*, Baden-Baden: Nomos.

Prem, H. J. (2008), *Geschichte Altamerikas*, 2nd edn, Munich: Oldenbourg.

Price, B., ed. (2002), *Francis Bacon's New Atlantis: New Interdisciplinary Essays*, 129–55, Manchester and New York: Manchester University Press.

Priddat, B. P. (1988), *Das Geld und die Vernunft: Die vollständige Erschliessung der Erde durch vernunftgemässen Gebrauch des Geldes—Über John Lockes Versuch einer naturrechtlich begründeten Ökonomie*, Frankfurt am Main: Lang.

Priddat, B. P. (1998), *Theologie, Ökonomie, Macht: Eine Rekonstruktion der Ökonomie John Lockes*, Marburg: Metropolis Verlag.

Quijano, A. (2000), "Coloniality of Power, Eurocentrism, and Latin America," *Nepantla Views South*, 1 (3): 533–80.
Quijano, A. (2014), "Colonialidad del poder y clasificación social," in A. Quijano, *Cuestiones y horizontes: De la dependencia histórica-estructural a la colonialidad/descolonialidad del poder*, 236–72, ed. D. Assis Clímaco, Buenos Aires: CLASCO.
Rabin, S. J. (2007), "Pico on Magic and Astrology," in M. V. Dougherty (ed.), *Pico della Mirandola: New Essays*, 152–78, Cambridge: Cambridge University Press.
Ramos, S. (1985), "Historia de la filosofía en México (1943)," in Samuel Ramos, *Obras completas*, vol. 2, 97–231, 2nd edn, Mexico City: Universidad Nacional Autónoma de México.
Randles, W. G. L. (1993), "Classical Models of World Geography and their Transformation following the Discovery of America," in W. Haase and R. Meyer (eds), *The Classical Tradition and the Americas*, vol. 1, 5–76, Berlin and New York: de Gruyter.
Rapp, C. (2004), "Grenzen des Seins: Die Diskussion um die Grenzen des Seienden in der Ontologie der vorsokratischen Philosophien," in W. Hogrebe and J. Bromand (eds), *Grenzen und Grenzüberschreitungen: XIX. Deutscher Kongress für PhilosophieVorträge und Kolloquien*, 40–53, Berlin: Akademie-Verlag.
Redondo Redondo, M. L. (1992), *Utopia vitoriana y realidad indiana*, Madrid: Fundación Universitaria Española.
Rehg, W. (1997), *Insight and Solidarity: The Discourse Ethics of Jürgen Habermas*, 2nd edn, Berkeley: University of California Press.
Reibstein, E. (1958), *Völkerrecht: Eine Geschichte seiner Ideen in Lehre und Praxis*, vol. 1: *Von der Antike bis zu Aufklärung*, Freiburg im Breisgau: Alber.
Reinhardt, H. (1987), "Die Lehre vom Willen bei Richard von St. Viktor und bei Giovanni Pico della Mirandola," *Zeitschrift für philosophische Forschung*, 41: 383–407.
Reinhardt, H. (1989), *Freiheit zu Gott: Der Grundgedanke des Systematikers Giovanni Pico della Mirandola (1463–1494)*, Weinheim: VCH-Verlagsgesellschaft, Acta Humaniora.
Reschke, R., ed. (2004), *Nietzsche—radikaler Aufklärer oder Gegenaufklärer?* Berlin: Akademie-Verlag.
Rigolot, F. (1992), "What is Civilization? Montaigne's Response to Columbus, 1492, 1592, 1992," *Princeton University Library Chronicle*, 54: 8–23.
Rio, A. (2021), "Slavery in the Carolingian Empire," in P. Craig, D. Eltis, S. L. Engerman, and D. Richardson (eds), *The Cambridge World History of Slavery*, vol. 2: *AD 500–AD 1420*, 431–52, Cambridge: Cambridge University Press.
Roberts, J. (2004), "The Dialectic of Enlightenment," in F. Rush (ed.), *The Cambridge Companion to Critical Theory*, 57–73, Cambridge: Cambridge University Press.
Roetz, H. (1993), *Confucian Ethics of the Axial Age: A Reconstruction under the Aspect of the Breakthrough towards Postconventional Thinking*, Albany: SUNY Press.

Rogers, F. M. (1955), "The Vivaldi Expedition," *Annual Report of the Dante Society*, 73: 31–45.
Romm, J. (1992), *The Edges of the Earth in Ancient Thought: Geography, Exploration, and Fiction*, Princeton: Princeton University Press.
Rorty, R. (1989), *Contingency, Irony, and Solidarity*, Cambridge: Cambridge University Press.
Rorty, R. (1998), "Human Rights, Rationality, and Sentimentality," in R. Rorty, *Truth and Progress: Philosophical Papers*, 168–85, Cambridge: Cambridge University Press.
Roseman, C. H. (1994), *Pytheas of Massalia: On the Ocean—Text, Translation and Commentary*, Chicago: Ares.
Rosenthal, E. (1971), "'Plus ultra, non plus ultra', and the Columnar Device of Emperor Charles V," *Journal of the Warburg and Courtauld Institutes*, 44: 204–28.
Rossi, P. (1968), *Francis Bacon: From Magic to Science*, Chicago: University of Chicago Press.
Roth, H. I. (2016), "Peng Chun Chang, Intercultural Ethics and the Universal Declaration of Human Rights," in G. Collste (ed.), *Ethics and Communication: Global Perspectives*, 103–23, London: Rowman & Littlefield.
Rovira Gaspar, M. del C. (2004), *Francisco de Vitoria: España y América—El poder y el hombre*, Mexico City: Conocer para decidir—H. Cámara de diputados LIX legislatura.
Russell, J. B. (1991), *Inventing the Flat Earth*, New York: Praeger.
Ryan, A. (1984), *Property and Political Theory*, Oxford: Basil Blackwell.
Sabundus, R. (1966), *Theologia naturalis seu Liber creaturarum*, facsimile reprint of the Sulzbach edition 1852, ed. F. Stegmüller, Stuttgart-Bad Cannstatt: Frommann-Holzboog.
Salazar Bondy, A. ([1969] 1988), *¿Existe una filosofía de nuestra América?* 11th edn, Mexico City: Siglo XXI.
Sánchez, C. A. (2019), "Authenticity and the Right to Philosophy: On Latin American Philosophy's Great Debate," in K. Becker and I. D. Thomson (eds), *The Cambridge History of Philosophy, 1945–2015*, 679–90, Cambridge: Cambridge University Press.
Sartre, J.-P. (1963), "Preface," in F. Fanon, *The Wretched of the Earth*, trans. Constance Farrington, 8–30, New York: Grove Press.
Sartre, J.-P. (1976), *Black Orpheus*, trans. S. W. Allen, Paris: Présence Africaine.
Sayce, R. A. (1972), *The "Essais" of Montaigne: A Critical Exploration*, London: Weidenfeld & Nicolson.
Schäfer, C. (2002), "Juan Ginés de Sepúlveda und die politische Aristotelesrezeption im Zeitalter der Konquista," *Vivarium*, 40: 241–71.
Schärf, C. (1999), *Geschichte des Essays: Von Montaigne bis Adorno*, Göttingen: Vandenhoeck & Ruprecht.
Schelkshorn, H. (1992), *Ethik der Befreiung: Einführung in die Philosophie Enrique Dussels*, Freiburg im Breisgau, Basel, and Vienna: Herder.

Schelkshorn, H. (1997), *Diskurs und Befreiung: Studien zur philosophischen Ethik von Karl-Otto Apel und Enrique Dussel*, Amsterdam: Rodopi.

Schelkshorn, H. (2004), "Dialogische Vernunft und die Grundlagen interkultureller Ethik: Thesen zu einer Revision der Diskursethik," in N. Gottschalk-Mazouz (ed.), *Perspektiven der Diskursethik*, Würzburg: Königshausen & Neumann.

Schmid Noerr, G. (1997), *Gesten: Konstellationen der Kritischen Theorie*, Frankfurt am Main: Fischer.

Schmidt-Biggemann, W. (1983), *Topica universalis: Eine Modellgeschichte humanistischer und barocker Wissenschaft*, Hamburg: Meiner.

Schmitt, C. (2003), *The Nomos of the Earth in the International Law of the Jus Publicum Europaeum*, trans. G. L. Ulmen, New York: Telos.

Schnädelbach, H. (1989), "Die Aktualität der 'Dialektik der Aufklärung,'" in H. Kunnemann and H. de Vries (eds), *Die Aktualität der "Dialektik der Aufklärung": Zwischen Moderne und Postmoderne*, 15–35, Frankfurt am Main and New York: Campus.

Schnär, M. (1979), *Das Nachleben des Origenes im Zeitalter des Humanismus*, Basel and Stuttgart: Helbing & Lichtenhahn.

Schneewind, J. B. (1994), "Locke's Moral Philosophy," in V. Chappell (ed.), *The Cambridge Companion to Locke*, 199–225, Cambridge: Cambridge University Press.

Schockenhoff, E. (2012), "Die Wirkungsgeschichte des Origenes," in A. Fürst and C. Hengstermann (eds), *Autonomie und Menschenwürde: Origenes in der Philosophie der Neuzeit*, 47–68, Münster: Aschendorff.

Schofield, M. (1991), *The Stoic Idea of the City*, Chicago: University of Chicago Press.

Scholten, A. (1982), "Islamisches Denken und Geographie im Mittelalter," in M. Büttner (ed.), *Zur Entwicklung der Geographie vom Mittelalter bis Carl Ritter*, 9–19, Paderborn: Schöningh.

Schulz, R. (1993), *Die Entwicklung des römischen Völkerrechts im vierten und fünften Jahrhundert n. Chr.*, Stuttgart: Steiner.

Schulz, R. (2003), "Roms Eroberung des Mittelmeeres und der Vorstoss in den Atlantik: Reaktionen und Rückwirkungen auf die Ideologie, Geographie, Ethnographie und Anthropologie der späten Republik und frühen Kaiserzeit," in R. Schulz (ed.), *Aufbruch in neue Welten und neue Zeiten: Die grossen maritimen Expansionsbewegungen der Antike und frühen Neuzeit im Vergleich der europäischen Geschichte*, 29–50, Munich: Oldenburg.

Schulz, R. (2005), *Die Antike und das Meer*, Darmstadt: Primus.

Schumpeter, J. A. (1954), *History of Economic Analysis*, ed. and trans. E. B. Schumpeter, Oxford: Oxford University Press.

Schüssler, R. (2002), "Die humanitäre Intervention in der Doktrin des gerechten Krieges," in E. Müller, P. Schneider, and K. Thony (eds), *Menschenrechtsschutz: Politische Massnahmen, zivilgesellschaftliche Strategien, humanitäre Interventionen*, 200–17, Baden-Baden: Nomos.

Schütrumpf, E. (1982), "Einleitung," in Xenophon, *Poroi/Vorschläge zur Beschaffung von Geldmitteln oder über die Staatseinkünfte*, trans. and ed. E. Schütrumpf, 1–75, Darmstadt: Wissenschaftliche Buchgesellschaft.

Schütrumpf, E. (1991), *Aristoteles: Politik Buch I—Über die Hausverwaltung und die Herrschaft des Herrn über Sklaven*, trans. with commentaries E. Schütrumpf, Berlin: Akademie-Verlag.

Schwaetzer, H. (2002), "'Semen universale': Die Anthroplogie bei Nikolaus von Kues und Giovanni Pico della Mirandola," in M. Thurner (ed.), *Nicolaus Cusanus zwischen Deutschland und Italien*, 555–74, Berlin: Akademie-Verlag.

Schwoebel, R. (1967), *The Shadow of the Crescent: The Renaissance Image of the Turk (1453–1517)*, Nieuwkoop: de Graf.

Scott, J. B. (1934), *The Spanish Origins of International Law: Francisco de Vitoria and his Law of Nations*, Oxford: Clarendon.

Seagrave, S. A. (2016), "Locke on the Law of Nature and Natural Rights," in M. Stuart (ed.), *A Companion to Locke*, 373–94, Malden: Wiley-Blackwell.

Seaman, J. W. (1990), "Hobbes on Public Charity & the Prevention of Idleness: A Liberal Case for Welfare," *Polity*, 23 (1): 105–26.

Seliger, M. (1968), *The Liberal Politics of John Locke*, London: George Allen & Unwin Ltd.

Seneca, L. A. (1917), *Hercules Furens; Troades; Medea; Hippolytus; Oedipus*, trans. F. J. Miller, Cambridge, MA: Harvard University Press.

Seneca, L. A. (1932), *Moral Essays*, vol. 2: *De Consolatione ad Marciam; De Vita Beata; De Otio; De Tranquillitate Animi; De Brevitate Vitae; De Consolatione ad Polybium; De Consolatione ad Helviam*, trans. J. W. Basore, Cambridge, MA: Harvard University Press.

Seneca, L. A. (1933), *Moral Essays*, vol. 3: *De Beneficiis*, trans. John W. Basore, Cambridge, MA: Harvard University Press.

Seneca, L. A. (1971–2), *Naturales quaestiones/Natural Questions*, 2 vols, trans. T. H. Corcoran, Cambridge, MA: Harvard University Press.

Seneca, L. A. (1996), *Suasoriae*, ed. and trans. W. A. Edward, Bristol: Bristol Classical.

Sepúlveda, J. G. de (1997a), "Democrates segundo o sobre las justas causas de la guerra," in *Juan Ginés de Sepúlveda: Obras completas*, vol. 3, ed. and trans. A. Coroleu Lletget, 37–134, Pozoblanco: Ayuntamiento.

Sepúlveda, J. G. de (1997b), "Apologia pro libro De iusti belli causis," in *Juan Ginés de Sepúlveda: Obras completas*, vol. 3, ed. A. Moreno Hernández, trans. Á. Losada, 189–222, Pozoblanco: Ayuntamiento.

Sepúlveda, J. G. de (2001), "De Regno: Acerca de Monarquía," in *Juan Ginés de Sepúlveda: Obras completas*, vol. 6, ed. and trans. I. J. García Pinilla, 45–103, Pozoblanco: Ayuntamiento.

Sepúlveda, J. G. de (2003), "Cohortatio ad Carolum V," in *Juan Ginés de Sepúlveda: Obras completas*, vol. 7, ed. and trans. B. Cuart Monder, 327–46, Pozoblanco: Ayuntamiento.

Sepúlveda, J. G. de (2007), "*Epistolario: Cartas* (1459–1557), " in *Juan Ginés de Sepúlveda: Obras completas*, vol. 10.2, ed. I. J. García Pinilla, trans. I. J. Solana Pujalte, 76–139, Pozoblanco: Ayuntamiento.

Sepúlveda, J. G. de (2010), "Democrates," in *Juan Ginés de Sepúlveda: Obras completas*, vol. 15, ed. J. Solana Pujalte, trans. I. J. García Pinilla, 80–192, Pozoblanco: Ayuntamiento.

Serjeantson, R. (2002), "Natural Knowledge the New Atlantis," in B. Price (ed.), *Francis Bacon's New Atlantis: New Interdisciplinary Essays*, 82–105, Manchester and New York: Manchester University Press.

Serulnikov, S. (2013), *The Revolution in the Andes: The Age of Tupac Amaru*, Durham, NC: Duke University Press.

Sessions, W. A. (1996), *Francis Bacon Revisited*, London: Twayne.

Seubold, Günter (1986), *Heideggers Analyse neuzeitlicher Technik*, Freiburg im Breisgau: Alber.

Simek, R. (1992), *Erde und Kosmos im Mittelalter: Das Weltbild vor Kolumbus*, Munich: Beck.

Simmons, A. J. (1992), *The Lockean Theory of Rights*, Princeton: Princeton University Press.

Skinner, Q. (1978), *The Foundations of Modern Political Thought*, 2 vols, Cambridge: Cambridge University Press.

Skinner, Q. (2002), *Visions of Politics*, vol. 2: *Renaissance Virtues*, Cambridge: Cambridge University Press.

Skinner, Q. (2018), *From Humanism to Hobbes: Studies in Rhetoric and Politics*, Cambridge: Cambridge University Press.

Smith, M. J. (1986), *Realist Thought from Weber to Kissinger*, Baton Rouge: Louisiana State University Press.

Soder, J. (1955), *Die Idee der Völkergemeinschaft: Francisco de Vitoria und die philosophischen Grundlagen des Völkerrechts*, Frankfurt am Main: Metzner.

Spaemann, R. (1996), "Bürgerliche Ethik und nichtteleologische Ontologie," in H. Ebeling (ed.), *Subjektivität und Selbsterhaltung: Beiträge zur Diagnose der Moderne*, 76–96, Frankfurt am Main: Suhrkamp.

Spelman, E. V. (1994), "Who is Who in the Polis," in B.-A. Bar On (ed.), *Engendering Origins: Critical Feminist Readings in Plato and Aristotle*, 99–126, Albany: SUNY Press.

Starobinski, J. (1985), *Montaigne in Motion*, trans. A. Goldhammer, Chicago: University of Chicago Press.

Steiger, H. (1992), "Völkerrecht," in O. Brunner, W. Conze, and R. Koselleck (eds), *Geschichtliche Grundbegriffe: historisches Lexikon zur politisch-sozialen Sprache in Deutschland*, vol. 7, 97–140, Stuttgart: Klett-Cotta.

Strabo (1917–32), *Geography*, 8 vols, ed. and trans. H. L. Jones, Cambridge, MA: Harvard University Press.

Strauss, L. (1952), *The Political Philosophy of Hobbes: Its Basis and its Genesis*, trans. E. M. Sinclair, Chicago: University of Chicago Press.

Strauss, L. (1965), *Natural Right and History*, Chicago and London: University of Chicago Press.

Strunk, N. R. (2019),"Motion, Space, and Early Modern Re-formations of the Cosmos: Nicholas of Cusa's Anima Mundi and Henry More's Spirit of Nature," in S. J. G. Burton, J. Hollmann, and E. M. Parker (eds), *Nicholas of Cusa and the Making of the Early Modern World*, 307–35, Leiden and Boston: Brill.

Struve, T. (1978), *Die Entwicklung der organologischen Staatsauffassung im Mittelalter*, Stuttgart: Hiersemann.

Stückelberger, A. (1965), *Senecas 88. Brief*, Heidelberg: C. Winter.

Stückelberger, A. (1987), "Kolumbus und die antiken Wissenschaften," *Archiv für Kulturgeschichte*, 69: 331–40.

Stückelberger, A. (2000), "Klaudius Ptolemaios," in W. Hübner (ed.), *Geschichte der Mathematik und der Naturwissenschaften in der Antike*, vol. 2: *Geographie und verwandte Wissenschaften*, 185–208, Wiesbaden: Steiner.

Sudduth, M. (2007), "Pico Mirandola's Philosophy of Religion," in M. V. Dougherty (ed.), *Pico della Mirandola: New Essays*, 61–80, Cambridge: Cambridge University Press.

Suetonius, T. C. (1914), *The Lives of the Caesars*, vol. 1: *Julius; Augustus; Tiberius; Gaius; Caligula*, Cambridge, MA: Harvard University Press.

Szabó, A. (1992), *Das geozentrische Weltbild: Astronomie, Geographie und Mathematik der Griechen*, Munich: Deutscher Taschenbuchverlag.

Tacitus, P. C. (1914), "Germania," in P. C. Tacitus, *Agricola: Germania*, trans. M. Hutton and W. Peterson, rev. R. M. Ogilvie, E. H. Warmington, and M. Winterbottom, 118–219, Cambridge, MA: Harvard University Press.

Tarn, W. W. (1951), *Alexander the Great*, vol. 2: *Sources and Studies*, Cambridge: Cambridge University Press.

Taylor, C. (1989), *Sources of the Self: The Making of Modern Identity*, Cambridge, MA: Harvard University Press.

Tertullian, Q. S. F. (1931), "Apology," in Tertullian, Minucius Felix, *Apology: De Spectaculis: Minucius Felix: Octavius*, ed. and trans. T. R. Glover and H. Gerald H. Rendall, 2–229, Cambridge, MA: Harvard University Press.

Theobald, M. (2000), *Der Römerbrief*, Darmstadt: Wissenschaftliche Buchgesellschaft.

Thierney, B. (1982), *Religion, Law, and the Growth of Constitutional Thought 1150–1650*, Cambridge: Cambridge University Press.

Thomä, D. (2006), "Eine Philosophie des Lebens jenseits des Biologismus und diesseits der 'Geschichte der Metaphysik': Bemerkungen zu Nietzsche und Heidegger mit Seitenblicken auf Emerson, Musil und Cavell," in A. Denker, M. Heinz, J. Sallis, B. Vedder, and H. Zaborowski (eds), *Heidegger-Jahrbuch 2: Heidegger und Nietzsche*, 265–96, Freiburg im Breisgau: Alber.

Thomas Aquinas (1920), *Summa theologica: The Summa theologica of St. Thomas Aquinas*, trans. fathers of the Engl. Dominican province, 2nd edn, London: Burns & Washbroune.

Thomas Aquinas (1947), *On Kingship to the King of Cyprus*, trans. G. B. Phelan, rev. I. T. Eschmann, Westport, CT: Hyperion.

Thomas Aquinas (1980), *Opera omnia*, ed. R. Busa, Stuttgart-Bad Cannstatt: Frommann-Holzboog, http://www.corpusthomisticum.org/orp.html.

Thumfahrt, J. (2012), *Die Begründung der globalpolitischen Philosophie: Francisco de Vitorias Vorlesung über die Entdeckung Amerikas im ideengeschichtlichen Kontext*, Berlin: Kadmos.

Thumfart, A. (1996), *Die Perspektive und die Zeichen: Hermetische Verschlüsselungen bei Giovanni Pico della Mirandola*, Munich: Fink.

Tibullus (1995), *Elegies*, ed. and trans. G. Lee, 3rd edn, repr., Liverpool: Cairns.

Todorov, T. (1984), *The Conquest of America: The Question of the Other*, New York: Harper & Row.

Töpfer, B. (1999), *Urzustand und Sündenfall in der mittelalterlichen Gesellschafts- und Staatstheorie*, Stuttgart: Hiersemann.

Tolan, J. V. (1996), *Medieval Christian Perceptions of Islam*, New York: Routledge.

Toulmin, S. (1990), *Cosmopolis: The Hidden Agenda of Modernity*, Chicago: University of Chicago Press.

Tournon, A. (2000), *La Glose et l'essai*, 2nd edn, Paris: Champion.

Tricaud, F. (1988), "Hobbes' Conception of the State of Nature from 1640 to 1651: Evolution and Ambiguities," in G. A. J. Rogers and A. Ryan (eds), *Perspectives on Thomas Hobbes*, 107–23, Oxford: Clarendon.

Trinkaus, C. (1970), *In Our Image and Likeness: Humanity and Divinity in Italian Humanist Thought*, 2 vols, London: Constable.

Trinkaus, C. (1976), "Protagoras in the Renaissance: An Exploration," in E. P. Mahoney (ed.), *Philosophy and Humanism: Essays in Honour of Paul Oskar Kristeller*, 190–221, Leiden: Brill.

Truglia, C. (2010), "Al-Ghazali and Giovanni Pico della Mirandola on Human Freedom and the Chain of Being," *Philosophy East & West*, 60 (2): 143–66.

Tuck, R. (1979), *Natural Rights Theories: Their Origin and Development*, Cambridge: Cambridge University Press.

Tully, J. (1980), *A Discourse on Property: John Locke and his Adversaries*, Cambridge: Cambridge University Press.

Tully, J. (1993), *An Approach to Political Philosophy: Locke in Contexts*, Cambridge: Cambridge University Press.

Turner, D. (1995), *The Darkness of God: Negativity in Christian Mysticism*, Cambridge: Cambridge University Press.

Turner, J. (2011), "John Locke, Christian Mission, and Colonial America," *Modern Intellectual History*, 8 (2): 267–97.

Tuschling, B. (2005), "Recht? Gerechtigkeit? Cicero, Karneades, Hobbes pro et contra ius naturae," in D. Hüning (ed.), *Der lange Schatten des Leviathan: Hobbes' politische Philosophie nach 350 Jahren*, 109–42, Berlin: Duncker & Humblot.

Unruh, P. (2002), "Die Gleichheit der Menschen bei Antiphon dem Sophisten," in S. Kirste, K. Waechter, and M. Walther (eds), *Die Sophistik: Entstehung, Gestalt und Folgeprobleme des Gegensatzes von Naturrecht und positivem Recht*, 59–82, Wiesbaden: Steiner.

Urbach, P. (1987), *Francis Bacon's Philosophy of Science: An Account and Reappraisal*, La Salle, IL: Open Court.

Valéry, P. (1989), *The Outlook for Intelligence*, trans. D. Foliot and J. Mathews, Princeton: Princeton University Press.

Vansteenberghe, E., ed. (1910), *Le "De ignota litteratura" de Jean Wenck de Herrenberg contre Nicolas de Cuse*, Münster: Aschendorff.

Vaughn, K. I. (1980), *John Locke: Economist and Social Scientist*, Chicago: University of Chicago Press.

Velthoven, T. van (1977), *Gottesschau und menschliche Kreativität*, Leiden: Brill.

Vickers, B. (1968), *Francis Bacon and Renaissance Prose*, Cambridge: Cambridge University Press.

Vickers, B. (1984), "Bacon's So-Called 'Utilitarianism': Sources and Influence," in M. Fattori (ed.), *Francis Bacon: Terminologia e Fortuna nel XVII Secolo*, 281–313, Rome: Edizioni dell'Ateneo.

Villey, P. (1933), *Les Sources et l'Évolution des Essais de Montaigne*, 2nd edn, Osnabrück: Zeller.

Virgil (1916), *Eclogues; Georgics; Aeneid*, books 1–6, ed. and trans. H. Rushton Fairclough, rev. G. P. Goold, Cambridge, MA: Harvard University Press.

Vitoria, F. de (1960), *Obras de Francisco de Vitoria*, ed. T. Urdañoz, Madrid: Biblioteca de Autores Cristianos.

Vitoria, F. de (1967), *Relectio de Indis o Libertad de los Indios*, ed. and trans. L. Pereña and J. M. Perez Prendes, Madrid: Consejo superior de investigaciónes científicas.

Vitoria, F. de (1991), *Political Writings*, ed. A. Pagden, trans. J. Lawrance, Cambridge: Cambridge University Press.

Vitoria, F. de (1995–7), *Vorlesungen: Relectiones*, 2 vols, ed. and trans. U. Horst, H.-G. Justenhoven, and J. Stüben, Stuttgart: Kohlhammer.

Vlastos, G. (1981), *Platonic Studies*, 2nd edn, Princeton: Princeton University Press.

Vogel, H. U. (2013), *Marco Polo was in China: New Evidence from Currencies, Salts and Revenues*, Leiden: Brill.

Vogt, J. (1960), *Orbis: Ausgewählte Schriften zur Geschichte des Altertums*, Freiburg im Breisgau, Basel, and Vienna: Herder.

Waldron, J. (1988), *The Right to Private Property*, Oxford: Clarendon.

Waldron, J. (2002), *God, Locke, and Equality: Christian Foundations in Locke's Political Thought*, Cambridge: Cambridge University Press.

Wallerstein, I. (2006), *European Universalism: The Rhetoric of Power*, New York: New Press.

Waszink, J. H. (1980), "Die Vorstellungen von der 'Ausdehnung der Natur' in der griechisch-römischen Antike und im frühen Christentum," in E. Dassmann (ed.), *Pietas, Festschrift für B. Kötting*, 30–8, Münster: Aschendorff.

Watkins, J. W. N. (1973), *Hobbes's System of Ideas*, 2nd edn, London: Hutchinson.

Watts, P. M. (1982), *Nicolaus Cusanus: A Fifteenth-Century Vision of Man*, Leiden: Brill.
Weber, M. ([1921–2] 2019), *Economy and Society*, ed. and trans. K. Tribe, Cambridge, MA: Harvard University Press.
Weber, M. (1947), "Science as a Vocation," in *From Max Weber: Essay in Sociology*, ed. and trans. H. H. Gerth and C. Wright Mills, 129–56, London: Kegan.
Weinberger, J. (1985), *Science, Faith, and Politics: Francis Bacon and the Utopian Roots of the Modern Age*, Ithaca and London: Cornell University Press.
Wellmer, A. (1991), *The Persistence of Modernity*, Cambridge: Polity.
Westerwelle, K. (2002), *Montaigne: Die Imagination und die Kunst des Essays*, Munich: Fink.
White, H. B. (1968), *Peace among the Willows: The Political Philosophy of Francis Bacon*, The Hague: Martinus Nijhoff.
Whitney, C. A. (1986), *Francis Bacon and Modernity*, New Haven, CT: Yale University Press.
Wicke-Reuter, U. (2000), *Göttliche Providenz und menschliche Verantwortung bei Ben Sira und in der Frühen Stoa*, Berlin and New York: Walter de Gruyter.
Wiggershaus, R. (1994), *The Frankfurt School: Its History, Theories, and Political Significance*, Cambridge, MA: MIT Press.
Williams, M. C. (2009), *The Realist Tradition and the Limits of International Relations*, Cambridge: Cambridge University Press.
Williams, R. A. (1990), *The American Indian in Western Legal Thought: The Discourses of Conquest*, New York and Oxford: Oxford University Press.
Willms, B. (1987), *Thomas Hobbes: Das Reich des Leviathan*, Munich: Piper.
Wimmer, F. M. (2004), *Interkulturelle Philosophie*, Vienna: UTB.
Winterfeld, U. von (2006), *Naturpatriarchen: Geburt und Dilemma der Naturbeherrschung bei geistigen Vätern der Neuzeit*, Munich: oekom-Verlag.
Wolfers, B. (1991), *"Geschwätzige Philosophie": Thomas Hobbes' Kritik an Aristoteles*, Würzburg: Königshausen & Neumann.
Xenophon (1923), *Xenophon IV: Memorabilia, Oeconomicus, Symposium, Apology*, trans. E. C. Marchant, Cambridge, MA: Harvard University Press.
Xenophon (1971), "Ways and Means," in Xenophon, *Scripta Minora*, ed. and trans. E. C. Marchant, 191–232, Cambridge: Cambridge University Press.
Yates, F. A. (1964), *Giordano Bruno and the Hermetic Tradition*, London: Routledge & Kegan Paul.
Zagorin, P. (1998), *Francis Bacon*, Princeton: Princeton University Press.
Zavala, S. (1944), *Servidumbre natural y libertad cristiana según los tratadistas españoles de los siglos XVI y XVII*, Buenos Aires: Faculdad de Filosofía y Letras.
Zea, L. (1942–3), *El positivismo en México: Nacimiento, apogeo y decadencia*, 2 vols., Mexico City: Fondo de Cultura Económica.
Zea, L. (1945), *En torno a una filosofía americana*, Mexico City: Colégio de México.
Zea, L. ([1969] 1989), *La filosofía americana como filosofía sin más*, 13th edn, corrected, Mexico City: Fondo de Cultura Económica.

Zea, L. (1978), *Filosofía de la historia americana*, Mexico City: Fondo de Cultura Económica.

Zea, L. (2022), "Is a Latin American Philosophy Possible?" *British Journal for the History of Philosophy*, 30 (5): 874–96.

Zimmermann, A. (1979), "'Belehrte Unwissenheit' als Ziel der Naturforschung," in K. Jacobi (ed.), *Nikolaus von Kues: Einführung in sein philosophisches Denken*, 121–37, Freiburg im Breisgau and Munich: Alber.

Zimmermann, M. E. (1990), *Heidegger's Confrontation with Modernity: Technology, Politics, and Art*, Bloomington: Indiana University Press.

Zimmermann, M. E. (2006), "Die Entwicklung von Heideggers Nietzsche-Interpretationen," in A. Denker, M. Heinz, J. Sallis, B. Vedder, and H. Zaborowski (eds), Heidegger-Jahrbuch 2: *Heidegger und Nietzsche*, 97–116, Freiburg im Breisgau and Munich: Alber.

Zuckert, M. (1994), *Natural Rights and the New Republicanism*, Princeton: Princeton University Press.

Name Index

Aarsleff, H. 351
Abel, K. 144
Abimelech, King 370
Abizadeh, A. 314, 330
Abraham (biblical figure) 370
Acosta, J. de 151, 152
Adorno, Th. W. 4, 12, 24–31, 33, 35, 59, 69, 115, 258, 273, 297, 400
Aegidius Romanus 169
Aeschylus 154
Agricola, G. I. 147
Al-Afghani, J. 7
Alberdi, J. B. 49–51, 54, 55, 57
Alberti, L. B. 117
Alcidamas 153
Alcoff, L. 58
Alexander the Great 2, 147, 155, 156, 157, 206
Alexander VI (Pope) 173
Alfonso (general) 406n7
Alfonso VI 173
Al-Ghazali 78, 136–7, 405n6
Al-Idrisi, M. 148–9
Al-Masudi 148
Al-Muqaddasi 148
Alonso-Núñez, J.-M. 158
Álvarez-Gómez, M. 105
Ambrosius 405n2
Amyot, J. 242
Anaxagoras 80
Anaximander 141–2
Andrés Marcos, T. 195, 406n6, 407n11
Anghie, A. 172, 207, 208, 210, 212
Antiphon 153
Antonin of Florence 169
Antonino of Florence 186
Apel, K.-O. viii, 4, 12, 33–5, 41, 43, 45–8, 69, 394, 403n1 (Chapter 3)
Aquinas, Thomas 78, 102–3, 105, 121, 125–6, 135, 136, 167, 169–72, 174, 177, 183, 184, 187, 191, 192, 282, 346, 356
Arcesilaus 230

Arendt, H. 299, 300, 377
Argote, F. de 189, 406n6
Aristarchus (of Samos) 93, 144
Aristippus (of Cyrene) 230
Aristotle 23, 29, 78–82, 87–90, 92, 94, 95, 102, 111, 119, 123, 125, 127, 130–3, 136, 140, 143–5, 151, 153–7, 158, 162–3, 166, 167, 171, 172, 176, 181, 183, 189, 191, 192, 194, 196, 197, 198, 199, 203, 211, 220, 238, 259, 260, 275, 316, 317, 335–8, 340, 342, 344, 377, 378–82, 384, 385, 389, 400, 402
Armitage, D. J. 348, 363–5
Árnason, J. P. 7, 41, 42, 48, 398
Arneil, B. 363
Asclepius (the Athenian) 132
Ashcraft, R. 354, 358
Aspe Armella, V. 189
Assmann, J. 303
Atuahalpa 172
Aughterson, K. 292
Augustine 70, 94, 95, 100–4, 109–11, 148, 150, 162, 166, 167, 169–71, 187, 191, 206, 216, 221, 222, 226, 262, 282, 311, 315, 405n2
Augustus 159, 160, 172
Aujac, G. 146

Bacon, F. 3, 12, 13, 23–5, 28, 69, 72, 73, 152, 255, 257–98, 300, 302, 305–7, 311, 312, 332, 333, 340, 343, 344, 346–9, 359, 369, 383, 384, 385, 387, 391, 396–402, 408n1, 408n2, 409n3, 409n4, 409n5, 409n6
Bacon, R. 150
Baldry, H. C. 153, 154, 157, 159, 161
Ban Chao 164
Baraz, M. 407n4
Bartholomew of Lucca 167
Bayly, C. 1

Beestermöller, G. 170, 187
Beierwaltes, W. 85
Beitz, C. 328
Bell, A. F. G. 189
Bellah, R. 303
Bellers, J. 153
Beneyto Pérez, J. M. 172
Benhabib, S. 44
Beorlegui, C. 49
Berlinger, R. 105
Beuchot, M. 50, 189
Bianchi, L. 78
Bichler, R. 142
Binswanger, H. C. 367, 380, 401
Bippus, H.-P. 232
Bisaha, N. 193
Bishop, J. D. 365
Blumenberg, H. 2, 4, 8–9, 30, 70, 77–9,
    93–4, 100, 102, 114, 150, 226,
    262, 269, 347, 404n2
Blum, P. R. 120, 188
Boal, A. 57
Bodin, J. 2, 224
Boethius, A. M. S. 119, 405n7
Bohórquez, C. 50
Bonaventura 121, 122, 167
Borghesi, F. 404n1
Bormann, K. 107
Bosbach, F. 174, 194
Bös, G. 95, 99, 102
Bosworth, A. B. 156
Botermann, H. 162
Bouwsma, W. J. 117
Bovillus, Ch. de 118
Box, I. 271, 288, 409n5
Brahe, T. 93, 194
Bredow, G. von 82
Brett, S. F. 167
Brewer, H. 363
Brieskorn, N. 172, 188
Briggs, J. C. 288
Brincken, A.-D. von den 141, 148–50, 166,
    168
Brocker, M. 356, 357, 411n2
Bruni, L. 344
Bruno, G. 188
Brunschvicg, L. 215
Buchheim, T. 81
Buck, A. 118, 220
Buck, G. 311

Buckle, S. 347, 349, 356
Burckhardt, J. 117, 118, 129
Bürger, P. 216, 222
Burke, P. 60, 216
Burkert, W. 143
Burstein, S. M. 164
Busche, H. 344

Caesar 146–7, 159, 160, 217, 231
Cain 263
Callicles 286, 350
Calypso 129, 138
Campanella, T. 188, 290
Camus, A. 402
Cantillon, Ph. de 375
Capizzi, J. E. 174
Carneades 338
Carrasco, D. 209
Carraud, V. 215
Casale, G. 194
Casarella, P. 77
Casas, G. 404n3
Cassirer, E. 77, 118, 215
Cassius 157
Castany Prado, B. 245
Castilla Urbaño, F. 172, 193, 194
Cato 236
Cattaneo, A. 150
Cavallar, G. 183, 209
Cerutti-Guldberg, H. 57
César, A. 6
Charité, R. C. 407n4
Charlemagne 167, 217
Charles IX (of France) 408n6
Charles V of Spain 174, 175, 178, 189, 190
Charpentier, F. 222, 226–7
Cheneval, F. 319
Cheng, Peng-Chun 397
Chiusi, T. 356
Chrysippus 157–8
Cicero, M. T. 95, 96, 98–101, 113, 114,
    132, 144, 147, 160–4, 169, 170,
    177, 180, 186, 187, 206, 220,
    228, 235–6, 259, 326, 356, 361,
    404n2 (Chapter 5)
Clarke, K. 158
Clavijero, F. J. 54
Cleisthenes 381
Clement VI (Pope) 170
Colaeus 142

Colman, J. 344, 351, 352, 358
Colomer, E. 110
Columbus, C. 11, 60, 62, 71, 139–41, 151, 152, 173, 175, 182, 216, 236, 247, 266, 268–71, 293, 390, 391
Commodus 285
Comte, A. 2
Condorcet, J. A. N. de Caritat de 26, 139
Confucius 339
Cooter, W. S. 159
Copenhaver, B. P. 118, 132, 404n2
Copernicus, N. 11, 70, 78, 93, 194, 225, 343
Corcoran, P. 365, 366
Cortés, H. 56, 59, 61, 63, 69, 198, 200
Corti Varela, J. 172
Cosmas/ Indicopleusteus 141
Crates of Mallos / Mallus 144, 145, 148, 150, 151, 159
Craven, W. G. 124
Crombie, A. C. 265

D'Ailly, P. 150
Daly, H. E. 402
D'Angelo, J. 149
Daniélou, J. 134, 135
Dante Alighieri 149, 150, 171, 172, 174, 175, 265
Darius 142
Daston, L. 312
Davenport, F. G. 173
Davis, J. C. 409n6
De Buffon, G.-L. L. 54
Deckers, D. 177, 180, 181, 183
Defaux, G. 219
de la Vera Cruz, F. A. 188–9
Delgado, M. 188
De Lubac, H. 118, 119
Democrates 196, 201
Democritus 79, 80, 157, 259, 269
De Pauw 54
De Sade, M. 28
Desan, Ph. 217
Descartes, R. 3, 12, 17–21, 58, 62, 63, 69, 72, 112, 215, 238, 255, 257, 261, 276, 299, 312, 343
De Soto 209
Dewey, J. 397
Dicaearchus 144
Didymus 98

Dijksterhuis, E. J. 257–8
Dilke, O. W. A. 144
Diodorus 156
Dionysius Areopagite 127
Dougherty, M. V. 118, 119, 127, 130, 405n7
Drusus Germanicus 145, 147
Dulles, A. 119
Dunn, J. 344, 373
Dussel, E. viii, 8, 50, 57–65, 67–9, 72, 139, 189, 200, 207, 212, 299, 334, 399, 403n1 (Chapter 3)
Duval, E. M. 248, 249

Eggers, D. 319, 322, 410n2
Einstein, A. 7
Eisenstadt, S. N. 7
Ellis, J. 257
Ellis, R. L. 408n1
Elton, H. 159
Enders, A. 408n5, 408n6
Enders, M. 89
Ennius 161, 229
Enoch 129
Epictetus 132, 285
Epicurus 30, 231, 259, 332, 350
Epimetheus 122
Erasmus (of Rotterdam) 132, 189, 190, 191, 237, 328, 406n7
Eratosthenes (of Cyrene) 141, 144, 147
Erskine, A. 157
Esfeld, M. 308, 323, 410n2
Eudoxus of Cyzicus 146
Euler, W. A. 118, 127, 137
Eusebius (of Caesarea) 166
Euthymenes of Massilia 142
Evrigenis, I. D. 304

Fanon, F. 5, 6, 67
Farmer, S. A. 137
Faroqhi, S. 193, 195
Farrington, B. 258, 259, 260, 265, 408n1, 408n2
Farr, J. 363
Faulkner, R. K. 409n6
Faustus of Mileve 100
Feldmann, E. 100
Fernández-Santamaría, J. A. 189, 192, 197, 202, 206, 406n6, 407n11

Fichte, J. G. 3
Ficino, M. 120, 137, 405n5
Figueroa, D. 181, 183
Filmer, R. 347, 348, 354, 356, 357, 362
Findley, C. V. 195
Fink-Eitel, H. 245
Fisch, J. 170, 173
Flasch, K. 77, 105, 111, 112, 113
Fornet-Betancourt, R. viii, 7
Forschner, M. x, 158, 162, 163, 187, 405n2
Foucault, M. 3, 4, 290, 375
Fra Mauro 150
Frame, D. M. 222, 407n1
Freire, P. 57
Friedrich, H. 27, 231, 233, 408n5
Fukuyama, F. 41
Funke, G. 132
Fynn-Paul, J. 167

Galen 259
Galilei, G. 255, 257, 300, 343
Gandhi, M. 6
Gaos, J. 51, 52
Garin, E. 118, 119, 133, 404n1 (Chapter 6)
Gaskin, G. S. A. 410n1
Gattinara, M. 174, 179
Gatzemeier, M. 124
Gaukroger, S. 261, 265
Gehrke, H.-J. 142
Geismann, G. 314, 320
Georgescu-Roegen, N. 402
Gerard of Cremona 149
Gerl, H. B 123
Gert, B. 410n1
Gessmann, M. 225, 226
Geus, K. 156
Gillner, M. 170, 200, 202, 204
Gisinger, F. 142, 143
Glancy, J.-A. 165
Gog 148
Goldie, M. 371, 372
Gottschalk-Mazouz, G. 43, 47
Gournay, M. de 217
Gracia, J. E. 52
Grant, E. 78, 89
Grasmück, E. L. 171
Great Khan 168
Greenblatt, St. 117
Gregory the Great 166
Grosseteste, R. 265

Grotius, H. 164, 207, 345, 348, 356, 393, 406n4, 410n2 (Chapter 11), 411n2
Güngerich, R. 142

Habermas, J. 4, 9, 12, 27, 33–48, 58, 69, 72, 139, 299, 300, 314, 394, 396, 398
Hamann, G. 152
Hamilton, J. J. 286, 340
Hampton, J. 249, 314, 319
Hanke, L. 173, 175, 189, 195
Harries, K. 84, 85
Harrison, R. 354
Heath, D. D. 408n1
Hecataeus of Miletus 142
Hegel, G. F. W. 3, 6, 12, 17, 18, 20–1, 54, 57, 58, 62, 215, 304, 410n3
Heidegger, M. 3, 4, 9, 12, 17–24, 33, 34, 62, 63, 67, 69, 71, 115, 400
Heilen, S. 142, 146
Hellenes 155
Hengstermann, C. 135
Hennig, R. 147, 149
Henry of Segusio / Hostiensis 170
Henry the Navigator 151
Heraclitus (of Ephesus) 26, 128, 157–8, 259
Herb, K. 314, 320
Hercules (Pillars of) 142, 143, 145, 266, 291, 293
Herder, J. G. 4
Hermes Trismegisthos 120, 233, 337, 404n2 (Chapter 6)
Herodotus 142, 143, 154, 158, 160
Herold, N. 82, 85, 104
Hill, J. S. 79
Hindess, B. 348, 352
Hitler, A. 212
Hobbes, T. 3, 12, 13, 63–4, 69, 72, 73, 255, 299–343, 351–2, 353, 354, 372, 386, 391, 393, 394, 397, 410n1, 410n2
Hoekstra, K. 319
Höffe, O. 153, 265, 275
Hoff, J. 77
Höffner, J. 168, 169, 188
Hölderlin, F. 22–3
Holland, T. 156
Holzhey, H. 124
Homer 26, 29, 96, 99, 132, 141, 143

Hopkins, J. 82, 404n1 (Chapter 5)
Horace 163
Horkheimer, M. 4, 12, 24–31, 35, 59, 69, 115, 215, 258, 273, 297, 400
Horst, U. 175
Hossenfelder, M. 350
Hostiensis / Henry of Segusio 170, 173, 176
Hoyer, U. 89
Huitzilopochtli 210
Huntington 41
Husserl, E. 3, 39, 62

Ibn-Battuta 149
İhsanoğlu, E. 194
Innarone, A. 172
Innocent IV (Pope) 168, 170, 171, 186
Innocent VIII (Pope) 118
Irving, S. 291
Isermann, M. 307, 310
Isidor of Sevilla 148, 170
Jackson, P. 168
James I 305
Jamme, C. 41
Jardine, L. 259
Jaspers, K. 11, 36, 118, 212, 395
John VIII Palaeologus 179
Jowitt, C. 410n7
Justenhoven, H.-G. 182
Jütte, R. 107

Kahn, C. H. 142
Kant, I. 1, 3, 18, 28, 43, 44, 54, 129, 207, 212, 261, 393
Kaser, M. 164
Kavka, G. S. 312, 314
Keller, E. F. 258, 408n2, 409n4
Kepler, J. 93
Kersting, W. 333
Kettner, M. 41
Kleingeld, P. 393
Klempt, A. 3
Kobusch, T. 119, 133, 135
Koch, B. 300
Koch, J. 105
Kohl, K.-H. 245
Koselleck, R. 3
Koyré, A. 70, 77, 78
Krämer, H. J. 131
Kraynak, R. P. 304, 305

Kremer, K. 107
Kristeller, O. 137
Kritzman, L. D. 238, 407n4
Krohn, W. 258, 261, 268, 272, 276, 278, 290, 409n6

Labhardt, A. 95
La Boétie, E. de 218
La Charité, R. 407n4
Lactantius 141, 405n2
Lai, T. 89
La Mettrie, J. O. de 392, 393
Lantigua, D. M. 174
Las Casas, F. B. de 55, 56, 61–3, 67, 69, 72, 140, 173, 195, 197, 198, 200, 201, 204, 206, 209, 211, 212, 244, 247, 364, 406n9, 406n10, 407n10, 407n11
Laslett, P. 410n1 (Chapter 11)
Lawrence, J. N. H. 193
Leibniz, G. W. 6
Leinkauf, T. 86
Lenski, N. 167
Leo I. (Pope) 166
Léon-Portilla, M. 50, 200, 210, 211
Leo the Great 166
Léry, J. de 408n5
Leturia, P. 173
Liebig, J. von 257
Lindgren, U. 148
Livy 160
Lloyd, S. A. 311, 314, 327, 330
Locke, J. 12, 13, 72, 73, 255, 322, 342–80, 382–8, 391, 396–8, 400, 411n1 (Chapter 11), 411n2 (Chapter 11), 411n3
Lohlker, R. 194
Lombard, P. 405n4 (Chapter 6)
Lopéz de Gomara 408n5
Losada, A. 189, 190, 200, 211, 406n5, 407n11
Löwith, K. 9
Lubac, H. 118, 119
Lucian of Samosata 146
Lucifer 125
Lucretius 336, 337
Ludwig, B. 315, 326, 332
Lupher, D. A. 175
Luther, M. 28, 57, 58, 188, 406n7
Lyotard, J.-F. 4, 5, 58, 215

McEvoy, J. 121
McFarlane, I. D. 238
Machiavelli, N. 59–60, 192, 287, 300, 328
McKinley, M. B. 219
McKnight, S. 261, 296
MacLean, I. 224
McNeilly, F. S. 320, 410n2
Macpherson, C. B. 299, 318, 319, 334, 344, 373, 385
Macrobius 148
Magnus, Albertus 78, 150
Mahoney, E. P. 119, 133
Mair, John 173, 174
Malcolm, N. 328, 331, 410n1
Mall, R. A. 7, 8, 50
Malocelli, L. 149
Manetti, G. 110
Manning, C. E. 163
Maqbul, A. S. 149
Maravall, J. A. 192
Marchi, D. M. 215
Marcianus Capella 148
Marco Polo 149, 405n1
Marcus Aurelius 99, 101, 164
Marshall, J. 344, 346
Martí, J. 54
Martinet, J.-L. 232, 233, 242
Martinich, A. P. 339
Martin, R. W. 209
Marx, K. 2, 4, 24, 73, 377, 403n1
Maskell, D. 217
Mattox, J. M. 169
Méchoulan, H. 192
Mehmet II 194
Meier-Oeser, S. 78, 93
Meijer, M. S. 224
Meikle, S. 379, 380
Melissus 81
Mendieta, E. 49, 50, 65
Menéndez Pelayo, M. 406n5
Mengzi 336
Mensching, G. 167
Merchant, C. 258, 409n3, 409n4
Mesalla Corvinus 159
Metrodorus 230
Mette, H. J. 144
Mignolo, W. 50, 65–7, 69, 172, 207, 399
Mikhail, A. 194
Miller, C. L. 105
Mill, J. St. 402

Miltner, F. 156
Miquel, A. 148
Moctezuma 60, 200
Moctezuma, 61, 189
Molina, L. 188
Monnerjahn, E. 127, 133
Montaigne, M. de 12, 62, 72, 215–53, 260, 261, 287, 289, 292, 293, 300, 302, 311, 312, 320, 321, 325, 329, 349, 391, 392, 398, 407n1, 407n2, 407n3, 407n4, 408n5, 408n6
Montesinos, A. de 175
More, T. 118
Moretti, G. 146
Moses 122, 129
Muldoon, J. 168, 170, 171, 210
Müller, K. E. 142
Münkler, H. 172, 322
Muñoz Machado, S. 190, 192
Myers, K. A. 406n9
Myrdal, G. 33

Nagel, F. 90, 93
Nagl-Docekal, H. 258, 409n4
Navarro Reyes, J. 216
Necho (Pharoah) 142
Nemesis 402
Nero 285
Nezahualcóyotl 211
Nicholas of Cusa 12, 70, 77–9, 81–93, 102–15, 117, 137, 140, 152, 219, 223, 226, 234–7, 265, 275, 297, 307, 312, 348, 390–2, 403n1, 404n1, 407n3
Nicholas V (Pope) 173
Nicolet, C. 159, 160
Nidditch, P. H. 410n1 (Chapter 11)
Nietzsche, F. 3, 4–5, 17, 21, 28, 34, 62, 67, 72, 215, 392, 403n1
Niquet, M. 43
Nobel, Th. F. X. 168
Nonnenmacher, G. 322, 344
Norman, Y. A. 7
Nussbaum, M. C. 162
Nys, E. 172

Ockham, W. of 180, 346–7
Odysseus 25, 96, 149–50, 404n2 (Chapter 5)

Offermann, U. 82
Ohnsorge, W. 168
Olivecrona, K. 358, 410n2
Olsthoorn, J. 357
Oresme, N. 89
Origen 119, 130, 133–136, 405n2
Orpheus 129
Ortega y Gasset, J. 52
Osorio, J. 408
Ovid, P. O. N. 160
Oviedo, F. de 61, 63, 197, 200, 406n9
Owen, D. 41

Paganini, G. 310, 312
Pagden, A. 163, 165, 166, 167, 172
Palacios Rubios, J. L. de 174
Panaetius 160-1
Panaitios 196, 199, 211
Papio, M. 404n1 (Chapter 1)
Park, K. 312
Parmenides (of Elea) 81, 90, 144
Pascal, B. 401
Pauer, A. 406n4
Paul (apostle) 165, 174, 405n2
Paul III (Pope) 196
Pečar, A. 4
Pellat, C. 148
Pellegrin, P. 378
Penelope 150
Peréz-Ramos, A. 106, 276
Peters, J. T. 366, 378
Petrarch, F. 94
Philip II 189
Philo of Alexandria 404n3
Piano Carpini, John of / Pian di Carpine 168
Pico della Mirandola, Gianfrancesco 118, 131
Pico della Mirandola, Giovanni 12, 71, 110, 117–38, 202, 203, 212, 216, 287, 346, 385, 404n1
Pierson, C. 356
Pietschmann, H. 189
Pindar 143
Pio, A. 202
Plato 79, 84, 90, 92, 94–6, 107–11, 120, 122, 129, 132, 143, 144, 153–5, 157, 158, 220, 221, 246, 259, 260, 269, 337, 350, 380, 397, 404n3

Plautus 183
Pliny 273
Plotinus 111
Plutarch 146, 156, 157, 220, 221, 242, 259, 407n2
Pollock, F. 27
Polonos, B. 168
Polybius 158-60
Pomponazzi, P. 189, 202
Pomponius Mela 145, 146
Popkin, R. H. 215
Popper, K. 257
Porter, R. 2
Poseidonios 141
Posidonius 146, 147
Pouilloux, Y. 219
Preiser, W. 153, 169
Price, B. 290
Priddat, B. P. 341, 359, 370, 375, 377, 384
Prometheus 122, 309
Protagoras 20, 99, 111, 122, 123, 234–5, 237, 260, 336, 337, 405n5
Proteus 129, 132, 287–8
Ptolemy, C. 78, 90, 93, 144, 145, 147–51
Pufendorf, S. 345, 356, 393, 406n4
Pyrrho of Elis 220, 407n2
Pyrrhus 241, 259
Pythagoras 96, 260, 269
Pytheas 146

Quijano, A. 64, 65, 67

Rabin, S. J. 131
Ramos, S. 51
Randles, W. G. L. 149, 150, 151
Rapp, C. 81
Rawley, W. 409n5, 409n6
Redondo Redondo, M. L 208
Rehg, W. 44
Reibstein, E. 405n2
Reinhardt, H. 123, 131, 136
Renan, E. 7
Reschke, R. 5
Rigolot, F. 253
Rio, A. 167
Riva, M. 404n1 (Chapter 1)
Roetz, H. 336, 339
Roger II 148
Rogers, F. M. 149
Roig, A. A. 57

Romm, J. 143, 147
Rorty, R. 5, 133, 392
Roseman, C. H. 146
Rossi, P. 275, 276, 287
Roth, H. I. 397
Rousseau, J.-J. 4
Rovira Gaspar, M. del C. 176
Roy, Raman Mohan 6
Russell, J. B. 141
Ryan, A. 370

Sabundus, R. 231, 232
Salazar Bondy, A. 50, 52–7, 66, 67
Sánchez, C. A. 54, 55
Sappho 99
Sartre, J.-P. 5, 6, 8, 67, 118, 119, 129, 133, 392
Sassoferrato, B. 180
Saulnier, V.-L. 407n1
Sayce, R. A. 223
Schäfer, C. 189, 196
Schärf, C. 222
Schelkshorn, H. 9, 47, 403n1 (Chapter 3)
Schmid Noerr, G. 24
Schmidt-Biggemann, W. 259
Schmitt, C. 9, 66, 207, 299, 300
Schnädelbach, H. 26
Schnär, M. 133
Schneewind, J. B. 344
Schockenhoff, E. 130, 133
Schofield, M. 157
Scholten, A. 148
Schulz, R. 146, 147, 164
Schumpeter, J. A. 343
Schüssler, R. 187
Schütrumpf, E. 377, 378, 381
Schwaetzer, H. 137
Schwoebel, R. 193
Scipio Aemilianus, C. 158
Scott, J.B. 172
Seagrave, S. A. 358
Seneca, L. A. 95, 97–101, 113, 114, 132, 146, 147, 150, 158, 163, 165, 220, 233, 242, 259, 336, 337, 407n2
Senghor, S. L. 6
Sepúlveda, J. G. de 12, 55, 56, 61, 69, 72, 140, 141, 173, 189–213, 244, 247, 248, 289, 299, 302, 313, 315, 316, 325, 329, 348, 363, 364, 393, 394, 406n5, 406n6,
406n7, 406n8, 406n9, 406n10, 407n10, 407n11
Serjeantson, R. 291
Serulnikov, S. 50
Servius, M. 146
Sessions, W. A. 261, 287
Sigüenza y Gongoras, C. de 50
Simek, R. 141
Simmons, A. J. 359
Simon of Saint-Quentin 168
Skinner, Q. 300, 333
Skylax of Caryanda 142
Socrates 48, 78, 83, 101, 228, 236, 252, 286, 407n2
Soder, J. 172
Solomon (Biblical) 84, 261, 264, 296
Spaemann, R. 339
Spedding, J. 408n1
Spelman, E. V. 153
Spinoza, B. de 26
Starobinski, J. 218, 407n4
Steiger, H. 164, 170, 180
Strabo 145, 147, 149, 160, 164
Strauss, L. 299, 319, 344, 377
Strunk, N. R. 91
Struve, T. 171, 199
Stückelberger, A. 141, 144, 148, 149, 150
Sudduth, M. 129
Suetonius, T. C. 163
Szabó, A. 141

Tacitus, P. C. 145
Tagore, R. 7
Taylor, Ch. 4, 216
Tempier, E. 78
Tertullian 166
Tethys 147
Thales of Miletus 226, 269, 382
Theobald, M. 405n2
Theophrastus 237
Thierney, B. 300
Thomä, D. 403n1 (Chapter 1)
Thumfahrt, J. 208
Thumfart, A. 125, 175, 208
Tiberius 147
Tibullus 159
Tiening, G. 172
Tlacaélel 210–11
Todorov, T. 189
Tolan, J. V. 193

Töpfer, B. 167
Toulmin, S. 215
Tournon, A. 246, 407n2
Tricaud, F. 308, 410n2
Tricoire, A. 4
Trinkaus, C. 122, 405n4, 405n5
Truglia, C. 136, 405n6
Truman, H. L. 33
Tuck, R. 300
Tully, J. 358, 359, 363, 365, 370, 371
Túpac Amaru II 50
Turgot 26
Turner, D. 121
Turner, J. 387
Tuschling, B. 338, 339

Ulcurrun, M. de 175, 179
Unruh, P. 153
Urbach, P. 257

Valéry, P. 7
Vansteenberghe, E. 104
Vasco da Gama 11, 71, 141, 151, 152, 390
Vattel, E. de 365
Vaughn, K. I. 372, 375, 383
Velthoven, T. van 82, 109
Vickers, B. 259
Villey, P. 218, 231, 407n1, 407n2, 407n3, 408n5
Virgil 146, 159
Vitoria, F. de 12, 66, 67, 69, 71, 72, 140, 141, 152, 153, 172–3, 175–89, 192, 195–7, 200, 201, 203–13, 216, 219, 244, 252, 289, 293, 294, 316, 328, 329, 344, 363, 365, 385, 386, 390, 393, 396–9, 405n3, 405n4
Vivaldi, U. 149
Vivaldi, V. 149
Vivekananda, S. 7
Vives, J. L. 118, 119, 190
Vlastos, G. 153
Vogel, H. U. 405n1
Vogt, J. 160, 163, 166

Waldron, J. 344, 358, 364, 371, 387
Wallerstein, I. 189, 210
Warrender, H. 410n1
Waszink, J. H. 132
Watts, P. M. 105, 108, 112, 137
Weber, M. 3, 39, 377, 378
Weinberger, J. 290
Wellmer, A. 46
Wenck, J. 103, 104
Westerwelle, K. 238
White, H. B. 290
Whitney, Ch. A. 261, 265, 290, 291, 294
Wicke-Reuter, U. 130
Wiggershaus, R. 27
William III 363
William of Conches 150
William of Ockham *see* Ockham, W. of
William of Rubruck 168
Williams, M. C. 328
Williams, R. A. 210
William the Conquerer 383
Willms, B. 299
Wimmer, F. M. viii, 7, 8
Winterfeld, U. von 258, 409n3, 409n4
Wolfers, B. 335
Wolff, Christian 6

Xenophon 309, 381–2
Xunxi 336

Zagorin, P. 275, 283, 408n2
Zarathustra 129
Zavala, S. 167
Zea, L. 50, 51, 52, 54, 55, 56, 57, 66, 67, 205
Zenon of Citium 157, 158, 161
Zeno of Elea 99, 157
Zeus 123, 132, 337
Zimmerman, M. E. 17, 22
Zimmermann, A. 89
Zoroaster 120
Zuckert, M. 345, 348

Subject Index

absolute, the 18, 21, 85–7, 90–2, 103–5, 114, 115, 186, 193
   docta ignorantia, rule of 91
   and the finite 87, 89
   God as 88, 111
   knowledge of 226
   minimum and maximum concepts 86, 87
   of monarchy 362
   non-knowing thinking of 104
   philosophy of 103, 390
   as *posse ipsum* 112
   present in all things of creation 90–1
absolutism
   theocratic 352
   theological 78, 347
accumulation of capital 355
   limitless 344, 385, 388
Acosta, J. de 152
   Historia natural y moral de las Indias 151
Adorno, T. W. 4, 33, 35, 69, 115, 258, 273, 297, 400
   Dialectic of Enlightenment 12, 24–31, 59
Adv. Learn see under Bacon, F.
aesthetics 1, 18
Africa
   circumnavigation of 142, 151
   civilizing/civilized regions 160
   geographic worldviews 148–50, 151
   intercultural philosophy 7
   modernity discourses 6–7
   moral duties of peoples in 348
   and *oikumene* see oikumene (continent of Europe, Asia and North Africa)
   Portuguese exploration 151–2
age of discovery 62, 141–52
age of enlightenment 4, 9, 13, 213
   see also The Enlightenment; enlightenment
agricultural societies 360–1, 363, 365
   commercial agriculture 367, 368
   pre-monetary 383

Al-Ghazali 78, 136–7, 405n6
   Alchemy of Happiness 136
Al-Idrisi, M.
   Compendium of the Properties of Diverse Plants and Various Kinds of Simple Drugs 148
   world map 148–9
Al-Masudi, *Murudj al dhaba* 148
altruism 315, 319, 330, 351
Americas
   appropriation of land in see land, appropriation of
   Carolina, constitution of 365
   conquest of see Conquista of the Americas
   contemporary 293
   cultural backwardness that Europeans perceived in 293–4
   "discovery" of 2, 60, 70, 151, 219, 268, 269, 390
   age of discovery 141–52
   and Europe 250, 251, 252
   expansion of Iberian powers to 174
   Five Nations Confederacy 387
   independent civilization of 249
   Montaigne on 223, 245, 246–7, 252
   Oviedo's portrayal of 406n9
   as "a Pattern of the first Ages in Asia and Europe" 370
   peoples of 54, 235, 245, 246, 293, 312, 327, 355, 356, 365
      indigenous peoples of North America 363, 365, 368, 371
      moral duties of 348
   projections on 244–53
   slaves in see natural slavery of barbarians, alleged; slavery
   still to be discovered territories in 173
   see also Amerindians; indigenous peoples; land appropriation; nomadic peoples; tribal societies

Amerindians 12, 50, 56, 71, 205, 208, 390
　alleged inhuman barbarism of 198, 203, 247, 248
　Bacon on 289, 291
　barbarism of 198, 203, 302
　Christian preachers in societies 204
　conquering of peoples 60–1, 140
　cultures 55
　De Indis see under Vitoria, F. de
　denigrating views of 66
　devaluation of cultures 141
　dominion rights 177
　enslavement 196
　Hobbes on 327
　integration into the *Imperium Romanum* 251–2
　just war against 195
　Latin American philosophy 61, 62, 66
　law of nations and global ethics 172–5, 180, 183, 184
　in the "New World" 205
　productive nature 291–2
　and projecting of the Americas 248, 251–2
　rule of Spain over 205
　Sepúlveda's justification of conquest 189
　tribal societies 354
　violence against 175, 390
　see also barbarians; Conquista of the Americas; indigenous peoples; New World; nomadic peoples; tribal societies
anarchy
　international 201, 293, 329, 386
　social 24, 302, 333, 335, 337, 338, 339
　tribal societies 327
　and violence 228
Anaximander, world map of 141–2
Ancient Greece 141–2, 153
see also Greek city-states
ancient philosophy 25, 152–72, 221, 269
　classical 18, 71–2, 129, 268, 272, 273, 276–7, 302, 335, 342, 377, 395
　elitism of 338
　techné model 20
angels
　Aquinas on 125–6, 135, 136
　Bacon on 284
　dignity of 122, 127

　fall of 125–6, 129
　hierarchy of 404n3
　medieval angelology 125
　Montaigne on 241
　mundus intelligibilis (dwelling place of angels) 122
　nature of 118
　Origen on 136–7
　Pico's theory of human superiority over 119, 120–3, 127, 128
　Plato on 404n3
animals 47, 97, 125, 129, 132, 136–7, 177, 197, 237, 241, 298
　acts of feeding 357
　free-roaming 356
　and humans 124, 312
　　compared with 181, 234, 301, 309, 310–11
　　degeneration to animals 130
　　relationship with 223
　　as social animals 346
　　superiority over animals 120–1, 234, 235, 309, 336
　hunting 360
　incarnation into 135
　inner impulses of 235
　memory capacity of 309
　and nature 242
　nomadic life of 181
　self-preservation drives 320
　wild/savage 122, 360
anthropology
　ancient 130
　of Bacon 287
　Christian 105
　empirical 313
　and human nature 122
　microcosm 124, 125
　of Pico, in the *Oratio* 118, 119, 127, 129, 135, 287
　of Renaissance 117, 140, 202, 231–233, 239, 242, 287, 289, 301
　self-fashioning, anthropological idea of 216
　and self-transformative capacity of human being 122
Antichthones 145
Antioeci 144
　see also Antipodes; southern hemisphere

Antipodes 144, 146–8, 150, 151, 159, 165
　inhabitants of 146
　see also Antioeci; southern hemisphere
antiquity 29, 48, 58, 90, 91, 107, 111, 113
　and Cicero 186, 356
　classical 12, 71, 115
　cosmopolitanism 153, 169, 173
　and curioso 99, 391, 392
　disc theory *see* disc theory of the earth
　early 142, 143
　ethical and political universalism 152–72
　expeditions/voyages 142, 145, 390
　geographic worldviews 140–2, 144, 146, 150, 151
　international law 153, 169
　and interventionism 186
　late 146, 169
　literary imagination 146
　vs. modern times 18
　and natural resources 183
　oikumene, boundaries of *see oikumene* (continent of Europe, Asia and North Africa)
　political geography 177
　political philosophy 158, 337, 339
　Republican ideals 338
　teleological world view 389
　world empires in 159
　　see also Ancient Greece
Apel, K.-O. viii, 4, 12, 69, 394, 403n1
　on discourse ethics 45, 46
　and the Enlightenment 33–5, 41, 43, 45–8
　and Habermas 45–6
　justification of ethics 47
　on Socrates 48
　　see also Habermas, J.
appropriation 7, 163
　of cultural discoveries 65
　of goods 153, 177, 359–60, 372, 383
　by *historia* movement 52
　by labor 359, 387
　of land 360, 365, 367, 369–71
　of living space 368
　original, Cicero's theory of 356
　private 356
　of property 359–60
　unilateral 364

Aquinas, T. 78, 102–3, 105, 121, 169–72, 174, 177, 183, 184, 187, 192, 346, 356
　compared with Pico 136
　just war doctrine of 170
　natural law of 191
　on perfection 136
　on the status of the angels 125–6, 135, 136
　Summa theologiae 125, 167, 170, 172, 282, 326
Arab world 142, 148–9
　modernity discourses 6–7
Argentina 55, 57
Aristotle 23, 29, 78–82, 87–90, 92, 95, 111, 119, 125, 136, 153–7, 162, 167, 172, 189, 197, 203, 211, 220, 259, 260, 335–8, 344, 378–82, 384, 385, 389, 400, 402
　and Bacon, F. 275
　chrematistics, objections to 380, 382
　compared with Pico 123
　compared with Plato 380
　cosmology of 140, 149
　　hierarchically ordered cosmos 90
　　limited cosmos 78, 79–81
　　matter 80–1
　criticism of Democritus 79–80
　on democracy 382
　on divine reason 130–1
　economy 377–8
　on ethical virtues 131–2
　on *eudaimonia* 94, 128, 154, 166, 171, 340, 350, 377, 380
　on exchange relations 379
　on freedom 130–3
　geographic worldview 143–5
　on happiness 129
　on impossibility of multiple worlds 78
　on justice 317
　on limited cosmos 78, 79–81
　Locke, compared with 378–9
　loss of authority 151
　on matter 80–1
　metaphysics 78, 81–2, 87, 103, 154
　on multiplicity of worlds 79
　on natural slavery 61, 140, 158, 173, 174, 176, 196, 202, 205, 207
　on naturalness of urge for knowledge 102

oikonomia vs. unlimited money
  economy 377–88
ontology 82
opposition between Greeks and
  barbarians 131
Plato, compared with 153, 380
polis 153, 154, 163, 171, 192, 199, 337,
  338, 342
political philosophy of 183, 335, 337,
  342
potential infinite, concept of 81, 88, 89
praxis, concept of 300
principle of the natural rule of the
  perfect over the imperfect 196
on rationality 127
on reason 316–17
republicanism 194
substance ontology 274
teleological concept of knowledge 238
writings
  De Caelo 79, 80
  Eudemian Ethics 131
  *Historia natural y moral de las
    Indias* 151
  Metaphysica 81
  Nicomachean Ethics 130–2
  Physics 80, 81
  The Politics 131, 154, 155, 163, 181,
    199, 335–7, 342, 377–82
  zoon politikon claim 335
art
  autonomous 37
  chrematistics 380
  civic 337
  of conjecture 110
  of differentiation 247
  of engineering 249
  expressive 18
  of government 374
  institutionalized criticism 37
  materials of 387
  significance of 22
  and technology 22
  of war 155
Asia 158, 269
  civilizing/civilized regions 156, 160
  division of 142
  geographic worldview 142, 144, 148,
    149
  intercultural philosophy 7

modernity discourses 6–7
moral duties of peoples in 348
and Ottoman imperialism 190–5
peoples of 155
and Persian Empire 158
rulers 180
southeast 5, 57
trade 293
  see also China; Far East; India;
    Japan
astronomy
  astronomic worldview 70
  Copernicus, ideas of 93, 139
  early modern debates 78
  heliocentric model of Aristarchus of
    Samos 93
  metaphysics 81–6
  Ottoman Empire 194
  revolution of early modern period 150
  and speculative reason 79–93
  stars 90–2
  see also Aristotle; Augustine;
    cosmology; earth; Nicholas of
    Cusa
ataraxia, ethical ideal of 98, 99, 103, 114,
  132, 220, 229, 250
  Bacon on 280, 285, 286, 350, 392
Atlantis, Platonic legend of 245
Augustine 70, 109–11, 150, 162, 169–71,
  187, 191, 216, 221, 222, 226,
  262, 282, 311, 315, 405n2
  bondage, justification of 167
  criticism of curiosity 94, 95, 100–2
  just war doctrine of 169
  on knowledge and happiness 101
  and Montaigne 221–2
  on original sin 100, 121, 356
  writings
    Confessions 94, 100, 101, 221
    De civitate Dei 102, 148, 163, 166,
      167, 169, 206
    The Literal Meaning of Genesis 102
autarky 153, 154, 171
authoritarianism 48
avarice 28, 231, 340, 377, 378
  recasting as a virtue 378, 385
  see also greed
Axial Age 36, 37
Aztec Empire 2, 204, 209, 327, 371
  architectural achievements 250

barbarism of 198
conquest of 197, 199, 204, 394
criticism of Aztec culture 61
cultures 51
humanitarian intervention 213
and Incas 51, 56, 61, 178
rulers 200, 210
sacrifices in 203, 210, 211, 212, 364
and Spanish imperium 199
technological innovations 249
tyrannical imperium of 199
wisdom teachings 210, 211

Bacon, F. 3, 12, 13, 23–5, 28, 69, 72, 255, 300, 302, 305–7, 311, 312, 332, 333, 340, 359, 369, 383, 384, 387, 391, 396–402
and Adorno 297
on Amerindian peoples 289, 291
anthropology 287
and Aristotle 275
on *ataraxia*, ethical ideal of 280, 285, 286, 350, 392
on charity 282, 297
and Colombus 266, 268
on composed onlooker, image of 280
criticisms of ideas of 258, 297
criticisms of the classical philosophers by 259
on curiosity 280–1
difference between *scientia* and *potentia* 278–9
and Horkheimer 297
on House of Solomon 283, 290, 294, 295
inductive method of 257
Instauratio Magna (*The Great Instauration*) 255, 259–70, 267f, 270–3, 275, 282, 285, 297, 387, 397, 409n3
　Historia naturalis et experimentalis 271–2
　main sections 271–2
　The Masculine Birth of Time 258, 265
　and medicine 285
　modern science portrayed as independent institution 296
　moral orientation of science 279–88
　Novum organum (*N.O.*) see below
　Scala intellectus 272
　theological justification 279
　utopian vision of transformation 288–9
and Locke 343, 344, 346–9
on love 282–3, 284
on the mind 260–1, 271, 273, 288
and Montaigne 260, 261, 287
on moral philosophy 262, 284, 286, 297
on natural philosophy vs. theology 282
nature, concept of 272–3, 281
New Atlantis 259, 277, 283, 296
　Bensalem island 290–5
　colonialism, early modern period 291
　isolationism in 290–1, 294
　"merchants of Light" 290, 293
　and Old Atlantis 293
　opening scene 292
on "new" science 23–4, 152, 258–9, 385
Novum organum (*N.O.*) 257, 260, 265, 266, 269–71, 273–9, 282, 289, 387
　aphorisms, use of 271
　criticism by Popper 257
　"Idols of the Cave" 260
　"Idols of the Marketplace" 260
　"Idols of the Theatre" 260
　"Idols of the Tribe" 260–1
　knowledge and power 277
　language in 260
　new science, vision of 270
paradise/restoration of paradise narrative 258
　expulsion from paradise 263
　and other biblical motifs 264
　partial restoration of paradise 259–70, 296
　theological framework 261–5
and Pico 287, 288
on production of effects 275
and Proteus 287
scientia activa 280, 281
seen as founder of modern science 73, 257–8, 343
unity of *contemplatio* and *actio* 262–3, 284
vision of modern science/limitless technological progress 257–98
writings

De augmentis 269, 275, 280, 284–8
De fluxu et refluxu maris 272
Essays, or Counsels Civil and Moral
  (*Essays*) 280, 284, 286–9
Instauratio magna see above
New Atlantis see above
Novum organum (*N.O.*) *see* above
Parasceve 288
Of the Proficience and Advancement
  of Learning, Divine and Human
  (*Adv. Learn*) 262–4, 269, 271,
  273, 275, 279–83
Valerius Terminus of the
  Interpretation of Nature (*Val.*
  Term) 262, 263, 264, 281, 282
barbarians
  and the Greeks 153
  Montaigne's meanings of 246
  natural slavery 140, 155, 157, 163, 167,
    189, 196, 202, 207
  Near Orient peoples as 155
  and torture 249
  tribal societies perceived as 155
  violent humanization of 188–206, 348
  wars against 154, 155
barbarism
  alleged inhuman barbarism of the
    Amerindians 198, 203, 247, 248,
    302
  in the Americas 246
  Asian 156, 190–5
  of the Aztecs 198
  and civilization 244
  collective 212
  in Europe 248, 329
  of Germany/Nazi regime 52, 212
  Montaigne on 244, 246
  of oriental empires 154
  Pico on 203
  regression into 24, 35, 333
    preventing 302–17
  Sepúlveda on 198, 203, 212, 247, 248,
    329
bartering 365
Bartholomew of Lucca, *De regimine*
  principum (*On Kingship*) 167
Battle of Pydna (168 BCE) *see* Pydna,
  Battle of (168 BCE)
Bible 148, 187
  Abraham, story of 370

angels, accounts of 404n3
book of Daniel 270
Cain and Abel 263
charity commandment 182, 186
Christian pacifism 192
creation narrative 261–2, 383
division of time 3
Fall narrative 102, 261, 263
and the flood 263
Genesis, book of 119, 261, 263
God's self-revelation in 100, 111–13,
  391
and the gospels 166, 179
and humanity's place in the cosmos 120
interpretation of 258, 264–5, 338,
  354–5, 362
love one's enemies commandment 191,
  233
New Testament 165, 190, 292
Old Testament 130, 136, 292
paradise/restoration of paradise
  narrative 258
  expulsion from paradise 263
  and other biblical motifs 264
  partial restoration of paradise
    259–70, 296
  theological framework 261–5
  see also under Bacon, F.
prohibition on interest 344
Proverbs, book of 187
Revelation, book of 165
Second Coming 165, 170
and Solomon/House of Solomon 276,
  283, 290, 294, 295, 297–8
sources 265
tower of Babel narrative 263, 264
  see also creation
boundaries
  of *oikumene* 58, 66, 71, 144–5, 146
  of unknown world 146
boundless charity 279–88
Brincken, A-D., *Terrae Incognitae* 148,
  166
Britain 146, 147
Bruno, G., *The Ash Wednesday Supper* 188
Byzantium/Byzantine Empire 167–9, 173

Campanella, T. 188
  La città del Sole 290
Canary Islands, discovery of 149

cannibalism 185, 247, 248
  of the Amerindians 248
  and human sacrifice 186, 195, 200, 201, 203–4
  protection of the innocent from 203–4
  see also Montaigne, M. de
capacity, loss of, and lapse of dominion rights 177–8
capitalism 24, 344, 394
  colonial 73, 343
  market economy 65
  neo-Marxist critiques of 343
  racist colonial 343
  and science 29, 41–2
Carolingians 168
Cartesianism 215
Carthaginians 158
cartography 148, 150, 152
casus belli 201
certainty, absolute 18
chameleon-like nature of human being 119, 132, 136–8, 240, 243, 287–8
charity 161, 283
  Bacon on 282, 297
  biblical commandment of 182, 186
  boundless 279–88
  Christian teaching of 186, 282
  ethic of 282
  moral principle of 295
Cheng, Peng-Chun 397
China 3, 11, 36, 62, 291, 364, 395
  Christian mission 168
  civilization 244
  cultures 58, 60, 149
  discourse ethics 48
  expansion of 395–6
  genome-edited babies born in 399
  geography 149
  high culture, as 64
  intellectuals from 7
  and Latin America 49
  pre-axial monarchies 303
  reformists 6
  rise of 399
  and Rome 164–5
  trade 164, 293
chrematistics
  and accumulation of money 379, 400
  Aristotelian objections to 380, 382
  criticism of 380

  as greed 344
  institutionalizing of 379
  and Locke 377
  and trade 381
  use and exchange value, distinction between 380
Christianity 50
  and Augustine's criticism of *curiositas* 94, 95, 100–2, 109, 110, 226
  charity ethic 186, 282
  Christian theology of history 2
  claim of absolute truth 184
  claim to universality 61
  co-existence of Christian empires 205–6
  common good, concept of 315
  conflict in 179
  and curiosity 70
  and disc theory of the earth 141–3
  disputes between universal powers 169
  early communities 187
  early medieval 148
  ethical universalism of Early Christianity 169
  evangelization see evangelization
  four kingdoms 2–3
  and Hellenistic philosophy 57, 94
  in High Middle Ages 149, 150
  ideals of existence 221
  illegitimate secularization, alleged 9
  imperialism 210
  and law of nature 198
  love, ethic of 282–4, 296
  medieval, destruction of the universal powers of 178–85
  metaphysics 133
  missionizing 61
  and morality/moral theories 191, 229, 316
  natural law 179, 213
  Neoplatonism 78
  original sin 100, 121, 356
  pacificism 190, 192, 315
  perceived superiority of civilization 168
  philanthropy 295
  reconquering of former territories 170
  redemption 148
  salvation 148
  self-sacrifice 315

Stoic-Christian tradition 166, 196, 201, 207, 233, 282, 356
  ethics 175–8, 319
temporary sovereignty of Christians 196
theology 2, 128, 129, 147–8, 165–6, 167, 177, 209, 225, 301, 315, 316
  creation 348
  medieval 344
  time horizon 4
  see also Bible; Judeo-Christian tradition; Latin Christianity; Reformation; salvation
Cicero, M. T. 113, 114, 132, 147, 160–4, 170, 177, 180, 206, 220, 228, 235–6, 259, 326, 361, 404n2
  and antiquity 186, 356
  on curiosity 95, 98–101
  on immoderateness of human curiosity 96
  ius gentium see ius gentium (law of nations) doctrine
  just war doctrine 162, 169, 187
  on striving for knowledge and curiosity 95, 96
  theory of original appropriation 356
  writings
    De finibus bonorum et malorum 96, 97
    De Re Publica 95
    Somnium Scipionis 95, 144, 147
citizenship
  Aristotle's definition of the citizen 199
  customarily acquiring 183
  good citizen, virtues of 344
  happiness of citizens 340
  right of by naturalization 182, 183
  self-government model 155, 377
  virtuous 333
  see also polis
city-states *see* Greek city-states
civil wars
  compared with conflicts between states 328
  creedal 300
  curiosity, lack of 313
  early modern period 337
  English Civil War 301
  European 301, 302, 304, 327, 329
  Hobbes on 302, 304
  lack of curiosity 313
  morality and justice 326
  and pure natural condition 326–7
  religiously motivated 244, 305
  territorial state 327
  turmoil of 247
  and violence 304, 306, 338
civilization
  of the Americas 249
  axial 42
  Chinese 244
  civilizing process 61–2
  collective self-civilization through creative freedom 329–33
  defining 244–53
  European 7
  frameworks 41
  neolithic 58
  peoples of 250
  theory 7, 41
Clavijero, F. J., *Historia antigua de México* 54
C-M-C cycle *see* commodity-money-commodity (C-M-C) cycle
cogitare 19
coinage crisis, England 343
Colombus, C. 139–41, 266, 268
  Bacon on 266, 268
  importance for modern age 139
  partial restoration of paradise in age of 259–70
  voyages of 71, 139–40, 152, 216, 269
  see also voyages of discovery
colonialism
  colonial ideology vs. breakthrough to global cosmopolitanism 206–13
  colonial violence 63
  colonialist modernity, radical critique 61–2
  and coloniality 64, 65
  early modern period 291
  epistemic coloniality based on 65
  global neo-colonial power syndrome 53
  and humanism 66
  ideology 211
  and imperialism 10
  justifications 72
  labor theory of property 73, 354–66
  and modernity 207

neo-colonial Western dominance 292–3
sixteenth-century debates 55, 62, 141
coloniality
  and colonialism 64, 65
  and cosmopolitanism 140
  epistemic 65
  and Locke 343, 348, 364
  of power *see* coloniality of power
  racist ideology 66, 71, 208
  and reason/power 73, 343, 389
  Salamanca School 71, 152
  social identities 65
  Vitoria as founding figure 67, 69, 207
coloniality of power
  colonial matrix of power 67
  in India 62, 64
  Latin American philosophy 57–68
  origin of term/defining 64–5
comets 91, 97, 283
Committee on Intellectual Cooperation 7
commodity-money-commodity (C-M-C) cycle 366, 379
common good 162, 208–9, 315
common properties, right to use/enjoy 182
communication
  and community 181, 188
  global 183, 188
  international law 180
  media 38
  oikumene, concept of 143, 164
  and partnership 180, 182, 207
  post traditional everyday 40–1
  between scientists 290
  self-communicating 110
  severing of 182
  universal 185, 208
  Vitoria on 181
communicative action, theory of 36, 37, 39
communicative rationality 9, 35–6
conflicts 96, 122, 279, 305
  belligerent 294
  causes 311, 313, 321–5
  in Christianity 179
  civil 199
  East–West 7
  Greek city-states 154
  Hobbes on 300, 304, 311, 313, 321, 322–5, 328, 329, 334
  ideological 22
  of interests 46
  internal 164, 300
  in natural state 324–5
  between pope and emperor 168, 304
  power-political 159
  in Roman Empire 163
  societal 247, 326, 327
  state of nature 324, 329
  between states 328
  tribal societies 327
  violent 290
  and war 169
  see also violence; wars
Confucianism 6, 338–9
conjectures 105, 223, 266, 278
Conquest of the Americas *see* Conquista of the Americas
Conquista of the Americas ix, 7, 48, 58, 59, 139–213, 217, 291
  colonization of 139
  and Eurocentrism 65
  globalization 71
  and humanization of barbarians 188–206
  moral justification issues 289
  rationalization of European geographic worldviews 150, 151–2
  Sepúlveda's justification of 140
  see also Americas
consensus 43, 211, 363
  consensus-building process 386, 396
  discourse ethics theory 43, 46, 396
  established 38
  explicit 354
  general 356
  of humanity 184, 208, 209, 357
  imagined 177
  interpretative 208
  and international law 208
  international law 211
  interpretative 208
  ius gentium (law of nations) doctrine 180
  language formation 38
  law of nations doctrine, incorporation into 180, 184
  legal changes 363
  moral norms, justifying 357
  and natural law 313

political processes of 365
pre-monetary economy 354
principle 47, 355, 356, 357, 365
processes of 365, 386, 396
rational 320
tacit 208
theory of truth 46
and truth 46, 47
unanimous 356
universal, of all humans 208, 209
and validity claims 36
validity claims 36
consent 180, 263, 321, 336, 357, 361, 367
of indigenous peoples 365
mutual 366
of nomadic tribes 364, 371
tacit 355, 362, 368–9, 370
conservatism, nineteenth-century 2
contradiction, principle of 330
Copernicus, ideas of 93, 139
cosmology
of Aristotle 149
hierarchically ordered cosmos 90
limited cosmos 78, 79–81
matter 80–1
astral world 122, 124
classical ancient conception of 11, 89
comets 91, 97
comparison of Cusa with Copernicus and Ptolemy 93
and Conquista of the Americas 140
contradictions between systems 223
de-limitations of 12, 70, 77–115
heliocentric model of Aristarchus of Samos 93
humanity's place in 120, 122, 124, 127, 224
see also angels; human beings; Pico della Mirandola, Giovanni; spirit beings
ideal order of cosmos 90
infinite universe in 71, 72, 78, 79, 86–9
metaphysical 210
mundus intelligibilis (dwelling place of angels) 122
ontological hierarchy 123, 124
orbital movement of heavenly bodies 80

order of the cosmos 90, 95, 99, 103, 120–1, 134
hierarchical 138, 279
only God knowing 109–10
planets 91
potential infinite, concept of 81, 88, 89
stars 90–2
structure of cosmos 122
sublunar world 122, 124
see also Aristotle; astronomy; earth; Nicholas of Cusa
cosmopolitanism 140, 157, 186, 217, 394
in antiquity 153, 169, 173
of de Vitoria 71
global 12, 72, 206–13
of Hellenistic Roman philosophy 156
in Latin American philosophy 153
of Montaigne 217, 253
Stoic 163
of Vitoria 71, 201, 252, 329
Council of the Indies 175, 195, 200
Crates of Mallos, on *oikumene* 144
creatio ex nihilo 107, 108, 138
creation 25, 65, 78, 100, 105, 107, 216, 263, 358
absolute present in all things 90–1
biblical narrative of 261–2, 383
Christian theology 177, 348
divine order of 115
and God 110, 111, 112, 347
creative power of 25, 105
as the Creator 101, 105, 106, 109, 111, 122–4, 134–6, 174, 176–7, 283, 346, 348, 405n2
as origin and goal of creation 110
plan of creation 384
by humans 359
inquiry into 104
Locke on 358, 359
myth of 405n5
"now" of 125
order of 246, 346, 347
Pico on 122, 123, 125, 129–38, 289
as production of new objects 358
self-creation 70, 72, 118, 126, 289, 312, 392
modernity of Pico's theory 129–38
see also ius creationis (right of creation)
creativity
creative freedom 108, 124, 301

collective self-civilization through 329–33
Montaigne on 239
Pico on 119, 129, 137, 287, 288, 300, 332
Renaissance idea of 117, 239, 310, 332, 358
self-creative freedom 402
creative power of God 105
creative power of the mind 12, 105–13, 114, 137, 332
and productive nature 288–98
and the Renaissance *see under* Renaissance
creoles 56
critical theory 9
Cuban Revolution 57
cultural imperialism 10, 210, 212, 394, 399
cultural relativism 248
curiosity (*curiositas*) 98, 259
   affirmation of and de-limitation of the cosmos 70
   in antiquity 99, 391, 392
   Augustine's criticism of 94, 95, 100–2, 109, 110, 226
   boundlessness of 224
   Christian stances on 70
   classical ancient objections to 279
   concept, introduced by Cicero 95, 98–101
   creative power of the human mind 105–13
   dangers 311
   excessive 103, 106, 226
   and geometrical method 305–12
   and happiness 226
   of humans, compared with animals 310–11
   importance of Cusa in history of 103
   insatiable (limitless) 12, 13, 77–115
      Bacon on 280–1
      justification of in *De docta ignorantia* 70, 102–5
      problematizations of in ancient and medieval thought 94–102
   Montaigne on 216–17, 226, 227, 391
   natural 281
   Nicholas of Cusa on 102–5, 114
      significance in history of curiosity 103
   objections to 94, 95, 100–2, 109, 110, 226, 279
   and perfection 98
   preferred subjects of 226
   revaluating 339
   Roman problematizations of 95, 102, 222
   and striving for knowledge 95, 96, 106
   and unfathomableness of "natural" human 219–31
   see also knowledge
Cusa, Nicholas of *see* Nicholas of Cusa
cylindrical earth *see* disc theory of the earth; earth
Cynics 157

Dante Alighieri 171, 172, 174, 175
   De Monarchia 171
   Divine Comedy 149
   on Odysseus 149–50
   on purgatory 265
Dasein (everyday being-there), Heidegger on 17
De augmentis (Bacon) *see under* Bacon, F.
De corpore see under Hobbes, T.
De docta ignorantia (*DDI*) *see under* Nicholas of Cusa
De hominis dignitate (G), Pico della Mirandola *see under* Pico della Mirandola, Giovanni
De Indis see under Vitoria, F. de
decolonial theory 10
de-limitations
   of cosmos 12, 70, 77–115
   and dialectic of enlightenment 389–94
      early modern period 334–42
   of essentialist anthropology 70
   geocentric worldview 78
   geographic worldview 70
   global cosmopolitanism 393
   modern dialectic 393
   oikumene (continent of Europe, Asia and North Africa) 11, 71, 143, 216, 390
   politico-geographic 71–2
   Renaissance 72, 216, 259, 301
   terminology 11
democracy
   Aristotle on 382
   constitutional 11

deliberative democracy ideal 33–4, 395
  extreme 382
  German 33
  Greek 305
  Hellenic 57
  and human rights 2, 11, 22, 42, 211–12
  liberal 343
  and market economy 381
  modern 2
  twentieth-century 61
deontological ethics 37, 43
dependency theory 53
Descartes, R. 3, 12, 17–21, 58, 69, 72, 112,
    215, 238, 255, 257, 261, 276,
    299, 312, 343
  Cartesian subject 18, 20
  cogito/ego cogito 19, 20–1, 62, 63, 69
  doubt of 19
  on freedom 18–19
  Heidegger on 18, 20
  and Hobbes 63
dialectic of enlightenment 334–42, 389–94
Dialectic of Enlightenment (Adorno and
    Horkheimer) 12, 24–31, 59
dialogue, intercultural 7
dignitas hominis literature 118, 216,
    231–44, 287
dignity of humanity 8, 56, 216, 239, 242,
    316
  devaluation of 138
  and dignity of the angels 122, 127
  Pico on 117–19, 121, 122, 127, 138
  Renaissance tractates 118, 216
    see also dignitas hominis literature
disc theory of the earth 141–3
discourse
  argument-based 45, 395
  autonomous 6
  consensus through 396
  critical 5
  factual 397
  Frankfurt discourse theory 12, 394
  general/primordial principle of 45–6
  global ix, 6, 7, 8, 47, 396, 402
  intercultural 397
  legal 210
  liberation 57
  of modernity 2, 4–8, 10, 12, 67, 77,
      139, 401
  moral 45, 46, 47
  new rules of 6
  norms 44, 47
  paradigms 9
  practical 43, 46
  principle 44–7
  rules of 44, 46, 48
  theoretical 46
  truth theories 46
  world philosophies 7
discourse ethics 42, 43–8
  of Apel 45, 46
  consensus 46
  consensus theory 46
  correction of 47
  Eurocentrism 47
  European viii
  Habermasian 45
  and lifeworld 45, 46
  moral principle of 46
  universality of 45
divine will 346–7
doubt
  of Descartes 19
  self-doubt 52, 67
  theological 265
Dussel, E. viii, 8, 50, 57–65, 67–9, 72, 139,
    189, 200, 207, 212, 299, 334,
    399, 403n1
  known as "Hegel of Coyoacán" 58
  on Latin American philosophy 67
  philosophy of history, critique of
      57–8

early modern period 12
  astronomy debates 78
  colonial debate 118–19, 291
  de-limitations, dialectic of
      enlightenment 334–42
  territorial state 319
  voyages of discovery 12, 140, 141, 150,
      151, 269, 270, 306
earth
  axial rotation of 89–90
  comprehensive affirmative revaluation
      92
  as a disc, questioning of 143
  and heavenly bodies 92–3
  landmasses 142, 144
  limited resources of 346
  as limited terrain 143

ontologically inferior to the heavens, perceived as 80
speed of movement 91
spherical shape 93, 141, 143, 144, 156
stellarization of 89–93
zone theory 144–6, 150, 151, 156
see also disc theory of the earth; heavenly bodies
economic development of humankind 355
economy *see* market economy; political economy
Edict of Gülhane (1839) 194
Egypt 58, 64, 142, 156, 249, 293, 304
ancient 120, 153, 156, 305
Napoleon's campaign 6
neolithic civilizations 58
pre-axial monarchies 303
pyramids 223
Elements of Law, Natural and Politic (Elem.), Hobbes *see under* Hobbes, T.
elites
bourgeois 54
elitism of ancient philosophies 338
intellectual 54
liberal 57
small 338
England
Bacon on 291
coinage crisis in 343
exchange value 388
foreign trade 374–5
Hobbes on 302
intellectuals in 4
public opinion 383
scientific research in 257–8
seventeenth-century 305
English Works of Thomas Hobbes of Malmesbury (EW) see under Hobbes, T.
The Enlightenment 2, 12, 33–48, 139, 152, 213
defense of 5, 40
deliberative democracy ideal 33–4
discourse ethics 43–8
enlightened society based on communicative reason 35–43
ethical reason, Kant on 43–8
European 9, 10, 42, 48, 50
political ideals 33, 42
rational/reason-based morality of 42, 45, 48
social differentiation and rationalization of the life word 35–43
enlightenment
age of/new age of 4, 9, 13, 213
equivocal concept 394–5
Middle Ages 60
and modernity 4, 13
movements 11
normative concept of 1, 2
processes of 395
radical 2, 5, 395
see also The Enlightenment
Epicurean teaching 218, 231, 336, 338, 344, 350, 407n2
epicycles, theory of 90
epistemology 77, 78, 140, 238, 390
sensualist 343, 345, 348, 349, 351
equality 10, 44, 56, 83, 109, 163, 311, 317, 338–9, 352, 355, 360, 395
agreements made on principle of 164
Hobbes on 317, 337, 338–9
universal, of all humans 45, 165, 174, 196, 316, 317, 341, 347, 348, 360
see also inequality
equatorial zone 145, 150, 151, 172
Essais (E) (Montaigne) *see under* Montaigne, M. de
Essay Concerning Human Understanding (Essay), Locke *see under* Locke, J.
Essays, or Counsels Civil and Moral (Essays), Bacon *see under* Bacon, F.
ethical and political universalism
in ancient and medieval thought 152–72
classical Greek thought and Roman philosophy 153–65
in Latin Christianity 165–72
path to 153–65
see also ethical universalism
ethical relativism 212–13
ethical universalism 37, 71, 177, 207, 212–13, 316, 386
and cultural imperialism 212
and political universalism *see* ethical and political universalism

Stoicism 138, 155, 157, 158, 159, 160, 162, 163, 165–6
  see also ethics
ethics
  ancient theories 221
  ataraxia, ethical ideal of *see ataraxia*, ethical ideal of
  cognitive 43
  Confucian 6
  deontological 43
  discourse 43–8
  Epicurean teaching 231
  epistemological problems 192
  global 172–88
  of the good life 47
  hedonism 350
  history of 314–15
  of Kant 43
  and natural law 192, 351, 385
  post-traditional 37
  on reason 43–8
  Stoic-Christian 175–8, 319
  traditional 315
  universalistic 155, 161
  see also ethical and political universalism; ethical universalism
ethnocentrism 5, 245, 247
ethnographic research 142–3, 149
ethnological perspective, reversal 325–6
eudaimonia (fulfillment of highest capacities) 94, 128, 154, 166, 171, 340, 350, 377, 380
  see also Aristotle
eudemonism, theory of 369
Euro-American philosophy 5, 7, 9, 11, 255
Eurocentrism viii, 7, 10, 42, 212, 301, 313
  discourse ethics 47
  dogmatism 394–5
  epistemic coloniality based on 65
  Eurocentric bias 41
  in Habermas's thought 43
  maps of the world 66
  myths 65
  racism 65–6
  world system 65
Europe
  and the Americas 250, 251, 252

  and Asia 158
  civilizing/civilized regions 160
  colonial expansion of 13
  Eurocentrism *see* Eurocentrism
  impact of Second World War on 5
  international law in 140, 365
  modernity *see* modernity
  political philosophy of 155, 207, 390
  see also European Enlightenment; European philosophy
European Enlightenment 9, 10, 42, 48, 50
European philosophy ix, 5, 6, 11, 33, 50, 51, 53–6, 67, 68, 188, 215, 396, 398
  contemporary/modern 63, 391
evangelization 206
  efficiency of 204
  imperative to evangelize 204
  peaceful 204
  resistance to 189
  right to evangelize 170, 209
    violent enforcement of 184, 185
  see also Christianity
exchange value 371, 380, 388

Fanon, F., and Sartre 5–6
Far East 164, 168, 244
fascism, twentieth-century 2, 24, 212
feminist philosophy 258
Ficino, M. 120, 405n5
  Theologia Platonica 137
Filmer, R. 347, 348, 354, 356, 357
  Patriarcha: or the Natural Rights of Kings 362
filosofía americana 49, 55, 57, 67
filosofía de nuestra América 67
filosofía nahuatl 50
four kingdoms, in Christianity 2–3
Frankfurt discourse theory 12, 394
free movement, right of 182
free will 125, 126, 130, 131, 134, 135, 232, 235
freedom 6, 25, 61, 63, 77, 142, 192, 196, 197, 205, 218, 237, 285, 308
  absolute 109
  autonomous 117
  boundless 138
  Christian metaphysics of 133
  civil 194, 198, 199
  consciousness of 57, 304

creative 13, 105, 108, 119, 124, 129, 137, 138, 287, 288, 301, 329–33, 358
  Montaigne on 239, 242–3
  see also self-fashioning
  defending against new Asian barbarity 190–5
  Descartes on 18–19
  and Enlightenment 212
  essence of 126
  flexibility of 119, 137
  for good and evil 136–7
  of Greek *polis* 154, 155
  individual 29
  interpretation of 70–1, 138
  modern 18, 19, 57
  natura altera 132
  of nature's first laws 219, 244
  in the *Oratio* 132–3
  Origen on 133, 134
  Patristic teaching 135
  Pico on 118, 119, 125, 127, 130–3, 135–7, 287, 300
  of pure spirits 134–5
  revaluation of, in the doctrine of natural slavery 197
  scholasticism context 119
  scope of 288
  and self-creation 399
  as self-fashioning 357
  self-transformative power embedded in 138
  Stoics on 132, 194
  of subjectivity 17–18
  and subjugation 235
  of will *see* free will
  see also liberation
French Revolution 4, 24, 58

Generación 1837 (liberal reform movement) 54
Genesis, book of, Pico's philosophical commentary on 119
geocentric worldviews 70, 78, 91, 150, 151
geographic worldviews 141–52
  ancient geography 144
  Antioeci 144
  Antipodes 144, 146, 147
  of antiquity 140–2, 144, 146, 150, 151

  Arab geography 149
  and climate 142
  and Conquista of the Americas 140
  de-limitations 70
  earth
    landmasses 142, 144
    spherical shape 93, 141, 143, 144, 156
    zone theory 144–6, 150, 151, 156
  historiographical and ethnographical geography 148
  Latin Christianity 150
  mathematical geography 142, 147, 148, 150
  Perioici continent (northern hemisphere) 144
  Periplus literature 142
  physical geography of the pre-Socratics 142
  political geography 177
  and Ptolemy 144
  rationalization of 150, 151–2
  scientific geography 142, 143, 148
  sea route description, Arab Peninsula 142
  tripartite division of the continents 142
  world conception of Crates 148
  see also age of discovery; earth; *oikumene* (continent of Europe, Asia and North Africa)
geometric space 142
geometrical method
  and curiosity 305–12
  evidence of 311–12
  harmony of 144
  importance for Hobbes 306
  importance for universal science 307
  methodological model for moral philosophy 305–6
  see also Hobbes, T.
Germany
  democracy in 33
  lapse into barbarism 52, 212
  National Socialism/Nazi regime 22, 33, 52, 212
  occupation by the Allies 212
  post-war European philosophy 33
  and religion 2
Gibraltar, Strait of 142, 147, 149

global cosmopolitanism 13, 72, 141, 391
  breakthrough to vs. colonial ideology
    206–13
  challenges of 344
  de-limitations 393
  new 12, 71, 140
  paradigmatic conceptions 211
  principles 70
  Salamanca School, coloniality 152
  Vitoria's vision of 12, 195, 207–8, 390,
    393
global ethics, philosophical foundations
  172–88
global responsibility 393
  and humanitarian intervention 185–8
Global South 9, 34, 212
globalization 7, 41, 398
  Conquista of the Americas 71
God 87, 90, 102, 105–6, 109
  as the absolute 88, 104, 111
  and the angels 125
  annihilate, right to 360
  arbitrary will of 78
  and creation 110, 111, 112, 347
    creative power of God 25, 105
    God as origin and goal of creation 110
    God as the Creator 101, 105, 106,
      109, 111, 122–124, 134–136,
      174, 176–7, 283, 346, 348, 405n2
    plan of 384
  Cusa on 110–13
  debates on 1
  and desire 81–2
  divine will 346–7
  dominion of 121
  happiness in the knowledge of 101
  humans owing existence to 347
  infinity of 88, 114
  knowledge of 101, 105, 109–10
  man's likeness to 25
  mirror of self-knowledge for human
    beings 221
  mystical union with 119, 120–9
  omnipotence of 347
  order of the cosmos, knowing 109–10
  Plato on 111
  power of 88, 128
  presence of 121
  relationship with 57–8
  self-communicating 114

self-revelation 100, 103, 111–13, 391
universal dominion over nature 347
unknowability 223
world as book of 111
see also Christianity; creation; Islam;
  Judeo-Christian tradition;
  religion
"Golden Age" 355
goods
  in agrarian societies 369
  annihilation of 356, 360
  appropriation of 153, 177, 359–60, 372,
    383
  cheap 376
  claim to, in state of nature 352
  common 162, 183
  essential 379, 381, 387, 400
  exchange of 380, 382
  external 411n2
  import and export of 342, 381
  irrelevant for human flourishing 162
  life-sustaining 320
  manufactured 374
  material, pursuit of 340, 377
  natural 356, 358, 366
  vs. natural resources 183
  peace as greatest of all 312–17
  prices of 374, 376
  procuring of 325
  production and distribution of 375, 382
  sale of 375
  scarcity of 322, 336
  and Stoic-Christian morality 282
  storing of 378
  technological enhancement of 383
  trade in 183, 382
  unequal possession of 372
  unperishable 367–8
  useful 366, 388
  utility 379
  see also property
greed 139, 153, 224, 227, 230
  chrematistics as 344
  Spanish 183
  see also avarice
Greek city-states 153, 154, 164, 303, 385
  conflict 154
  see also Ancient Greece
Greek philosophy 19, 36, 304–5
  and Roman philosophy 153–65

Habermas, J. 4, 9, 12, 27, 34–48, 58, 69, 72, 139, 299, 300, 314, 394, 396, 398
  and Apel 45–6
  Eurocentrism in thought of 41, 43
  and Kant 43
  on the lifeworld 36, 45
  writings
    Between Facts and Norms 43, 44–5
    Theory of Communicative Action 35, 41
  see also Apel, K.-O.
happiness 39, 96, 113, 128, 225, 306, 311
  of all humankind 384
  Aristotle on 129
  Augustine on 101
  Bacon on 281–2
  of citizens 340
  and curiosity 226
  earthly 166
  Epicurean teaching 231
  and God/divine existence 95
    God as only source of true happiness 101
    knowledge of God 101
  and hedonism 285, 345, 346, 349, 351, 355, 370
  Hobbes on 398
  human desire for 281–2
  individual 340, 342
  infinite stages 350
  Jacob's ladder imagery 127
  and knowledge of the world 101
  Locke on 350
  maximizing, in utilitarian thought 48
  and morality 285
  and natural law 355
  and nature 128
  perfect 171, 191
  Pico on 127–9
  and pleasure 355
  sensual 350
  traditional definition, rejection 128–9
  and tranquillity 285
  and virtue 284–5
  without friction 94–5
heavenly bodies 95, 125, 129, 278
  circular motion 90
  and the earth 92–3
  orbital movement 80, 90
  see also earth

hedonism 29, 30, 378, 350, 369, 380, 382, 385
  and happiness 285, 345, 346, 349, 351, 355, 370
  and natural law 344, 345–51, 385
Hegel, G. F. W. 3, 6, 12, 54, 62, 215, 304, 410n3
  on America 49
  and Heidegger 17, 18
  Lectures on the History of Philosophy 62
  on modern subject 20–1
  oriental despotism stereotype 303
  philosophy of history, Dussel's critique of 57–8
  on unity of reality and reason 24
Heidegger, M. 3, 4, 9, 12, 17, 22, 33, 34, 62, 63, 67, 69, 115, 400
  and Descartes 18, 20
  and Hegel 17, 18
  and Nietzsche 17, 21
  and Pico 71
  on power 17–24
  on reason 21–2
  on technology 21, 22, 23, 24
  writings
    The Age of the World Picture 17
    Contributions to Philosophy 21–2
Hellenistic philosophy 219, 221, 395
  and Christianity 57, 94
  cosmopolitanism 156
  and curiosity 94
  and Roman philosophy 95, 103, 155–6, 350
Hermes Trismegisthos
  Asclepius 120
  Corpus hermeticum 120, 404n2
hierocrats 169, 180, 186
  hierocratic theology 174, 186, 201
  hierocratic warmongering 200
  justification of the Conquista 180
  on papal power 174
  papal world dominion, hierocratic notion of 173
  warmongering 200
high cultures 64
High Middle Ages 149, 172
Hispano-American philosophy *see* Latin American philosophy

historia de las ideas movement 9, 50–2, 54, 57
historical context 52
Hittites 153
Hobbes, T. 3, 12, 13, 63–4, 69, 72, 73, 255, 299–342, 354, 372, 386, 391, 393, 394, 410n1, 410n2
  on Amerindian peoples 327
  on civil war 302, 304
  on conflicts 300, 304, 311, 313, 321, 322–5, 328, 329, 334
  criticism of 299–300
  and Descartes 63
  ethnological perspective, reversal 325–6
  and geometrical method 305–12
  on history of ethics 314–15
  on law of nature 314–18, 324, 326, 328, 331, 339
  and Locke 351–4
  on the mind 312, 320
  modern politics, foundations 299–343
  and Montaigne 311, 312, 320–1
  on morality 316, 317
  on natural law 300, 314, 315, 319–20, 354
  and Pico 333
  political philosophy of 299, 300–3, 306, 319, 332, 334, 335, 337–9, 397
  reversal of ethnological perspective 325–6
  scientia iustitiae (science of justice) 301, 308, 335, 337, 341, 397
  and self-preservation principle 314, 315
  social contract of 333, 338, 339
  on state of nature 299, 300, 314, 317–29, 331, 333, 334, 336–9, 353
  on states and empires 327–8
  Stoics, compared with 314, 319
  on violence/war 318, 334
  writings
    Behemoth or the Long Parliament 305
    De cive 300, 303, 306, 308, 313, 318, 334, 339, 340
    De corpore 299, 304–7, 312, 313
    De homine 305, 307, 310, 340
    The Elements of Law, Natural and Politic (*Elem.*) 300, 315, 317, 318, 328, 410n1

The English Works of Thomas Hobbes of Malmesbury (*EW*) 299, 304, 306, 307, 312, 318, 410n1
    Leviathan (*Lev.*) 73, 300, 302–5, 307–18, 321–6, 328–32, 333, 334, 340, 342, 354
  see also barbarians
Horkheimer, M. 4, 35, 69, 115, 215, 258, 273, 297, 400
  The Authoritarian State 24
  and Bacon 297
  Dialectic of Enlightenment 12, 24–31, 59
  "Materialism and Morality" 24
human beings
  ancient motif as *contemplator mundi* 122, 123
  angels, in relation to 118, 119
  and animals 124
    compared with 181, 234, 301, 309, 310–11
    degeneration to 130
    humans as social animals 346
    relationships 223
    superiority over 120–1, 234, 235, 309, 336
  belief in the unity of humankind 201
  claim to power over nature 123
  and creation *see*
  creators of ideas, actions and labor 359
  curiosity of, compared with animals 310–11
    see also curiosity (*curiositas*)
  dignity of *see* dignity of humanity
  disabilities, born with 134
  human–nature relationship 258
  intermediary position, Pico on 123–5, 127, 131
  mind, creative power of 12, 105–13
  mystical union with God 120–9
  Protagoras myth relating to 122–3
  reborn into the divine 130
  recognition, need for 324–5
  self-creation 312
  self-transformation into the divine 240, 241
  socio-economic evolution of humankind 344–5
  status in Renaissance philosophy 216

stellarization of the earth, enhancing position through 89–93
Stoicism on unity of human species 180
unfathomableness of "natural" human 219–31
universal community between 201
upright position 309
vulnerability of 122, 216, 321
zoon politikon claim 335
see also human nature; human rights
human nature 18, 71, 100, 120–9
chameleon-like 119, 132, 136–8, 240, 243, 287–8
and law of nature 202
moral qualities 319
see also Hobbes, T.
human rights 2, 5, 9, 73, 141, 213
declarations of 213
and democracy 2, 11, 22, 42, 211–12
ethics of 10, 59, 61, 213
individual 343
modern 69, 343, 394
secular 213
Universal Declaration of Human Rights 396–7
violation of 211
humanism 19, 133, 191, 202
alphabetical literate culture 66
and colonialism 66
and the Ottoman Empire 194
Renaissance 60, 67, 70, 199, 334, 335
of Sepúlveda 189, 192, 197
Spanish Renaissance 60
studies 220
humanitarian intervention 185–8, 203, 207
in Aztec Empire 213
mandate, extending by Security Council 211
part of international law 211
problems carrying out 209–10
to save the innocent 253
seen as aggressive cultural imperialism 212
Sepúlveda's justifications of 209
susceptible to exploitation and abuse 210
Vitoria's idea of 211
hunter-gatherer societies 355, 360, 363, 364

imagination 107, 115, 143, 221, 276, 278, 311, 320, 387
fantasies (phantasms) produced by 222, 237, 238, 239, 246
literary 146
Montaigne on 238, 239
of poets and generals 152
imperialism 10, 175
Christian 210
cultural 10, 210, 212, 394, 399
of great European powers 294
justifying 293
Ottoman 190–5
racist 66
Roman Empire 157, 162, 164–7, 334, 336
Spanish 185
Inca Empire 51, 56, 61, 178, 250, 327, 371
see also Aztec Empire
India 11, 36, 156, 173, 303, 395, 399
coloniality of power 62, 64
and Enlightenment 48, 49
and European geographic worldviews 141–3, 145–7, 149, 151
gold in 143
neolithic civilizations 58
New India 289
sea route to 139
Indians 12, 54, 65, 66, 175, 189, 195, 302, 407n11, 408n6
alleged inferiority of 66, 196–200
in America 355
exclusion of 208
idealization of 252
naturalness of 248, 249, 250
at war 247
see also Amerindians
indigenous peoples 50, 51, 56, 178, 182, 370
of the Americas 245, 250, 356, 386
North America 363, 365, 368, 371
appropriation of land 363, 365
campaigns to exterminate 55
before the Conquista 49–50
cultures 51, 54
knowledge traditions 396
Latin American context 57
Locke on options open for 368, 369
negotiations with for purchase of land 365

nonviolent Christian missionizing 386
philosophy of 50
sovereignty of 365
spiritual traditions 402
struggles of 399
violence against 55, 363
"waste land" inhabited by 369, 371, 387, 400
see also Amerindians; nomadic peoples; tribal societies
inequality 10, 167, 317, 338, 368
  extreme 290–1
  social 135, 372
  unequal exchange 26
  unequal land appropriation 371
  see also equality
inferior status 347, 357
  and animal nature of humans 234
  base senses 107
  of earth in relation to the heavens 80
  of humans in relation to celestial beings 95
  Indians seen as inferior 66
  "inferior" peoples taking a stand on their subservience 200
  inhabitants of the *oikumene* in relation to the Antipodes 146
  of slaves, perceived as 197
  Tawantinsuyu and Anáhuac peoples seen as inferior 207
  of world in geocentric worldview 91
infidels, right to rule 170
infinity of being concept (Melissus) 80
innocent persons, right to intervene to save 185–6
intellect 82, 103–4, 108–9, 111, 260, 392
  achievements of 237
  and the mind 237, 268
  and reason 126
  and the senses 236, 238
  see also mind
intercultural philosophy 7, 8
interest rates 374–5
international anarchy 201, 293, 329, 386
international law 155, 158, 289, 290, 390, 393, 399, 406n4
  in antiquity 153, 169
  communications theory of 184
  and consensus 208
  in Europe 140, 365

founders of 211
global 66
history of 172
and medieval theology 169
and natural law 180, 182
norms 182, 183, 208, 209, 211, 386, 396
order based on 165
origins 207
participants 208
philosophical theory 164
practice 153, 164, 169
Sepúlveda, as founder 211
theories 153, 164, 169, 184, 398
Vitoria as founder 140, 172, 180, 207
intersubjectivity, of moral norms 47
inwardness 58
Islam 6, 58, 185
  mathematical geography 148
  stereotypes 193
  theology 78
ius creationis (right of creation) 346, 347, 357, 358
  see also natural law
ius gentium (law of nations) doctrine
  and Christian evangelization 184
  concept 164, 170
  consensus element 180
  and global ethics 172–5, 180, 183, 184
  humanity of Amerindians, affirming 66
  incorporation of consensus into 180, 184
  and international trade 344
  introduction into political philosophy 180
  and *ius inter gentes* doctrine 175
  and *ius naturale* doctrine 164
  as a *jus publicum Europaeum* 66
  philosophical foundations 172–88
  of Vitoria 140, 172, 180, 207, 208, 209, 328, 344
  see also Vitoria, F. de
ius in omnes et omnia 330, 331
ius inter gentes doctrine, and *ius gentium* (law of nations) doctrine 175
ius naturale doctrine, and *ius gentium* doctrine 164

Jacob's ladder imagery 127–8
Japan 60, 149, 291
  imperial 33
  Kyoto School 6

Judaism
    Jewish hope of rebuilding the temple 261
    Judeo-Christian tradition 25, 36, 65, 165
    see also Kabbalah
just war doctrine 164, 174, 179, 190
    alleged inferiority of the Indians 196–200
    of Aquinas 170
    of Augustine 169
    Christian evangelization, efficiency 204
    and Christianity 171, 184
    of Cicero 162, 169, 187
    and humanitarian intervention 187
    medieval theology 171
    and natural law 204
    pagans 179
    protection from cannibalism and sacrifice 203–4
    of Sepúlveda 190, 192, 195, 200–1
    sins against nature 200–3
    and violence 162, 163
    of Vitoria 184, 189
    and world empires 169
justice 161, 175, 199, 241, 325
    administration of 336
    archaic knowledge of 304
    commutative 316, 317
    distributive 155, 316, 317
    divine 302
    idea of 303, 304, 313, 316, 332
    and morality 47, 326, 332
    and peace 337
    principles of 155
    science of 301, 308
    and shame 123
    of social institutions 39
    virtue of 95, 109

Kabbalah 118, 120, 137
Kant, I. 3, 28, 54, 129, 207, 212, 261, 393
    categorical imperative 43, 47
    Critique of Pure Reason 1
    ethics of 21
    and Habermas 43
    on rational subject 5
    on reason 1, 18, 19
    reconstitution of ethical reason 43–8
killing, prohibition of 347, 357

knowledge 34, 64, 92, 295, 307, 349, 391, 396
    of the absolute 226
    of the ancients 151
    archaic 302, 304
    Aristotle's teleological concept of 238
    attainable through interaction with others 181
    Augustine on 100, 101
    autotelic of 275
    of belief 107
    cognitive 350
    colonializing 65
    as a comparative operation 82–3, 85, 86
    and creativity 108
    and curiosity 103
    degree of 99
    of the divine 95, 96, 98, 101
    dormant 271
    of empires in the Far East 164
    empirical 312–13
    of equatorial zone *see* equatorial zone
    ethnographic 142–3, 149
    of Europe's northern regions 149
    faculties of 348
    of foreign cultures 51
    forms of 65
    geographical 146, 342
    geological 3
    geometrical 307
    of God 101, 105, 109–10
    of heavenly conditions 97
    of ideas 107
    imprecision in 84
    infallible 348
    innovations/inventions 142, 295
    limits of or limitless 25, 78, 114
    mathematical 82, 84–5, 108
    of nature/natural law 348, 349, 351
    new 270
    of new kingdoms 149
    particulars of 161
    perspectival 84, 85, 90
    philosophy of 115, 348–9
    and power 28, 69, 277–8, 297
    precise 103
    process of gaining 114
    progressive 115
    provisional 104

questionable 98
and reality 46, 47
scientific 290, 343, 360
scope of 106
search for provisional general concepts and causes 225
secrecy of 296
self-knowledge 104, 221, 232, 392
Socratic/Socratic-Platonic knowing 78, 85
sources 142
and stellarization of the earth 90
superior 394
systematic 106
technological 329
transgenerational 97
of truth 276, 277
urge for/striving for 71, 78, 81, 82, 109, 123, 224–5, 226, 230
  ceasing of 103
  and curiosity 95, 96, 106
  Cusa's positive revaluation of 104
  innate 86
  insatiable, for knowledge of the world 94, 101
  limitless 93–115
  misuse of 100, 104, 222
  as natural 95, 100, 102, 103
  as never-ending 103
  philosophical 95
  restlessness resulting from 103
  of the truly valuable 96, 98
  vs. "vain" inquisitiveness 102
  see also Nicholas of Cusa
valid 306
of the world 94, 101, 103, 106, 109, 115, 223, 349
see also curiosity
knowledge society 290, 294
Kyoto School, Japan 6

labor theory of property (Locke) 73, 344–5
  agricultural societies 360–1, 363
  colonial applications 354–66
  consensual elements in justification of property 357
  development of concept 360
  and hedonistic concept of happiness 355
  justification of English settlers' property rights, questioning 364–7, 386
    without consent of indigenous population 365, 371
  land rights 361
  mixing argument 358
  modes of production 360
  and natural law 182, 355, 356
  relations between agricultural and hunter-gatherer societies 363
  spoilage proviso 360
  sufficiency proviso 360–2, 364, 368
  transition to territorial states 362–3
  see also land, appropriation of; Locke, J.; property
land, appropriation of 360–1, 365, 369–71
  by European settlers in North America, without consent 365, 371
  money-based expansion of land possession 367–8
  unequal 371
  "waste land" inhabited by indigenous peoples 369, 371, 387, 400
  see also under Americas; appropriation; goods; indigenous peoples; labor theory of property (Locke); nomadic peoples; property; tribal societies
landmasses theory 142, 144
Las Casas, F. B. de 55, 56, 61–3, 67, 69, 72, 140, 195, 197, 198, 200, 201, 204, 206, 209, 211, 212, 247, 364, 406n9, 406n10, 407n10, 407n11
  debate with Sepúlveda 61
  on peaceful proselytization 244
Latin American philosophy 12, 49–68
  alienation of 53, 54
  and Amerindians 61, 62, 66
  authenticity of 55
  Bondy and Zea debate ("Great Debate") 50, 51–6, 66–7
  and Christian theology of history 2
  coloniality of power 57–68
  and Conquista of the Americas 139
  cosmopolitanism in 153
  decolonial 66
  defining 49–50
  Dussel on 67

epigonic character 53
of the future 52
importing of European philosophies 54
intercultural 7
of liberation viii, 9, 50, 57, 63
Mexican 51, 54
modernity discourses 6–7
part of global neo-colonial power syndrome, seen as 53
post-Second World War 51
Salazar Bondy on 53
social revolutionary movements 57
universal political ideas 152
see also Salazar Bondy, A.: on Latin American philosophy
Latin Christianity 2, 58, 71, 179, 304
ethical universalism and world empire 165–72
geography 147, 149, 150
political ideas 152
law
international *see* international law
of nations *see ius gentium* (law of nations) doctrine
natural 165, 319, 344, 348, 349, 351, 354
philosophical justification of global order based on 180
positive 37
see also law of nature
law of nature 161, 183, 186, 203, 206, 313–14, 346–7, 353
Christian view 198
ethical standards 178
Hobbes on 314–18, 324, 326, 328, 331, 339
and human nature 202
mutuality principle 191
and New Testament 191
offences against 201
and reason 166
vs. self-interest 326
social contract theory 177
Stoicism 165, 314
validity 328, 353
see also natural law; nature
League of Nations 7
learned ignorance, rule of 78, 88, 89, 104
Leitideen (guiding ideas) 13, 42, 48
lex naturae 191

liberalism 55, 57
liberation
discourse 57
ethics of 403n1
Latin American philosophy of viii, 9, 50, 57
limitless 273
from pain or pleasure 350
Philosophy of Liberation philosophy 59
theologies 49, 57
theories 57
see also freedom
lifeworld 37–39, 41, 61, 142
colonization of 40, 342, 380
and discourse ethics 45, 46
Habermas on 36, 45
rationalization of 35–43
structures of 40, 45
Locke, J. 12, 13, 72, 73, 255, 322, 342, 355, 382–8, 391, 396–8, 400
Aristotle, compared with 378–9
and Bacon 343, 344, 346–9
British colonialism, involvement with 363–4, 367, 371
on creation 358
criticized as defender of racist colonialism and slavery 363–4
on economic cycles 375–6
and Hobbes 351–4
and introduction of "money" 366–70
labor theory of property *see* labor theory of property (Locke)
on law of nature 345, 346–8, 352, 354
moral philosophy 343, 345–54
on natural law 346, 349, 351, 353, 354, 357, 376, 377, 383, 386
on "New World" 365
on political economy and social policy 370–6
political philosophy of 343, 345–6, 351, 352, 353–4, 357
on poverty
beggars vs. families with many children 373
children, treatment of 373
combating through policy 373–4
seen as idleness 371–2
and pre-monetary economy 354–66
on state of nature 353, 354, 384–5

on theological absolutism 347
Two Treatises of Government (TTG)
    343, 345, 347, 349, 351–7, 358,
    360, 361–4, 366–72, 374, 383–5,
    387, 388, 410n1
  First Treatise 362–3
  Second Treatise 255, 352
unlimited market economy
  vs. Aristotelian economy 377–88
  justification of 343–80
on war 353
writings
  Essay Concerning Human
    Understanding (Essay) 343, 345,
    347–51, 358, 359
  An Essay on the Poor Law 371, 372
  Essays on the Law of Nature 345,
    348
  For a General Naturalization
    (unpublished) 375, 383
  Notes on Trade (unpublished) 382
  Reasonableness of Christianity 345
  Two Treatises of Government (TTG)
    see above
  Venditio (unpublished) 376
Lucifer, fall of 125
maps of the world 66, 145f, 148–9
market economy
  capitalist 65
  economic cycles 375–6
  embedding the market system 370–6
  foreign trade 374, 375
  global market system, emergence of
    366–70
  Habermas on 38, 39
  introduction of "money" 366–70
  labor theory of property 73, 344–5,
    354–66
  moral right to secure subsistence 357
  pre-monetary 354–66
  prices and interest rates 374–5
  subsystems of modern societies 12
  unlimited, justification (Locke) 343–88
  see also labor theory of property
    (Locke); Locke, J.; monetary
    economy; property

Martí, J., "Nuestra América" 53
Marx, K. 2, 24, 73, 377, 403n1
  compared with Nietzsche 4

mathematical geography 142, 147, 148,
    150
matter, Aristotelian theory of 80–1
Mayans 51
M-C-M cycle see money-commodity-
    money (M-C-M) cycle
Mecca 148
medieval period
  angelology 125
  Christian theology 169, 344
  curiosity, problematizing 94–102
  destruction of the universal powers of
    Christianity 178–85
  ethical and political universalism
    152–72
Mesoamerica 54, 61, 197, 198
Mesopotamia 58, 153, 156, 303
metaphysics 1, 81–6
  of antiquity 296
  Aristotelian 78, 79, 82, 154
  Aristotelian-Scholastic 127
  Christian 133, 296
  of Cusa 81
  and Nietzsche 17
  Platonic-Aristotelian 270
  post-metaphysical thought 37, 41, 42, 44
  of Sepúlveda 189
  "twisting" with technology 22
Mexican philosophy 51
microcosm anthropology 124, 125
Middle Ages 1
  enlightenment processes 60
  High Middle Ages 149, 150
  intellectual debates of late Middle Ages
    77
  late 106
  Late Middle Ages 265
  theology of 121
Mignolo, W. 50, 65–7, 69, 172, 207, 399
  The Darker Side of the Renaissance
    65–6
migrate, global right to 182–3
mind 25, 83–4, 95, 96, 98, 101, 109, 117,
    154, 167, 208, 226, 228, 234,
    237, 259, 277–8, 284, 391
  Bacon on 260–1, 271, 273, 288
  capricious 218
  cognitive faculties 223–5
  colonial 55
  contraction of 229

control of 239
creative power of 12, 105–13, 114, 137, 332
daily examination of cognitive faculties 238
European 8
finiteness of 85
Hobbes on 312, 320
human and divine 107
idols of 258, 260
inhuman 108
and the intellect 237, 268
and mathematical ideas 108
Montaigne on 220–1, 237–8, 261
and nature 312, 313
ordering 25
perfectior esse posset principle 103
philosophy of 70, 103, 110, 113, 115
power of 223–4
projections of 247
rational, weakness of 237–8
restless 281
as a tormenter 220–1
variable 281
volatility of 241–2
weaknesses of 261, 287
see also knowledge
Modernism 1
modernity
and colonialism 207
colonialist ideology of 299
radical critique 61–2
cultural 38
definitional issues 1–2
descriptive theories 1–2
destructive dimensions of 23
discourses of 2, 4–8, 10, 12, 67, 77, 139, 401
emancipatory and power-driven dimensions 59–60
and enlightenment 4
founding figures of 62
future of 389–402
genesis of European modernity 11
global, three levels (Habermas) 41–2
globalization 41
Heidegger on 17
intercultural theory of 7
legitimacy of European modernity, defending 9

multiple modernities, question of 41, 397–9
philosophical founding figures/sources ix, 73
as a process of enlightenment 13
and rationality 37–8
sacrifice myth of 63, 64, 72
self-creation concept 129–38
self-critical reinterpretation 1–13
theories of viii, 10
three motif complexes 69–72
transmodernity 63
universal claims of 394–7
universalist morality of 22
victim myth of 61
Western 5
modernization 54
classical theories 7
processes of 5
theories 33–4, 397
tools 398
monarchy
and the absolute 362
enlightened, Sepúlveda's ideal of 200
pre-axial 303
universal *see* universal monarchy
monetary economy
in civil society 371
introduction of "money" 366–70
limitless 355
Locke's defense of 377, 382, 388
and natural law 366, 371, 373–4, 386
and precious metals 366, 367
pre-monetary economy 344–5, 354–66
money-commodity-money (M-C-M) cycle 366
Mongols 58, 149, 168
monism, materialistic 310, 312
Montaigne, M. de 215–53, 289, 292, 293, 311, 312, 320, 321, 325, 329, 349, 392, 398, 407n1, 407n2, 407n3, 407n4, 408n6
on the Americas 223, 245, 246–7, 252
and Augustine 221–2
and Bacon 260, 261, 287
on barbarism 244, 246
contemplation by 219–20
cosmopolitanism of 217, 253
on creative freedom 239, 242–3
on curiosity 216–17, 226, 227, 391

and Cusa 236, 237
dignitas hominis literature 231–44
discourse with Brazilians in *Of Cannibals* 249–50, 302, 408n6
on diversity of the universe 223
Essais (*E*) 72, 223, 240
    "Bordeaux copy" 217, 222
    civilization and barbarism in 244
    curiosity theme 226, 227–9
    editions 217, 218
    on nature 234
    overall interpretation of 216
    philosophical hermeneutics of 215–19
    seen as a personal portrait 218, 219
    self-understanding of 217
    on sensory pleasures 230–1
    uncompleted 222
on freedom vs. subjugation 235
and Hobbes 311, 312, 320–1
on the imagination 238, 239
and limitedness of human cognitive faculties 223
on the mind 220–1, 237–8, 261
on "New World" 244, 300, 408n5
on reason 239
on self-deification 233, 234, 241, 242
and Sepúlveda 248
on subjectivity 12
travel by 227–8
on truthfulness 219, 240
Villey's interpretation of 218–19
writings
    Apologia for Raymond Sebond 216, 218, 232, 233, 247
    Of Cannibals 62, 217, 244–51, 302, 408n6
    Of Coaches 249, 250
    Education of Children 217
    Essais (*E*) see above
    Of Giving the Lie 219
    To the Reader 217–18
    Theologia naturalis 231
    On Vanity 229, 234
moral philosophy 177, 345–54, 397, 398
    of Bacon 262, 284, 286, 297
    of European Enlightenment 48
    geometry as methodological model for 305–6
    history of 305
    of Hobbes 300, 301, 306, 308, 313–17, 330, 339
    iustitia commutativa and *iustitia distributiva*, distinguishing between. 316
    of Locke 343, 345–54
    methodological model for 305–6
    new 308
    occidental 188, 231
    of Pico 127–8
    and rationality 339
    traditional 279, 301, 314, 316, 330, 340
    virtues 284, 315
morality
    Christian 191, 282, 316
    concept 315
    discourse 45, 46, 47
    discriminating minimum standard of 47
    Golden Rule 317
    and happiness 285
    and hedonism 382
    Hobbes on 316, 317
    Horkheimer on 24
    intersubjectivity of moral norms 47
    moral orientation of science 279–88
    moral self-determination 133
    moral standards in state of nature 351–4
    Nietzsche on 4–5
    and rationality 4–5, 34, 35, 42, 47, 48
    and self-preservation 314
    sensualist 313
    subject matter of 312–17
    universalist, of modernity 22
    see also moral philosophy
More, T.
    Life of Pico 118
    Utopia 290
myths 18, 26, 36, 56, 61, 65, 304, 327
    creation 405n5
    "noble savage" and "savage beast" 245, 247, 248, 249, 251, 289
    Protagoras myth 122–3
    sacrifice myth of modernity 63, 64, 72

Napoleonic Wars 56
National Socialism/Nazi regime 22, 33, 52, 212
natural labor 378

natural law 300, 319, 324, 332, 344, 349, 351
  and Amerindians 203
  ancient theories 405n2
  Aquinas on 191
  autonomy over *ius divinum* 316
  Christianity 179, 213, 313
  classical ancient and medieval theories 326
  and consensus 313
  contravening 186
  dismantling of 338
  duties 228
  equality of all humans principle 360
  and ethics 192, 351, 385
  failure of 348
  and happiness 355
  and hedonism 344, 345–51, 385
  Hobbes on 300, 314, 315, 319–20, 354
  humanistic doctrine 313
  institutionalizing 206
  internalizing 205
  and international law 180, 182
  and just war 204
  knowledge of 348
  Locke on 346, 349, 351, 353, 354, 357, 376, 377, 383, 386
  and monetary economy 366, 371, 373–4, 386
  morals based on 192, 204
  norms 191, 202
  practices contrary to 204
  principles 204
  and property theory 182, 356
  and reason 202–3, 329
  and saving of the innocent 185
  secular rule 169, 170
  self-preservation principle 330, 331, 356
  Sepúlveda on 192, 195, 202, 316, 406n7
  and servitude 167
  and state of nature 319, 344, 354
  state-sanctioned transgressions of 364
  Stoics' theory of 338
  violating 186, 200, 201
  see also nature; state of nature
natural slavery of barbarians, alleged 155, 157, 163, 167, 189
  Aristotelian doctrine 61, 140, 158, 173, 174, 176, 196, 202, 205, 207

  concept 202
  contradiction of Christian teaching 176
  economic factors 197
  neopagan teaching 189
  rejecting 177
  revaluation of freedom in doctrine of 197
  Sepúlveda on 196
  Vitoria's criticism of teaching 185
  see also barbarians; slavery
naturalize, right to 183
nature 82, 83, 97
  of the angels 118
  and animals 242
  chaotic 30
  compulsion of 26
  and culture 36
  cycle of 26
  desacralization of 36
  destruction of 73
  disenchanted 25
  divided from itself 30
  and ethical virtues 131–2
  greatness of 96
  and happiness 128
  holistic concept of 30
  hostile 122
  human *see* human beings
  investigating 102
  inward and outward 25, 59
  law of *see* law of nature
  lifeless 19–20
  mastery of 25
  mechanistic philosophy of 299–300, 307, 308
  and mind 312, 313
  moral 46
  of non-humans 126
  potentiality of 297–8
  power of 24
  productive 13, 270–9
    and human creativity 288–98
  rational 121
  reconciliation with 27
  remembrance within the subject 27
  second nature 133–4
  secrets of 100
  spirit-nature 92
  and status of human 18

studying 96, 98, 99, 101, 102
subjugation of 115, 123
technological domination of 11, 22
violations of 200–1
zoon politikon claim 335
see also human nature; law of nature; natural law; state of nature
nature, law of 161
négritude movement 5, 6, 8
neoconservatism 33–4
neolithic civilizations 58
Neoplatonism 78, 90, 121, 137
neo-positivism 34
Netherlands, the 375
New Testament 165, 190, 191, 292
New World 58, 62, 63, 66, 147, 149, 176, 183, 195, 197, 200, 205, 228, 251, 268, 302, 365
   bans on emigration to 188
   barbarians of 175, 196
   Montaigne on 244, 300, 408n5
   and Old Word 269
   peoples of 244, 245–6, 248, 252
   provinces of 269
   Sepúlveda on 195, 197, 200
   Spanish rule 205, 206
   Vitoria's engagement with 172–3, 176, 177, 178, 183
   see also Conquista of the Americas; Old World
Nicholas of Cusa 12, 81–93, 102–15, 117, 140, 152, 219, 226, 234–7, 265, 275, 297, 307, 312, 348
   ancient cosmo-ontology of 93
   and Aristotelian metaphysics 78, 81–2, 87, 103
   on coincidence of opposites 86
   compared with Pico 137
   on creation of concepts 107
   on curiosity 102–5, 114
   definition of knowledge 82–3
   on the earth 91–2
   on God 110–13
   on indissoluble dissimilarity between finite things 83–4
   limitless universe, idea of 390–2
   metaphysics of 81
   minimum and maximum concepts 86, 87
   and Montaigne 236, 237

   philosophical theology 223
   querying of classical ancient cosmology 89
   on reason 112
   on Socrates 78
   transformation of Aristotelian metaphysics 78
   unlimited universe concept 71, 72, 78, 79, 86–9, 114, 115
   writings
      Compendium 106–9, 111
      De apice theoriae 112, 113
      De coniecturis 103, 105, 106, 109–11, 113, 115, 137
      De docta ignorantia (*DDI*) 70, 78, 81–6, 89–92, 102–6, 111–14
      De visione Dei 111
      Idiota dialogues 70, 105–9, 110, 111, 113
   see also Aristotle; astronomy; Augustine; cosmology; Nicholas of Cusa
Nietzsche, F. 3, 17, 28, 34, 62, 67, 72, 215, 392, 403n1
   compared with Marx 4
   critique of morality and reason 4–5
   Heidegger on 17, 21
   will to power 21
nihilism 21, 22
Nile, sources of 146
"noble savage" image/myth 245
   and "savage beast" 247, 248, 249, 251, 289
nomadic peoples 178, 197, 354, 360, 364–6, 368, 384
   and agricultural societies 362, 368
   consent to land appropriation 364, 371
   evolution of humanity from 354
   inefficient, seen as 384
   and labor theory of property 364
   natural labor 378
   sale of land to 371
   squeezing out 369
   subjugation of 197
   subsistence rights of 365, 399
   suppression of 370
   trade 366
   "work-shy" 378
   see also hunter-gatherer societies; indigenous peoples
North America *see* Americas

Odysseus, Dante on 149–50
Of the Proficience and Advancement of Learning, Divine and Human (*Adv. Learn*) *see under* Bacon, F.
oikumene (continent of Europe, Asia and North Africa)
  boundaries 58, 66, 71, 144–5, 146
  classical ancient conception of 11
  conquest of 147
  Crates of Mallos on 144
  de-limitation of 11, 71, 143, 216, 390
  and the earth 141
  geographical horizon 149
  habitable world of 156
  Herodotus on 143
  incorporation of other *oikumene* 159–60
  inhabitants of 146
  loss of power within 164
  nations of 120
  notion of others 150–1, 152
  power-political conflicts in 159
  previously independent 58
  Ptolemy on 144
  and Roman Empire 158–9, 162
  salvation history 148
  and scientific geography 143
  and voyages of discovery *see* voyages of discovery
  in the West 143
okeanos
  ability to cross 146
  earth as disc surrounded by 141, 143
  questioning by Ptolemy 144
  Persian kings on 156
Old Testament 130, 136, 292
Old World 49, 51, 53, 250, 269
  see also New World
On Airs, Waters, and Places (treatise) 142
ontology 30, 36, 63, 81–3, 88, 91, 123, 124, 211, 222, 340, 350, 389
  Aristotelian 82, 274
  body
    deterministic 332
    materialist 301, 306, 308, 310, 312, 319
    mechanistic 397
  cosmo-ontology 93
    earth and heavens 80
    ontological structure of the cosmos 377

humans
  and angels 121
  animal nature 124, 310
  in relation to God 347
  materialist 312, 319
  of the body 301, 306, 308, 310
  perfection 93
  perfectior esse posset, ontological formula 85
  principles 82, 211
  substance 274
  teleological 81, 82, 140, 390
  see also deontological ethics; *perfectior esse posset* principle
Oratio de hominis dignitate (Pico della Mirandola) *see under* Pico della Mirandola, Giovanni
orbis terrarium, concept of 163
Origen
  De principiis 119
  on freedom 133, 134
  on second nature 133–4
original sin 100, 121, 225, 356
Ottoman Empire 198, 199, 200, 384
  imperialism 190–5
  Ottoman Wars 140, 190, 192, 199
  Sepúlveda on 193
Oveido, F. de, *Historia general y natural de las Indias* 197

pacificism 190, 192, 315
pagans 170, 173, 179, 184, 185, 191
  lack of jurisdictional authority over 184, 186
  legitimate masters over their own lands 200, 206
pain, and pleasure 350, 351
Parthians 163, 164, 166
Paul III (Pope), *Sublimis Deus* 196
peace, as greatest of all goods 312–17
peaceful coexistence, fiction of 352
Peace of Westphalia 180
perfection 79, 98, 128, 384, 389
  absolute 124, 242
  apostolic 191
  Aquinas on 136
  attaining 87
  degrees of 83, 84
  divine 233
  of human spirit-nature 92

individual and collective 285
moral-practical 98–9
ontological 93
Pico on 127, 138
self-perfection 94, 284
striving for 85
perfectior esse posset principle 84, 85, 87, 88, 103
Perioici continent (northern hemisphere) 144
Periplus literature 142
Persia/Persian Empire 156, 158, 160, 163, 166, 179, 192, 193
philanthropy 295
philosophia perennis 129
philosophy
  of the absolute 103, 390
  ancient 20, 25, 221, 269
    classical 18, 129, 268, 272, 273, 276–7, 302, 335, 342, 377, 395
  Bacon's criticisms of classical philosophers 259
  civil 307
  decolonial 9
  Euro-American 5, 7, 9, 11, 255
  European ix, 5, 6, 11, 33, 50, 51, 53–6, 67, 68, 188, 215, 396, 398
    contemporary/modern 63, 391
  feminist 258
  Greek 19, 36, 153–65, 304–5
  Hellenistic schools 219, 221
  hermeneutics *see* philosophical hermeneutics
  history of 118
  intercultural 7, 8
  of knowledge 115, 348–9
  and language 307
  Latin American *see* Latin American philosophy
  law of nations and global ethics, philosophical foundations 172–89
  metaphysics *see* metaphysics
  moral 305–6, 345–54
  of nature 307
  philosophical anthropology 12
  philosophical hermeneutics 72, 215–19
  philosophical postmodernism 5, 34, 215
  political 180

  post-war European 33
  Renaissance 12, 13, 31, 60, 69, 73, 77, 216, 231, 242, 259, 273, 279, 287, 297, 300, 301, 312, 333, 339
  Roman 95, 103, 132, 153–65, 350
  schools of 305
  seen as an ideology of domination 53
  seventeenth-century 8, 12–13, 72
  of the state 308
  studies of 99, 397
  of technology 17, 21
  see also philosophical anthropology; philosophical hermeneutics
Pico della Mirandola, Giovanni 12, 110, 203, 212, 216, 385
  anthropology 118, 119, 127, 129, 135, 287
  on barbarism 203
  compared with Aquinas 136
  compared with Aristotle 123
  compared with Cusa 137
  compared with Hobbes 333
  on creation 122, 123, 125
  on dignity 117–19, 121, 122, 127, 138
  existentialist misunderstandings of the *Oratio* 126
  as founder of modern freedom, rejection of image 118
  on freedom 125–7, 130–3, 135–7, 287, 288, 333
    creative 119, 129, 137, 287, 288, 300, 332
    as developed in *the Oratio* 119
    scholasticism context 119
  on happiness 127–9
  Heidegger on 71
  human superiority over angels, theory of 119, 120–3, 125–6, 127, 128
  on intermediary position of humans 123–5, 127, 131
  and Islamic theology 137
  medium, concept of 124–5
  Oratio as speech on dignity of humanity 117–18
  publication of text of *Oratio* 118
  on reason and the intellect 126
  on self-creation 289, 392–3
  modernity of 129–38
  writings
    Commentary on a Poem of Platonic Love 126

De hominis dignitate (G) 124, 125,
  127–9, 311, 404n1, 410n1
Heptaplus 119, 123–5, 127–9, 137,
  138, 404n1
Oratio de hominis dignitate 71,
  117–38, 202, 216, 233, 243, 346,
  404n1
Pillars of Hercules 142, 143, 145, 266, 291
Plato 5, 79, 84, 90, 92, 94–6, 107–11, 120,
  122, 129, 132, 144, 153–5, 157,
  220, 246, 260, 269, 337, 350, 397
  on the angels 404n3
  Aristotle, compared with 153, 380
  Bacon on 259
  compared with Aristotle 380
  doctrine of forms 274
  on the earth 143
  on man and God 221
  polis 153, 158
  on transmigration 135
  writings
    Gorgias 286
    Laws 154
    Republic 153, 154
  see also Neoplatonism
Platonic-Aristotelian metaphysics 270
pleasure
  as absence of pain 231
  in acts of conquest 322, 326
  defining 231
  forbidden by the Stoics 225
  and happiness 355
  increase of 345–51
  intellectual 225
  intensifying 286
  of the mind 275
  and pain 350
  principle of 286
  pure 286
  and reason 231
  satiety 280
  and self-preservation 319, 322
  of the senses 231
  sensory 230, 231
  sensual 231, 248
  striving for 224, 322
  in technological devices 283–4
polis 207, 342, 378
  of Aristotle 153, 154, 163, 171, 192,
    199, 337, 338, 342

as artificial entity 335
autarkic 171
disorganized 153
economic foundations 381
vs. empire 199
good citizen, virtues of 344
Greek 154, 155
ideal 153, 154, 163, 381
loss of importance 219
organized 155
perfect 381
of Plato 153, 158
rights of citizen 199, 338
see also citizenship
political economy 381, 382, 384
  and social policy 370–6
political philosophy 11, 49, 140, 152, 153,
  180, 189, 206, 305–8, 318, 401
  in antiquity 158, 337, 339
  of Aristotle 183, 335, 337, 342
  classical 300, 337
  of Europe 155, 207, 390
  of Hobbes 299, 300–3, 306, 319, 332,
    334, 335, 337–9, 397
  of Locke 343, 345–6, 351, 352, 353–4,
    357
  modern 61, 69, 73, 299, 333, 394
  new 255, 299
  of the Occident 172
  of Plato 337
  and power 393–4
  Renaissance 333
  Roman Empire 164
  of Sepúlveda 211
  shortcomings 409n6
  and totalitarianism 261
Political Writings (LP) *see under* Vitoria,
  F. de
polycentric history 58
Polylog (journal) viii
Pomponazzi, P. 189
  On the Immortality of the Soul 202
Pomponius Mela, *De Chorographia* 145,
  146
positive law 37
positivism 2, 19, 25, 26, 28
  neo-positivism 34
  positivist-oriented dictatorships 53
post-colonial theory 10
post-idealism 216

postmodernism 4, 58, 64, 219
  philosophical 5, 34, 215
postmodernity 4
post-structuralism 34
potential infinite, concept of 81, 88, 89
poverty 245, 246
  and access to precious metals 375
  criticism of measures to combat 373–4
  extreme 382
  ideal 191
  Locke on
    beggars vs. families with many children 373
    children, treatment of 373
    combating through policy 373–4
    seen as idleness 371–2
power
  and coloniality/colonial matrix of power 57–68, 343, 389
  creative *see under* creativity
  extension of 323
  of God 88, 105, 128
  hegemonic 157, 163
  Heidegger on 17–24
  and knowledge 28, 69, 277–8, 297
  loss of 164
  of the mind 223–4
  and modernity 59–60
  and natural philosophy 277
  of nature 24, 123
  Nietzsche on 4, 21
  papal 174
  and political philosophy 393–4
  power-political conflicts 159
  racist relations of 65
  of reason 4, 5, 17–31, 107–9
  self-transformative, of freedom 138
  and state of nature 320
  and subjectivity 64
  syndromes of 13, 19, 22, 53, 63, 69, 72, 258
  theories of 10
  of truth 112
  universal augmentation of 331
  universal powers of Christianity, destruction of 178–85
  see also will to power
precious metals 366, 367, 375
prisca theologia 129, 130, 131

productive nature 13
  Bacon on 270–9, 288–98
  and human creativity 288–98
property
  common, of humanity 364–5
  consensual elements in justification of 357
  labor theory of *see* labor theory of property (Locke)
  organization of ownership 198
  private, consensual justification 356
  rights *see* property rights
  see also goods; labor theory of property; Locke, J.
property rights 358, 362
  of creation *see ius creationis* (right of creation)
  of English settlers, questioning 364–7, 371
  to private property 364
  see also labor theory of property (Locke); property
Protagoras 99, 234–5, 237, 336, 337, 405n5
  homo mensura theorem 20, 111, 260, 360
  myth of 122–3
  politiké téchne 337
Ptolemaic system 225
Ptolemy, C. 78, 90, 93, 147–51
  Almagest 149
  Geographia 149
  on inland seas 144
  map of the world 145f
  mathematical geography 150
  on *oikumene* 144
  rediscovery of writings 150
Pydna, Battle of (168 BCE) 158

Ramos, S., *Historia de la filosofía en México* 51
ratio (power of reason) 107, 108, 109, 236
  see also reason
rationality 26, 34, 40, 46, 64, 66, 102, 141, 197, 207, 297, 300, 364, 378, 385, 388, 398
  advances in 11, 73, 339
  Aristotle on 127
  communicative 9, 35–6
  dual condition of 317

gains in 39, 337, 388, 389, 394, 396, 398, 400
material 377–8
and modernity 37–8
and morality 4–5, 34, 35, 42, 45, 47, 48
purposive 38, 311
radical breakthroughs toward 395
theories 1, 69
types 13, 41, 42, 48, 72, 398
reason
ahistorical concept of (Kant) 55
Aristotle on 316–17
autonomy of 62
communicative, enlightened society based on 35–43
and creative power of God 105
Cusa on 112
disengagement from religious authority 18
divine 130–1
emancipative 63
"enlightened" 4
Habermas on 37
Hegel on unity with reality 24
Heidegger on 21–2
and intellect 126
Kant on 1, 18, 19, 55
and law of nature 166
Montaigne on 239, 248
moral/practical 297, 300
and natural law 202–3, 329
and order of creation 347
and pleasure 231
power of 4, 5, 17–31, 107–9
pure 44
rules of 62, 248
self-critical defense of heritage of 4
self-incapacitation in name of 354
sociocultural situatedness of 55
speculative, astronomical revolution through 79–93
tabula rasa conception of 373
theory 9
universality of 52
utopia of 40
Zea on 52
see also ratio (power of reason)
redemption 148
Reformation 1, 3, 57, 58

Relectiones de Indis (*De Indis*) *see under* Vitoria, F. de
religion
Abrahamic religions 78
civil wars, religiously motivated 244, 305
disengagement of reason from religious authority 18
Judeo-Christian tradition 25, 36, 65, 165
salvation, certainty of 18
world pictures 37
see also Bible; Christianity; Islam; Judaism; Reformation; soul
Renaissance viii, 2, 48, 58, 77, 120, 132
anthropology of 117, 140, 202, 231–3, 239, 242, 287, 289, 301
counter-Renaissance 215
creativity/creative freedom 117, 239, 310, 332, 358
culture 250
de-limitations 72, 216, 259, 301
dignitas hominis literature 118, 216, 232, 287
ending of 12, 215
humanism 60, 67, 70, 199, 334, 335
Italian 60
motif complexes of 13, 219, 222, 255
neo platonic thought of 137
philosophy of 12, 13, 31, 60, 69, 73, 77, 216, 231, 242, 259, 273, 279, 287, 297, 300, 301, 312, 333, 339
proponents of the *Quattrocento* 59
Spanish 60
spirit of 117
studies of 8, 138
and theology 130
thinkers 118
re-presenting 19, 21, 115
rivalry 168, 169, 290, 303, 304, 321
Roman Empire 160, 161, 164, 166, 167, 206
civilizing achievements of 169
conflict 163
cultural substance of 163
domination over the barbarians 196
eastern 168
expansions of 145, 146–7, 151, 159, 304
hegemonic power 157, 163

idealization of 252
imperialism 157, 162, 164–7, 334, 336
late period 164
and the *oikumene* 187
rise of 158
Roman Imperium 163
sacralization of 165
western, collapse of 147–8
see also Ancient Greece; Greek city-states; Roman philosophy
Roman philosophy 132
and classical Greek thought 153–65
and Hellenistic philosophy 95, 103, 155–6, 350
Romanus Pontifex (papal bull) 173

Sabundus, R., *Theologia naturalis* 231, 232
sacrifice
in Aztec Empire 203, 210, 211, 212, 364
and cannibalism 186, 195, 200, 201, 203–4
protection from cannibalism and sacrifice 203–4
protection of the innocent from 203–4
sacrifice myth of modernity 63, 64, 72
self-sacrifice 28, 315, 330
Salamanca School, coloniality 71, 152, 207
Salazar Bondy, A.: on Latin American philosophy 50, 52–7, 66, 67
criticism of history 54, 55
debate with Zea on 50, 51–6, 66–7
salvation 100, 184, 282, 296
eternal 18, 185, 316
history 148
specific doctrines 36, 37
of the subjugated 205
'sancta respublica' 166
Sartre, J.-P.
and Fanon 5–6
freedom, philosophy of 6
on intercultural philosophy 8
on Third World 6
writings, *The Wretched of the Earth* 5
Sasanian Empire 163, 164
"savage beast" myth/image 247, 248, 249, 251, 327
Schelkshorn, H., *Diskurs und Befreiung* viii

Schmitt, C. 9, 207, 299, 300
The Nomos of the Earth 66
school divinity 304
science
ambivalent character 23
Bacon's vision of 257–98
and capitalism 29, 41–2
Habermas on 37
"historical-philosophical" place of 258–9
Leitideen (guiding ideas) of 13, 42
and loss of meaning 39
moral orientation of 279–88
natural sciences 139, 320
"new" 23–4, 258–9
part of natural philosophy 277
scientific geography 142, 143, 148
subsystems of modern societies 12
and technology 3, 4, 13, 18, 22–4, 257, 265, 281, 282, 284, 286, 297, 344, 402
see also Bacon, F.
scientia iustitiae (science of justice) 301, 308, 335, 337, 341, 397
self-creation 70, 72, 118, 126, 312, 382, 392
and freedom 399
modernity of 129–38
Pico on 289, 392–3
see also creation
self-defense 191, 192, 324, 326
self-deification 118, 233, 234, 241, 242
self-determination 131, 308
free 353
moral 133
rational 197, 198
restrictions on 369–70
right of 317
self-fashioning 300, 392
anthropological idea of 216
creative 70, 117, 240, 288, 358, 390
experimental 344
freedom as 127, 357
and mystical union with God 120–9
and perceived superiority of humankind 119
self-legislation, and rational subject 18
self-limitations, new, search for 400–2
self-preservation principle
and animals 320

Hobbes on 314, 315
Locke on 352
and morality 314
natural law 330, 331, 356
and pleasure 319, 322
self-rule 181
self-sacrifice 28, 315, 330
Seneca, L. A. 97–101
   Epistles 409n6
   Medea 147
   Quaestiones naturales (QNat) 97–8, 146, 147, 163, 242, 337
sensualist epistemology 343, 345, 348, 349, 351
Sepúlveda, J. G. de 12, 55, 56, 72, 141, 173, 189–213, 244, 247–248, 289, 299, 302, 313, 315, 316, 325, 329, 348, 363, 364, 393, 394
   on barbarism 198, 203, 212, 247, 248, 329
   compared with Vitoria 201
   criticism of Aztec culture 61
   debate with Las Casas 61
   humanism of 189, 192, 197
   ideal of an enlightened monarchy 200
   just war doctrine of 190, 192, 195, 200–1
   justification of Spanish colonialism 190
   justification of the Conquista 140
   metaphysics 189
   and Montaigne 247
   on natural law 192, 195, 202, 316, 406n7
   on natural slavery 196
   on "New World" 197, 200
   political philosophy 69
   Sermon on the Mount 190, 191
   Stoicism of 206
   on violations of nature 200–1
   writings
      Apologia 189
      Apologia pro libro de iustis belli causis 195
      Cohortatio ad Carolum V 190, 192, 193, 406n5
      De regno 190, 193, 196, 197, 199, 205, 206, 406n8
      Democrates alter (DS) 189, 191, 195–206, 406n5, 406n8
      Democrates primus 190, 195

Democrates secundus 189, 190–1, 193, 195, 205
Democrates sive de convenientia militiae cum Christiana religio dialogus (DP) 190, 191
servitude 175, 196, 246
   Christian/Ottoman 192
   distinction between master and servant 361
   and natural law 167
   philosophical idea of 197
settled farmers 378
   see also nomadic peoples
Seven Sages 304
sin
   depravation of 165–6
   hereditary 166, 167
   mortal 176, 201
   nature, against 200–3
   original 100, 102, 121, 356
Six Nation Confederacy 365
slavery
   abolition 158
   in Greek *polis* 155
   institution of 153, 158, 163, 165
   juristic concept 197
   natural *see* natural slavery
   see also servitude
social anarchy 24, 104, 302, 333, 335, 337–9
social animal theory 181–2
social contract 177, 329–33, 338, 339, 354
social differentiation 1, 35–43
social policy 370–6
sociology, Western 7
Socrates 83, 101, 228, 236, 252, 407n2
   Apel on 48
   Cusa on 78
   dispute with Callicles 286
   pre-Socratics 80, 94, 124, 142, 259
Sophism 153, 157, 259, 332, 379
soul 1, 98–100, 125, 126, 221, 226, 236
   cognizing 112
   desires of 231
   harmony of 99
   human 121
   living and rational 347
   tranquillity of 340
   transmigration of 135
   world 90

southern hemisphere 144, 145, 146, 147, 159
  see also Antioeci; Antipodes
Spain 144–5, 147, 151, 174, 179, 369, 375
  Apologia pro libro de iustis belli causis, banning of 195
  Comunidades uprisings 193
  early sixteenth-century 200
  and expansion of Imperial powers 140
  flight of Jews from 194
  imperial ideology 140
  Late Scholasticism 300, 386
  and the Netherlands 375
  "New World," rule of 205, 206
  people of 51
  poverty in 197
  rule over Amerindians 205
  Spanish Renaissance 60
speculative reason 79–93
spirit beings
  decisions of 134
  freedom of pure spirits 134–5
  human superiority over, Pico's theory of 119, 120–3, 127, 128
  perfection of human spirit-nature 92
  Pico on superior status of humans over 125–6
  pure 126
  see also angels; heavenly bodies
Sri Lanka 146
Stalinism 24
stars 90–2
state of nature 65, 329, 352, 393, 410n2
  belligerent 353
  conflict 324
  and diffidence 322
  Hobbes on 299, 300, 314, 317–29, 331, 333, 334, 336–9, 353
  indigenous peoples living in 365
  international nature 328
  Locke on 353, 354, 384–5
  moderate vs. immoderate 323
  moral standards in 351–4
  and natural law 319, 344, 354
  and power 320
  pure 326, 327
  theory 299, 334
  see also Hobbes, T.; law of nature; natural law; nature

Stoic-Christian tradition 138, 166, 196, 201, 207, 233, 282, 356
  ethics 175–8, 319
Stoicism 104, 132–5, 225–6
  Chrysippus as founder 157–8
  cosmopolitanism 163
  on equality 163
  and ethics 155–7
    early Stoics 165
    ethical particularism 158
    ethical universalism 138, 155, 157, 159, 160, 162, 163, 165–6
    and imperial geography 160
    of old Stoics 160, 161
  founders of school 157–8
  and freedom 132
  and Hobbes 314, 319
  law of nature 165, 314
  nullus est servus natura 176
  of Sepúlveda 206
  single human genus concept 163
  and slavery 158
  on unity of human species 180
  Zenon of Citium as founder 157
  see also Stoic-Christian tradition
Strabo 145, 147, 164
  Geography 149
  Historika Hypomnemata 160
subjectivity
  essence of 21
  freedom of 17–18
  historical events establishing principle of 58
  Montaigne on 12
  and power 64
  subjective inwardness, Luther on 58
  universal power syndrome emanating from 22
subsystems of modern societies 12–13, 69
  and value spheres 40, 48
suicide, prohibition of 347, 357
Sumerian Empire 156

T'ang dynasty (621–907 CE) 164
technology 235, 349, 399, 400
  ambiguity of 23
  and art 22
  and destruction of nature 24
  Heidegger on 21, 22, 23, 24

human 275
innovations 268
maritime 24
military 59
nihilism of 22
philosophy of 17, 21
reform-orientation 22
and reform-oriented movements 22
and science 3, 4, 13, 18, 22–4, 257, 265, 281, 282, 284, 286, 297, 344, 402
"twisting" with metaphysics 22
teleology, philosophical anthropology 12
telos 127
Tenochtitlán (Aztec capital) 198
territorial states 13, 168, 180, 255
  civil wars 327
  early modern period 319
  emerging European 327
  subsystems of modern societies 12
  transitions to 362
Third World 6–7
Thucydides, *History of the Peloponnesian War* 304
Thule, island of 146
torture 247, 248–9, 258, 409n3
totalitarianism 10, 24, 29, 33, 210, 212, 261
  see also fascism, twentieth-century; National Socialism/Nazi regime
Toulmin, S., *Cosmopolis: The Hidden Agenda of Modernity* 215
trade, right to 182, 183
tranquillity of the soul 279, 281, 340
translatio imperii doctrine 2–3
transmodernity 63, 399
transoceanic expansion, first debates 172–88
travel, global right to 182–3
Treaty of Tordesillas 173
tribal societies
  conflict 247, 327
  nomadic *see* nomadic peoples
  perceived as barbarians 155
  primitive 196, 197
  temporary guardianship over 197
  see also Amerindians; barbarians; indigenous peoples
truth 23, 44, 82, 83, 97, 100, 110, 186
  absolute 18, 184
  and Christian evangelization 204
  claims 46, 168

concept 84, 85
consensus theory 46, 47
of creation 100
difficult to determine precisely 84
divine 85
of historical accounts 143
and intellect 103
knowledge of 276, 277
measuring 85
power of 112
propositional 36
search of 154
theories of 46
truthfulness 45, 143, 248
  Montaigne on 219, 240
  validity claims 35, 37, 38, 45, 46, 210, 395
Two Treatises of Government (TTG) see under Locke, J.

United Nations Security Council (UNSC) 211
United States *see* Americas
Universal Declaration of Human Rights 396–7
universal monarchy 172, 174, 175, 178, 179, 354
universalism
  ethical and political *see* ethical universalism
  violent 189
universality 6
  Christianity 61, 148
  claims to 9, 61
  communication 185
  discourse ethics 45
  ethical reason 34
  principle of 44
  of reason 34, 52, 55, 396
  violent 189
universalization principle 43, 44
universe
  diversity of 272–3
  infinite and limitless 71, 72, 78, 79, 86–9, 91, 114, 115
  potential infinite, concept of 81, 88, 89
  teleological order of 82
  see also cosmology
unlimited market economy, justification (Locke) 343–80
  vs. Aristotelian economy 377–88

utilitarianism 43, 283
  materialist 284, 296
  see also happiness

Valerius Terminus of the Interpretation of Nature (*Val. Term*) see under Bacon, F.
verum factum principle 25, 106, 276, 297, 307
victim myth of modernity 61
Vienna Society for Intercultural Philosophy viii
violence 4, 33, 59, 61–63, 66, 155, 171, 176, 184, 186, 187, 318
  against the Amerindians 175, 390
  and anarchy 228
  and the barbarians 188–206
  belligerent 162, 163
  Christianity, violent imposition of 171
  colonial 63–4
  enforcement of right to evangelize 184, 185
  extreme 33, 71
  imperialist 163, 184, 209
  just war doctrine 162, 163
  renunciation 44, 45
  resistance to evangelization 189
  wars 122, 169, 184, 200
    civil wars 304, 306, 338
  see also just war doctrine; wars
Virgil, *Aeneid* 146
virtues 95, 109, 191, 197, 205, 333, 335, 406n8
  citizenship 344
  civic 342
  ethical 131–2
  Greek and Roman 251
  and happiness 284–5
  magnanimity 344
  moral philosophy 284, 315
  moral quality 315
  natural 131
  necessary 155
  rational 131
  self-control 230
  Stoic-Christian ethics 282
  temperance 230
  and vices 340
Vitoria, F. de 12, 72, 141, 153, 192, 195–7, 200, 203–13, 216, 219, 244, 252, 289, 294, 316, 328, 329, 344, 363, 365, 385, 386, 390, 393, 396–9, 405n3, 405n4
  compared with Sepúlveda 201
  cosmopolitanism of 71, 201, 252, 329
  as founding figure of coloniality 66, 67, 69, 207
  ius gentium doctrine 140, 172, 180, 207–9, 328, 344
  lectures on Amerindians 71
  philosophical foundations of law of nations and global ethics 172–89
  Salamanca School, coloniality 71, 152
  on world society 293
  writings
    De Indis 71, 173–87, 195, 196, 207–8, 405n3
    Political Writings (LP) 175, 176, 177–87, 197, 405n3
    Relectio de Potestate civili 172, 177, 181, 185
voyages of discovery 150, 152, 269
  to the Antipodes 146
  in antiquity 142, 145, 390
  early modern 12, 140, 141, 150, 151, 269, 270, 306
  to Thule 146
  transoceanic expeditions 150
  see also Colombus, C.
vulnerability
  of human beings 122, 216, 321
  in interpersonal relations 324–5
  and need 181
  psychological 321
  to savage animals 122

wars 62, 122, 153, 200, 201
  against the barbarians 154, 155, 205
  flower wars 211
  of independence 52, 53
  Napoleonic Wars 56
  Ottoman Wars 140, 190, 192, 199
  and violence 122, 169, 184, 200
  see also civil wars; just war doctrine
Westphalia, Peace of 180
will 22, 30, 43, 44, 78, 224, 262
  see also free will; will to power
will to power
  Bacon on 297

ego cogito as 17–24
European 63
Heidegger's repressive interpretation of 403n1
nature as an object of 138
Nietzsche on 21
radical reversal of 27
technocratic 20
William III, Board of Trade and Foreign Plantations 363
world community, self-ruling 181
world dominion 66, 156, 159, 160, 163–9, 188, 206, 323, 324, 325
Christian 173
papal 173, 179–80
rejection by Vitoria 178
Roman 174, 175
Spanish 174
see also world empires
world empires 156, 157, 159, 160, 163, 169, 172, 393
in Latin Christianity 165–72
oriental idea of 158, 207
Roman 162, 390
see also world dominion
world history 57, 58
world maps 141–2, 145f, 148–9
world pictures 36, 37
"worldlessness" 377

Zea, L. 50, 57
debate with Salazar Bondy on Latin American philosophy 50, 51–6, 66–7
on reason 52
writings
El positivismo en México 54
La filosofia americana como filosofia sin más 54
Toward a Latin American Philosophy 51–2
zone theory 144, 146, 156
equatorial zone 145, 150, 151, 172
temperate zone 155

www.ingramcontent.com/pod-product-compliance
Lightning Source LLC
Chambersburg PA
CBHW071232300426
44116CB00008B/1001